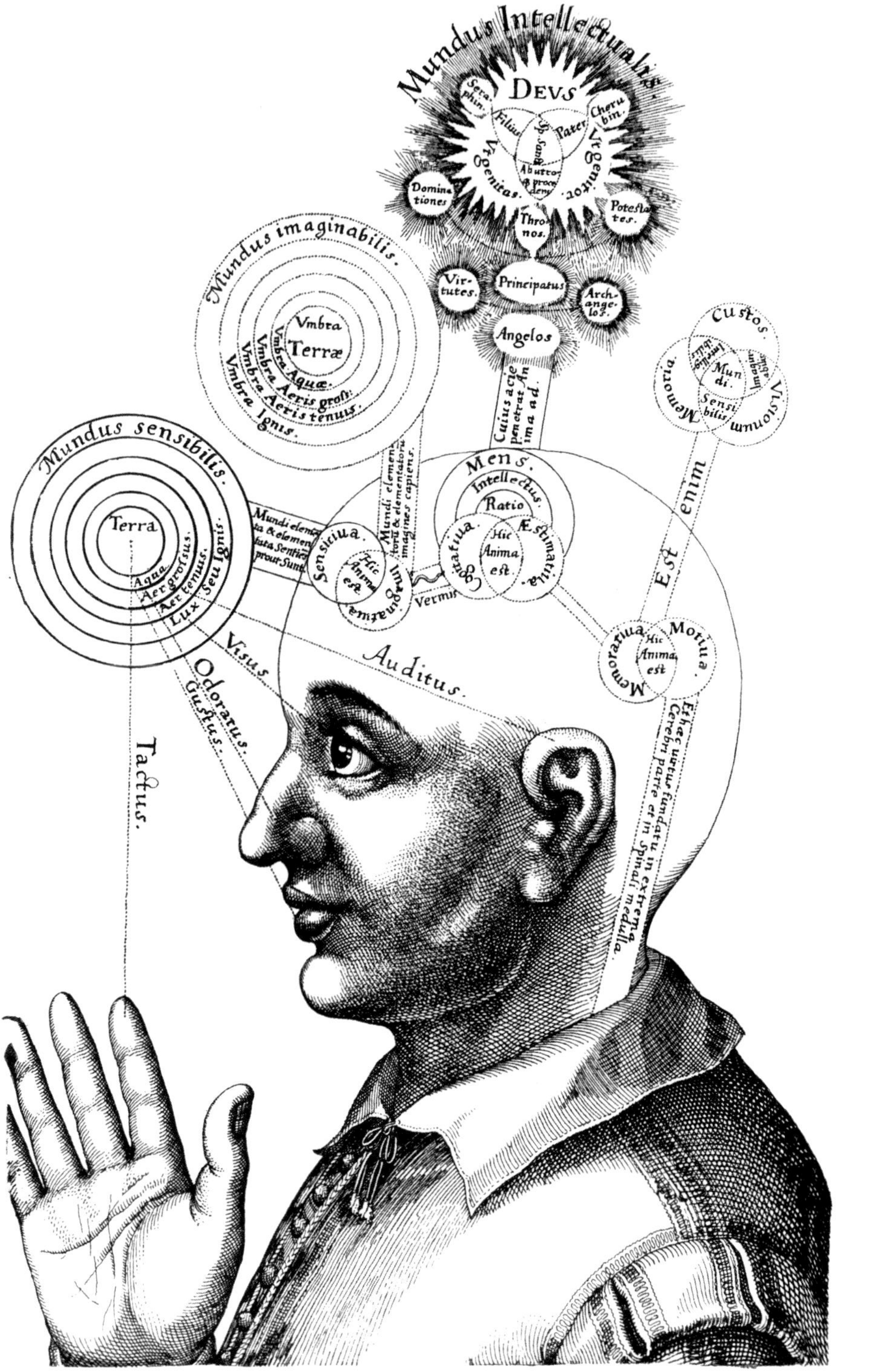

Mundus Intellectualis.
Devs
Sera phin.
Cheru bin.
Filius
Pater
Sp. Sanct.
Vrgenitas.
Vrgenitor.
Domina tiones
Potesta tes.
Thro nos.
Vir tutes.
Principatus
Arch angelos.
Angelos
Cuius acie penetrat Anima ad.
Mundus imaginabilis.
Vmbra Terræ
Vmbra Aquæ.
Vmbra Aeris grossi.
Vmbra Aeris tenuis.
Vmbra Ignis.
Mundus sensibilis.
Terra
Aqua
Aer grossus.
Aer tenuis.
Lux Seu Ignis
Mundi elementorum & elementatorum imagines capiens.
Mens.
Intellectus.
Ratio
Sensitiva.
Hic Anima est.
Imaginativa.
Vermis
Cogitativa.
Hic Anima est.
Æstimativa.
Custos.
Memoria
Mun di.
Sensi bilis.
Visionum
Est enim
Memorativa.
Hic Anima est
Motiva.
Et hæc virtus fundatur in extrema Cerebri parte et in Spinali medulla.
Visus.
Auditus.
Odoratus.
Gustus.
Tactus.

Der Mensch als Industriepalast

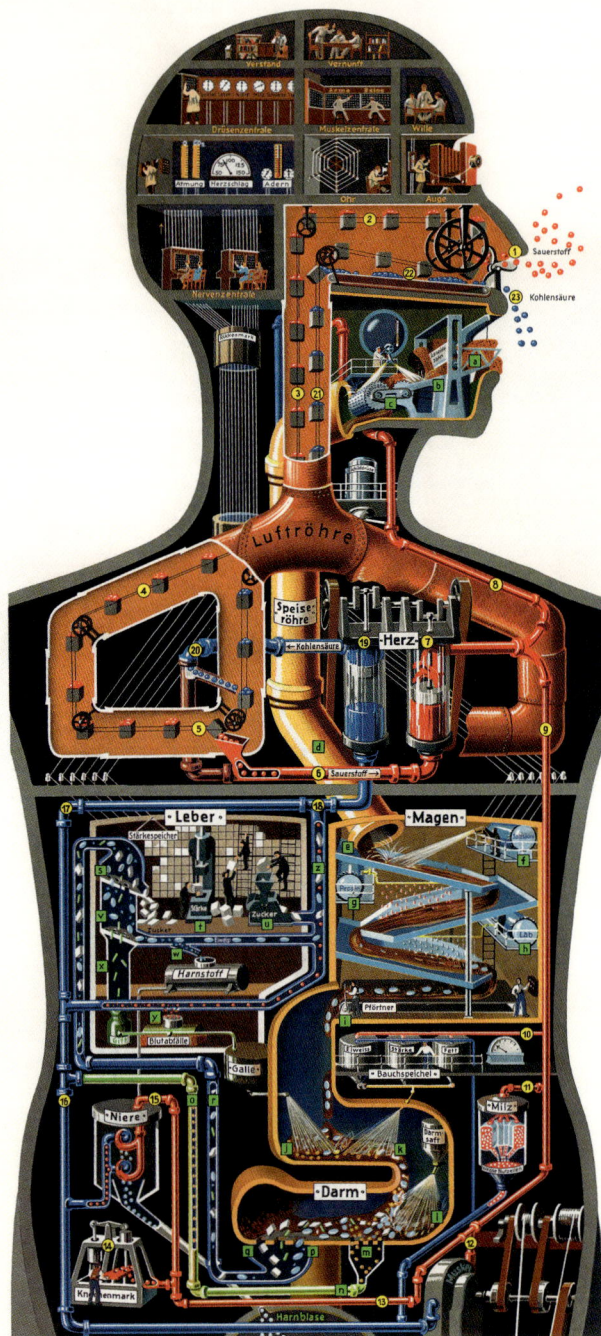

Beilage zu Kahn, DAS LEBEN DES MENSCHEN /Franckh'sche Verlagshandlung, Stuttgart /

Sandra Rendgen
Ed. Julius Wiedemann

Information Graphics

TASCHEN

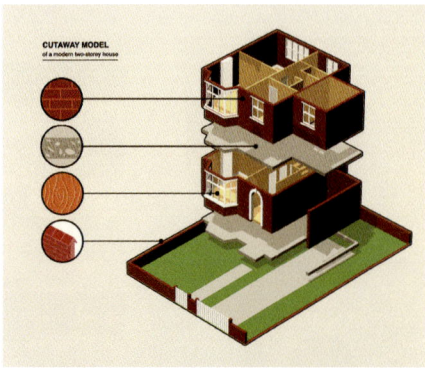

CUTAWAY MODEL
of a modern two-storey house

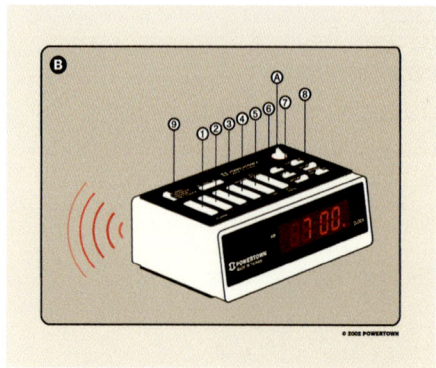

B

© 2002 POWERTOWN

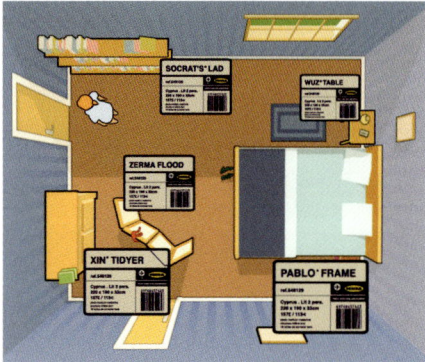

SOCRAT'S* LAD

WUZ*TABLE

ZERMA FLOOD

XIN' TIDYER

PABLO' FRAME

SUBURBAN STATION

1 2 3

KEY TO

Stairs
City bus terminal
Parking space
Taxi
Information

130

PROJECT OVERVIEW

London Transit
www.londontransit.uk

■ Single-track tunnel
■ Exploration tunnel lateral adit
■ Tunnel exclusively for ventilation

Exhaust ventilation centre

Operations centre

West tunnel

East tunnel

Inlet ventilation centre

CONFERENCE FLOOR

Lifts

Meeting Room

Lifts

LOWER GROUND FLOOR

Lobby

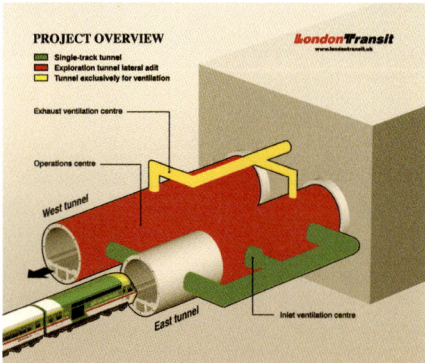

Welcome
Screen(portal)

Knowledge Base

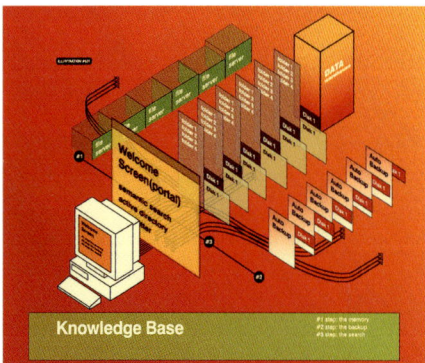

1,53
998
1,74
279
218
170

E MARKETS & STOCKS. Market data & world indices

Essays

Projects

Contents

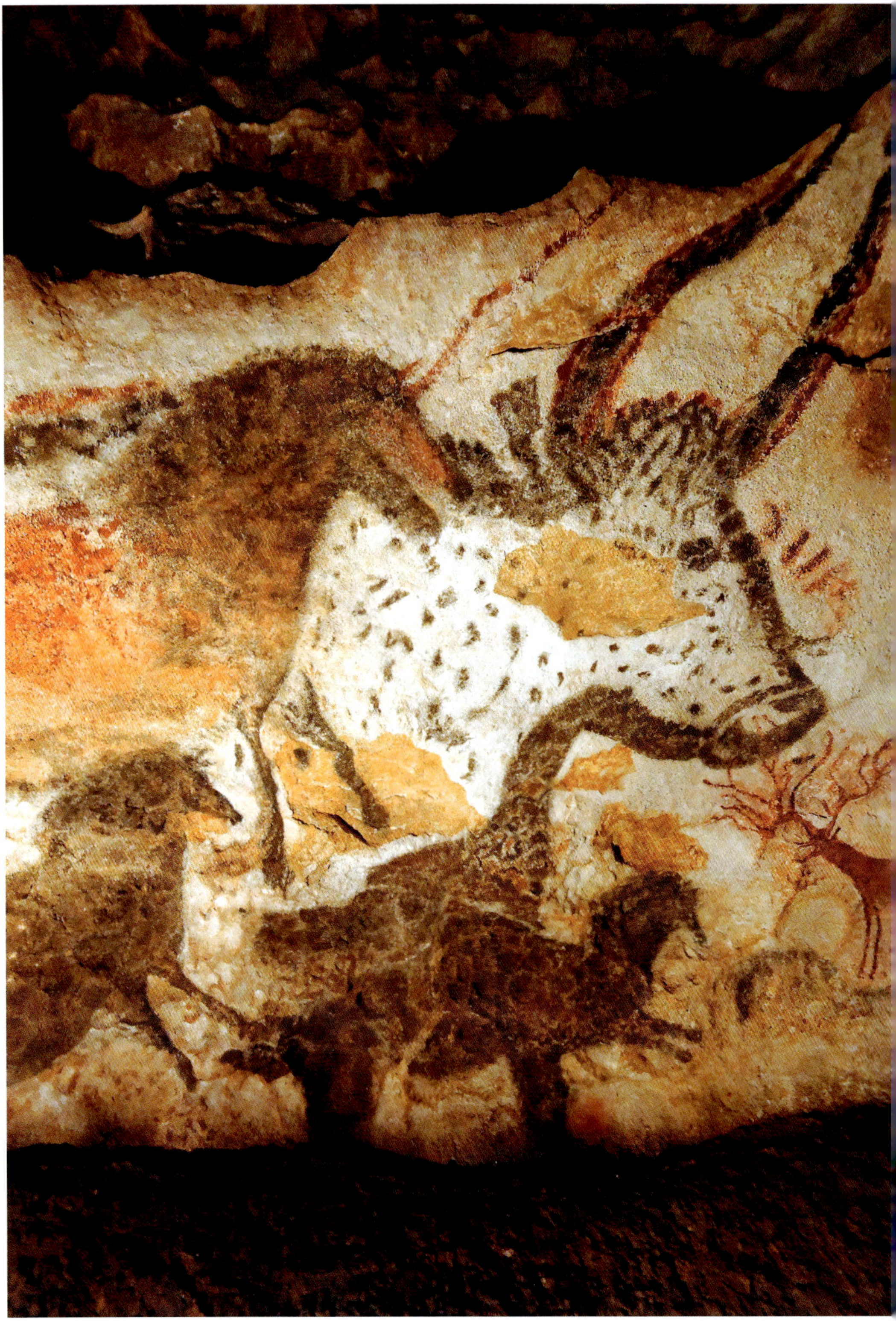

Sandra Rendgen

7—40

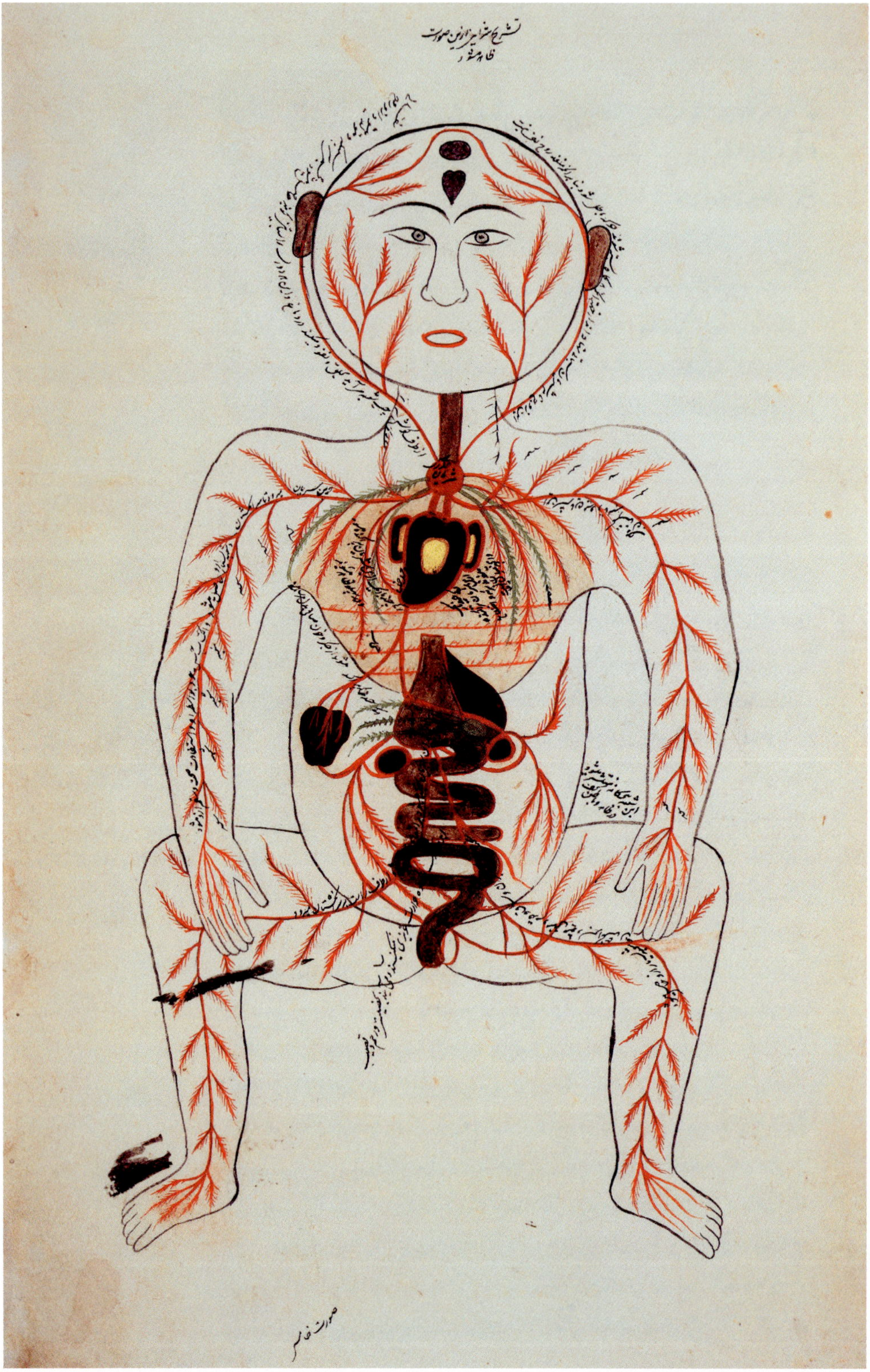

Introduction

Sandra Rendgen

Today, infinite amounts of information and data can be accessed in seconds and across large distances. However, raw data in themselves are of negligible value – they need to be filtered and evaluated. That's why professional data and information management will be a central cultural tool in the decades to come.

The graphic representation of data and information has been around for a long time, and not just in the world of science. Newspapers regularly publish statistics in chart form; magazines make use of infographics to explain anything from natural phenomena to the latest technology. In business, economic data are communicated in the form of diagrams. User manuals and safety instructions frequently make use of schematic drawings.

For a long time the genre tended to attract little attention, even though infographics have been almost omnipresent for decades. Of the innumerable examples, only a few had much thought and work put into their design. In contrast to other areas of graphic design, infographics had few style-defining precursors. Added to this, there is always a certain amount of tension between graphic design and the accurate depiction of data. On the one hand, infographics are supposed to convert complex problems into images that are easy to understand, but on the other, there is traditionally a suspicion that "beautiful" graphics may tell lies.

Since the turn of the millennium there has been a renewed interest in the visualisation of data and information in many different areas, including journalism, science, art and design.

The new trend has even penetrated pop culture: the Norwegian music duo Röyksopp released a music video in 2002 which consisted solely of animated infographics (p.4). The video depicts the life of a young woman in London and segments an entire day into infographics.

There are a number of reasons for this renewed interest. More and more statistical data are freely available and there is more demand for them to be processed. Visual interactive user interfaces are required to access digital archives, whilst the introduction of digital devices in general is changing our reading habits. Communication is shifting towards generally shorter texts in combination with charts and images; hence information graphics are taking centre stage.

This book documents the recent upswing of information graphics and data visualisation. Key issues are discussed by the authors of the essays, such as the aims of data visualisation or the professional handling of information. The historical images accompanying the introduction and essays, on the other hand, demonstrate that there is an old tradition of depicting knowledge in diagrams and charts.

Information graphics are hybrids and hence difficult to define. Text, image and geometric shapes are indissolubly interlaced to produce single entities. This does not follow automatically from the data, but has to be developed. The French cartographer and theoretician Jacques Bertin commented that, "A graphic representation is not merely a drawing, but often entails a heavy responsibility when deciding on how to proceed. One does not 'draw'

Page 6 / ca. 17,000 BC

The cave paintings of Lascaux consist of approximately 2,000 images of men, animals and abstract signs. Although the exact interpretation is still being disputed, it seems certain that the creators of the paintings included extensive information in their images.

Page 8 / 1390

Illustrations have always played a cardinal role in the passing-on of medical knowledge. This schematic drawing of the circulation of the blood originates from the so-called *Anatomy of Mansur*, assembled in the late 14th century in Iran.

1144 BC

In Ancient Egyptian tombs, walls were completely covered with symbols and hieroglyphs in order to record information on the life of the deceased. This was supplemented with images of deities (here from the tomb of Ramses VI).

a graphic representation in a solid form; instead one constructs it and rearranges it until every relationship between the data has been revealed."[1]

In 1967 Bertin wrote a standard work on the graphic means available for depicting data. In addition to the two dimensions of the (paper's) surface on which points, lines and planes can be drawn there are six other options for visually representing data: size, value, texture, colour, orientation and form. Every possible visual construction is composed out of this basic vocabulary combined with text labels.[2]

Various tendencies can be discerned within the hybrid field of information graphics and data visualisation, even though it may not be possible to subject it to a strict division into groups. On the one hand, *visualisation* is the process of visual conversion. On the other hand, the term *visualisation* separates interactive dynamic representations from static *charts*. A distinction is also made between *qualitative information* and *quantitative data*. Data are numerical, and their traditional representation is the abstract diagram devoid of figurative images. By contrast, information graphics present

qualitative relationships – for example, how an oil rig works. Schematic drawings are often used in this context.

A major difference between individual works also consists in their specific purpose. Many are aimed at a broad audience and seek to provide clear explanations. Conversely there are other depictions that serve above all as scientific tools to aid analysis. In these cases, the main concern is to recognise patterns in data or to arrange information in a clear way. For a long time, diagrams, sketches and maps have been used for such functions, as can be seen from the following historical examples.

The Legible World

Maps, for instance, afford an overall view. They allow us to recognise and order the world. In the cartography of the Middle Ages, as opposed to its later developments, there was no separation between the geographic features of the Earth's surface and the landscape's historic and religious character. Hence the Ebstorf Map, which was made in ca. 1300 in northern Germany, shows all of the then known world on an area 3.5 metres in diameter (p.18). Aligned towards the east, this map is centred on Jerusalem and based on the medieval tripartite division of the world into Europe (below left) / Africa (below right) / Asia (centre top).

The world is overlaid upon the figure of Christ (head, hands and feet), and there is a depiction of the Garden of Eden to the left of his head. In the bottom right, the Mediterranean Sea is shown in a vertical direction. Innumerable animals, people, buildings and narrative scenes enrich the geographic arrangement with strategically placed information about the world's religions and cultures. The map is a visual display, an arrangement of knowledge into a single image.

Anatomical atlases also create an overview of things that cannot be captured by the eye (p.8). Early anatomical works had already availed themselves of schematic drawings of the human body in order to record medical knowledge. Abstract figures show the position and function of various organs. Several Renaissance artists in turn revisited these schematic drawings; Leonardo da Vinci (p.23) and Albrecht Dürer, for instance, investigated human proportions in order to achieve realistic representations of the body.

ca. 1090

The embroidered Bayeux Tapestry from the Middle Ages shows the Norman conquest of England over a length of 68 metres. The historic events are narrated in 58 individual scenes which include additional text explanations.

Following spread / **ca. 1190**

The monk Joachim of Fiore used diagrams to represent his theory of the three ages which correlate to the Holy Trinity. The age of the Father (recounted in the Old Testament of the Bible) was followed by that of the Son (as told in the New Testament). According to Fiore's prediction, this was in turn to be followed by the celestial age of the Holy Spirit.

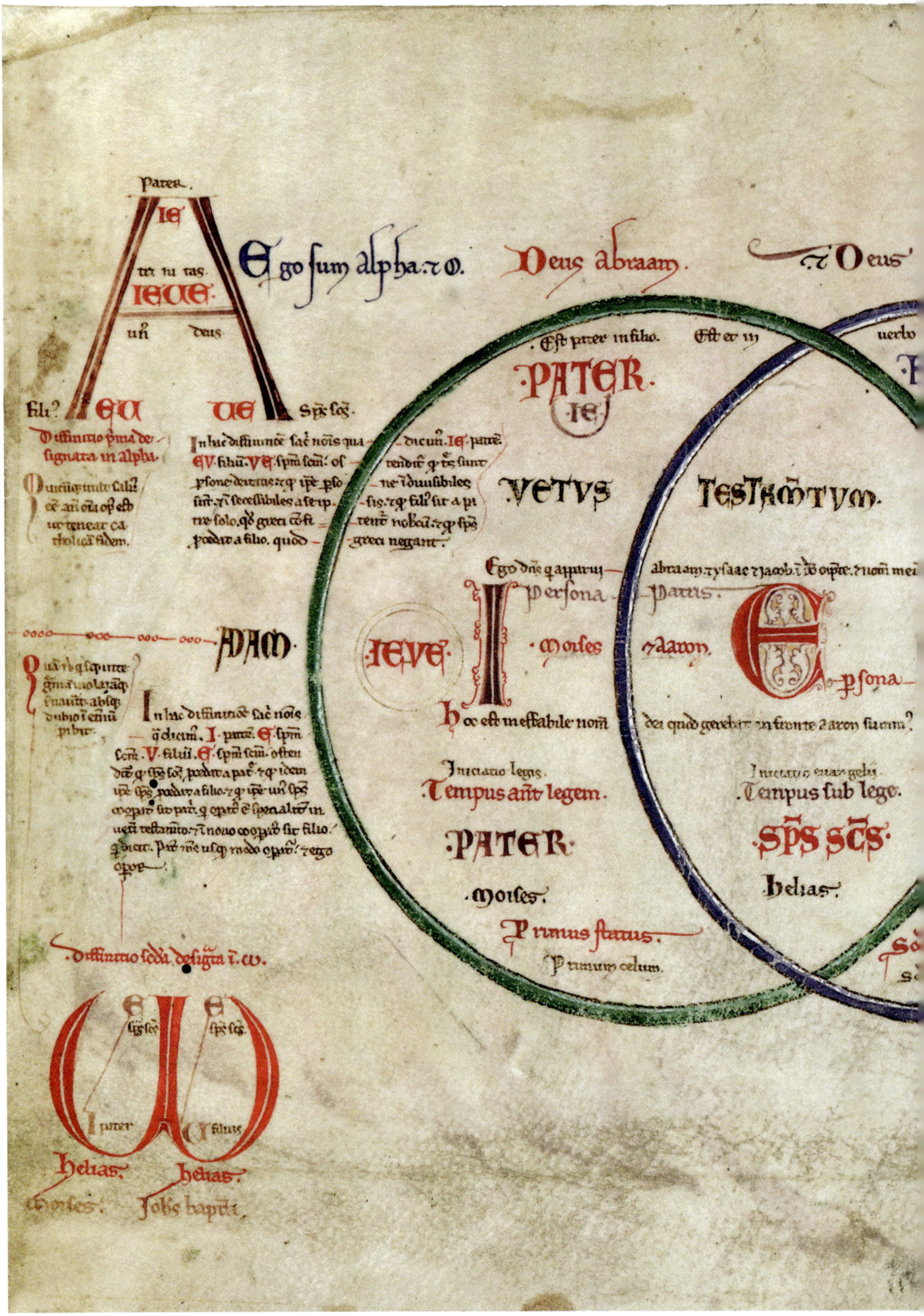
Pater.
Ego sum alpha et O.
Deus abraam.
PATER
VETUS
ADAM
IEVE
Tempus ante legem.
Tempus sub lege.
PATER
moises.
helias.
Primus status.
Primum celum.
helias.
helias.
Johs bapta.

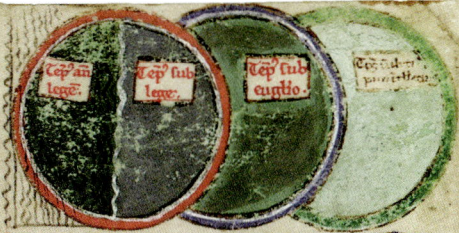

Tenebre eut fup
facis abissi qa ca
cliui illd indicui q
regnum meos ab dam
usq; ad amser. yna
leuib tenebs iusta
ne. dilui & usq;
& positi.

Tep an
lege.

Tep sub
lege.

Tep sub
euglio.

Tep sub
pmittesis.

⁊ Deus Jacob.

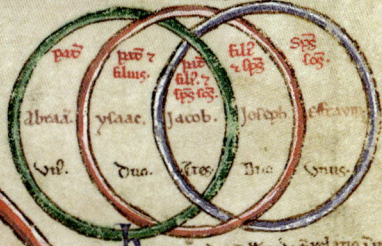

pat̄

pat̄ ⁊
filius.

filₐ
⁊ ꝑs.

sꝑs
scs.

abraa.

ysaac.

Jacob.

Joseph

⁊ esau.

vii.

duo.

tres.

duo.

unus.

His quoq̄ modis i telliḡ di ē relatio i pso ie
durang. suo singulari atq̄ ad alteru.
suo simul duau ad una. siue enī cōte
i pus. tum ad bona sp̄ula. ut eut ad
officu ata etuau.

sp̄s. ab utroq; pcedens.

SPS SCS.
Ue.

NOVVM   TESTAMTVM.

non   in   di   ca   u   e   i   s.

Ypsona   sp̄s scī.

ꝓlens   tempus.

pr qd ra groce teīgnatory noiat.

filiꝯ.

sccpiu quatuor litis i hac pagina i signatus.

Juicatio tipica intellectus.
Tempus sub euangelio.

Juicatio anagogica intellec.
Temp sub tipico inccllciu.

FILIVS.

SPS SCS.

Johs baptista.

helias.

Tcrciuf status.

Terciuu celum.

FINIS MVNDI.

His septe modis dicuntr ad se plene di
ratiō sui singillati. siue sint due.
uel tres.

pat̄ d̄s.
singul̄
abraam.

filꝰ d̄s.
s̄ingulꝰ
ysaac.

sꝑs scs d̄s.
s̄ingulꝰ
Jacob.

pat̄ ⁊filꝰ.
s̄ul uī due
abra̅ ⁊Jacob.
s̄ul uā due

pat̄ ⁊filꝰ.
s̄ul uā d̄s.
abra̅ ⁊ysaac.
s̄ul una due

filꝰ ⁊ꝑs.
s̄ul uā due
ysaac ⁊Jacob.
s̄ul una

pat̄ ⁊filꝰ ⁊ꝑs.
s̄ul uī due
abra̅ ysaac ⁊Jacob.
s̄ul una due

1280

The English scholar Roger Bacon tried to establish exact mathematics and empirical natural research as the foundation of all science. He is also known for his research in the field of optics: this plate shows a study on the nature of light.

The role of the structure of the cosmos was as central in late Renaissance thought as that of the properties of the body. Many scientists used diagrams to explain their cosmological theories. The English philosopher and physician Robert Fludd, for instance, designed a diagram in 1618 in which he presented the universe as the stretched chord of a monochord – tuned by the hand of God (p.37). The musical notes A, B, C, D, E, F and G are inscribed on the neck of the instrument, as are, from the bottom up, the four elements and the seven celestial bodies: the Moon, Mercury, Venus, the Sun, Mars, Jupiter and Saturn.

At this level cosmic reality ends, and above it are the supernatural regions. The dotted circles represent the harmonic proportions that rule the cosmos. This scheme reflects the belief that the universe was organised in line with numerical proportions, and that music mirrored this cosmic order. Diagrams were suitable for illustrating such theories because the scientists could use them to show the complex reference systems they could see in the cosmos.

In parallel with the development of cartography, which from the early modern period was experiencing a golden age, there had been since the 17th century attempts at expanding geographic maps by adding extra information. As an example, in 1741 the German linguist Gottfried Hensel designed four maps showing the then known continents along with the languages spoken in them (p.50). The individual areas are annotated with characters from their respective alphabets, and there are also tables of all the characters. The maps are designed to provide a full tableau of all the linguistic signs of the world, and thereby substantiate a universal theory of human language. Hensel's designs are among the first examples in which colour was deployed to demarcate geographic areas by theme.[3]

Statistical Patterns

Politicians need aids to help them make decisions. With the development of the modern state in the late 18th century came an increased need to base political decisions on reliable data. For this reason, statistics – the science of the systematic treatment of demographic and economic data – was developed. Unlike today, such numbers were initially accessible only to a small circle of officials and politicians. However, even these experts found that statistics were abstract and not highly descriptive. It is therefore no coincidence that graphic representations were soon developed.

The simplest way of noting data was by means of tables, but by 1786 the Scottish engineer and economist William Playfair had developed diagrams to depict economic figures (p.53). He represented imports and exports to and from England in a time-series chart, and showed England's foreign trade balance in bar charts. In 1820 August Crome developed a comprehensive graphic overview of statistical data for the King of Prussia (p.54). The large tableau compares all the German states on the basis of a series of data, which includes area, state income, military budget and number of army troops.

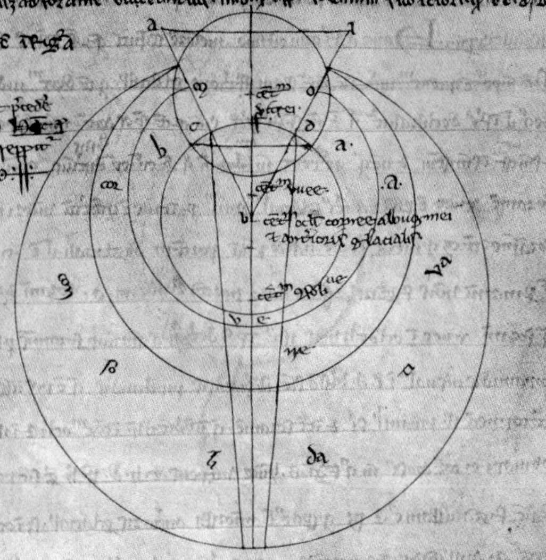

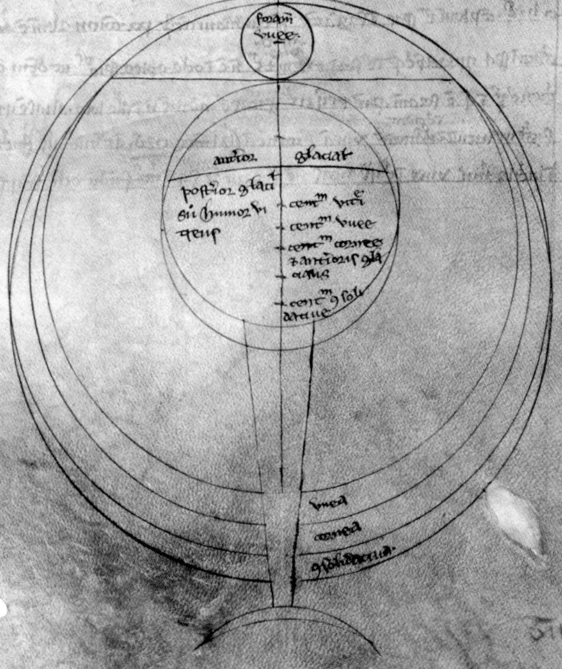

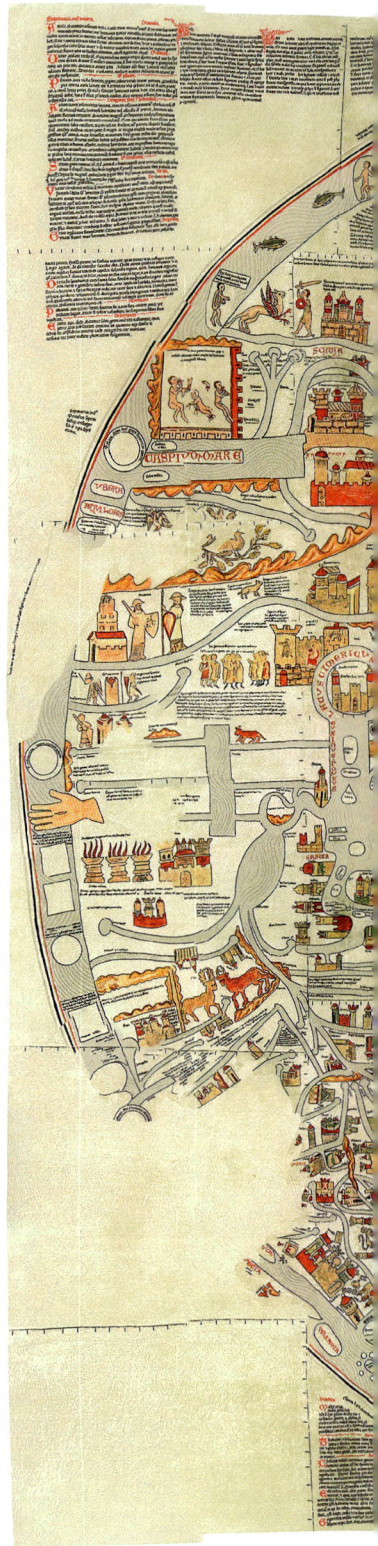

1300

This medieval world map from around 1300 shows the then known continents Europe (below left) / Africa (below right) / Asia (centre top). The geographical rendering is supplemented by mythological stories and creatures as well as historical facts.

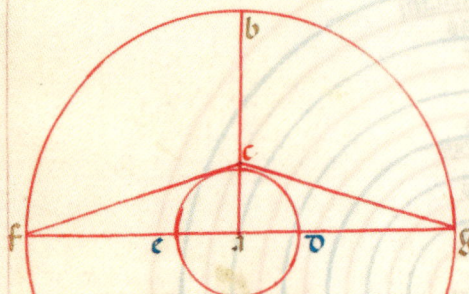

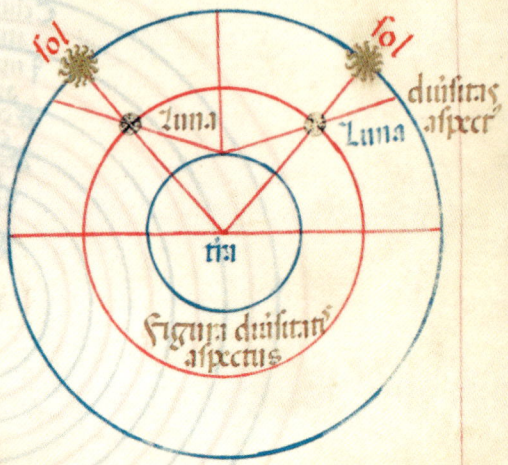

meridies

fol · Luna · fol

diuisitas aspect'

tra

figura diuisitati aspectus

Igit̄ cœls exiēns ī cent̄ tc̄. Sīc semi diamet̄ ad sc̄t diamet̄. sīc circul̄ ad circulū ⁊ spā a spā. sā. c. lineę ad a.b, n̄ c sesibilis cōntās ḡ n̄ circlī c.c. d. ad p. b tc̄.
Circulū sensibilis erit quantitas tc̄.

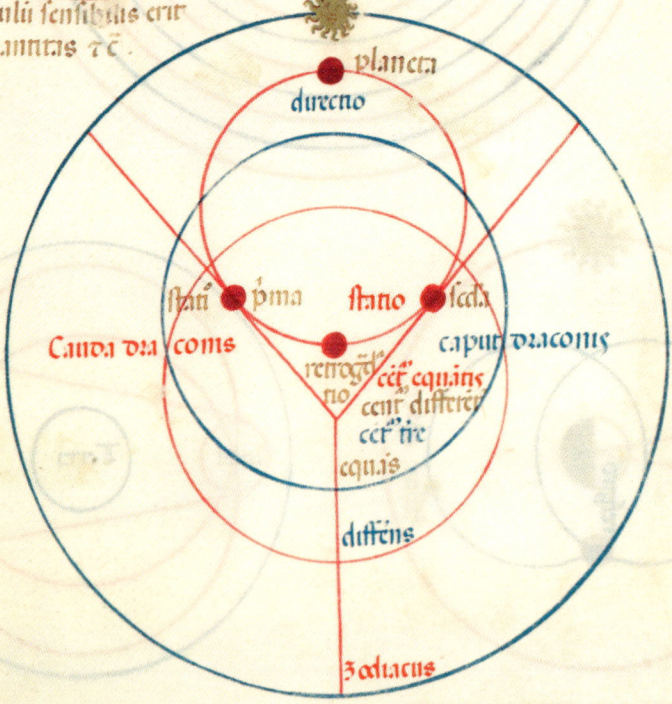

Sol

planeta

directio

stanō pma   stanō secda
        retrogradatio
caput draconis
cauda dra comis

cēt' equāns
cēt' differēt'
cēt' tre
equās

differns

zodiacus

1460

The Italian manuscript *De sphaera* is a lavishly illustrated volume on astrology. Aside from many detailed illustrations, the codex comprises several diagrams showing the structure of the universe and the system of the planets.

Another graphic innovation, the flow map, was developed by the French engineer Charles Joseph Minard. Flow maps are a cross between maps and flow charts, and visualise the movement of objects. Minard produced dozens of such maps during the course of his professional life. In 1869 he applied the principle to a historic subject and created one of the most famous of all infographics: a map of Napoleon's catastrophic Russian campaign (p.70). Napoleon had set out for Russia with 422,000 soldiers and returned with only 10,000. The map links numerous variables including the army's direction, declining size, dates and a temperature diagram. Another format was developed by the English nurse and statistician Florence Nightingale. After her harrowing experiences in the Crimean War, where many soldiers fell victim to the abysmal health care provided, she described the mortality of soldiers over a period of two years in a polar area diagram (p.72). The vast majority of soldiers, shown in blue, died from avoidable infections. Despite scattered criticism of its partly disproportional representation, this diagram is a famous example of the visual expressiveness of statistical graphics.

The Well-Informed Public

The widespread availability of newspapers and magazines is an innovation of the last century. New printing techniques permitted the mass distribution of printed products and made it easier to include images in texts. As this was happening, the popularisation of information and data graphics became unstoppable. At the same time graphic design became generally more professional, not just in the print media but also in public spaces for which guidance systems and aids to orientation were invented.

In 1920s Vienna, the philosopher and economist Otto Neurath sought ways of providing workers and employees with information about societal conditions. To do this he conceived posters that depicted statistical relationships (p.84–85). His posters used standardised pictographs and were designed to be understood by anyone, anywhere in the world. Proportions are denoted by varying the number of particular pictographs. One of the people who worked with Neurath on the design of the posters and pictographs was the graphic designer Gerd Arntz. Thanks to the modern style and progressive attitude of Otto Neurath's pictorial statistics, they continue to serve as a major reference for designers who are concerned with the representation of information and data.

A famous example of the spread of infographics in everyday life is the London Underground map devised by Harry Beck. The starting point was provided by the realisation that the map's primary function was to help people find their way around the Underground network and it therefore did not need to be geographically accurate. Earlier versions had depicted the actual course of the Underground lines within the city and were therefore visually unclear. Beck significantly modified the map by designing a diagrammatic version (p.86). All lines run parallel to the page edges or at a 45-degree angle. Distances between stations are always of equal length, while the stylised course of the Thames is the sole visual

1487
Leonardo da Vinci visualises the ideal human proportions as described by the Roman architect Vitruvius in this famous drawing from the late 15th century. The ideal male body is inscribed in the forms of a square and a circle.

reference to the city. To this day the design provides a model on which many of the world's public transport maps are based.

A further example of the spread of information graphics is its increasing use in newspapers and magazines. While statistics in newspapers were often enough represented just with numbers, some magazines like *McCall's* or *Fortune* introduced a lively graphic language for statistical charts (p.92). The popularisation of information and data graphics also spread to business communication. Business reports and presentations often require numbers to be represented graphically. Equally, over the course of the 20th century we have come to take for granted all kinds of pictorial instructions, such as how to assemble furniture, use electrical appliances, and how to behave in the event of emergencies.

Suspicious Data
Information graphics are intended to explain how things really are. Thanks to their scientific aura they found acceptance in the mass media and advertising, and they continue to stand for objectivity and accuracy of information. Whereas in earlier centuries only scientists worked with data and information graphics, they were joined in the 20th century by editors and advertising professionals. However, general popularisation brings with it a level of degeneration, and content-related weaknesses are frequently found in graphic representations.

Since the 1950s several authors, including John Tukey, Jacques Bertin and Edward Tufte, have grappled with the accuracy of graphic representation. In 1954 Darrell Huff published the entertaining book, *How to Lie with Statistics*. He noted numerous cases from advertising and the media in which distorted statistical information was used to emphasise particular statements. His criticism of graphic representations included charts that lacked labelling, and insufficient comparative data to allow a proper evaluation of figures.

The political scientist and statistician Edward Tufte systematically developed these observations and published a series of standard works in which he criticised distortions in graphic representations, for instance, his book *The Visual Display of Quantitative Information*, first published in 1982. Tufte analysed graphics published in major daily newspapers and criticised the tendency to enrich statistical diagrams with pictorial metaphors. Although graphic designers were trying to make abstract numbers easier to understand, they also frequently let themselves get carried away by the pictorial metaphor and so created a visual distortion of the data.

As a reaction to this negligence, Tufte developed his own, strictly minimalist design code for data visualisation. He made a plea for labelling to be complete, for restraint in design and a reduction of superfluous "ink". Every dot and line should contain information. Anything more he considered superfluous adornment. He gave excessively decorated graphics the term *chartjunk*.

These analyses have been a significant factor in leading major Western newspapers to practise a certain level of restraint in their

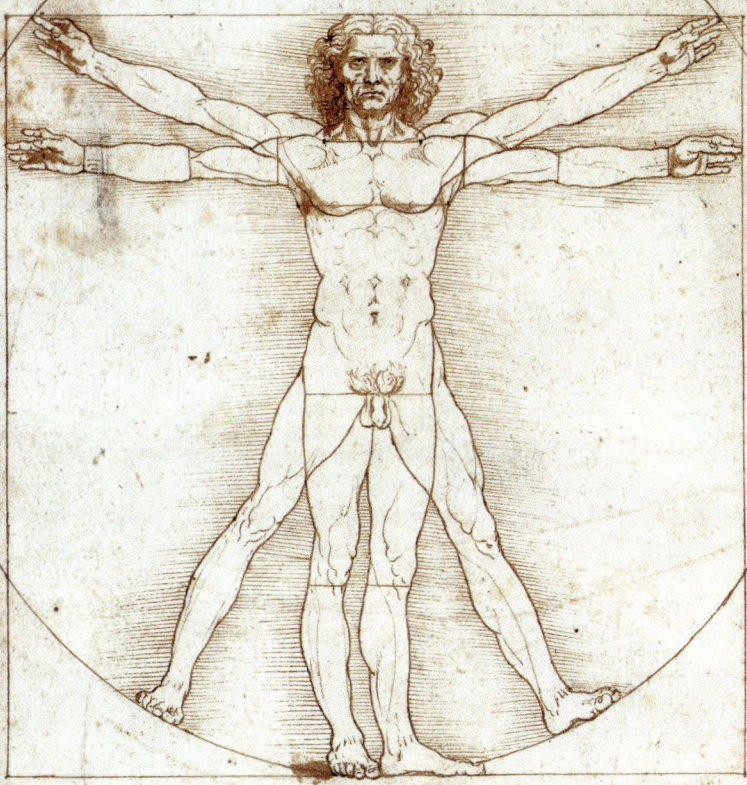

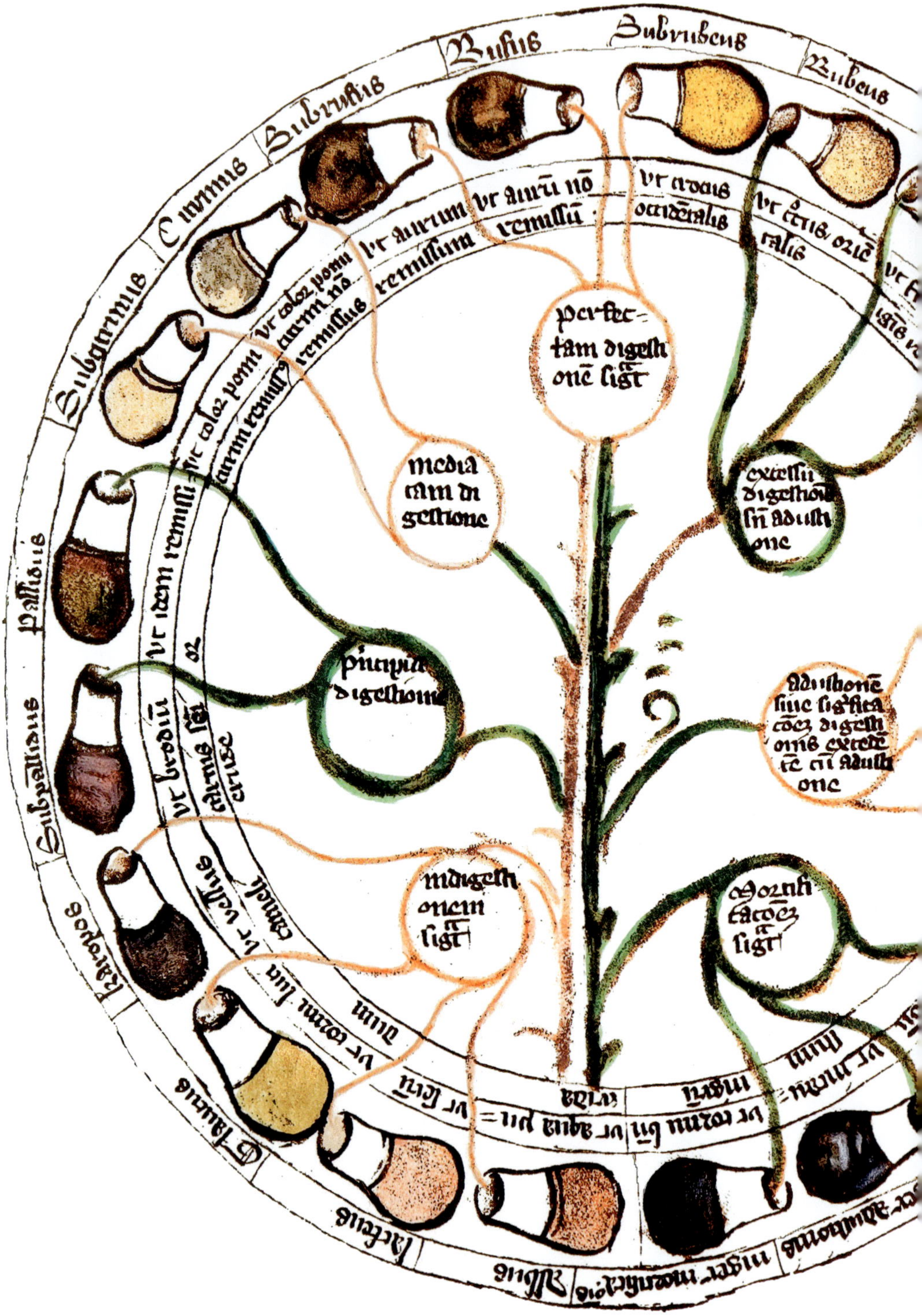

1491

Already in Antiquity and the Middle Ages the colour of urine served as an important piece of evidence for the diagnosis of various ailments. This so-called uroscopy wheel shows urine flasks in different colours, indicating various diseases.

infographics design in order to avoid jeopardising the seriousness of their statements. By way of contrast, magazines tend to be more open to pictorial representations. Nigel Holmes, Peter Grundy and John Grimwade are among the designers who have shaped a new and unconventional style (compare their works in this volume). Furthermore, studies have shown that the use of images helps readers remember infographics for longer.[4]

The architect and designer Richard Saul Wurman has been studying the effective transmission of information since the 1960s. Starting with the "data explosion" that came with the development of computer technology, he coined the term "information architecture". In numerous publications he developed ways of clarifying complex relationships by means of structured design. In an essay in this book he introduces his LATCH information-structuring system.

In Wurman's dictum "Understanding is Power" we discern an idea which also resonates in the information pyramid made up of *data*, *information*, *knowledge* and *wisdom*. This concept comes from information science and describes the hierarchical relationships between the individual levels: *data* are the unprocessed symbols; *information* is the processed data, which in turn produces *knowledge* in the reader. The last level of *wisdom* implies not only a deeper understanding, but also the possibility of *acting* in line with this understanding. Therefore, whoever has processed the data and has achieved wisdom via information and knowledge knows what needs to be done. In this model, which is still seen as a point of reference in information

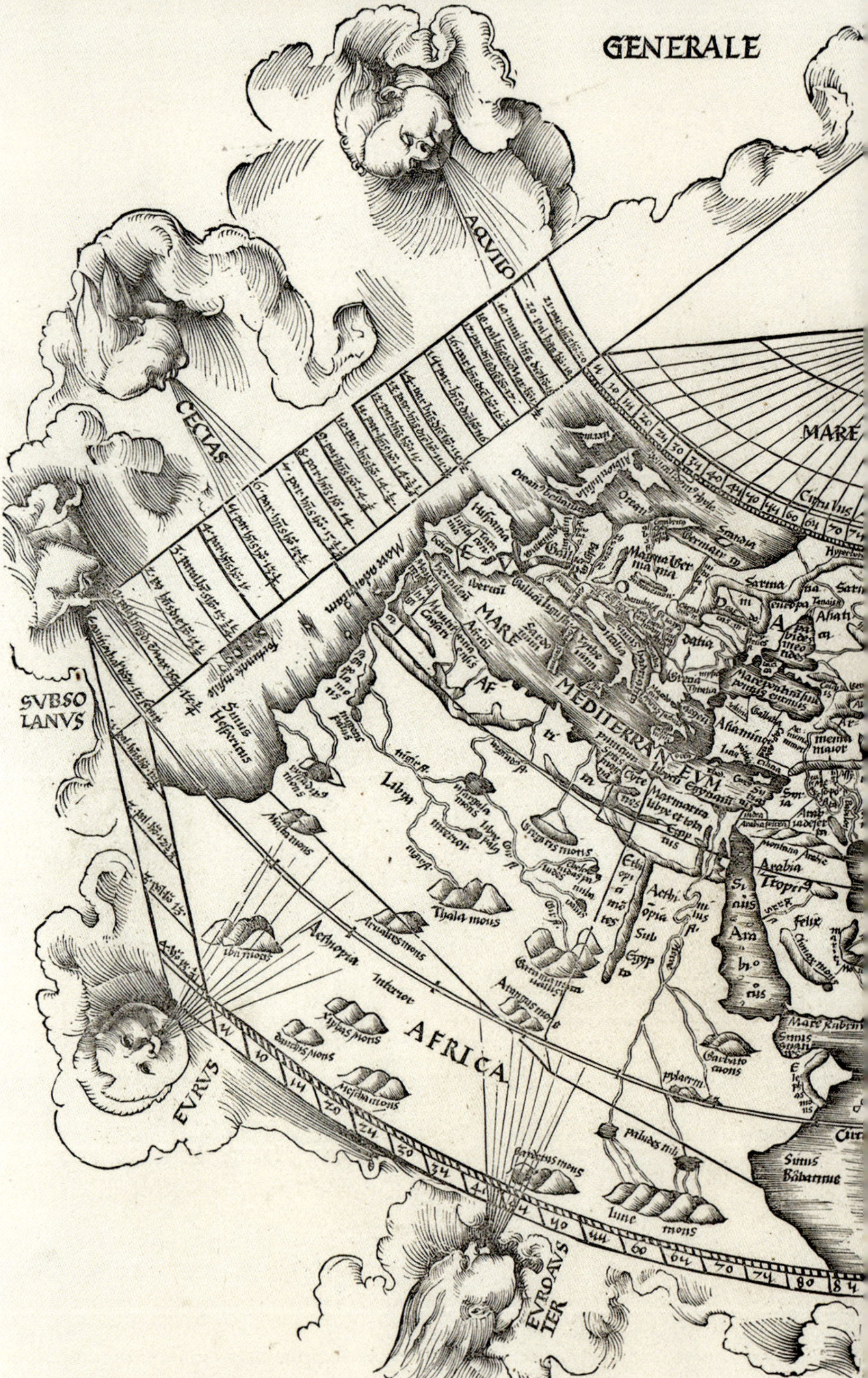

GENERALE

MARE

AQVILO

CECIAS

SVBSO
LANVS

MARE
MEDITERRAN EVM

AF

Libia

Aethiopia Interior

AFRICA

EVRVS

EVRO AVS
TER

PTHOLEMEI

CIRCINVS

CAVRVS

FAVONIVS

CONGELATVM

Serica Regio

Scythia

Asia

India

Sinus Gangeticus

Sinus Magnus

RE INDICVM

Taprobana insula

AVSTER AFRICVS

AFRICVS LIBS

MEXICO.

MEXICO REGIA
ET CELEBRIS
HISPANIÆ NO
VAE CIVITAS.

Cum Privilegio.

Previous spread / **1520**

The teachings of the ancient geographer Ptolemy were widely accepted during the Renaissance. He had invented perspective for projection and plotted longitudes and latitudes. This map also includes additional information on major winds.

ca. 1600

This Mexican city view comes from the atlas *Cities of the World*, which was published between 1572 and 1617 in Cologne. The atlas collects numerous city views from four continents. Many maps additionally feature figures in local costumes.

28

1523

In his book *Summa de Arithmetica*, Franciscan friar Luca Pacioli collected the mathematical knowledge of his time. This table displays his doctrine of proportions and shows different types of proportional relations, particularly in geometry.

HOROSCOPION APIANI

GENERALE DIGNOSCENDIS HORIS CVIVSCVMQVE

generis aptiſsimum, neq̃ id ex Sole tantum interdiu, ſed & noctu ex Luna, aliiſq̃ Pla=
netis & Stellis quibuſdam fixis, quo per vniuerſum Rhomanum imperium atq̃ adeo
vbiuis gentium vti queas, adiuncta ratione, qua vtaris, expeditiſ=
ſima, nunc ab illo primum & inuentum & æditum.

His accedit diſtantiarꝫ, altitudinum, & profunditatum per idem hoc inſtrumentum
dimetiendarum ratio longè accuratiſsima & ingenioſa. Similiter in quam altitu=
dinem aqua naturaliter citrà omne artis beneficium, Deinde quanto ſublimius
ſcaturigine ſua adminiculo artis per cannales deduci poſsit.

Nocturna quoq̃ adnexa eſt obſeruatio horaria ex digitis manuum, priori illa
quæ ſuperiori anno vnà cũ Quadrante ædita eſt, tũ promptior tũ expeditior.

1533
Petrus Apianus was a German mathematician and astronomer.
This book title page features a solar quadrant for measuring
the sun's angle of elevation and thus the time of day. The
scale is a mesh of intersecting date lines (vertical) and hour
lines (horizontal).

visualisation, there resonates the progressive idea that information can motivate action.

Data Future
Today the users themselves have become the authors. With the spread of personal computers, almost everyone has the tools needed to produce graphics. The best-known example of this is Microsoft's PowerPoint presentation software which has been distributed on a huge scale and which any office worker can use to visualise his own statistics. The enormous number of badly prepared charts with which we have since been inundated has no doubt contributed to the bad reputation of pie charts and bar charts. In 2003, Colin Powell achieved dubious fame with his evidence to the UN regarding Iraq's weapons of mass destruction – which significantly contributed to the start of the Iraq war. Among other things he gave a poorly prepared presentation, which included information graphics and labelled satellite photographs.

The plethora of badly designed visualisations coincides with a growing need to deal with the flood of information with a certain degree of professionalism. No longer is data secret knowledge. With a general freedom of information, which has now become legally anchored in many countries, comes a public culture of information. At a time when everyone is swamped by information it is necessary firstly to subject data to precise analysis and secondly to prepare it in an intelligent and appealing way. This requires a general *visual literacy*.

Graphic designers are reacting to this and are increasingly interested in developing a visual language for information and data. They do not want graphic representations merely to be factually accurate; they must also reflect good design. Theoreticians are looking at the way in which visual design impacts on the cognitive comprehension of graphic representations. For instance, the architect and design researcher Paolo Ciuccarelli argues in his essay in this book for improving the way in which scientific research is communicated to the public. He pleads for a stronger integration of narrative elements into abstract graphics in order to increase understanding.

Interaction designers, on the other hand, develop interactive data visualisations so that users can independently discover, compare and comment on data. New software solutions provide an opportunity for visualising and publishing data in a variety of basic patterns. Online comment functions allow users to discuss and hence control the different visualisations. The interpretation of statistical data becomes a cooperative process.

Journalists in turn consider the wealth of data as a new source for balanced reporting. Simon Rogers from the London-based *Guardian* describes under the heading of *data journalism* the way in which the availability of statistics on the Internet has massively expanded journalistic practice in the last ten years. In his essay, a moment of democratisation can be heard; journalists can evaluate political events with greater nuance when alternative sources of information are available to them.

1583

The German physician Georg Bartisch published a book on ophthalmology containing 92 full-page woodcuts. Here, the inner brain is shown. The woodcut contains several overlays to reveal the layers of the brain's anatomy.

This book portrays the recent changes in information graphics on the basis of 200 projects from a variety of different fields. Scientists, journalists and designers are represented, as are freelance artists who have their own ways of interpreting the genre. The culture of information visualisation that was created in this period will continue to grow and differentiate. We keenly await future developments.

1   Bertin, Jacques: *La graphique et le traitement graphique de l'information*. Paris: Flammarion, 1977. Translation 1981, *Graphics and graphic information-processing* by William J. Berg and Paul Scott.
2   Bertin, Jacques: *Sémiologie Graphique. Les diagrammes, les réseaux, les cartes*. Paris: Gauthier-Villars, 1967. Translation 1983, *Semiology of Graphics* by William J. Berg.
3   Robinson, Arthur H.: *Early Thematic Mapping in the History of Cartography*. Chicago and London: Chicago University Press, 1982, p.54.
4   Bateman, Scott et al.: *Useful Junk? The Effects of Visual Embellishment on Comprehension and Memorability of Charts*. University of Saskatchewan, Department of Computer Science. Paper Presented on CHI, April 2010.

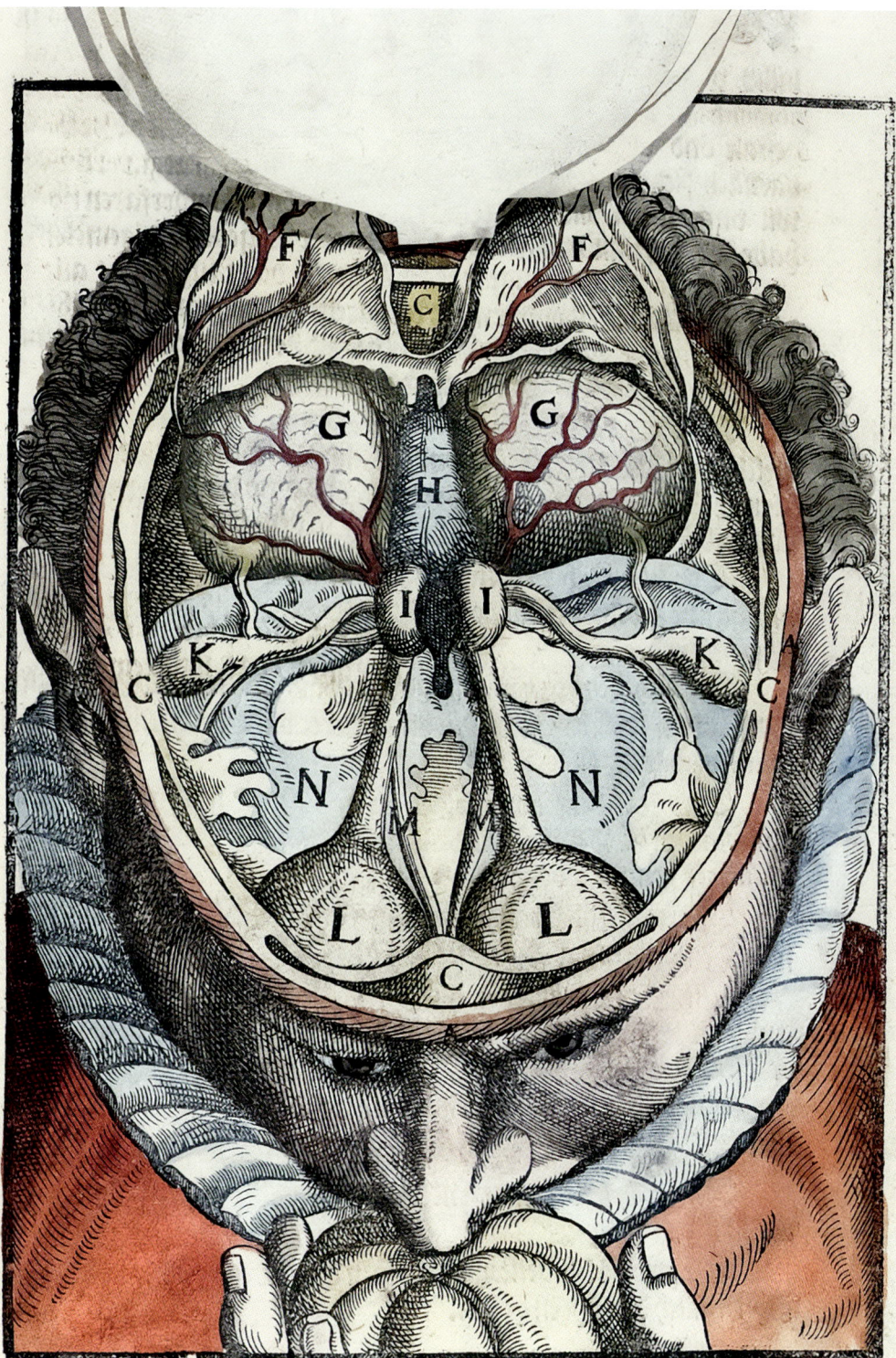

Encyclopedie, ou la suite & liaison de tous les Arts & sciences.

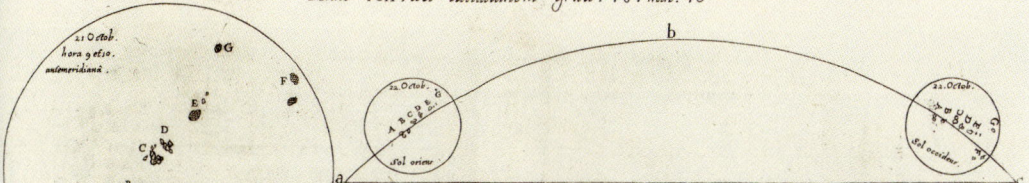

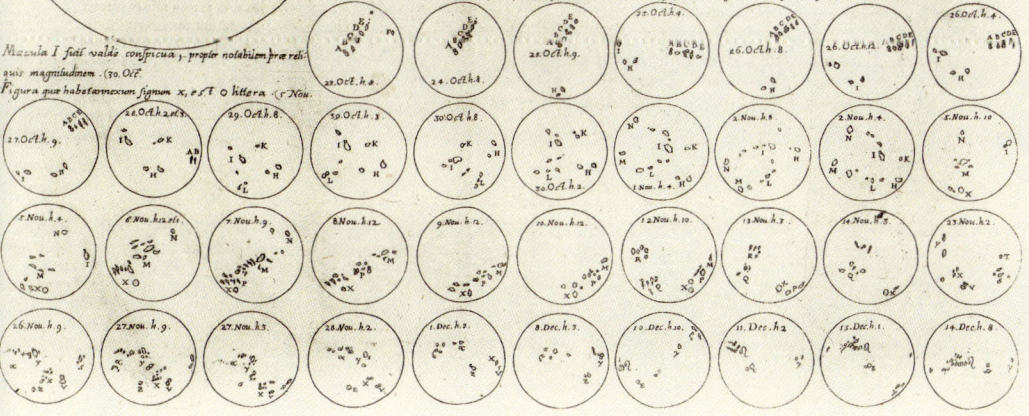

1587

In his book *Tableaux accomplis de tous les arts libéraux*, the French humanist Christophe de Savigny created an encyclopaedic overview of all the sciences of his time. It contains many "organigrams" which show the break-down of all the individual scientific disciplines.

1613

In the course of his research, the Italian scientist Galileo Galilei found various proofs for heliocentrism. One of them was the discovery and description of sun spots which he documented in a series of drawings.

Lauf der Sonnenflecken vom 11. bis 23. Mai 1625.
»Rosa Ursina« Seite 211.

1626

Parallel to his contemporary Galileo, the German Christoph Scheiner also worked on exploring the nature of sun spots. In his book *Rosa Ursina sive Sol* he described his observations and drew the course of the sun spots over the period of one year.

1618

In his book *De musica mundana*, the English scientist Robert Fludd described the ordering principle of the universe based on musical harmonies. Musical notes as well as the four elements and seven celestial bodies are inscribed on the neck of the instrument.

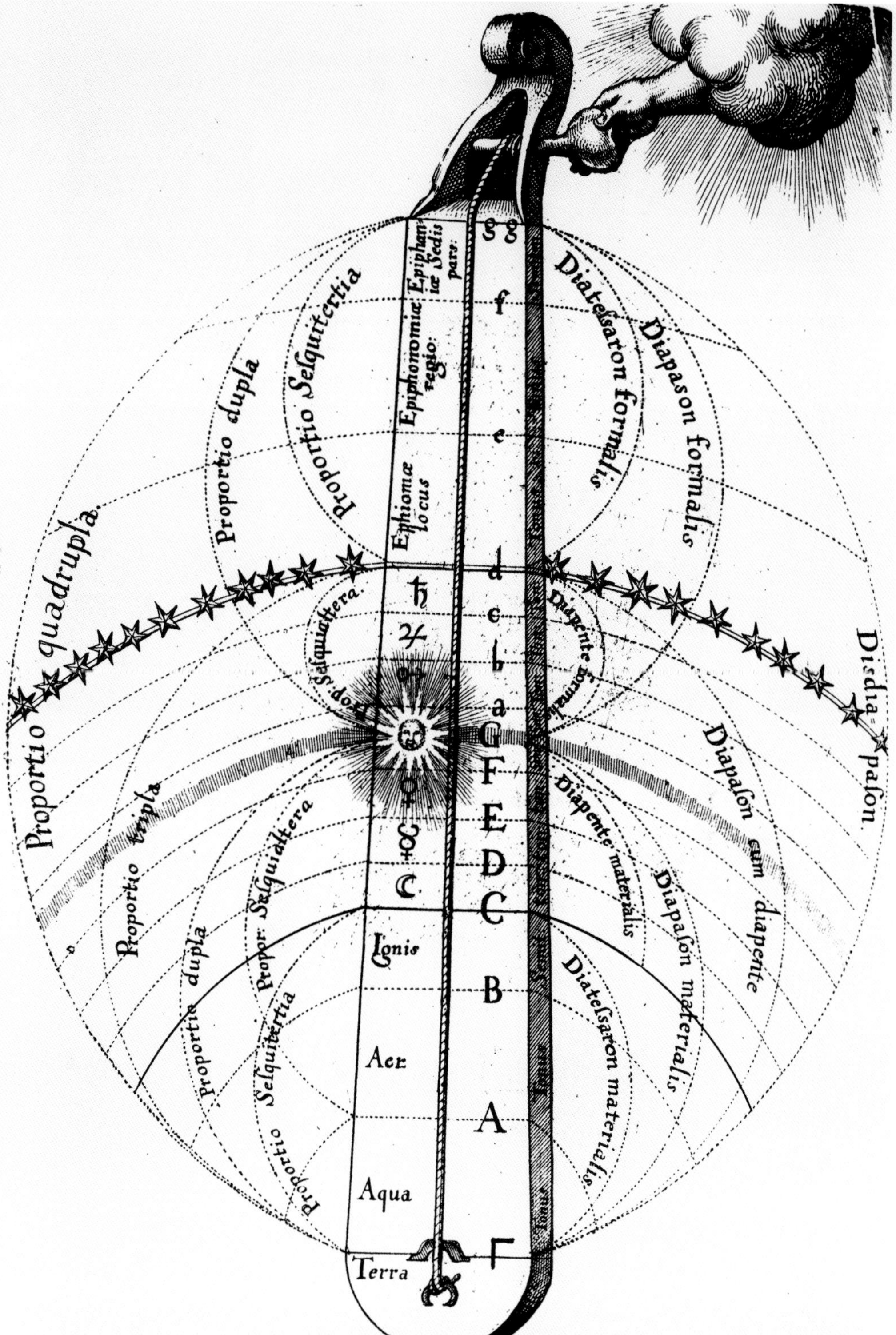

Proportio quadrupla
Proportio dupla
Proportio Sesquitertia
Epiphaniæ Sedis pars
Epiphonomiæ regio
Epiphomæ locus
Diatessaron formalis
Diapason formalis
Disdiapason
Proportio Sesquialtera
Diapente formalis
Prop: Sesquialtera
Proportio tripla
Diapason cum diapente
Diapente materialis
Proportio dupla
Propor: Sesquialtera
Diapason materialis
Diatessaron materialis
Proportio Sesquitertia
Ignis
Aer
Aqua
Terra
gg
f
e
d
c
b
a
G
F
E
D
C
B
A
Γ

Zelotypia.

Democritus Abderites.

Solitudo.

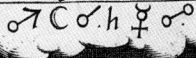

THE
ANATOMY OF
MELANCHOLY.

*What it is, With all the kinds causes,
Symptomes, Prognostickes, & severall cures of it.*

*In three Partitions, with their severall
Sections, members & subsections.*

*Philosophically, Medicinally,
Historically, opened & cut vp.*

BY.

Democritus Junior.

*With a Satyricall Preface, Conducing
to the following Discourse.*

*The thirde Edition, corrected and
augmented by the Author.*

Omne tulit punctum, qui miscuit vtile dulci.

Inamorato.

Hypocondriacus.

Superstitiosus.

Democritus   Junior

Maniacus.

Oxford
Printed for
Henry Cripps.

1628   Blon fe.

Borago.

Helleborus.

1628

In *The Anatomy of Melancholy*, Robert Burton collected all the knowledge of his time on the subject of depression. The emblems in the frontispiece symbolise various aspects of melancholy, like hypochondria, superstition or madness.

1636

Musical theory was one of the research fields of the French monk Marin Mersenne. In his book *Harmonicorum Libri XII*, he analysed the nature of sound. The work contains numerous diagrams, amongst others about the tuning of various instruments.

A. Munero.	B. Auxilium fero.	C. Irascar.	D. Demonstro non habere.
E. Castigo.	F. Pugno.	G. Confido.	H. Impedio.
I. Recommendo.	K. Officiosè duco.	L. Impatientiā prodo.	M. Sollicitè cogito.
N. Pudet.	O. Adoro.	P. Conscientèr affirmo.	Q. Pœnitentiā ostendo.
R. Indignatione timeo.	S. Data fide promitto.	T. Reconcileo.	V. Suspicionē et odiū noto.
W. Honoro.	X. Reservatione saluto.	Y. Furacitatem noto.	Z. Benedico.

Richard Saul Wurman 41—60

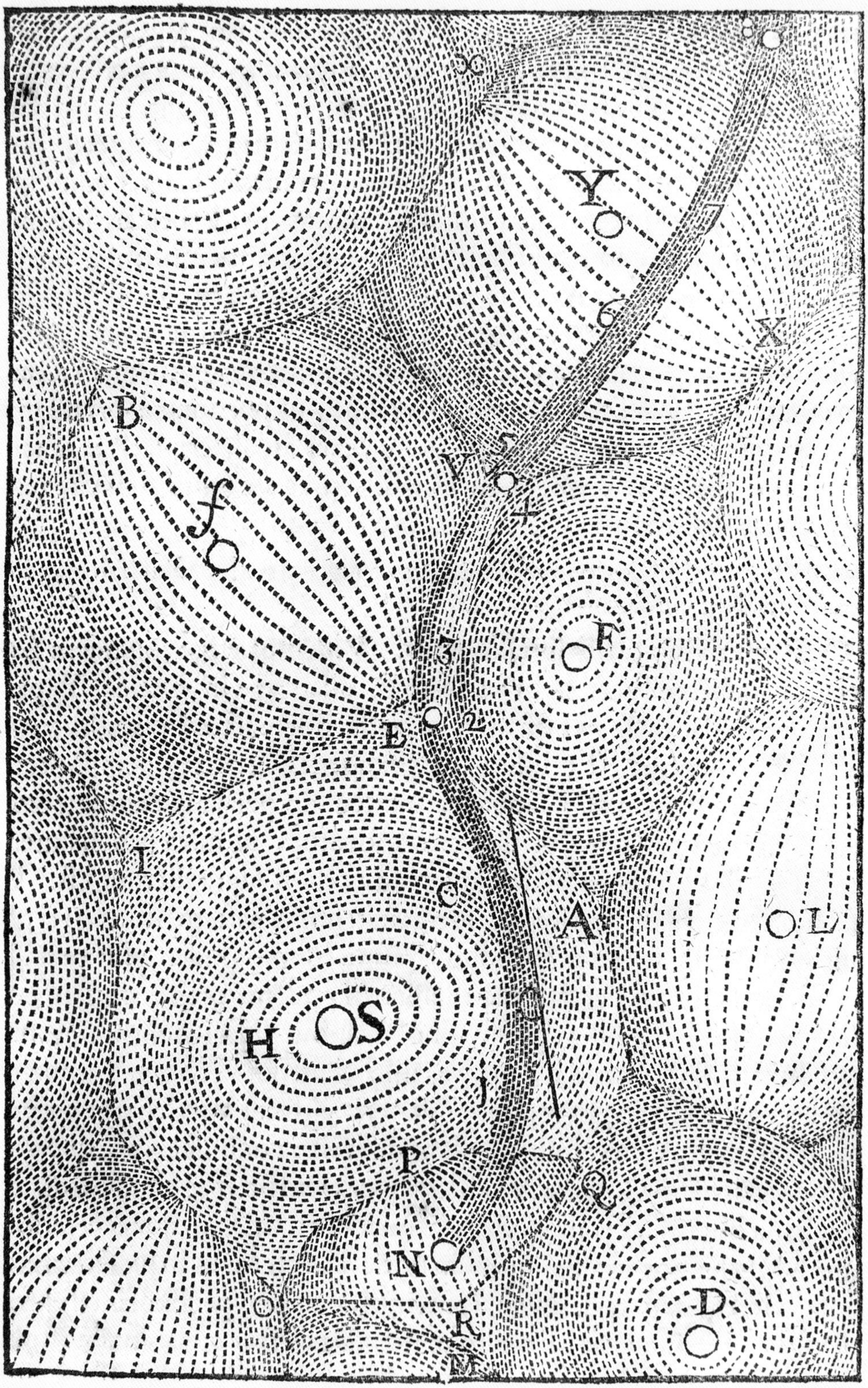
Y
7
6
X
B
S
V
f
4
F
3
E
2
I
C
A
L
S
H
P
Q
N
D
R
M

How I strive to understand what it is like not to understand

Richard Saul Wurman

There is a tsunami of data that is crashing on to the beaches of the civilized world. This is a tidal wave of unrelated, growing data formed in bits and bytes, coming in an unorganized, uncontrolled, incoherent cacophony of foam. It's filled with flotsam and jetsam. It's filled with the sticks and bones and shells of inanimate and animate life. None of it is easily related; none of it comes with any organizational methodology.

As it washes up on our beaches, we see people in suits and ties skipping along the shoreline, men and women in fine shirts and blouses dressed for business. We see academics, designers and government officials, all getting their shoes wet and slowly submerging in the dense trough of stuff. Their trousers and slacks soaked, they walk stupidly into the water, smiling – a false smile of confidence and control. The tsunami is a wall of data – data produced at greater and greater speed, greater and greater amounts to store in memory, amounts that double, it seems, with each sunset. On tape, on disks, on paper, sent by streams of light bouncing off the cloud, careening through the ether of Wi-Fi, 3G, 4G, G squared. Faster, more and more and more Twitters, texts and Facebooking. They nod their heads and say, "Yes, this is important, this is good stuff. The person sitting next to me, sitting in the next office down the aisle, they understand it, so I will smile, making believe I understand it too."

These same people read their newspapers, their iPhone, iPad, their smart-this or smart-that, thinking they understand the issues of the day, whether it's the recession, depression, windfall or downfall, the healthcare debacle, national debt or international debt, taxes, the balance or the imbalance, trade, the dollar more valuable-good? Less valuable-good? They nod their heads, knee-jerking to key words in headlines, but unable to tell anybody else, including themselves, the essence of any issue.

All day, from morning at home, to workday lunches to dinner at night, out loud or to themselves, they "uh-huh, uh-huh, uh-huh", making believe they understand a reference to a name, a reference to a fact, the references to knowledge that supposedly makes the world coherent. They "uh-huh" some friend, some teacher, a boss, a peer when a book or movie or magazine article, or piece of machinery, or software, or hardware is discussed. They "uh-huh" everybody because they were taught when they were young that it is not good to look stupid, that it is not good to say "I don't know", it is not good to ask questions, not good to focus on failure. Instead, the rewards come from acknowledging or answering everything with "I know". So they ask each other "keepin' busy"?

You're supposed to look smart in our society. You are supposed to gain expertise and to sell it as the means of moving ahead in your career. You are supposed to focus on what you know how to do, and then do it better and better. You're supposed to revel in some niche of ability. That is where the rewards are supposed to come from.

Of course, when you sell your expertise – and what I mean by sell is to move ahead in a corporation, or sell an idea to a publisher, or a script to a producer, or sell an ability to a client – when you sell your expertise, by definition, you're

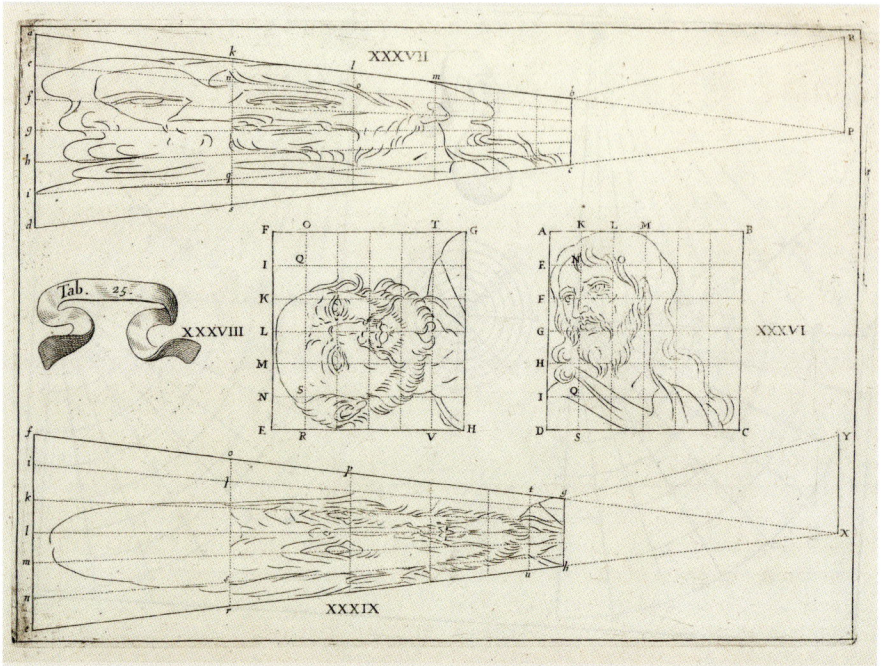

selling from a limited repertoire. However, when you sell your ignorance, when you sell your desire to learn about something, when you sell your desire to create and explore and navigate paths to knowledge and understanding, when you sell your *curiosity* – you sell from a bucket with an infinitely deep bottom that represents an unlimited repertoire. And, you sell in a way that's not intimidating, in a way that joins the explanation to the fascination that comes with that understanding.

How opposite is our life from what we have been taught. Our educational system is based on the memorization of things we're not interested in, bulimically spewed out on a paper called a test, and then forgotten. We learn to use our short-term memory rather than long-term memory. Many of our interests are shunted aside. The teenagers' interest in music, movies, games, cars and sports are looked on as second-rate themes for their lives instead of embraced as connections to all knowledge and wisdom. The car connects to the history of transportation, to our road systems, to our cities and our highways. It connects to the balance of payments and economics around the world.

To steel and iron, and steel construction, and plastics and design. It connects to physics and mathematics and chemistry. It connects to foreign languages and culture. To medicine and governmental policy. And, all the things the car connects to connect to everything else. So do sports. And so does entertainment, which connects to technologies of all sorts, to design and hardware and software and information. Information is validated by understanding. We are what we understand.

We remember what we are interested in. That is the definition of learning.

If I throw 140,000 words randomly on the floor, I wouldn't call it a dictionary. However, if I attach a phrase of meaning to each word, and organize them alphabetically, I could. In addition, if I group those words by meanings on the same subject, it is the beginning of an encyclopedia: a book organized both by alphabet and category. The ability to find something goes hand-in-hand with how well it's organized and the way by which it is organized. We choose to organize the dictionary alphabetically, and for most of us, most of the time, that's a useful organizing principle.

1638

In his book about the applications of perspective, the French mathematician Jean François Niceron described the construction of distorted images. The illustration shows the perspectival transformation of two portraits into an anamorphosis.

Page 40 / **1644**

The English physician John Bulwer published a treatise on gestures, which he considered a universal expression of human reason. The graphics each show one example and label it with what it expresses, like remorse, shame or confidence.

Page 42 / **1668**

The philosopher René Descartes was convinced that there is no empty space and that the universe is filled with matter. This graphic illustrates how elementary particles gather around the fixed stars. The thick line shows the course of a comet.

In fact, the alphabet is the only organizing principle that we actually have to learn. Because the alphabet was not given to us by God. Alphabets change with languages: the Russian alphabet is different from English, in Japan it is different again. For us, the alphabet is a learned order of 26 letters. The 26 letters have no functional sequence, but have proved useful in the evolution of our literate society. It really works quite well and it is one of our acceptable ways of organizing information. Now we could organize dictionary words by groups. All words that have to do with climate or weather could be together, all words that have to do with automobiles or speed or traffic could be together, all words about health and well-being could be lumped in a group. Therefore, great groups of these words could have one or another category as their organizing principle. In turn, the categories could be organized alphabetically, with words about automobiles in that category in the beginning under the "A's", and words about animals and zoology under "A" and "Z".

Some things are best organized by where they are. The thousands of roads and sites and towns and bodies of water are best organized by location on a map. We want to be able to find those places that are immediately around us as we look on a map. We certainly don't want to drive across France alphabetically. We don't want the United States in an atlas organized with Alabama first, and Alaska next, and Washington last, because we don't drive that way. That's not how we find where we're going, or how we find something.

1658

The Bohemian philosopher Comenius developed a pictorial system of education. His book *Orbis sensualium pictus* was the first illustrated children's encyclopaedia. Individual elements in the images are labelled and explained, e.g. musical instruments in this example.

1704

In his treatise *Opticks*, Isaac Newton demonstrated among other things that sunlight consists of coloured components. The diagrams above show the refraction of beams of white light in prisms and the succession of the spectral colours.

ca. 1724

In 1715, Edmond Halley succeeded in precisely predicting a solar eclipse. He produced a map with the expected path of the moon's shadow over England. Later, this map was augmented with data about a second eclipse which took place in 1724.

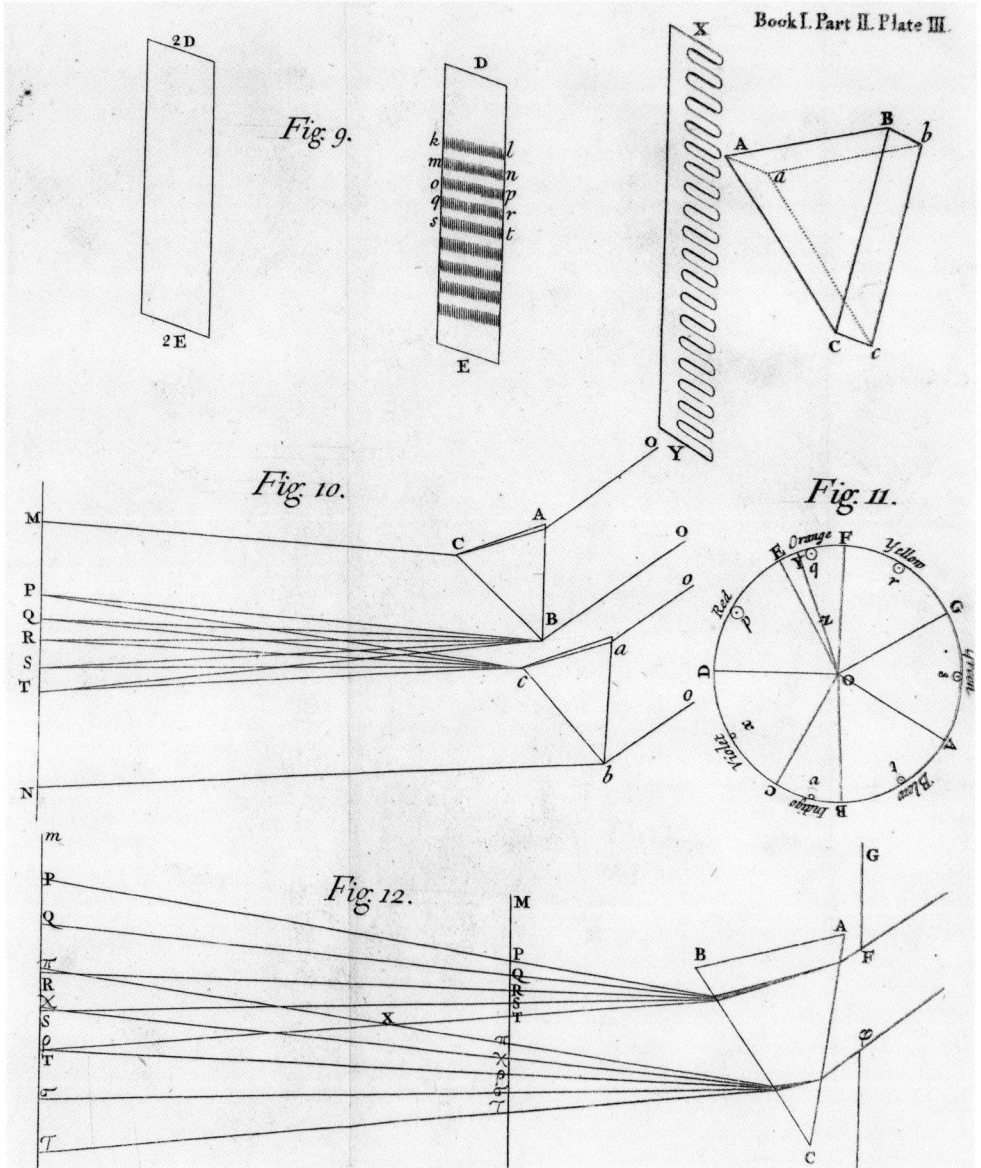

A Description of the Passage of the Shadow of the Moon over England

In the Total Eclipse of the Sun on the 11th day of May 1724 in the Evening. Together with the Passage of the Shadow as it was Observ'd in the last Total Eclipse of 1715. By Dr E. Halley, R.S.S. Astr. Roy.

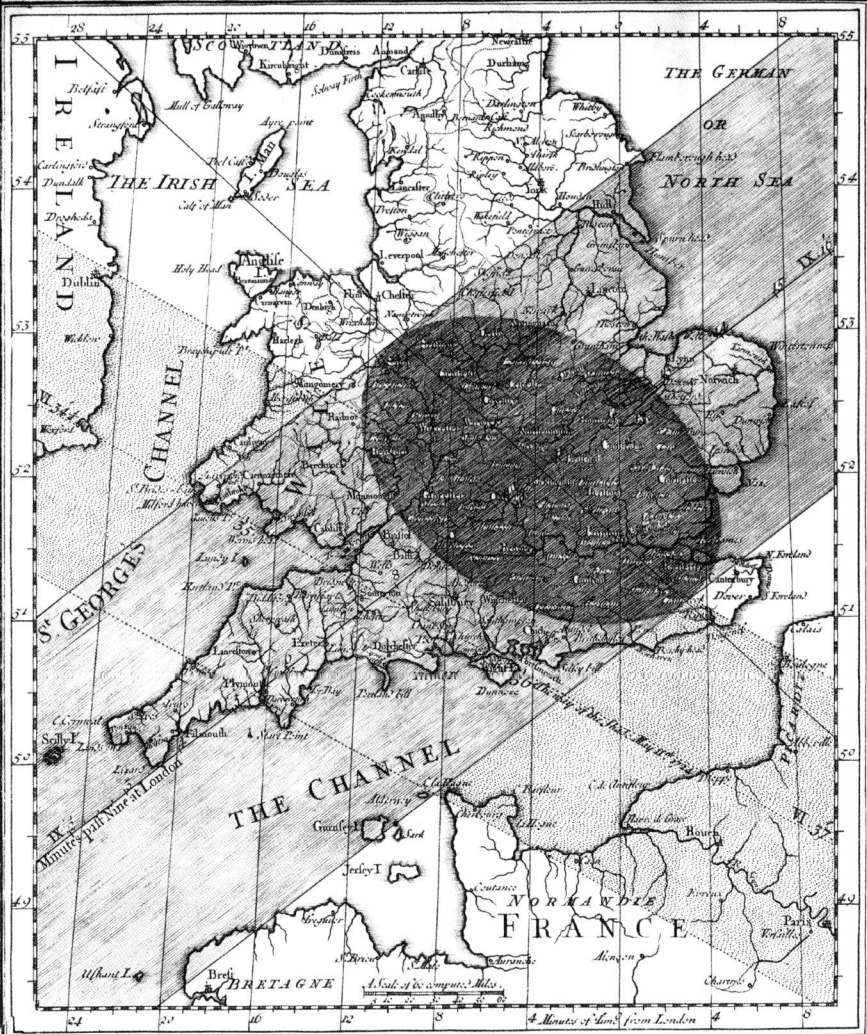

THE GERMAN OR NORTH SEA

IRELAND

THE IRISH SEA

SCOTLAND

ST GEORGES CHANNEL

THE CHANNEL

NORMANDIE FRANCE

BRETAGNE

A Scale of 60 English Miles.

Minutes past Nine at London

Minutes of Time from London

Since the Publication of our Predictions of this Eclipse has had the desired effect, and many curious Persons have been excited thereby to communicate their Observations from most parts of the Kingdom, we thought it might not be unacceptable to represent after the same manner the passage of the Shade as it really happened; whereby it will appear that tho' our Numbers pretend not to be altogether perfect, yet the correction they need is very small.

At London the Eclipse was carefully Observed to begin at 8h. 6' mane, and to become Total at 9h. 9'. It continued Total 3' 23", and ended at 10h. 20'. And by the Accounts we have received from abroad, the Center of the Shade past nearly over Plymouth, Exeter, Buckingham and Huntingdon, leaving Bath and Lynn a little on the left, and Oxford and Ely on the right. The Southern limit past over Cranbrook in Kent, leaving Newhaven and Canterbury a very little without: And the Northern limit entered on the Coast of Wales in St Bride's-bay, & left England near Flamborough-head, all which the Map more particularly describes. The greater diameter of y Shade having been 180 English Miles or Minutes, and y lesser 110.

The Numbers on the middle parallel lines in our former, denote y place of y Center of y Shade at so many minutes past Nine at London. By help of this and of y other diameter of y shaded Oval conjugate to y on y y Center moved passing over y places where the greatest Obscurity was at y same instant as at London, we may very nearly find y time of y greatest darkness at any other place in y Map. For drawing a line parallel to this conjugate diameter thro' y proposed place, it will cross y way of y Shade at y minute of y greatest Obscurity reckon'd as at London, and by allowing y difference of Meridians, at y place itself. Thus for example, the greatest Eclipse will be found at York at 9h. 10', at Dublin 8h. 42¼', at Brest 8h. 43¾'. After y same manner may y time of Total Darkness be had, by drawing a line parallel to y way of y Shade by y Place proposed. For as much of that line as falls within y shadowed Oval, measur'd on the Scale of minutes, will shew how long that place continued within the true Shade quam proxime.

We give you likewise y transit of y Shade, as it will pass over y West of England in y Eclipse y will be this June 1724 May 11. P.M. in w y Northern limit passes very near Dublin & Oxford. But it will scarce reach London where it begins at 6h. 39', is greatest at 6h. 55', & ends at 7h. 27' in y Evening.

Tab: Perspective

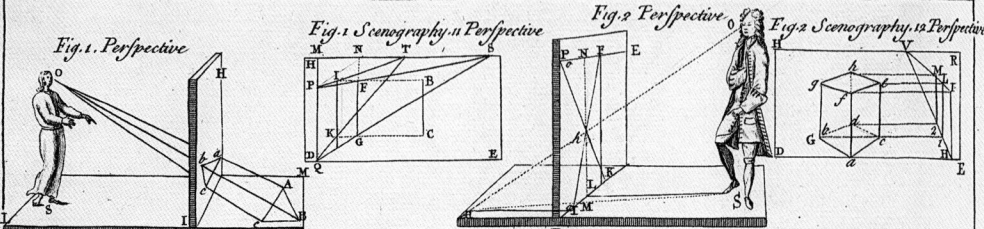

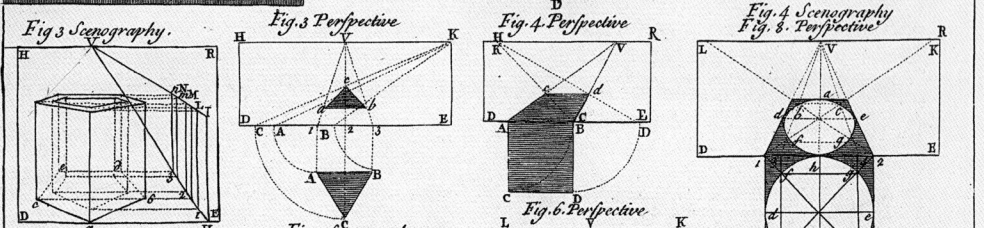

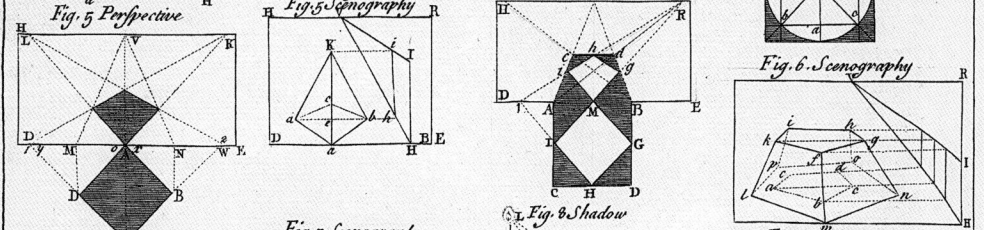

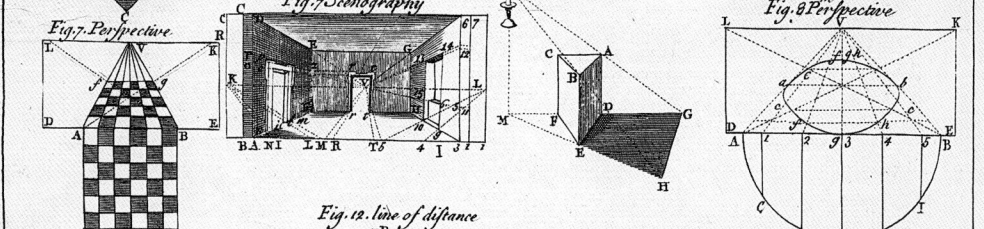

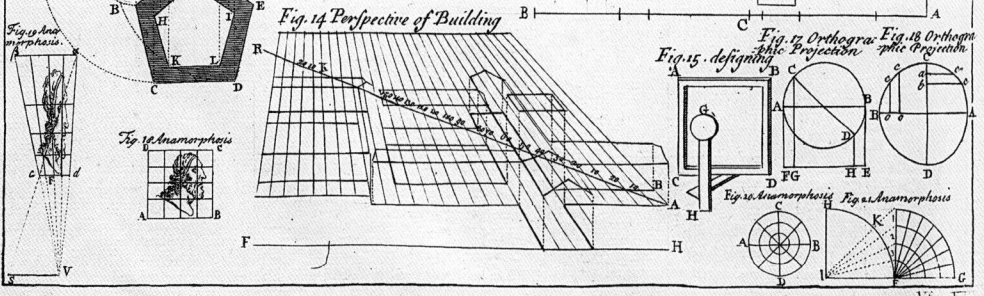

Fig. 1. Perspective

Fig. 1. Scenography. 11 Perspective

Fig. 2. Perspective

Fig. 2. Scenography. 12 Perspective

Fig. 3. Scenography.

Fig. 3. Perspective

Fig. 4. Perspective

Fig. 4. Scenography
Fig. 8. Perspective

Fig. 5. Perspective

Fig. 5. Scenography

Fig. 6. Perspective

Fig. 6. Scenography

Fig. 7. Perspective

Fig. 7. Scenography

Fig. 8. Shadow

Fig. 9. Perspective

Fig. 10. Perspective.

Fig. 12. line of distance

Fig. 13. Orthography of Building

Fig. 19. Anamorphosis

Fig. 14. Anamorphosis

Fig. 14. Perspective of Building

Fig. 15. designing

Fig. 17. Orthographic Projection

Fig. 18. Orthographic Projection

Fig. 20. Anamorphosis

Fig. 21. Anamorphosis

1728

The *Cyclopedia*, published by Ephraim Chambers from 1728, was the first comprehensive dictionary written in English. It contained several tables with graphics and diagrams. This example demonstrates the mathematical construction of perspectival depictions.

As I looked into the organization of information, I realized that there were only five ways to do it. They can be remembered by the acronym LATCH: (L) by location, (A) by alphabet, (T) by time (many museum shows are organized by timeline; the famous timeline by Charlie Eames, created for his film *The World of Franklin and Jefferson*, was probably one of the best ever devised), (C) by category (the way department stores are organized), and (H) by hierarchy, from the largest to the smallest of something, from the reddest to the lightest red, from the densest to the least dense, and so on.

These are all examples of information architecture: the building of information structures that allow others to understand. But the structures of information go well beyond basic organization. Many principles of clarity can be employed. For example, you only understand something new relative to something you already understand, whether visually, verbally, or numerically. Something will have an understandable size if it is related to the size of something you know. This is easy to see when viewing a photograph of a building that seems to have no human scale. Or visiting a painting and being surprised by its size, because all the reproductions of it are not relative to a human being. Scale always relates to us.

Well, why am I going into the organization of information in such detail? Just to show that thoughtful structuring of information is an essential skill that a graphic designer, information architect, or information designer needs to have in his or her repertoire. There is not a single school with a degree program called *Understanding* or *The Question*.

In 1962, nearly 50 years ago, I produced my first book with plans of 50 of the world's cities, all drawn to the same scale. Nobody had done that before. Five years later I created an urban atlas, again with all maps and legends and statistical analysis in the same scale, the same weighing of information. Now in 2011, I am revisiting the comparative information that affects the 51% of the world's population that live in urbanized areas (according to the United Nations), which is predicted to increase to 70% in the next few decades. This move to urbanization is undoubtedly the greatest megatrend of the 21st century, which makes the inability of city-to-city conversation even more inexplicable.

It is understandably counterintuitive to believe any of the following:

- No two cities in the world draw their maps to the same scale.
- No two cities in the world use the same map legends.
- There is no standardized method for collecting information or what is collected.
- The names of land use on legends vary widely. Actually there are hundreds of different names relative to residential, commercial, light commercial, recreational and cemetery uses.
- There are no standard ways to display information which break it down according to category or by incidence of occurrence. In verbal language (if this information were

EVROPA
Poly Glotta

Linguarum Genealogiam exhibens, una cum Literis, scribendiqz modis, Omnium Gentium.

Gothica
Atta unsak ψu in himinam veihnai namo ψein

Norwegica
Fader uor þu som ert a himnum, helgest hitt Nafn. Gothica

Picto Scotica
Vpen ja a þen hic anþ in heofe naf.

Anglo Saxon
Fæder ure þe eart on heofenum.

Wallica

Belgica
Onse Vader dit dastu in de Hemelen uwen naam werde gehey ligt.

GALLICA
Nostre Pere, qui es és Cieux. Ton Nom soit Sanctifié.

Foro-Juliana
Pari nestri chees in Cyl. See sanctificad la to Nom.

Helvetia
Deutsch

ITALICA
Padre nostro, sei ne cieli. Sanctifi...

Biscaina Cantabrica
Cure aita cerne tan aicena. Sanctifica bedi sure Icena. Tarracon:

O HISPANICA
Padre nuestro, que estas en los cielos. Sanctificado sea el tu Nombre.

LVSITANIA
Padre nosso, que...

Mauritania

Olyssippo — Fret: Herculeum — Mare Cantabricum — Majorca — Corsica — Sardinia — **MARE**

Alphabet tables (column headers)

Litt. Scythica.	Graeca vetus.	Littera.	Marcomannorum.	Runica.	Moeso Gothica.	Picto Hybernica.
N. a	A.	—	a
b	B.	—	b
g	—	c
d	—	d
h	—	e
v	—	f
s	—	z. h
ch	—	h
i	—	i
c	—	l
L	—	m
m	—	n. x. x
n	—	o
s	—	p
o	—	q
p	—	r
k. q	—	s
r	—	t
s	—	y. u
T	—	z. v
x	—	y. th

Latinae vers. m. Angl. Sax.

A.		A.
B.		B.
C.		C.
D.		D.
E.		E.
F.		F.
G.		G.
H.		H.
I.		I.
K.		K.
L.		L.
M.		M.
N.		N.
O.		O.
P.		P.
Q.		Q.
R.		R.
S.		S.
T.		T.
U. V.		U.
W.		X. ch.
X.		Y.
Y.		Þ.
Z.		Z.

PR O G EN I (map region)

Lower alphabet table

Hunorum elementa	a.	b.	cz. cs.	d. e. he	f.	gh. gr.	h.	i. k.
Sclavonico Cyrillica.	a. d.	b.	v. c.	d. e. sh.	ph.	g.	ch.	i.
Glagolitico Illyrica.	a.		v. c.	d. sh. e	ph.	g.	ch.	i.
Hetrusco Eugubina.	a.	b.	c.	d.	e.	v. s.	g. ch.	i.

Opera Godofr. Henselii delineata

Lapponica
Isa meidhen joko
oledh tajuahitza
uhetta olkohon sun
Rimesi
ca

NOVA
ZEMBLICÆ
ОꙂ Ф Е Н Ц Ч
Ц Р Ϩ Е Ц П Н Х Н Е
Б Е Ϩ П О Ц Ч Л Ꙋ Ϩ Е П
М Е Ϩ О Ꙗ Е.
Otse naz icse zi na
nebey pozuetytze ime
ture.

Finnonica
Isa meiden joca
olet tai Maisa
Pyhittetty stolcon
sinum Nymes

RVSSICA
ОꙋꙂ Н Х Ш П Ꙁ Ж Е
Ѥ С Ц П Ꙋ Н Е Ϩ Е Ꙑ Ц
П О Ꙁ Ꙋ Ϩ Ꙁ Н Ц Ꙋ Е И М Е Ϩ О Ꙋ Е.
h.e.
Otse nash ishe
jeszi unebeszih.
Posuetysze ime
toye.

SCLAVONICA

Tartarica

Tewe musukurseyesi
dangus Szveskis
vardas Tawo.

POLONICA
Oicze nász, ktorys
jest v niebiesiech.
Swiec Ise imie
tvoie.

Bohemia HVNGARICA
MiAlyanckivagyaz
mennyekben.

Vien
SKLAVONICA

GRÆCA

TARTARIA Voci-
bus Teutonicis
Sclavonicis
mixta.

PONTVS EVXINVS

Græca Barbara
ΠΑΤΕΡΑ ΜΑΝ Ο ΡꙊ
ΕΙΣΑΙ ΕΙΣ ΤΟΥΣ ΘΥΡΑΝΟΥΣ
Α Σ ΕΙΝΑΙ ΑΓΙΑϹϺΕΝΟΝ
ΤΟ ΟϺΟΜΑ ΣΟΥ,

ASIA intra TAVRVM ab IONIBVS
HELLENICA Posteris
inhabitata.

Cyprus

Creta

MEDITERRANEVM

Excusa prostat in Officina Homanniana

Charact. Ruteniæ Ling.

Charact.	Rutenicæ	Ling.					
Λ λ.	A	О.о.	o	Ѣ	æ		
Б.b.	b	П π. П.	p	С.С.	ie		
К.ш.	w	Р.ρ.	r	Ю.Ꙋ.	iu		
Г Г.	g	G.C.	s	Ж.Ꙅ.	ius		
Д.д.	d	Ꙗ.Ϩ.	t	Ꙗ λ.	ia		
Е.Е.	e	У.ꙋ.ѵ.	u	ꙃ	ks		
Ж.Ѱ.sch		Ф.Ꙃ.	ph		x		
З.ς.	s	Х.	ch	Ψ.Ѱ.	ps		
Ꙁ.ᵹ.	sf	Ѿ.Ꙍ.	o	Ѳ.Ꙍ.	ph		
Ин.	i	Ц.Ϥ.Ϩ.	z	Ѵ.	i		
I.i.	i	Ч.ч.	tz		ѵ y		
К.к.	k	Ш.ш.sch		Господи			
Λ.Ʌ.	l	Щ.щ.tsch		Поми			
И.М.Ᵹ. m.		Ѣ.ь.	je	лꙋ́			
Н.н.	n	Ꙑ.	ü				

Previous spread / **1741**
This early thematic map shows the geographical distribution of various languages, together with the characters of their alphabet. European countries are labelled with the Lord's Prayer written in their respective languages.

being described in text) category would correspond to a noun and incidence would be represented by a verb.
· And now to cap it all off, as every major city spills over its political borders, there exists no standard method for establishing these new edges.
· If you don't have a border or defined area, you can't collect data and describe density, you can't compare. Cities can't talk to each other, learn or understand each other.
· Understanding precedes action.

My last point is a somewhat apocryphal look at movies, which in their earliest form archived stage shows. My iPad archives books and magazines and occasionally shows me a trumped-up version of a page turning. I am still waiting for the new modality – an iPad that can nod, that I can talk to, that upon my request automatically changes its degree of difficulty or intensity of content, that has nuance, that talks back and suggests links and connections that help me in my waking dream: my journey to understanding.

My waking dream is to have a network of 20, 50, 100 urban observatories around the world. They would show live, real-time exhibitions of understandable information from city to city.

Imagine walking into such a place, and the first experience is to be immersed in whatever great festival or parade or light show that is occurring someplace else in the world. Then to the room of complete information about land use, economics, growth, displayed on a globe which shows the changes of our blue planet:

its urbanization, interaction, weather patterns, earthquakes, floods, pestilence, war, but also the migration of people to the largest cities around the world. And this globe would also be animated by changes in borders and explorations. An aquarium, a planet earth focused on people as opposed to frogs in the wilderness. Of course as urbanization grows, wilderness diminishes, so that yang will not be forgotten.

I believe we are at this cusp.

A first toe in the warm bath of this new modality.

Richard Saul Wurman is an architect, information architect, author of dozens of books and founder of the TED, TEDMED and eg conferences.

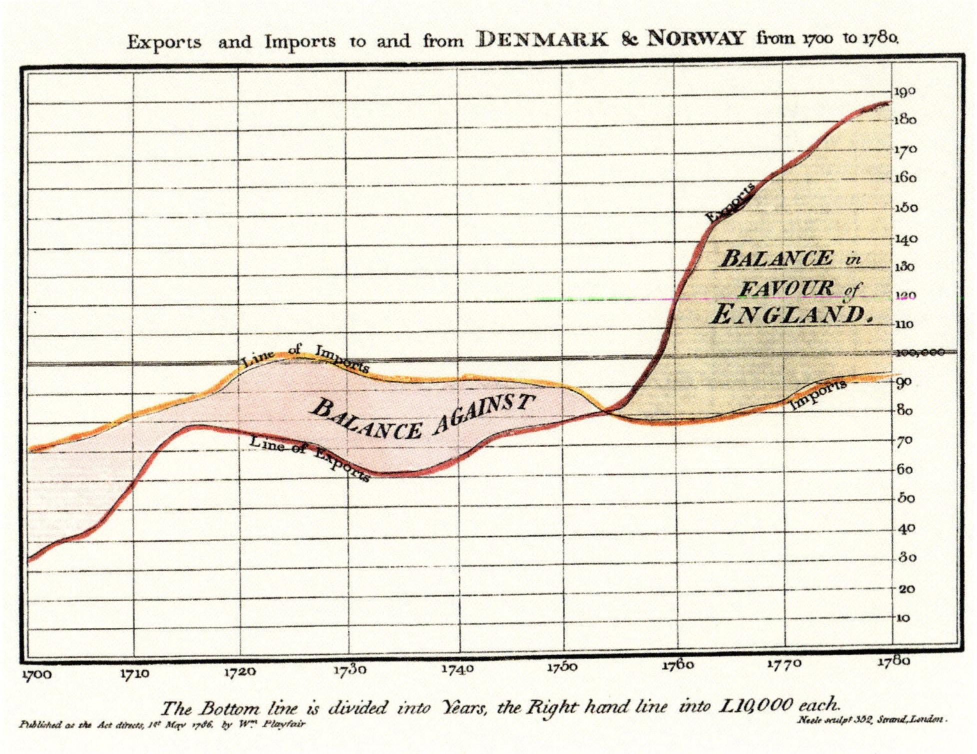

Exports and Imports to and from DENMARK & NORWAY from 1700 to 1780.

BALANCE in FAVOUR of ENGLAND.

Line of Imports

BALANCE AGAINST

Line of Exports

Imports

The Bottom line is divided into Years, the Right hand line into L10,000 each.

Published as the Act directs, 1st May 1786, by Wm Playfair.

Neele sculpt 352, Strand, London.

1786

The Scottish economist and engineer William Playfair is considered to be one of the inventors of statistical bar and pie charts. This example from his 1786 *Commercial and Political Atlas* shows the English foreign trade balance with Norway and Denmark.

Following spread / **ca. 1820**

With this "relational map" from ca. 1820, the statistician Friedrich August Crome developed a display format to compare the very different German federal countries in regard to their size, economical and military power.

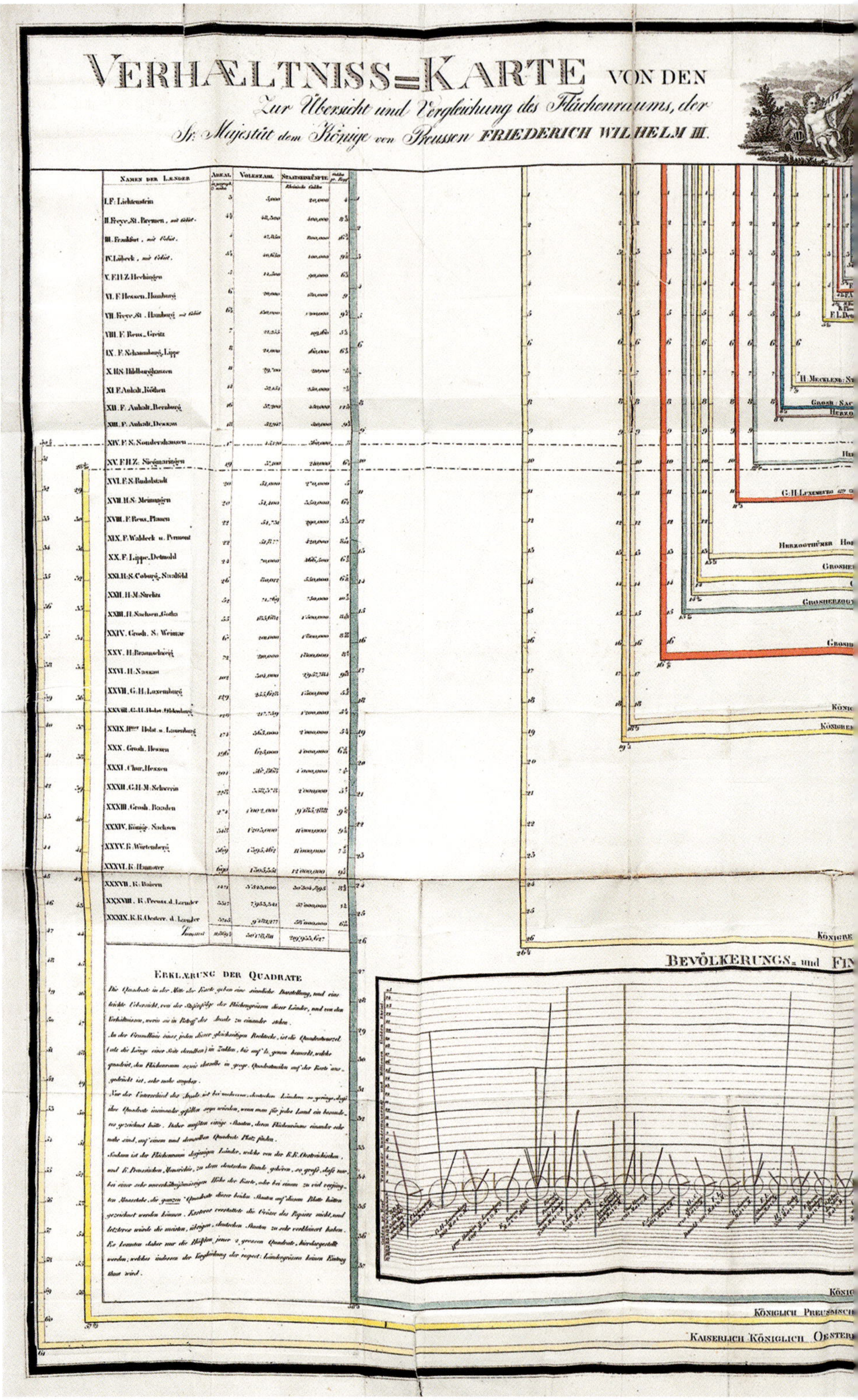
VERHÆLTNISS=KARTE VON DEN
Zur Übersicht und Vergleichung des Flächenraums, der
Sr. Majestät dem Könige von Preussen FRIEDERICH WILHELM III.
NAMEN DER LÆNDER
AREAL
VOLKSZAHL
STAATSEINKÜNFTE
I. F. Lichtenstein
II. Freye St. Bremen, mit Gebiet.
III. Frankfurt, mit Gebiet.
IV. Lübeck, mit Gebiet.
V. F. H. Z. Hechingen
VI. F. Hessen Homburg
VII. Freye St. Hamburg mit Gebiet
VIII. F. Reus Greitz
IX. F. Schaumburg Lippe
X. H. S. Hildburghausen
XI. F. Anhalt Köthen
XII. F. Anhalt Bernburg
XIII. F. Anhalt Dessau
XIV. F. S. Sondershausen
XV. F. H. Z. Siegmaringen
XVI. F. S. Rudolstadt
XVII. H. S. Meiningen
XVIII. F. Reus Plauen
XIX. F. Waldeck u. Pyrmont
XX. F. Lippe Detmold
XXI. H. S. Coburg Saalfeld
XXII. H. M. Strelitz
XXIII. H. Sachsen Gotha
XXIV. Grosh. S. Weimar
XXV. H. Braunschweig
XXVI. H. Nassau
XXVII. G. H. Luxemburg
XXVIII. G. H. Holst. Oldenburg
XXIX. Hert. Holst. u. Lauenburg
XXX. Grosh. Hessen
XXXI. Chur Hessen
XXXII. G. H. M. Schwerin
XXXIII. Grosh. Baaden
XXXIV. König. Sachsen
XXXV. K. Wirtemberg
XXXVI. K. Hannover
XXXVII. K. Baiern
XXXVIII. K. Preuss. d. Lænder
XXXIX. K. K. Oesterr. d. Lænder
Summa
ERKLÆRUNG DER QUADRATE
Die Quadrate in der Mitte der Karte geben eine sinnliche Darstellung, und eine leichte Uebersicht, von der Stufenfolge der Flächengrössen dieser Länder, und von den Verhältnissen, worin sie in Betreff der Areale zu einander stehen.
An der Grundlinie eines jeden dieser gleichseitigen Rechtecke, ist die Quadratwurzel (als die Länge einer Seite derselben) in Zahlen, bis auf ¼ genau bemerkt, welche quadrirt, den Flächenraum so wie derselbe in geogr. Quadratmeilen auf der Karte ausgedrückt ist, sehr nahe angeben.
Nur der Unterschied der Areale ist bei mehreren deutschen Ländern so gering, daß ihre Quadrate ineinander gefallen seyn würden, wenn man für jedes Land ein besonderes gezeichnet hätte. Daher mußten einige Staaten, deren Flächenräume einander sehr nahe sind, auf einem und demselben Quadrate Platz finden.
Sodann ist der Flächenraum derjenigen Länder, welche von der K.K. Oestreichischen, und K. Preussischen Monarchie, zu dem deutschen Bunde gehören, so groß, daß nur bei einer sehr unverhältnißmäßigen Höhe der Karte, oder bei einem zu viel verjüngten Maasstabe, die ganzen Quadrate dieser beiden Staaten auf diesem Blatte hätten gezeichnet werden können. Ersteres verstattete die Grösse des Papiers nicht, und letzteres würde die meisten, übrigen, deutschen Staaten zu sehr verkleinert haben. Es konnten daher nur die Hälften jener 2 grossen Quadrate, hierdargestellt werden; welches indessen der Vergleichung der respect: Ländergrössen keinen Eintrag thun wird.
H. MECKLENB. STR
GROSH. SAC
G. H. LUXEMBURG
HERZOGTHÜMER HOL
GROSHERZOGT
BEVÖLKERUNGS= und FIN
KÖNIGLICH PREUSSISCH
KAISERLICH KÖNIGLICH OESTERR

DEUTSCHEN BUNDESSTAATEN

Bevölkerung, der Staatseinkünfte u.s.w. dieser Länder.

alleruntertänigst zugeeignet von dem Verfasser, Dr. Aug. Fried. Wilh. Crome.

	Namen der Bundesstaaten	Militair Etat	Grundsläche in Dörfer	Grundsläche in Städte	Wahlstimmen in Plenar
1	I. K.K. Oestr. deutsche Länder	154,000	84,811	101,935	4
2	II. K. Preuss. deutsche Länder	1,30,000	79,334	108,300	4
3	III. K. Bayern	60,000	23,630	32,843	4
4	IV. K. Sachsen	16,000	11,650	18,263	4
5	V. K. Hanover	13,055	13,655	13,20	4
6	VI. K. Würtemberg	13,955	13,953	10,953	4
7	VII. Groh. Baden	10,000	10,010	11,000	3
8	VIII. Chur. Hessen	10,000	3,679	8,411	3
9	IX. Groh. Hessen	9,000	6,250	9,535	3
10	X. H Holstein u Lauenburg	4,700	3,610	4,843	3
11	XI. G.H. Lauenburg	7,700	7,216	7,070	3
12	XII. G.H. S. Weimar	1,600	1,000	3,003	
13	XIII. H. Sachsen. Gotha	1,600	1,636	2,783	
14	XIV. H. S. Meiningen	800	811	806	
15	XV. H. S. Hildburghausen	800	733	816	
16	XVI. H. S. Coburg. Saalfeld	630	860	1,000	
17	XVII. H. Braunschweig	2,000	2,096	3,111	2
18	XVIII. H. Nassau	3,000	3,630	4,160	2
19	XIX. G.H. M. Schwerin	7,323	3,024	3,376	2
20	XX. G.H. M. Strelitz	300	717	807	1
21	XXI. G.H. Holstein. Oldenburg	1,600	2,218	3,086	1
22	XXII. F. Anhalt. Dessau	800	839	794	1
23	XXIII. F. Anhalt. Bernburg	400	570	636	1
24	XXIV. F. Anhalt. Köthen	400	524	486	1
25	XXV. F. Schw. Sonderhausen	300	434	616	
26	XXVI. F. Schw. Rudolstadt	300	539	606	
27	XXVII. F.H. Z. Hechingen	270	141	116	
28	XXVIII. F.H. Z. Sigmaringen	180	370	386	
29	XXIX. F. Lichtenstein	80	90	83	
30	XXX. F. Reuss. Greiz	80	135	35,8	
31	XXXI. F. Reuss. Plauen	80	127	200	1
32	XXXII. F. Lippe. Detmold	500	700	1030	1
33	XXXIII. F. Lippe. Schaumburg	280	240	360	
34	XXXIV. F. Waldeck u. Pyrmont	500	710	773	
35	XXXV. F.H. Hamburg	80	600	600	
36	XXXVI. Frankfurt, mit Gebiet	300	179	75	
37	XXXVII. Lübeck, mit Gebiet	300	630	700	1
38	XXXVIII. Bremen, mit Gebiet	300	435	733	1
39	XXXIX. Hamburg, mit Gebiet	300	800	1,960	
	Summa	551,700	308,780	414,610	4

ERKLÄRUNG DER BEVÖLKERUNGS= UND FINANZ=
ÜBERSICHT VON DEUTSCHLAND.

Die unten auf die Karte befindlichen illuminirte Kreise, bezeichnen die Dichtigkeit der Bevölkerung, indem in der Flächenverhältniß der Raume angibt, auf welchem im Durchschnitt jedem einzelnen Staate, zum Menschen wohnen. Diese steht im vergleichbaren Verhältniss mit der Population, d.h. je grösser der Bevölkerung ist, desto kleiner ist der Kreis. z.B. für das G.H.Baum 2½ mal kleiner, als für das O.H.K. Stelle, ...

(weiterer erläuternder Text, teilweise unleserlich)

...ICHT von DEUTSCHLAND

... □ meile.
...UTSCHLAND 3307 □ meile.
...ER in DEUTSCHLAND 375 □ meile.

Fig. 1.

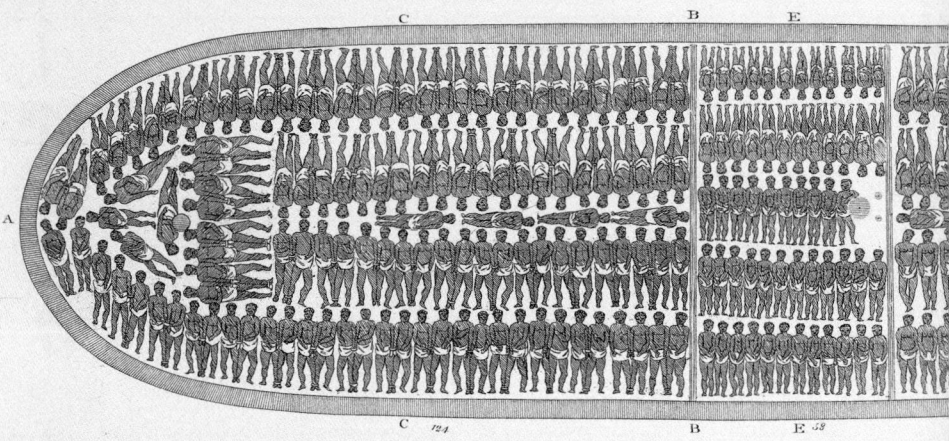

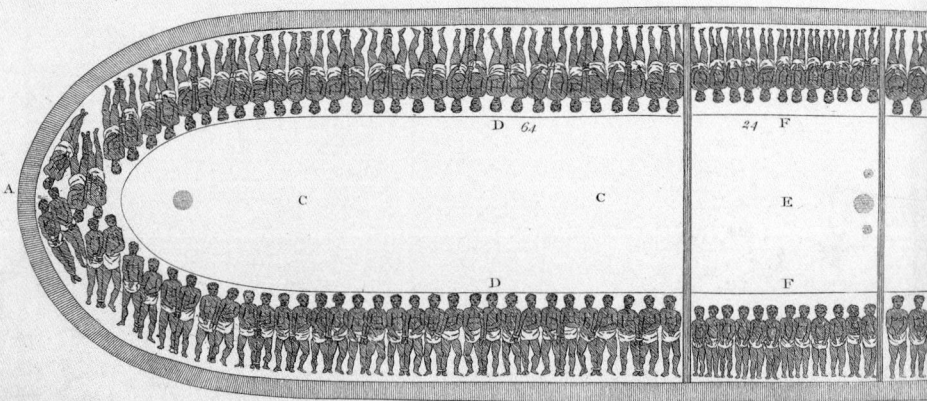

Pub. by J.

1808

English politician Thomas Clarkson was active in the fight against the slave trade and collected evidence for the inhumane treatment of slaves. In this diagram he illustrates how they were penned up for transportation.

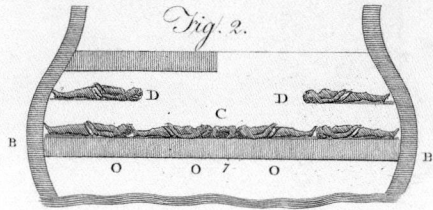

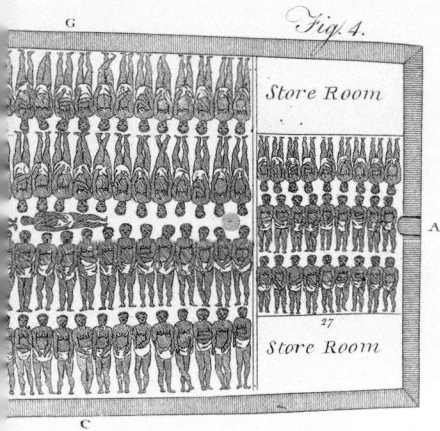

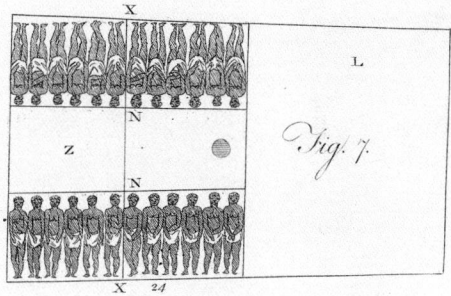

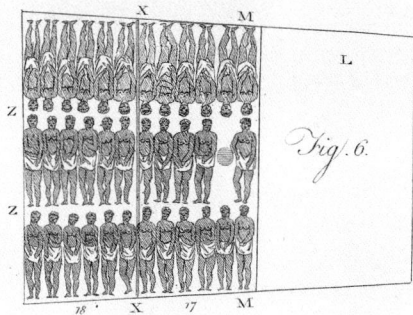

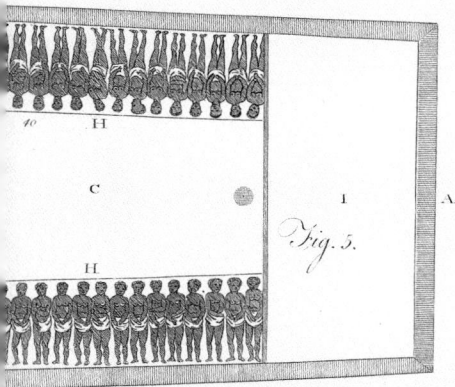

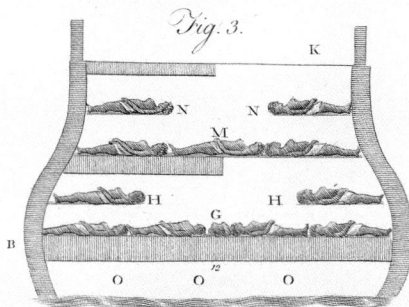

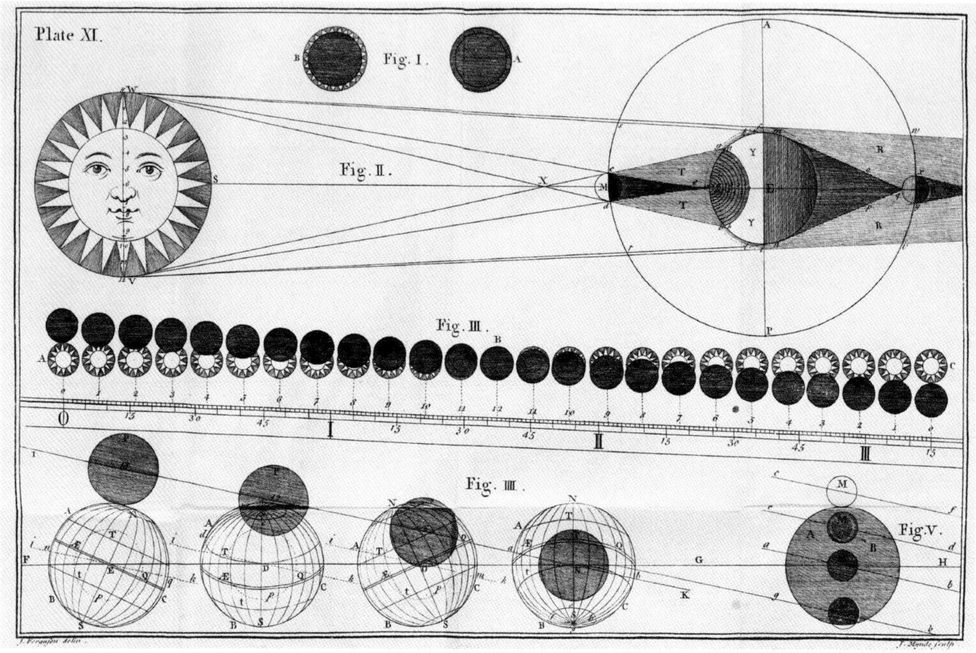

1756

This etching was published in the popular book *Astronomy Explained upon Newton's Principles* by the Scot James Ferguson. The diagrams show the alignments responsible for solar and lunar eclipses on Earth.

1760

In a magic square the sums of all rows, columns and diagonals are equal. It is constructed by systematically writing down ordered numerical sequences. This example by Benjamin Franklin dates from around 1760.

Pl. I.

A Magic Square of Squares.

200	217	232	249	8	25	40	57	72	89	104	121	136	153	168	185
58	39	26	7	250	231	218	199	186	167	154	135	122	103	90	71
198	219	230	251	6	27	38	59	70	91	102	123	134	155	166	187
60	37	28	5	252	229	220	197	188	165	156	133	124	101	92	69
201	216	233	248	9	24	41	56	73	88	105	120	137	152	169	184
55	42	23	10	247	234	215	202	183	170	151	138	119	106	87	74
203	214	235	246	11	22	43	54	75	86	107	118	139	150	171	182
53	44	21	12	245	236	213	204	181	172	149	140	117	108	85	76
205	212	237	244	13	20	45	52	77	84	109	116	141	148	173	180
51	46	19	14	243	238	211	206	179	174	147	142	115	110	83	78
207	210	239	242	15	18	47	50	79	82	111	114	143	146	175	178
49	48	17	16	241	240	209	208	177	176	145	144	113	112	81	80
196	221	228	253	4	29	36	61	68	93	100	125	132	157	164	189
62	35	30	3	254	227	222	195	190	163	158	131	126	99	94	67
194	223	226	255	2	31	34	63	66	95	98	127	130	159	162	191
64	33	32	1	256	225	224	193	192	161	160	129	128	97	96	65

B. Franklin inv. I. Ferguson delin.   J. Mynde sc.

The great Square is divided into 256 small squares; in which, all the numbers from 1 to 256 are so placed, as to have the following Properties.

1. The sum of all the 16 numbers, in any column, horizontal or vertical, is 2056.
2. The sum of half a column, either horizontal or vertical, is 1028, the half of 2056.
3. The sum in any oblique line ascending, added to that in the oblique line descending from it, is 2056.
4. The sum of all the numbers added together, in the 4 little squares next the 4 corners, is 2056.
5. If a square hole (as below) be cut in a piece of paper, of such a size as to take in just 16 of the small squares, and be laid upon any part of the great Square; the sum of all the 16 numbers seen through the hole will be 2056, the same as in any column.

The Hole

244	13	20	45
14	243	238	211
242	15	18	47
16	241	240	209

2056

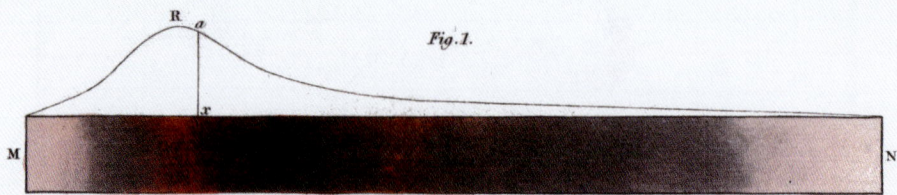

Fig.1.

Fig.2.

Fig.3.

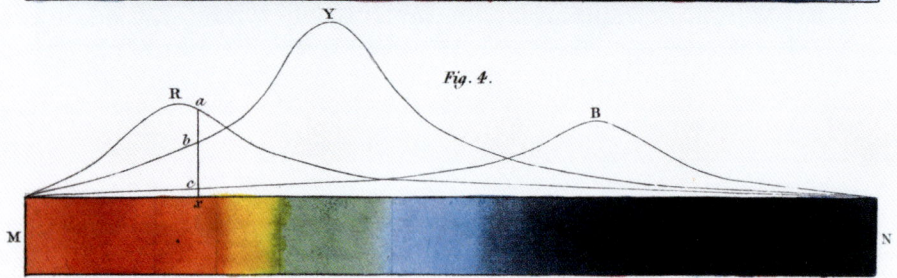

Fig.4.

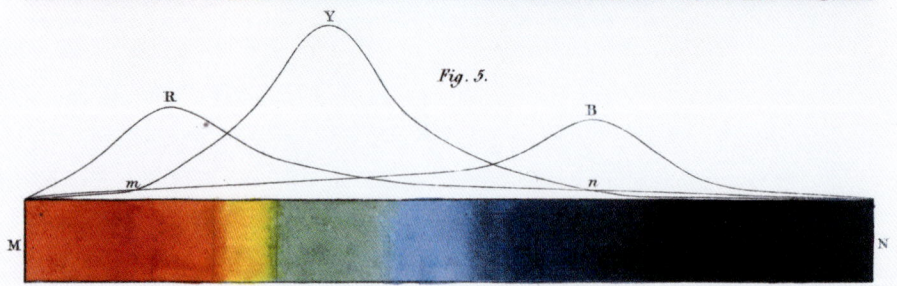

Fig.5.

Simon
Rogers
61—80

◦ Star

SUN

THE MOON'S ANGULAR DISTANCE
FROM A CERTAIN STAR $= 40°$
The Moon and Star are observed (allowance being made for parallax and refraction) at the required distance apart.
From Station B at 9 p.m. Local time
„ „ A . 6 . . . .
Difference 3 hours.
Consequently B is 45° (3×15 = 45) East of A.

Diurnal Rotation of the Earth on its Axis

in 24 hours — 360°

ECLIPSE OF THE MOON
Seen at C at 12(midnight) Local time
„ „ A . 6 . p.m. „ „
Difference 6 hours.
A therefore is 90° West of C.

MOON

OCCULTATION OF A STAR
BY THE MOON
Observations corrected for parallax
Seen from E at 6 a.m. Local time
„ „ D . 3 . . . .
Difference 3 hours.
Consequently E is 45° East of D.

The Planet
JUPITER

Satellite

◦ Star

THE LONGITUDE of a place is determined by comparing relative times under two different meridians. In consequence of the Earth's rotation upon its axis the Sun appears to move round the Earth from East to West in 24 hours. Places, therefore, to the Eastward of a given meridian have noon sooner, and those to the Westward later, by so much time as the Sun requires to pass over the interval between their meridians.

Each of the phenomena shown upon the diagram is seen *at the same instant* from all parts of the Earth at which it may be visible. The exact moment of the occurrence can be calculated in advance, and is stated in the Nautical Almanac in the local time of the meridian of Greenwich. So, then the difference between the observer's local time when any of these appearances happen and that stated in the Almanac will be the time required by

the Sun to pass between his meridan and that of Greenwich ; and being turned into degrees at the rate of 15° for 1 hour, will give his longitude East or West according as the local time may be the greater or the less. For example, suppose an eclipse of the Moon to begin according to the Almanac at 10 p.m., and that at the place of observation when the phenomenon happens, the *local* time is 6 p.m., the difference is 4 hours, or 60 degrees of longitude, and Westward of Greenwich. Again, an eclipse of one of Jupiter's Satellites is observed at 4 a.m., local time, when it occurs the time at Greenwich, as stated in the Almanac, is 2 a.m. The difference turned into degrees gives the observer's longitude thirty degrees East of Greenwich.

The longitude is also found by comparing *local* time with that of an accurate chronometer set to, and keeping, Greenwich time.

LONDON: JAMES REYNOLDS & SONS, 174, STRAND.

How data changed journalism

Simon Rogers

"Data journalism" or "computer-assisted reporting"? What is it? How do you describe it? Is it even real journalism? These are just two terms for the latest trend in journalism, a field combining spreadsheets, graphics, data analysis and the biggest news stories to dominate reporting in the last two years.

The WikiLeaks releases on Afghanistan, Iraq and the US embassy cables; the UK MPs' expenses scandal; the global recession; even the swine flu panic... reporting on all of those events was arguably only possible because of (and irrevocably changed by) the existence of reporters who are not afraid of maths, know how to use a spreadsheet, work with the latest web visualisation tools and – crucially – know what questions to ask.

What is data journalism? It reflects the new transparency movement spreading across the globe, from Washington DC to Sydney, via California, London, Paris and Spain. It's hard to know what came first: the data or the demand for it. Or maybe the two have grown symbiotically. But it seems there was a tipping point where a number of factors combined to form an unstoppable movement. I would argue they were:

- the widespread availability of data via the Internet
- easy-to-use spreadsheet packages on every home computer
- a growing interest in visualising data, to make it easier to understand
- some huge news stories we might never have heard of without data-based reporting

A crucial early step was taken when President Barack Obama, as one of his first legislative acts, announced the US government would launch a new site: data.gov. This was not a million years ago – only 2009.

Data.gov would be a single portal for government datasets, the spreadsheets hitherto published to deafening silence by individual government departments. Go to data.gov today and you will find an enormous amount of datasets covering everything from crime rates through agricultural planning to the latest population estimates. Some of the stuff is esoterically weird – you can get live data for US river levels, for instance; and some of it is dramatically interesting – the FBI's homicide data gives a breakdown of firearm murders by each US state, with details of which kind of gun was responsible.

The US was followed by countries across the world: Australia, New Zealand and in the UK data.gov.uk, launched by inventor of the worldwide web Sir Tim Berners-Lee. At a more local level, cities and state governments joined the race too: London, Toronto, Vancouver, New York, San Francisco, as well as a good number of US states. More recently, non-English language sites have been launched: from Catalonia in Spain and Paris in France, for instance.

But you'd be wrong to think this process was entirely led by governments. There's the pioneering work of enthusiasts like the Swedish physician Hans Rosling with his Gapminder project (p.452). Or the huge impression made by Al Gore's use of charts in his lectures on climate change.

Page 60 / **1834**

This drawing by David Brewster shows the then known spectrum of solar radiation, including infrared light, visible light and UV radiation (from top). The bottom bars show the complete radiation spectrum including the colours of the visible light.

Page 62 / **1850**

This educational chart drawn by John Emslie shows three different methods for determining longitude on the Earth. In contrast to latitudes, the determination of longitudes proved very complicated up until the eighteenth century.

1847

Luke Howard played an important role in establishing meteorology as a science. This plate from his work *Barometrographia* visualises weather data collected in Tottenham, London, in 1817. The circular graph shows barometric pressure and lunar phases over the course of the year.

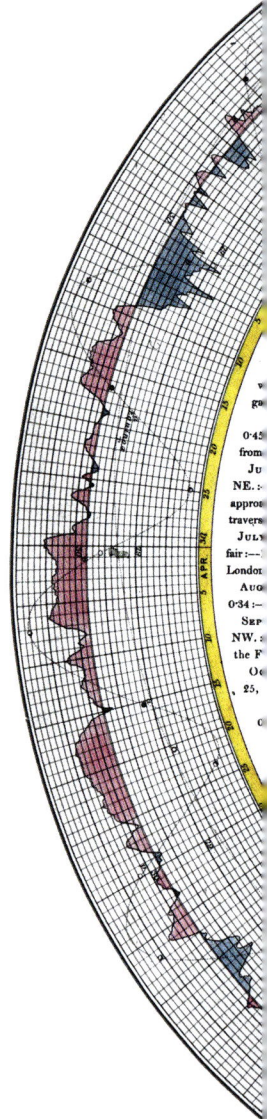

Then there are transparency campaigners like the *Guardian*'s Free our Data movement, which has long called for governments to release the data they charge for. We have, after all, paid for it – why can't we have access to massive datasets such as post-code data and Ordnance Survey geography. Thanks to those campaigns, the UK's official mapmaker Ordnance Survey has been forced to release its data.

Locally, those big campaigns have translated to thousands of ultra-local journalists, reporters who might write about an area only a few miles wide. These reporters either hunt down the data they need or demand their local governments give it to them through Freedom of Information legislation. This is the Open Data movement in action.

There are still some rules, of course: crucially, the data has to be available in a form you can manipulate – as an Excel spreadsheet or a CSV file. Why does that matter? Well, traditionally, statistics were published in the least accessible format possible: books, and then later as Adobe PDF files. PDF files look like books, read like books and may as well be books; they're of absolutely no use to anyone wanting to analyse the data for themselves or to visualise that data. In the past, when we all relied on official bodies to tell us what we needed to know, it didn't matter if the data was aggregated and analysed for us. But now we trust governments very little, and traditional media outlets even less. We want to know the numbers behind the story for ourselves – to see if we're being told the truth and discover our own stories.

TOTTENHAM, 1817.

Barom.—max. 30·57 in.: min. 28·43 in.: mean 29·82 in.: range 2·14 in.: spaces traversed by Curve 95·5 in. Therm.—max. 86° (June), NE., SE.: min. 17° (March), N.: mean of the year 47°·86: Rain 24·83 in. on 187 days.

JAN. 1-3, S., SW., S.,1·07 in. :—4, 5, W., 1·46 :—6, SW., 0·14 :—7-9, NW., NE.:—10-16, var., S'ly, 1·03 :—17-20, S., SW., 0·14 :—21-26, SW., 0·09 :—27, var., 0·06 :—28-31, E. to N'ly. On the 2nd snow after rain; again snow on 15th from SE., followed by sleet, after which more snow and frost: decided thaw with rain 16th : gales of wind 3, 7, 17,19-23 : Fair, with frost 7-12. Rain gauge 3·99 in. on 21 days.

FEB. 1-4, NW. to SW., 0·02 :—5-9, NW., NW., 0·04 :—10, 11, var., 0·34 :—12, NW., 0·07 :—13, 14, SW., 0·42 :—15, NW., 0·03 :—16-18, W., 0·03 :—19-22, SW., NW., 0·06 :—23, W., 0·04 :—24-28, NW., W., NW., SW., 0·24. Gales of wind 4, 5, 7, 8, 11, 14, 15, 20, 27 : snow 11th, Nimbus 21, 27. Rain gauge 1·29 in. on 17 days : on the 8th an Aurora borealis was very perceptible about 10 P.M., through the clouds which overspread : a windy night with a little rain followed.

MARCH. 1—2, 3, SW., 0·64 :—4, 5, NW., W., 0·25 :—6-8, W., NW., 0·55 :—9-12, NW., SW., W., 0·01 :—14-17, NE., E'ly.:—18, var. :—19-21, NW., N.:—22, S'ly, var., 0·07 :—26, var., 0·13 :—27, var.:—28-31, SW. to NW., 0·04. Gales of wind 2, 3, 5, 6, 20, 30 : snow 8th in flakes of about an inch and Nimbus (mostly affording hail) 4, 5, 8, 9 : Frost 14-24. Rain gauge 1·69 in. on 16 days. See Clim. Lond., the copious notes under T. cxxviii.

APRIL. 2, E.:—4-10, N'ly, E'ly, 0·01 :—11-15, NW., 0·06 :—16-18, N., 0·02 :—19-21, NE.:—22, SE. :—23-26, NE.:—27, 28, var., W.:—29, 30, NW., W., NE., 0·10 : snow along gale from NW. and N., with rain and hail 16th. Swallows appeared 22nd. Hygrom. receded to 32° on 23rd. A gale at NE. with Nimbus and hail 30th. Rain 2 days. Vegetation has been peculiarly slow : for some account of the change in the currents producing the extraordinary dryness of this month, see the Notes.

MAY. W. :—4-7, var., ending SE., 0·04 :—8, var., 0·08 :—9-11, var., 0·15 :—12, 13, W., SW., 0·13 : a W'ly gale on 12th in the forenoon after rain in the night :—14, W., 0·01 :—18, SE., 0·11 :—19-22, NE., SW., 1·44 :—24, 25, NE., SE., 0·47 :—26-30, E., NE., 0·23. On 5th the hygrom. receded to 32°, the wind after it going high we had Cirrocumulus with Nimbus, after which a thunder-storm about 4 P.M. : on 25th also distant thunder, and Stratus 27th. Rain 3·11 in. on 19 days.

JUNE. 5, SW., 0·11 :—6-9, SW., 0·70 : thunder 7th, and a stormy wet day and night 9 :—10, NW., 0·06 :—11-13, SW., var., 0·39 :—14, NW., 0·01 :—16-22, E., SE., NE.: thunder ; very heavy rain :—28-30, W., SW., 1·07. Rain 2·34 in. on 12 days. The usual solstitial disturbance (of the electric state of the atmosphere) but the rain did not come till the 24th, the hygrom. being actually at 36° before the storm. Electrical manifestations on 7, 20, 22, 24, 27 : on the last a Waterspout ? See Notes.

JULY. NW., 0·58 :—6-9, SW. :—10, 11, S. :—12, 13, NW., SW., 0·13 :—14, NW., 0·72 :—15, SW. (Swithin), 0·18 : the night was stormy, the next day cloudy, calmer and W., 0·02 :—21-24, SW., 0·11 :—25, 26, SE., S., 0·20 :—27-30, W., 0·40. Thunder to S. and SW. on 5th, and thrice in the latter ten days : a heavy storm of hail in . on 16 days.

AUG. 3 :—5, 6, NE. :—7, NW. :—8-10, SW., W., 0·10 : thunder-showers prevail :—11, 12, NW., 0·45 :—14, 15, W., 0·07 :—16, S., 0·02 :—17, W., 0·06 :—18, 19, SW., :—22, 23, E., SE. :—24, 25, S., SW., 0·29 :—26, S., 0·15 :—27, 28, SW., 0·15 :—29, 30, W., SW., 0·18 :—31, SW. Nimbus on 25, 26. Rain 2·16 in. on 18 days.

SEPT. :—4-6, var. :—7-9, SE., E., NE. :—10, 11, N., NE. :—12-14, var., SE., NE., 0·17 :—15-17, NE. and SE. :—18, N., 0·04 : slight showers, with wind :—19, 20, W., SE. :—25-27, SW., 0·27 :—28, 29, W., NW. :—30, NE. A gale from SW. with rain 25th. Except about three days after New Moon, and the same space after been fair. Rain 0·48 in. on 7 days.

OCT. chiefly NE. :—11, 12, NE., 0·05 :—13-15, NE., N., 0·06 :—16, 17, NE., 0·35 :—18, E., 0·17 :—19, 20, N., 0·03 :—21, E., :—22, N. :—23, 24, NE., 0·04 :—SW., 0·36 :—30, 31, S., 0·28. Ice appeared by the 2nd, temperature by night 24°. Squalls of wind occurred about the 30th. Rain 1·34 in. on 6 days.

NOV. :—6, S., 0·06 :—7, 8, SW., 0·18 :—9, 10, W., SW. :—11, SE., 0·14 :—12, 13, NE., 0·76 :—15, W., 0·10 :—16-24, NW., W'ly, fair :—25, W., 0·27-30, SW., 0·08. A gale at SW. on 7 : squally 8: strong wind P.M. 5 : wind fell in the neighbourhood 18: temperature next night 30° : 96°, as it had done before to 100° on the 12th. On the 25th, after Hoar-frost, a steady gale through the day : Nimbus on 29th. Rain days.

DEC. , 0·51 :—2, NW., 0·02 :—3, NE., 0·05 :—4, 5, E., S., 0·27 :—6, 7, NW., SW., 0·13 :—8, var., 0·48, after a gale of wind by night, which was se next:—9, 10, NW., NE. :—12-14, SE., 0·64 :—15, SW., 0·72 :—16, SW., 0·32 :—17, SW., 0·67 : in the night a most violent gale, increasing in force by slow intervals, with much rain :—18, SW., 0·02 :—19, var., 0·15 :—20-22, NE., N. :—23, SE. :—24, 25, NE. :—26, var., 0·10 :—S'ly, 0·05 :—30, var., 0·06. Nimbus on 3 and 8: snow 10, 22, 25, 28 : gales 7, 8, 13, 14, 16, 17, 27. The month had more than twenty nights, the rain by day notwithstanding. The gauge afforded 4·19 in. fallen on 18 days.

The mean temperatures of the several months have been as follows, viz.—JAN. 38°·67 : FEB. 42°·91 : MARCH 40°·25 :

APRIL 43°·25 : MAY 49°·11 : JUNE 61°·21 : JULY 59°·55 : AUG. 57°·84 : SEPT. 56°·90 : OCT. 43°·16 :

NOV. 46°·68 : DEC. 34°·55 : Clim. Lond. Tab. A 2, Temperature.

C. F. Cheffins, Lith. Southampton B^d. London.

SCALE 30 INCHES TO A MILE.

If a dataset is published as a spreadsheet it's suddenly easier to use. If that data is properly formatted, i.e. country names have codes on them so you can tell the difference between "Burma" and "Myanmar", or "Congo" and "Congo, Dem Rep" – well, suddenly you can start mashing data together, combining poverty rates with carbon emissions or crime figures with economic growth, for instance. Then you can start to create journalism which either works in words or even graphics – or both. Sometimes just reproducing a table tells you a story.

A lot of this isn't new – it's just easier now for us to all find. In fact what governments have

offered have been, for the most part, portals to collections of data they all offered anyway. But there is new information out there too. In the UK, the coalition government elected in 2010 has committed itself to releasing a "tsunami of data" as part of its transparency agenda. And, only a few months in, we have seen huge datasets released: every government item of spending over £25,000; salaries of senior civil servants; detailed Treasury spending records; street-by-street crime data and individual hospitals' performance.

Very soon, every local authority in England will have published every individual item of

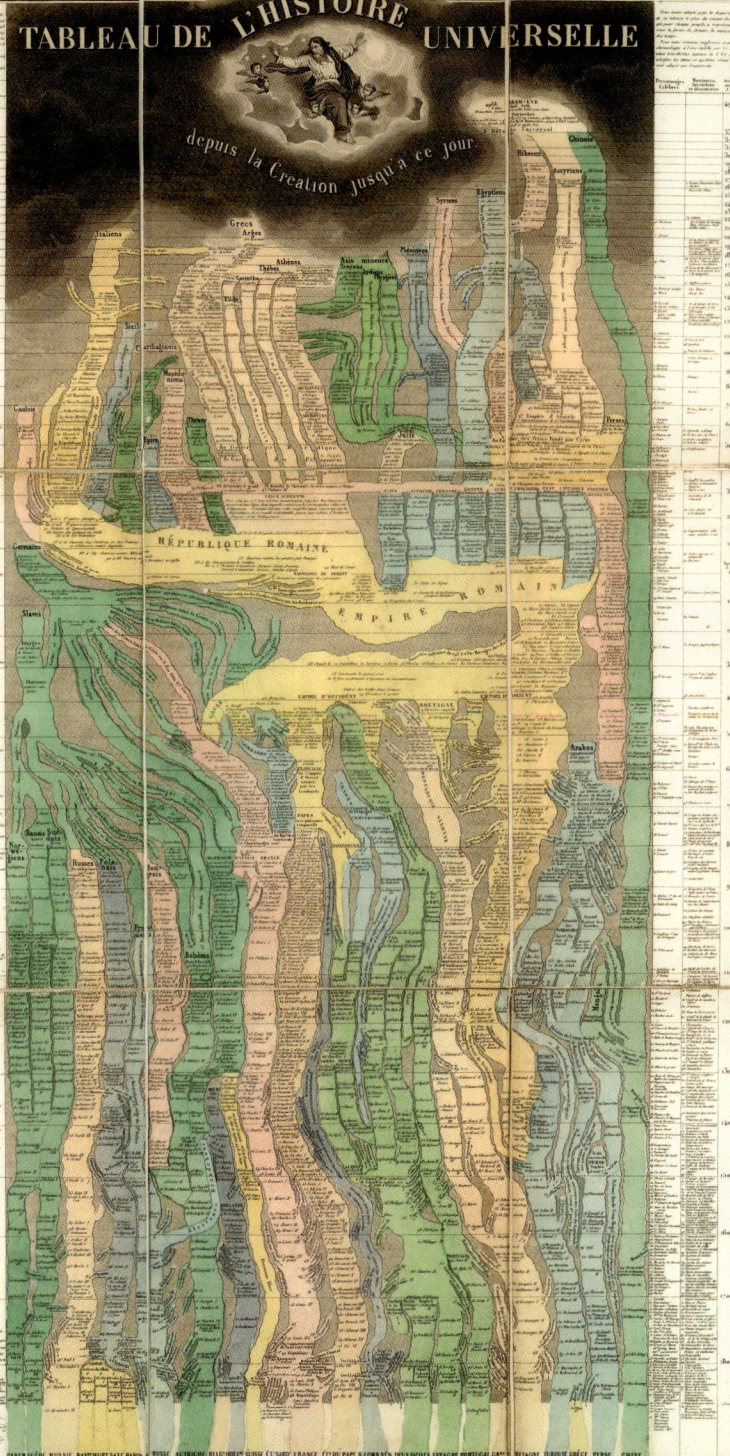

TABLEAU DE L'HISTOIRE UNIVERSELLE

depuis la Création jusqu'à ce jour.

RÉPUBLIQUE ROMAINE

EMPIRE ROMAIN

EMPIRE D'OCCIDENT

Grecs
Arabes
Athènes
Thèbes

Italiens

Carthage

Gaulois

Épire

Juifs

Perses

Asie mineure

Phéniciens

Syriens
Égyptiens
Assyriens
Babel
Chinois

ADAM-ÈVE

Slaves

Russes
Polonais

Normandie

BRETAGNE

Arabes

Bohème

DANEMARCK SUÈDE RUSSIE BAV^{ère} WURTE SAXE HAND PRUSSE AUTRICHE BELGHOLL SUISSE ÉT^S SARD^S FRANCE ÉT^S DU PAPE R. LOMB VEN DEUX SICILES ESPAGNE PORTUGAL GR BRETAGNE TURQUIE GRÈCE PERSE CHINE

Page 66 / **1854**

The London physician John Snow held the novel view that cholera was caused by polluted drinking water. In this map he proved that the accumulation of cases was centred around a contaminated well during a cholera epidemic in 1854.

Page 67 / **1858**

This *Table of Universal History* was published in Paris. It visualises the complete history of humankind, top down, from the creation of Adam and Eve to the then present day. Individual cultures are depicted as rivers.

spending over £500. Some commentators worry about the end of local journalism with the closure of newspapers around the country. But here is an endless source of stories just waiting to reward reporters hungry enough to find them.

In the new industry, all of that data has combined with a feeling, maybe even a hunch, that no one trusts or likes their news source very much any more. At a time when established news organisations have to fight with bloggers and citizen journalists for their very existence, there has been a move towards explaining the news, to being open about the sources of our stories. One of the hits has been the independent website *Where Does My Money Go?* Its main purpose is simply to explain how the British government spends its money.

At the *Guardian*, we launched our first official foray into data journalism at the same time as we launched our Open Platform API. The *Guardian Datablog* was to be a small blog offering the full datasets behind our news stories. In just two years it has become a portal to world data and data visualisation bringing in around a million page impressions a month. Now it consists of a front page (guardian.co.uk/data); searches of world government and global development data; data visualisations by *Guardian* graphic artists and others (including Information is Beautiful's David McCandless) and tools for exploring public-spending data.

As a news editor and journalist working with graphics, for me it was a logical extension of work I was already doing. Every day I was accumulating new datasets and wrangling with them to try to make sense of the news stories

of the day. In turn, my professional life has been bookended by war. My first day on the paper's newsdesk was September 10, 2001. After the events of the following day, the results have been reverberating through the newspaper's pages ever since.

Gradually, the Datablog's work reflected and added to the stories we faced. We crowdsourced 458,000 documents relating to MPs' expenses and we analysed the detailed data of which MPs had claimed what. We helped our users explore detailed Treasury spending databases and published the data behind the news.

But the game-changer for data journalism happened in spring 2010. It began with a spreadsheet: 92,201 rows of data, each one containing a detailed breakdown of a military event in Afghanistan. This was the WikiLeaks war logs. Part one, that is. There were to be two more episodes to follow: Iraq and the cables. The official term for the first two parts was SIGACTS: the US military Significant Actions Database. A recent article in the *New York Times* explained how US soldiers were drowning under the weight of detailed datasets. SIGACTS was one of these. Recorded by soldiers in the field, this was war as it was fought, complete with military jargon and incredible detail.

With the WikiLeaks files we had two criteria for success: help our journalists access the information, break down and analyse the data – and make it available for our users. The Afghanistan and Iraq data came to us as huge spreadsheet files, over 92,000 rows of data in the first, nearly 400,000 rows in the second. Iraq and Afghanistan are now the

1862

This diagram visualises time differences seen from Washington, D.C. (centre). Numerous smaller clocks symbolise places around the globe. Each clock face shows the local time and names place, country and the distance to Washington in miles.

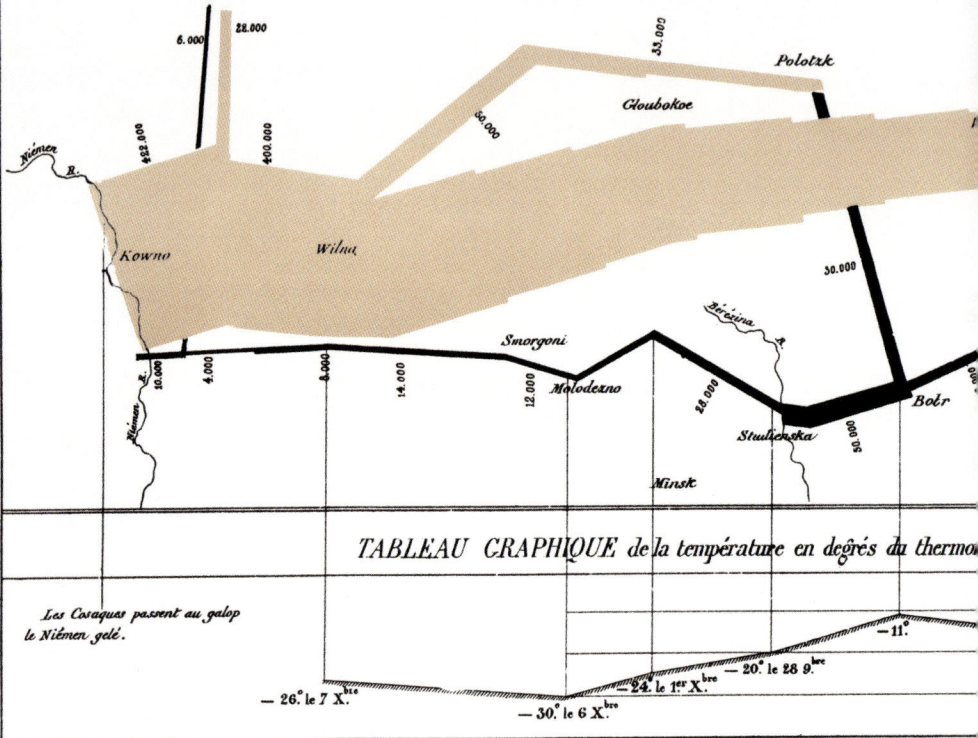

1869

The development of the so-called flow map is based on the work of the French engineer Charles Joseph Minard. This famous example visualises the casualties during Napoleon's invasion of Russia as a narrowing flow of soldiers.

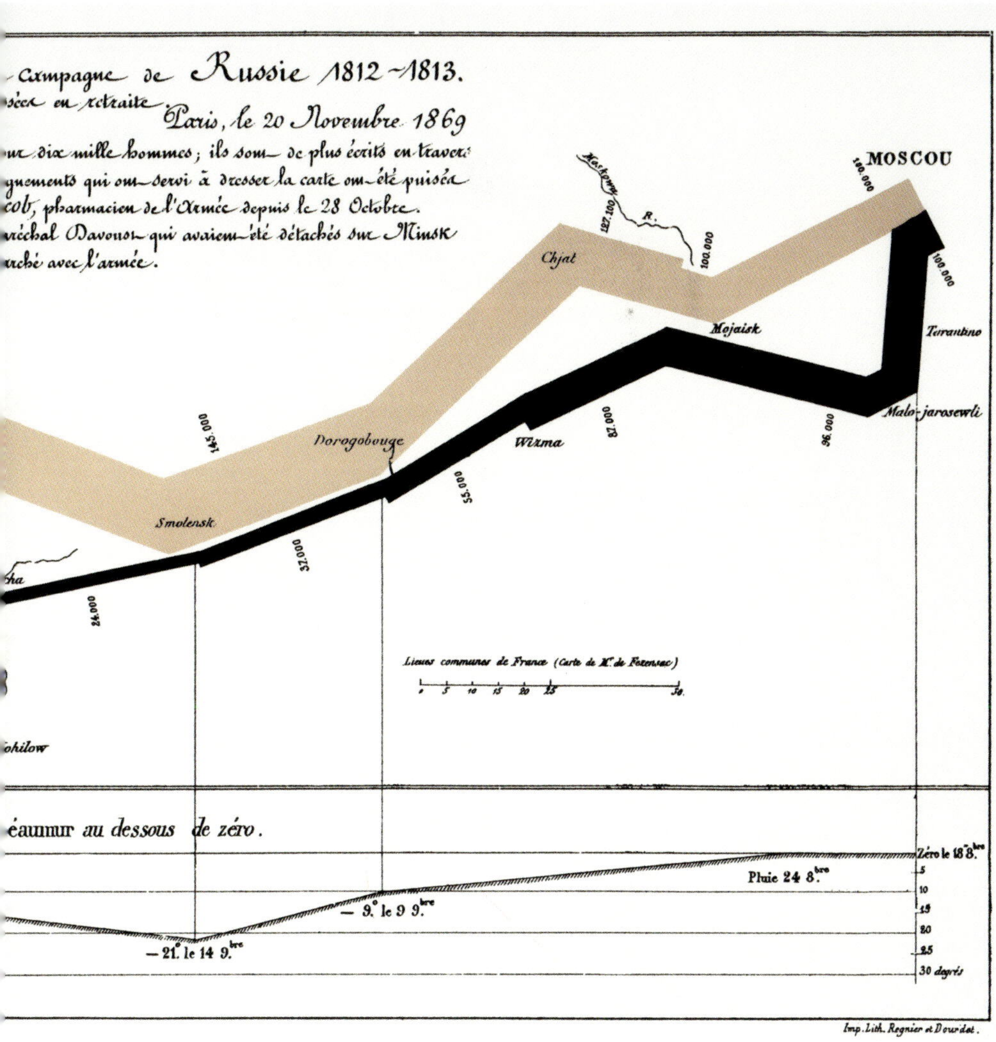

Campagne de *Russie 1812 – 1813.*

...sée en retraite

Paris, le 20 Novembre 1869

...ur dix mille hommes; ils sont de plus écrits en travers

...gnements qui ont servi à dresser la carte ont été puisés

...COB, pharmacien de l'Armée depuis le 28 Octobre.

...réchal Davoust qui avaient été détachés sur Minsk

...rché avec l'armée.

MOSCOU
112.000

100.000

100.000

Kaluga R.

127.100

Chjat

Mojaisk
Terantino

Dorogobouge
Wixma
87.000
96.000
Malo-jarosewli

145.000
55.000

Smolensk
37.000

...ha
24.000

...ohilow

Lieues communes de France (Carte de M. de Fezensac)

1   5   10   15   20   25   50.

...éaumur au dessous de zéro.

Zéro le 18 8.bre

Pluie 24 8.bre
5
10

— 9.° le 9 9.bre
15
20

— 21.° le 14 9.bre
25
30 degrés

Imp. Lith. Regnier et Dourdet.

71

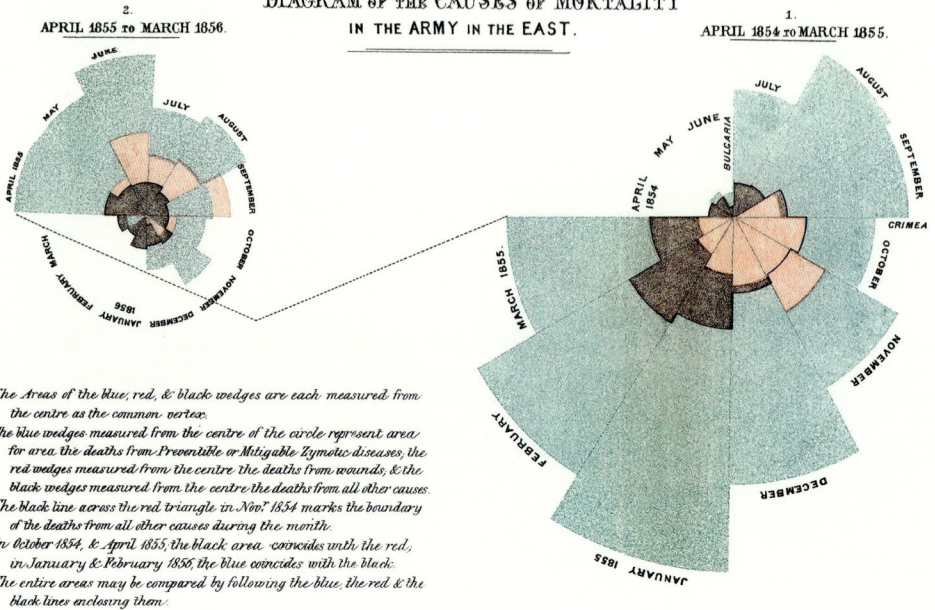

DIAGRAM of the CAUSES of MORTALITY
IN THE ARMY IN THE EAST.

2.
APRIL 1855 to MARCH 1856.

1.
APRIL 1854 to MARCH 1855.

The Areas of the blue, red, & black wedges are each measured from the centre as the common vertex.

The blue wedges measured from the centre of the circle represent area for area the deaths from Preventible or Mitigable Zymotic diseases, the red wedges measured from the centre the deaths from wounds, & the black wedges measured from the centre the deaths from all other causes.

The black line across the red triangle in Nov.r 1854 marks the boundary of the deaths from all other causes during the month.

In October 1854, & April 1855, the black area coincides with the red, in January & February 1856, the blue coincides with the black.

The entire areas may be compared by following the blue, the red & the black lines enclosing them.

most-documented wars in history. By contrast, the Vietnam war revealed in 1972 by the Pentagon papers was only 7,000 pages.

The data was well structured: each event had the following key data: time, date, a description, casualty figures and – crucially – detailed latitude and longitude. The cables, by contrast, were a mess – a huge text file, with fields running into one another and merging together. The work to clean up that database of 251,000 records was immense.

In the data team we started filtering the numbers to help us tell the key stories of the war: in Afghanistan it was the rise in IED (improvised explosive device) attacks. This data allowed us to see that the south, where the British and Canadian troops are, was the worst-hit area – which backed up what our reporters who had covered the war knew. In Iraq it was breaking down the huge casualty numbers – over 109,000 people's deaths were detailed in the dataset.

The casualties data brought its own challenges, repeated again when we dealt with the Iraq data. It was often inaccurately compiled

and incomplete – we compared Nato-recorded casualties too, to test the veracity of the data, and the results varied.

Using developers to help map the data, we created a map of every IED explosion in Afghanistan, the data team working with graphic artists to work out what needed to be displayed and the best way of doing it. Online, this translated into an interactive graphic where users could play out the attacks over time. With the Iraq table we opted to use a free tool – Google Fusion Tables – to map out each one of the 66,000 incidents where someone died. It was not perfect, but a start in trying to map the patterns of destruction which had ravaged Iraq.

Guardian developers including Alastair Dant created online interactives, showing attacks over time, or a single day's worth of events. We allowed users to download selected sets of the data to see for themselves how the story unfolded. And we provided interactive guides and data breakdowns for key documents.

That is just one set of stories, a single high-point in data journalism's road to acceptance. There are still reporters out there who don't

1858

The English nurse Florence Nightingale conceived of this polar area diagram to display the high mortality rate in British military hospitals during the Crimean War. Shown in blue is the large majority of soldiers who died of infectious diseases.

Following spread / **1872**

This diagram by American economist Francis A. Walker visualises the development of the US budget from 1789 up to 1870. On the left, revenues are broken down into sources. The central column demonstrates the public debt, while on the right, expenditures are shown.

get what all the fuss is about, who really don't want to know about maths or spreadsheets. But for others, this new wave represents a way to save journalism. A new role for journalists as a bridge and guide between those in power who have the data (and are rubbish at explaining it) and the public who desperately want to understand the data and access it but need help. We can be that bridge.

In future our role may even be in supplying data as trusted sources, as a "safe" location of quality information. Sometimes people talk about the Internet killing journalism. The WikiLeaks story was a combination of the two: traditional journalistic skills and the power of the technology, harnessed to tell an amazing story. In future, data journalism may not seem amazing and new; for now it is. The world has changed and it is data that has changed it.

Simon Rogers is an award-winning data journalist, writer and speaker. Data editor at Google, he is director of the Sigma Data Journalism Awards and teaches Data Journalism at Medill-Northwestern University in San Francisco.

Legend

- From Public Lands
- " Bank Stock
- " Internal Revenue
- " Customs
- " Direct Tax
- " Postage
- " Miscellaneous

FISC.
OF THE U

SHOWING THE COURSE OF TH
TOGETHER WITH T

R
FROM EACH PRI
AND THE

EXP
FOR EACH PRIN
PU
Compiled from the Report of

FRA.

1.-REVENUE.

2-P
In
Jan.

Year	In millions and tenths (00,000 omitted)
May 4. 1789 to Dec. 31. 1791.	4.4
1792	3.7
1793	4.7
1794	5.4
1795	6.1
1796	8.4
1797	8.7
1798	7.9
1799	7.5
1800	10.8
1801	12.9
1802	15.0
1803	11.1
1804	11.8
1805	13.6
1806	15.6
1807	16.4
1808	17.1
1809	7.8
1810	9.4
1811	14.4
1812	9.8
1813	14.3
1814	11.2
1815	15.7
1816	47.7
1817	33.1
1818	21.6
1819	24.6
1820	17.8
1821	14.6
1822	20.2
1823	20.5
1824	19.4
1825	21.8
1826	25.3
1827	23.0
1828	24.8
1829	24.8
1830	24.8
1831	28.5
1832	31.9
1833	33.9
1834	21.8
1835	35.4
1836	50.8
1837	24.9
1838	26.3
1839	30.0
1840	19.4
1841	16.9
1842	20.0
Jan. 1 1843 to June 30. 1844	37.6
1845*	29.9
1846	29.7
1847	26.4
1848	35.7
1849	30.7
1850	43.6
1851	52.6
1852	49.8
1853	61.5
1854	73.8
1855	65.4
1856	74.1
1857	69.0
1858	46.7
1859	52.8
1860	56.1
1861	41.5
1862	51.9
1863	112.1
1864	262.7
1865	323.1
1866	619.6
1867	489.9
1868	405.6
1869	370.9
1870	411.3

1862
1863
1864
1865
1866
1867
1868
1869
1870

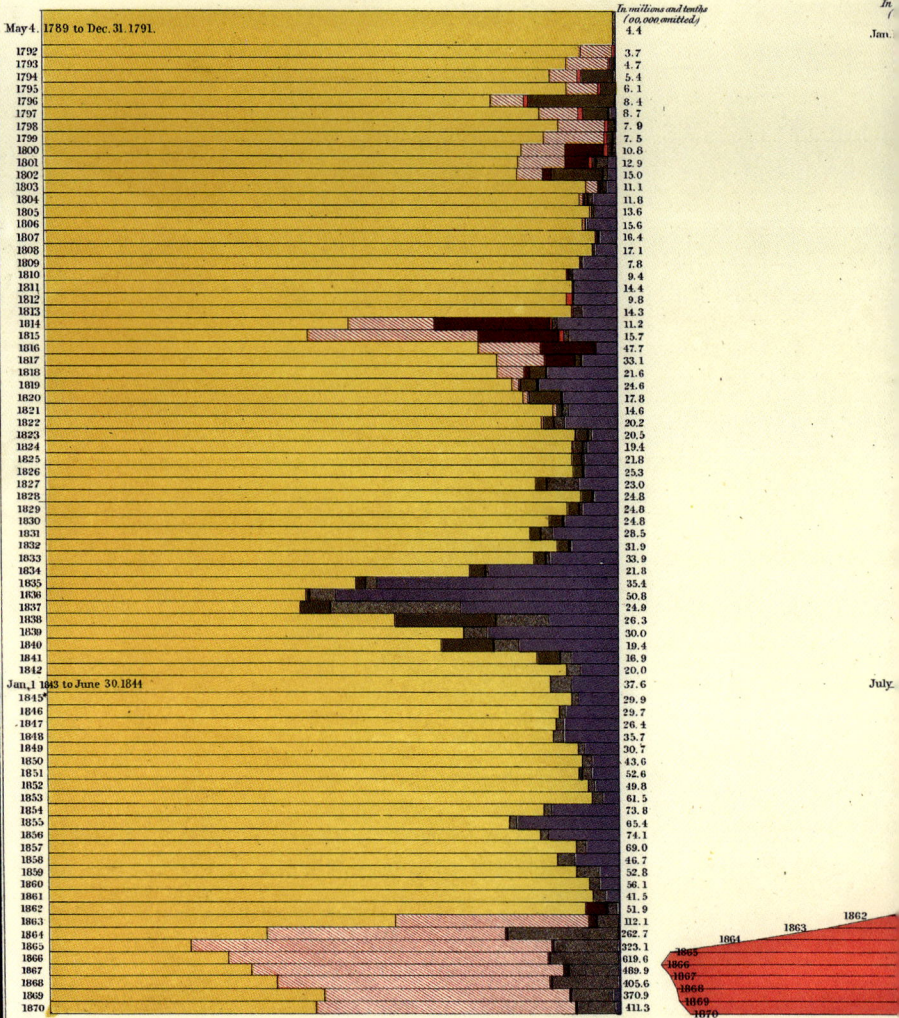

*Fiscal Year ending June 30.

July

The Public Debt

HART

O STATES

DEBT BY YEARS 1789 TO 1870.
RTION OF THE TOTAL

TS

RCE OF REVENUE
N OF TOTAL

URES

ARTMENT OF THE
VICE.

f the Treasury for the year 1872,

ALKER.

T.

3-EXPENDITURES.

In millions and tenths
(00,000 omitted.)

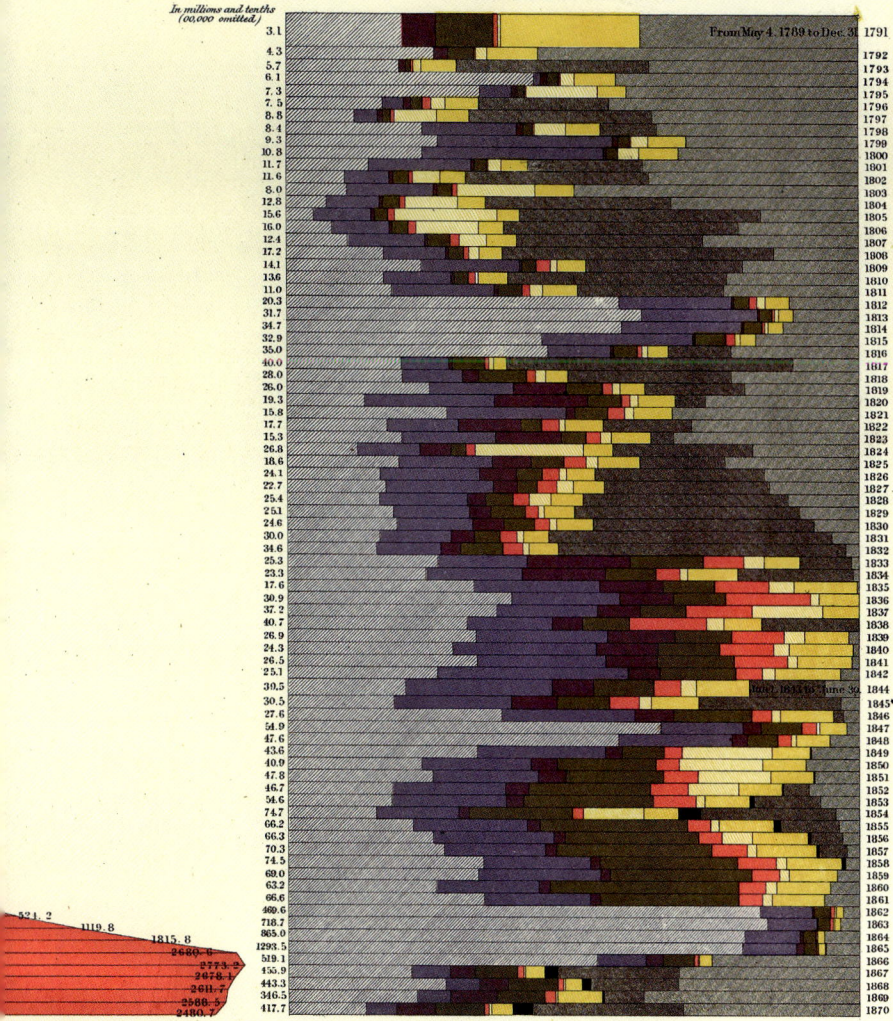

Legend	
Army	
Navy	
Pensions	
Civil	
Indians	
Foreign	
Miscellaneous	
Premium on Pub. Debt.	
Principal of Pub. Debt.	
Interest on Pub. Debt.	

Value	Year
3.1	From May 4. 1789 to Dec. 31 1791
4.3	1792
5.7	1793
6.1	1794
7.3	1795
7.5	1796
8.8	1797
8.4	1798
9.3	1799
10.8	1800
11.7	1801
11.6	1802
8.0	1803
12.8	1804
15.6	1805
16.0	1806
12.4	1807
17.2	1808
14.1	1809
13.6	1810
11.0	1811
20.3	1812
31.7	1813
34.7	1814
32.9	1815
35.0	1816
40.0	1817
28.0	1818
26.0	1819
19.3	1820
15.8	1821
17.7	1822
15.3	1823
26.8	1824
18.6	1825
24.1	1826
22.7	1827
25.4	1828
25.1	1829
24.6	1830
30.0	1831
34.6	1832
25.3	1833
23.3	1834
17.6	1835
30.9	1836
37.2	1837
40.7	1838
26.9	1839
24.3	1840
26.5	1841
25.1	1842
39.5	1844
30.5	1845*
27.6	1846
54.9	1847
47.6	1848
43.6	1849
40.9	1850
47.8	1851
46.7	1852
54.6	1853
74.7	1854
66.2	1855
66.3	1856
70.3	1857
74.5	1858
69.0	1859
63.2	1860
66.6	1861
469.6	1862
718.7	1863
865.0	1864
1293.5	1865
519.1	1866
455.9	1867
443.3	1868
346.5	1869
417.7	1870

1843 to June 30. 1844

521. 2
1119. 8
1815. 8
2680. 6
2773. 2
2478. 1
2611. 7
2586. 5
2480. 7

835, was $ 37.513.

*Fiscal Year ending June 30.

PEDIGREE OF MAN.

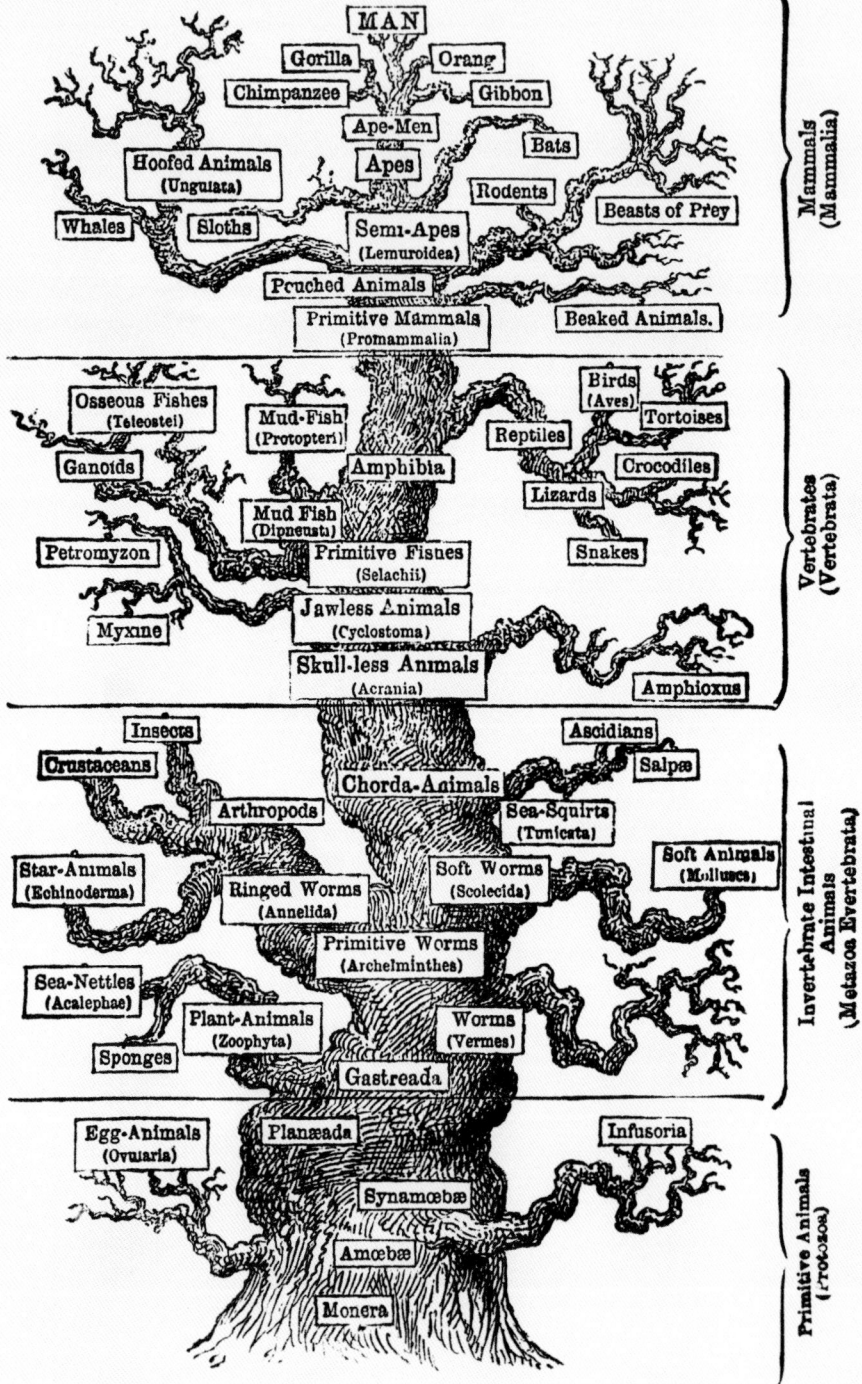

MAN

Gorilla   Orang

Chimpanzee   Gibbon

Ape-Men

Apes   Bats

Hoofed Animals (Ungulata)   Rodents

Whales   Sloths   Semi-Apes (Lemuroidea)   Beasts of Prey

Pouched Animals

Primitive Mammals (Promammalia)   Beaked Animals.

Mammals (Mammalia)

Osseous Fishes (Teleostei)   Birds (Aves)   Tortoises

Mud-Fish (Protopteri)   Reptiles   Crocodiles

Ganoids   Amphibia   Lizards

Mud Fish (Dipneusti)   Snakes

Petromyzon   Primitive Fishes (Selachii)

Myxine   Jawless Animals (Cyclostoma)

Skull-less Animals (Acrania)   Amphioxus

Vertebrates (Vertebrata)

Insects   Ascidians

Crustaceans   Salpæ

Arthropods   Chorda-Animals   Sea-Squirts (Tunicata)

Star-Animals (Echinoderma)   Ringed Worms (Annelida)   Soft Worms (Scolecida)   Soft Animals (Molluscs)

Primitive Worms (Archelminthes)

Sea-Nettles (Acalephae)   Plant-Animals (Zoophyta)   Worms (Vermes)

Sponges

Gastreada

Invertebrate Intestinal Animals (Metazoa Evertebrata)

Egg-Animals (Ovularia)   Planæada   Infusoria

Synamœbæ

Amœbæ

Monera

Primitive Animals (Protozoa)

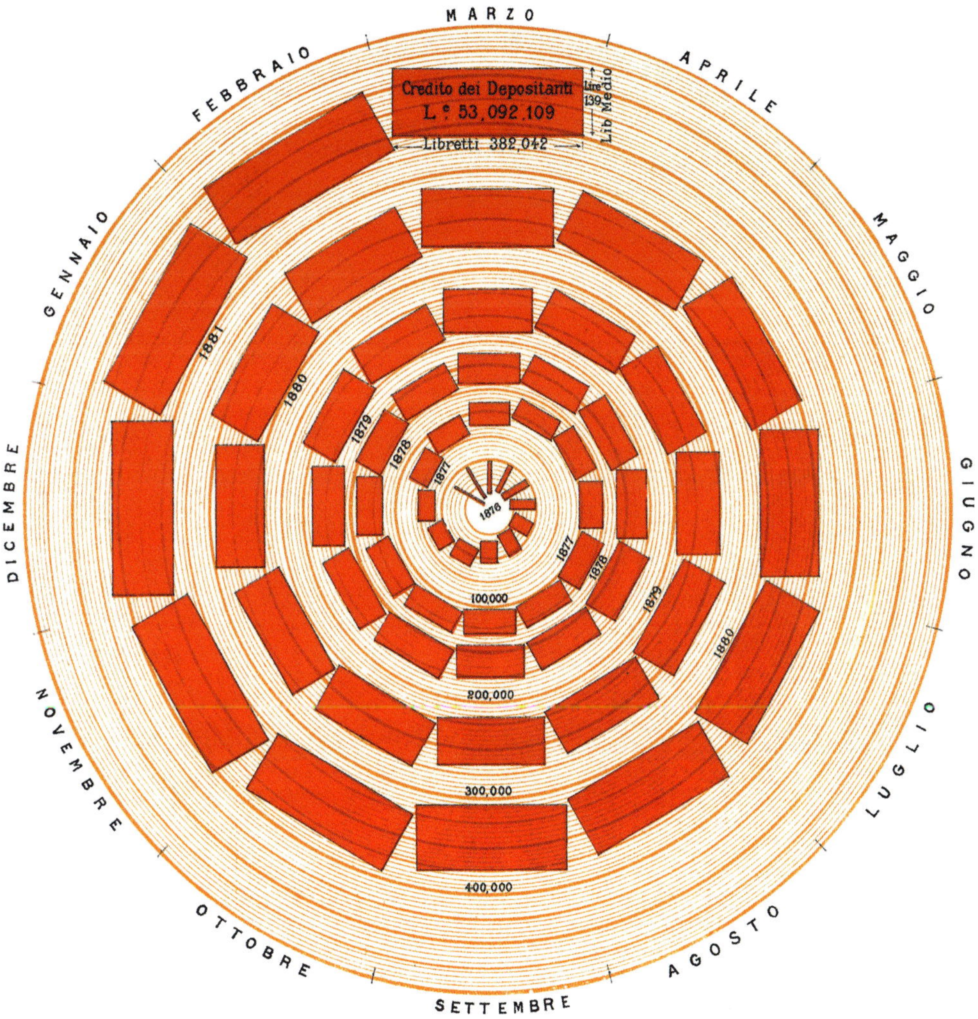

Credito dei Depositanti
L.ᵉ 53,092,109
Libretti 382,042

Lire 139 Medio
Lib Medio

1879

The German biologist Ernst Haeckel advocated Charles Darwin's theory of evolution and expanded it to his own theory of origin. He used a tree to visualise his idea of the evolution of man starting with the most primitive organisms.

1888

This chart by the Italian statistician Antonio Gabaglio provides both a historical and a quantitative display. It shows the monthly savings deposits at the Italian Post in the period from 1876 to 1881.

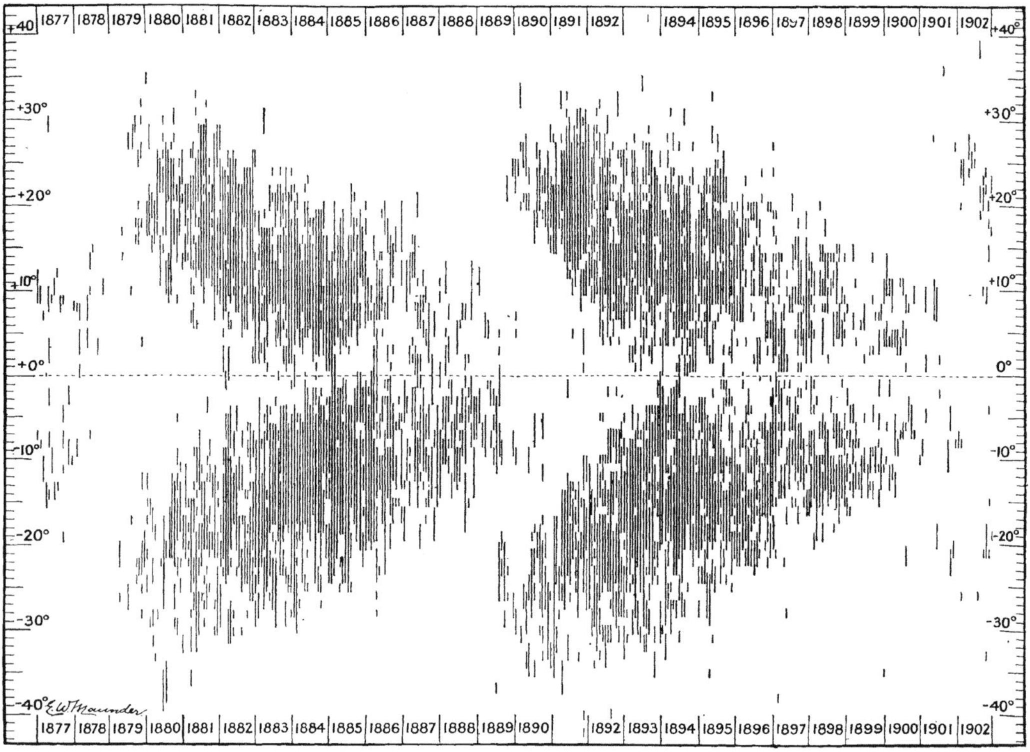

FIG. 8.—DISTRIBUTION OF SPOT-CENTRES IN LATITUDE, ROTATION BY ROTATION, 1877–1902.

1904

The English astronomer Edward Maunder discovered that sun spots reappear at certain latitudes of the Sun in a regular cycle of eleven years. Because of their shape, his records are popularly known as "butterfly diagrams".

1912

This diagram visualises the official statistics on casualties and people saved during the sinking of the *Titanic*, broken down into different categories. It was published in the British magazine *The Sphere*.

THE LOSS of the "TITANIC."

The Results Analysed and Shown in a Special "Sphere" Diagram

Drawn from the Official Figures Given in the House of Commons

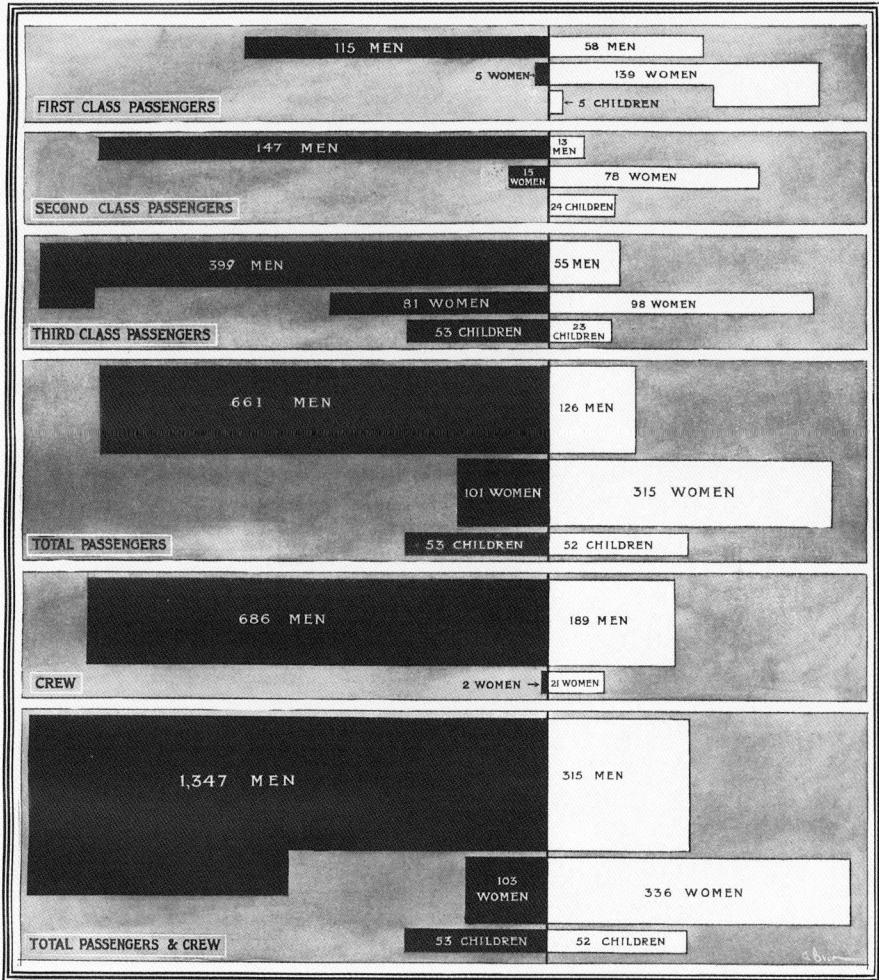

FIRST CLASS PASSENGERS
- 115 MEN — 58 MEN
- 5 WOMEN — 139 WOMEN
- 5 CHILDREN

SECOND CLASS PASSENGERS
- 147 MEN — 13 MEN
- 15 WOMEN — 78 WOMEN
- 24 CHILDREN

THIRD CLASS PASSENGERS
- 399 MEN — 55 MEN
- 81 WOMEN — 98 WOMEN
- 53 CHILDREN — 23 CHILDREN

TOTAL PASSENGERS
- 661 MEN — 126 MEN
- 101 WOMEN — 315 WOMEN
- 53 CHILDREN — 52 CHILDREN

CREW
- 686 MEN — 189 MEN
- 2 WOMEN → 21 WOMEN

TOTAL PASSENGERS & CREW
- 1,347 MEN — 315 MEN
- 103 WOMEN — 336 WOMEN
- 53 CHILDREN — 52 CHILDREN

SPECIALLY DRAWN FOR "THE SPHERE" BY G. BRON

The Black Indicates Passengers and Crew NOT SAVED, the White Indicates the SAVED

The official figures given last week show that the first figures (as given in "The Sphere" of last week) were in excess of the real numbers on board by about 132. The actual figures are as above. The actual numbers of the saved and lost are given above ; the percentage is shown below

NUMBERS OF SAVED		FIRST CLASS				SECOND CLASS				THIRD CLASS				THE CREW				PASSENGERS AND CREW			
	Per cent.		Carried	Saved	Per cent.		Carried	Saved	Per cent.		Carried	Saved	Per cent.		Carried	Saved	Per cent.		Carried	Saved	Per cent.
First class	63	Men	173	58	34	Men	160	13	8	Men	454	55	12					Men	1,662	315	19
Second class	42	Women	144	139	97	Women	93	78	84	Women	179	98	55	Men	875	189	22	Women	439	336	77
Third class	25	Children	5	5	100	Children	24	24	100	Children	76	23	30	Women	23	21	91	Children	105	52	49
Crew	23		322	202	63		277	115	42		709	176	25		898	210	23	Totals	2,206	703	32

c

P

P

C 2p

C 3p
C 4p

C 5-8p

R.int.de D2-7p
Acc du brach.
cut. interne
N intercosto-
-huméral
Br perf later de I3
R.int de D2-7p

Ram. ext. de
S1 3p.

Circonflexe

Radial

Branche sus
claviculaire

Branches sus
claviculaires

R sensitif du conduit
auditif externe

C 3p
C 4p

C 5-8p

R int de D2-7p
Filet scapulaire de
l'acc du brach
cut int.
N intercosto-
-huméral

B.perf lat de I3
R int de D2-7p

N cutané
de l'épaule

Gr et p⁴ nerf
abdomino genital
N. honteux
interne

N.cut.post.
de la cuisse

N. fémoro-cutané

Nerf crural

N.cut. ant. de l'abdomen.
N N. abdominaux -
latéraux

N. fémoro-cutané

Br cut saphène
int.

N.musculo cutané
N. plantaire ext
N. plantaire
interne

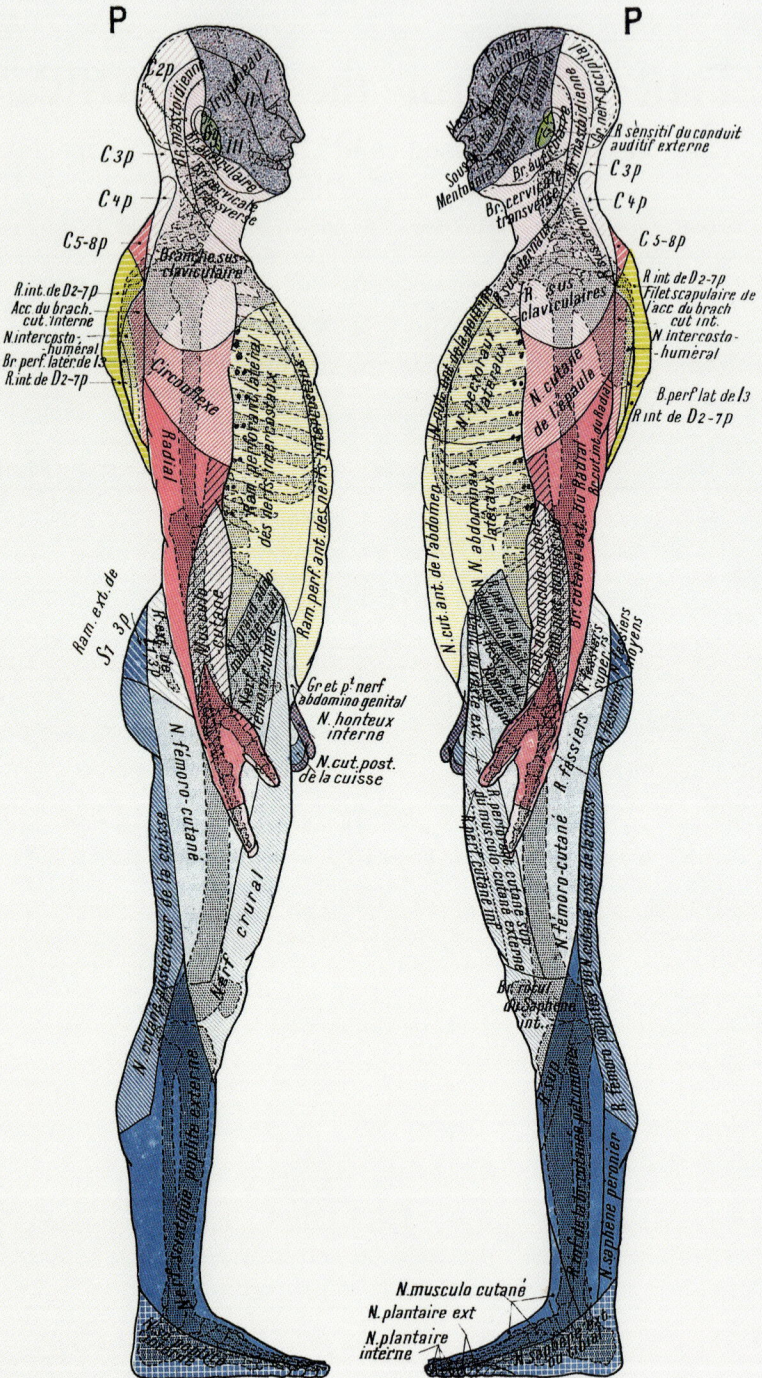

Fig. 381 et 382. — Topographie sensitive périphérique de la peau de la face latérale du corps. Le
profil droit représente la distribution cutanée des gros troncs nerveux périphériques ; le profil
gauche les territoires de chacun de leurs rameaux cutanés.

Paolo Ciuccarelli 81—100

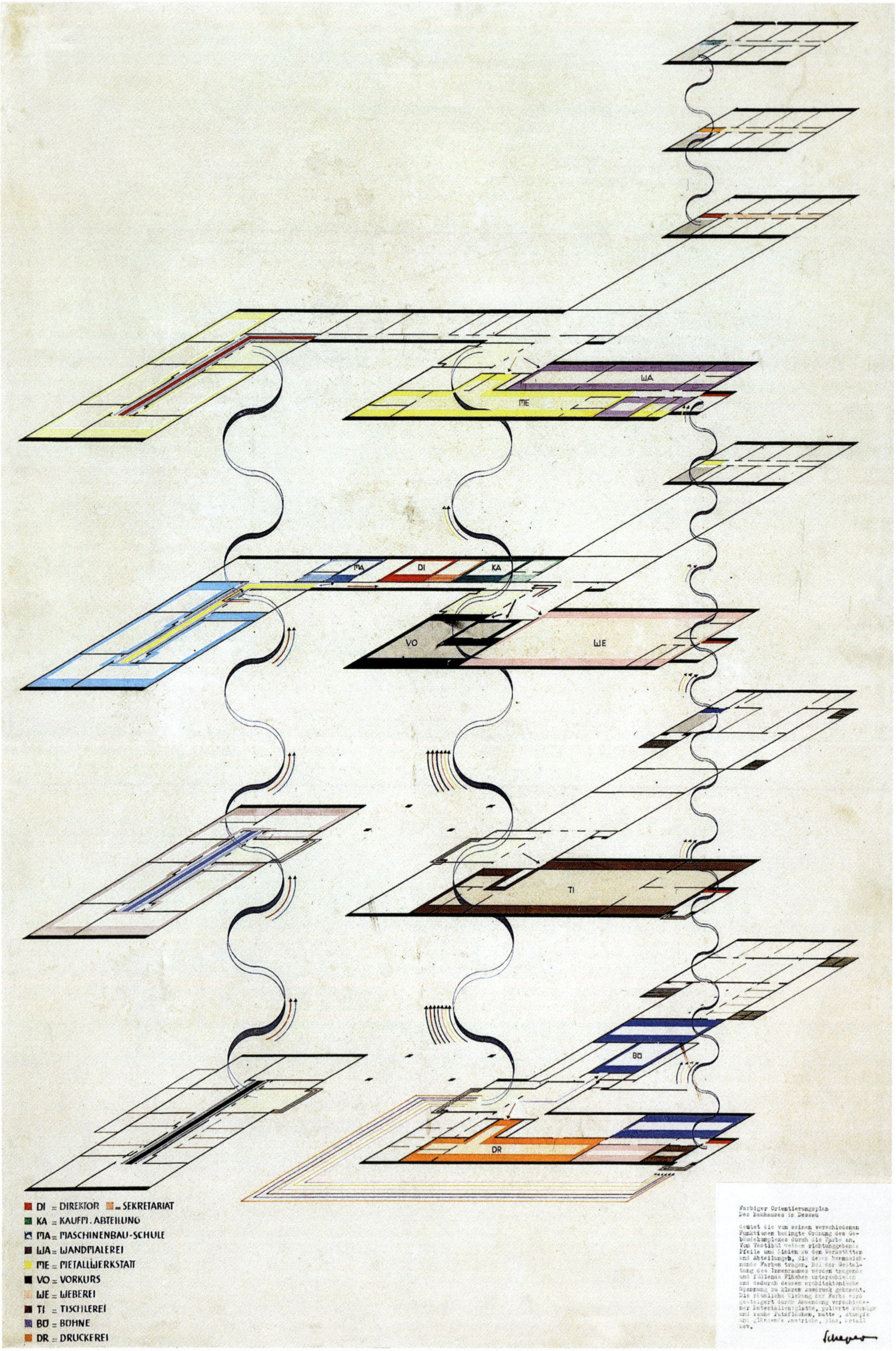

Farbiger Orientierungsplan
des Bauhauses in Dessau

Gezeigt ist von seinen verschiedenen
Funktionen bezeigte Ordnung des Ge-
bäudekomplexes durch die Farbe an.
Zum Vorbild wurde ein richtungsgebender
Pfeile und Linien an dem Verkehrten
und Abteilungen, die beim Termsmich-
munde Farben tragen, bei der Darstellung des Innenraumes wurden trägende
und fallende Flächen unterschieden
und dadurch seiner architektonische
Ordnung im klaren Ausdruck gebracht.
Die rämliche Wirkung der Farbe wird
gesteigert durch Anwendung verschieden-
tiger Materialoberfläche, polierte Anzüge
und raube Materfarben, matte, stumpfe
und glänzende Anstriche, Glas, Metall
usw.

DI = DIREKTOR   SEKRETARIAT
KA = KAUFM. ABTEILUNG
MA = MASCHINENBAU-SCHULE
WA = WANDMALEREI
ME = METALLWERKSTATT
VO = VORKURS
WE = WEBEREI
TI = TISCHLEREI
BÜ = BÜHNE
DR = DRUCKEREI

Turning visualisations into stories and "big pictures"

Paolo Ciuccarelli

The amount of socially relevant data that reaches the public through various media is increasing: epidemics, wars, technological innovations, natural disasters, financial crises and genomic discoveries are all examples of information being released in our ever-expanding cycle of news reporting. Social and economic issues are more often narrated nowadays with numbers complementing text, frequently also accompanied by visual representations of data. This is a major step forward in the human quest for knowledge, but does it really contribute to public understanding of socio-economic phenomena?

It is clear that there is room for improvement, especially in the visual communication of data and information generated by research organisations. These institutions are experiencing an unprecedented opportunity to fill the critical historical debt they have toward society. While scientists have earned recognition and a measure of autonomy, they are still generally considered distant and elitist. They must cope with a public sense of distance and scepticism, and a lack of interest and appreciation. Sometimes they are faced with fierce opposition, despite the relevance of their research for both human and societal development. This gap between sciences and the public has widened over the years, partly because scientists tend to use a specific and often impenetrable language, even on the rare occasions where a clear comment to the public was necessary.

Now, to be granted the resources (money and personnel) and freedom (political independence) necessary to carry on their research,

scientific organisations need, more than ever, a close relationship with society; political support, based on broad public consensus, is of utmost importance. Moreover, decisions that affect the activity of research bodies are taken outside of the scientific community more often. Non-experts have the means and the will to participate in decision-making processes in place of experts. The very method of even defining the *expert* is a challenge.

Scientists must nurture a constructive relationship with society. The need for trust is particularly evident when controversial issues are discussed, especially when not even the researchers have a universal consensus. Nuclear energy, global warming, electromagnetic pollution and Genetically Modified Organisms (GMOs) are just a few examples of the many ongoing debates which include strong irrational components.

For these reasons, the marriage between the scientific community and society may be uneasy, but it is certainly necessary. It has not yet been openly celebrated because of a basic communication problem: the sciences and the public do not speak the same language. As the European Commission states in its document "Communicating Science":[1] "The same data that for scientists are another piece to add to a well-known picture of knowledge (and emotions), for the public are only an isolated fragment of information, with almost no meaning."

When the aim is to let the public *see* social or economic problems, simple data visualisations are not enough. People need visual orientation tools. The most important condition for

Page 80 / **1914**

Joseph Jules Dejerine was a French neurologist whose book *Sémiologie des affections du système nerveux* is considered a classic of his discipline. Amongst other things, he described in it the anatomy of the nervous system, using coloured graphics.

Page 82 / **1926**

This orientation map was created by Bauhaus teacher Hinnerk Scheper and visualises the room layout in the Bauhaus building in Dessau, Germany. Single floors are shown one upon the other. Colours signify the functions of individual parts of the building.

Mächte der Erde

Jede Figur 25 Millionen Menschen

1930

With the objective of promoting national education, Austrian economist Otto Neurath created many display boards in which social and economic issues were explained in a simple way. Quantities are displayed through a varying number of icons.

Großstädter unter je 25 Personen

Europa 1930

Grossbritannien und Irland

Frankreich

Italien

Deutsches Reich

Österreich

U d S S R

Amerika 1930

U S A

Argentinien

Asien 1930

Indien

China

Australien 1930

Römisches Reich um Chr. Geb.

Mittelamerikan. Altkulturbereich 13. Jahrhdt.

Großstadt von 100 000 Einwohnern aufwärts
Rot: Großstädter

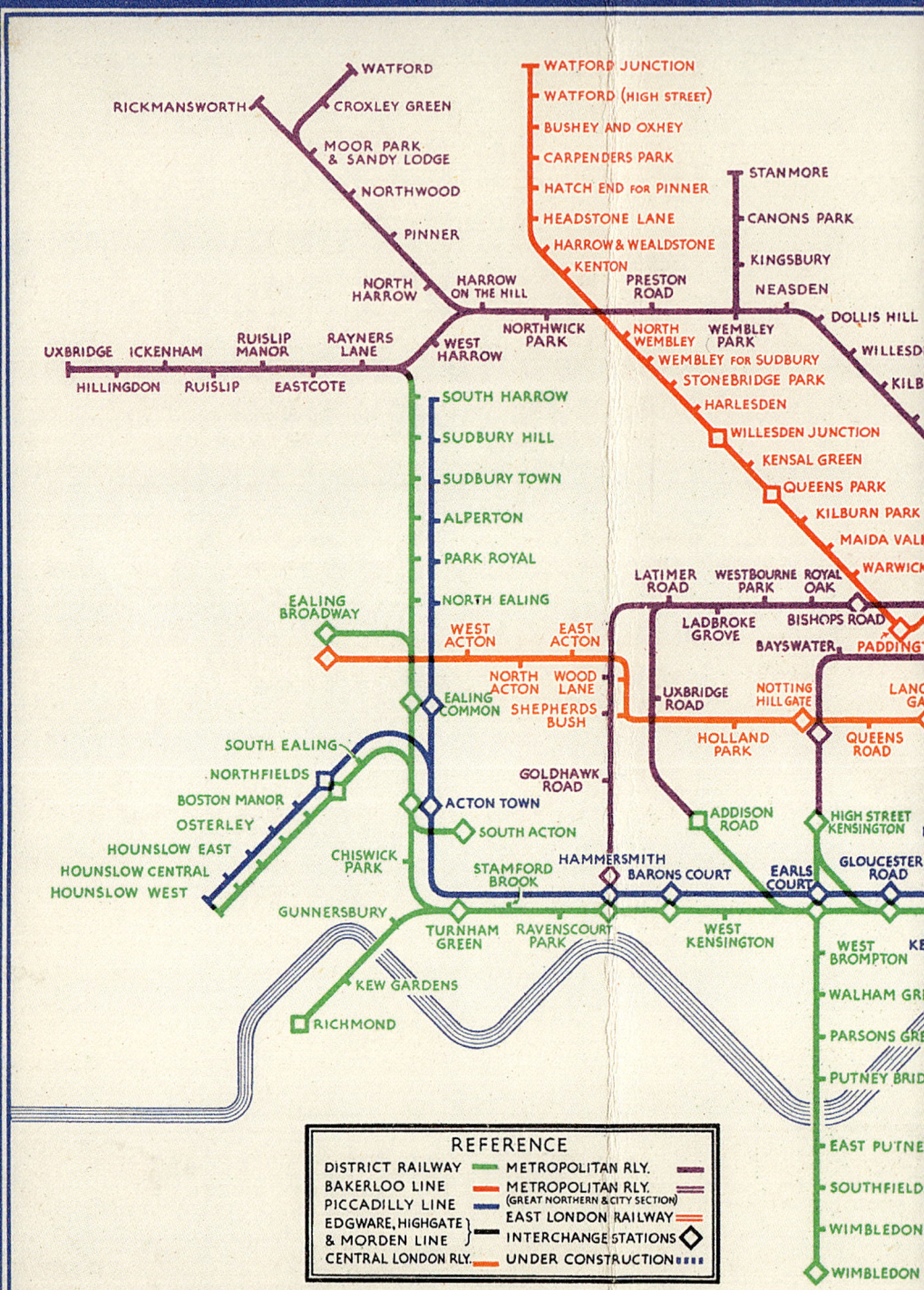

WATFORD
RICKMANSWORTH
CROXLEY GREEN
MOOR PARK & SANDY LODGE
NORTHWOOD
PINNER
WATFORD JUNCTION
WATFORD (HIGH STREET)
BUSHEY AND OXHEY
CARPENDERS PARK
HATCH END for PINNER
HEADSTONE LANE
HARROW & WEALDSTONE
KENTON
STANMORE
CANONS PARK
KINGSBURY
NEASDEN
NORTH HARROW
HARROW ON THE HILL
PRESTON ROAD
DOLLIS HILL
WILLESD
UXBRIDGE ICKENHAM RUISLIP MANOR RAYNERS LANE
WEST HARROW
NORTHWICK PARK
NORTH WEMBLEY
WEMBLEY PARK
WEMBLEY for SUDBURY
STONEBRIDGE PARK
KILB
HILLINGDON RUISLIP EASTCOTE
SOUTH HARROW
HARLESDEN
WILLESDEN JUNCTION
KENSAL GREEN
QUEENS PARK
SUDBURY HILL
SUDBURY TOWN
ALPERTON
KILBURN PARK
MAIDA VAL
WARWICK
PARK ROYAL
NORTH EALING
EALING BROADWAY
WEST ACTON
EAST ACTON
LATIMER ROAD
WESTBOURNE PARK
ROYAL OAK
LADBROKE GROVE
BISHOPS ROAD
BAYSWATER
PADDING
EALING COMMON
NORTH ACTON
WOOD LANE
SHEPHERDS BUSH
UXBRIDGE ROAD
NOTTING HILL GATE
LANC
GA
SOUTH EALING
NORTHFIELDS
BOSTON MANOR
OSTERLEY
HOUNSLOW EAST
HOUNSLOW CENTRAL
HOUNSLOW WEST
HOLLAND PARK
QUEENS ROAD
GOLDHAWK ROAD
ACTON TOWN
SOUTH ACTON
ADDISON ROAD
HIGH STREET KENSINGTON
CHISWICK PARK
STAMFORD BROOK
HAMMERSMITH
BARONS COURT
EARLS COURT
GLOUCESTER ROAD
GUNNERSBURY
TURNHAM GREEN
RAVENSCOURT PARK
WEST KENSINGTON
WEST BROMPTON
KE
KEW GARDENS
WALHAM GR
RICHMOND
PARSONS GRE
PUTNEY BRID
EAST PUTNE
SOUTHFIELD
WIMBLEDON
WIMBLEDON

REFERENCE
DISTRICT RAILWAY
BAKERLOO LINE
PICCADILLY LINE
EDGWARE, HIGHGATE & MORDEN LINE
CENTRAL LONDON RLY.
METROPOLITAN RLY.
METROPOLITAN RLY. (GREAT NORTHERN & CITY SECTION)
EAST LONDON RAILWAY
INTERCHANGE STATIONS
UNDER CONSTRUCTION

H.C.BECK

WATERLOW

COCKFOSTERS

OPEN MIDSUMMER 1933

ENFIELD WEST

SOUTHGATE

ARNOS GROVE

BOUNDS GREEN

WOOD GREEN

TURNPIKE LANE

MANOR HOUSE

T OAK (WATLING)
OLINDALE
HENDON CENTRAL
BRENT
GOLDERS GREEN
DESBURY
HAMPSTEAD
STEAD
BELSIZE PARK
EY ROAD
CHALK FARM
SS COTTAGE
MARLBORO ROAD
ST. JOHNS WOOD
MARYLEBONE

HIGHGATE
TUFNELL PARK
KENTISH TOWN
CAMDEN TOWN
MORNINGTON CRESCENT
EUSTON

FINSBURY PARK
ARSENAL (HIGHBURY HILL)
DRAYTON PARK
HOLLOWAY ROAD
HIGHBURY & ISLINGTON
CALEDONIAN ROAD
CANONBURY & ESSEX ROAD
KINGS CROSS ST. PANCRAS

TO
BOW ROAD
BROMLEY
WEST HAM
PLAISTOW
UPTON PARK
EAST HAM
BARKING
UPNEY
BECONTREE
HEATHWAY
DAGENHAM
HORNCHURCH
UPMINSTER
& SOUTHEND

RE
BAKER STREET
GREAT PORTLAND ST.
REGENTS PARK
BOND STREET
OXFORD CIRCUS
PICCADILLY
R STREET
ORNER
DGE
ON

EUSTON SQUARE
WARREN STREET
GOODGE STREET
TOTTENHAM COURT ROAD
BRITISH MUSEUM
LEICESTER SQUARE

ANGEL
FARRINGDON ALDERSGATE
RUSSELL SQUARE
CHANCERY LANE
POST OFFICE
HOLBORN
ALDWYCH
COVENT GARDEN
MANSION HOUSE

OLD STREET
MOORGATE
LIVERPOOL STREET
BANK
ALDGATE
MONUMENT
ALDGATE EAST

SHOREDITCH
ST. MARYS
STEPNEY GREEN
WHITECHAPEL
MILE END

STRAND
BLACKFRIARS
CANNON STREET
TEMPLE
CHARING CROSS
MARK LANE

TRAFALGAR SQUARE
WESTMINSTER
VICTORIA
WATERLOO
LAMBETH NORTH
LONDON BRIDGE
BOROUGH
ELEPHANT & CASTLE

SHADWELL
WAPPING

ROTHERHITHE
SURREY DOCKS

SLOANE SQUARE
ST. JAMES PARK

KENNINGTON
OVAL
STOCKWELL
CLAPHAM NORTH
CLAPHAM COMMON
CLAPHAM SOUTH
BALHAM
TRINITY ROAD (TOOTING BEC)
TOOTING BROADWAY
COLLIERS WOOD
SOUTH WIMBLEDON (MERTON)
MORDEN

NEW CROSS GATE
NEW CROSS

UNDERGROUND

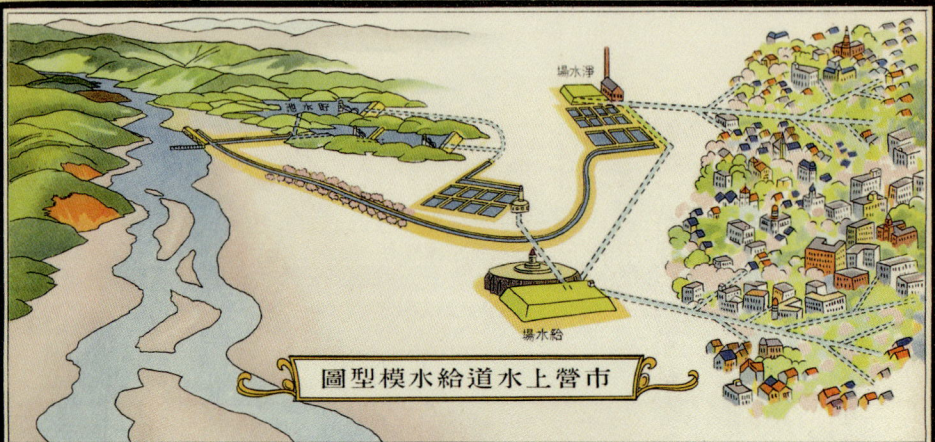

市營上水道給水模型圖

市營上水道總配水量
（二億四千一百八十七萬四千八百二十立方米）

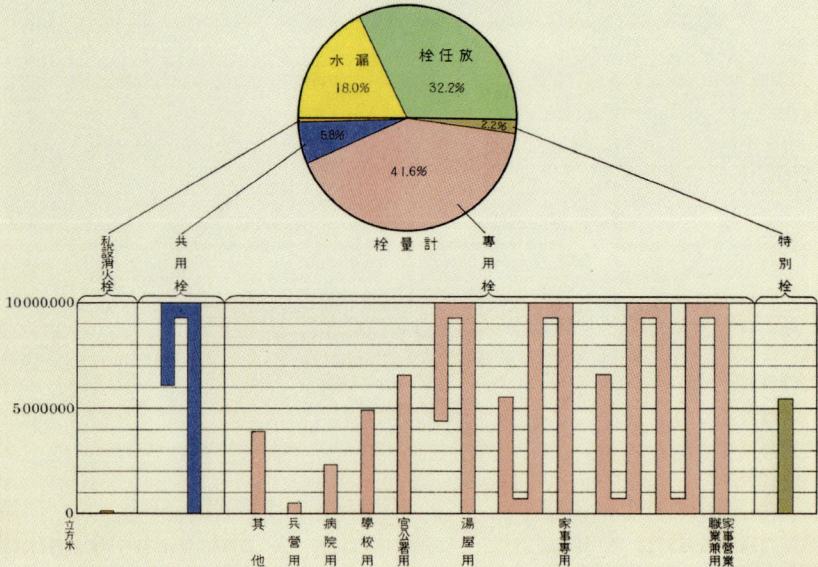

放任栓 32.2%
水漏 18.0%
5.8%
41.6%
2.2%

私設消火栓　共用栓　計量栓　專用栓　特別栓

其他　兵營用　病院用　學校用　官公署用　湯屋用　家事專用　職業兼用家事專用

10000000
5000000
0 立方米

水道事業

東京市内ニ於ケル水道事業ハ本市ノ經營ニ屬スルモノ、外會社經營ノ三水道ガアリマス。然シ乍ラ其ノ給水人口ハ何レモ僅少デアリ右ノ中玉川水道株式會社ノ經營ニ屬スル水道ハ其ノ特許年限ノ滿了ト同時ニ之ヲ本市ニ買收スルノ目下萬般ノ準備ヲ進メテ居リマス又大東京ノ圓滑ナル給水ハ一ニ懸ツテ市營水道事業ニ依ルノデアリマス。

本市ノ水道ハ多摩川江戸川掘川ノ三種デアリマシテ多摩川ハ東京府西多摩郡羽村ニ於テ江戸川ハ金町淨水場カラ掘井ハ善福池畔カラ夫々取入レ淨化セラレテ給水場ニ至リ鐵管タ以テ市内ニ配水スルノデアリマス。又渇水期ニ於ケル給水ノ安定ヲ圖ル爲メ貯水池ノ設備ハ必要缺クベカラザルモノデアリマシテ而カモ其ノ構造規模ハ數百萬ノ市民ヲ對象ト致シマスノデ當然互大ナラザルヲ得ナイノデアリマス。現在ノ村山山口兩貯水池ハ貯水量

Previous spread / **1933**
Harry Beck was the first to draw a diagrammatical map of
London's Underground system. His version served as a model
for many other maps worldwide. The individual lines are sim-
plified in order to render junction points more clearly.

1935
The diagrams in this print break down the water consumption
in Tokyo by various users. In the lower diagram, some bars are
bent in order to provide correct representations of the very
different consumption rates (given in cubic metres of water)
within the limited scale.

effective participation is to know and understand the context: who are the participants,
what are their points of view, which feelings
and interests are involved, and which positive
and negative forces influence the evolution of
the phenomena.

Scientists should try to humanise, if not
popularise their communication. If they want
to be trusted and gain public legitimacy, they
must also be authentic and honest about their
limits, insecurities and weaknesses. It is not
only a matter of economic survival, it is their
ethical duty towards society. Socio-economic
issues are by nature complex; one cannot understand them if considering only one aspect.
They are ambiguous and blurred; they cannot
be measured, and can only be represented
in qualitative terms. They are observed using
methods having inherent errors and approxi-
mations. Data never exactly correspond to the
phenomena they are supposed to synthesise.

Information design and, more specifically,
narrative visualisations, can play an important
role. Narrative visualisation uses communica-
tive elements that are not limited to the purpose of conveying facts. These elements go
beyond the mere visualisation of data, they
draw the bigger context of the phenomena. At
the visualisation research lab DensityDesign
in Milan which I directed for several years,
we therefore talked of complex works of data
visualization as *visual macroscopes*. This term
describes visualisations as tools that allow
people to see not the infinitely small or the infinitely distant, as *microscopes* and *telescopes*
do, but the infinitely complex.[2] Agreeing with

John Thackara, visualisations are understood as
"Tools and aesthetic notions, that help us understand – and act mindfully – in the big picture."

In close cooperation with statistics researchers, we recently worked on the visualisation of
poverty as a complex socio-economic problem.
The project was guided by a common belief: in
order to really make people understand what
poverty is about, a nuanced or *fuzzy* perspective
is needed. The general aim was to go beyond
the conventional, non-exhaustive, *0-1*, *yes-no*,
included-excluded pattern of communication.
This approach led to visualisations in which
multiple dimensions and uncertainties were
taken into account. The visualisation of uncertainty in the field of Digital Humanities is also
the core topic of a collaboration with the
Stanford Humanities Center. This joint project is to map the written exchanges between
the greatest thinkers of the Enlightenment.
One of the very first subjects of conversation
was discussing the traditional visualisation
modes for such flows and exchanges: does the
visualisation of the path of a letter sent from
Sender A to Recipient B with a simple, straight
line really convey the meaning of dispatching
that letter at that time, within the social and
cultural context? The awareness of the story
behind the data is fundamental to having a real
understanding of the phenomena. Moreover,
there is also a degree of uncertainty and incom-
pleteness in the database that must be reflected
in the visualisation.

The approach presented here (i.e. to amend
data visualisation by using a narrative dimension) does not only affect the communication

1936

MoMA's director Alfred H. Barr sketched the history of modern art on this famous cover of an exhibition catalogue. He conceived of a sort of family tree of styles. External influences like *Machine Esthetic* or *Japanese Prints* are marked in red.

between researchers and society. It also offers opportunities to foster relationships between different disciplines and research groups. Scientists must deal with increasingly complex issues which cannot be tackled by just one discipline. Experts from a wide range of scientific domains, each with different knowledge backgrounds, collaborate on joint projects. It is crucial to build a shared body of information, together with the possibility of sharing hypotheses and ideas: that's exactly where information design and narrative visualisation can play their role.

Just like sciences, governmental institutions often face the same risks – distance, distrust, scepticism and unmotivated opposition; their quest for accountability and trust is very similar. Many projects that go under the label of *open data* publish a growing source of information on socio-economic phenomena, without any explanation. So, is *open data* really *open*? How much can people really understand when they just collect, from a gigantic data warehouse, small slices of a pie whose size they are totally unaware of? Can you get an idea of a phenomenon's big picture just by playing with chunks of data? What can you learn if the story behind the data is hidden?

Governments that dare to face the sea of open data explore how they can go beyond understanding and *encourage* their citizens to become involved. The same goes for sciences and research organisations. The use of narrative elements in data visualisation can fuel commitment. Narrative elements cannot be considered as mere embellishments, they have a specific function in that they build the story – the narration – that is necessary to re-create the context and make sense of the data. To do so, one must leave the protected realm of research domains, and play with issues like *beauty* and *pleasure*. In other fields of design research it is quite established that *emotion* is a cognitive force which contributes to sense-making, facilitates interaction and enables a better user experience. Usability and aesthetics are no longer in opposition to each other: attractive things, says Donald Norman, often work better![3]

There was a time when complaints were made about embellishment in data visualisation being a common practice, recalling the traditional tensions – now relegated to history – between form and function (with an extremely strict position taken by Adolf Loos in his "Ornament and Crime"). Today at least there is room for debating a possible function for non-data ink,[4] denying in fact the very definition of embellishment as a purely ornamental and useless – or even detrimental – addition.

One could even overturn the argument and wonder whether plain, minimalist charts really do convey the right message, appropriate to the nature of the observed phenomenon. Any picture conveys a message, if not a story, and can be considered a narrative in a broad sense. Collaborating with statisticians on a regular basis, one learns that a simple table with numbers and decimals in its very simplicity conveys a notion of accuracy that may not be consistent with the methods used to gather the data. Statistical processes are less accurate and precise than the representation of their results

1890 JAPANESE PRINTS Gauguin d. 1903 Cézanne Provence d. 1906 Seurat d.1891 1890
SYNTHETISM NEO-IMPRESSIONISM
Van Gogh d. 1890 1888 Pont-Aven, Paris 1886 Paris

1895 Redon Paris d. 1916 Rousseau Paris d. 1910 1895

1900 NEAR-EASTERN ART 1900

1905 FAUVISM NEGRO SCULPTURE CUBISM 1905
1905 Paris 1906-08 Paris

1910 (ABSTRACT) EXPRESSIONISM FUTURISM MACHINE ESTHETIC ORPHISM SUPREMATISM 1910
1911 Munich 1910 Milan 1912 Paris 1913 Moscow

1915 Brancusi Paris CONSTRUCTIVISM 1915
1914 Moscow
(ABSTRACT) DADAISM DE STIJL and NEOPLASTICISM
Zurich Paris PURISM
1916 Cologne 1918 Paris Leyden Berlin
Berlin 1916 Paris

1920 BAUHAUS 1920
MODERN ARCHITECTURE Weimar Dessau
1919 1925

1925 (ABSTRACT) SURREALISM 1925
1924 Paris

1930 1930

NON-GEOMETRICAL ABSTRACT ART GEOMETRICAL ABSTRACT ART
1935 1935

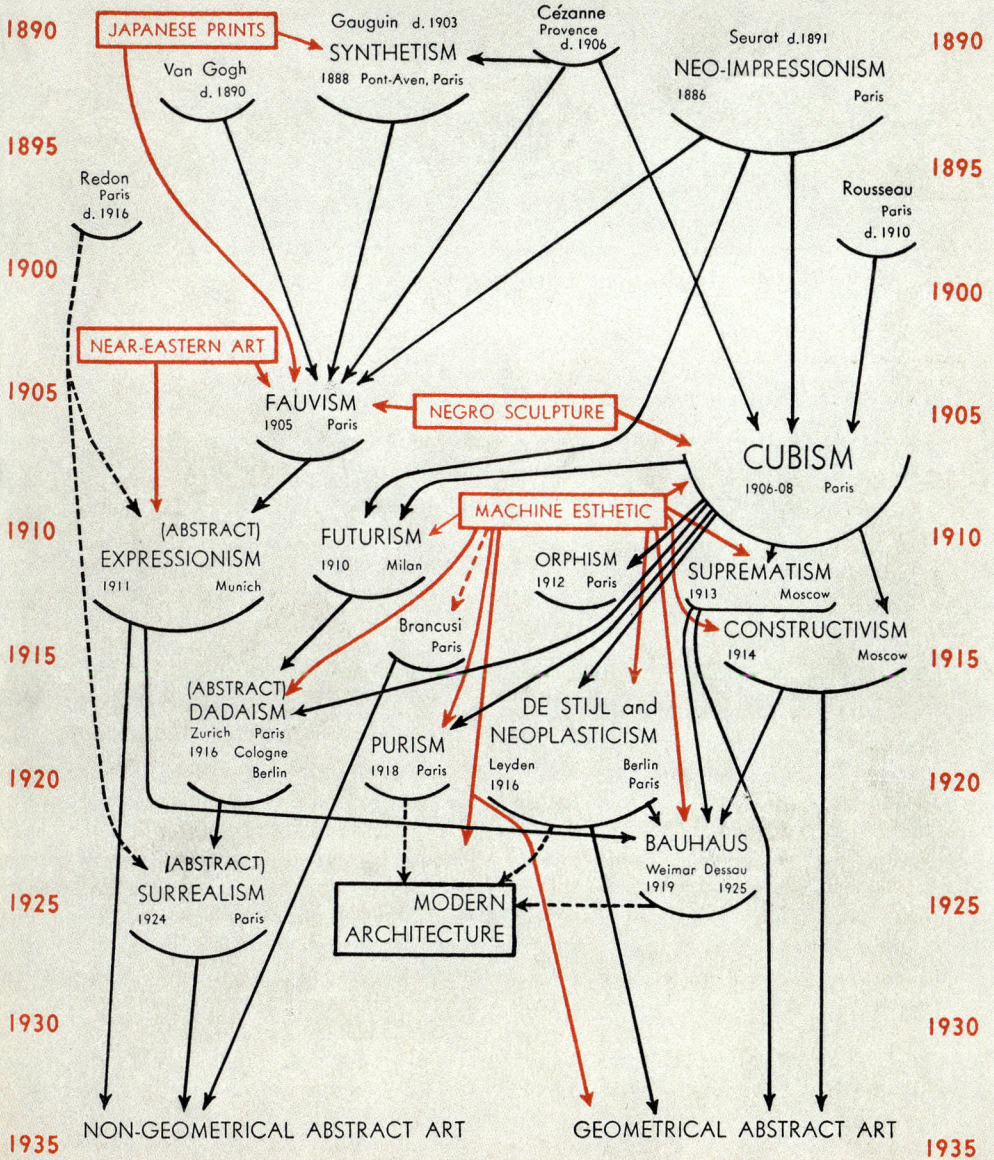

CUBISM AND ABSTRACT ART

OUR WORLD.....OU

$\frac{1}{2}$ OF THE GLOBE.....

THE PEOPLE: WHITE 170,000,000—BLACK 36,000,000—INDIAN 25,000,000—MIXED 39,000,00
270,000,000

would suggest. On the other hand, turning visualisation into a story – revealing the background, building up a context – asks for a designer's point of view. It goes far from neutrality and demands responsibility. Any visualisation is an interpretation, and it is the designer's responsibility to be fully aware of the intentionality of any communication artefact.

If storytelling is "the world's second-oldest profession,"[5] it is because it reflects a fundamental need of every human being. It is related to the human desire for knowledge, the need to understand and make sense of the phenomena we face. We want to know what the story is, and possibly be able to tell others what we have discovered and learned. These days, this fundamental need seems to become more apparent to institutions dealing with collecting and communicating social data: "It is indisputable that successful communication with the increasingly important group of non-professional customers requires that statistical offices go

far beyond the simple provision of tables and other purely static information. The visual presentation of data through comprehensible and flexible graphical tools, possibly embedded in a storytelling environment and connected with maps for the presentation of spatial data, crucially contributes to meeting the needs of the non-expert."[6]

We can probably all agree that if we do not understand statistics at all, we cannot know what is going on, as stated by Clive Thompson in an article in *Wired US*,[7] but are we really sure that the solution is, as Thompson proposes, to make statistics a core part of general education? Is statistics really the new grammar? It probably makes more sense to encourage researchers and scientists to partner with designers, in order to represent data in the language of the people, and not in the language of data.

LAND.....OUR PEOPLE

29% OF THE
EARTH'S SURFACE.....

$\frac{1}{8}$ OF THE WORLD'S
POPULATION.

FOOD — HOUSES — HEALTH
136,000,000, BELOW THE SAFETY LINE

Paolo Ciuccarelli is Professor of Design at North-eastern University in Boston. In his 20 years at the Politecnico di Milano he founded the DensityDesign Research Lab, an award winning laboratory for data visualization and information design.

1   Carrada, G.: *Communicating Science*. European Commission. Directorate-General for Research, 2006.

2   De Rosnay, J.: *The Macroscope*. New York: Harper & Row, 1979.

3   Norman, D.: "Emotion and design: Attractive things work better", *Interactions* magazine, ix (4), 2002, 36–42.

4   Bateman, Scott et al.: *Useful Junk? The Effects of Visual Embellishment on Comprehension and Memorability of Charts*. University of Saskatchewan, Department of Computer Science. Paper Presented on CHI, April 2010.

5   Gershon, N. and Page, W.: "What storytelling can do for information visualization". *Communications of the ACM*, 44 (8), 2001, 31–37.

6   Mittag, H.: "Educating the Public, The Role of E-Learning and Visual Communication of Official Data". Invited paper at the Statistical Commission and Economic Commission for Europe, Conference of European Statisticians, Paris, 12–15 June 2006. United Nations, Economic and Social Council, ECE/CES/2006.

7   Thompson, C.: "Why We Should Learn the Language of Data", *Wired US*, April 2010.

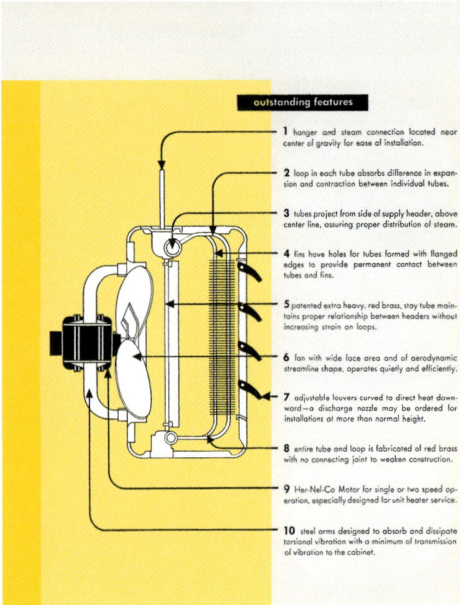

The Herman Nelson Corporation

Previous spread / **ca. 1940**

In the 1930s, magazines like *Fortune* or *McCall's* developed a vivid visual language for statistical data. In this graphic for *McCall's*, Irving Geis visualised data concerning the population of the Americas, e.g. an ethnic breakdown and the number of poor people.

ca. 1950

Czech designer Ladislav Sutnar focused on the clear structuring of information, both in the creation of exhibits as well as in his graphic designs. Exemplary are the industrial catalogues he designed for various clients.

1939

Herbert Bayer was an influential designer, architect and typographer, who studied and taught at Bauhaus Dessau in Germany. His work is considered an inspiring example in the field of information design to this day. This piece was created after his emigration to the US.

The human eye—a living camera

With its covering layers, its muscles and blood vessels, the eye is infinitely more delicately made than the finest camera. But its principle is the same. The crystalline lens throws an inverted image on the retina in exactly the same way that the camera lens forms an image on a film. Unlike the camera, however, the eye is focused by muscles which change the focal length of the lens, making it thicker for close objects, thinner for far ones. To compensate for changes in light intensity, the eye's pupil is "stopped down" or opened up like a lens diaphragm.

herbert bayer 39

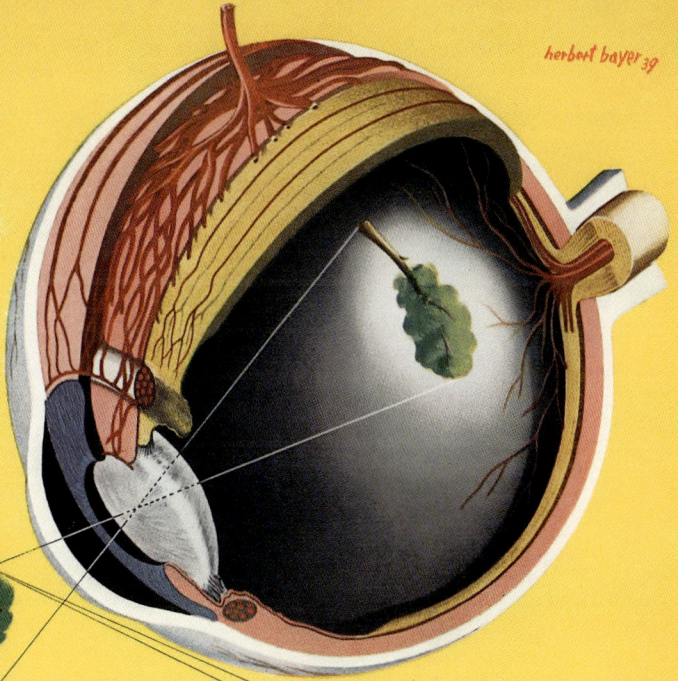

IN THE BRAIN THE INVERTED IMAGES, FORMED ON RETINAS OF TWO EYES, ARE BROUGHT TOGETHER TO FORM AN UPRIGHT STEREOSCOPIC VISUAL OBJECT

TO SCAN SUBJECTS, THE EYES ARE EQUIPPED WITH SIX PAIRS OF MUSCLES WHICH PERMIT THE EYES TO BE TURNED IN ANY DIRECTION OR CONVERGED

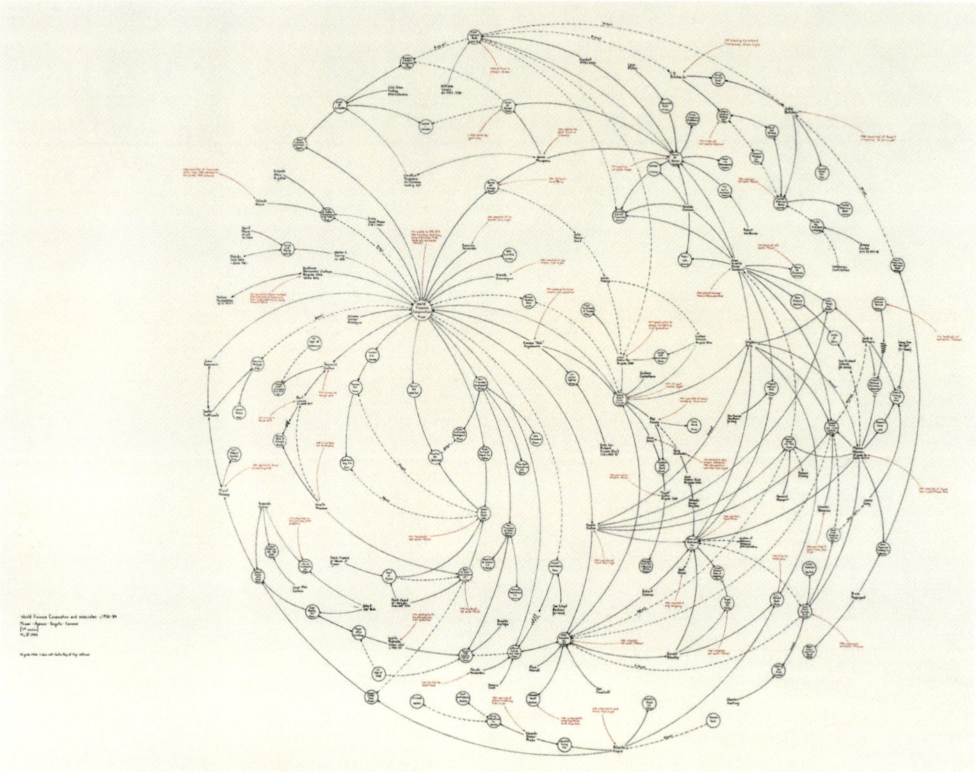

1999

The artist Mark Lombardi became known for his "sociograms" describing scandalous ties between economy and politics. This example focuses on the World Finance Corp. that laundered money for the Colombian drug mafia in the 1970s.

1955

Starting in the 1940s, artist Ad Reinhardt created a series of "art comics". This "art mandala" ironically shows the relationships between art, nature, economy and politics. Many "godly incarnations" of the artist surround the central diagram.

JOKE *by Ad Reinhardt*

A PORTEND OF THE ARTIST AS A YHUNG MANDALA

The Art World was recreated in 4 Days in 4 Sections, 40 years ago, and originally in 4001 b.c. Today minor Artists have 400 Disciples and more favored mediocre Artists have 44,000 Devotees approximately. There are 4,040 Rules of Art Conduct. The Ten Thousand Things are Four. Art History has Four Sides. There are Four Art Publications and Four Canons of Art Criticism. Judgment Days are Four Seasons.

The Four Sacred Art Texts are Confusionist, Doughist, Tantrumist and Sham-Buddhist. The Four Art Castes are Purehatpriests, Guruteacherhats, Sunnyascetichats and Bighatdevotees. The Four Mu-eums are the Four Mirrors of the Western Paradises.

Artistbuddies are Four Animals, half-hero, half-save, Holy-Naga-Beasts of the Four-Horse-Sacrificial-Ceremonies, whose entrails feed the Four Bird-Monsters.

Criticbuddies are Four Birds, half-harpy, half-deity, Garudabuzzards and Localpalies, who fly the Four Winds, who make the Music of the Art-Spheres.

Curatorbuddies are the Four Guardians of the Four Directions and the Four Pillars of the Milky Ways, Lotus-Eaters and Boom-Pickers, the Collecting Unconscience of the Art-Race.

The Art Universe is Square. Art is a Big, Booming Flux-Phenomena and Abyss. Your Soul's a sold-circle in the company-square. The Art-House is not a Home.

ART AND GOVERNMENT
The Human Animal
THE SORDID PRESENT

ART AND EDUCATION
The Human Machine

ART AND NATURE
The Human Eye

ART AND BUSINESS
The Human Vegetable
THE SICK PRESENT

Advertising Art, Cartooning & Sculpture
AMERICAN ACADEMY OF ARTS & EQUITIES, INC.

Magazine & Fashion Illustration
AMERICAN MERCURY & PAGE PAINTERS, INC.

Industrial Design & Architecture
ASSOCIATION OF AMERICAN ART PROFESSORS, INC.

Show Business, Poetry, Theater, Opera
NEW YORK SCHOOL, CHAMBER OF ART COMMERCE, INC.

Artist as Recorder — *Artist as Explainer* — *Artist as Cathartic* — *Artist as Commodity*

NORTH · SOUTH · EAST · WEST
THERE-NOW · HERE-NOW
YESTERDAY · TOMORROW
THE GLORIOUS PAST · THE GLORIOUS FUTURE
1900 · 1950

KEY:
Iconograph: Animal-in-the-Bird's-Mouth-Motif
Iconology: Square-Soul left in the Life-Circle outside
History: Clockwise, circle from S.E. to S.W.
  Asburn to Abstraction to Ashcan, Etc.
  Romanticism Up, Down, North, South.
  Classicism Old, New, Across, East, West.
  Intellectualism North-West.
Instinctivism: South-East.
Philistinism: North, East, South, West.
Sodden Ratmanland Haits Eden North-West.
Middy Brownland Pave Land South-East.
Emily Genuhed Happy Hunting Ground North, East, South.
Tawny Hrugupper Blessed Stable Clockwise, circle from S.E.
Clammy Greenland Blue Heaven South-East.
Howling Rosenbird Green Pastures Up, Down, North, South.
WHITNEY FISH-FRY VALHALLA North-East.
METROPOLITAN PEPSI-COLA NIRVANA North-West.
MUSEUM OF MODE EDEN ART UTOPIA South-West.
GUGGENHEIM ASPIDISTRA ELYSIUM South-East.
Action: Pin, Spin, Tear, Stomp, Burn Pin, Spin, Etc.

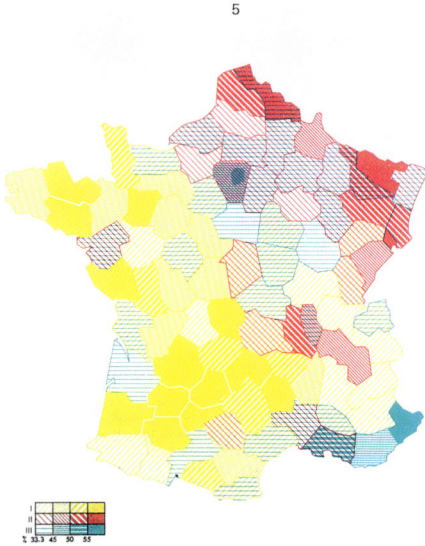

1967

In 1967 the French cartographer Jacques Bertin wrote a standard reference on the graphic depiction of quantitative data. These maps of France for example show how multi-dimensional quantitative data can be mapped on a geographical arena.

1960

This poster by British Railways shows the congestion of trains during rush hour and suggests passengers take earlier or later trains instead. The timeline runs top down, the bars showing the proportion of passengers and available seats.

EVENING BUSINESS TRAINS
from VICTORIA STATION

P.M.
4·00-4·14
4·15-4·29
4·30-4·44
4·45-4·59
5·00-5·14
5·15-5·29
5·30
to
6·15
6·15-6·29
6·30-6·44
6·45-7·00

= 250 STANDING PASSENGERS
= 250 SEATED PASSENGERS
= 1000 SEATS

THERE ARE MORE SEATS

SOUTHERN
BRITISH RAILWAYS

BEFORE 5·30 p.m. and AFTER 6·15 p.m.

STUDIO SEVEN

Periodic Table of Swearing

MODERN TOSS

2010

The Periodic Table combines several classifications, dividing the elements by nuclear charge (ordering number), periodically recurring attributes (rows) and groups (columns). Modern Toss ironically adapted this system for swear-words.

LATCH

The classification of infographics and data visualisations is not a simple matter. Many works are complex, and they all differ according to topic, in the form of their expression or in their tone, which can range from scientific gravitas to tongue-in-cheek humour. Classifications are rarely clear and there are many overlapping areas.

Graphics and visualisations serve to communicate information. The way in which data are arranged is the critical factor in enabling readers to understand them quickly. According to Richard Saul Wurman, there are five ways in which information can be structured. He termed this system "LATCH", which stands for:

Since infographics make less use of text there are fewer alphabetical examples, which is why this book does not include a section entitled "Alphabet". In many works, however, data is organised by combining several criteria. This is the case, for example, when timelines and weather data are added to maps.

This kind of combined representation is particularly found in animated and interactive visualisations. Nowadays, digital records can be organised flexibly by location, time or other criteria. The projects in this book have been allocated to individual chapters according to their dominant structural feature.

Location
Elements are organised spatially

Alphabet
Elements are organised alphabetically

Time
Elements are organised against a timeline

Category
Elements are divided into classes

Hierarchy
Elements are ranked in order of priority

Location
102-223

Location
Elements are organised spatially

Everything that happens occurs somewhere. To find one's bearings in the world one must first orient oneself spatially: where do things happen? By organising objects spatially, one obtains an overview and can place side by side the items that occur concurrently within a space. Cartography is the science of depicting geographical information. For centuries it revolved around the question of how to project the curvature of the Earth on to paper. Topographical maps deal with the correct depiction of the Earth's surface, whereas thematic maps supplement spatial information with additional data (*The Geotaggers' World Atlas*, p.196).

Unlike photographically precise satellite images, maps use graphic means to make generalisations about the world. Maps are selective and standardise characteristic features, and therein lies their strength. Although they are a medium of simultaneity, some maps introduce a time element: for instance, in the context of a journey, the traversing of space can be depicted within a certain time-frame (*Flight AF447*, p.131).

Until recently maps were the main medium for storing geographical data, but a fundamental change is on the horizon thanks to the digital revolution. Space-related data can now be stored in databases, which in turn provide the starting point for complex visualisations. In addition, there are some works that do not place spatially sorted data on maps, but list them by name of country. These relate to the mental map of the world that we all hold in our heads (*A_B_ peace & terror etc.*, p.104).

Visualising information in maps goes beyond real spaces; imagined spaces can also be mapped. Mental maps show how relationships are arranged spatially in the imagination. For instance, Hugleikur Dagsson's map of Iceland uses the island's contours as the template for a mental image of his homeland (*The Land of Ice*, p.198). Esther Aarts arranges violent street names so that together they form the shape of a skull (*Map to Ghost Town*, p.156).

The organisation of information by place does not end with maps. Spatial arrangements can also be found in schematic drawings, which depict technical facilities or natural phenomena such as underground volcanoes (cf. *Sleeping Giant*, p.184). The human body, too, has repeatedly been considered as a spatial arrangement. Medicine is subdivided into specialisations based on different areas of the body, and each different body-part has its own monetary value (*Body Parts*, p.114). Geometry as a branch of mathematics is also concerned with spatial arrangements; its subject is the projection of multi-dimensional structures on to a two-dimensional surface (*Real Magick in Theory and Practise*, p.168).

Project Info: Dual-sided screen print, 2008, UK
Data Source: Global Peace Index; SIPRI; Happy Planet Index;
Subjective Well-Being Index; Political Terror Scale
Design: Peter Crnokrak (The Luxury of Protest)
Awards: AIGA 365, 2009

A_B_peace & terror etc.

This diagram surveys how the 192 member states of the UN contribute to global peace or terror. The inner circle lists all states in alphabetical order. The outer circles visualise various indices for contributions to peace or terror. Peace is shown in black and is derived from the Global Peace Index, the Happy Planet Index and the Subjective Well-Being Index (from the centre outwards). The terror contributions of each country are shown in white and are derived from the Political Terror Scale, Weapon Holdings per Capita and Military Expenditure per Capita (from the centre outwards). Originally this diagram was issued as a double-sided transparent poster, with peace printed on the A-side and war on the B-side.

An American Watershed

Five decades after authorizing the building of canals and levees to control flooding, Congress has acted to restore the flow of freshwater that sustains the United States' only subtropical preserve.

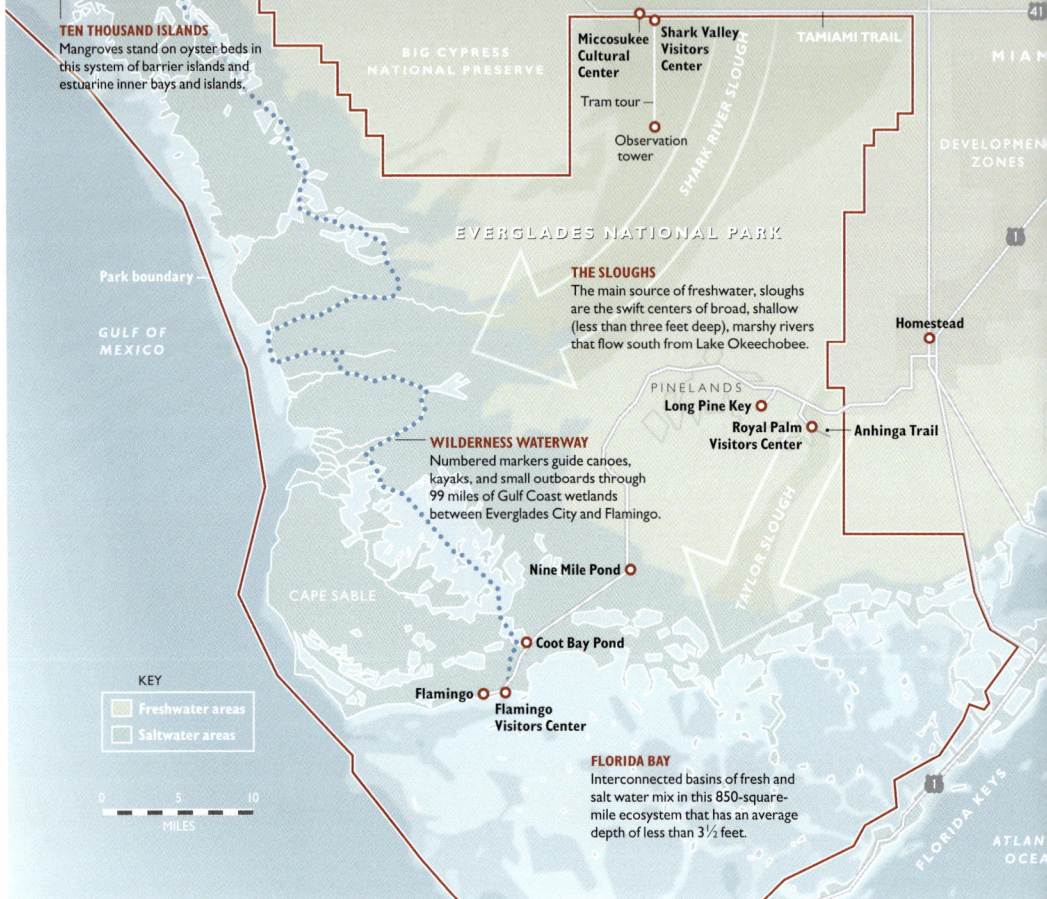

Gulf Coast Visitors Center

Everglades City

TEN THOUSAND ISLANDS
Mangroves stand on oyster beds in this system of barrier islands and estuarine inner bays and islands.

Miccosukee Cultural Center

Shark Valley Visitors Center

TAMIAMI TRAIL

BIG CYPRESS NATIONAL PRESERVE

Tram tour

Observation tower

SHARK RIVER SLOUGH

MIAMI

DEVELOPMENT ZONES

EVERGLADES NATIONAL PARK

Park boundary

GULF OF MEXICO

THE SLOUGHS
The main source of freshwater, sloughs are the swift centers of broad, shallow (less than three feet deep), marshy rivers that flow south from Lake Okeechobee.

Homestead

PINELANDS

Long Pine Key

Royal Palm Visitors Center

Anhinga Trail

WILDERNESS WATERWAY
Numbered markers guide canoes, kayaks, and small outboards through 99 miles of Gulf Coast wetlands between Everglades City and Flamingo.

TAYLOR SLOUGH

Nine Mile Pond

CAPE SABLE

Coot Bay Pond

Flamingo

Flamingo Visitors Center

FLORIDA BAY
Interconnected basins of fresh and salt water mix in this 850-square-mile ecosystem that has an average depth of less than 3½ feet.

FLORIDA KEYS

ATLANTIC OCEAN

KEY
Freshwater areas
Saltwater areas

0   5   10
MILES

Ecosystems under threat

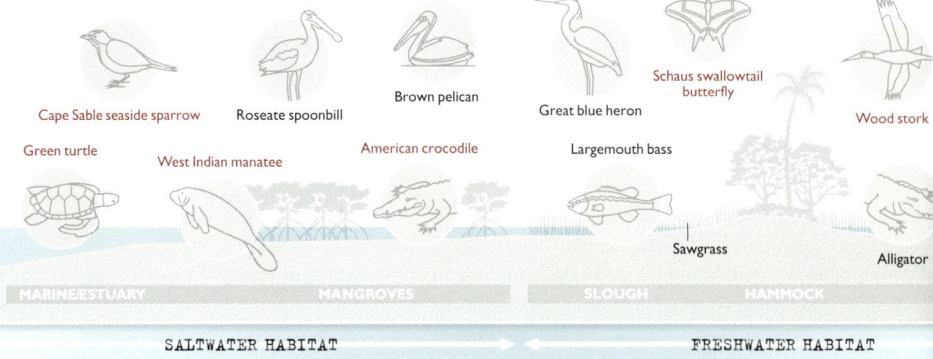

Cape Sable seaside sparrow

Roseate spoonbill

Brown pelican

Great blue heron

Schaus swallowtail butterfly

Wood stork

Green turtle

West Indian manatee

American crocodile

Largemouth bass

Sawgrass

Alligator

MARINE/ESTUARY   MANGROVES   SLOUGH   HAMMOCK

SALTWATER HABITAT ⟶   ⟵ FRESHWATER HABITAT

Graphics by John Grimwade

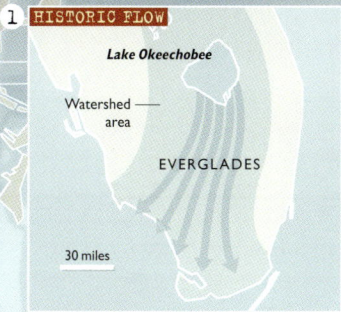

1 HISTORIC FLOW

Lake Okeechobee

Watershed area

EVERGLADES

30 miles

2 CURRENT FLOW

75

Lake Okeechobee

West Palm Beach

Fort Myers

Everglades Agricultural Area

Naples

Water Conservation Area

Miami

Everglades National Park

3 PLANNED FLOW

Lake Okeechobee

West Palm Beach

Fort Myers

Naples

Miami

Everglades National Park

White ibis

Everglades kite

Florida panther

Red =Endangered species

Bluegill

CYPRESS

PINELANDS

An American Watershed

The Everglades in Florida are a system of sub-tropical wetlands, fed by fresh waters from Lake Okeechobee in the north which form a very wide slow-moving river. After decades of draining, a major restoration plan for the Everglades was agreed by US Congress in 2000. This map shows the Everglades National Park, which safeguards the southern part of the wetlands. The sequence of historical maps on the right demonstrate how the water-flows had been modified in the past for the fresh-water supplies of cities in the area, and how the plans were to restore much of the natural water-flow to preserve the Everglades. The panorama at the bottom lists endangered species living in the area.

Project Info: *Condé Nast Traveler*, magazine article, 2003, USA
Design: Robert Best
Illustration: John Grimwade

AS MAIORES CURIOSIDADES DO CORPO HUMANO

Você sabia que a pele é a mais pesada que os ossos?
Que o sangue passa por algumas artérias a mais de 100 km/h?
Pois é, não faltam fatos intrigantes sobre nossa anatomia.
Fique por dentro deles entrando numa superconsulta médica,
capaz de curar qualquer curioso!

YURI VASCONCELOS / GABRIEL SILVEIRA / ALESSANDRA KALKO / FABIO VOLPE

O HOMEM É O ANIMAL COM MAIS NEURÔNIOS?

Definir o número de neurônios não é tarefa fácil. Estima-se que cada ser humano tenha cerca de 100 bilhões dessas células nervosas. Perto de animais pesquisados em laboratórios, como macacos e ratos, de fato somos os campeões. Mas o problema é que não existem estudos sobre a quantidade de neurônios em animais de grande porte, como ursos, elefantes ou baleias.

REI DOS MACACOS (E DOS RATOS)

HOMEM
100 bilhões de neurônios

MACACO RHESUS
6 bilhões de neurônios

CAMUNDONGO
71 milhões de neurônios

POR QUE A GENTE PISCA?

A gente dá cerca de 25 mil piscadas por dia, e todo esse esforço serve para espalhar lágrimas pelos olhos. Eles precisam ser mantidos úmidos e lubrificados o tempo todo para se protegerem de corpos estranhos, como poeira. As lágrimas são produzidas por glândulas e se espalham pelos olhos por meio de dois pequenos canais, os dutos lacrimais. Por dia, uma pessoa adulta produz de 1 a 2 litros de lágrimas – sem contar as derramadas no choro. Haja piscada para dar vazão a esse aguaceiro!

DO QUE É FEITA A REMELA?

A remela surge da desidratação da lágrima, que é composta de uma parte mucosa, uma de gordura e outra líquida. O excesso de lágrima vai para o canto dos olhos, levando consigo todo tipo de sujeira. Ali, a parte líquida evapora ou é absorvida pelo duto lacrimal e o que sobra é a remela.

QUAL É O MÚSCULO QUE MAIS TRABALHA?

Os músculos mais ativos são os oculares, responsáveis pelos movimentos dos olhos. Eles se mexem mais de 100 mil vezes por dia. É claro que não estamos considerando o coração, que nunca para de bater, mas que não é controlado pela gente. Já os músculos oculares obedecem aos comandos do cérebro. O curioso é que boa parte da atividade deles ocorre com os olhos fechados, durante a fase de sono REM, que indica que estamos sonhando.

DO QUE É FEITA A CERA DO OUVIDO?

A cera de ouvido é uma mistura de gorduras e óleos, produzidos por glândulas no canal do ouvido. Ao contrário do que muita gente pensa, ela não é sujeira, não, pois tem uma importante função protetora: além de reter poeira e outras impurezas, suas enzimas protegem os ouvidos de microrganismos invasores. >>

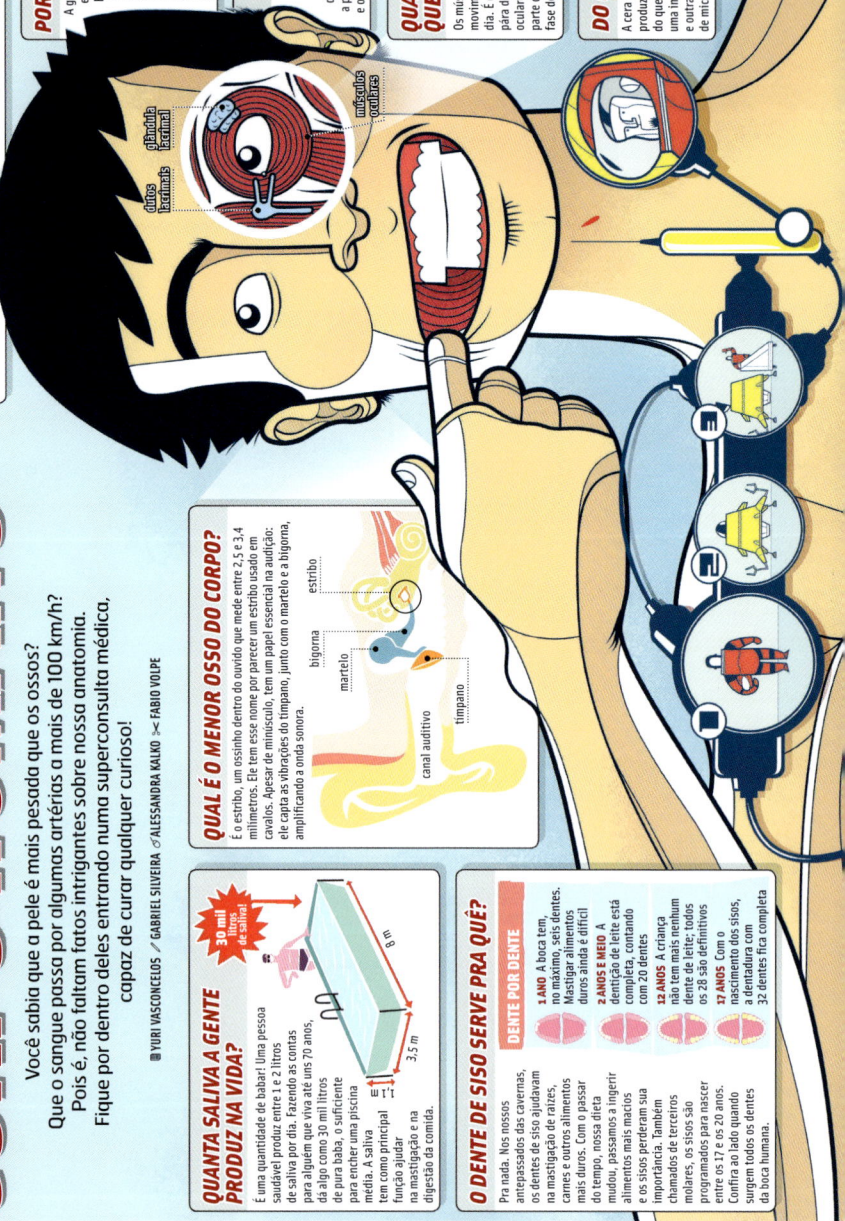

QUAL É O MENOR OSSO DO CORPO?

É o estribo, um ossinho dentro do ouvido que mede entre 2,5 e 3,4 milímetros. Ele tem esse nome por parecer um estribo usado em cavalos. Apesar de minúsculo, tem um papel essencial na audição: ele capta as vibrações do tímpano, junto com o martelo e a bigorna, amplificando a onda sonora.

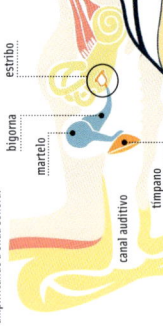

estribo
bigorna
martelo
canal auditivo
tímpano

QUANTA SALIVA A GENTE PRODUZ NA VIDA?

É uma quantidade de babar! Uma pessoa saudável produz entre 1 e 2 litros de saliva por dia. Fazendo as contas para alguém que viva até uns 70 anos, dá algo como 30 mil litros de pura baba, o suficiente para encher uma piscina média. A saliva tem como principal função ajudar na mastigação e na digestão da comida.

30 mil litros de saliva!

1,1 m
8 m
3,5 m

O DENTE DE SISO SERVE PRA QUÊ?

Pra nada. Nos nossos antepassados das cavernas, os dentes de siso ajudavam na mastigação de raízes, carnes e outros alimentos mais duros. Com o passar do tempo, nossa dieta mudou, passamos a ingerir alimentos mais macios e os sisos perderam sua importância. Também chamados de terceiros molares, os sisos são programados para nascer entre os 17 e os 20 anos. Confira ao lado quando surgem todos os dentes da boca humana.

DENTE POR DENTE

1 ANO A boca tem, no máximo, seis dentes. Mastigar alimentos duros ainda é difícil

2 ANOS E MEIO A dentição de leite está completa, contando com 20 dentes

12 ANOS A criança não tem mais nenhum dente de leite; todos os 28 são definitivos

17 ANOS Com o nascimento dos sisos, a dentadura com 32 dentes fica completa

QUAL É A MAIOR ARTÉRIA?

É a aorta, uma supra-artéria com 3 centímetros de diâmetro e 50 de comprimento. Começando no coração perto da região genital, ela leva o sangue oxigenado a todas as partes do corpo. Em comprimento, porém, a aorta perde para uma supra-veia que fica na perna. Com cerca de 70 centímetros num homem de altura mediana, a veia safena magna é o maior vaso sanguíneo do corpo.

aorta
safena
magna

POR QUE A ARÉOLA DO SEIO TEM COR E PELE DIFERENTES?

Esta região tem a córnea – subcamada mais superficial da epiderme – muito fina, o que torna a pele da aréola do seio bem mais lisa do que a do resto do corpo. Já a cor é mais forte porque nesta região há maior atividade dos melanócitos, células produtoras de melanina, um pigmento de cor marrom-escura.

UM CORTE NA PELE

EPIDERME É a camada mais externa, que vive "descascando". Aqui ficam os melanócitos e a córnea, subcamada mais superficial da epiderme.

DERME Camada rica em vasos sanguíneos e nervos. Mantém a pele hidratada e flexível, produzindo substâncias como colágeno e elastina.

HIPODERME Camada mais profunda, formada principalmente de gordura para proteger o corpo contra o frio.

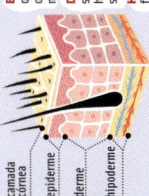

camada
córnea
epiderme
derme
hipoderme

QUANTAS VEZES TROCAMOS DE PELE?

As células da pele se renovam a cada 20 ou 30 dias. Isso significa que ao longo da vida "trocamos" de pele umas mil vezes! Mas a troca só envolve a camada mais externa, a epiderme.

Apesar de quase imperceptível, essa renovação dá um trabalho danado, afinal, a pele é o maior órgão do corpo humano, com cerca de 2 m². Com exceção dos olhos, mucosas, unhas e orifícios alimentares e genitais, toda nossa superfície corporal é coberta por esse super-revestimento.

QUANTOS MÚSCULOS A GENTE TEM?

O corpo humano tem mais de 600 músculos. Apesar de ser sinônimo de força, o bíceps, músculo da parte da frente do braço, não leva o título de mais forte do corpo. O grande campeão é o masseter, músculo responsável pela mastigação. Graças a ele, uma mordida de dois segundos é capaz de exercer uma pressão equivalente a 124 quilos.

As centenas de músculos que temos fazem desse tipo de tecido o mais pesado na composição do corpo humano. Veja como o nosso peso é distribuído:

MÚSCULOS 40% do peso	PELE 16%	OUTROS ÓRGÃOS* 15%	OSSOS 14%	SANGUE 7%	OUTROS COMPONENTES** 8%

*CÉREBRO, CORAÇÃO, PULMÕES, RINS, FÍGADO, ESTÔMAGO, INTESTINOS, BAÇO, PÂNCREAS E BEXIGA
**TENDÕES, LIGAMENTOS, CARTILAGENS, GLÂNDULAS, NERVOS, DENTES E OUTROS TECIDOS
OBS.: VALORES ESTIMADOS PARA UM ADULTO

POR QUE SÓ OS HOMENS TÊM GOGÓ?

Por causa da maior quantidade do hormônio testosterona. É ele que faz crescer o gogó, o nome popular da cartilagem tireóide e região que os homens têm. E cheia de receptores de testosterona. Essa cartilagem fica um pouco acima da glândula tireóide, que produz hormônios que regulam boa parte do organismo.

O outro nome popular do gogó, pomo-de-adão, tem origem bíblica e faz alusão ao fato de Adão ter comido o fruto proibido no paraíso e um pedaço dele ter ficado entalado na sua garganta.

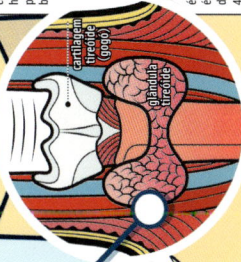

cartilagem
tireóide
(gogó)

glândula
tireóide

QUANTO AR CABE NOS PULMÕES?

Os pulmões comportam uns 5 litros de ar, mas apenas meio litro é renovado a cada respiração. Como nossa frequência respiratória é de cerca de 15 movimentos por minuto, respiramos 7,5 litros de ar a esse intervalo de tempo. Fazendo as contas, respiramos 450 litros de ar em uma hora; 10 800 litros em um dia; 3,9 milhões de litros em um ano; e por volta de 276 milhões de litros de ar ao longo de 70 anos!

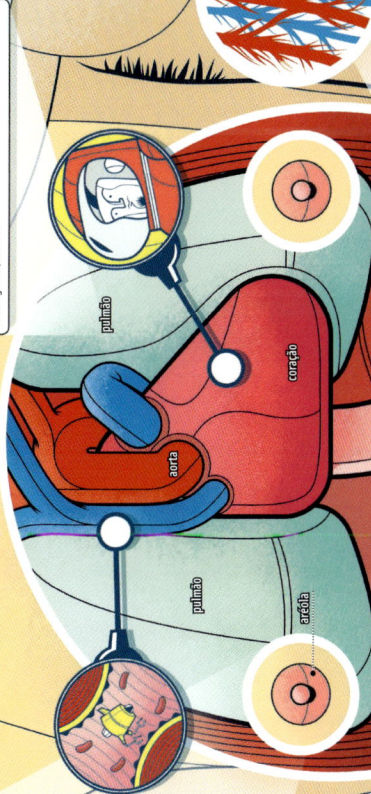

pulmão

coração

aorta

pulmão

aréola

O CORAÇÃO É DO TAMANHO DO PUNHO?

Sim. O coração de um adulto tem cerca de 12 centímetros de comprimento por 8 ou 9 centímetros de largura, o que corresponde ao tamanho aproximado de um punho fechado. Mas as proporções mais exatas no corpo humano estão nos ossos da mão e são vitais para que ela possa exercer a função de pegar as coisas. Veja como essas proporções funcionam:

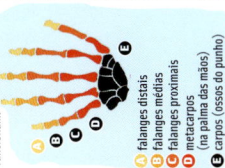

A falanges distais
B falanges médias
C falanges proximais
D metacarpos
E carpos (ossos do punho)

E
D
C
B
A

1ª PROPORÇÃO: a soma do comprimento da falange distal com a falange média é igual ao tamanho da falange proximal do dedo (A + B = C)

A
B
C
D

E
D
C
B
A

2ª PROPORÇÃO: a soma da falange média à proximal é igual ao tamanho do metacarpo (B + C = D)

QUANTO SANGUE CIRCULA NO CORPO?

Cinco litros, em média. Para distribuir o sangue pelo organismo, o coração bate cerca de 70 vezes por minuto. A cada batida, ele bombeia 90 mililitros de sangue, que percorrem o corpo em apenas um minuto. No caso de um acidente que provoque hemorragia grave, o máximo de sangue que o corpo pode perder antes que a pessoa morra é 2 litros. >>

mundo estranho 29

QUAL É O ÓRGÃO MAIS DISPENSÁVEL DO CORPO?

Se você tiver o azar de lesionar um órgão, torça pra ser o baço. Ele tem lá suas funções, como remover os glóbulos vermelhos velhos de vírus e bactérias. Mas tá para viver sem ele - o que não rola sem coração, pulmões, fígado, estômago, pâncreas ou intestino - sem os dois rins também não dá.

Quando alguém sofre uma pancada forte na barriga e danifica o baço, a ponto de ele precisar ser removido, o fígado se encarrega da "limpeza" dos glóbulos vermelhos. Já a imunidade da pessoa fica debilitada com a menor produção de anticorpos. >>

QUAL É A PRODUÇÃO DIÁRIA DE PUM?

Entre 1 litro e 1,5 litro! A maior parte da matéria-prima para os puns são gases que engolimos enquanto falamos ou comemos.

O ar ingerido vai até o estômago. Parte dele pode voltar pela boca, na forma de arroto. O resto ou é absorvido pelo organismo ou segue para o intestino, onde se junta com gases malcheirosos produzidos pela ação das bactérias sobre a comida. O pum produzido se acumula no reto até ser liberado. Quando prendemos um "rojão", o gás fedorento volta para o intestino até ter uma oportunidade mais discreta para escapar...

QUANTO COCÔ UMA PESSOA PRODUZ POR DIA?

São 150 gramas, em média. As fezes produzidas se acumulam na porção final do intestino grosso, onde fica o reto. Quando o "estoque" atinge uns 30 gramas, automaticamente se abre o esfíncter interno, uma musculatura que libera o cocô pra sair. Ao mesmo tempo, o cérebro manda um sinal dizendo que é hora de sentar no trono. Ainda bem que uma outra parte da musculatura do reto, o esfíncter externo, é controlada pela gente. É ele que nos dá tempo suficiente para ir até uma privada antes de soltar a porqueira toda.

baço
estômago
intestino grosso
fígado
intestino delgado
esfíncter
cocô
reto

QUAL É O MÁXIMO DE COMIDA QUE CABE NO ESTÔMAGO?

Com um formato parecido ao da letra J, o estômago é um órgão elástico. Quando vazio, tem um volume de apenas 50 mililitros. Mas, se você comer sem parar, ele pode aumentar em 80 vezes sua capacidade, o equivalente a entuchar 3 ou 4 litros de comida.

Se a pessoa insistir em continuar ingerindo rango além desse volume, pode acabar vomitando. Ao lado você confere a "tradução" dessa capacidade em lanches do tipo fast food:

2 Big Mac + 2 refrigerantes de 500 ml + 2 porções grandes de batata frita + 2 milk shakes de 500 ml = **4 litros**

QUAIS SÃO OS MAIORES ÓRGÃOS INTERNOS?

Nas páginas anteriores você já viu que a pele é o maior e o mais pesado órgão do corpo. Mas, se a gente for considerar apenas os órgãos internos, temos outros dois campeões. Em peso, ninguém mais que o fígado, que tem entre 1,3 e 1,5 quilo. Agora, se o critério for comprimento, o título fica com o intestino, que, somando o grosso e o delgado, tem uns 7,5 metros de extensão. O delgado, que começa no estômago, mede cerca de 6 metros e tem 2 ou 3 centímetros de diâmetro. O grosso tem 1,5 metro e diâmetro de até 8 centímetros. Enquanto o intestino delgado continua a digestão iniciada no estômago, o grosso é responsável pela produção do cocô.

PRA QUE SERVE O CÓCCIX?

Esse ossinho, que fica na base da nossa coluna, parece não ter nenhuma utilidade hoje em dia. Mas, num passado remoto, ele devia fazer parte da cauda de nossos ancestrais, que sumiu com a evolução. Basta ver ao lado, no esqueleto de um babuíno, como a cauda é uma simples continuação da coluna dos macacos.

O cóccix humano é na verdade uma fusão de quatro pequenas vértebras. Veja como se dividem os ossos da nossa coluna vertebral:

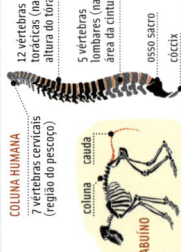

COLUNA HUMANA
7 vértebras cervicais (região do pescoço)
12 vértebras torácicas (na altura do tórax)
5 vértebras lombares (na área da cintura)
osso sacro
cóccix

coluna
cauda
BABUÍNO

QUEM É MAIS RÁPIDO: OS ESPERMATOZOIDES OU O SANGUE?

Movendo-se a cerca de 45 km/h, um espermatozoide deixaria pra trás os melhores atletas do mundo nos 100 metros rasos - que atingem no máximo 37 km/h. Mas numa "corrida orgânica" ele perderia feio para a circulação sanguínea e outros velocistas do corpo. Confira como seria essa racha:

CORRIDA MALUCA

IMPULSO NERVOSO 360 km/h
SANGUE 108 km/h*
ESPERMATOZOIDE 45 km/h*
ESPARRO 150 km/h

*NA AORTA, AO SAIR DO CORAÇÃO

QUAL FOI O MAIOR OSSO HUMANO JÁ ENCONTRADO?

Foi um fêmur de 76 centímetros, que pertenceu a um "gigante" alemão chamado Constantine. O fêmur se estende da bacia ao joelho e é o maior osso do corpo – ele tem quase o dobro do tamanho do úmero, o maior osso do braço. Na média, o fêmur corresponde a 27,5% da altura da pessoa. Em um adulto de 1,80 m, portanto, ele mede por volta de 50 centímetros. Por essa proporção, o tal alemão Constantine teria impressionantes 2,76 metros de altura!

úmero 30 cm
fêmur 50 cm
altura 1,80 m

É VERDADE QUE O NÚMERO DE OSSOS DIMINUI AO LONGO DA VIDA?

É verdade, sim! Quando nascemos, nosso esqueleto tem cerca de 300 ossos, mas, na idade adulta, são apenas 206. Mas pode ficar tranquilo, você não vai perder nenhum osso... O que acontece é que alguns deles se fundem à medida que crescemos. O melhor exemplo é na bacia. Em bebês, cada lado dela é formado por três ossos: ísquio, ílio e púbis. Com o passar do tempo, eles se juntam, dando origem a um só grande osso, chamado ilíaco.

BEBÊ
ílio
púbis
ísquio

ADULTO
ilíaco

AS UNHAS DOS PÉS CRESCEM NA MESMA VELOCIDADE QUE AS UNHAS DAS MÃOS?

Não, as unhas das mãos crescem quatro vezes mais rápido do que as dos pés. No dia-a-dia, nem dá para perceber tanto, mas, se você descuidasse de corta-las durante um ano, ia ver uma diferença e tanto! O curioso é que as unhas da mão dominante – a direita dos destros e a esquerda dos canhotos – também crescem mais rapidamente do que as da outra mão.

UM ANO DEPOIS...
UNHA DO DEDÃO ~0,9 cm
UNHA DO POLEGAR ~3,6 cm

QUANTOS QUILÔMETROS DE "VEIAS" HÁ NO CORPO?

Se a gente pudesse unir-los em linha reta, conseguiríamos algo como 100 mil quilômetros de vasos sanguíneos! Isso é o suficiente para dar mais de duas voltas e meia em torno da Terra. Existem cinco tipos de vasos sanguíneos, como mostra o infográfico abaixo:

ARTÉRIAS
Levam o sangue rico em oxigênio do coração para o resto do corpo

ARTERÍOLAS
Artérias pequenas, que cumprem a mesma função que suas "irmãs" maiores

VEIAS
Carregam o sangue até o coração e os pulmões, onde ele recebe oxigênio

VÊNULAS
São veias pequenas, que cumprem a mesma função que suas "irmãs" maiores

CAPILARES
Unem vênulas e arteríolas; neles ocorrem as trocas gasosas com as células

POR QUE TEMOS REFLEXO NO JOELHO?

Quando o médico dá uma "martelada" no nosso joelho, ele aciona um intricado mecanismo que faz com que a perna se mova para a frente. Esse movimento, conhecido como reflexo patelar – de patela, o osso do joelho –, é uma resposta involuntária a um estímulo sensorial. Veja como ele ocorre:

medula espinhal
nervo motor
nervo sensorial
musculatura da coxa

1 A "martelada" no joelho estimula receptores sensitivos, gerando um sinal nervoso. Esse sinal não chega até o cérebro. Por isso a reação é automática, não depende da nossa vontade.

2 O sinal segue por um nervo sensorial – que transmite sensações captadas pelo corpo – até chegar à medula espinhal.

3 Na medula, o sinal passa do nervo sensorial para um nervo motor – que transmite estímulos de movimento.

4 O nervo motor leva o sinal de movimento até a musculatura da coxa. O sinal manda os músculos contraír, o que faz a perna se deslocar para a frente.

POR QUE O PÊLO DA PERNA CRESCE MENOS QUE O FIO DE CABELO?

A única explicação que os especialistas têm é evolutiva. Os pêlos que cobriam nossos antepassados primatas tinham várias funções, entre elas a proteção tanto contra o frio como contra os raios solares. Quando os primeiros hominídeos passaram a caminhar sob duas pernas, o sol passou a incidir menos fortemente sobre a cabeça e menos sobre o resto do corpo. Assim, o pêlo do corpo perdeu sua função e rareou. Já os pêlos da cabeça passaram a ser mais necessários para a proteção e cresceram com mais vigor, dando origem ao cabelo. :–P

PÊLO
Tem um folículo piloso (estrutura onde nasce o fio) mais afilado

CABELO
O fio é mais grosso – tem 0,6 mm de diâmetro

folículo piloso

COMO O SANGUE QUE CHEGA AOS PÉS SOBE DE VOLTA AO CORAÇÃO?

1 A grande velocidade com que o sangue desce até os pés já dá o primeiro embalo para a subida.

2 Os músculos da panturrilha também ajudam a bombear o sangue. Suas contrações comprimem as veias e empurram a circulação

3 Mas o grande segredo da subida é o sistema de válvulas dentro das veias. Elas abrem quando o sangue bombeado passa e fecham em seguida, impedindo que ele volte pra baixo

válvulas
sangue subindo
sangue bloqueado

CONSULTORIA: ANDRÉ HEDISSDEIAN, PROFESSOR DE EDUCAÇÃO FÍSICA, DANIEL BARANCHUSKOY, ORTOPEDISTA, FERNANDO D'AGNOLUD, ENDOCRINOLOGISTA, FLÁVIO DAVINI, CLÍNICO GERAL, LUCIANO BASSANT, MÉDICO TRICOLOGISTA – ESPECIALISTA EM CABELO, MARCELO MACHADO, ODONTOLOGISTA, MÁRCIA MAMANA, ODONTOLOGISTA, MARCOS MAIA, DERMATOLOGISTA, NADIM ZARRAN HOMAIN, GASTROENTEROLOGISTA, NEWTON M. BARROS JUNIOR, CIRURGIÃO VASCULAR, RENATO NEVES, OFTALMOLOGISTA, ROBERTA VENTURA, DERMATOLOGISTA, SÉRGIO SCHER II, HEMATOLOGISTA, SUZANA HERCULANO-HOUZEL, NEUROCIENTISTA, VANDERLI MANCHOEMI, NUTRICIONISTA

Previous spreads

The Greatest Curiosities of the Human Body

This series of four double spreads presents the human body and its countless little secrets. In the middle of each spread, a part of the human figure is laid out as one of four sequential sections, like a map representing an unknown territory. The bubbles show a tiny figure in a funny little spacecraft – he explores the unknown territory, gliding through blood vessels, falling into the intestines, exiting through the penis. Other bubbles at key points on the body work like magnifying glasses, facilitating an X-ray view into the body. Text boxes along both sides add interesting details: how you could fill an ordinary swimming-pool with the saliva produced during an average human life-span, or how fingernails grow faster than toenails.

Project Info: *Mundo Estranho*, magazine article, 2008, Brazil
Research: Fabio Volpe, Yuri Vasconscelos
Design: Alessandra Kalko
Illustration: Gabriel Silveira

Crusin for Brusin

With piracy having become a modern phenomenon around Somalia, this piece gains a slightly ghoulish relevance. It refers to the pirate codes that captains set for their crew members in earlier times. Besides setting up rules of conduct, these codes governed the distribution of stolen goods and the compensation a pirate would receive in the event of injury. In this graphic, Michael Spitz quotes Article 8 of Captain John Phillips' code from 1724. Around the skeleton, price tags show how much compensation was due to a pirate should he lose a body part in the course of battle. Prices are given in Spanish dollars, a historical currency widely used in the 18th century.

Project Info: Screen print, 2006, USA
Data Source: Captain John Phillips: "Pirate Code of Conduct", 1724
Design: Michael Spitz

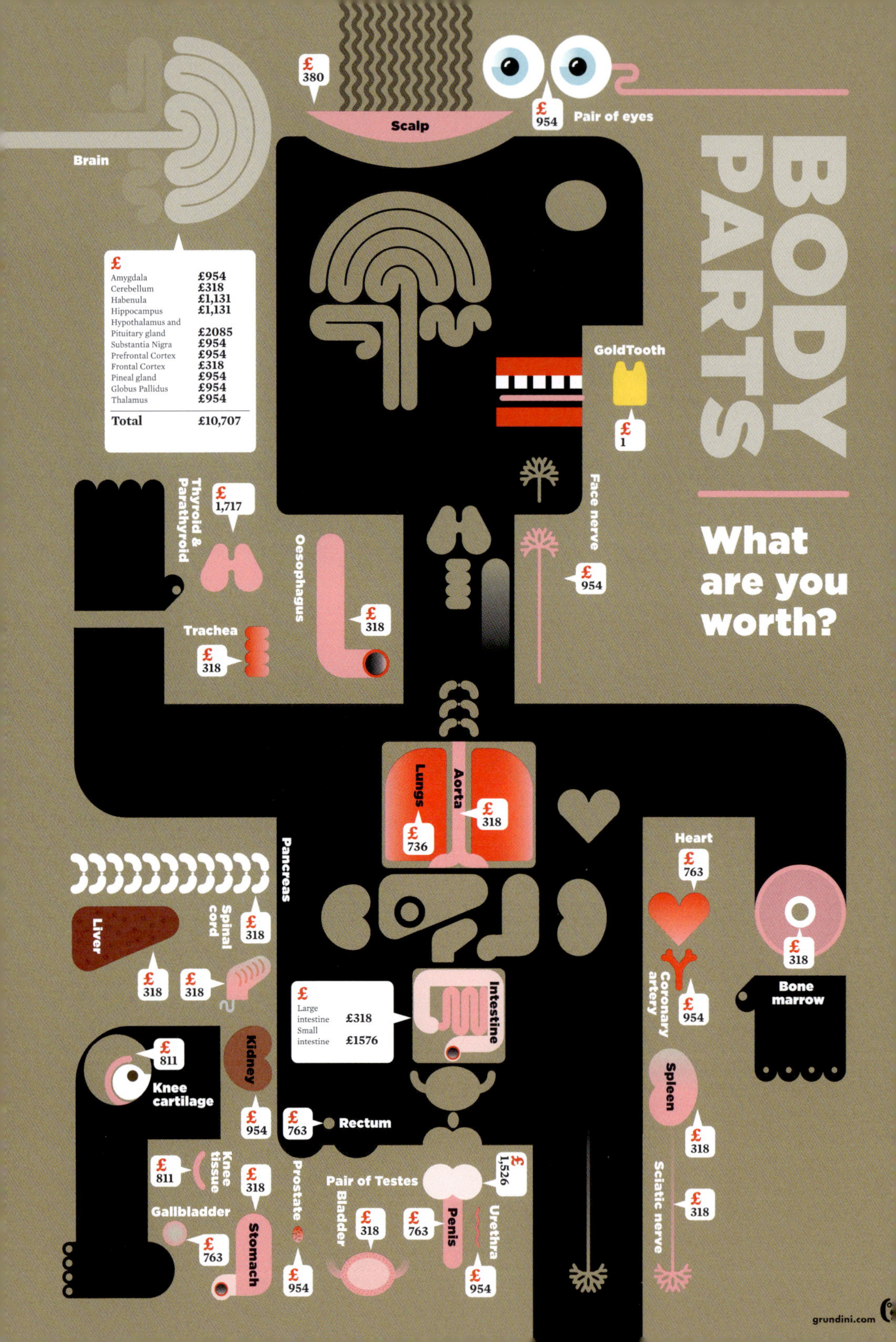

BODY PARTS

What are you worth?

Brain

£ 380 — Scalp

£ 954 — Pair of eyes

GoldTooth — £ 1

Face nerve — £ 954

£	
Amygdala	£954
Cerebellum	£318
Habenula	£1,131
Hippocampus	£1,131
Hypothalamus and	£2085
Pituitary gland	£954
Substantia Nigra	£954
Prefrontal Cortex	£318
Frontal Cortex	£954
Pineal gland	£954
Globus Pallidus	£954
Thalamus	£954
Total	**£10,707**

Thyroid & Parathyroid — £ 1,717

Oesophagus — £ 318

Trachea — £ 318

Lungs — £ 736

Aorta — £ 318

Heart — £ 763

Coronary artery — £ 954

Bone marrow — £ 318

Pancreas

Liver

Spinal cord — £ 318

£ 318 — £ 318

Kidney — £ 954

£	
Large intestine	£318
Small intestine	£1576

Intestine

Spleen — £ 318

Sciatic nerve — £ 318

Knee cartilage — £ 811

Knee tissue — £ 811

Rectum — £ 763

Prostate — £ 954

Gallbladder

Stomach — £ 763

Bladder — £ 318

Pair of Testes

Penis — £ 763

Urethra — £ 1,526

£ 954

£ 318

grundini.com

Body Parts

With the option of replacing dysfunctional body-parts through surgery, replacement human organs have become a somewhat creepy commodity. This piece does the maths and shows the market value of all body parts and organs. As this is more of a financial issue, designer Peter Grundy didn't opt for a medical type of illustration, but located each organ on an abstract body map and tagged it with its open-market price. The funny graphical body conception serves as an effective antidote to the uncomfortable idea of us being worth roundabout as much as a small car.

Project Info: *Esquire*, magazine article, 2006, UK
Design: Peter Grundy (Grundini)
Art Direction: Alex Breuer
Awards: AOI Images 2007

Right and following spread

Circos

The sequencing of the dog genome, completed in 2005, revealed large overlaps between the dog and human genomes – a similarity arising from shared ancestry. This diagram charts some of these similarities in genes by arranging chromosomes – organised structures of DNA containing many genes – around a circle. Selected human chromosomes are shown – each marked by its own colour – along the top (blue outer band), dog chromosomes are shown along the bottom (orange outer band). Where DNA in a dog chromosome matches human DNA, colour-coded stripes on the inner ring indicate the corresponding human chromosomes. Some of the patterns in dog-human homology are indicated by bands connecting similar regions. This visualisation was created using Circos, software which allows the showing of multidimensional relations between objects in a circular layout.

American Scientist

SEPTEMBER–OCTOBER 2007   THE MAGAZINE OF SIGMA XI, THE SCIENTIFIC RESEARCH SOCIETY

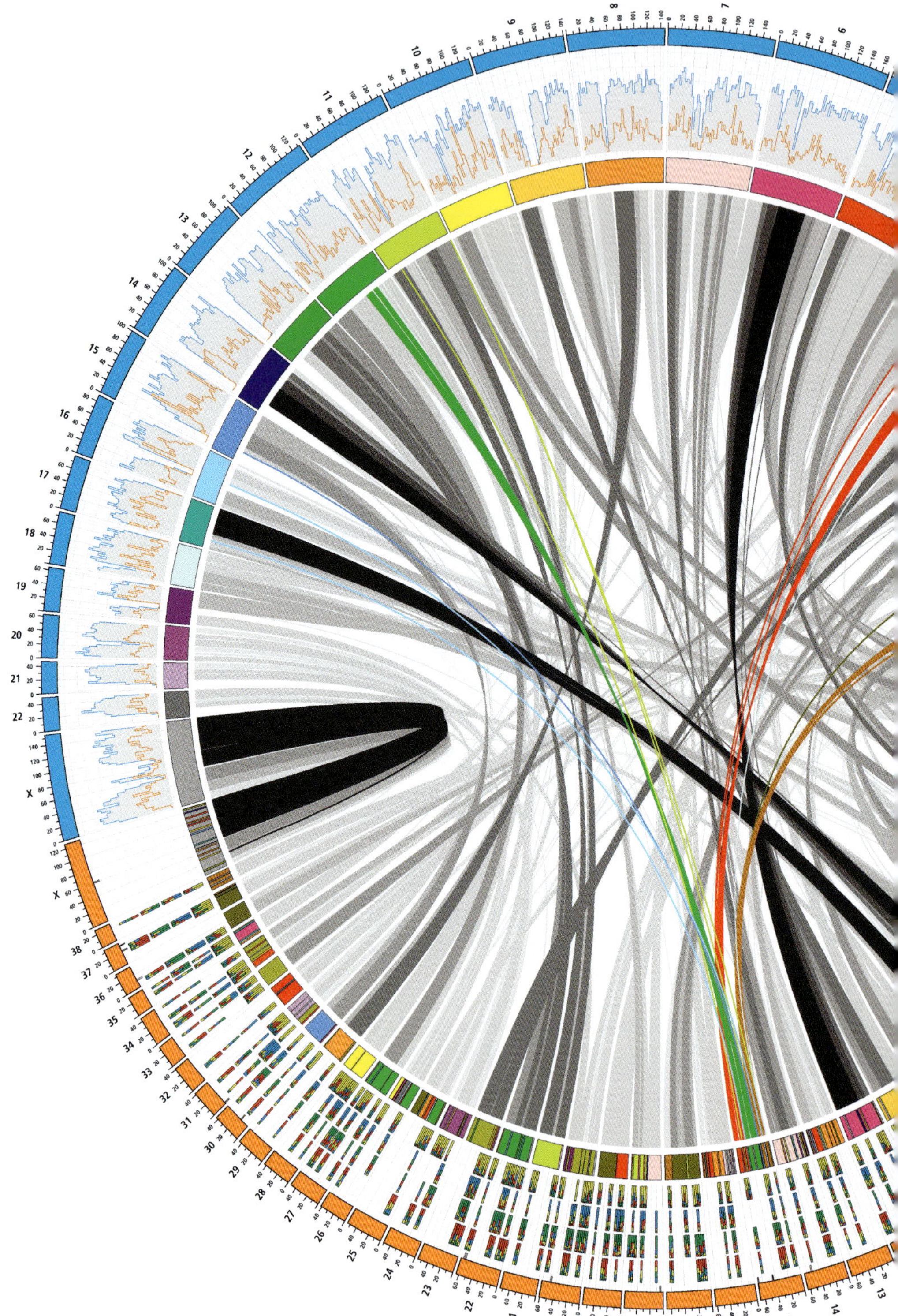
10
11
12
13
14
15
16
17
18
19
20
21
22
X
X
38
37
36
35
34
33
32
31
30
29
28
27
26
25
24
23
22
21
20
19
18
17
16
15
14
13

Project Info: "Genetics and the Shape of Dogs", *American Scientist*, magazine article, 2007, USA
Data Source: Broad Institute of MIT and Harvard University: Dog Genome Project
Design: Martin Krzywinski
Art Direction: Barbara Aulicino
Article: Elaine Ostrander
Awards: Association Media & Publishing EXCEL Award 2008, Silver

Following spreads

City Railway System

Subway maps are not intended to express correct geographical relations. In their abstract language they also do not reveal any cultural features concerning the city they correspond to. Seoul-based design studio Zero Per Zero developed a series of subway maps using cultural symbols in order to reveal cultural identity even in diagrammatic maps. The London map is a combination of the British flag and the six London Underground zones, shown in rectangular shape. The Union Jack is continued in pale patterns throughout the map. In the Seoul map the centre is occupied by the Han River whose meandering course has been shaped to mimic the curve of the Tae Guk mark which forms the centre of the South Korean flag.

Project Info: Series of folded maps, 2010, South Korea
Design: Sol Jin, Ji-hwan Kim (Zero Per Zero)

Chesham · Chalfont & Latimer · Amersham · Chorleywood · Rickmansworth · Croxley · Watford

Bushey · Watford High Street · Watford Junction

Kings Langley / Apsley / Berkhamsted · Hemel Hempstead / Tring / Cheddington · Leighton Buzzard / Bletchley

Moor Park

Hatch End · Radlett / St. Albans City / Harpenden · Luton Airport Parkway / Bedford / Luton · Leagrave / Harlington / Flitwick · Elstree & Borehamwood

LONDON RAILWAY S...
THIS IS NOT THE OF...
DESIGN © PRODUCE F...
WWW.ZEROPERZERO...

Great Missenden / Wendover · Stoke Mandeville / Aylesbury · Aylesbury Vale Parkway · Aylesbury

Northwood · Northwood Hills · Pinner · North Harrow

Headstone Lane · Harrow & Wealdstone · Stanmore · Canons Park · Edgware · Burnt Oak · Colindale · Hendon C...

Harrow-on-the-Hill · Kenton · Preston Road · Queensbury · Kingsbury · Mill Hill Broadway

West Harrow · Rayners Lane · Northwick Park · South Kenton · North Wembley · Wembley Central · Wembley Park · Neasden · Dollis Hill · Willesden Green · Brent Cro... · Golders Green · Hampstead...

Sudbury Hill · Sudbury Town · Alperton · Stonebridge Park · Harlesden · Willesden Junction · Kensal Rise · Brondesbury · Brondesbury Park · Kilburn · Finchley Road & Frognal · Kentish Town W...

Ruislip Manor · Eastcote · South Harrow · Sudbury Hill Harrow · Kensal Green · Queen's Park · Finchley Road · West Hampstead · Belsize Park · Chal...

West Ruislip · Ruislip · Ruislip Gardens · Kilburn Park · Kilburn High Road · South Hampstead · Swiss Cottage · St. John's Wood

Ickenham · Northolt Park · Maida Vale · Great Portla...

Hillingdon · South Ruislip · Warwick Avenue · Edgware Road · Marylebone · Baker Street · Regent's Park · War... Stre...

Uxbridge · Northolt · Royal Oak · Paddington · Edgware Road

Greenford · Perivale · Hanger Lane · Westbourne Park · Bayswater · Marble Arch · Selfridges · Bond Street · Oxford Circus

Park Royal · Ladbroke Grove · Latimer Road · East Acton · Shepherd's Bush · Holland Park · Queensway · Lancaster Gate · Marble Arch · Erro · Piccadilly Circus · Leic... Sq...

North Acton · White City · Wood Lane · Notting Hill Gate · Hyde Park Corner · Green Park · National Ga...

North Ealing · West Acton · Acton Main Line · Acton Central · Shepherd's Bush Market · High Street Kensington · Knightsbridge · Westminster · Embank...

Ealing Broadway · Ealing Common · Goldhawk Road · Kensington (Olympia) · Natural History Museum · South Kensington · Buckingham Palace

Hounslow Central · Osterley · Northfields · South Ealing · Acton Town · Chiswick Park · Turnham Green · Stamford Brook · Ravenscourt Park · West Kensington · Victoria · St. James's Park

Heathrow Terminals 1,2,3 · Heathrow Terminal 4 · Hounslow West · Hounslow East · Boston Manor · Hammersmith · Barons Court · Earl's Court · Gloucester Road · Sloane Square · Tate Britain · Big Ben · Londo...

Heathrow Terminal 5 · HEATHROW INT'L AIRPORT · West Brompton · Pimlico

Gunnersbury · Stamford Bridge · Fulham Broadway · Saatchi Gallery · Vauxhall

Kew Gardens · Parsons Green · Imperial Wharf · Oval

Craven Cottage · Putney Bridge · CLAPHAM JUNCTION · Stockwell · Clap...

Richmond · East Putney · BALHAM · Clap... · Clap...

Wimbledon Park · Southfields · WIMBLEDON · Dundonald Road · Merton Park · Toot... · Toot... · Colli...

Morden · Phipps Bridge · Belgra... Walk · South Wimb...

RIVER THAMES

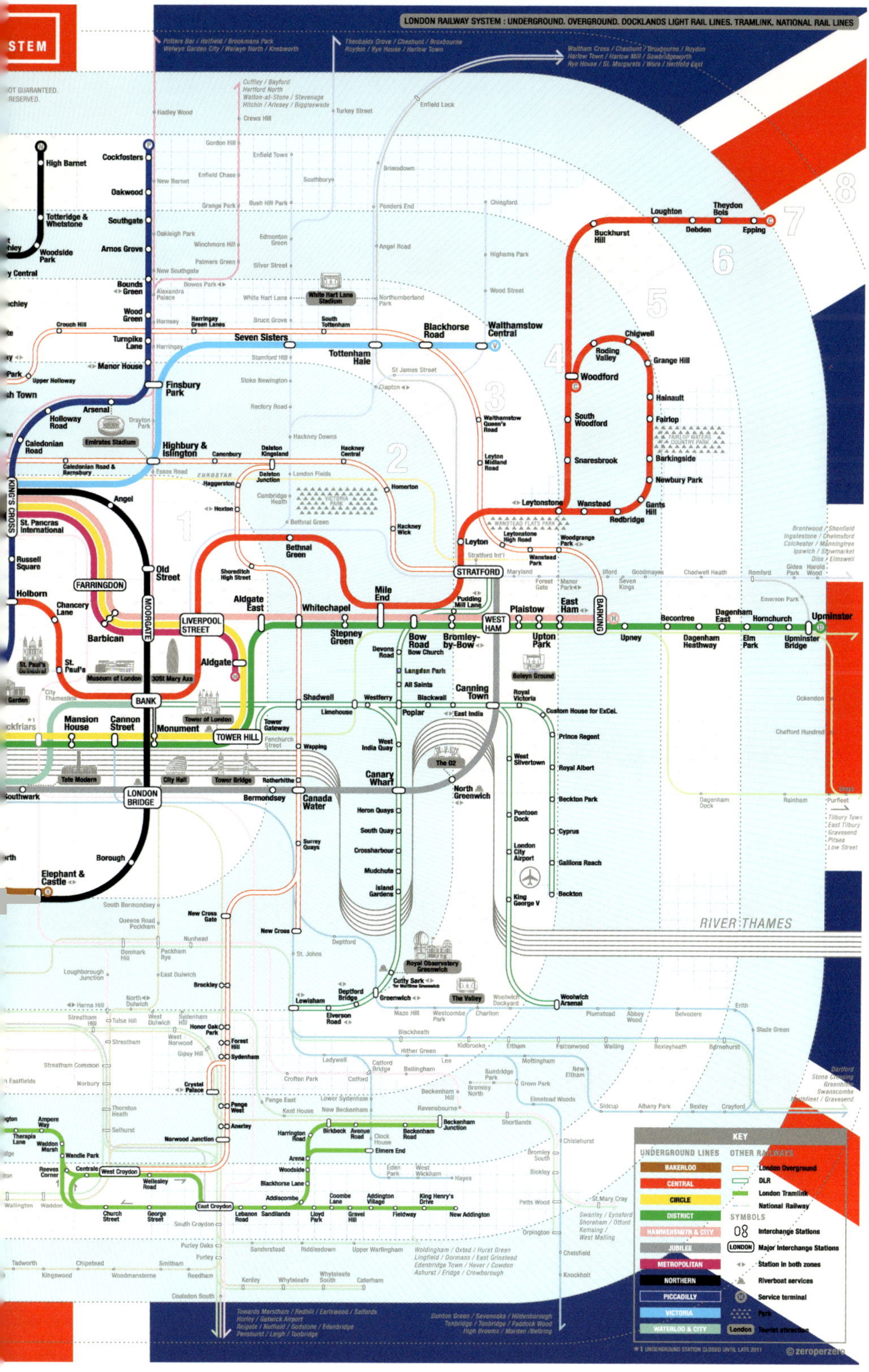

LONDON RAILWAY SYSTEM : UNDERGROUND. OVERGROUND. DOCKLANDS LIGHT RAIL LINES. TRAMLINK, NATIONAL RAIL LINES

RIVER THAMES

KEY

UNDERGROUND LINES
- BAKERLOO
- CENTRAL
- CIRCLE
- DISTRICT
- HAMMERSMITH & CITY
- JUBILEE
- METROPOLITAN
- NORTHERN
- PICCADILLY
- VICTORIA
- WATERLOO & CITY

OTHER RAILWAYS
- London Overground
- DLR
- London Tramlink
- National Railway

SYMBOLS
- 08
- Interchange Stations
- LONDON — Major Interchange Stations
- Station in both zones
- Riverboat services
- Service terminal
- Pier
- London — Tourist attraction

© zeroperzero

HAN RIVER 한 강

AREX AIRPORT LINE

Incheon Int'l Airport 인천국제공항
Incheon Int'l Airport Cargo Terminal 공항화물청사
Incheon Int'l Airport 인천국제공항
Unseo 운서
Geomam 검암
Gyeyang 계양
Gyuhyeon 귤현
Bakchon 박촌
Imhak 임학
Gyesan 계산
Gyeong-in National Univ. of Education 경인교대입구
Jakjeon 작전
Galsan 갈산

Banghwa 방화
Gaehwa 개화
Gaehwasan 개화산
Gimpo Int'l Airport 김포공항
Airport Market 공항시장
Sinbanghwa 신방화
Magongnaru 마곡나루
Yangcheon Hyanggyo 양천향교
Gayang 가양
Jungmi 증미
Deungchon 등촌
Yeomchang 염창
Sinmok-Dong 신목동
Seonyudo 선유도
Dangsan 당산

Gaehwa 개화
Gimpo Int'l Airport 김포공항
Songjeong 송정
Magok 마곡
Balsan 발산
Ujangsan 우장산
Hwagok 화곡
Kkachisan 까치산
Sinjeong 신정
Mok-Dong 목동
Omokgyo 오목교
Yangpyeong 양평
Yeongdeungpo-Gu Office 영등포구청
Mullae 문래
Sindorim 신도림

Gimpo Int'l Airport
Airport Market 공항시장
Sinbanghwa 신방화

Gaewha 개화
Tanhyeon 탄현
Unjeong 운정
Geumneung 금릉
Geumchon 금촌
Wollong 월롱
Paju 파주
Ilsan 일산
Pungsan 풍산
Baekma 백마
Goksan 곡산
Daegok 대곡
Neunggok 능곡
Haengsin 행신
Gangmae 강매
Hwajeon 화전
Susaek 수색
Digital Media City 디지털 미디어 시티
Dokbawi 독바위
Bulgwang 불광
Yoonsinnae 연신내
Gupabal 구파발
Jichuk 지축
Samsong 삼송
Wondang 원당
Hwajeong 화정
Daehwa 대화
Juyeop 주엽
Jeongbalsan 정발산
Madu 마두
Baekseok 백석

World Cup Stadium 월드컵경기장
World Cup Stadium 서울 월드컵 경기장
Mapo-Gu Office 마포구청
Mangwon 망원
Hapjeong 합정
Hongik Univ. 홍대입구
Sangsu 상수
Gwangheung-chang 광흥창
Daeheung 대흥
Gongdeok 공덕
Mapo 마포
Yongsan 용산

Digital Media City
Sinchon(Gyeongui) 신촌(경의선)
Gajwa 가좌
Sodaemun 서대문
Chungjeongno 충정로
Ahyeon 아현
Ewha Womans Univ. 이대
Sinchon 신촌
Hongik Univ. 홍대입구

Nokbeon 녹번
Hongje 홍제
Muakjae 무악재
Eungam 응암

Gyeongbok-Gung 경복궁
Gyeongbok-Gung 경복궁
Gwanghwamun 광화문
Anguk 안국
Jongno 종로
Jonggak 종각
City Hall 시청
Euljiro-Ilga 을지로입구
Myeong-Dong 명동
Hoehyeon 회현
Seoul Station 서울역
Sookmyung Women's Univ. 숙대입구
Namyeong 남영

Soonae 소내
Samgak 삼각
Sinyongsan 신용산
Yongsan 용산
Ichon 이촌

Yeomni 염리
Gongdeok 공덕
Hyochang Park 효창공원앞

Seoul 서울(경의선)
Seoul Station 서울역

Yeouinaru 여의나루
National Assembly 국회의사당
Yeouido 여의도
Yeongdeungpo Market 영등포시장
Yeongdeungpo-Gu Office 영등포구청
Yeongdeungpo 영등포

Saetgang 샛강
Singil 신길
Yeongdeungpo 영등포

Norangjin 노량진
Daebang 대방
Sindaebang 신대방
Boramae 보라매
Sinpung 신풍
Daerim 대림
Guro 구로

Gyeong-in National Univ. of Education 경인교대입구
Ganseok 간석
Juan 주안
Dohwa 도화
Jemulpo 제물포
Dowon 도원
Dongincheon 동인천
Incheon 인천

Bupyeong-Gu Office 부평구청
Bupyeong Market 부평시장
Bupyeong 부평
Baegun 백운
Dongam 동암
Ganseok 간석
Bupyeong Samgeori 부평삼거리
Ganseogogeori 간석오거리
Incheon City Hall 인천시청
Arts Center 예술회관
Incheon Bus Terminal 인천종합터미널
Munhak Sports Complex 문학경기장
Seonhak 선학
Sinyeonsu 신연수
Woninjae 원인재
Dongchun 동춘
Dongmak 동막

Sosa 소사
Bucheon 부천
Jung-Dong 중동
Songnae 송내
Jungni 중리
Singil-Oncheon 신길온천
Ansan 안산
Gojan 고잔
Jungang 중앙
Hanyang Univ. at Ansan 한대앞
Sangnoksu 상록수
Banwol 반월
Daeyami 대야미
Surisan 수리산
Geumjeong 금정

Yeokgok 역곡
Onsu 온수
Dryu-Dong 오류동
Gaebong 개봉
Guil 구일
Guro 구로

Gwangmyeong Sageori 광명사거리
Cheolsan 철산
Gasan Digital Complex 가산디지털단지
Doksan 독산
Geumcheon-Gu Office 금천구청
Gwangmyeong 광명
Seoul Grand Park 서울대공원
Gwacheon 과천
Daegongwon 대공원
Gyeongmachi-won 경마공원
Seonbawi 선바위
Namtaeryeong 남태령

Gwangmyeong 광명
Sovieksu 소요산

Guro Digital Complex 구로디지털단지
Sillim 신림
Sinpung 신풍
Songcheon 송천

Sinjeong Negeori 신정네거리
Yangcheon-Gu Office 양천구청
Dorimcheon 도림천

Jeongwang 정왕
Oido 오이도

Sinchang 신창
Onyang Oncheon 온양온천
Baebang 배방
Asan 아산
Ssangyong 쌍용
Bongmyeong 봉명
Cheonan 천안

Incheon 인천
Incheon 인천

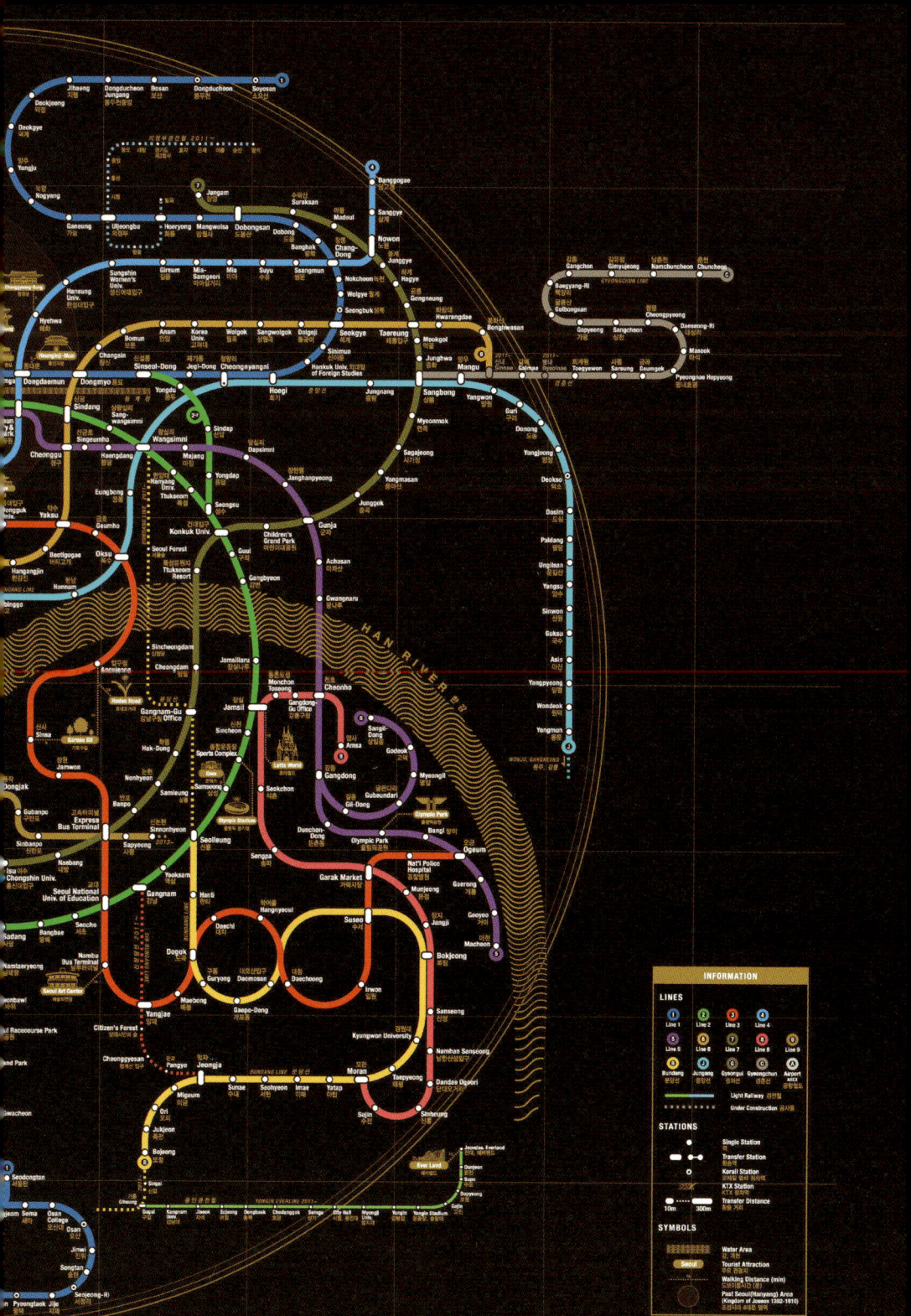

HAN RIVER 한강

INFORMATION

LINES

1 Line 1	2 Line 2	3 Line 3	4 Line 4
5 Line 5	6 Line 6	7 Line 7	8 Line 8	9 Line 9
Bundang 분당선	Jungang 중앙선	Gyeongui 경의선	Gyeongchun 경춘선	Airport AREX 공항철도

— Light Railway 경전철
▪▪▪▪▪ Under Construction 공사중

STATIONS

○ Single Station
◐ Transfer Station
⊙ Korail Station 코레일 영차 정차역
KTX Station KTX 정차역
Transfer Distance 환승 거리
10m 300m

SYMBOLS

Water Area 강, 하천
Seoul Tourist Attraction 주요 명소지
Walking Distance (min) 도보이동시간 (분)
Past Seoul(Hanyang) Area (Kingdom of Joseon 1392-1910) 조선시대 서울권 (조선 1392-1910)

Death Row

Last week, Michael Rosales, who murdered 67-year-old Mary Felder in 1997, became the thirteenth person executed this year—in Texas. Whether or not you believe in the death penalty, it's important to know that the United States is one of 59 countries that still executes its citizens on a regular basis (we currently have more than 3,000 inmates on death row). This is a look at where, around the world, the death penalty is still used and where it has been abolished.

UNITED STATES OF AMERICA

CUBA
BAHAMAS
GUATEMALA
BELIZE
JAMAICA
GUYANA

ANTIGUA AND BARBUDA
BARBADOS
DOMINICA
SAINT KITTS AND NEVIS
SAINT LUCIA
ST. VINCENT AND THE GRENADINES
TRINIDAD AND TOBAGO

GUINEA
SIERRA LEONE

EQUITOR

MAP KEY

✸ **DEATH PENALTY ABOLISHED** (92)

✸ **UNOFFICIALLY ANTI-DEATH PENALTY** (36)
NO EXECUTIONS IN THE LAST 10 YEARS

✸ **DEATH PENALTY ONLY IN
EXCEPTIONAL CASES** (10)
LIKE TREASON OR WAR CRIMES

✸ **DEATH PENALTY STILL IN USE** (59)

✸ Albania, Andorra, Angola, Argentina, Armenia, Australia, Austria, Azerbaijan, Belgium, Bhutan, Bosnia-Herzegovina, Bulgaria, Cambodia, Car Estonia, Finland, France, Georgia, Germany, Greece, Guinea-Bissau, Haiti, Holy See, Honduras, Hungary, Iceland, Ireland, Italy, Kiribati, Liecht Nepal, Netherlands, New Zealand, Nicaragua, Niue, Norway, Palau, Panama, Paraguay, Philippines, Poland, Portugal, Romania, Rwanda, Samo Switzerland, Timor-Leste, Turkey, Turkmenistan, Tuvalu, Ukraine, United Kingdom, Uruguay, Uzbekistan, Vanuatu, Venezuela ✸ Algeria, Benin, Malawi, Maldives, Mali, Mauritania, Morocco, Burma, Nauru, Niger, Papua New Guinea, Russia, South Korea, Sri Lanka, Suriname, Swaziland,

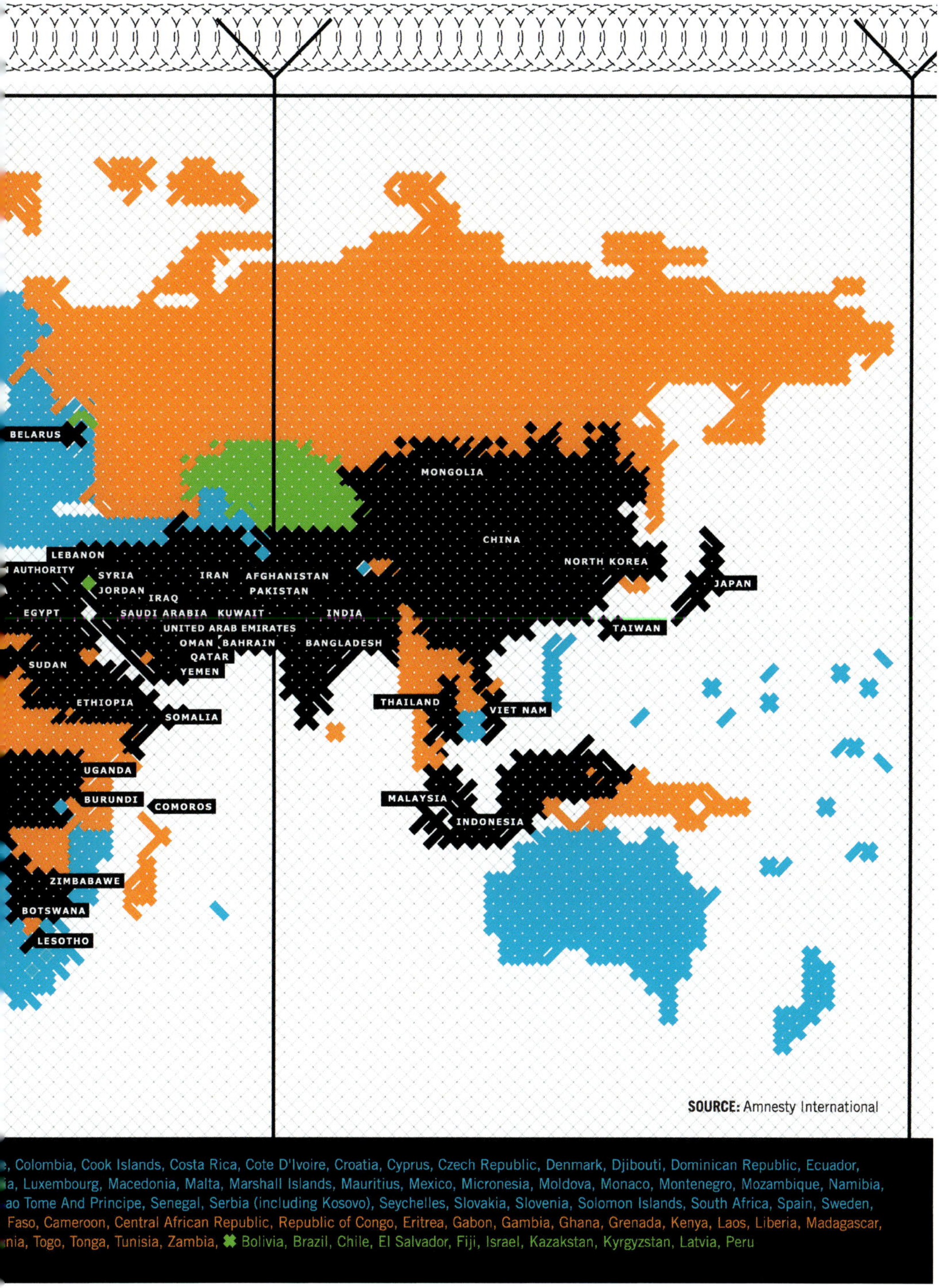
BELARUS
MONGOLIA
CHINA
NORTH KOREA
JAPAN
LEBANON
AUTHORITY
SYRIA
JORDAN
IRAN
IRAQ
AFGHANISTAN
PAKISTAN
EGYPT
SAUDI ARABIA
KUWAIT
INDIA
UNITED ARAB EMIRATES
TAIWAN
OMAN
BAHRAIN
BANGLADESH
QATAR
SUDAN
YEMEN
THAILAND
ETHIOPIA
VIET NAM
SOMALIA
UGANDA
MALAYSIA
BURUNDI
COMOROS
INDONESIA
ZIMBABAWE
BOTSWANA
LESOTHO

SOURCE: Amnesty International

, Colombia, Cook Islands, Costa Rica, Cote D'Ivoire, Croatia, Cyprus, Czech Republic, Denmark, Djibouti, Dominican Republic, Ecuador,
a, Luxembourg, Macedonia, Malta, Marshall Islands, Mauritius, Mexico, Micronesia, Moldova, Monaco, Montenegro, Mozambique, Namibia,
ao Tome And Principe, Senegal, Serbia (including Kosovo), Seychelles, Slovakia, Slovenia, Solomon Islands, South Africa, Spain, Sweden,
Faso, Cameroon, Central African Republic, Republic of Congo, Eritrea, Gabon, Gambia, Ghana, Grenada, Kenya, Laos, Liberia, Madagascar,
nia, Togo, Tonga, Tunisia, Zambia, ✖ Bolivia, Brazil, Chile, El Salvador, Fiji, Israel, Kazakstan, Kyrgyzstan, Latvia, Peru

Previous spread

Death Row

In this thematic world map, countries are coloured according to whether they still use the death penalty or not. 92 countries have officially abolished it, and these are shown in blue; orange and green haven't formally abolished executions, but don't carry them out on a regular basis. All these countries are listed below the map in their respective colours. The 59 countries which do execute citizens on a regular basis are shown in black and are named on the map. As a symbolic layer, the world map is shown behind a high fence topped with barbed wire.

Project Info: "The Death Penalty Around the World", *GOOD*, online article, 2009, USA
Data Source: Amnesty International
Research: Morgan Clendaniel

Design: Joshua Covarrubias (Kiss Me I'm Polish)
Art Direction: Agnieszka Gasparska
(Kiss Me I'm Polish)

Dry Well-Bores

Since oil was discovered in Norwegian waters in the late 1960s, the quest for gas and oil sources has driven the Norwegian economy. This series of maps reports all the futile test-drillings, showing every "dry" well-bore from the start of Norwegian oil exploitation in 1966 to 1984. By then, the exploitation of North Sea sources had peaked and a major new gas field further north was discovered. The 150 bores are numbered and connected by lines, thus showing the chronology of testing various sites and the push to look further north. Using a number of maps, Torgeir Husevaag provides an alternative historical record. He doesn't focus on the successes of Norwegian oil exploitation, but describes how much effort these have taken.

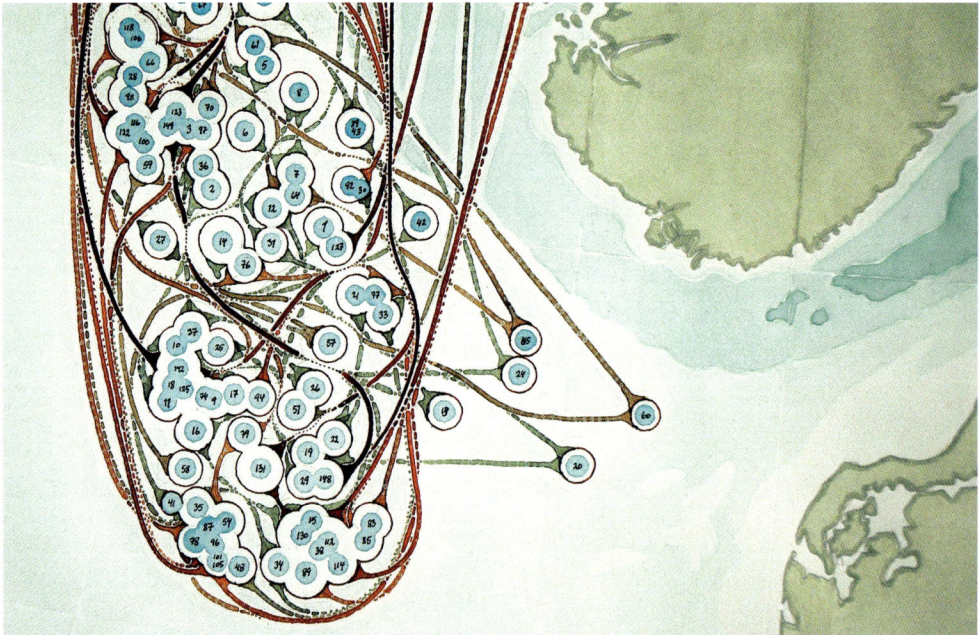

ny written skiltet in Norwegian sector 1966 Mw 1990 (26 7 98)

Project Info: Series of drawings,
Arctic Princess / Höegh LNG,2005, Norway
Data Source: Norwegian Petroleum Directorate
Design: Torgeir Husevaag

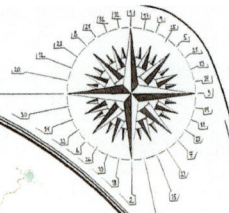
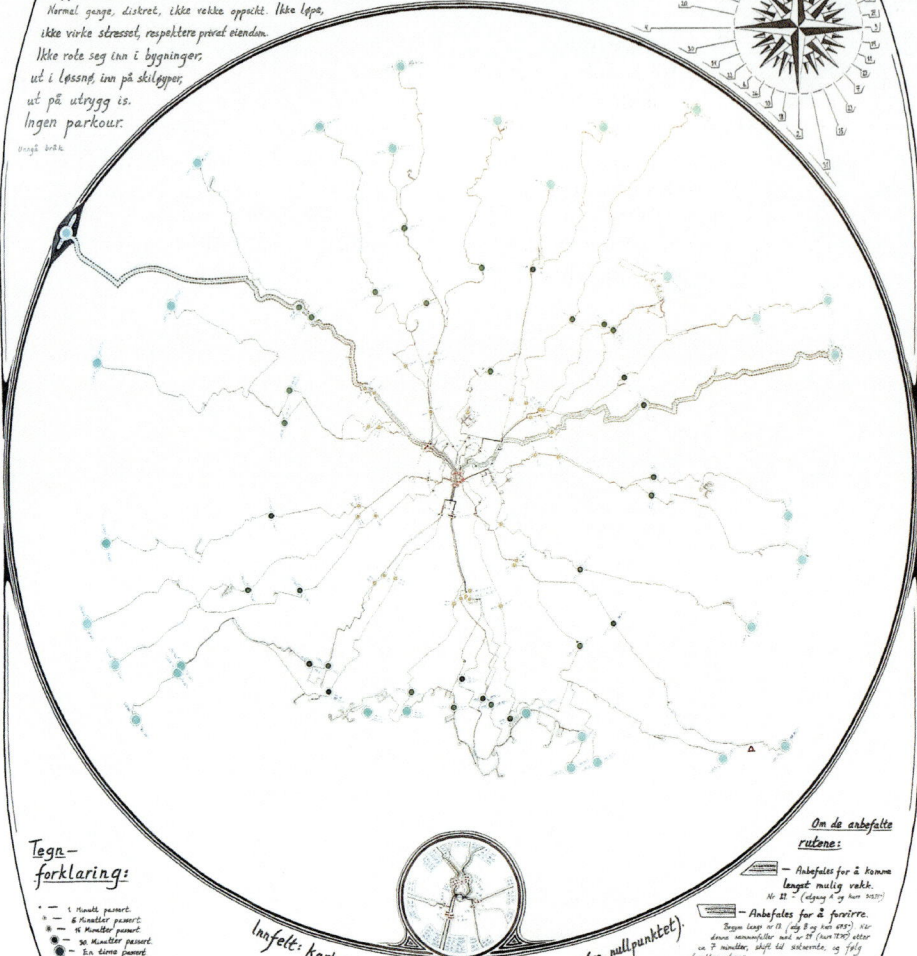
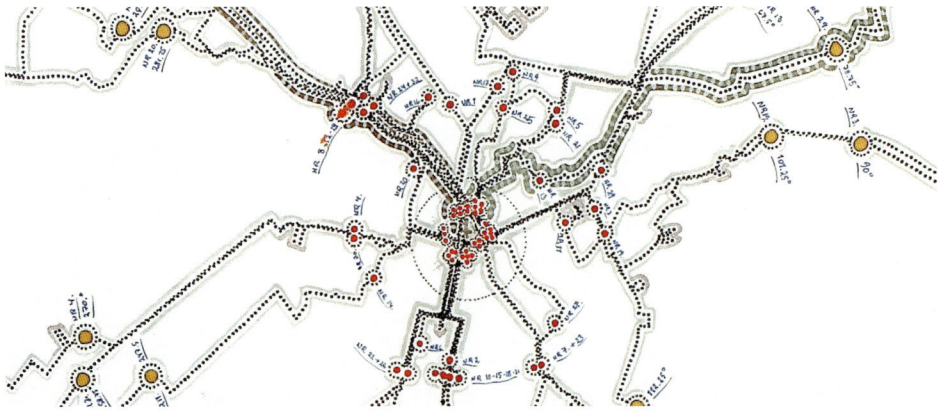

Escape Routes

Torgeir Husevaag plotted escape routes from a given point by following these rules: "A study of escape routes by foot, in all directions. Upto an hour. Wintertime. Moving discreetly, not getting noticed, not running, staying cool. No trespassing. Keeping outdoors, avoiding ski tracks, deep snow, thin ice..." One drawing shows all 32 resulting routes, without any clue to specific location. Two tracks are marked as the most suitable. The second drawing maps points which are reached within specific time intervals (one minute / five minutes etc.) from point zero. The circles are coloured and sized according to how long it takes to get there. Within the circles, details of the underlying map are shown. In the event that someone really was fleeing along these routes, he could easily be spotted in these areas.

Project Info: Series of drawings, 2010–2011, Norway
Design: Torgeir Husevaag

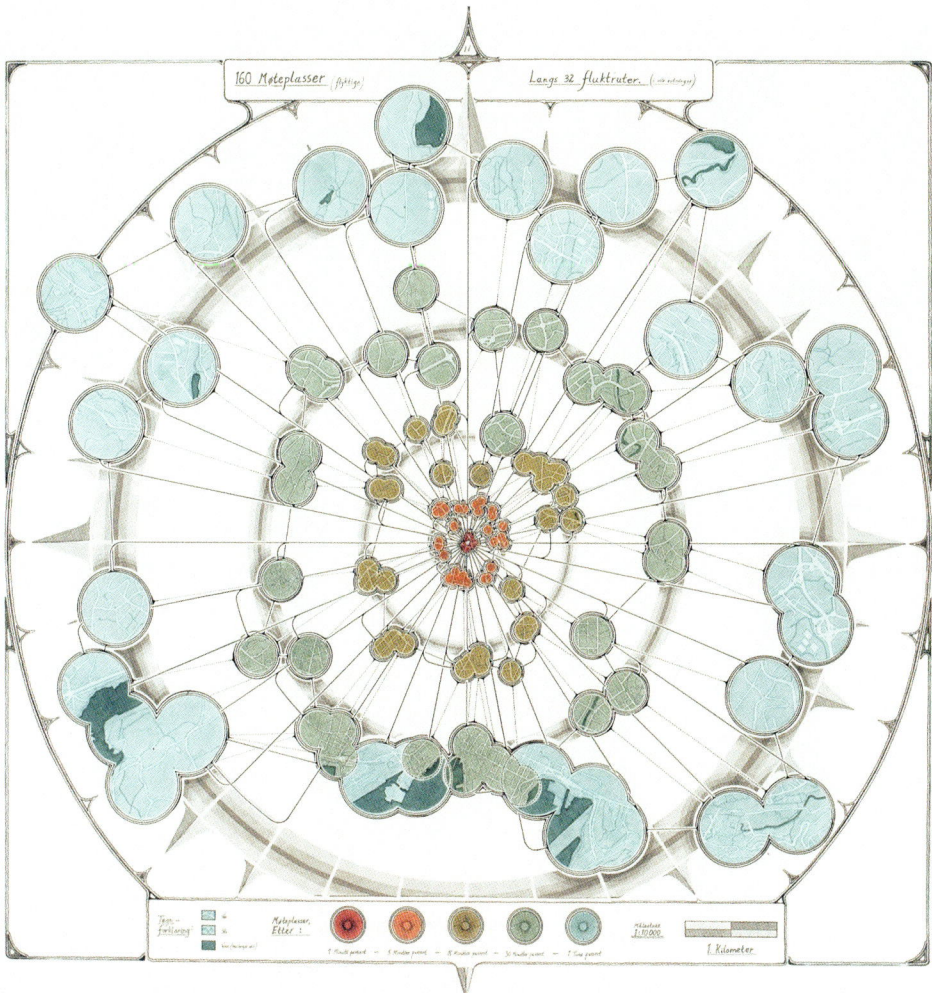

456
BDFV
NQRW
JMZ
AC
23
WORST MEAL
UNIVERSITY HOSPITAL BURGER KING
SALT LAKE CITY
BLUE RIBBON
PARK CITY
OISHI
WORST MOMENT
SAN RAFAEL
FAVORITE LUNCH WITH DAD
MILL VALLEY
BEST BRUNCH
OAKLAND
SEATTLE
LAKE UNION CREW
MOST LIP SYNCING
BEST MACKEREL
ACADEMY OF SCIENCES
SAN FRANCISCO
MICHAEL POLLAN LECTURE
FIRST HOCKEY GAME
BEAT GRAND THEFT AUTO
GRAND THEFT AUTO IV
JANUARY MILES
FEBRUARY MILES
MARCH MILES
APRIL MILES
MAY MILES
JUNE MILES

THE FELTRON
2008 ATLAS

ISLANDERS HOCKEY GAME

LONG ISLAND

PALAFRUGELL   TAMARIU   JELLYFISH STING

MUSEU FREDERIC MARES

BOHAN   BARCELONA   PORTLAND

CALELLA DE
PALAFRUGELL   TURISMO SHOWROOM   DUKES   NEWPORT
                                                              BEST FRIED OYSTERS
BROOKLYN   ALGONQUIN
                         MOST SPECTACULAR CRASH

                                                    GOLD BEACH   RIVERVIEW RESTAURANT

                         BROKER   EUREKA   SHASTA LAKE
                                                    BEST HIKES
                                                              GARBERVILLE

                                                              POINT ARENA

MCMINNVILLE   MILL VALLEY
        AEROSPACE HIGH POINT

            HEATHER & MARK'S WEDDING
        MOUNT ANGEL   PORTLAND

FIRST ICE   SECRET   OBAMA   AMADOR'S
CREAM OF   SERVICE   ELECTED   APPENDIX
SUMMER   VISITS   REMOVED
                    OFFICE

Relationships

Reporting on the reporters.

Activities

The length and habits of an encounter.

FIGURE 3. RELATIONSHIPS REPORTED

FRIEND   WORK   FAMILY   MORE THAN FRIENDS

ACQUAINTANCE   OTHER   PEER

JAN   FEB   MAR   APR   MAY   JUN   JUL   AUG   SEP   OCT   NOV   DEC

FIGURE 5. AVERAGE LENGTH OF AN ENCOUNTER

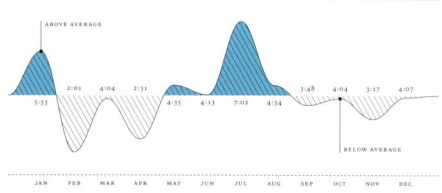

ABOVE AVERAGE

5:53   2:01   4:04   2:31   4:35   4:13   7:02   4:34   3:48   4:04   3:17   4:07

BELOW AVERAGE

JAN   FEB   MAR   APR   MAY   JUN   JUL   AUG   SEP   OCT   NOV   DEC

FIGURE 6. FREQUENTLY REPORTED ACTIVITIES

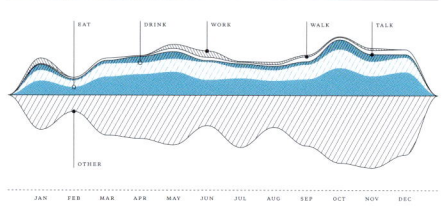

EAT   DRINK   WORK   WALK   TALK

OTHER

JAN   FEB   MAR   APR   MAY   JUN   JUL   AUG   SEP   OCT   NOV   DEC

SHORTEST RELATIONSHIP
5 Mins
ERIC, MAY 15

LONGEST RELATIONSHIP
Forever
ELISE, JAN 7

FIGURE 4. DEGREES OF FRIENDSHIP

6 FRIEND OF A FRIENDS

234 FRIENDS

AVERAGE RELATIONSHIP DURATION
About 3 Years
3 YEARS, 3 MONTHS AND 22 DAYS

MOST COMMON RELATIONSHIP
Friend
234 REPORTS

STUDENT TO TEACHER RATIO
3:1
6 STUDENTS, 1 TEACHER AND
1 BIRDING INSTRUCTOR

1 FRIEND OF A FRIEND
OF A FRIEND OF A FRIEND

DISTINCT RELATIONSHIPS
179

NO RELATIONSHIP REPORTED
Eight

1 FRIEND OF A
FRIEND OF A FRIEND

CUMULATIVE REPORTING TIME
Three Months
99 DAYS, 6 HOURS AND 17 MINUTES

MOST FREQUENT ACTIVITY
Dinner
105 REPORTS

AVERAGE ENCOUNTER LENGTH
Four Hours
4 HOURS, 15 MINUTES AND 15 SECONDS

MOST ACTIVITIES IN A MONTH
157
OCTOBER

DJING TO DANCING RATIO
5:4

AVERAGE ACTIVITIES PER ENCOUNTER
2.3

INSTANCES OF LAUGHTER
14

Project Info: Booklet and poster, 2008, USA
Design: Nicholas Felton

Previous spread and above

Feltron Annual Report

While data visualisation is mostly considered as a tool for coping with inscrutable problems, Nicholas Felton has employed it in a very personal way: to keep track of his life. Since 2005, he has published an annual report of his life, visualising meticulously logged facts relating to his travel, dining, drinking and personal experiences. The image (previous spread) shows the 2008 poster with various maps, featuring details from Felton's travels from that year. The piece is a collage of 13 maps in 20 equilateral triangles, reminiscent of Buckminster Fuller's Dymaxion world maps. Put together, the polyhedron forms the "cosmos" of Felton's life in 2008. The timeline beneath demonstrates how many miles were travelled during the year and is complemented by personal highlights.

Flight AF447

This graphic combines data about location and time, with the globe providing the overall map motif. It depicts the journey of Air France flight AF447, which crashed into the Atlantic on the night of June 1st, 2009 on its way from Rio de Janeiro to Paris. The names along the flight route include real places on the ground, such as Natal in Brazil, as well as names of abstract aviation waypoints which have artificial five-letter names. Orange clouds across the Atlantic mark an area with heavy thunderstorms at the time of the disaster. White lines show civilian flight-paths, dark lines mark sectors of controlled air space.

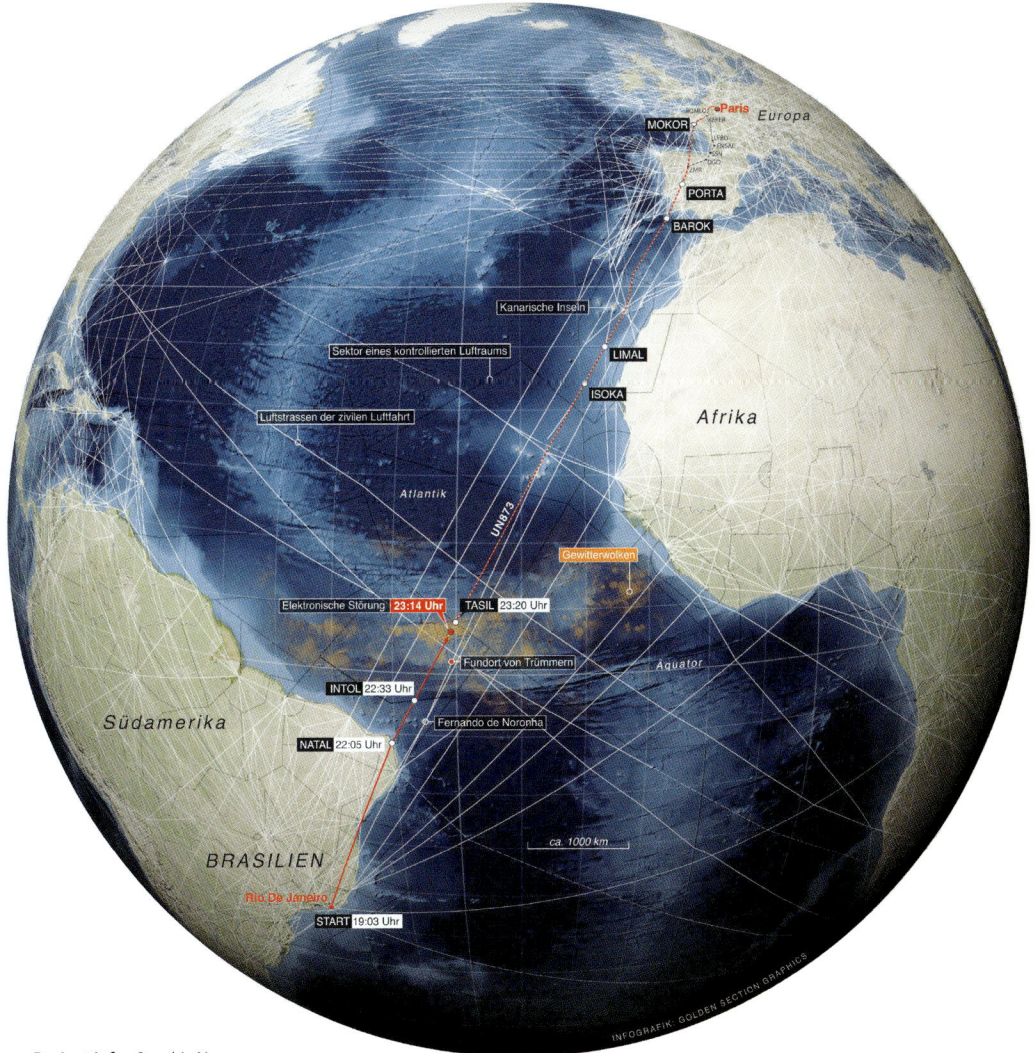

Project Info: *Graphic News*, newspaper article, 2009, Germany
Data Source: Air France; Meteo France; BEA
Design: Jan Schwochow (Golden Section Graphics)

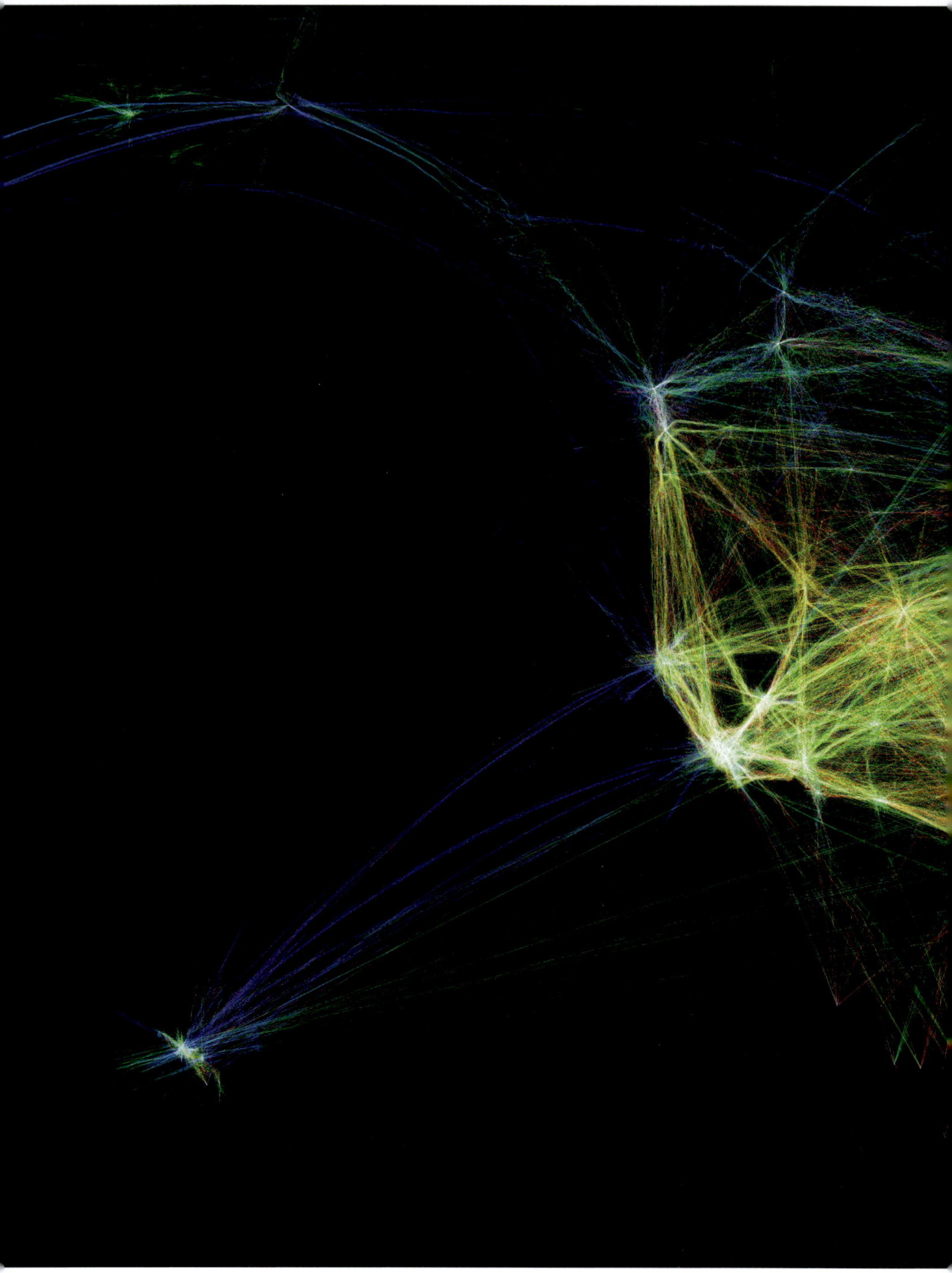

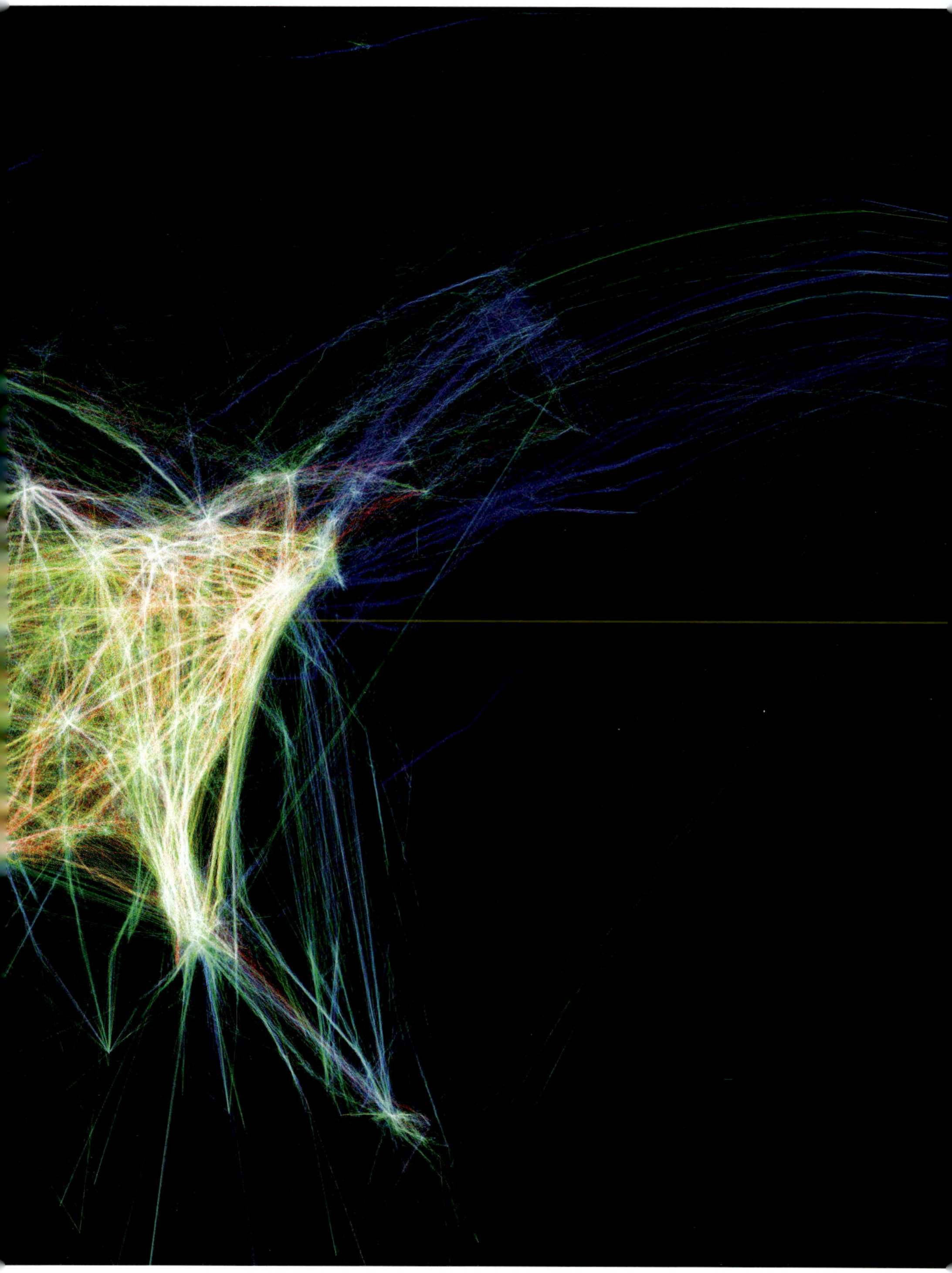

Previous spread and below

Flight Patterns

This series of visualisations developed by Aaron Koblin shows air-traffic paths over North America in coloured linear networks. The Federal Aviation Administration, the US government agency for monitoring civil air traffic, provided flight data for a 24-hour period. These were analysed and plotted using the Processing programming environment.

Without seeing the underlying US map, patterns and paths nevertheless appear. Intersections at major airports are easily visible. In continuative studies, Koblin researched into altitude, aircraft type and manufacturer. Colour coding was used to distinguish flights according to this enriched information.

Project Info: Website and poster, 2008, USA
Data Source: Federal Aviation Administration
Design: Aaron Koblin
Awards: NSF Science Visualisation

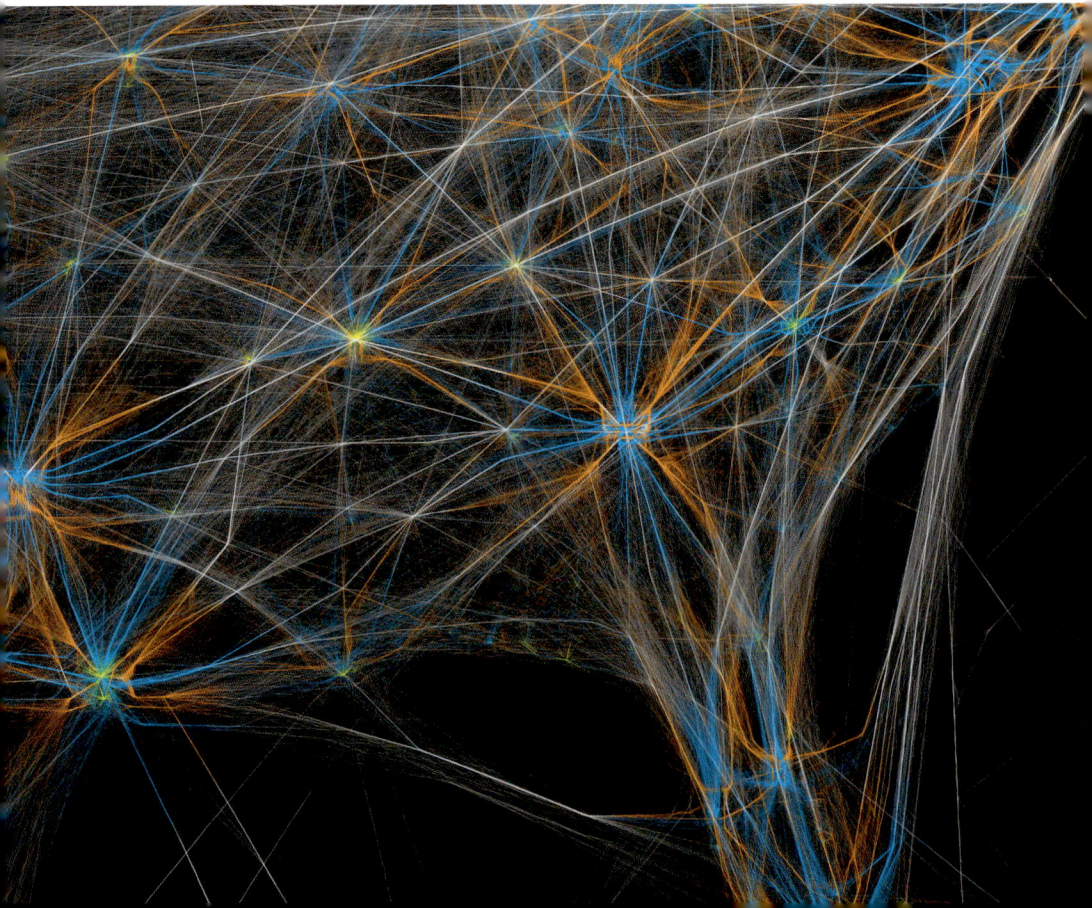

Gaming Injuries

This piece, developed for Swedish news-paper *Svenska Dagbladet* in 2003, humor-ously focuses on the physical impacts of the excessive playing of computer games. It is structured around body features, using as its centre a somewhat creepy wire-frame graphic of a toddler holding a gun.

Linked to individual body-parts, possible injuries are listed and described, mimicking the language of the now omnipresent tobacco warnings: uninterrupted gaming for years on end can lead to traumatic separations and a broken heart.

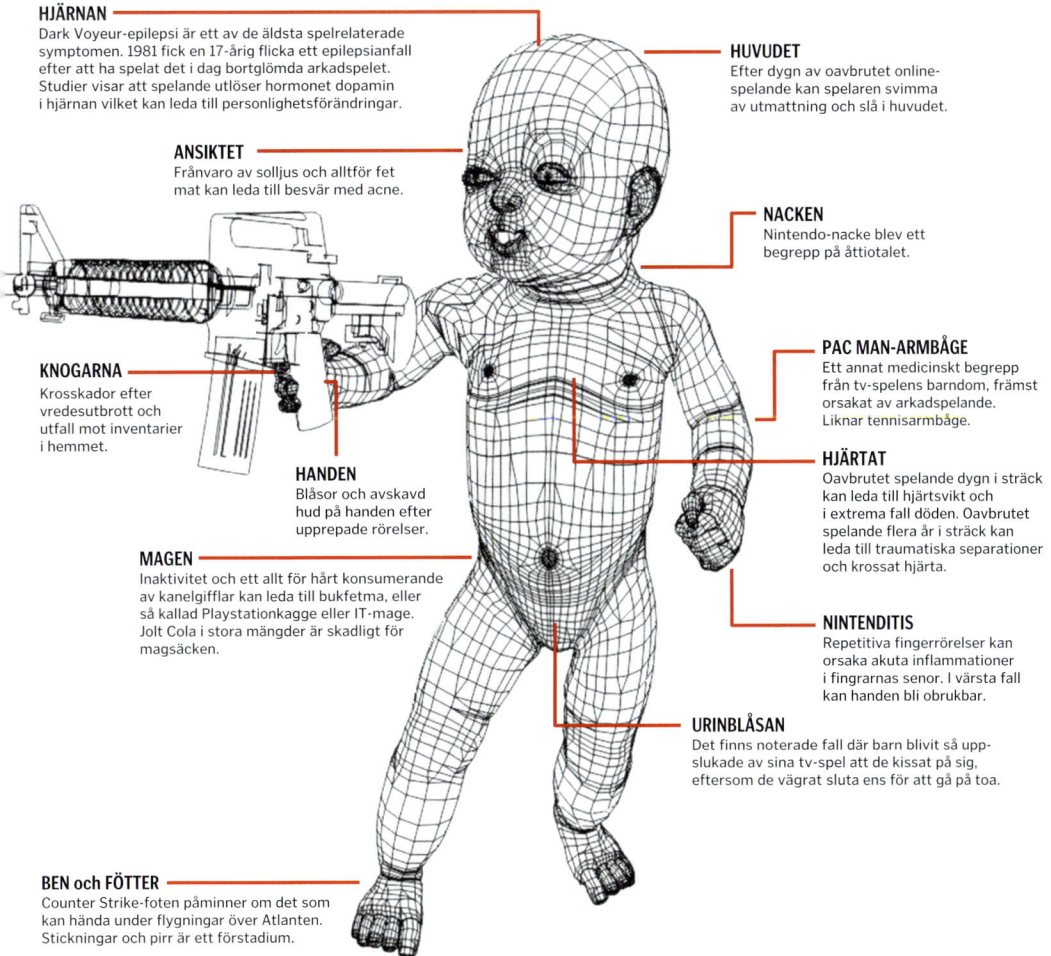

HJÄRNAN
Dark Voyeur-epilepsi är ett av de äldsta spelrelaterade symptomen. 1981 fick en 17-årig flicka ett epilepsianfall efter att ha spelat det i dag bortglömda arkadspelet. Studier visar att spelande utlöser hormonet dopamin i hjärnan vilket kan leda till personlighetsförändringar.

ANSIKTET
Frånvaro av solljus och alltför fet mat kan leda till besvär med acne.

KNOGARNA
Krosskador efter vredesutbrott och utfall mot inventarier i hemmet.

HANDEN
Blåsor och avskavd hud på handen efter upprepade rörelser.

MAGEN
Inaktivitet och ett allt för hårt konsumerande av kanelgifflar kan leda till bukfetma, eller så kallad Playstationkagge eller IT-mage. Jolt Cola i stora mängder är skadligt för magsäcken.

BEN och FÖTTER
Counter Strike-foten påminner om det som kan hända under flygningar över Atlanten. Stickningar och pirr är ett förstadium.

HUVUDET
Efter dygn av oavbrutet online-spelande kan spelaren svimma av utmattning och slå i huvudet.

NACKEN
Nintendo-nacke blev ett begrepp på åttiotalet.

PAC MAN-ARMBÅGE
Ett annat medicinskt begrepp från tv-spelens barndom, främst orsakat av arkadspelande. Liknar tennisarmbåge.

HJÄRTAT
Oavbrutet spelande dygn i sträck kan leda till hjärtsvikt och i extrema fall döden. Oavbrutet spelande flera år i sträck kan leda till traumatiska separationer och krossat hjärta.

NINTENDITIS
Repetitiva fingerrörelser kan orsaka akuta inflammationer i fingrarnas senor. I värsta fall kan handen bli obrukbar.

URINBLÅSAN
Det finns noterade fall där barn blivit så upp-slukade av sina tv-spel att de kissat på sig, eftersom de vägrat sluta ens för att gå på toa.

Project Info: *Svenska Dagbladet*, newspaper article, 2003, Sweden
Research: Lars Berge
Design: Thomas Molén

IS THERE A DOCTOR
IN THE HOUSE?
COUNTRY PATIENTS : DOCTOR RATIO
KEY
COUNTRY
CA 470:1
US 390:1
CU
MX 500:1
IS 280:1
NO 320:1
SE 310:1
NL 320:1
DK 310:1
GB 440:1
IE 360:1
BE
DE
CZ
FR 300:1
CH
AT
SK
HU
PT 290:1
ES 300:1
MC 172:1
IT 240:1
JM 1200:1
DO 1408:1
PA
VE
CO 750:1
EC 650:1
BR 900:1
BO 800:1
PE 850:1
PY 900:1
AR 330:1
UY 270:1
CL 900:1

M
LS
LT
LV
LY
MC
MD
MK
MN
8.7 LITHUANIA_
8.7 LATVIA_
3.9 LIBYA_
* MOROCCO_
19.5 MONACO_
6.7 MOLDOVA_
* MADAGASCAR_
4.8 MACEDONIA_
* MALI_
11.5 MONGOLIA_
* MAURITANIA_
1.3 MALAWI_
* MEXICO

Global Healthcare

In this typographic world map, Michael Spitz looks at healthcare resources around the world. Countries are represented by their ISO code, which is scaled in size according to how many doctors are available to the general population. The scaling thus distorts the geographical relations. Cuba tops the list with a ratio of one doctor per 170 inhabitants. Countries with more than 5,000 people per doctor have a fixed scale to account for extreme variations in developing countries. The map is completed by the line along the bottom which shows the number of hospital beds per 1,000 people. The country codes are listed alphabetically, and again are scaled according to the availability of hospital care.

Project Info: Poster, 2008, Croatia
Data Source: The World Bank
Design: Michael Spitz

Following spread

Help! Cries Noah

On the occasion of the 2010 International Year of Biodiversity, this double spread surveyed the subject around the globe. Maps and diagrams on the left chart general facts concerning the richness of species – with a distribution world map, numbers of endangered species, an outlook to the future as well as in a historical chart covering 600 million years of evolution. For five of the continents, more detailed information is set out. For each region, three examples of endangered animals are described. Icons indicate the reasons for their vulnerability, with all reasons explained at the top of the spread. The green line of text to the lower left reports that as of 2007, 34% of Europeans had not even heard the term "biodiversity".

Project Info: *Intelligence in Lifestyle*, magazine article, 2010, Italy
Data Source: IUCN Red List 2008; Global Biodiversity Outlook; WWF; *Nature*: "Biodiversity: Extinction by Numbers"
Research: Daniele Lorenzetti
Design / Art Direction: Francesco Franchi
Illustration: Laura Cattaneo

TUTTE LE CAUSE DI ESTINZIONE
Sono indicate anche nelle schede di queste pagine in riferimento ai 15 animali di cui parliamo

URBANIZZAZIONE
– La crescita delle aree cittadine danneggia e frammenta molti habitat.

INQUINAMENTO
– Un serio problema per specie marine, anfibi e insetti, sensibili agli agenti chimici.

SPECIE ALIENE
– L'introduzione artificiale di una specie in un ecosistema può distruggerne gli equilibri.

CAMBIAMENTO CLIMATICO
– Investe specie marine sensibili alla temperatura e gli uccelli migratori.

Aiuto, chiamate Noè

Il 2010 è l'anno mondiale della biodiversità. Ricordiamoci che se scompare una specie, l'intero ecosistema può subire danni irrimediabili: senza api non avremmo frutta, caffè, cotone. La "lista rossa" degli animali a rischio è lunga. Ecco una mappa sintetica e alcuni casi-simbolo... Ma ve lo immaginate un mondo senza elefanti?

– di **Francesco Franchi** e **Daniele Lorenzetti** | illustrazioni di **Laura Cattaneo**

CHE RICCA LA BARRIERA

Nella mappa, i luoghi dove la ricchezza di specie viventi (marine e terrestri) è maggiore. Alti livelli di biodiversità si registrano soprattutto nelle foreste equatoriali e lungo la Grande barriera corallina

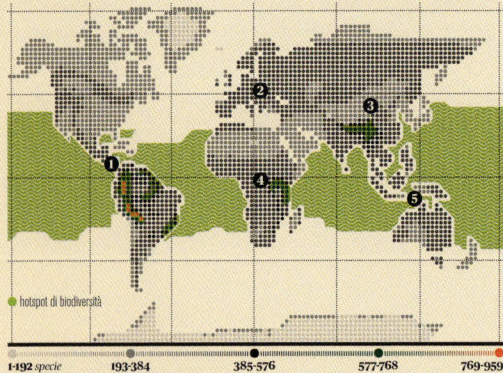

- hotspot di biodiversità

| 1-192 specie | 193-384 | 385-576 | 577-768 | 769-959 |

COSA SUCCEDERÀ SE CONSERVIAMO...

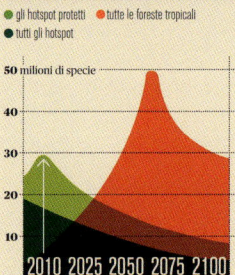

- gli hotspot protetti
- tutti gli hotspot
- tutte le foreste tropicali

50 milioni di specie
2010 2025 2050 2075 2100

FAMIGLIE CHE NASCONO E MUOIONO

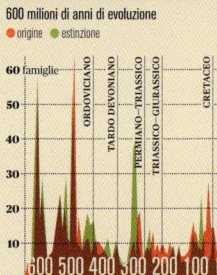

600 milioni di anni di evoluzione
- origine
- estinzione

60 famiglie
ORDOVICIANO — TARDO DEVONIANO — PERMIANO–TRIASSICO — TRIASSICO–GIURASSICO — CRETACEO
600 500 400 300 200 100

① Americhe – Epidemia silenziosa dal polo ai tropici

Ⓐ LONTRA DI MARE
Enhydra lutris
La riduzione delle popolazioni di lontra marina causa il proliferare dei ricci, una delle loro prede principali. Troppi ricci depaurano le riserve di kelp e macroalghe.

Ⓑ ARMADILLO GIGANTE
Priodontes maximus
Un mammifero simbolo dell'ecosistema amazzonico, classificato come *endangered* nella lista rossa Iucn. La caccia indiscriminata e la riduzione degli habitat lo minacciano.

Ⓒ ORSO GRIZZLY
Ursus arctos horribilis
Negli ecosistemi sub-polari come l'Alaska l'orso grizzly è al vertice della catena alimentare. È una "specie ombrello": dalla sua sopravvivenza dipende quella di molte altre.

ATTENZIONE, INSETTI VULNERABILI

L'Iucn (Unione mondiale per la conservazione della natura) valuta periodicamente le specie potenzialmente a rischio. Ecco le percentuali di quelle minacciate secondo la Red List del 2008

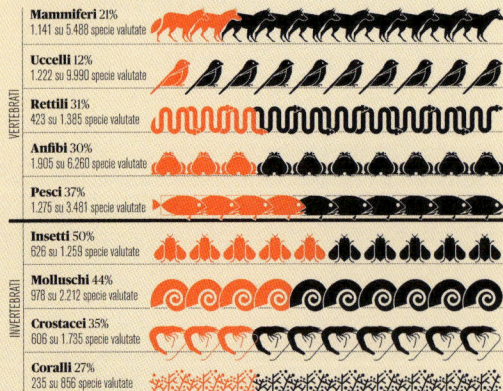

VERTEBRATI

Mammiferi 21%
1.141 su 5.488 specie valutate

Uccelli 12%
1.222 su 9.990 specie valutate

Rettili 31%
423 su 1.385 specie valutate

Anfibi 30%
1.905 su 6.260 specie valutate

Pesci 37%
1.275 su 3.481 specie valutate

INVERTEBRATI

Insetti 50%
626 su 1.259 specie valutate

Molluschi 44%
978 su 2.212 specie valutate

Crostacei 35%
606 su 1.735 specie valutate

Coralli 27%
235 su 856 specie valutate

MEDICINA ALTERNATIVA
– La medicina tradizionale cinese usa ancora parti di animali: soprattutto ossa e corna.

PERDITA HABITAT
– La deforestazione e la riduzione di habitat strangolano la biodiversità.

SVILUPPO AGRICOLO
– L'espansione di aree agricole causa la perdita di foreste e specie indigene.

CACCIA E PESCA
– Bracconaggio e traffico illegale di parti di animale sono una piaga globale.

---

❷ Europa – Tornano gli ululati, soffrono le rane

Ⓐ APE
Apis mellifera

Non ancora a rischio, ma in rapido declino: tra le cause l'inquinamento, i pesticidi e le epidemie parassitarie. La loro scomparsa sarebbe un disastro per l'impollinazione, da cui dipende la vita di fiori e frutti.

Ⓑ LUPO ITALICO
Canis lupus italicus

Caso esemplare di successo delle strategie di tutela, il lupo è tornato a popolare gli Appennini e vaste aree europee. Il bracconaggio è stata la prima minaccia per la specie.

Ⓒ PELOBATE FOSCO
Pelobates fuscus insubricus

La sottospecie del pelobate italico, tipica della Pianura padana, soffre come molti altri anfibi la distruzione di habitat umidi e viene predata da specie introdotte artificialmente quali tartarughe e rane toro.

❸ Asia – Là dove regnavano le tigri

Ⓐ TIGRE
Panthera tigris

È la specie simbolo della lotta per la biodiversità: ne restano 3mila esemplari adulti. Estinte tre delle nove sottospecie. Una curiosità: il 2010, secondo il calendario cinese, è proprio il suo anno.

Ⓑ PANDA GIGANTE
Ailuropoda melanoleuca

La popolazione totale si attesta tra i mille e i duemila individui. È giudicato "in pericolo di estinzione". Le minacce: distruzione dell'habitat e caccia per la preziosa pelle.

Ⓒ ANTILOPE TIBETANA
Pantholops hodgsonii

La popolazione di questa specie che vive sugli altopiani del Tibet si attesta sui 100mila capi. Viene cacciata per la fine lana, lo *shatoosh*. Le corna sono utilizzate nella medicina cinese.

---

❹ Africa – Il destino delle specie "carismatiche"

Ⓐ RINOCERONTE NERO
Diceros bicornis

Fino a metà del XX secolo diffusissimo nelle savane africane, questo mammifero è arrivato sulla soglia dell'estinzione. Il corno viene usato nella medicina tradizionale cinese.

Ⓑ LEONE
Panthera leo

Il suo areale, un tempo esteso all'intera Eurasia, si è ridotto all'Africa subsahariana. L'Iucn lo considera "vulnerabile": la sua riduzione minaccia l'equilibrio dell'ecosistema.

Ⓒ ELEFANTE AFRICANO
Loxodonta africana

Gli esperti ne stimano in natura circa 400mila esemplari rispetto agli 1,3 milioni degli anni Settanta. Il bracconaggio per commercio di avorio mostra una recrudescenza.

❺ Oceania – Se cambia la geografia degli atolli

Ⓐ CORALLI
Scleractinia

L'ordine comprende 26 famiglie. Il degrado della Grande barriera minaccia un intero ecosistema: pesci, molluschi, cavallucci marini. Effetti anche sulla geografia degli atolli.

Ⓑ CASUARIO
Casuarius casuarius

Non solo i predatori, ma anche gli erbivori possono essere in pericolo: il casuario è fondamentale perché disperde, attraverso le feci, i semi delle piante di cui si nutre.

Ⓒ DIAVOLO DELLA TASMANIA
Sarcophilus harrisii

Questo marsupiale, un tempo diffuso anche in Australia, vive oggi solo in Tasmania. In pericolo per la caccia e la diffusione del tumore facciale infettivo, è a rischio estinzione.

FONTI: Iucn Red List 2008; Global Biodiversity Outlook; WWF; Nature, *Biodiversity: extinction by numbers* | HA COLLABORATO – **Prof. Maurizio Casiraghi** (*Università Milano Bicocca*)

Historic Shift

Developed in the wake of the 2010 US mid-
term elections, this map indicates the shift in
votes for each individual district in the US,
compared with the results of the 2008 elections. Shifts towards Republican votes are
shown by red arrows pointing right, blue arrows
to the left represent shifts towards Democrat
votes. The length of the vectors corresponds
to the percentage points in voting results (cf.
the legend to the right of the map). The motion
visually implied in the arrows is a symbol for
the political changes brought about by these
shifts in voting results. The piece ran both in
the printed edition of the *New York Times* as
well as an interactive feature online.

Project Info: *The New York Times*, newspaper and
online article, 2010, USA
Data Source: Associated Press; Dave Leip's Atlas of
US Presidential Elections; Edison / Mitofsky Exit Polls
Design: Amanda Cox, Kevin Quealy, Amy Schoenfeld,
Archie Tse
Graphics Director: Steve D

Following spread

Hot Spots – the Carbon Atlas

In a cross between a hierarchy and a world
map, this piece visualises how much each
country produces in carbon dioxide emissions
from the consumption of energy. Countries
are represented by a circle, scaled according to how many tons of CO_2 they emit. All the
circles are placed on the map according to
their location in the world. Bar charts along
the bottom indicate for selected countries
how much emissions have grown since 1995
(left) and how much CO_2 is emitted per capita
(right). Since this graphic appeared in 2007,
new figures from the US Energy Information
Administration show that China has become
the biggest emitter.

Project Info: *The Guardian*, newspaper article, 2007, UK
Research: Simon Rogers
Design: Mark McCormick
Art Direction: Michael Robinson

Districts

In a sign of dis

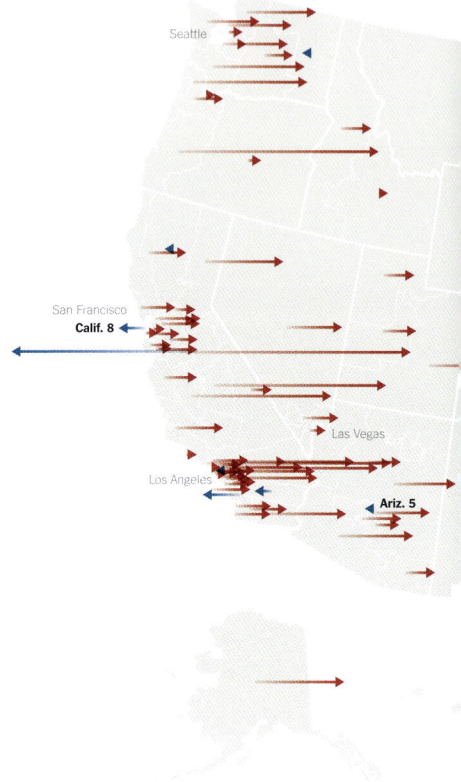

Seattle

San Francisco
Calif. 8

Las Vegas

Los Angeles

Ariz. 5

While Republicans increased their
share of the vote in **California 8**,
Nancy Pelosi's lead still increased
in the absence of a strong
third-party candidate.

Arizona 5 shifted right abo
points — enough to switc
seat to Republicans. Davi
Schweikert defeated the
Democrat he lost to in 200

Previous Shifts **From 2002 to 2004**

NO. OF DISTRICTS: 260 | 175

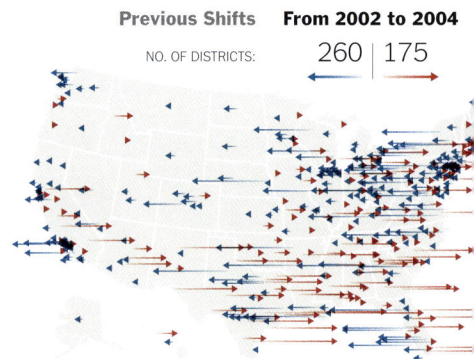

With President George W. Bush up for his second
term in a close race against John Kerry, most
districts voted more Democratic.

the party in power, 9 of every 10 House districts voted more Republican than they did in 2008.

The length of each arrow represents how much the vote in that House district shifted from 2008 to 2010.

Wis. 7

Detroit

Chicago

Ill. 17

New York

Del.

Washington

N.C. 2

Dallas

Atlanta

Houston

Miami

From 2008 to 2010

NUMBER OF DISTRICTS THAT VOTED MORE:

DEMOCRATIC	REPUBLICAN
42	**393**

+20 +10 | +10 +20 pct. pts.

The average shift toward Republicans from 2008 to 2010 was 20 percentage points.

e shift in **Wisconsin 7** was out average for an open race. re, Sean P. Duffy, a Republican trict attorney, won by 8 centage points.

One of the largest shifts was in **Illinois 17**, where Republican Bobby Schilling, a pizza business owner, beat Phil Hare, a two-term Democratic incumbent.

Only a few districts voted more Democratic. In **Delaware**, the shift helped John Carney defeat Glen Urquhart for the seat held by Michael N. Castle since 1993.

Renee Ellmers delivered one of the Republican Party's narrowest gains in **North Carolina 2**, a district that Democrats won by 36 percentage points in 2008.

From 2004 to 2006

353 | 82

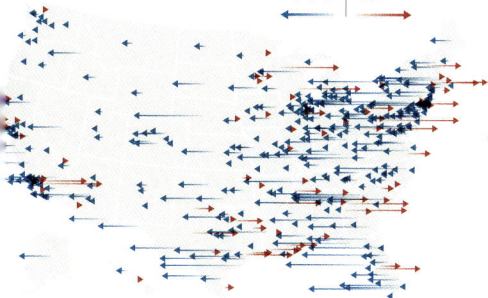

Discontent with President Bush, the war in Iraq and the handling of Hurricane Katrina helped the Democrats take control of the House and Senate.

From 2006 to 2008

245 | 190

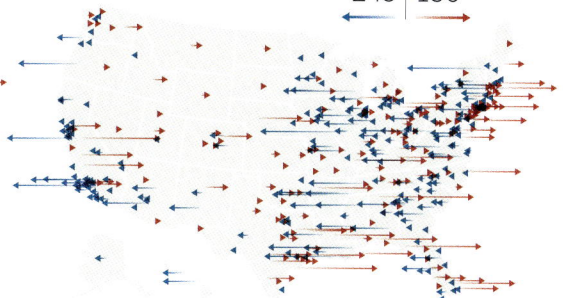

A majority of districts, riding the wave of Barack Obama's campaign, moved toward the Democrats, but the shift was less widespread than in 2006.

Hot spots - the carbon atlas

This week's Bali meeting highlighted just how difficult it will be to secure an international agreement to reduce greenhouse gas levels by enough to save the earth from catastrophic temperature rises. This map, showing countries according to their emissions, shows why an international deal is needed — and why only one binding the big polluters can succeed

Europe
4.67bn tonnes of CO2
9% growth in carbon emissions, 1990-2005

For the first time, there is hard scientific evidence of climate change affecting Europe, said the Intergovernmental Panel on Climate Change recently. Freak weather events, such as the heatwaves of 2003, will become ever more common

7 Canada 631.26

1 United States 5,957 million tonnes of carbon dioxide

6 Germany 844.17

23 Netherlands

8 United Kingdom 577.17

13 France 415.27

10 Italy 466.64

17 Spain 387.11

16 Mexico 398.25

27 Egypt

12 South Africa 423.81

North America
6.99bn tonnes of CO2
14% growth in carbon emissions, 1990-2005

The US as a major producer of greenhouse gases has been reluctant to accept that man-made climate change even existed — and refused to accept the Kyoto protocol. But freak weather events and an avalanche of scientific evidence have forced it to rethink its position

Central & South America
1.10bn tonnes of CO2
29% growth in carbon emissions, 1990-2005

Increased freak weather events mean the IPCC is concerned South America will be hard-hit by climate change. Agriculture, water supplies and the unique natural habitat could be affected by a temperature increase of up to 4C by the end of the century

Africa
1.04bn tonnes of CO2
28% growth in carbon emissions, 1990-2005

Its carbon emissions may be small but this is the continent most vulnerable to the effects of climate change, hitting food and water supplies, causing coastal flooding and an increase in tropical diseases such as malaria — as well as destroying parts of the ecosystem

These latest UN figures for climate change emissions are from 2005, but are already dated. Reliable, but provisional estimates for 2006 by Dutch government researchers suggest China's CO2 emissions increased by 9% in 2006 and have now overtaken the US emissions, which declined by 1.4% in 2006. US emissions per person are nearly three times as great as Chinese

29 Venezuela

18 Brazil 360.57

30 Argentina

CO2 emission growth of the highest 20 emitters, 1995 to 2005

87%	76%	73%	69%	56%	43%	35%	32%	26%	25%	25%	23%	14%	13%	12%	9%	5%	4%	-4%	-18%
China	Saudi Arabia	Iran	Indonesia	Spain	Australia	India	South Korea	Brazil	Mexico	Canada	South Africa	Japan	US	France	Italy	Russia	UK	Germany	Ukraine

The carbon list

Rank	Country	Tonnes per person	Million tonnes CO2
North America			
1	United States	20.40	5,956.98
7	Canada	20.00	631.26
16	Mexico	3.70	398.25
176	Bermuda	9.50	0.62
207	St Pierre & Miquelon	13.30	0.08
Central & South America			
18	Brazil	1.80	360.57
29	Venezuela	5.45	151.29
30	Argentina	3.70	146.64
48	Chile	3.90	66.19
53	Colombia	1.35	58.80
67	Puerto Rico	10.00	39.02
69	Trinidad & Tobago	25.00	38.18
73	Cuba	2.90	32.98
74	Peru	1.10	31.31
77	Ecuador	1.70	23.90

Rank	Country	Tonnes per person	Million tonnes CO2
83	Dominican Republic	1.90	17.77
88	Virgin Islands, U.S.	117.50	16.05
89	Panama	4.30	14.33
94	Bolivia	1.30	11.96
96	Jamaica	4.40	11.55
97	Netherlands Antilles	55.40	11.05
98	Guatemala	0.90	10.96
108	Honduras	1.00	7.13
113	El Salvador	1.00	6.16
114	Uruguay	1.80	6.01
115	Costa Rica	1.40	5.69
126	Nicaragua	0.80	4.30
127	The Bahamas	13.50	4.06
131	Paraguay	0.67	3.85
145	Martinique	5.90	2.29
148	Guadeloupe	5.00	2.02
150	Suriname	4.70	1.86
151	Haiti	0.20	1.75
153	Guyana	1.70	1.58
154	Barbados	5.40	1.44
161	French Guiana	6.10	1.04
163	Aruba	10.35	1.03
166	Belize	3.35	0.93
179	Antigua and Barbuda	7.25	0.59

Rank	Country	Tonnes per person	Million tonnes CO2
183	Cayman Islands	8.60	0.38
185	St Lucia	2.30	0.37
192	Grenada	2.25	0.24
193	Antarctica	7.00	0.24
195	St Vincent/Grenadines	2.00	0.20
200	Saint Kitts & Nevis	3.00	0.13
202	Dominica	1.70	0.11
206	Virgin Islands, UK	4.00	0.09
208	Montserrat	2.20	0.07
210	Falkland Islands	12.00	0.04
212	Turks & Caicos Is	0.40	0.01
Europe			
6	Germany	10.20	844.17
8	United Kingdom	9.50	577.17
10	Italy	8.00	466.64
13	France	6.60	415.27
17	Spain	9.00	387.11
21	Netherlands	16.50	269.66
23	Turkey	3.30	230.04
31	Belgium	13.00	135.81
32	Czech Republic	11.00	112.83

Rank	Country	Tonnes per person	Million tonnes CO2
38	Greece	9.50	103.16
39	Romania	4.60	99.34
43	Austria	9.50	78.17
50	Portugal	6.10	64.97
52	Hungary	5.50	59.84
54	Sweden	6.30	58.77
57	Serbia & Montenegro	5.00	52.56
58	Norway	11.10	52.35
59	Finland	10.00	52.25
60	Denmark	9.80	50.96
61	Bulgaria	6.50	50.54
64	Switzerland	6.00	45.92
65	Ireland	10.60	44.10
71	Slovakia	6.90	37.81
79	Croatia	4.80	21.46
84	Bosnia & Herzegovina	4.50	17.45
86	Slovenia	8.15	16.77
92	Luxembourg	26.50	12.55
102	Cyprus	11.60	8.81
104	Macedonia	3.90	8.05
124	Albania	1.40	4.35
125	Gibraltar	151.35	4.34
132	Iceland	11.75	3.39
133	Malta	7.75	3.02

Rank	Country	Tonnes per person	Million tonnes CO2
174	Faroe Islands	13.90	0.68
178	Greenland	11.20	0.59
Eurasia			
3	Russia	11.70	1,696.00
20	Ukraine	7.10	342.52
26	Kazakhstan	12.90	198.01
35	Uzbekistan	4.40	117.97
55	Belarus	5.50	57.11
63	Turkmenistan	10.40	49.64
72	Azerbaijan	4.30	37.03
81	Estonia	13.70	18.89
90	Lithuania	4.00	13.94
101	Armenia	3.00	9.61
103	Latvia	3.60	8.39
107	Tajikistan	1.80	7.16
118	Kyrgyzstan	1.00	5.28
121	Georgia	1.00	4.72
Middle East			
11	Iran	6.60	450.68

World carbon emissions are up from 18.3bn tonnes in 1980 – and with rapid industrialisation in the developing world, those numbers will climb higher. The effect is delayed, which means even if we stopped emitting carbon now, it would go on increasing in the atmosphere

20 Ukraine 342.57
3 Russia 1,696
81
51
90
103
107
121
101
72
63
26 Kazakhstan
35
106 118

Eurasia
2.58bn tonnes of CO2

Russia's carbon emissions dropped from 583 million metric tonnes of carbon in 1992 to 405 million metric tonnes in 1998, due to its then-deteriorating economic situation. Now, the energy giant may make clean up trading carbon credits

25 Turkey

11 Iran 450.68
87 62
49
82 40
45
14 Saudi Arabia 412.35
76
85
75 56
31

Middle East
45bn tonnes of CO2

The region is a major contributor to global greenhouse gas emissions, through an oil and gas industry which produces over 30 percent of world oil supply and over 10 percent of its gas

2 China 5,323 million tonnes of carbon dioxide
4 Japan 1,230
47
9 South Korea 499.63
22 Taiwan
105
34
134
5 India 1,166
187
66
91
24 Thailand
42
46
44
33
28 Malaysia
19 Indonesia 359.47
147 155
197 205
199
177
214 209 168
189
123
198 139
157
211
201
93
172
15 Australia 406.64
70

Asia & Oceania
10.36bn tonnes of CO2

Rapid industrialisation combined with greater numbers of people moving to cities has provoked a huge rise in carbon emissions – with China rapidly moving to become the world's greatest carbon emitter in the next two years – some scientists say this has happened already

WORDS: SIMON ROGERS. GRAPHIC: MARK McCORMICK

Highest per person CO2 emissions, Top twenty plus UK, 2005, tonnes

Qatar	Bahrain	Trinidad & Tobago	UAE	Kuwait	Singapore	Lux-embourg	Australia	US	Canada	Netherlands	Saudi Arabia	Estonia	Bahamas	Belgium	Kazakhstan	Taiwan	Russia	Norway	Czech Republic	UK (36th)	World
61.94	36.58	35.51	33.73	32.84	30.25	26.79	20.24	20.14	19.24	16.44	15.61	14.17	13.46	13.10	13.04	12.53	11.88	11.40	11.02	9.55	4.37

4	Saudi Arabia	412.35	99	Sudan	10.79	156	Guinea	1.34
	United Arab Emirates	137.82	100	Kenya	9.88	158	Niger	1.23
	Iraq	98.13	109	Cameroon	6.81	159	Sierra Leone	1.18
	Kuwait	76.69	110	Ghana	6.67	160	Burkina Faso	1.17
	Israel	65.01	116	IvoryCoast	6.42	161	Swaziland	1.14
	Qatar	53.45	116	Senegal	5.49	167	Seychelles	0.92
	Syria	49.78	117	Congo	5.31	169	Malawi	0.86
	Oman	29.72	119	Gabon	4.95	170	Rwanda	0.86
	Bahrain	25.18	120	Equatorial Guinea	4.87	171	Eritrea	0.78
	Jordan	18.67	122	Ethiopia	4.37	173	Somalia	0.75
	Yemen	17.15	128	Mauritius	4.01	175	Mali	0.66
	Lebanon	16.17	129	Tanzania	3.92	181	Liberia	0.53
			130	Botswana	3.50	182	Burundi	0.41
			135	Namibia	2.67	184	Guinea-Bissau	0.38
Africa			136	Reunion	2.65	186	Central African Rep	0.34
	South Africa	423.81	137	Mauritania	2.63	188	The Gambia	0.30
	Egypt	161.79	138	Madagascar	2.54	190	Cape Verde	0.28
	Algeria	105.39	140	Zambia	2.45	191	Western Sahara	0.28
	Libya	88.10	141	Togo	2.38	194	Lesotho	0.21
	Morocco	53.47	142	Dem Rep Congo	2.37	196	Chad	0.19
	Tunisia	38.89	144	Mozambique	2.30	203	Comoros	0.10
	Angola	22.24	146	Benin	2.27	204	Sao Tome & Principe	0.10
	Zimbabwe	20.39	149	Djibouti	1.95	215	St Helena	0.01
		11.78	152	Uganda	1.62			

Asia & Oceania			134	Nepal	2.95
2	China	5,322.69	139	New Caledonia	2.51
4	Japan	1,230.36	147	Guam	2.35
5	India	1,165.72	155	Wake Island	2.18
9	South Korea	499.63	157	Fiji	1.36
15	Australia	406.64	162	Laos	1.34
19	Indonesia	359.47	168	Afghanistan	1.06
22	Taiwan	284.40	168	French Polynesia	0.98
24	Thailand	234.16	172	Maldives	0.87
28	Malaysia	155.51	177	American Samoa	0.76
33	Singapore	133.88	180	Cambodia	0.60
34	Pakistan	121.49	187	Bhutan	0.57
42	Vietnam	80.38	189	U.S. Pacific Islands	0.32
46	North Korea	73.50	197	Solomon Islands	0.29
47	Bangladesh	39.82	198	Nauru	0.19
70	New Zealand	37.82	199	Samoa	0.18
91	Burma	13.87	201	Tonga	0.16
93	Sri Lanka	12.38	201	Vanuatu	0.13
105	Mongolia	7.87	209	Cook Islands	0.09
110	Brunei	6.44	211	Kiribati	0.07
123	Papua New Guinea	4.35	214	Niue	0.03
					0.003
			World	4.37	28,192.74

HOW THE WORLD FE

Corporate environmental consciousness ha
influencing not only public perception of a comp
how this trend is developing around the

MOST POPULAR GREEN BRANDS IN THE WORLD
ACCORDING TO A PENN SCHOEN BERLAND SURVEY

APPLE

DOVE

GOOGLE

IKEA

PERCENT OF RESPONDENTS

— 100

UNITED STATES

UNITED KINGDOM

FRANCE

GERMANY

— 50

— 0

ARE PEOPLE MORE CONCERNED ABOUT THE ENVIRONMENT OR ECONOMY?

ECONOMY

ENVIRONMENT

IMPORTANCE OF BUYING PRODUCTS FROM GREEN COMPANIES

○ NOT IMPORTANT

○ SOMEWHAT IMPORTANT

○ VERY IMPORTANT

Data based on survey responses of consumers from the eight countries

Project Info: *GOOD*, website, 2010, USA
Data Source: Cohn & Wolfe; Esty Environmental Partners;
Landor; Penn Schoen Berland

Research: Colin Dobrin
Design: Andrew Effendy (Column Five Media)
Art Direction: Ross Crooks

SOURCE:

Cohn & Wolfe
Esty Environmental Partners
Landor
Penn Schoen Berland

issue of increasing concern in our society,
consumers' buying habits. Here we take stock of
ich popular brands are on the forefront.

MICROSOFT

NIVEA

NOKIA

TOYOTA

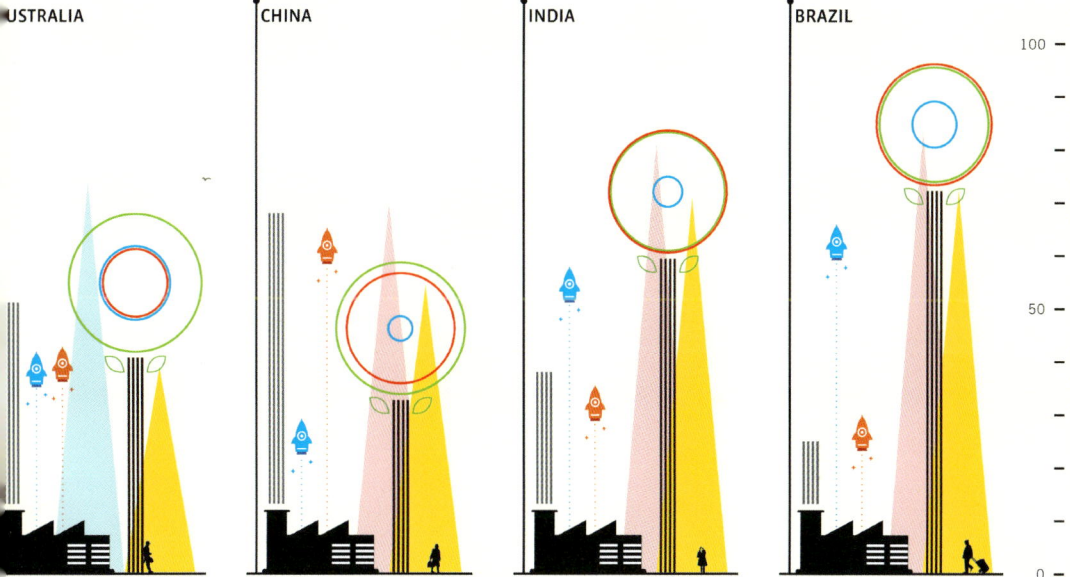

USTRALIA

CHINA

INDIA

BRAZIL

100

50

0

SENTIMENTS ABOUT THE DIRECTION OF THE ENVIRONMENT

RIGHT TRACK   WRONG TRACK

MOST IMPORTANT THINGS FOR A COMPANY TO OFFER

GOOD VALUE
TRUSTWORTHINESS
ENVIRONMENTAL CONSCIOUSNESS

a collaboration between GOOD and COLUMN FIVE

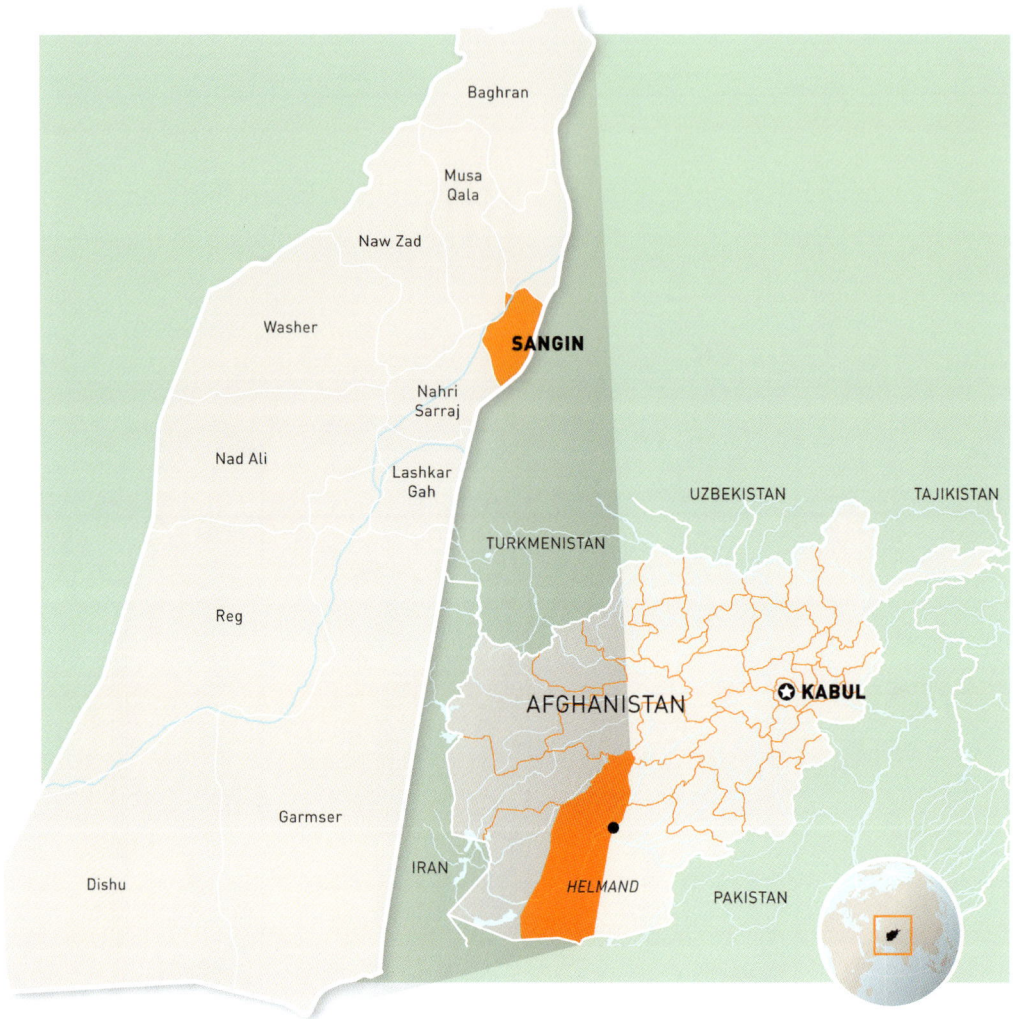

Previous spread

How the World feels about Green Brands

Many consumers today are keen to support companies that show social and ecological responsibility. This diagram was developed by Column Five as part of *GOOD* magazine's Transparency series. It highlights how people in several leading countries feel about the economy and environment. The data visualised are based upon responses to a series of survey questions. The heights of the bars correspond to the percentage of respondents, and thus shows the very high concern Brazilians have for the environment, whereas the majority of people in the US are more worried about the economy. The tiny rockets indicate how positively people estimate the state of the environment, with China clearly leading there.

Project Info: *Esquire*, magazine article, 2010, UK
Design: Infomen

Improvised Explosive Devices

Sangin in the province of Helmand has been one of the most hard-fought areas in the Afghanistan war. British troops who have been stationed in the region from 2006–2010 experienced the fighting as the most brutal they have been involved in since the Korean War. This series of graphics explains roadside bombs, a weapon frequently used against the coalition troops in the area. One graphic shows the device, while another explains the setting: how bombs are placed and detonated in the road. A schematic shows the Dragon Runner, a small robot deployed for the reconnaissance of unsecured territory. The motion sequence along the bottom elucidates how it removes explosive devices. The soldier silhouette in the background points up the small size of the robot.

IL | **GREEN REPORT** – ANALISI GRAFICA

CORSA SENZA FRENI

Design avveniristico e materiali tecnologici: la sperimentazione sulle bici non conosce sosta. Ecco alcuni modelli

Senza catena

Trek District Bike: al posto della catena monta una cinghia in fibra di carbonio.
725 euro ⊕ trekbikes.com

Pieghevole

Mµ Uno: una bici pieghevole con ruote da 16" e freno posteriore a pedale.
450 euro ⊕ dahon.com

È la bicicletta che

"Bike sharing" e investimenti per le piste ciclabili, integrazioni con autobus e metropolitane e domeniche chiuse al traffico: si moltiplicano nel mondo le iniziative per promuovere l'uso della bicicletta. Un mezzo di trasporto ecologico, economico e "city friendly". Insomma, il mezzo del futuro

– di **Francesco Franchi**

DUE RUOTE RADDOPPIANO LE QUATTRO

La produzione mondiale di biciclette ha toccato quota **130 milioni** nel 2007: più del doppio rispetto ai **52 milioni** di auto immesse sul mercato. Il boom registrato dopo il 2004 è in parte dovuto alla crescente domanda di **bici elettriche**

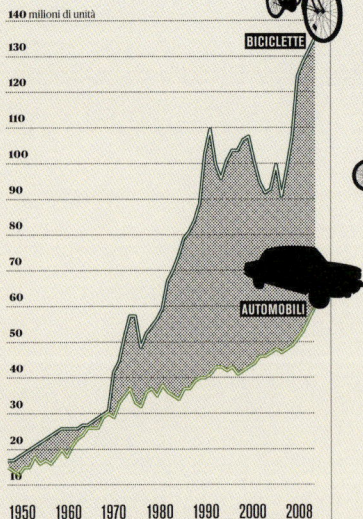

140 milioni di unità
130
120 — **BICICLETTE**
110
100
90
80
70
60 — **AUTOMOBILI**
50
40
30
20
10

1950 1960 1970 1980 1990 2000 2008

FONTE: Worldwatch, Bike Europe, Global Insight

Canada

Montreal la rete ciclabile copre 180 km. Nel 2007 la città ha lanciato un piano da **6,3 miliardi** di euro che include il raddoppio delle piste per le bici

Stati Uniti

L'obiettivo della città di **Chicago** per il 2015 è di raggiungere gli **800 km** di piste ciclabili e che il 5% dei viaggi sotto gli 8 km avvenga sulle due ruote

Colombia

Bogotà ha una rete ciclabile di **300 km**. In città, nelle domeniche e nei giorni festivi vengono chiusi al traffico automobilistico **120 km** di strade

Messico

Dal 2007 **Città del Messico** ha iniziato il suo programma di *Ciclo-Paseos*: nelle domeniche le auto non possono circolare dalle 7 alle 14 nel centro cittadino

Stati Uniti

Il piano di sostenibilità del sindaco Bloomberg porterà a **New York** entro il 2030, oltre **2.800 km** di piste ciclabili. 700 km sono già stati costruiti

Gran Bretagna

Il **London Cycle Network** (LCN +) prevede 900 km di corsie ciclabili entro il 2010. Dal 2000 a oggi i ciclisti in città sono aumentati dell'**83%**

Francia

A **Parigi** nel 2007 fu introdotto il sistema di bike-sharing **Vélib**, che oggi conta 20.600 biciclette e 1.451 stazioni. Esempi simili anche in altre città europee

BIANCHI, ATALA, BOTTECCHIA, COLNAGO

Nella classifica dei maggiori produttori mondiali di biciclette l'Italia si piazza alle spalle di Cina e Taiwan: due colossi che riforniscono i mercati di mezzo globo. I maggiori importatori sono gli Stati Uniti

biciclette esportate

biciclette prodotte

Stato
10 milioni

biciclette importate

7 10,15 milioni di biciclette esportate

Stati Uniti
0,3 milioni

18,12 milioni di biciclette importate

Francia
1,1 milioni

German[ia]
2,4 milioni

Italia
2,5 milioni

0,57 milioni

0,90 milioni

1,32 milioni di biciclette esportate

28,1 metri: è quanto misura la bici più lunga del mondo

IL

Luci nel telaio

Da un progetto di Bortolani e Righi, la Plus Bike: il telaio incorpora i fanalini anteriori e posteriori. ● **dovetusai.it**

Artigianato italiano

Modello Fuga di Abici, prodotta artigianalmente in Italia, ricorda le bici da pista. 950 euro ● **abici-italia.it**

fa girare il mondo

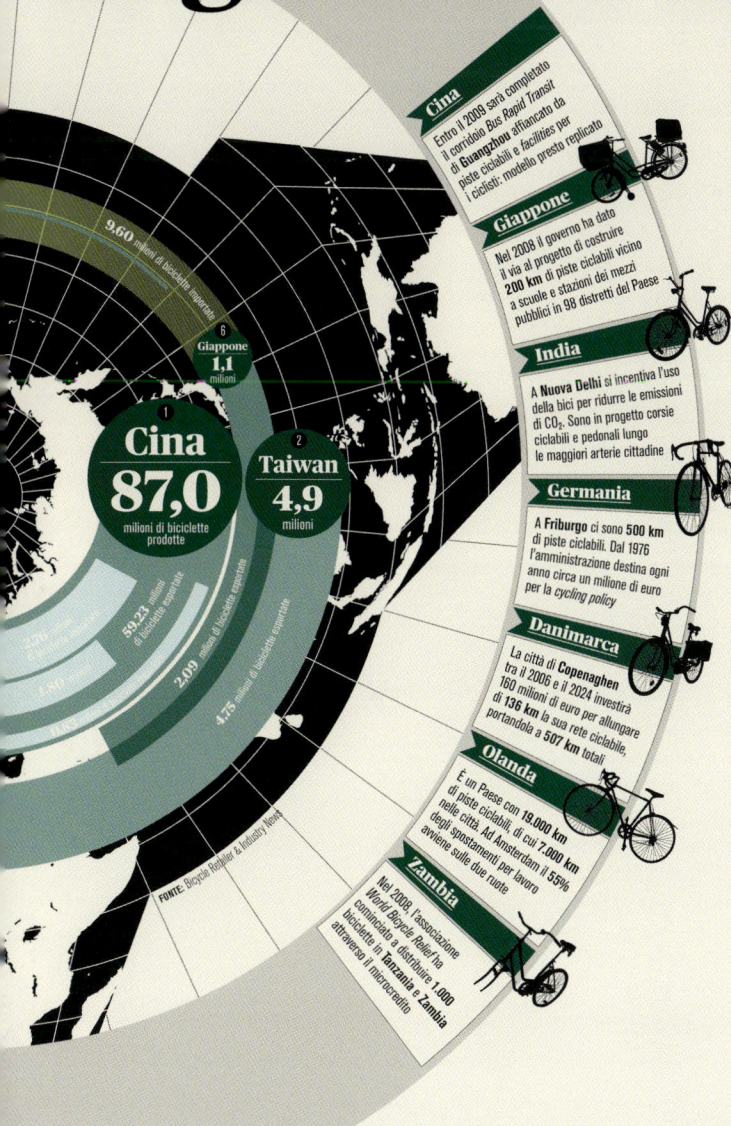

Cina
Entro il 2009 sarà completato il corridoio *Bus Rapid Transit* di **Guangzhou** affiancato da piste ciclabili e *facilities* per i ciclisti: modello presto replicato

Giappone
Nel 2008 il governo ha dato il via al progetto di costruire **200 km** di piste ciclabili vicino a scuole e stazioni dei mezzi pubblici in 98 distretti del Paese

India
A **Nuova Delhi** si incentiva l'uso della bici per ridurre le emissioni di CO_2. Sono in progetto corsie ciclabili e pedonali lungo le maggiori arterie cittadine

Germania
A **Friburgo** ci sono 500 km di piste ciclabili. Dal 1976 l'amministrazione destina ogni anno circa un milione di euro per il *cycling policy*

Danimarca
La città di **Copenaghen** tra il 2006 e il 2024 investirà 136 milioni di euro per allungare di 136 km la sua rete ciclabile portandola a 507 km totali

Olanda
È un Paese con 19.000 km di piste ciclabili, di cui 7.000 km nelle città. Ad Amsterdam il 55% degli spostamenti per lavoro avviene sulle due ruote

Zambia
Nel 2008 l'associazione *World Bicycle Relief* ha cominciato a distribuire 1.000 biciclette in **Tanzania** e **Zambia** attraverso il microcredito

9,60 milioni di biciclette importate

6
Giappone
1,1
milioni

① **Cina**
87,0
milioni di biciclette prodotte

② **Taiwan**
4,9
milioni

4,26 milioni di biciclette esportate

59,23 milioni di biciclette esportate

1,60 milioni di biciclette importate

2,09 milioni di biciclette esportate

4,75 milioni di biciclette esportate

FONTE: Bicycle Retailer & Industry News

MADE IN ITALY A MARCIA INDIETRO

Nonostante i trend mondiali di crescita generale, in Italia la produzione di biciclette è andata calando negli anni

— biciclette **prodotte**   — biciclette **importate**   — biciclette **esportate**

7,0 milioni di biciclette

6,0
5,0
4,0
3,0
2,0
1,0

1993 1995 1997 1999 2001 2003 2005 2007

FONTE: Ancma

PEDALA RAGAZZO, PEDALA

In Italia la metà delle bici prodotte è costituita da modelli da bambino. Le mountain bike rappresentano un quarto degli ordini

MTB 25%
51% BAMBINI
CORSA 4%
CITY BIKE 20%

FONTE: Ancma

SUL SELLINO CHE NOI PORTIAMO

Oltre al prodotto finito, il nostro Paese produce anche molti componenti per biciclette. I pezzi più esportati (per valore commerciale) sono cambi, selle e cerchi

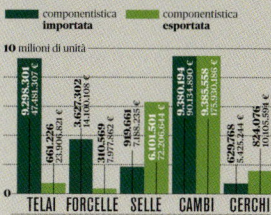

■ componentistica **importata**   ■ componentistica **esportata**

10 milioni di unità

	TELAI	FORCELLE	SELLE	CAMBI	CERCHI
importata	9.298.301 — 47.481.307 €	3.622.302 — 14.006.108 €	916.661 — 7.877.862 €	9.380.494 — 90.134.890 €	629.768 — 5.425.244 €
esportata	661.226 — 23.906.823 €	310.569 — 7.877.862 €	6.141.207 — 72.506.644 €	9.265.558 — 175.500.186 €	824.076 — 3.465.594 €

FONTE: Ancma

149

Previous spread

It's the Bike that Makes the World Go Round

This circle diagram looks at the use and production of bicycles around the world. The centre is occupied by a map of the northern hemisphere, with three wings swung outwards. Selected countries are marked on this map with circles, figures indicating the number of bicycles produced in each one. Dark-green stripes show the number of bicycles exported. Imports of bicycles are shown with light-green stripes. The map is surrounded by small notes explaining local policy towards upgrading the bicycle traffic infrastructure in various countries. The chart on the left compares global production figures for cars and bikes, while the charts on the right give further key data for the Italian market.

Project Info: *Intelligence in Lifestyle*, magazine article, 2009, Italy
Data Source: Worldwatch Institute; Bike Europe; Global Insight; Bicycle Retailer & Industry News; Associazione Nazionale Ciclo Motociclo Accessori
Design: Francesco Franchi

Literary Madrid

This graphic shows a collection of literary quotes about the city of Madrid, taken from the works of famous Spanish and international writers. The circle represents an abstract map of the inner city, with Puerta del Sol in the centre, the Calle Gran Via floating as a grey streak up towards the top left and Parque del Retiro taking up most of the lower right side. The quotes are allocated either to the place where the writer lived or to where the story took place, thus creating a net of literary references across the city.

Project Info: *La Información*, website, 2010, Spain
Design: Raul Arias
Art Direction: Mario Tascon, Antonio Pasagali

EL JARAMA

PLAZA CASTILLA

EL OTRO DÍA LES ROGÓ ANDRÉS QUE MUDASEN DE SITIO Y SE ALEJASEN DE MADRID, PORQUE TENÍA QUE SER RECONOCIDO SI ALLÍ ESTABA.

Cuatro Caminos

TRISTANA

BENITO PÉREZ GALDÓS

FRANCISCO UMBRAL

LUIS MARTÍN SANTOS

ARTURO SORIA Y MATA LA CIUDAD LINEAL

MALASAÑA

BILBAO

ALONSO MARTÍNEZ

ORELLANA

CALLE

FRANCISCO UMBRAL, "LA LEYENDA DEL CÉSAR VISIONARIO"

VENTAS

PUÉRTOLAS

LA GRAN VÍA

LEOPOLDO ALAS

MINGUEZ

MAX AUB

MADRID PUERTA DEL SOL

CIBELES

PUERTA ALCALÁ

BENITO PÉREZ GALDÓS

RAMÓN GÓMEZ DE LA SERNA GREGUERÍAS

BENITO PÉREZ GALDÓS

CALLE MAYOR

ISMAEL GRASA

ARTURO BAREA

DE JUAN VENET

ATOCHA

LA PUERTA DE ATOCHA

LA FORJA DE UN REBELDE

RAMÓN MESONERO ROMANOS

DE JUAN GARCÍA HORTELANO

ERNEST HEMINGWAY

CERVANTES

"EL BUSCÓN" FRANCISCO DE QUEVEDO

LA GITANILLA, NOVELAS EJEMPLARES, MIGUEL DE CERVANTES

151

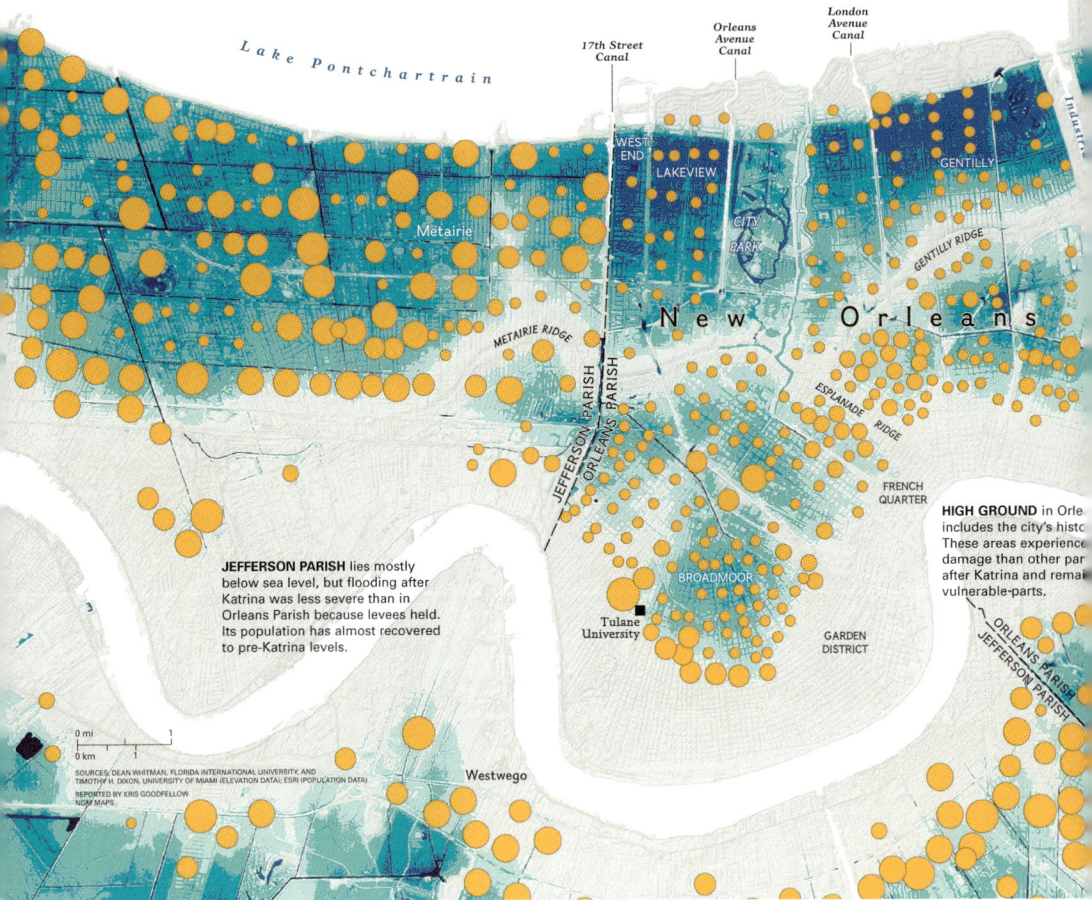

LIVES STILL AT RISK

In New Orleans and adjoining parishes, 500,000 people now live at or below sea level, as shown in a map giving population for low-lying neighborhoods. Some of these areas lay underwater for weeks after Katrina; all face serious risk of flooding in future storms. Jefferson and Orleans Parishes have the nation's highest number of properties with repeated flood losses.

POPULATION AT OR BELOW SEA LEVEL

10 50 100 250 500 1,000 1,500 2,000 2,500

Estimates for July 2007

ELEVATION in feet

0   -2   -4   -6   -8   -10

Sea level

Lake Pontchartrain

17th Street Canal

Orleans Avenue Canal

London Avenue Canal

WEST END

LAKEVIEW

GENTILLY

Metairie

CITY PARK

N e w   O r l e a n s

METAIRIE RIDGE

GENTILLY RIDGE

JEFFERSON PARISH

ORLEANS PARISH

ESPLANADE RIDGE

FRENCH QUARTER

HIGH GROUND in Orle includes the city's histo These areas experience damage than other par after Katrina and rema vulnerable-parts.

JEFFERSON PARISH lies mostly below sea level, but flooding after Katrina was less severe than in Orleans Parish because levees held. Its population has almost recovered to pre-Katrina levels.

BROADMOOR

Tulane University

GARDEN DISTRICT

ORLEANS PARISH
JEFFERSON PARISH

0 mi   1
0 km   1

SOURCES: DEAN WHITMAN, FLORIDA INTERNATIONAL UNIVERSITY, AND TIMOTHY H. DIXON, UNIVERSITY OF MIAMI (ELEVATION DATA); ESRI (POPULATION DATA)
REPORTED BY KRIS GOODFELLOW
NGM MAPS

Westwego

Lives Still at Risk

This thematic map from 2007 looks at how many people living in New Orleans are exposed to the danger of flooding. After Hurricane Katrina devastated New Orleans in 2005, large parts of the city stood under water for weeks. The key part of the geo-graphical data featured in this map is elevation – areas that are at or below sea level are marked in blue. This geographical information is enriched with population data – yellow dots show where and how many people live below sea level and are thus greatly exposed to the danger of flooding in future storms.

SWAMPLAND in Orleans
including New Orleans East
between Lake Pontchartrain
igh ground to the south,
xtensively after Katrina
al levees failed.

NEW ORLEANS
EAST

Gulf Intracoastal Waterway

Bayou Bienvenue

*Lake
Borgne*

ORLEANS
PARISH

ST. BERNARD
PARISH

*Mississippi River
Gulf Outlet (MRGO)*

**THE LOWER NINTH WARD
AND ST. BERNARD PARISH**
were heavily flooded after Katrina
breached levees along MRGO and
the Industrial Canal. Rebuilding
has been limited.

ORLEANS PARISH
ST. BERNARD PARISH

DECOMINE DR.

Mississippi River

Below Sea Level
ORLEANS PARISH AND ST. BERNARD PARISH

POPULATION	BUILDING PERMITS
Thousands of people	*Thousands of addresses*

POPULATION: 25 20 15 10 5

BUILDING PERMITS: 5 10 15

Sea level
-1 ft.
-2
-3
-4
-5
-6
-7
-8
-9
-10
-11
-12
-13
-14
-15

*Roughly 120,000
permits have
been issued for
addresses
between sea
level and ten feet
below sea level.*

*More than 32,000
people still live
ten feet or more
below sea level.*

Project Info: *National Geographic*, magazine article, 2007, USA
Data Source: Dean Whitman (Florida International University);
Timothy H. Dixon (University of Miami); ESRI
Research: Kris Goodfellow
Design: William McNulty
Art Direction: Charles M. Blow

DEUTSCHLANDKARTE

HEILIGER BUCHMARKT

Wo verkauft
sich die Bibel wie gut?

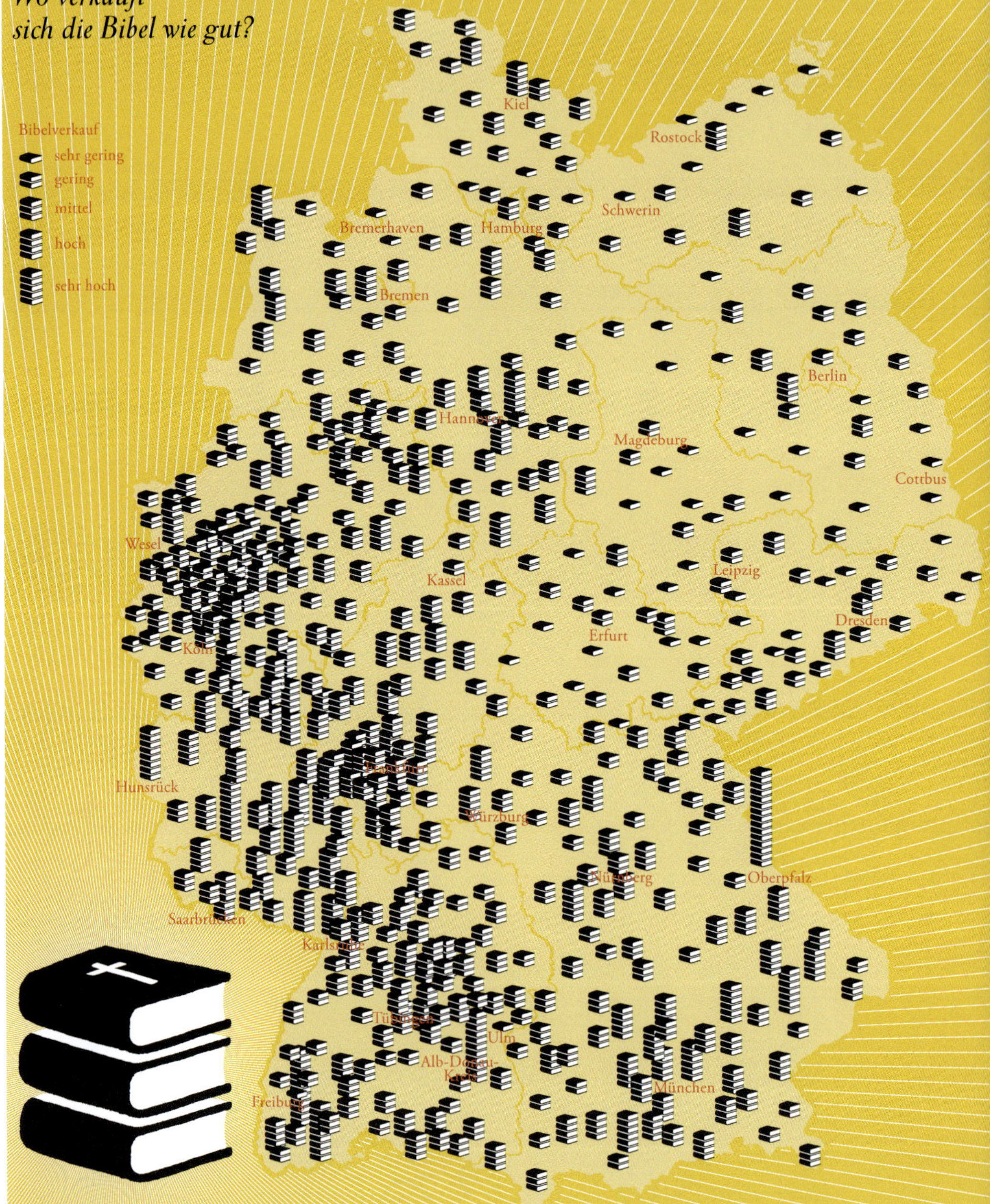

Bibelverkauf

sehr gering
gering
mittel
hoch
sehr hoch

Kiel

Rostock

Bremerhaven Hamburg Schwerin

Bremen

Berlin

Hannover

Magdeburg

Cottbus

Wesel

Kassel Leipzig

Köln Erfurt Dresden

Hunsrück

Nürnberg Oberpfalz

Saarbrücken

Karlsruhe

Tübingen Ulm

Alb-Donau-
kreis München

Freiburg

Würzburg

Maps of Germany

This series of thematic maps of Germany is a continuous single-spread feature in the weekly magazine supplement of German newspaper *Die Zeit*. Created by various designers, they cover all kinds of everyday topics: from top hairdressers' names, the distribution of lidos across the country, down to which regions have the highest divorce rates. The visual design always makes a reference to the map's theme. The examples shown here were designed by Ole Häntzschel. "Holy book market" records sales figures for the Bible. "Exonyms" lists German cities with their names in other languages. "Fish or Meat" shows in separate maps how much fish and meat is eaten according to gender (men shown left). "Genetically modified corn" maps the regions in which GM corn is cultivated.

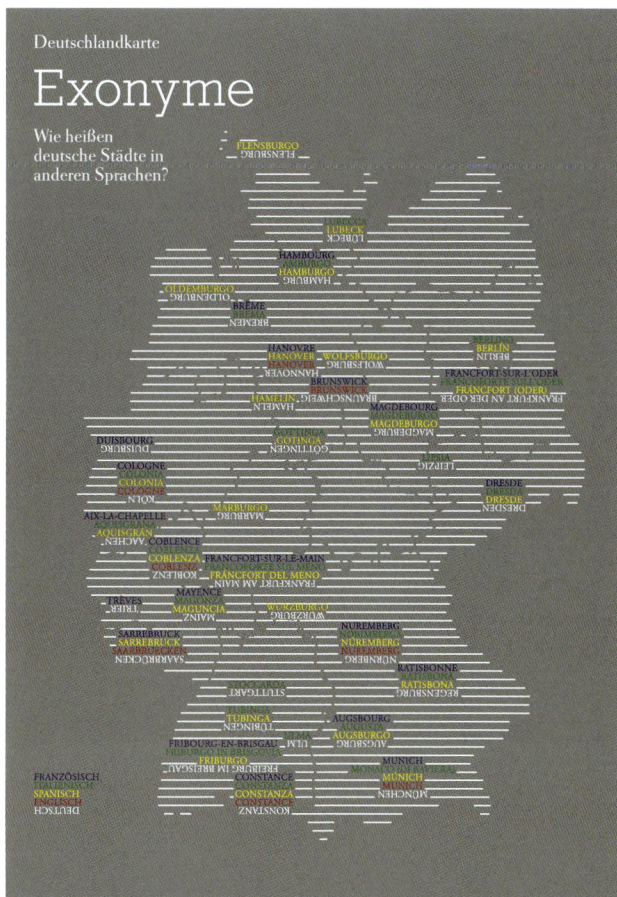

Deutschlandkarte

Exonyme

Wie heißen deutsche Städte in anderen Sprachen?

Project Info: *ZEITmagazin*, magazine article, 2008, Germany
Data Source: Initiative Neue Soziale Marktwirtschaft; Amazon; Nationale Verzehrstudie (2008); Greenpeace
Research: Matthias Stolz, Nele Heinevetter (*Die Zeit*)
Design: Ole Häntzschel
Additional Info: Series also published in a book by Knaur
Awards: Malofiej 2009

Map to Ghost Town

This map was developed as a T-shirt design and shows the fictional place of "Ghost Town", laid out in the shape of a skull. Like a traditional tourist map, it features street names and prominent attractions, using cute little pictorial elements typical for this sort of map. All names and places were made up as horror-themed wordplay, drawing on famous references to crime and murder. The graphic mimics the format of thematic maps.

Project Info: Threadless.com, T-shirt design, 2010, USA
Design: Esther Aarts

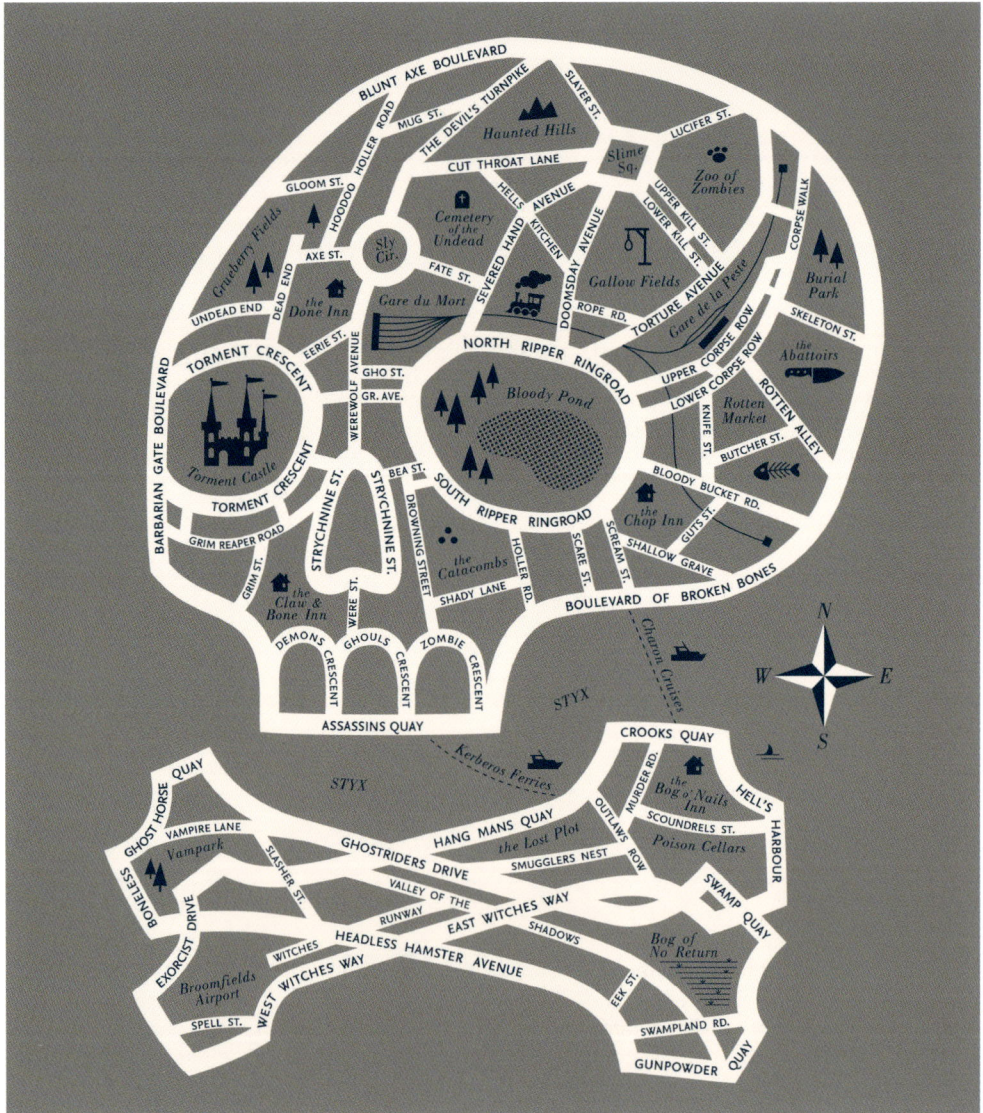

Project Info: Interactive visualisation, since 2008, USA
Data Source: Electronic Enlightenment Project;
Packard Humanities Institute; Edizione nazionale delle
opere di Antonio Vallisneri; The Athanasius Kircher
Project (Stanford University)

Design: Nicole Coleman,
Dan Edelstein, Paula Findlen, Kofi Ohene-Adu
(Stanford Humanities Center)
Tools: Protovis (Mike Bostock, Jeff Heer); Polymaps
(SimpleGeo, Stamen); CloudMade; OpenStreetMap

Above and following spread

Mapping the Republic of Letters

The term "Republic of Letters" refers to the intellectual network across Europe and the Americas during the Enlightenment, which relied primarily on the exchange of handwritten letters. Drawing on digital archives of such letters, this project visualises the correspondence of some leading historical figures. Each letter is plotted according to its author, date and where it was sent from and received. Data can be filtered via a menu. The clockwise bending of a line from A to B indicates the letter was sent in that direction. The combination of map and timeline also allows the plotting of those letters for which information on either date or location is missing. The project is a work in progress, and aims to facilitate the use of digital archives of the letters for scholars. The image above visualises Voltaire's correspondence during the years he spent near Geneva. Grey bars in the timeline indicate that most of his communication is not mapped, as many letters contain no indication of where they were written. In the correspondence of Benjamin Franklin (following spread), many letters contain no date. These are mapped with grey lines. Franklin spent some years as US ambassador in France, which is why many of the letters were sent from Paris.

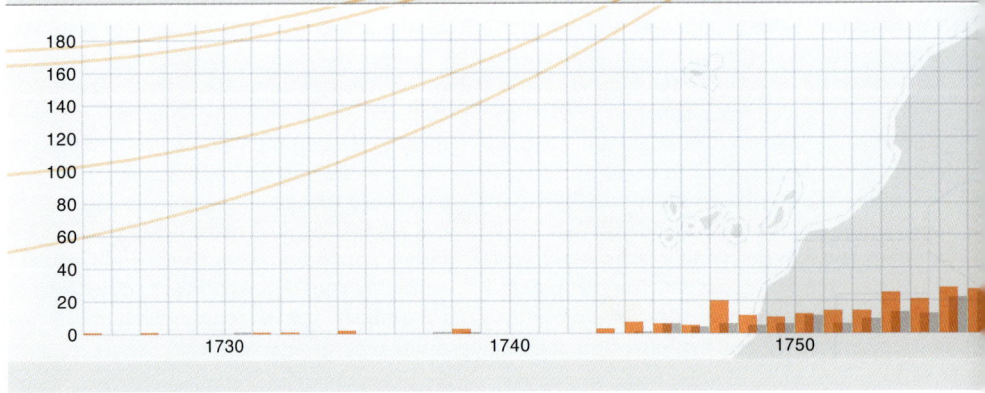

180
160
140
120
100
80
60
40
20
0

1730   1740   1750

Medallandssandur

During a stay in Iceland, Norwegian artist Torgeir Husevaag stumbled upon a series of old maps. One piece struck his imagination – the sheet showed a tiny little strip of land along the south coast of Iceland. The larger part of the map, on the other hand, shows the great blue void of the sea. Thrilled by the apparent lack of information conveyed in the map, Husevaag decided to enhance the sheets by hand-drawn visuals of invented phenomena. Referring to an old cartographic habit to fill the blank areas of unknown territory with imaginative decorations, he added pseudo-information pertaining to what happens in this large blue area which is supposed to represent the sea.

Project Info: Series of drawings, 2010, Norway / Iceland
Design: Torgeir Husevaag
Additional Info: original size each 58 x 54 cm

Missile Defence Shield

The US National Missile Defense Program, supported by President George W. Bush, was intended to destroy attacking missiles before they actually hit American soil. The map shows the northern hemisphere, with the US in red on the left, and Iran and North Korea as assumed aggressors in green. NATO member states are orange, whilst Russia is shown in yellow.

The ballistic trajectory of the missile is sketched out like a process in a number of steps. Black symbols mark the main projected components, such as ship-based defence systems in the oceans, as well as ground bases in Poland and the US. Various radar stations worldwide were to support the identification of an attacking missile.

Project Info: *Süddeutsche Zeitung Wissen*, magazine article, 2008, Germany
Design: Jens Uwe Meyer
(United States of the Art)

Globe Encounters

In the Information Age, the flow
of Internet traffic between
locations is nearly ubiquitous.
Globe Encounters visualizes the
volumes of Internet data flowing
between New York and cities
around the world over the past
24 hours. The size of the glow
on a particular city location
corresponds to the amount of IP
traffic flowing between that
place and New York City. A
larger glow implies a greater
IP flow.

IP traffic | total
outgoing from new york

12:00

new york time | night | morning | afternoon | evening

Following spread

New York Talk Exchange

NYTE was developed by the MIT SENSEable
City Laboratory for the "Design and the Elastic
Mind" exhibition at MoMA. The project illustrates global telephone communication in and out
of New York City. Data provided by the AT&T
network were used to measure the volume of
Internet protocol (IP) and voice traffic at a given
time. This data was plotted in three different
modes. "Globe Encounters" locates on a globe
the places New Yorkers are talking to. "Pulse of
the Planet" includes time as a dimension of the
map: it shows how phone calls shift through the
day as time zones sweep over the planet. The
third visualisation zooms inside New York City's
five boroughs: colour coding reveals the destinations called from particular neighbourhoods.

Nuclear Energy Worldwide

This thematic map for German *Greenpeace*
magazine shows nuclear reactors worldwide.
Colour coding denotes then current policy
towards nuclear power in each country, with
yellow indicating that it is to be expanded,
whereas green countries had developed exit
strategies which have been postponed. Striped
countries were planning to re-adopt the nuclear generation of electricity. Icons show the
geographical distribution and status of all 437
reactors worldwide, as of 2010. Pie charts show
the percentage of nuclear power out of the
total national energy production. The bar chart
to the lower right breaks down the age of all
reactors, showing that the majority were built
at least 25 years ago.

Project Info: Museum of Modern Art,
interactive installation, 2008, USA
Data Source: AT&T
Research: Assaf Biderman, Francesco Calabrese,
Francisca Rojas, Andrea Vaccari,
Margaret Ellen Haller (MIT SENSEable City Lab)
Design: Kristian Kloeckl, Aaron Koblin
(MIT SENSEable City Lab)

Project Info: *Greenpeace*, magazine article, 2010, Germany
Data Source: IAEA; *World Nuclear Industry Handbook* 2009;
World Nuclear Association; Greenpeace Media
Design: Carsten Raffel (United States of the Art)

City Ranking
Flushing, Queens

Seoul, KR **11.19%**

Porto, PT **8.19%**

Toronto, CA **5.91%**

Keelung, TW **3.93%**

Shanghai, CN **3.52%**

Santo Domingo, DR **3.00%**

Ho Chi Minh, VN **2.51%**

Quevedo, EC **1.81%**
Fuzhou, CN **1.80%**
Montreal, CA **1.67%**
Guangzhou, CN **1.62%**
Stockholm, SE **1.61%**
Kingston, JM **1.43%**
Moncton, CA **1.31%**
Manila, PH **1.14%**
Cuenca, EC **1.01%**
Geneva, CH **1.00%**
London (Outer City), GB **0.94%**
Halifax, CA **0.92%**
Belize City, BZ **0.84%**
Delhi, IN **0.80%**
Mumbai, IN **0.79%**
Munich, DE **0.74%**
Palermo, IT **0.68%**
Tokyo, JP **0.67%**
Frankfurt Am Main, DE **0.67%**

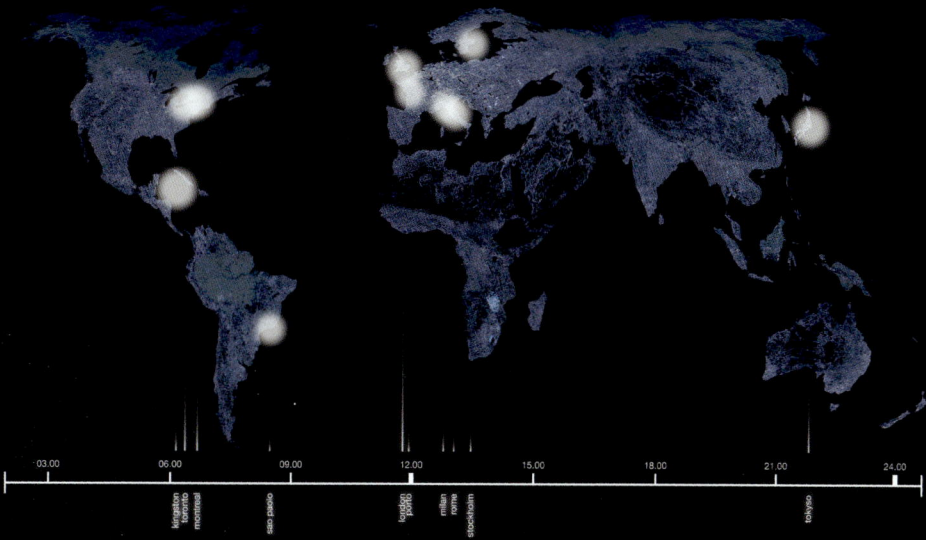

The Bronx

Manhattan

Queens

Brooklyn

Staten Island

World Within New York

World Within New York shows how different neighborhoods reach out to the rest of the world via the AT&T telephone network. The city is divided into a grid of square pixels where each pixel is colored according to the regions of the world wherein the top connecting cities are located. The heights of the color bars represent the proportion of world regions in contact with each neighborhood. Encoded within each pixel is also a list of the top ranking world cities that account for the communications with that particular area of New York.

03.00   06.00   09.00   12.00   15.00   18.00   21.00   24.00

kingston
toronto
montreal

sao paulo

london
paris

milan
roma
stockholm

tokyo

Pulse of the Planet

Time zones influence the global rhythm of communications. Pulse of the Planet illustrates the volume of international calls between New York City and 255 countries over the twenty-four hours in a day. Areas of the world receiving and making fewer phone calls shrink while areas experiencing a greater amount of voice call activity expand. International cities with the most call activity to and from New York are highlighted according to time zone.

165

Atomkraft weltweit

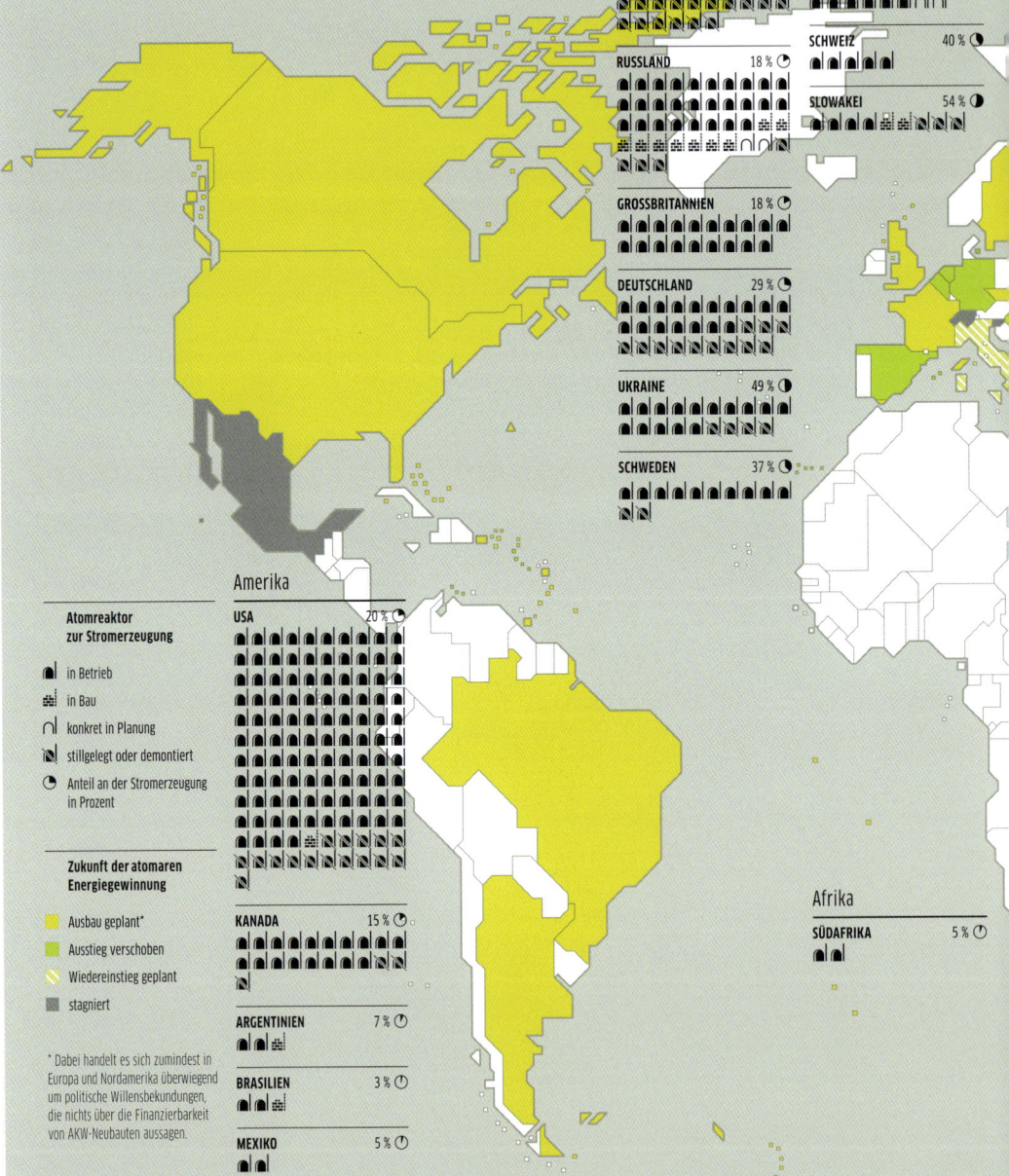

Europa

FRANKREICH	75 %	SPANIEN	18 %
BELGIEN	52 %
TSCHECHIEN	34 %
RUSSLAND	18 %	SCHWEIZ	40 %
		SLOWAKEI	54 %
GROSSBRITANNIEN	18 %
DEUTSCHLAND	29 %
UKRAINE	49 %
SCHWEDEN	37 %

Amerika

USA	20 %
KANADA	15 %
ARGENTINIEN	7 %
BRASILIEN	3 %
MEXIKO	5 %

Afrika

| SÜDAFRIKA | 5 % |

**Atomreaktor
zur Stromerzeugung**

- in Betrieb
- in Bau
- konkret in Planung
- stillgelegt oder demontiert
- Anteil an der Stromerzeugung in Prozent

**Zukunft der atomaren
Energiegewinnung**

- Ausbau geplant*
- Ausstieg verschoben
- Wiedereinstieg geplant
- stagniert

* Dabei handelt es sich zumindest in
Europa und Nordamerika überwiegend
um politische Willensbekundungen,
die nichts über die Finanzierbarkeit
von AKW-Neubauten aussagen.

FINNLAND 33 %

RUMÄNIEN 21 %

SLOWENIEN 38 %

UNGARN 43 %

ARMENIEN 45 %

ITALIEN 0 %

BULGARIEN 36 %

NIEDERLANDE 4 %

LITAUEN 0%

JAPAN 29 %

SÜDKOREA 35 %

INDIEN 2 %

CHINA 2 %

TAIWAN 21 %

PAKISTAN 3 %

IRAN 0 %

KASACHSTAN 0 %

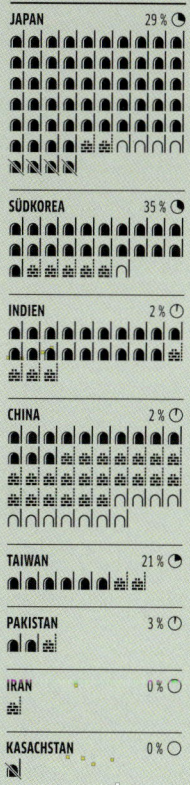

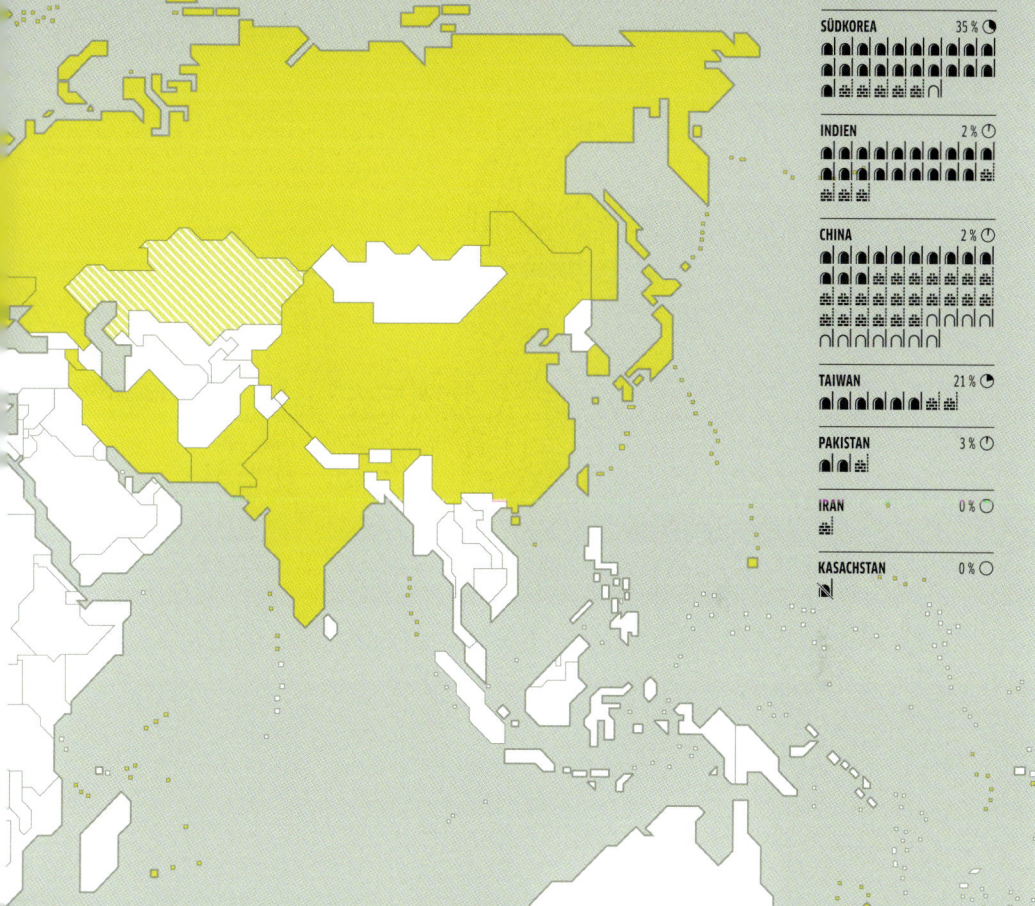

Marode Meiler

Der globale AKW-Bestand ist überaltert: Die meisten Reaktoren gingen vor 25 Jahren und mehr ans Netz.

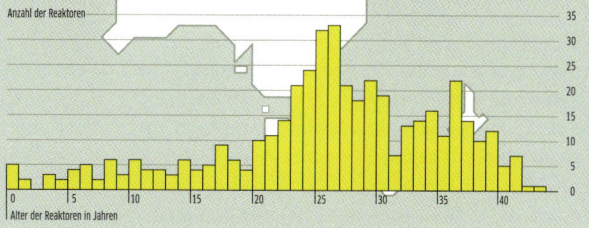

Anzahl der Reaktoren

35
30
25
20
15
10
5
0

0   5   10   15   20   25   30   35   40

Alter der Reaktoren in Jahren

Quellen:
IAEA, World Nuclear Industry Handbook 2009,
World Nuclear Association, eigene Recherche

Project Info: Print, 2010, UK
Design: Peter Crnokrak (The Luxury of Protest)
Additional Info: Silk screen print on clear
plastic, hand-applied 23 carat rouge gold foil,
gold powder gilding

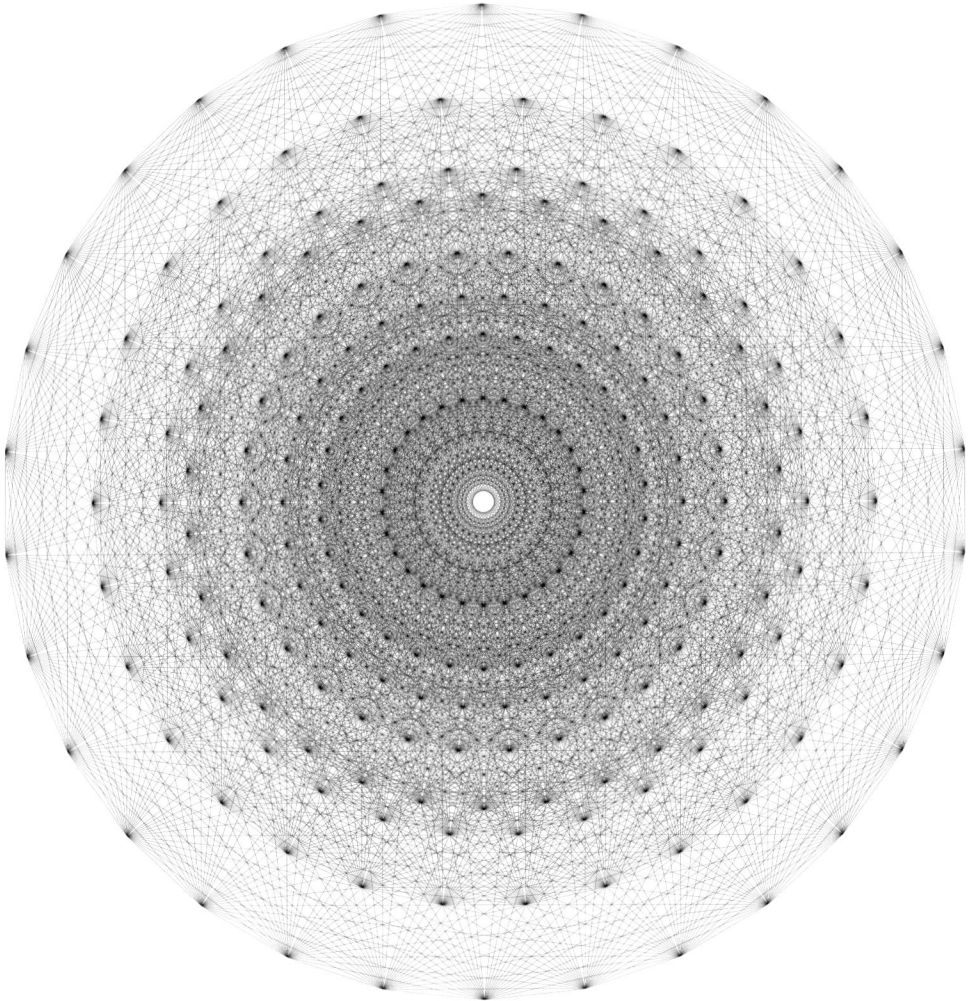

Real Magick in Theory and Practise

The 4_21 polytope is the algebraic form at the centre of a universal theory of everything. The theory attempts to unify quantum physics and gravitation in hopes of ultimately explaining the universe. 4_21 models particle transformations through geometry. Visualisation is a key measure for understanding the polytope – it must be drawn to see how it works. Its dimension-within-dimension structure creates a lattice that predicts all known and postulated particles and forces in the universe as it folds in space-time. Each intersection represents an element. This visualisation by Peter Crnokrak is the most accurate to date and was hand-drawn in Illustrator to an accuracy of 1/10,000 mm. Previous attempts were limited by the inability of graphics engines to construct perfect circles.

Following spread

Pirates off Somalia

With the massive rise in pirate attacks, the waters off the coast of Somalia have been the most dangerous area for shipping worldwide in recent years. This graphic lists some of the major pirate attacks over the course of two years and charts these incidents on a map of the region. The large-scale relief map is completed by a detailed list of the incidents, providing additional information regarding the type of ship, ransom paid or number of crew members.

Project Info: *In Graphics*, magazine article, 2010, Germany
Data Source: IMB Piracy Reporting Centre;
UNOSAT; Ecoterra Report on Piracy in Somalia
Design: Jan Schwochow (Golden Section Graphics)

Pages 172/173

Pynchon's L.A.

Jan Kallwejt created this fresh take on a thematic map for American magazine *Wired*. It shows an abstract version of Los Angeles, with various references to the American writer Thomas Pynchon. Born in 1937, he lives the life of a recluse; he was reported to have lived in Los Angeles for many years, from the 1960s onwards. Some parts of the map are marked in dark blue – these refer to places Pynchon has reportedly visited or which are described in his novels and stories. They are explained by text boxes placed over the ocean. The two-colour map itself is flat, with symbols marking natural and man-made features. Covering the whole map, the little icons form a carpet of landscape features.

Project Info: *Wired*, magazine article, 2010, USA
Design: Jan Kallwejt

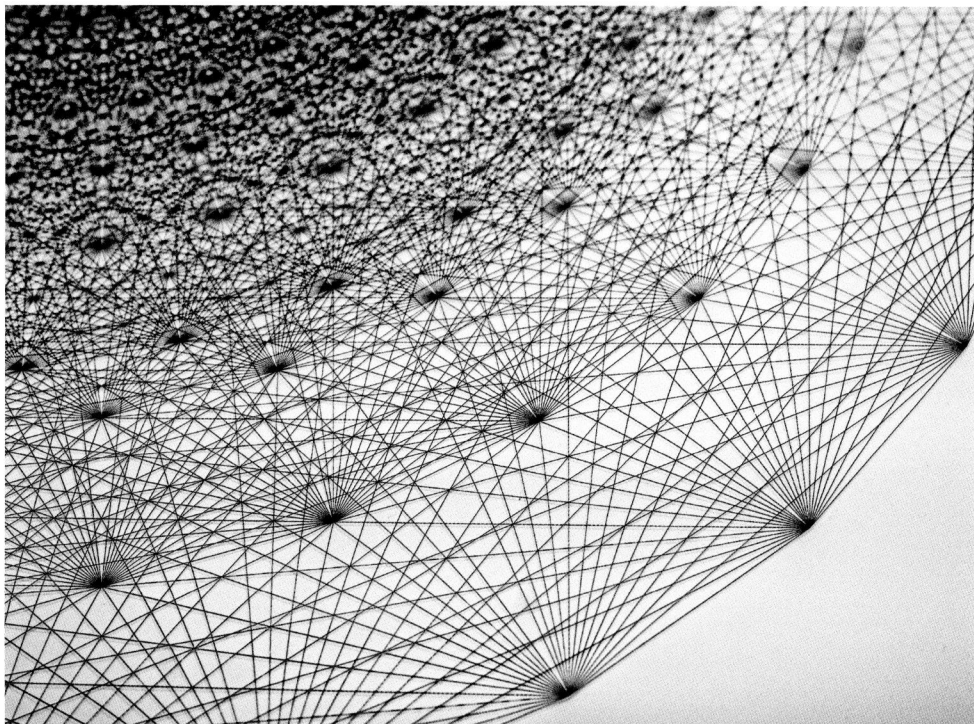

PIRATES off SOMALIA

// DIE PIRATEN VOR SOMALIA

Somalia's governing power has been fragmented since the beginning of the 90s, and is currently divided between competing local clans, warlords and militias. Here in the Horn of Africa a civil war is going on. The transitional rule of the government has failed, especially in tackling the issue of piracy at sea. By the end of October 2010, Somali pirates had seized control over more than 30 vessels and held more than 500 crew members hostage. A well-known example is the British couple Chandler. Fortunately Paul (60) and Rachel (56) were finally released on the 14th of November 2010. Pirates stormed their yacht in October 2009, which was the beginning of 388 days in captivity. At the time of printing, there are only rumors and speculation as to the exact amount of money paid for their release, and from where it came. // Seit Anfang der 1990er Jahre sind die Machtverhältnisse in dem Land am Horn von Afrika unübersichtlich. Es herrscht Bürgerkrieg: lokale Clans, Kriegsherren und Milizen kämpfen um Macht. Die Übergangsregierung im Land ist hingegen machtlos, auch gegen das Treiben der Piraten auf See. Ende Oktober 2010 haben die Piraten von Somalia rund 30 Schiffe und deren über 500 Besatzungsmitglieder in ihrer Gewalt. Ein bekannter Fall ist der des britischen Ehepaars Chandler. Paul (60) und Rachel (56) wurden am 14. November 2010 freigelassen, nach einer 388 Tage dauernden Gefangenschaft. Diese begann, als Piraten im Oktober 2009 ihre Yacht überfielen. Zum Zeitpunkt der Drucklegung gibt es nur Spekulationen über die Höhe und Herkunft des Lösegeldes.

	DATE OF ATTACK //ANGRIFFS-DATUM	DAYS IN CAPTIVITY // TAGE IN GE-FANGENSCHAFT	NAME	TYPE OF SHIP // SCHIFFSTYP	CREW	FLAG // FLAGGE	OWNER // BESITZER	STATUS	RANSOM (ESTIMATED) in US $ // LÖSEGELD (GESCHÄTZT) in US $
1	2009-01-01	63	Blue Star	Cargo ship	28	SKN	EGY		1 mil.
2	2009-01-04	58	MV Longchamp	LPG tanker	13	BAH	GER		6 mil.
3	2009-04-04	126	MV Hansa Stavanger	Cargo ship	25	GER	GER		2.7 mil.
4	2009-04-14	153	MV Irene	Cargo ship	22	VIN	GRE		2 mil.
5	2009-04-18	70	Pompei	Dredger	10	BEL	BEL		2.8 mil.
6	2009-05-03	221	MV Ariana	Cargo ship	24	MLT	GRE		3 mil.
7	2009-07-08	89	MV Horizon-1	Cargo ship	23	TUR	TUR		2.75 mil.
8	2009-10-15	74	MV Kota Wajar	Container	21	SIN	PAK		4 mil.
9	2009-10-19	70	De Xin Hai	Bulk Carrier	25	CHN	CHN		4 mil.
10	2009-10-22	110	MV Al-Khaliq	Bulk Carrier	26	PAN	IND		3.4 mil.
11	2009-10-23	388	S/Y Lynn Rival	Yacht	2	GBR	GBR		0.4 mil. + unknown ransom
12	2009-11-05	12	Almezaan	Cargo ship	18	PAN	VIN		15 000 (3 mil. demanded)

KEY // LEGENDE

▪ hijacking 2010 // Entführungsfälle 2010

● hijacking 2009 // Entführungsfälle 2009

☠ base of the pirates // Stützpunkte der Piraten

▪ border territorial waters // Grenze Hoheitsgewässer

▪ border economic zone // Grenze Wirtschaftszone

DEVELOPMENT // ENTWICKLUNG

RANSOM PAID // LÖSEGELDZAHLUNGEN: >55   >60 $ mil.

■ incidents // Fälle

■ hijacking // Entführungen

2003 2004 2005 2006 2007 2008 2009 Nov. '10

D.R.CONGO   SUDAN

UGANDA

Lake Victoria

Addis Abeba ■

KENYA   ETHIOPIA

Mombasa ■   SOMALIA

Mogadishu ■

HARADHEERE ☠

TANZANIA   22

23

3

14

13

10   8

11

6   5

MADAGASCAR

SEYCHELLES

17

#	DATE OF ATTACK // ANGRIFFS-DATUM	DAYS IN CAPTIVITY // TAGE IN GE-FANGENSCHAFT	NAME	TYPE OF SHIP // SCHIFFSTYP	CREW	FLAG // FLAGGE	OWNER // BESITZER	STATUS	RANSOM (ESTIMATED) US $ // LÖSEGELD (GESCHÄTZT) in US $
13	2009-11-05	42	MV Delvina	Bulk Carrier	21	MHL	GRE	🚩 $	unknown
14	2009-11-16	120	MV Theresa VIII	Chemical tanker	28	KIR	VGB	🚩 $	3.5 mil.
15	2009-11-30	50	MV Maran Centaurus	Tanker	28	GRE	GRE	🚩 $	5.5 - 7 mil.
16	2009-12-28	26	MV St James Park	Chemical tanker	26	GBR	ISR	🚩 $	3 mil.
17	2009-12-28	62	MV Navios Apollon	Cargo ship	19	PAN	GRE	🚩 $	unknown, 20 mil. demanded
18	2010-04-04	216	Samho Dream	Super Tanker	24	MHL	KOR	🚩 $	9.5 mil.
19	2010-04-05	1	MV Taipan	Container ship	13	GER	GER	Hijacking failed, ten pirates captured. They are being tried in Hamburg, Germany	
20	2010-06-28	>125	MV Golden Blessing	Chemical tanker	19	CHI	SIN	🏴	Vessel and crew are said to be held off Bargaal at the tip of the Horn of Africa
21	2010-07-04	>119	MT Motivator	Chemical tanker	18	MHL	GRE	🏴	
22	2010-10-10	>21	MV Izumi	Cargo ship	20	PAN	JPN	🏴	Anchored near Harardheere
23	2010-10-23	>8	MV York	LPG Tanker	17 (1 German)	SIN	GER	🏴	Commandeered towards Harardhere and Hobyo, possible final holding ground off Garacad
24	2010-10-24	1	MV Beluga Fortune	Cargo ship	16	ATG	GER	🚩	

Legend:
- CAPTURED // IN GEFANGENSCHAFT
- RELEASED // FREIGELASSEN
- $ RANSOM PAID // LÖSEGELD GEZAHLT

AREA OF DETAIL // KARTENAUSSCHNITT

TRADE ROUTES OF VESSELS // HANDELSROUTEN DER SCHIFFE

Mediterranean

Suez Canal

EGYPT

IRAQ

SAUDI ARABIA

KUWAIT

IRAN

RED SEA

Sana'a

Aden

DJIBOUTI

YEMEN

Al Mukallah

SOMALILAND

BOSASO

CALULA

PUNTLAND

GARACAD

EYL

U.A.E.

OMAN

2008-08-28 until 2009-01-31
MSPA Security Zone, with security ensured by sailing in convoys // Maritime Security Patrol Area, in der Kriegsschiffe in Convoys fahrend Schutz bieten

Since 2009-02-01
New International Recommended Transit Corridor (IRTC) for vessels // Neue IRTC-Schiffsdurchquerung

SOCOTRA (YEMEN)

INDIAN OCEAN

approximately 500 km

N

EQUATOR

500 km

1000 km

1500 km

101

1

Malibu

Manhattan Beach
The hero of Inherent Vice lives in Gordita Beach, home to surfers, flight attendants, and aerospace engineers. It's easily identifiable as Manhattan Beach, where Pynchon reportedly lived at various addresses for many years.

Aerospace Alley
This was home base for the Cold War defense industries that drove the Southern California economy. Pynchon worked for Boeing after college and later lived in the area.

Bel Air
Pynchon paid a well-documented visit to Beach Boys founder Brian Wilson, who resided here in the late '60s. The writer was a fan of the Pet Sounds album, but once they started smoking dope, he had very little to say.

Topanga Canyon
One nutty thread in Inherent Vice involves a Beach Boys-like band holed up in Topanga Canyon, LA's hippie hideaway and real-life home at the time to rockers like Neil Young.

Bradbu
This 18°
buildin
ultimat
tourist
additio
in Blad
D.O.A.,
China C
in Pync
Rainbo
the Day

San Narciso
Yoyodyne, the aerospace firm Pynchon created for The Crying of Lot 49, is in fictional San Narciso, just east of LA. The sinister company went on to appear in Star Trek: TNG, Buckaroo Banzai, and more.

UCLA
A hacker in Inherent Vice taps into what sounds like the Internet. But was that possible in 1970? Arpanet, the progenitor of the Internet, was kick-started by the Defense Department in late '69. Its first message originated at ... UCLA.

Watts
In 1966, Pynchon pondered the six-day race riot here in a New York Times Magazine essay. "Illusion is everywhere," he wrote, and violence lies just beneath the surface.

Benedict Canyon
The 1969 Charles Manson murders, which began in Topanga and continued with the Tate-LaBianca slaughter in Benedict Canyon, shut the door on LA's psychedelic '60s and ushered in a Pynchonesque era of fear and anxiety.

20th Ce
Pyncho
Hollyw
cartoor
his unfa
a reclus
voiced
The Sin

101

HOLLYWOOD

5

LA

LA

?

LA

10

Santa Monica

110

Downtown

405

LA

Original Tommy's Hamburgers
In Inherent Vice, everyone has the perpetual munchies, and they refuel at this "burger navel of the universe." (See also Pink's on La Brea.)

1

Long Beach

405

Pacific Palisades

Orpheus Theatre
Gravity's Rainbow ends apocalyptically with an ICBM screaming toward a fictional movie palace on Melrose, managed by the doppelganger of SoCal native Richard M. Nixon.

Roadtrip 2009

Moving home and visiting north-western Europe   13th - 22nd July

A visual explanation of a travel by car, measured in distance, time and cost

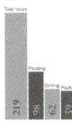
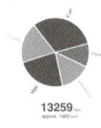

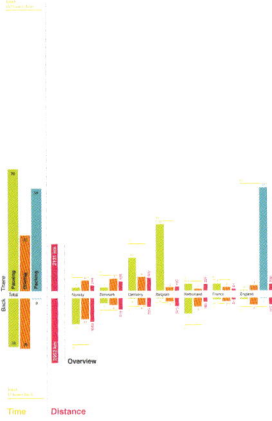

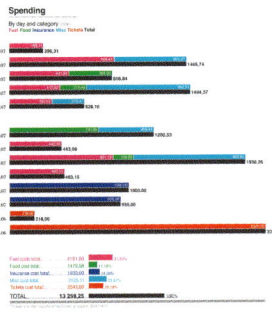

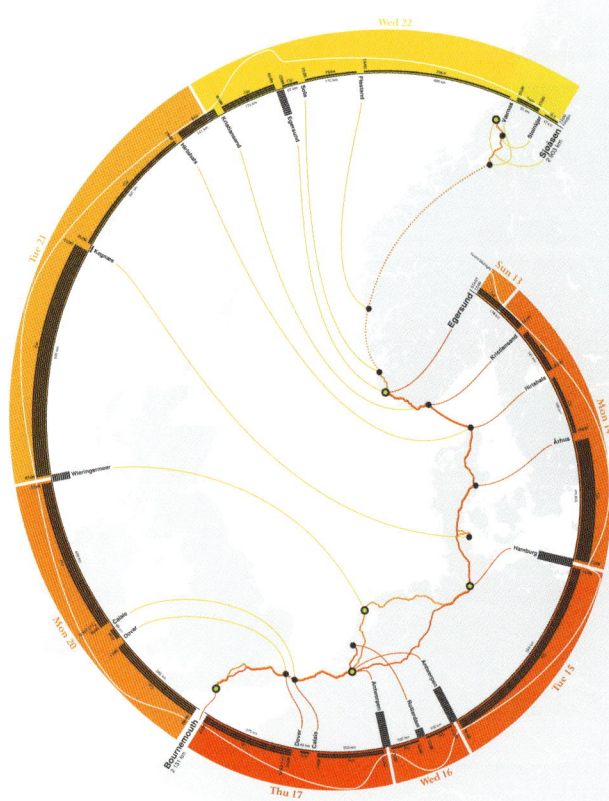

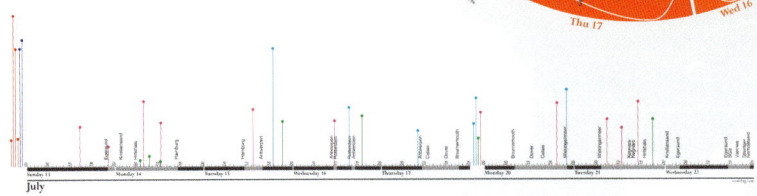

Project Info: Poster, 2009, Norway
Design: Ole Østring

174

Roadtrip 2009

With this poster, Ole Østring collected together a visual report of his road-trip through Europe, from summer 2009. In the central image he presents a particular mixture of map and time-line. The route of his journey is shown on the map, with individual stop points linked to a thick timeline, which bends around outside the actual itinerary. This facilitates two ways of reconstructing the journey: by following it on the map, or by reading the continuous timeline. The latter provides further data as to the time of day and the type of transport used. Additional statistics on the poster provide detailed information regarding the equipment, team members and money spent on this trip.

Following spreads

See the Bigger Picture

In his series "See the Bigger Picture", Austrian designer Michael Paukner explores the aesthetic side of visualising theory. The range of thinking he draws upon is vast and varies from ancient Inca or Celtic knowledge to scientific as well as pseudo-scientific thinking, conspiracy theories and hard mathematical or physical facts. For each theory, he tries to discern the appropriate visual structure, employing a clean and minimal style. The series presents a whole array of world knowledge, exploring how it is possible to communicate something about the mysteries of the cosmos by finding beautiful ways to visualise how people reflect on them. *Trembling Giants* (p.176) interlaces a world map with a hierarchy of the world's oldest trees. *Capital of Atlantis* (p.177) is a map of the main city of the mythical Atlantis, with its circular islands and canal system. Tags show Atlantis' wealth in metals. *Solar Eclipse* (p.178) shows the celestial alignment which causes a solar eclipse on Earth. *Hollow Earth* (p.179) visualises the old hypothesis that the Earth is a hollow sphere.

Project Info: Series of posters, 2009–2011, Austria
Design: Michael Paukner

The Earth's Oldest Trees

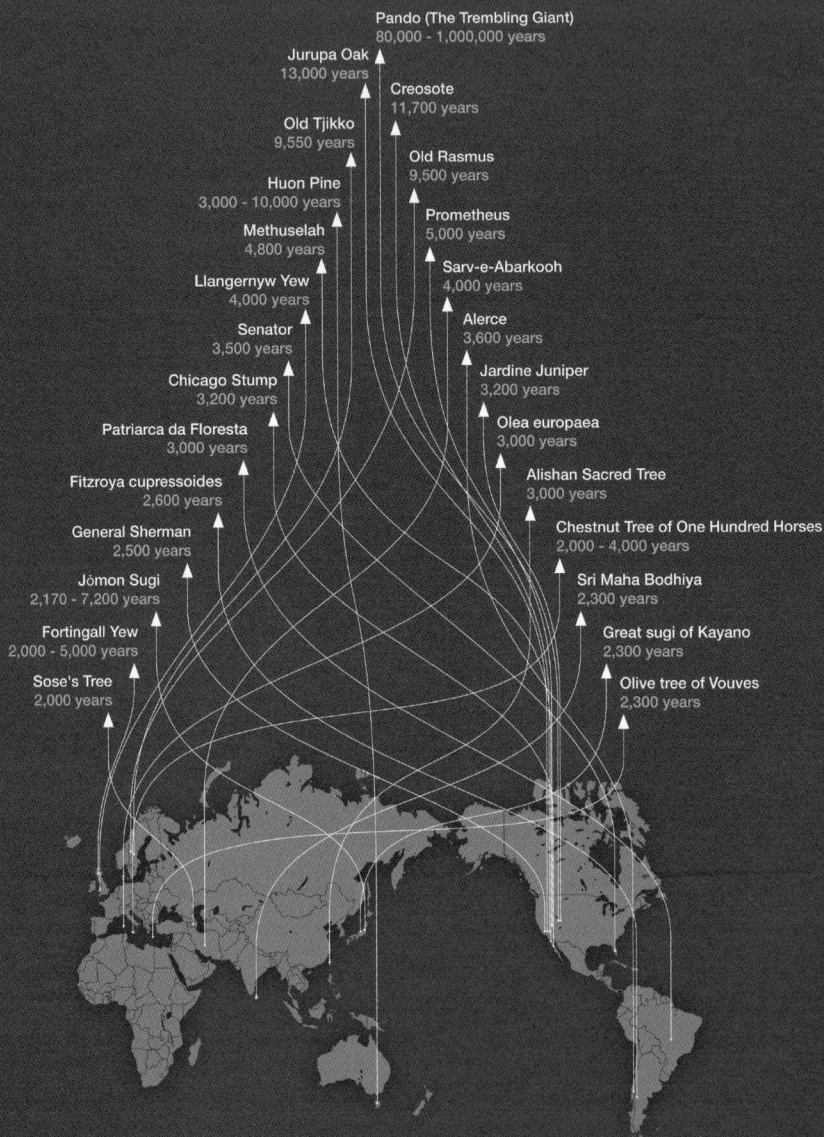

Pando (The Trembling Giant)
80,000 - 1,000,000 years

Jurupa Oak
13,000 years

Creosote
11,700 years

Old Tjikko
9,550 years

Old Rasmus
9,500 years

Huon Pine
3,000 - 10,000 years

Prometheus
5,000 years

Methuselah
4,800 years

Sarv-e-Abarkooh
4,000 years

Llangernyw Yew
4,000 years

Alerce
3,600 years

Senator
3,500 years

Jardine Juniper
3,200 years

Chicago Stump
3,200 years

Olea europaea
3,000 years

Patriarca da Floresta
3,000 years

Alishan Sacred Tree
3,000 years

Fitzroya cupressoides
2,600 years

Chestnut Tree of One Hundred Horses
2,000 - 4,000 years

General Sherman
2,500 years

Sri Maha Bodhiya
2,300 years

Jōmon Sugi
2,170 - 7,200 years

Great sugi of Kayano
2,300 years

Fortingall Yew
2,000 - 5,000 years

Olive tree of Vouves
2,300 years

Sose's Tree
2,000 years

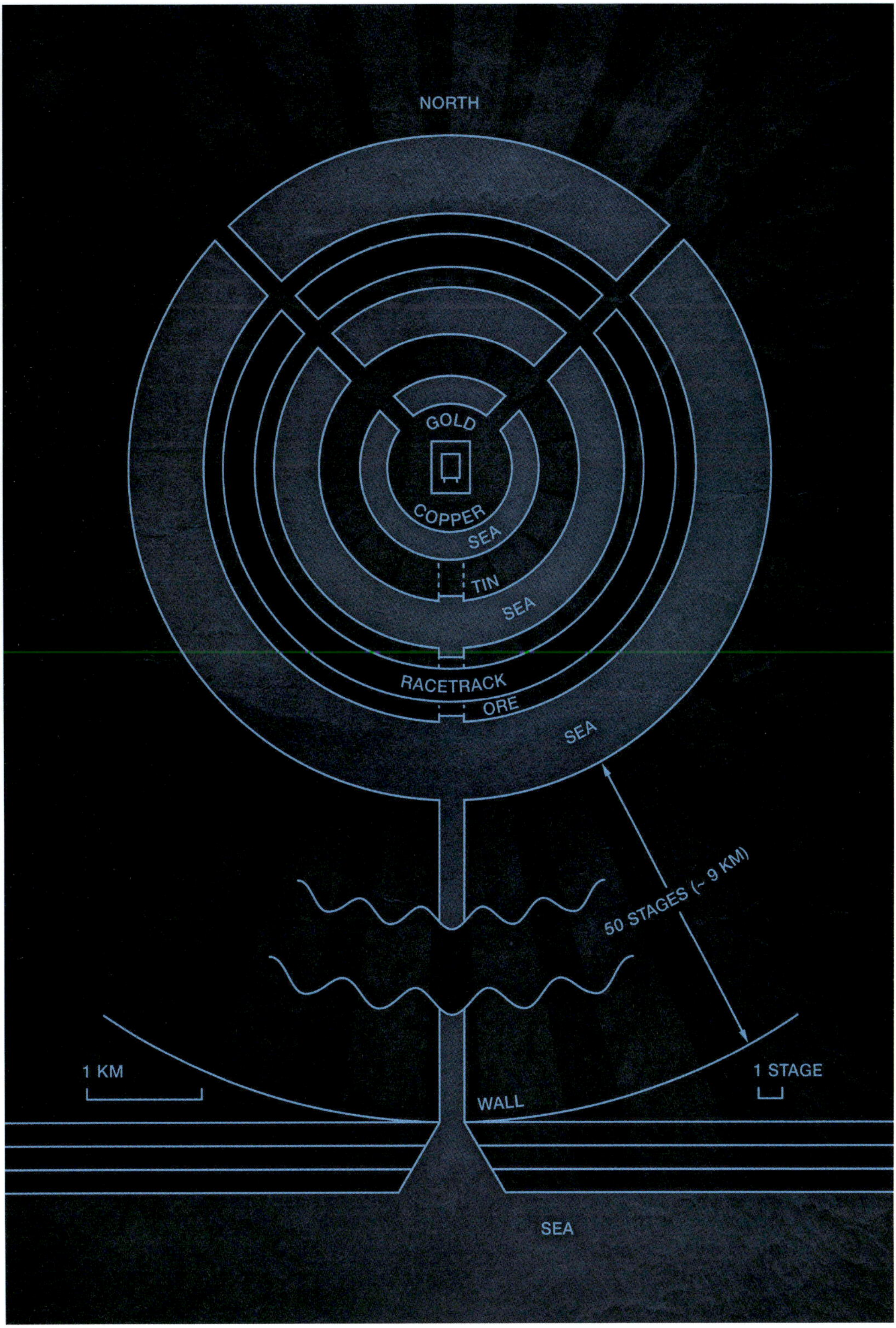

NORTH

GOLD

COPPER

SEA

TIN

SEA

RACETRACK

ORE

SEA

50 STAGES (~ 9 KM)

1 KM

1 STAGE

WALL

SEA

SUN

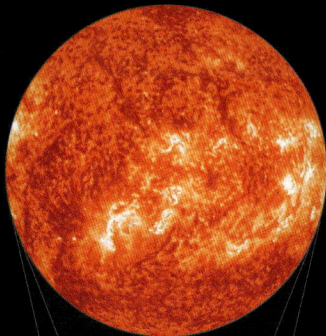

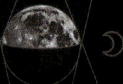
MOON

PENUMBRA   UMBRA

TOTAL ECLIPSE   PARTIAL ECLIPSE
VISIBLE HERE   VISIBLE HERE

EARTH

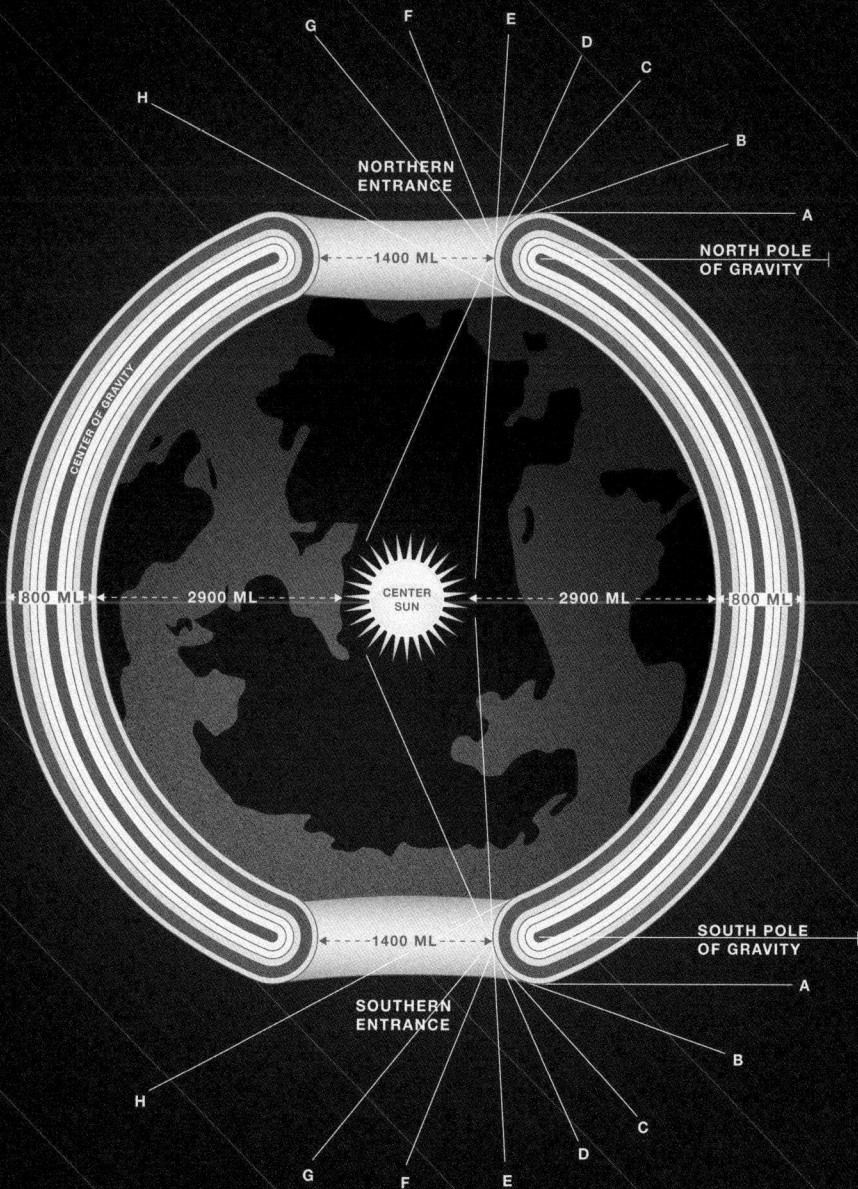

Setouchi Perfect Guide   Casa BRUTUS September・2010

A

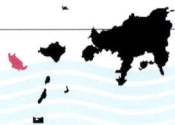

1 宮浦エリア

100m

三菱マテリアル直島生協

山本うどん店 P.96

大竹伸朗＜I♥湯＞ P.78   レンタサイクル

至 本村(約2km)↗

宮浦港

SANAA＜海の駅なおしま＞ P.78   総合福祉センター

草間彌生＜かぼちゃ＞ P.78

2 本村エリア

100m

石橋   木村港

茶寮 おおみやけ P.96   本村ラウンジ＆アーカイヴ

きんざ   碁会所

はいしゃ   角屋

家プロジェクト P.79   護王神社

直島町役場

南寺

至 宮浦(約2km)

至 地中美術館(約3.7km)↗

宮浦エリア

大竹伸朗＜I♥湯＞

SANAA＜海の駅なおしま＞

草間彌生＜かぼちゃ＞

直島
Naoshima

本村エリア

きんざ

碁会所

角屋

護王神社

地中美術館   李禹煥美術館

ベネッセミュージアム

3 ミュージアムエリア

100m

広木池

地中美術館
チケットセンター

至 宮浦(約1.8km)

地中美術館 P.80

李禹煥美術館 P.80

テレジータ・フェルナンデス
光の棺

パーク

ベネッセホテル P.81

至 本村(約3km)↗

オーバル

ビーチ

草間彌生
＜黄色かぼちゃ＞

テラスレストラン 海の星
エトワール・ド・ラ・メール P.94

ベネッセミュージアム P.80

Project Info: Setouchi International Art Festival 2010,
Casa Brutus, magazine article, 2010, Japan
Design: Tokuma, Noriyuki Tatemori (Bowlgraphics)

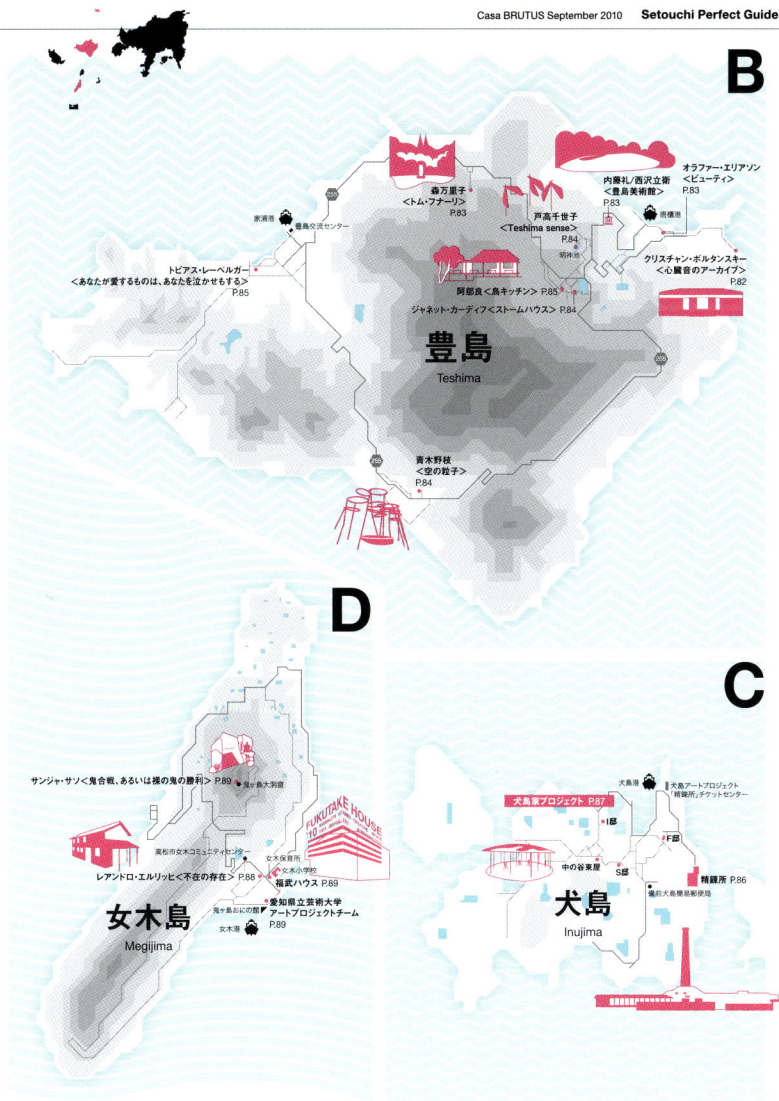

B

桑万里子
＜トム・フナーリ＞
P.83

内藤礼/西沢立衛
＜豊島美術館＞
P.83

オラファー・エリアソン
＜ビューティ＞
P.83

戸高千世子
＜Teshima sense＞
P.84

クリスチャン・ボルタンスキー
＜心臓音のアーカイブ＞
P.82

トビアス・レーベルガー
＜あなたが愛するものは、あなたを泣かせもする＞
P.85

阿部良＜島キッチン＞ P.85

ジャネット・カーディフ＜ストームハウス＞ P.84

豊島交流センター

家浦港

朝神池

唐櫃港

豊島
Teshima

青木野枝
＜空の粒子＞
P.84

D

サンジャ・サソ＜鬼合戦、あるいは裸の鬼の勝利＞ P.89

女木島女木コミュニティセンター

FUKUTAKE HOUSE

女木保育所

レアンドロ・エルリッヒ＜不在の存在＞ P.88

福武ハウス P.89

愛知県立芸術大学
アートプロジェクトチーム
女木港 P.89

鬼ヶ島おにの館

女木島
Megijima

C

犬島港

犬島アートプロジェクト
「精錬所」チケットセンター

犬島家プロジェクト P.87

I邸

F邸

中の谷東屋

S邸

精錬所 P.86

備前犬島築製郵便跡

犬島
Inujima

Setouchi Perfect Guide

The Seto Inland Sea is Japan's largest body of water, separating the three main islands and spotted with lots of tiny islands. In 2010, the Setouchi Art Festival was held on seven neighbouring islands. This series of maps shows the individual venues of the festival. A little icon at the top of each spread works as a guide as to which of the islands is depicted on each page. The islands are shown as stylised shapes, with grey shades giving an impression of geographical elevation on each one. Pink icons refer to venues or artworks in the festival. Additional inserts show detailed maps. For each island, the designer Tokuma developed a varying water pattern to depict the ocean.

Shell's Big Dig

Extracting oil from fields in deep seas is one
of the most technically advanced and often
dangerous undertakings. In this piece, John
Grimwade and Bryan Christie explain Perdido,
the floating platform atop the deepest offshore
production well to date, run by Shell. The main
3D illustration provides a look into the construction of the platform, indicating relative
size by the addition of a ship and a helicopter.
The map to the left shows the location in the
Gulf of Mexico, while a small inset strip to the
right gives an impression of the actual depth
at which the platform is drilling for oil, indicating that the oil-fields themselves lie very deep
beneath the ocean floor.

Project Info: *Condé Nast Portfolio*,
magazine article, 2009, USA
Research: Jeff VanDam
Design: John Grimwade, Grace Lee
Art Direction: Robert Priest
Illustration: Bryan Christie

Shell's
BIG DIG

The energy giant is installing an
oil rig in the Gulf of Mexico that can reach
depths never before tapped. An advance
look at how it's going to work

by Jeff VanDam

Graphics by **John Grimwade**
Illustration by **Bryan Christie Design**

Derrick
This houses and
supports drilling lines.

Living space
Crew members will live
above sea level in
blast-resistant quarters.

Spar
At 555 feet long, the spar (including
the cylinder, open truss, and ballast)
supports the topsides. The cylinder
contains plumbing and tanks that give
the platform buoyancy.

555
feet

Perdido spar

Drilling
Perdido's wells will be
drilled 6,000 feet below the
ocean floor, penetrating
the earth's lower tertiary
from the Paleogene period,
which began to form 65
million years ago, as
dinosaurs were becoming
extinct. The wells will
be drilled by the fixed
platform above the
spar and by a
remote rig.

Seafloor:
7,817 ft.

Pumping oil
Powerful (1,500-
horsepower) electric
pumps will bring oil
to the surface against
extreme pressure
from three undersea
fields with a combined
area the size of
downtown Houston.

Maximum
depth:
14,000 ft.
below
sea level

Oil

**Empire State Building
to the same scale**

Two hundred miles
off the coast of Texas, Royal Dutch Shell is building an
offshore energy platform that will operate deeper than any
other oil and gas production facility ever constructed. The
nearly 600-foot-long Perdido Regional Development Host
Spar—and the 80-person crew that will live onboard—will
float on the Gulf of Mexico's surface and be connected to

a network of more than 30 oil and natural-gas wells on
the seafloor nearly 8,000 feet below. The wells will drill
a half-mile deeper than any existing project's, reaching a
level of the earth's crust never before tapped for commercial energy production. Shell, which has partnered with
Chevron and BP on the venture, expects the spar to go fully
online by 2010 and yield about 100,000 barrels of oil and
200 million standard cubic feet of natural gas a day. While
Shell hasn't announced the project's total cost, the pipeline
system alone will cost $480 million.

New Orleans

Houston

U.S. OIL SECTORS

PERDIDO

Maritime border

GULF OF MEXICO

MEXICO

CUBA

0   300
MILES

Territorial Dispute
Because the spar will be just eight miles from
the U.S.'s maritime border with Mexico,
the Mexican government is concerned that
the project will siphon away its oil.

Mooring lines
Made of polyester
rope and chains, the
mooring lines represent
a technological
breakthrough for Shell.

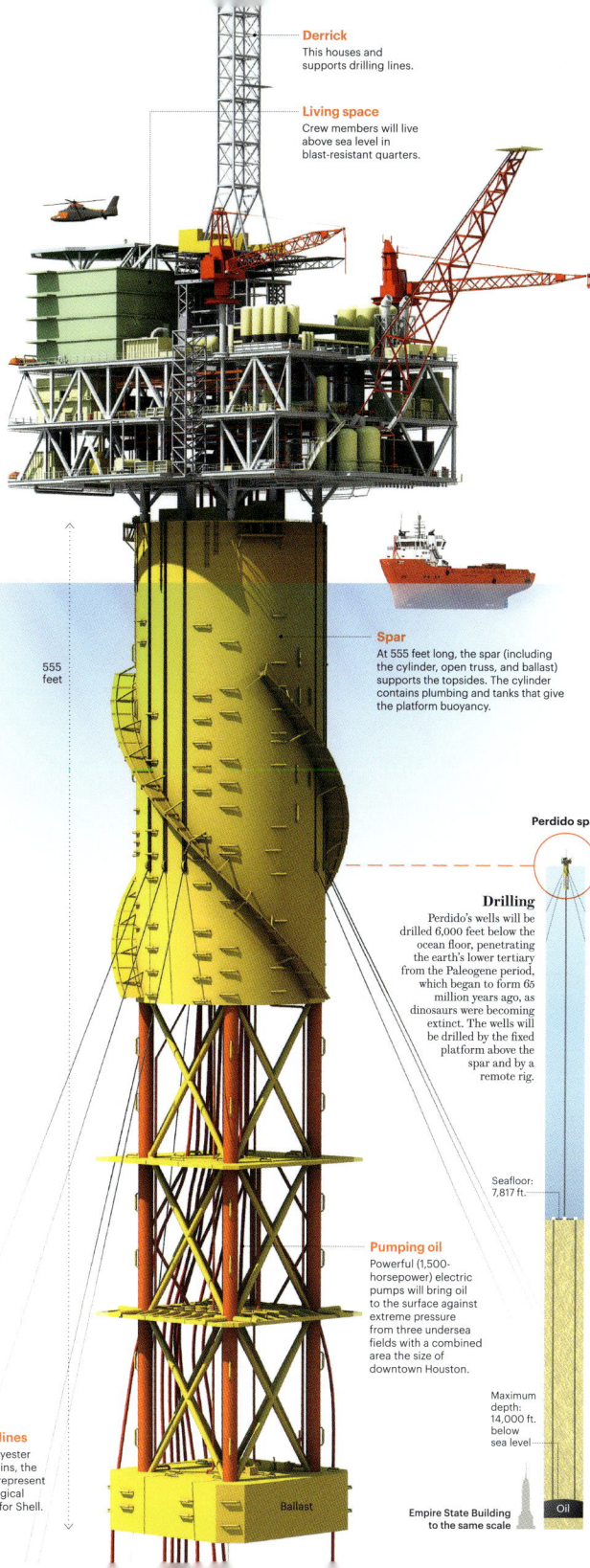

Ballast

Sleeping Giant

Below Yellowstone, a hellish column of super-heated rock—mostly solid, some viscous, some molten—rises from hundreds of miles within the Earth. Current stirrings may be remnants of a past eruption, or early harbingers of a still far-distant cataclysm.

AREA ENLARGED

Earthquake Swarm
In just 11 days starting last December, 1,000 quakes hit an area that averages 2,000 a year.

3+ Perceptible
0.3 Imperceptible
Magnitude

Yellowstone
National Park

Magma
chamber

MILES
0

CRUST

25

UPPER
MANTLE

Caldera
Buoyed by an expanding magma chamber, the caldera, formed during the last major eruption, has risen as much as 2.8 inches a year over the past decade.

2500°F

Plume
Beneath the caldera, a vast rocky zone of primordial heat emanates from the mantle. This plume feeds a magma chamber brimming with volcanic fuel just a few miles below the surface.

270

MANTLE

3500°F

Hot Pockets
Current seismic data and geological conditions suggest there may be smaller pockets of hot rock associated with the Yellowstone plume.

400

LOWER MANTLE

DETAIL

Crust 25 mi
Mantle 1,800 mi
Outer core 2,200 mi
Inner core 950 mi

Columns of ash may rise 25 miles high, then fall

What Happens the Next Time?

Scientists can anticipate the stages of a super eruption (below). Widespread ecological devastation would follow, and consequences would be felt for years.

Before the Eruption
Warning signs may appear years in advance. Pressure builds from below, driving seismic activity and doming of the land over the hot spot.

Magma
chamber

The Earth Fractures
Gas-filled magma explodes upward; ash and debris soon rain down across hundreds of miles. Fiery ash flows clog rivers and carpet landscapes near and far.

Eruptions Continue
Periodic blasts go on for weeks or even months, emitting pollutants and causing acid rain. Eventually the land collapses and a new caldera is born.

New
caldera

Sleeping Giant

In this piece, *National Geographic* cuts open
the Earth beneath Yellowstone National Park,
showing the giant column of magma resting
there, about 400 miles deep. The upper square
shows the Earth's surface with the National
Park marked in red. A surface detail is cut out
and elevated to show the seismic activity recently increasing in the area, by way of dots on
a map. Seismic activity data were drawn from
USGS and GIS mapping. Below, the magma
column is shown in detail. If the super-volcano
erupts again, widespread devastation would
follow. The 3D modelling of the column was
created by specialists at the University of Ohio.
Along the bottom, a series of schematic drawings shows scenarios for the near future.

Project Info: "When Yellowstone Explodes",
National Geographic, magazine article, 2009, USA
Data Source: Geodynamics of the Yellowstone
Hotspot Project (University of Utah); USGS Yellowstone
Volcano Observatory; Open University
Research: Shelley Sperry
Design: Alejandro Tumas, John Baxter
Art Direction: Juan Velasco
Illustration: Hernán Cañellas
Awards: Malofiej 2010; Society for News Design 2010

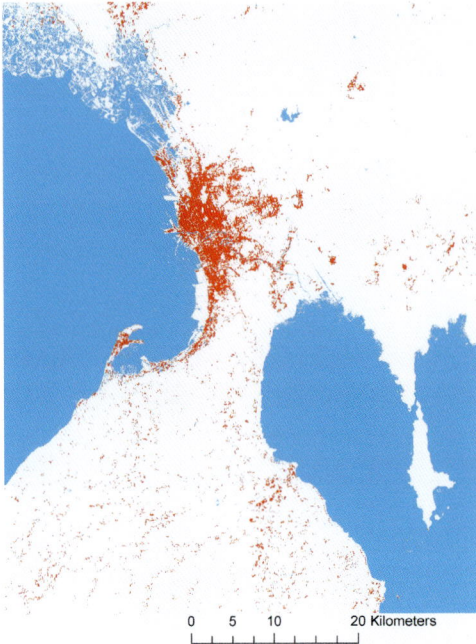

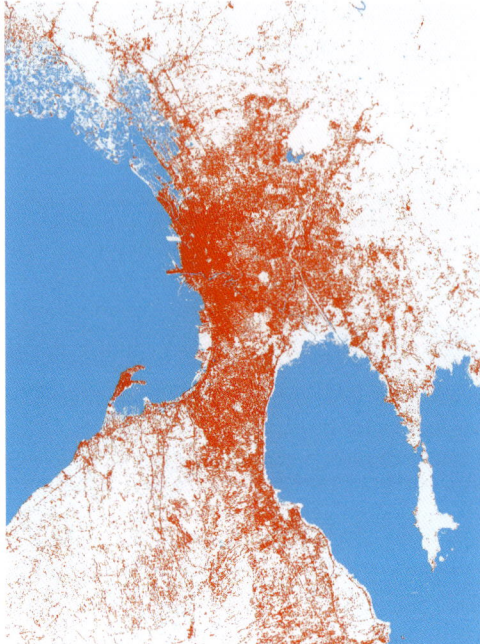

Spatio-Temporal Analysis of Mega-City Growth

Based on research from the German Aerospace Center, this project uses remote sensing data to measure and analyse the effects of urbanisation throughout the world. Satellite data are transformed into a series of maps, in which urban areas and water are marked in colour. The series shown here demonstrates the urban sprawl in the city of Manila, Philippines in three time-steps from 1975 to 2010. The exceptional spatial expansion is caused by the specific one-family-per-house architecture employed in large parts of the city. The project exemplifies how satellite data are transferred to enhanced maps in order to analyse large-scale geographical phenomena.

Project Info: Series of maps, 2010, Germany
Data Source: German Remote Sensing Data Center; Earth Observation Center; German Aerospace Center
Research / Design: Prof. Dr. Stefan Dech, Dr. Hannes Taubenböck, Dr. Thomas Esch (German Aerospace Center)

Following spread

The Babel of Beers

Beer is a drink available in many countries. Like a display board, this double spread presents an international status report on beer consumption and how it is regulated around the world. Each bottle represents one country, with the crown cap showing the national flag. On the bottle neck the price per half litre is given in $. All bottles are labelled "beer" in the respective national languages, while the percentage figure beneath indicates the tax rate on alcohol in each country. Shaded bars behind each bottle show how much beer is consumed in each country, with a record per capita consumption in the Czech Republic. Symbols beneath each bottle illustrate in which public places alcohol is banned by law.

Project Info: *Intelligence in Lifestyle*, magazine article, 2010, Italy
Data Source: World Health Organization
Research: Alessandro Giberti
Design / Art Direction: Francesco Franchi
Illustration: Laura Cattaneo

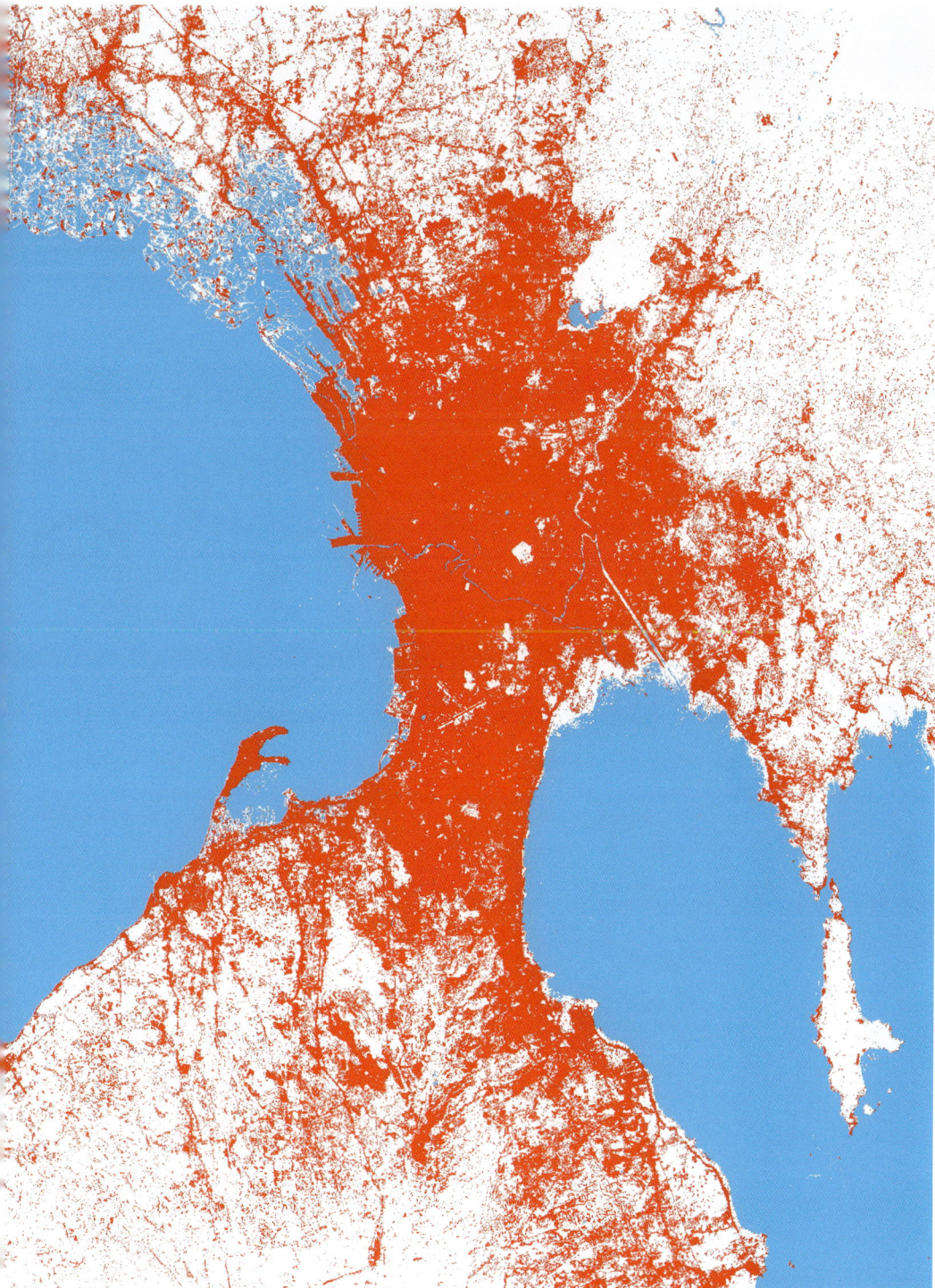

SCHIUMA, PROFUMO, CREMA: SCEGLIETE IL BICCHIERE GIUSTO

La vulgata associa le "bionde" al boccale o al calice a tulipano e le "scure" alle coppe. È vero, ma non basta. Oltre alla forma si deve considerare tipo di vetro e spessore.

Calice a tulipano
330 ml
La bocca svasata impedisce un'eccessiva schiumatura e favorisce l'olfatto. Adatto alle birre belghe d'abbazia.
A

Boccale
400 ml
Il "classico". Quello in vetro tedesco, il "Mass", è perfetto per le "Märzen" per le "Pale ale" ci vuole il vetro britannico.
B

Colonna conica
330 ml
Vetro di spessore medio, a imboccatura larga per controllare la schiuma. È l'ideale per le vivaci e profumate birre danesi.
C

Altglass
425 ml
Cilindrico, per non esaltare né mortificare la schiuma. Il vetro, molto sottile, lo rende adatto alle ambrate "Alt".
D

La babele delle birre

CHI TANTO, CHI POCO. IL BORSINO DEI BEVITORI

I cechi bevono come spugne; irlandesi, tedeschi e australiani non scherzano; mentre in Gran Bretagna esagerare con "Lager" e "Stout" potrebbe ridurvi rapidamente sul lastrico. Consumi, costi, tasse e proibizioni: radiografia del mercato della birra nei cinque continenti.

consumo pro capite
0,00 — prezzo per 500 ml (in $)
— nazione di provenienza
BIRRA — come si scrive "birra" nella lingua nazionale
0% — IVA sull'alcol

LUOGHI PUBBLICI E ALCOL

- OSPEDALI
- SCUOLE E UNIVERSITÀ
- EDIFICI GOVERNATIVI
- TRASPORTI PUBBLICI
- PARCHI E STRADE
- EVENTI SPORTIVI
- CONCERTI
- LUOGHI DI LAVORO

AAA ALCOLICO. TEMPI DURI PER PUBBLICIZZARE UNA MEDIA

Dai "Niet" assoluti – e assolutistici – iraniani, egiziani e algerini, al "tutto è lecito" per la pubblicità in Brasile, Cina e Sudafrica.

- illegale
- legale
- discrezionale

	TV	RADIO	STAMPA	MANIFESTI	EVENTI SPORTIVI	EVENTI DAL VIVO
ALGERIA						
IRAN						
GIORDANIA						
EGITTO						
VENEZUELA						
DANIMARCA						
FRANCIA						
SVEZIA						
ITALIA						
INDIA						
CANADA						
BRASILE						
CINA						
CROAZIA						
SUDAFRICA						

CONSUMO PRO CAPITE

1. Stati Uniti — 0,74 — 81,6 litri — *Beer* — 8,0%
2. Canada — 0,89 — 68,3 — BEER — 19%
3. Venezuela — 0,38 — 58,6 — CERVEZA — 14,5%
4. Messico — 0,81 — 51,8 — Cerveza — LA CERVEZA MAS FINA — 15%
5. Brasile — 0,35 — 47,6 — CERVEJA — 25%
11. Sudafrica — 0,38 — 59,2 — BIER — 14%
12. Gabon — 0,56 — 55,8 — Bière — 18%
13. Malawi — 0,32 — 8,0 — MOWA — 20%
14. Algeria — 1,91 — 3,8 — قربية — 17%
15. Australia — 1,29 — 109,9 — BEER REED — B — 10%

Weizenbecker
500 ml
Capacità di mezzo litro. La svasatura serve a controllare l'abbondante schiuma delle birre di grano, le "Weissbier".

Calice a chiudere
330 ml
La sua forma rastremata alza la sua schiuma, impedendole di traboccare. Il suo vetro sottile valorizza le "Lager".

Coppa
250 ml
Forma emisferica, ideale per abbassare progressivamente la schiuma ed esaltare il profumo.

Colonna biconica
425 ml
Forma allargata al centro, bocca a chiudere. Per "Pils" belghe e per chi vuole la schiuma decapitata dalla spatola.

Pinta
473 ml
La forma a cono rovesciato neutralizza la schiuma delle "Bitter ale" e valorizza la Cream delle Stout.

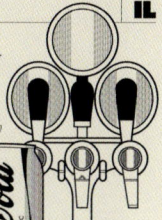

E — F — G — H — I

QUANTA COCA-COLA PER UNA BIRRA

Rapporto tra il prezzo di una birra e di una Coca-Cola: in Australia al costo di una birra media si compra poco più della metà di una Coca da 500 ml. In Iran una "bionda" costa 22 volte di più.

Conosciuta già ai tempi dei Sumeri, la birra ha dissetato l'uomo per 5mila anni prima di consacrarsi, nel mondo contemporaneo, come bevanda universale

– di **Francesco Franchi** e **Alessandro Giberti** | illustrazioni di **Laura Cattaneo**

Birre (fila 1)

- **156,9** — Repubblica Ceca — 0,22 — *Pivo* — 5%
- **131,1** — Irlanda — 2,07 — *BEOIR* — 21%
- **115,8** — Germania — 0,79 — *Bier* — 16%
- **99,0** — Gran Bretagna — 2,61 — *BEER* — 17,5%
- Italia — 1,64 — *BIRRA* — 20% — **29,4**

Birre (fila 2)

- **51,3** — Giappone — 2,02 — ビール — 5%
- **38,5** — Corea del Sud — 1,5 — 맥주 — 10%
- **22,1** — Cina — 0,6 — 啤酒 — 17%
- **20,0** — Malesia — 1,31 — *Bir* — 20%
- **1,5** — Giordania — 1,03 — بيرة — 13%

#	Paese	Valore	#	Paese	Valore
1	AUSTRALIA	0,61	100	IRAN	22
2	MONGOLIA	0,66	99	ALGERIA	10,13
3	MALESIA	0,67	98	GUATEMALA	5,25
4	ROMANIA	0,67	97	BOLIVIA	5,07
5	UNGHERIA	0,67	96	PERÙ	4,22
6	PARAGUAY	0,7	95	ITALIA	3,88
7	BIELORUSSIA	0,78	94	LITUANIA	3,75
8	COSTA RICA	0,8	93	SEYCHELLES	3,68
9	CROAZIA	0,8	92	NORVEGIA	3,47
10	PORTOGALLO	0,87	91	ARGENTINA	3,29
11	VENEZUELA	0,87	90	CANADA	3,02
12	GUINEA	0,88	89	UCRAINA	3
13	DANIMARCA	0,89	88	KAZAKHSTAN	3
14	BULGARIA	0,91	87	GUYANA	3
15	REP. CECA	0,93	86	COREA DEL SUD	3
16	MALAWI	0,94	85	AZERBAIJAN	3
17	STATI UNITI		84	COLOMBIA	2,82
18	POLONIA		83	THAILANDIA	2,78
19	SLOVACCHIA		82	ISRAELE	2,78
20	REP. CENTRAFRICANA	1,02	81	NICARAGUA	2,7

BIRRA E SOFT DRINK: IN EUROPA VINCE IL LUPPOLO

Consumo pro capite di birra (A), bibite analcoliche gassate (B) e bibite analcoliche non gassate (C). Dati riferiti al 2008.

- **73,7** CONSUMO PRO CAPITE (litri) — A
- **57** CONSUMO PRO CAPITE (litri) — B
- **15** CONSUMO PRO CAPITE (litri) — C

FONTE PRINCIPALE – *World Health Organization* (Global Status Report: Alcohol Policy)

Food Science
MORE COUNTRIES ARE GROWING
GENETICALLY MODIFIED CROPS

- GM CROPS GROWN
- GM CROPS BANNED
- NO COMMERCIAL GM CROPS

The farmscape is changing.
In the Americas, insect- and
herbicide-resistant corn, soy,
and canola—all genetically
modified—are taking root.
Even GM-phobic Europe is
letting down its guard. In
Africa, where crop yields are
among the lowest anywhere,
GM crops have yet to make
an impact. But convention-
ally bred New Rice for Africa
(Nerica) is helping boost
yields south of the Sahara;
and other new strains, including genetically enhanced
Golden Rice, are in the works
in Asia. —*Thomas Hayden*

+

Sources: Africa Rice Center; International
Service for the Acquisition of Agri-Biotech
Applications; National Center for Biotechnology
Information; *Science*

- ALBANIA ......
- AUSTRIA ......
- CZECH REP....
- FRANCE ......
- GERMANY ....
- GREECE ......
- POLAND ......
- PORTUGAL ...
- SLOVAKIA ...
- SPAIN ......
- SWITZERLAN
- ROMANIA ....

- CANADA.....................17.3 MILLION ACRES
- EL SALVADOR ....BANNED
- HONDURAS............LESS THAN 123,500 ACRES
- MEXICO ....247,000 ACRES
- U.S. ....142.5 MILLION ACRES

- ARGENTINA....................47.2 MILLION ACRES
- BOLIVIA ....BANNED
- BRAZIL.........................37.1 MILLION ACRES
- CHILE....................LESS THAN 123,500 ACRES
- COLOMBIA ....LESS THAN 123,500 ACRES
- PARAGUAY ....6.4 MILLION ACRES
- URUGUAY ....1.2 MILLION ACRES

- NERICA Benin
of the Congo, Eritr
Mauritania, Mozam
Republic of Tanzar

GENOME PROJECTS AROUND THE WORLD, RESEARCHERS ARE SEQUENCING THE GENOMES OF HUNDREDS   OF AGRICULTURALLY SIGNIFI

Cassava (*Manihot esculenta*)
Department of Energy Joint Genome
Institute, Walnut Creek, California
A root crop that, like bananas,
grows from cuttings—not seeds—
making it hard to breed. Highly tol-
erant of drought and poor soils.

Red flour beetle
(*Tribolium castaneum*)
Human Genome Sequencing Center,
Baylor College of Medicine, Houston
A thief, feeding on grains and flour.
Insights into its insecticide resis-
tance may help combat other pests.

Bovine (*Bos taurus*)
Human Genome Sequencing Center,
Baylor College of Medicine, Houston
Understanding milk and beef production as well as diseases like mad cow
could lead to higher productivity and
smarter breeding practices.

Chicken (*Gallus*
Genome Sequencir
School of Medicine
University in St. Lo
Missouri The first bi
sequenced was the
Jungle Fowl breed

Above and following spreads

The Future of Food

This series of three double spreads addresses
trends in global food-supply. One focuses on
current eating habits, with pie charts showing what and how much people eat in various
countries. The map top left indicates how far
supermarket produce in the US has travelled
on average, based on the example of Des
Moines, Iowa. One world map locates political and social events which affect the global
food-supply. The bar diagram beneath it shows
food imports and exports in selected regions,
demonstrating that Africa depends heavily on
importing food. The other world map (bottom
right) looks at states that develop genetically
modified food. They are marked in green, with
their height projection indicating the total area
of farm-land used.

Gene Banks
WHERE THE WORLD SAVES GENETIC MATERIAL

❶ Native Seeds/Search Seed Bank Tucson, Arizona Nothing high tech—just freezers with 2,000 food, fiber, and dye plant varieties from the Southwest.

❷ Ambrose Monell Collection for Molecular and Microbial Research New York City Samples of everything from lizards to whales. The goal is to figure out how the diversity of life evolved.

❸ Millennium Seed Bank Project West Sussex, UK Large underground vaults with more than 1 billion seeds, the most in the world. Wants 10 percent of the world's wild species by 2010.

❹ Svalbard Global Seed Vault Longyearbyen, Norway Built well above sea level and almost 400 feet into a mountain. Contains food crop seeds as insurance against catastrophe.

○ GOLDEN RICE Philippines
● TRADITIONALLY BRED NEW VARIETIES Bangladesh; South Korea

● AUSTRALIA............247,000 ACRES
● CHINA.............9.4 MILLION ACRES
● INDIA.............15.3 MILLION ACRES
● PHILIPPINES........247,000 ACRES
● THAILAND...................BANNED

● ALGERIA...........................BANNED
● BENIN............................BANNED
● SOUTH AFRICA.... 4.4 MILLION ACRES
● SAUDI ARABIA....................BANNED
● UGANDA..........................BANNED
● ZAMBIA...........................BANNED

...meroon, Central African Republic, Chad, Côte d'Ivoire, Democratic Republic ... Ghana, Guinea, Guinea-Bissau, Kenya, Liberia, Madagascar, Malawi, Mali, ...public of the Congo, Rwanda, Senegal, Sierra Leone, Sudan, Togo, Uganda, United

D ANIMALS TO LEARN HOW THEY WORK.

Sclerotinia sclerotiorum
Broad Institute, Cambridge, Massachusetts This fungal plant pathogen has a broad range of targets, causing everything from sunflower head rot and white mold on canola to soybean stem rot.

Coffee (*Coffea arabica*)
São Paulo (Brazil) Research Foundation; Brazilian Agricultural Research Corporation, Brasília, Brazil This cash crop could benefit from increased yield and resistance to disease and bad weather.

Project Info: "How Science Will Solve the Next Global Crisis", *Wired*, magazine article, 2008, USA
Data Source: UN FAO; Leopold Center for Sustainable Agriculture; Jamais Cascio; Stockholm University; ETH Zurich; US EIA; US EPA; African Rice Center; ISAAA; US NCBI; *Science*
Design: Carl De Torres
Art Direction: Maili Holiman
Creative Direction: Scott Dadich
Design Director: Wyatt Mitchell
Awards: Society of Publication Designers, Gold

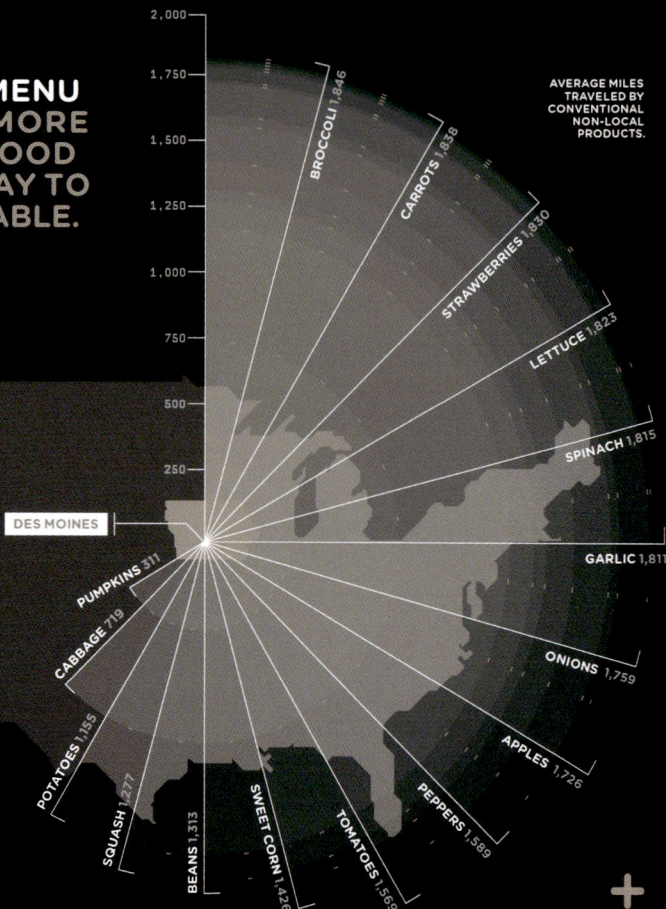

THE GLOBAL MENU
EVERYONE WANTS MORE TO EAT—AND THAT FOOD TRAVELS A LONG WAY TO GET FROM FARM TO TABLE.

AVERAGE MILES TRAVELED BY CONVENTIONAL NON-LOCAL PRODUCTS.

2,000
1,750
1,500
1,250
1,000
750
500
250

BROCCOLI 1,846
CARROTS 1,838
STRAWBERRIES 1,830
LETTUCE 1,823
SPINACH 1,815
GARLIC 1,811
ONIONS 1,759
APPLES 1,726
PEPPERS 1,589
TOMATOES 1,569
SWEET CORN 1,426
BEANS 1,313
SQUASH 1,277
POTATOES 1,155
CABBAGE 719
PUMPKINS 311

DES MOINES

Food From Afar
Attention, Iowa shoppers: If you eat standard super-market produce, figure an average transport distance of 1,500 miles (and that's just for stuff grown in the US). Such is the price you pay in cash and carbon emissions—not to mention the tax dollars spent on repairing highways chewed up by behemoth trucks. In general, a longer, more global supply chain is also vulnerable to strikes, gas hikes, political turmoil, and contamination. All so you can eat what you want when you want it. —Ben Paynter

Sources: Food and Agriculture Organization; Leopold Center for Sustainable Agriculture

PROP STYLIST: STUART POLASKY/MARK EDWARD INC

WHO'S EATING WHAT? MOST COUNTRIES ARE CONSUMING MORE FOOD; OTHERS SHOULD CUT BACK.

Once-hungry nations now have more to eat: In these 10 countries, selected from different regions and levels of economic development, almost everyone is eating better, increasing their intake of energy-dense (if energy-intensive) meat and dairy. But while developed, satiated nations like the UK consume only a little more per capita per day than they did 30 years ago, Americans have bumped up calorie intake by a piggish 24 percent, increasing global demand and making food that much more expensive for others. —B.P.

1969-1971

BRAZIL — 2,430 CALORIES
CHINA — 1,990
ICELAND — 2,950
INDIA — 2,040

2001-2003

BRAZIL — 3,110 CALORIES
CHINA — 2,930
ICELAND — 3,270
INDIA — 2,470

- CEREALS
- VEGETABLE OILS
- MEAT
- SUGAR & SWEETENERS
- MILK & PRODUCTS
- ANIMAL FATS
- OTHER*
- FRUITS/ VEGETABLES

Increased wealth (for some) means meat consumption has more than doubled.

The Chinese now eat as much meat as the English, and rice consumption is down.

Icelanders have stuck to their traditional diet of protein and fat.

A growing economy hasn't changed the menu much; there's just more of it.

Whole wheat bread 6 slices	
Canned spinach 12 oz	
Great northern beans 2 cups	
Powdered skim milk 8 oz	
Potato flakes 6 oz	
Tomato paste 6 oz	
Nondairy cheese 4 oz	
Raw carrots 4 oz	
Seedless raisins 4 oz	
Vegetable oil 4 Tbsp	

INSIDE NUTRALOAF

Could science build a completely nutritious space food? Sure, but it'd be a lot like nutraloaf, a substance served to prisoners in solitary in some states. It's so unpalatable that it's the subject of several lawsuits. The ingredients (at left) are ordinary enough, and Vermont's version of the recipe (this makes three 1,000-calorie loafs) is balanced for fat, protein, carbs, and vitamins. So how could such a harmony of food and science constitute cruel and unusual punishment? Because it tastes like cardboard, smells like rotten eggs, and looks like baked vomit. —THOMAS HAYDEN

AQUACULTURE (2006 TOTAL: 56.8 MILLION TONS)
WILD CAPTURE (2006 TOTAL: 101.1 MILLION TONS)

160

MILLION TONS

1950   2006

The Rise of Aquaculture

As humans worldwide consume more fish, wild-caught supplies cannot keep pace. That's where aquaculture—a factory farm approach to fish raising—comes in. But it's not all good: Fish farms pollute surrounding waters and cause disproportionate ecological damage. —T.H.

191

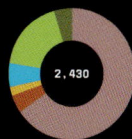

MADAGASCAR — 2,430

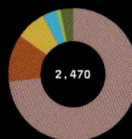

MOROCCO — 2,470

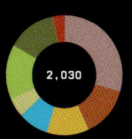

SAINT LUCIA — 2,030

UAE — 2,990

UK — 3,300

USA — 3,040

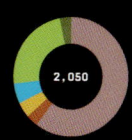

2,050

Political upheaval has forced the country into a subsistence diet.

3,110

Moroccans are eating more produce—and getting a bump in calories overall.

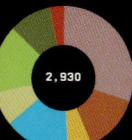

2,930

Party time in paradise: There's a lot of alcohol hidden in that "Other" category.

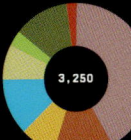

3,250

Recently arrived South Asian workers favor vegetable oils over animal fats.

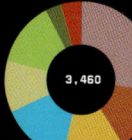

3,460

Brits have cut sugar and swapped butter for products like margarine.

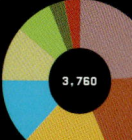

3,760

We love sweets, and we're lapping up the cooking oil. Fried Twinkie anyone?

*"OTHER" INCLUDES SEAFOOD, ALCOHOL, STARCHY ROOTS, AND OIL SEED CROPS. NOTE: FIGURES SHOW FOOD AVAILABILITY AND MAY INCLUDE HOUSEHOLD WASTAGE.

● Saudi Arabia
Forced to import most of its food, Saudi Arabia now purchases farmland in poorer countries like Pakistan, Thailand, and Sudan.

The global food market is in disarray: Commodity speculation and rising fuel costs are driving up prices, the world relies too heavily on too few crops, farm subsidies in rich countries give those growers an advantage over poor farmers in developing nations, man-made and natural disasters are reducing supply, and recently some countries have taken to hoarding, which clogs up free-flowing trade. Fixing this mess will require a mix of food diversification, trade incentives, and smarter, globally minded polices. —Erin Biba

Sources: "The Cheese-burger Footprint," Jamais Cascio; *Energy Use in the Food Sector: A Data Survey 2000*, Stockholm University and Swiss Federal Institute of Technology; Energy Information Administration; Environmental Protection Agency; Food and Agriculture Organization

✗ ● Argentina
The country is normally a major global food supplier, but shortages caused by striking farmers and high import prices led to rationing in Buenos Aires this year.

✗ ✗ ✗ ● U.S.
Talks between China, India, and the U.S. that may have boosted worldwide crop and meat exports recently fell apart because of America's refusal to scrap its farm subsidies.

✗ Egypt
High food prices are devastating the country's poor. Rioting among factory workers broke out in April after the price of some staples (like rice) nearly doubled.

GLOBAL IMPORTS AND EXPORTS   MAJOR PRODUCERS (EXPORT AT LEAST 80 MILLION TONS)

The more food trade there is across the world, the better, especially when countries maintain a balance of exports and imports. The good news: Overall, we are making and trading more. Plus, China and India finally export more than they import—a sign that those countries' agricultural industries are getting better. The bad news: Places like Africa that should be breadbaskets are relying more and more on imported food. —P.D.J.

■ Imports   ■ Exports

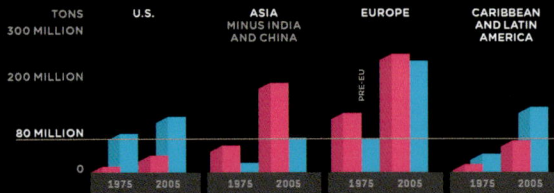

TONS
300 MILLION

200 MILLION

80 MILLION

0

	U.S.	ASIA MINUS INDIA AND CHINA	EUROPE	CARIBBEAN AND LATIN AMERICA
	1975 2005	1975 2005	1975 2005	1975 2005

PRE-EU

XX● **China**
Desertification and
population growth
are eating up arable
land. And due to
rising rice prices,
the government has
started restricting
exports drastically.

XX **India**
Four years of
severe drought
have prevented
adequate irrigation
and slashed food
production. Mal-
nutrition is ram-
pant, particularly
in small villages.

X **Cambodia**
Usually a major
rice seller (460,000
tons last year),
Cambodia's govern-
ment moved to
combat rising
prices by imposing
a two-month
ban on exports this
past March.

McCarbon

Two all-beef patties, special sauce*, lettuce, cheese, pickles, onions ... and a crapload of carbon. All on a sesame-seed bun. Where does the carbon come from? The fertilizer to grow the produce, the diesel in the delivery trucks, and the electricity to power the bakeries, for starters. Spend $2.87 on a Big Mac (the national average) and $0.54 goes to energy. In return you are responsible for producing 4.83 pounds of greenhouse gasses. —PATRICK DI JUSTO

|||||||||||||||||||||||||||||||||||||||||||||||

Disasters
PROBLEMS THAT REDUCE THE GLOBAL FOOD SUPPLY

X Drought
X Storms and/or flooding
X Strife
X Reduction of farmland by bad
 WTO and World Bank policies
X Subsumption of arable land
 to biofuel crops
X Population explosion

Trade Issues
PROBLEMS THAT DISTORT THE GLOBAL FOOD MARKET

● **HOARDING**
Countries attempting to combat
rising food prices and fears of
shortages by curbing or banning
the export of certain crops—
which drives up futures prices.
● **SUBSIDIES**
Wealthy countries subsidizing
food to offset a higher cost of
production, resulting in skewed
prices and less opportunity for
farmers in poorer countries.
● **IMPORT-DEPENDENCE**
Nations importing most of their
food because they are in arid
regions, have insufficient land for
crops, or are too poor to develop
farming infrastructure.

X **Australia**
Six years of drought
in Australia is
affecting the entire
planet. Instead of
exporting 28 million
tons of grain a year,
the country now
produces a mere
10 million.

BIG MACS SOLD
EACH YEAR IN THE U.S.:

550
MILLION

ENERGY COST:

$297
MILLION

POUNDS OF CARBON DIOXIDE/
METHANE RELEASED:

2.66
BILLION

Production stage	Energy cost	Methane/CO$_2$ released (pounds)
Crop/feed production	$0.27	1.5
Cow burping/flatulence	n/a	0.07
Transport	$0.02	0.13
Milling	$0.01	0.15
Baking	$0.03	0.37
Milking/making cheese	$0.01	0.12
Slaughtering/cutting	$0.04	0.52
Grinding/freezing	$0.005	0.06
Freeze-drying	$0.002	0.03
Pickling	$0.001	0.01
Frying	$0.03	0.37
Storage	$0.12	1.5
Total per Big Mac	**$0.54**	**4.83** pounds

*Since few know what's in
the special sauce, infor-
mation on its carbon and
energy cost is not available.

MINOR PRODUCERS (EXPORT LESS THAN 80 MILLION TONS) 1 9 5

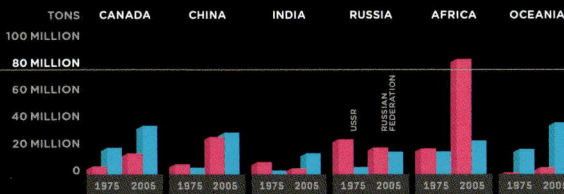

TONS	CANADA	CHINA	INDIA	RUSSIA	AFRICA	OCEANIA
100 MILLION						
80 MILLION						
60 MILLION						
40 MILLION				USSR / RUSSIAN FEDERATION		
20 MILLION						
0	1975 2005	1975 2005	1975 2005	1975 2005	1975 2005	1975 2005

Project Info: Series of maps, 2010, USA
Data Source: Flickr and Picasa search APIs; OpenStreetMap
Design: Eric Fisher

The Geotaggers' World Atlas

This is a large series of maps showing major cities of the world. Eric Fisher collected geographical data from geotagged images that were posted on Flickr and Picasa and placed them on maps. For various cities, the maps show the distribution of the spots where these images were taken. All are scaled to the same size, oriented on the central New York cluster to fit in. In this enhanced version, "Locals and Tourists", Fisher tried to discern which pictures were taken by tourists (red) and which by locals (blue). Yellow indicates when this distinction was unknown. The maps in this series are compelling examples of thematic maps, highlighting the most favourite places in each city. Clockwise from above right: New York, Tokyo, London and San Francisco.

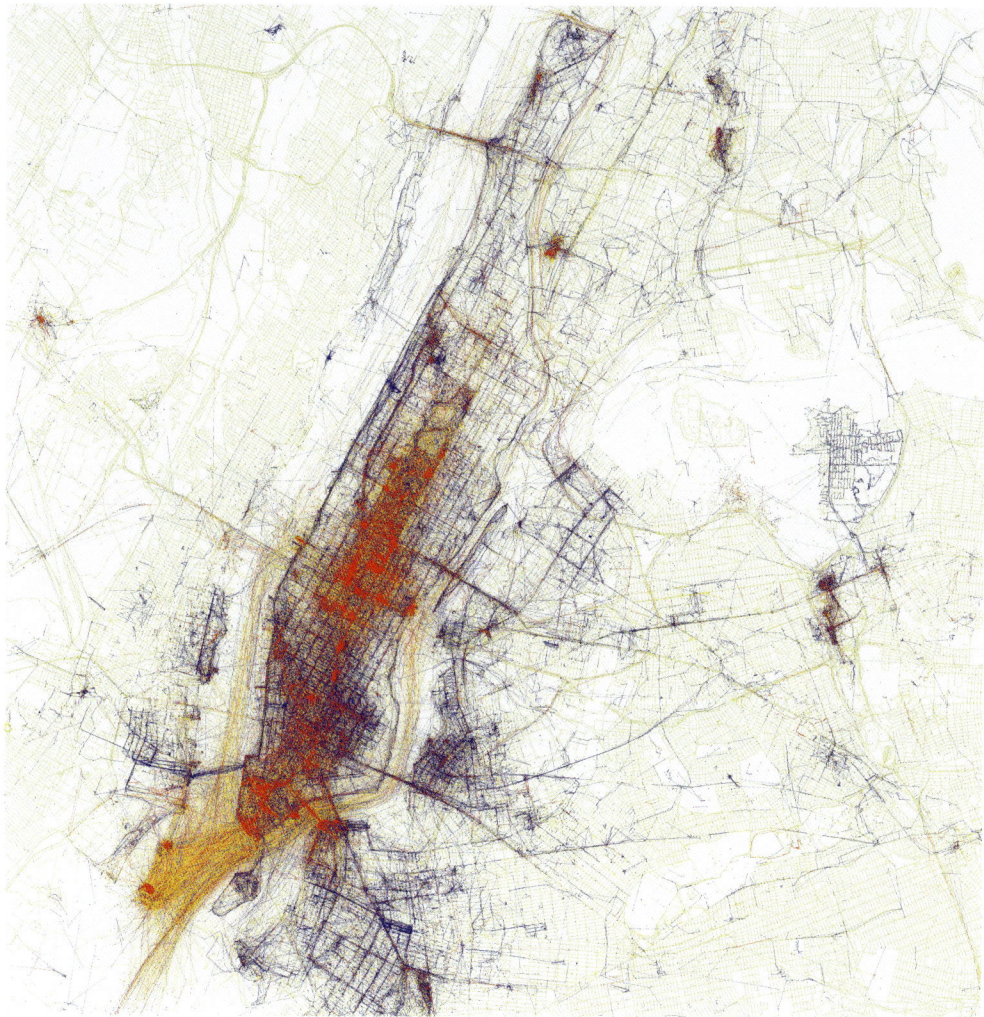

Following spreads

The Land of Ice

Until the financial crisis of 2009, Iceland had the reputation of being one of the world's happiest nations. According to the UN, it belongs amongst the most developed countries in the world. When asked for a contribution to an issue of the *Reykjavik Grapevine* magazine with the theme: "Iceland, happiest nation in the world", Hugleikur Dagsson drew this narrative map. Locating information on a map is not the key issue in this piece, instead, Dagsson used the island's outlines and stuffed it brimful with micro-stories. He turned it into a mental map of his home country.

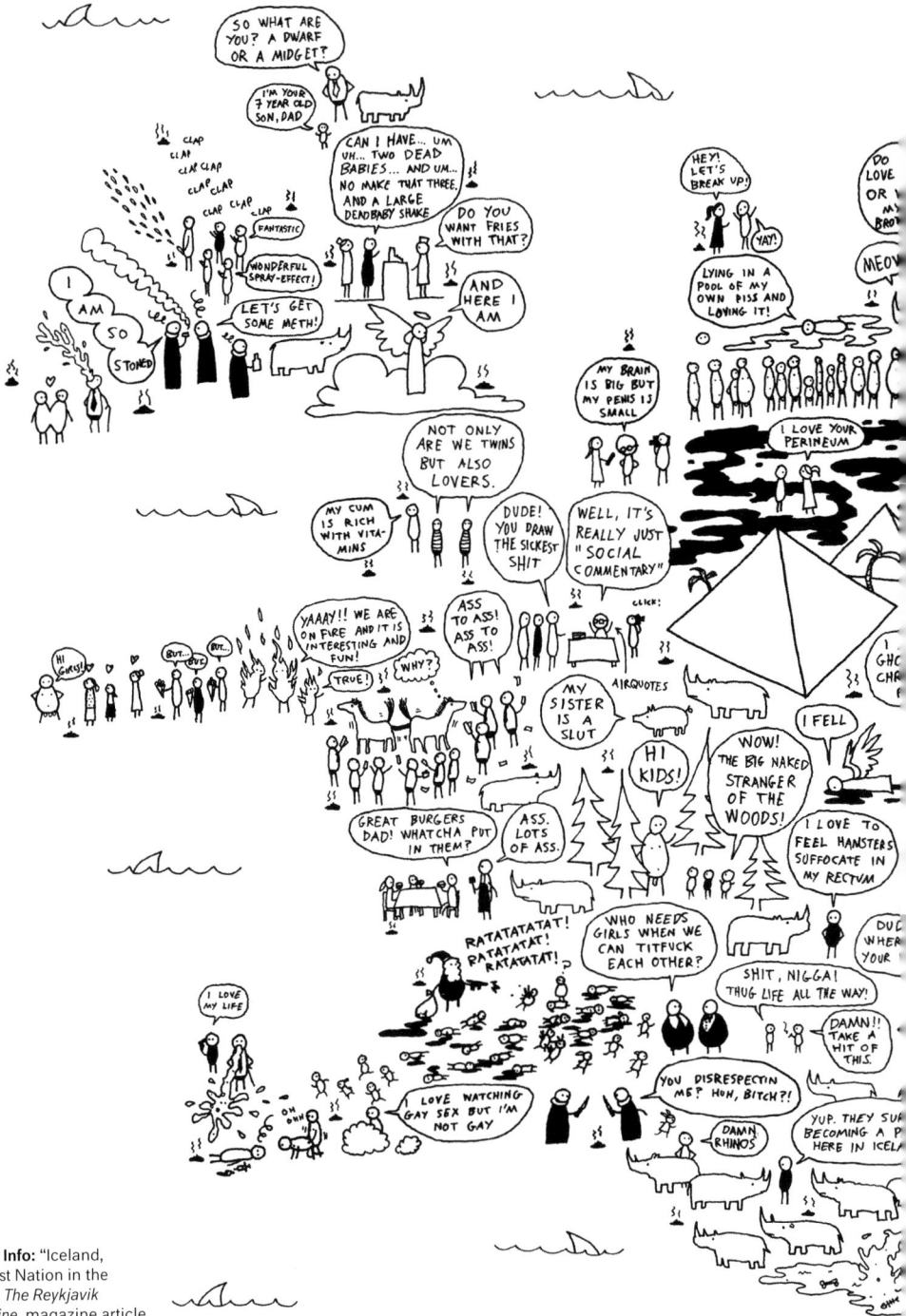

Project Info: "Iceland, Happiest Nation in the World", *The Reykjavik Grapevine*, magazine article, 2006 / 2010, Iceland
Design: Hugleikur Dagsson

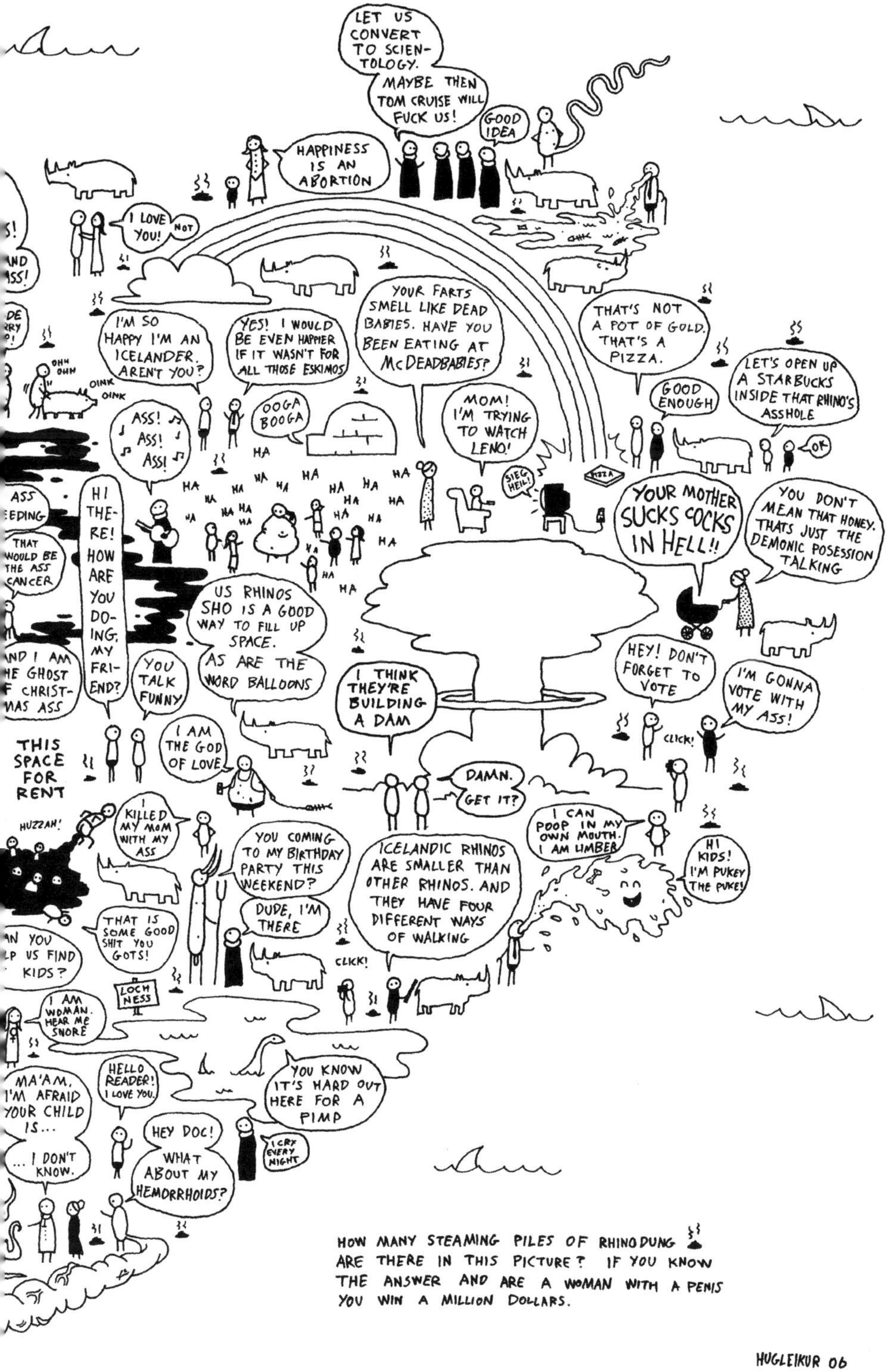
LET US CONVERT TO SCIENTOLOGY.
MAYBE THEN TOM CRUISE WILL FUCK US!
GOOD IDEA
HAPPINESS IS AN ABORTION
I LOVE YOU!
NOT
YOUR FARTS SMELL LIKE DEAD BABIES. HAVE YOU BEEN EATING AT McDEADBABIES?
THAT'S NOT A POT OF GOLD. THAT'S A PIZZA.
LET'S OPEN UP A STARBUCKS INSIDE THAT RHINO'S ASSHOLE
I'M SO HAPPY I'M AN ICELANDER. AREN'T YOU?
YES! I WOULD BE EVEN HAPPIER IF IT WASN'T FOR ALL THOSE ESKIMOS
OHH OHH
OINK OINK
OOGA BOOGA
MOM! I'M TRYING TO WATCH LENO!
GOOD ENOUGH
OK
ASS! ASS! ASS!
HA HA HA HA HA HA HA HA HA HA HA HA HA HA HA HA HA HA HA HA
SIEG HEIL!
PIZZA
YOUR MOTHER SUCKS COCKS IN HELL!!
YOU DON'T MEAN THAT HONEY. THATS JUST THE DEMONIC POSESSION TALKING
HI THERE! HOW ARE YOU DOING, MY FRIEND?
THAT WOULD BE THE ASS CANCER
US RHINOS SHO IS A GOOD WAY TO FILL UP SPACE.
AS ARE THE WORD BALLOONS
YOU TALK FUNNY
I THINK THEY'RE BUILDING A DAM
HEY! DON'T FORGET TO VOTE
I'M GONNA VOTE WITH MY ASS!
CLICK!
THE GHOST OF CHRISTMAS ASS
THIS SPACE FOR RENT
I AM THE GOD OF LOVE
DAMN. GET IT?
HUZZAH!
I KILLED MY MOM WITH MY ASS
YOU COMING TO MY BIRTHDAY PARTY THIS WEEKEND?
DUDE, I'M THERE
ICELANDIC RHINOS ARE SMALLER THAN OTHER RHINOS. AND THEY HAVE FOUR DIFFERENT WAYS OF WALKING
I CAN POOP IN MY OWN MOUTH. I AM LIMBER
HI KIDS! I'M PUKEY THE PUKE!
THAT IS SOME GOOD SHIT YOU GOTS!
CLICK!
LOCH NESS
I AM WOMAN. HEAR ME SNORE
MA'AM, I'M AFRAID YOUR CHILD IS...
... I DON'T KNOW.
HELLO READER! I LOVE YOU.
YOU KNOW IT'S HARD OUT HERE FOR A PIMP
HEY DOC! WHAT ABOUT MY HEMORRHOIDS?
I CRY EVERY NIGHT
HOW MANY STEAMING PILES OF RHINODUNG ARE THERE IN THIS PICTURE? IF YOU KNOW THE ANSWER AND ARE A WOMAN WITH A PENIS YOU WIN A MILLION DOLLARS.
HUGLEIKUR 06

ICELAND.

FAR IN THE NORTH LIES A SMALL ISLAND. SURROUNDED BY ICY SHARK INFECTED SALTWATER. ICELAND. THE LAND OF EMPTY PROMISES AND BROKEN DREAMS. SCANDINAVIA'S BASTARD CHILD. KNOWN TO THE NATIVES AS "ÍSLAND", WHICH MEANS "THE COUNTRY OF SNOW".

WHEN NORWAY ACCEPTED CHRISTIANITY IN THE DARK AGES, ALL THE COOL NORWEGIANS DECIDED TO DITCH THE JOINT, LEAVING ALL THE DORKS BEHIND. THEY MADE A PIT STOP IN IRELAND TO PICK UP SOME SLAVES.

THEN THEY WENT TO ICELAND AND RAPED ALL THE SLAVES. THUS, A PROUD NATION WAS BORN. A PROUD NATION OF PEOPLE AND SHEEP. AND A RARE HYBRID OF THE TWO CALLED "SHEOPLE". OR "PEEP". A SMALL NATION IN A SMALL LAND. TODAY, THERE ARE MORE THAN A THOUSAND ICELANDERS. AMONG THOSE PEOPLE, THERE IS ONE NOBEL PRIZE WINNER, THREE MISS WORLDS AND OVER A HUNDRED EVIL BANKERS. COME TO ICELAND! FIND OUT IF THE LEGENDS ARE TRUE. DO ICELANDERS REALLY EAT SHEEP? IS THEIR WATER REALLY COLD? DID THEY REALLY EVOLVE FROM APES?

HISTORY OF ICELAND.

874 — OMG! LAND!

930 — CHECK DIS! WE JUST FOUNDED DA MUTHAFUCKIN PARLIAMENT / DAAIMN!

1000 — AND NOW WE, LIKE, CHRISTIAN! / WHUUT SO WE BELIEVE LIKE, JESU AND SHI'

1262 — YO BITCHES! WE BE NORWAY AND NOW WE RULE YO ASS! / AW, SHEEIT!

1314 — I JUST INVENTED THE INTERNET, YO! / SURF FOR SOME PORN, YO!

1402 — FUCK! IT'S THE BLACK PLAGUE!! / DON'T BE RACIST

1662 — HEY FUCKAS! WE BE DENMARK AND WE GONNA RULE THA SHIT OUTTA YA BITCHES! / UNLIKE

1944 — FINALLY! MUTHAFUCKAS BE INDEPENDENT! / INDEPENDENT LIKE A MUTHAFUCKA!

1962 — SHIIT! IT'S THE BEE-PEOPLE! / BZZZ / BZZ

1985 — YO WE GOT OUR FIRST MISS WORLD! / MISS WORLD CLASS TOP CHOICE GRADE-A MEAT!

2008 — OH NO! WE LOST ALL OUR FAKE MONEY! / FUCK THIS SHIT.

2010 — FUUUUCK.

TOP FIVE ICELANDIC MOUNTAINS.

#5 ÖXNAVÖRÐUFELL

#4 ALLSKOSTARÞJÁNINGARSTÓLL

#3 DEYJAFJALLAJÖKULL

#2 ÞINGSÁLYKTUNARTILLAGA

#1 ÉYNLSÞÐÆNKFKÖSÐÐ

GREAT TOURIST ATTRACTIONS.

GULLFOSS.
IT MEANS "THE GOLDEN WATER FALLS" BUT IT'S NOT REALLY GOLDEN. IT'S JUST REGULAR-ASS CLEAR WATER. BUT IF YOU PHOTOSHOP A PICTURE OF IT, YOU CAN PROBABLY MAKE IT LOOK GOLDEN.

GEYSIR.
ICELAND'S MOST CELEBRATED NATURAL LANDMARK. IT WAS ONCE BELIEVED THAT IT WAS THE DEVIL EJACULATING FROM HIS UNDERGROUND LAIR. LATER IT WAS DISCOVERED THAT IT'S NOT THE DEVIL. OBVIOUSLY. IT'S JUST SOME GUY NAMED PHIL.

THE BLUE LAGOON.
A BIG WARM POOL OF LIGHT-BLUE WATER AND WHITE MUD. SOME GEOLOGICAL THING. I DON'T KNOW. I WAS GOING TO DO A CUM JOKE HERE. BUT I ALREADY DID IT WITH GEYSIR.

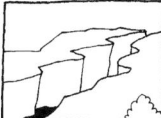

ALMANNAGJÁ.
A CANYON WHERE THE EURASIAN AND NORTH AMERICAN TECTONIC PLATES MEET. INTERESTINGLY ALMANNAGJ IS ALSO A WORD FOR "SLUT". THE DIRECT TRANSLATION IS "ALL-MENS-GAP".

JÖKULSÁRLÓN.
JUST A LAKE WITH SOME ICE IN IT. NOTHING SPECIAL. BUT HEY, UHM... REMEMBER THAT BOND MOVIE, "A VIEW TO A KILL"? THE OPENING SCENE WAS SHOT THERE.

ICELANDIC ANIMALS.

LAZER WALRUS

HE ONLY ANIMAL IN THE
RTHERN HEMISPHERE THAT CAN
OOT LAZERS OUT OF IT'S EYES.

SCREAMING SHEEP.

ZKREEE!

ZKREE!

FOR SOME REASON, THEY
ONLY SCREAM AT CHILDREN.

ICELANDIC HORSE.

E ICELANDIC HORSE LIKES
IE MOVIE "NOTEBOOK" AND
NG WALKS ON THE BEACH.

HATE OWL.

THE HATE OWL IS EXACTLY LIKE
IT'S COUSIN, THE SNOW OWL.
EXCEPT FOR THE FACT THAT IT'S
HEART IS FULL OF HATE.

E ASS-MOUTHED POLAR BEARS

IS POOR ANIMAL HAS ANUSES
BOTH ENDS. HENCE, IT IS
RED TWICE AS MUCH AS OTHER
AR BEARS.

BIG WHOOP WHALE.

THIS IS THE LARGEST WHALE
IN THE WORLD. BIG WHOOP.

WHIMBREL.

E ICELANDIC WHIMBREL IS
DELY CONSIDERED SEXIER
AN OTHER WHIMBRELS.

PAIN DEER.

YOU DON'T FUCK WITH THE
PAINDEER. YOU JUST DON'T.

REYKJAVÍK
"THE CITY OF FEAR"

1. MUSEUM OF ANCIENT HISTORY.
2. YOU CAN GET GREAT HOT DOGS HERE.
3. "THE POND" 50% WATER. 50% NOT WATER.
4. DOWNTOWN.
5. THE SWAMP OF DEFEATED DREAMS.
6. COCKSUCKER HOTEL.
7. THE NATIONAL MUSEUM OF SOMETHING.
8. HILLBILLY COUNTRY.
9. DINOSAUR FOREST.
10. WHOREHOUSE FOR DOGS.
42. THE FINAL RESTING PLACE OF JACK THE RIPPER.

ÖkebutOkur 2010©HUGLEIKUR DAGSSON www.okei.is – okei@okei.is

ELANDIC PROTESTS.

AR IN IRAQ.

STOP WAR

VIRONMENTAL ISSUES.

STOP RAPING EARTH

LEAVE NATURE ALONE

NO MORE POLLU TION

SING MONEY.

I AM SAD

THINK ABOUT THE CHILDREN!

NOW WE'RE KINDA POORS

WHERE'S MY MONEY?

FUCKIN BANKS

ICELAND

"THE LAND OF ICE"

HUGLEIKUR DAGSSON

THE **WORST OIL SPILL**

EXXON VALDEZ
271,210 Barrels
1989

17

ODYSSEY
968,711 Barrels
1988

11

DEEPWATER HORIZON
4,928,100 Barrels
2010

2

IXTOC I OIL WELL
3,423,110 Barrels
1979

3

ATLANTIC EMPRESS
2,023,080 Barrels
1979

5

WORST IN
U.S. HISTORY

TOTAL AMOUNT OF OIL SPILLED:

4,500,000+

In tonnes, since 1967.

TOTAL NUMBER OF TANKER SPILLS:

9,522

82% of spillages were under 7 tonnes.

TIME IT TAKES A SPILL TO CLEAR UP:

50 YEARS

For the average spill of around 35,000 tonnes.

N
HISTORY

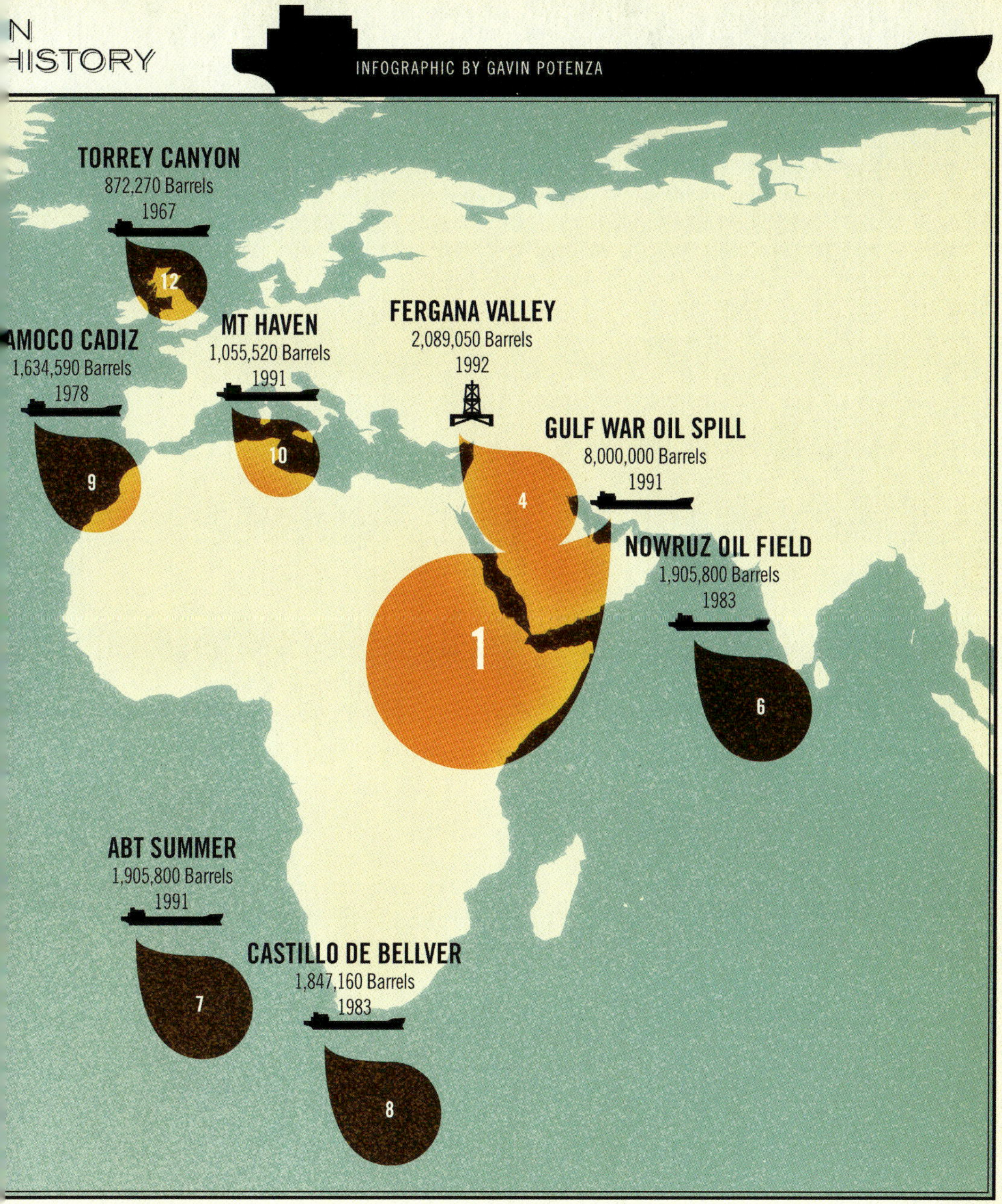

INFOGRAPHIC BY GAVIN POTENZA

TORREY CANYON
872,270 Barrels
1967

12

MT HAVEN
1,055,520 Barrels
1991

10

FERGANA VALLEY
2,089,050 Barrels
1992

GULF WAR OIL SPILL
8,000,000 Barrels
1991

4

AMOCO CADIZ
1,634,590 Barrels
1978

9

NOWRUZ OIL FIELD
1,905,800 Barrels
1983

6

1

ABT SUMMER
1,905,800 Barrels
1991

7

CASTILLO DE BELLVER
1,847,160 Barrels
1983

8

Previous spread

The Worst Oil Spills in History

The extraction and transportation of crude oil has repeatedly led to major accidents, which contaminate coastlines and oceans with sometimes unimaginable quantities of oil. This piece locates and ranks some of the biggest incidents on a thematic world map, indicating as well the year and how much oil was spilled. In comparison with other previous spills, the Deepwater Horizon disaster in April 2010 ranks second behind the total oil spills that occurred during the Gulf War. One tonne of oil equals about 7.3 barrels.

Project Info: Website, 2010, USA
Data Source: International Tanker Owners Pollution Federation
Design: Gavin Potenza

Tour de France 2010

Held annually since 1903, the Tour de France sets a course with a huge total distance for riders to complete in the quickest possible time. The illustrated map shows the outline of France, filled with all kinds of symbols related to the individual regions or to the race in general. Starting up north in the Netherlands the sequence of stages is marked for 2010, with tagged stops in between, up to the final destination in Paris. Whilst using the motif of a map, the piece isn't meant to locate actual specific places. Rather, it celebrates the popular event and the incredible efforts cyclists from around the world put into this road-trip.

Project Info: *Bicycling*, magazine article, 2010, USA
Design: I Love Dust

Following spread

Twilight of the Arctic Ice

With this look at the North polar region, *National Geographic* tackles the melting of the polar ice caps. The centrepiece maps the current ice sheet, with coloured lines showing its extension in 2007 and in 1980. The series of maps along the bottom form a timeline, showing the shrinking in several time steps. The schema atop the central map explains the chain reaction caused by the melting – while the ice used to reflect the sunlight, the latter is now absorbed by land-masses or the ocean and causes a further warming. The bar chart top right adds to the piece with average temperature deviations for latitudes above 60 degrees, for the time period 1900–2008.

Project Info: *National Geographic*, poster, 2009, USA
Data Source: National Snow and Ice Data Center; National Oceanic and Atmospheric Administration; Cooperative Institute for Research in Environmental Sciences
Research: Kaitlin Yarnall
Design: Alejandro Tumas
Art Direction: Juan Velasco
Illustration: Pablo Loscri, Hernán Cañellas
Awards: Malofiej; Society for News Design

TDF
2010
2010 TOUR DE FRANCE

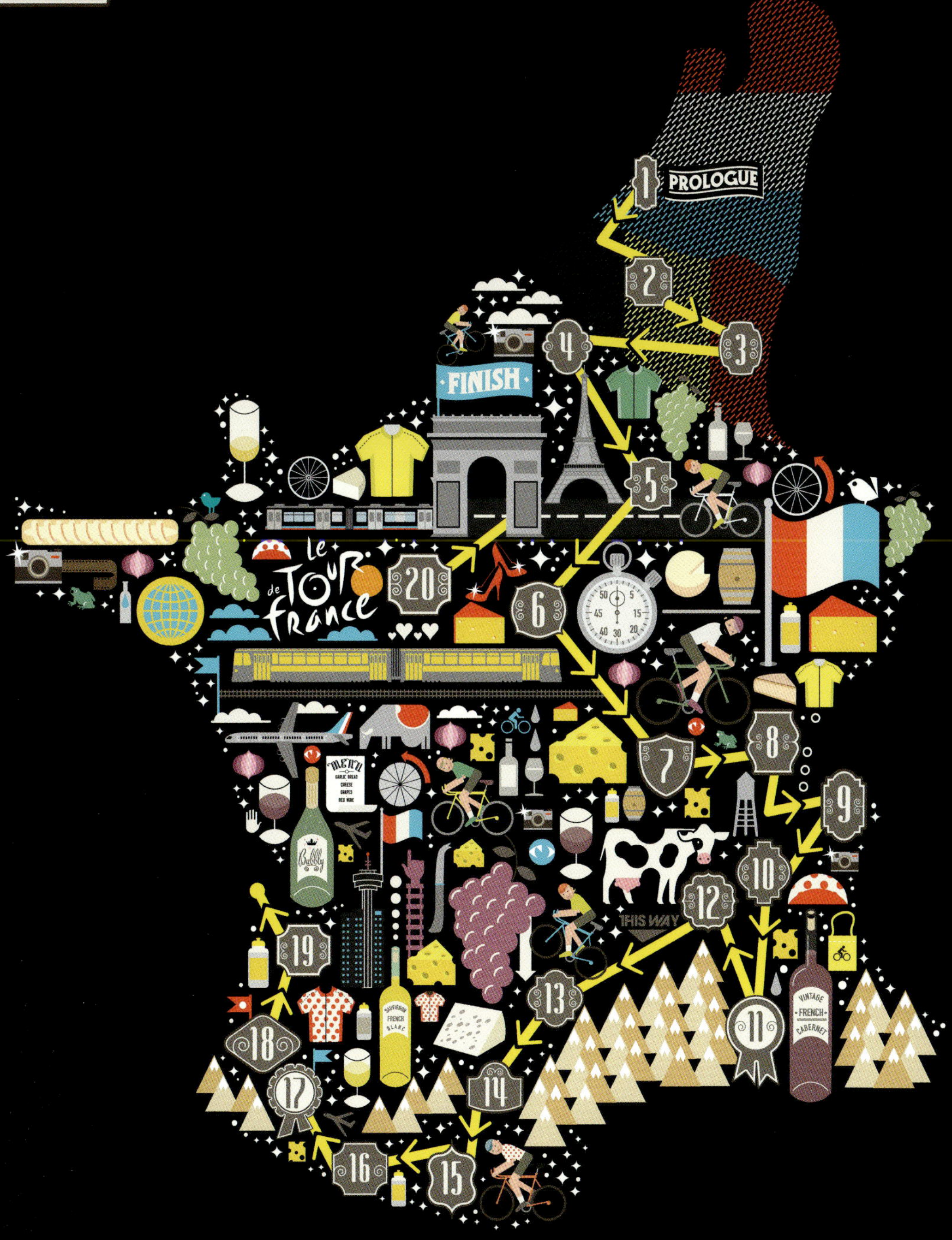

Twilight
of the
Arctic Ice

The empire of ice at the top of the world is shrinking. The Arctic Ocean's summer ice pack covers little more than half its former reach, as a sweeping satellite image from September 2008 documents. Atop Greenland's formidable ice sheet, melting has also quickened. Sea ice, naturally expanding and contracting with the seasons, has covered this ocean year-round for most of the past three million years. But the Arctic is uniquely sensitive to climate change (right). Ten years ago global-warming models predicted the Arctic Ocean could be ice free in summer by 2100. Then the date dropped to 2050, and now to 2030—or sooner. As climate scientist Mark Serreze puts it, "Reality is exceeding expectations."

Ice Sustains Ice

The brilliant white of ice and snow reflects more than 80 percent of incoming sunlight. This reflective quality is called albedo. The high albedo of an ice-covered Arctic helps keep its temperatures low and preserves its ice.

A Balance of Warmth

Some of the solar energy reflected by ice or reradiated as heat returns to space. Some is absorbed into the atmosphere by greenhouse gases like carbon dioxide and water vapor, whose heat-trapping qualities make life on Earth possible.

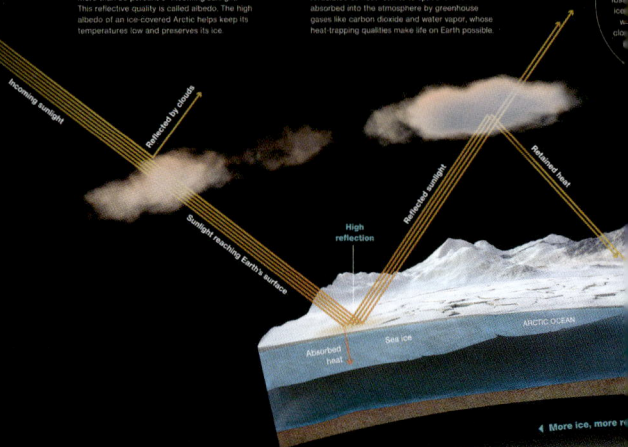

Incoming sunlight

Reflected by clouds

Reflected sunlight

Retained heat

Sunlight reaching Earth's surface

High reflection

Absorbed heat

Sea ice

ARCTIC OCEAN

◀ More ice, more re

Northern Hemisphere

Land 39.4%

Ocean 60.6%

Sea ice* 6.5%
5.8 million sq mi

*Average maximum extent
Winter 1978-2002

Southern Hemisphere

Land 18.5%

Ocean 81.5%

Sea ice* 7.1%
6.9 million sq mi

North and South

The Northern Hemisphere has experienced a greater temperature rise than the Southern, in part because it has more land, which warms faster than open ocean. Yet troubling signs of warming in Antarctica—where the vast continental ice sheet holds 85 percent of Earth's freshwater ice—make clear that the bottom of the world is also vulnerable.

Minimum extent
September 2008

Minimum extent
September 1980

Minimum extent
September 2007

RUSSIA

ALASKA (U.S.)

AR

CANADA

Relief vertically exaggerated

Arctic Retreat

Measured at the end of summer, the sea-ice minimum in September 1980 spanned an area slightly smaller than the contiguous United States. The September 2008 minimum was just over half that size. Regional weather patterns contributed to the even greater decline in 2007.

Higher reflection

| Year | Summer sea-ice extent | 1980 | 3.01 million sq mi | 1985 | 2.66 million sq mi | 1990 | 2.39 million sq mi | 1995 | 2.36 million sq mi |

Chain Reaction Melting

Open water and bare ground absorb more than 90 percent of incoming sunlight. When increased melting exposes more dark surface, the Arctic gets warmer—causing more ice to melt and expose even more dark surface.

An Opening Ocean

In a warmer ocean, ice forms later in the fall and melts earlier in the spring. The ice is also thinner and may be less reflective. The volume of ice that survives summer to thicken into multiyear ice has dropped by perhaps half.

Temperature Impact

Losing its reflective ice cover causes the Arctic to warm faster than any other region on Earth. For lower latitudes, a reduced Arctic ice pack will potentially contribute to warmer winters. Storm tracks could shift, affecting precipitation.

Temperatures have trended upward for two decades. Patterns of high or low air pressure over the Arctic create periods of below- or above-average readings. Now the driver is a rise in greenhouse gases.

Annual deviations from average surface air temperature over land in latitudes above 60°N, just outside the Arctic Circle

+2°C = 3.6°F

Past 20 years

+1.5°C
2.7°F

+1.0°C
1.8°F

+0.5°C
0.9°F

Above average
Below average

Average temperature
−6.8°C = 18.8°F
1961–2000

| 1900-1919 | 1920-1939 | 1940-1959 | 1960-1979 | 1980-1999 | 00-09 |

−0.5°C
0.9°F

−1.0°C
1.8°F

−1.5°C
2.7°F

-1.7°C = 3.06°F

Chain reaction labels

More summer clouds
Less heat returned to space
More heat retained
Less sunlight reflected
Less reflection
Open water
More heat absorbed and reradiated
GREENLAND

..., less reflection ▶

OCEAN

GREENLAND
(Denmark)

ICELAND

BAFFIN BAY

ARCTIC CIRCLE

Area of surface melt 1980
Area of additional surface melt 2007

Greenland's Slide

Greenland's ice sheet is so massive—a mile thick on average—that it creates its own weather. But new snowfall can no longer replace the ice the world's largest island is losing each year. Glaciers that carry inland ice to the sea have accelerated, in part because of greater surface melt. Meltwater flowing down through cracks lubricates the base of glaciers. A warming ocean also plays into the ice sheet's thaw. Sea levels aren't affected by melting Arctic Ocean ice, already afloat, but the pace of Greenland's melt could help raise sea levels five feet by 2100.

NATIONAL GEOGRAPHIC

Lower reflection ➡

2.43 million sq mi | 2005 | 2.16 million sq mi | 2007 | 1.67 million sq mi | 2008 | 1.81 million sq mi

SUPPLEMENT TO NATIONAL GEOGRAPHIC, MAY 2009

GRAPHICS EDITOR: ALEJANDRO TUMAS. DESIGN: PABLO LOICA AND R. EUNGEO TUMAS. ART: HERNÁN CAÑELLAS AND MAÑU LOCUS. MAP RESEARCH: PATRICIA R. FARRELL. TEXT: JANE VESSELS. PRODUCTION: NEVILLE BAKER. SATELLITE IMAGE: ROBERT SIMMON.

Transatlantic Superhighway

This piece, developed for *Condé Nast Traveler*, visualises the air-traffic system for the North Atlantic. Based on a strip from an abstract map oriented from North America towards Europe, the graphic shows scheduled trans-atlantic flight-paths, in which aircraft travel at safe distances from each other while keeping constant speed and altitude. The "safety envelope" at the top left is a detail taken from the scheduled track-system beneath and shows the minimum distances which must be kept between two aircraft. The overall layout, with the map aligned towards the top right into the dark blue, supports the association of east-ward bound night-flights across the Atlantic.

The Transatlantic Super

EVERY DAY, ABOUT 900 AIRCRAFT FLY
INSIDE THE NORTH ATLANTIC
ORGANIZED TRACK SYSTEM

60 miles

80 m

60 miles

2,000 feet

80 miles (10 min.)

2,000 feet

FLIGHT LEVELS (FEET)
39,000
37,000
35,000
33,000
31,000
29,000

ORGANIZED TRA

T

U

V

W

1 GETTING IN LINE
Taking into account airlines' preferred routes, oceanic controllers at Gander, Newfoundland, organize aircraft approaching from different directions into position for the Atlantic crossing. This flight is entering the system on track V at 35,000 feet.

232

Project Info: *Condé Nast Traveler*, magazine article, 1996, USA
Design: Robert Best
Illustration: John Grimwade

/ay

The Concorde flies between 50,000 and 60,000 feet, far above the main traffic flow.

4 HALFWAY POINT
At 30°W, responsibility for the flight is transferred from Gander to Prestwick Oceanic Air Traffic Control in Scotland.

Some flight levels are reserved for aircraft flying in the direction opposite the peak flow.

360 MILES

3 POSITION CHECK
Aircraft in oceanic airspace are out of radar contact for about four hours. Position reports are made by radio at every 10 degrees of longitude, and the information is used to update displays at the oceanic control centers.

Aircraft crossing the main traffic flow (for example, Madrid to Los Angeles) are routed above or below the track system.

UNITED KINGDOM
Prestwick

SHANWICK OCEANIC
CONTROL AREA

ICELAND

Shannon

IRELAND

NVELOPE
t keep minimum
m one another
system, while
constant altitude

GREENLAND

WESTBOUND (DAY)

EASTBOUND (NIGHT)

30°W

GANDER OCEANIC
CONTROL AREA

EAST INTO THE NIGHT
As a result of passenger demand, time zone differences, and airport noise restrictions, North Atlantic air traffic has two peak flows: eastbound, leaving North America in the evening, and westbound, leaving Europe in the morning. Every 12 hours a new track system is prepared, to allow as many aircraft as possible to follow the most economical flight paths. Because of changing weather conditions, the track positions are rarely identical.

A B C D E
T U V W X

CANADA

Gander

NEWFOUNDLAND

JET STREAM

NORTH ATLANTIC OCEAN

Graphics by
JOHN GRIMWADE

233

Following spread and page 212

Typographic Maps

This series of posters developed by Axis Maps accurately depicts the streets and highways, parks, neighbourhoods, coastlines and physical features of several major cities in the US, using nothing but typographic characters. They omit all the pictorial elements maps usually consist of. The full picture of the city emerges only by weaving together thousands upon thousands of carefully placed words. Every single character was manually placed, making the design of each map an extremely time-consuming process. The city is transformed into a complex series of interwoven letters and words.

CHICAGO

DOWNTOWN, INCLUDING THE NEIGHBORHOODS OF
CABRINI GREEN · CHINATOWN · DEARBORN PARK · EAST PILSEN · FULTON RIVER DISTRICT · GOLD COAST · GOOSE ISLAND · GREEKTOWN · LINCOLN PARK · THE LOOP · NEAR EAST SIDE · NEAR NORTH · NEAR WEST SIDE · NOBLE SQUARE · OLD TOWN · OLD TOWN TRIANGLE · PILSEN · PRINTER'S ROW · RANCH TRIANGLE · RIVER NORTH · RIVER WEST · SHEFFIELD NEIGHBORS · SOUTH LOOP · STREETERVILLE · UNIVERSITY VILLAGE / LITTLE ITALY · WEST LOOP GATE · WEST TOWN

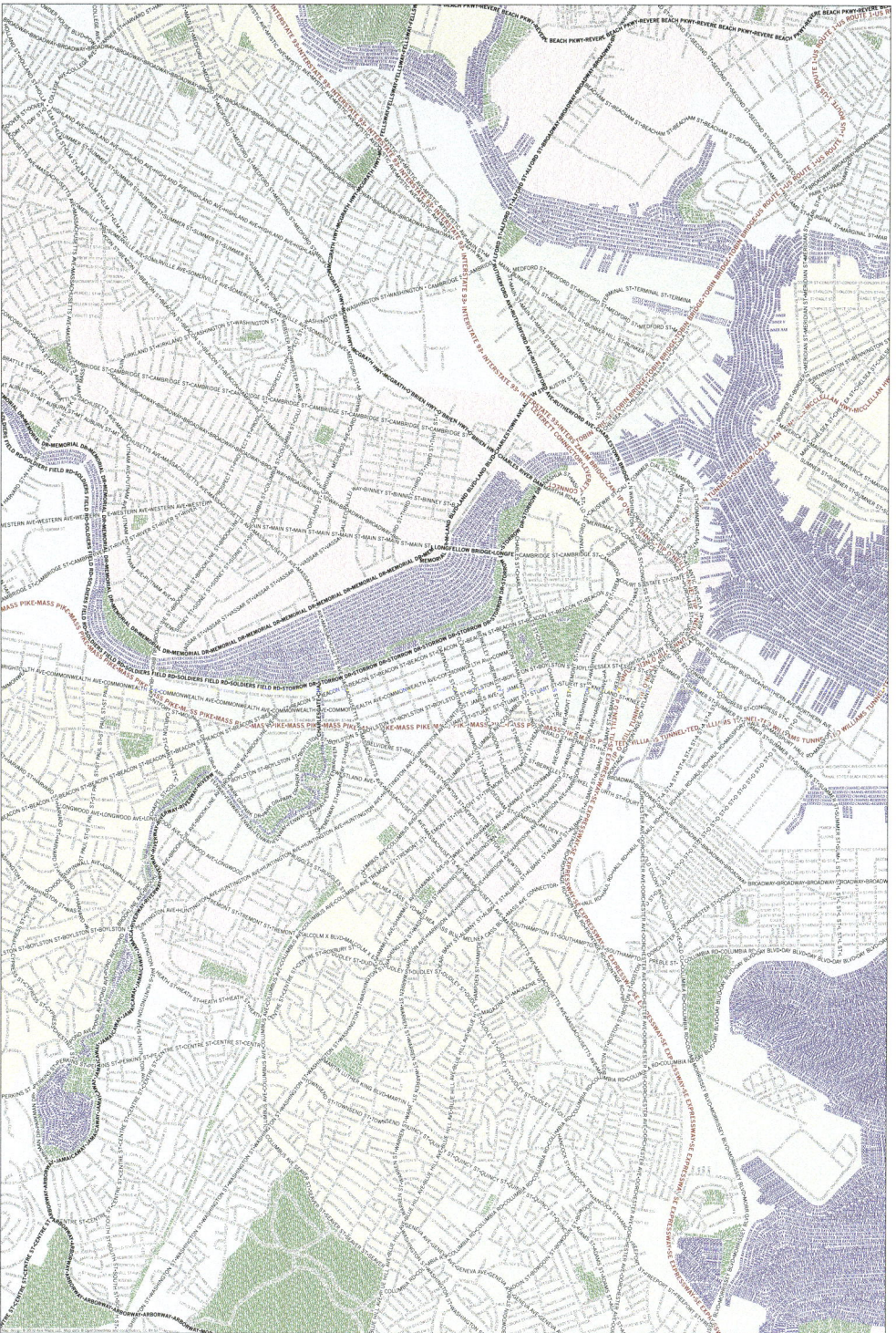

BOSTON

THE CITY CENTER, INCLUDING THE NEIGHBORHOODS OF
ALLSTON • BACK BAY • BAY VILLAGE • BEACON HILL • CHARLESTOWN • CHINATOWN • DORCHESTER • DOWNTOWN • EAST BOSTON • FENWAY-KENMORE • JAMAICA PLAIN • LEATHER DISTRICT • MISSION HILL • NORTH END • ROXBURY • SOUTH BOSTON • SOUTH END • WEST END
AND PARTS OF BROOKLINE • CAMBRIDGE • CHELSEA • EVERETT • MEDFORD • SOMERVILLE

Project Info: Series of posters, 2010, USA
Data Source: OpenStreetMap
Design: Andy Woodruff, Ben Sheesley,
Mark Harrower (Axis Maps)

VAR500 Map (2005)

VAR500 is a ranking of the 500 highest-valued technology companies in the US and Canada, started by *VAR Business* magazine. In the manner of a classical thematic map, this graphic shows the geographical distribution of the top businesses across North America. The height of each building indicates the value of each company. Placing the map on the globe with the sunlight casting long shadows adds a dramatic visual effect – the graphic doesn't even really look like a map in the first place.

Project Info: *VAR Business*, magazine article, 2005, USA
Design: Bryan Christie
Art Direction: Scott Gormley

Voting Patterns in the Eurovision Song Contest

The Eurovision Song Contest is an international competition held annually in Europe. Each country presents one song. The winner is determined through a voting system in which every country rates the other participants, while they are not allowed to rate themselves. Following the rumour that Eastern European countries were only voting for each other, this graphic looks into the voting patterns.

The circular diagram visualises all connections between countries. Eastern Europe is shown in blue, Western Europe is marked orange. Line thickness indicates exactly how many points were granted. And it shows: Eastern European countries mostly voted for each other, but so did the Western countries. The online interactive version allowed people to look up the voting separately for each country.

Vem röstade på vem?

Orange för västländer
Blått för östländer

Strecken visar poängen landet gav
Ju tjockare streck – desto högre poäng
Sverige gav ●━━━━ 12 poäng till Finland
                  10 poäng
Tunnaste strecken:
Övriga poäng: 1, 2, 3, 4, 5, 6, 8

Alla länder

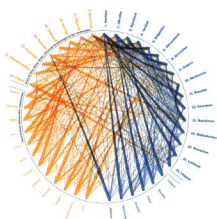

Västländernas röstning

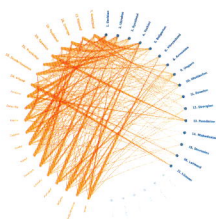

Östländernas röstning

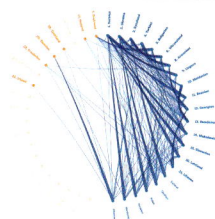

Vem röstade på vem av östländerna...

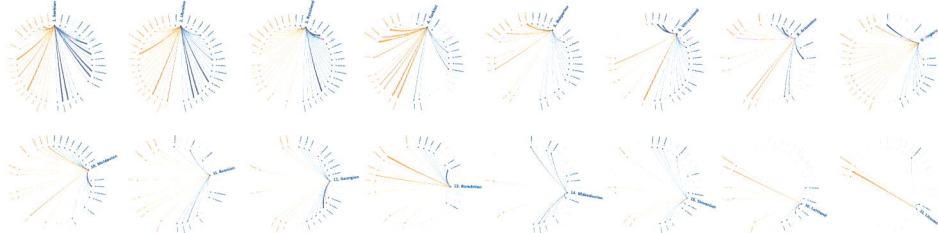

Vem röstade på vem av västländerna...

Project Info: *Svenska Dagbladet*,
interactive visualisation, 2008, Sweden
Data Source: Eurovision Song Contest
Design: Thomas Molén
Awards: Malofiej 2009

In Case of Emergency, Pray

Most US cities are ill-equipped to handle a mass evacuation.

Atlas

SEATTLE

PORTLAND

SAN FRANCISCO

SACRAMENTO

SAN DIEGO

LOS ANGELES

LAS VEGAS

PHOENIX

DENVER

AUSTIN

SAN ANTONIO

DALLAS

The lesson of New Orleans is clear: When disaster strikes, you're on your own. If the Big One shakes St. Louis or a dirty bomb blows up in Atlanta, residents and tourists alike will have to get themselves out of Dodge as best they can. Not that it'll be easy. Geographic barriers restrict some evacuation routes, and many highway systems aren't equipped to handle a major load. A new report from the American Highway Users Alliance evaluated the emergency exit capacity of 37 major US cities, half of which got a failing grade. Here's a look at the best—and worst—places to flee when the sirens begin to wail. —PATRICK DI JUSTO

LOS ANGELES

Almost all Angelenos have cars, and they're going to use them. The problem? They won't get anywhere. Imagine the worst SoCal rush hour—but with drivers fueled by Red Bull and panic.

Above and following spreads

Wired Start Atlases

The well-known American technology magazine *Wired* has created an established format with its "Start" atlases. At the beginning of each issue, a double spread tackles current topics in a thematic map. The design varies in each case and is aligned with the problem the map discusses. The maps in this selection were created by Carl De Torres between 2007 and 2008.

OR CATASTROPHE IN A MASS EVACUATION OF CITY RESIDENTS   LOW ● ● ● ● ● HIGH

MINNEAPOLIS MILWAUKEE DETROIT PHILADELPHIA
INDIANAPOLIS CLEVELAND BALTIMORE
CINCINNATI
COLUMBUS

PITTSBURGH BOSTON
WASHINGTON, DC NEW YORK CITY
ATLANTA ORLANDO
CHICAGO PROVIDENCE
MEMPHIS TAMPA
NEW ORLEANS VIRGINIA BEACH
MIAMI

AS CITY rbecue capital ccountry is likely to have soothest ation, thanks ent traffic flow, ous highways, a absence of natural barriers.

MIAMI With water on two sides and the Everglades on a third, a swamp boat might be the best way out. Come disaster time, cars will get stuck in the automotive quicksand that is I-95.

NEW YORK CITY The area's superb mass transit means most people here don't own cars. In an emergency, your best option will probably be a sturdy pair of sneakers (unless you have a helicopter waiting on your roof).

02|2007 0 3 7

Project Info: *Wired*, magazine article, 2007–2008, USA
Data Source: American Highway Users Alliance; International Communication Union; Bruce G. Charlton (New Castle University); *Medical Hypoteses*; US Department of Transportation
Design: Carl De Torres
Creative Direction: Scott Dadich
Design Director: Wyatt Mitchell

Access Denied

Broadband service is available worldwide, but it's beyond most people's budgets.

United States

■ $0.49/100 Kbps

The nearly 60 million broadband subscribers in the US typically pay 0.01 percent of their average monthly salary for a connection.

Nicaragua

■ $14.65/100 Kbps

No wonder this Central American country has only 6,600 high-speed customers—access costs a fifth of the average monthly paycheck.

Bolivia

■ $39.06/100 Kbps

There are only about 11,000 broadband customers here, but each forks over nearly half of the average monthly wage to get online.

Handing out $100 laptops to kids in rural African villages is great, but it won't bridge the digital divide. That's because it's so hard to find reasonably priced, high-speed Web access. Only about 3 percent of the world's population has broadband, and prices vary wildly. In Japan, DSL or cable averages 6 cents per 100 Kbps, with users typically paying 0.002 percent of their monthly salary for high-speed access. But in Kenya, that same hookup speed costs $86.11—nearly twice the average monthly income. Here's a look at where you can—and cannot—expect to find new *World of Warcraft* buddies. —FRANK BURES

Kazakhstan

$52.68/100 Kbps

The broadband prices, it's niiice? Not so much. The 2,000 Kazakhstani users must sacrifice one-fifth of the average monthly salary for access.

Netherlands

$0.14/100 Kbps

Tiptoe through the tulips and you'll find 4.1 million broadband customers enjoying some of the lowest prices on the planet.

Russia

$28.13/100 Kbps

The 1.6 million users who may want to stream President Putin's latest judo moves surrender 8 percent of the average pay for the privilege.

Price per 100 Kbps of broadband access

$0-$0.32	
$0.33-$0.66	
$0.67-$0.99	
$1-$9.99	
$10-$49.99	
$50-$99.99	
$100-$499.99	
$500+	
N/A	

South Korea

$0.08/100 Kbps

South Korea boasts 12.2 million broadband users, some of the world's highest speeds, and low prices, second only to Japan.

Pakistan

$106.98/100 Kbps

Local bloggers incensed over President Pervez Musharraf's support of the US must pay nearly twice the average income to have their say.

Mozambique

$361.83/100 Kbps

The nation's civil war is long over, but a high-speed connection costs as much as a private army: 1,400 times the average monthly wage.

Saudi Arabia

$571.82/100 Kbps

Expect to shell out 58 percent of the average monthly salary for DSL. Not surprisingly, only about 0.1 percent of the population has a connection.

Atlas

Are We Airborne Yet?

Airport delays are getting worse. Don't forget to pack your patience.

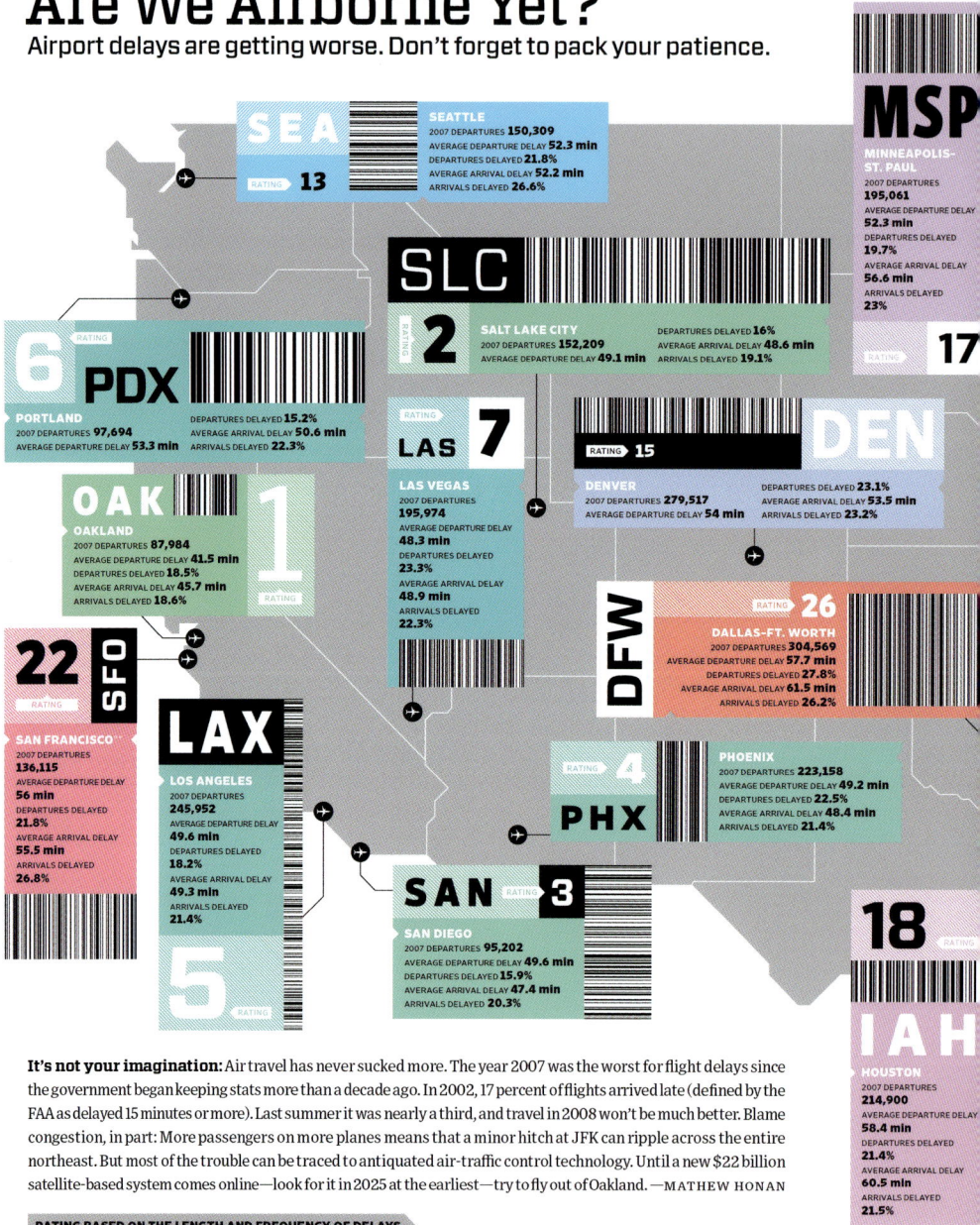

SEA
RATING 13
SEATTLE
2007 DEPARTURES **150,309**
AVERAGE DEPARTURE DELAY **52.3 min**
DEPARTURES DELAYED **21.8%**
AVERAGE ARRIVAL DELAY **52.2 min**
ARRIVALS DELAYED **26.6%**

MSP
MINNEAPOLIS–ST. PAUL
2007 DEPARTURES
195,061
AVERAGE DEPARTURE DELAY
52.3 min
DEPARTURES DELAYED
19.7%
AVERAGE ARRIVAL DELAY
56.6 min
ARRIVALS DELAYED
23%
RATING **17**

SLC
RATING **2**
SALT LAKE CITY
2007 DEPARTURES **152,209**
AVERAGE DEPARTURE DELAY **49.1 min**
DEPARTURES DELAYED **16%**
AVERAGE ARRIVAL DELAY **48.6 min**
ARRIVALS DELAYED **19.1%**

6 RATING
PDX
PORTLAND
2007 DEPARTURES **97,694**
AVERAGE DEPARTURE DELAY **53.3 min**
DEPARTURES DELAYED **15.2%**
AVERAGE ARRIVAL DELAY **50.6 min**
ARRIVALS DELAYED **22.3%**

RATING **7**
LAS
LAS VEGAS
2007 DEPARTURES
195,974
AVERAGE DEPARTURE DELAY
48.3 min
DEPARTURES DELAYED
23.3%
AVERAGE ARRIVAL DELAY
48.9 min
ARRIVALS DELAYED
22.3%

RATING **15**
DEN
DENVER
2007 DEPARTURES **279,517**
AVERAGE DEPARTURE DELAY **54 min**
DEPARTURES DELAYED **23.1%**
AVERAGE ARRIVAL DELAY **53.5 min**
ARRIVALS DELAYED **23.2%**

OAK
1 RATING
OAKLAND
2007 DEPARTURES **87,984**
AVERAGE DEPARTURE DELAY **41.5 min**
DEPARTURES DELAYED **18.5%**
AVERAGE ARRIVAL DELAY **45.7 min**
ARRIVALS DELAYED **18.6%**

22 SFO
RATING
SAN FRANCISCO
2007 DEPARTURES
136,115
AVERAGE DEPARTURE DELAY
56 min
DEPARTURES DELAYED
21.8%
AVERAGE ARRIVAL DELAY
55.5 min
ARRIVALS DELAYED
26.8%

LAX
LOS ANGELES
2007 DEPARTURES
245,952
AVERAGE DEPARTURE DELAY
49.6 min
DEPARTURES DELAYED
18.2%
AVERAGE ARRIVAL DELAY
49.3 min
ARRIVALS DELAYED
21.4%
RATING **5**

DFW
RATING **26**
DALLAS–FT. WORTH
2007 DEPARTURES **304,569**
AVERAGE DEPARTURE DELAY **57.7 min**
DEPARTURES DELAYED **27.8%**
AVERAGE ARRIVAL DELAY **61.5 min**
ARRIVALS DELAYED **26.2%**

RATING **4**
PHX
PHOENIX
2007 DEPARTURES **223,158**
AVERAGE DEPARTURE DELAY **49.2 min**
DEPARTURES DELAYED **22.5%**
AVERAGE ARRIVAL DELAY **48.4 min**
ARRIVALS DELAYED **21.4%**

SAN RATING **3**
SAN DIEGO
2007 DEPARTURES **95,202**
AVERAGE DEPARTURE DELAY **49.6 min**
DEPARTURES DELAYED **15.9%**
AVERAGE ARRIVAL DELAY **47.4 min**
ARRIVALS DELAYED **20.3%**

18 RATING
IAH
HOUSTON
2007 DEPARTURES
214,900
AVERAGE DEPARTURE DELAY
58.4 min
DEPARTURES DELAYED
21.4%
AVERAGE ARRIVAL DELAY
60.5 min
ARRIVALS DELAYED
21.5%

It's not your imagination: Air travel has never sucked more. The year 2007 was the worst for flight delays since the government began keeping stats more than a decade ago. In 2002, 17 percent of flights arrived late (defined by the FAA as delayed 15 minutes or more). Last summer it was nearly a third, and travel in 2008 won't be much better. Blame congestion, in part: More passengers on more planes means that a minor hitch at JFK can ripple across the entire northeast. But most of the trouble can be traced to antiquated air-traffic control technology. Until a new $22 billion satellite-based system comes online—look for it in 2025 at the earliest—try to fly out of Oakland. —MATHEW HONAN

RATING BASED ON THE LENGTH AND FREQUENCY OF DELAYS
1 2 3 4 5 6 7 8 9 10 11 12 13 14 15 16 17 18 19 20 21 22 23 24 25 26 27 28 29 30 31 32
BEST
WORST

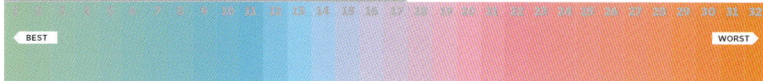

SOURCE: US DEPARTMENT

MDW RATING **9**

CHICAGO¹
2007 DEPARTURES **103,977**
AVERAGE DEPARTURE DELAY **51.8 min**
DEPARTURES DELAYED **26.2%**
AVERAGE ARRIVAL DELAY **52.4 min**
ARRIVALS DELAYED **20.7%**

ORD **31** RATING

CHICAGO
2007 DEPARTURES **404,828**
AVERAGE DEPARTURE DELAY **62.8 min**
DEPARTURES DELAYED **29.9%**
AVERAGE ARRIVAL DELAY **70.9 min**
ARRIVALS DELAYED **30.4%**

RATING **12**

STL

ST. LOUIS
2007 DEPARTURES **114,399**
AVERAGE DEPARTURE DELAY **55.3 min**
DEPARTURES DELAYED **21.3%**
AVERAGE ARRIVAL DELAY **52.8 min**
ARRIVALS DELAYED **24%**

CLT **16** RATING

CHARLOTTE
2007 DEPARTURES **216,190**
AVERAGE DEPARTURE DELAY **49.6 min**
DEPARTURES DELAYED **31%**
AVERAGE ARRIVAL DELAY **47.6 min**
ARRIVALS DELAYED **30.9%**

ATL
22 RATING

ATLANTA¹¹
2007 DEPARTURES **438,999**
AVERAGE DEPARTURE DELAY **53.1 min**
DEPARTURES DELAYED **26.6%**
AVERAGE ARRIVAL DELAY **57.9 min**
ARRIVALS DELAYED **22.5%**

MCO **14**

ORLANDO
2007 DEPARTURES **153,504**
AVERAGE DEPARTURE DELAY **56.8 min**
DEPARTURES DELAYED **22.1%**
AVERAGE ARRIVAL DELAY **54.3 min**
ARRIVALS DELAYED **24.4%**

TPA RATING **9**

TAMPA¹
2007 DEPARTURES **98,644**
AVERAGE DEPARTURE DELAY **56.9 min**
DEPARTURES DELAYED **19.4%**
AVERAGE ARRIVAL DELAY **52.8 min**
ARRIVALS DELAYED **24.2%**

DTW RATING **21**

DETROIT
2007 DEPARTURES **210,143**
AVERAGE DEPARTURE DELAY **51.9 min**
DEPARTURES DELAYED **22.1%**
AVERAGE ARRIVAL DELAY **54.9 min**
ARRIVALS DELAYED **24.9%**

BWI RATING **9**

BALTIMORE¹
2007 DEPARTURES **118,600**
AVERAGE DEPARTURE DELAY **52.9 min**
DEPARTURES DELAYED **23%**
AVERAGE ARRIVAL DELAY **53.4 min**
ARRIVALS DELAYED **22.3%**

CVG RATING **8**

CINCINNATI
2007 DEPARTURES **149,850**
AVERAGE DEPARTURE DELAY **50.4 min**
DEPARTURES DELAYED **21.3%**
AVERAGE ARRIVAL DELAY **54.1 min**
ARRIVALS DELAYED **21.7%**

IAD RATING **27**

WASHINGTON DC
2007 DEPARTURES **139,086**
AVERAGE DEPARTURE DELAY **64.4 min**
DEPARTURES DELAYED **23.3%**
AVERAGE ARRIVAL DELAY **60.8 min**
ARRIVALS DELAYED **25.1%**

RATING **29**

PHILADELPHIA
2007 DEPARTURES **208,977**
AVERAGE DEPARTURE DELAY **60.7 min**
DEPARTURES DELAYED **30%**
AVERAGE ARRIVAL DELAY **59.4 min**
ARRIVALS DELAYED **32.4%**

PHL

DCA RATING **19**

WASHINGTON DC
2007 DEPARTURES **130,432**
AVERAGE DEPARTURE DELAY **55.8 min**
DEPARTURES DELAYED **21.7%**
AVERAGE ARRIVAL DELAY **51.3 min**
ARRIVALS DELAYED **27%**

FLL RATING
FORT LAUDERDALE
2007 DEPARTURES **89,003**
AVERAGE DEPARTURE DELAY **58.3 min**
DEPARTURES DELAYED **22.9%**
AVERAGE ARRIVAL DELAY **53.5 min**
ARRIVALS DELAYED **27.7%**
20

MIA **24** RATING
MIAMI
2007 DEPARTURES **81,663**
AVERAGE DEPARTURE DELAY **59.1 min**
DEPARTURES DELAYED **26.3%**
AVERAGE ARRIVAL DELAY **56.1 min**
ARRIVALS DELAYED **28.8%**

BOS RATING **25**

BOSTON
2007 DEPARTURES **167,648**
AVERAGE DEPARTURE DELAY **60.4 min**
DEPARTURES DELAYED **23.3%**
AVERAGE ARRIVAL DELAY **57.4 min**
ARRIVALS DELAYED **29.4%**

LGA

NEW YORK
2007 DEPARTURES **179,687**
AVERAGE DEPARTURE DELAY **60.6 min**
DEPARTURES DELAYED **23%**
AVERAGE ARRIVAL DELAY **58.3 min**
ARRIVALS DELAYED **35.1%**
RATING **28**

JFK RATING **30**

NEW YORK
2007 DEPARTURES **138,947**
AVERAGE DEPARTURE DELAY **62.8 min**
DEPARTURES DELAYED **30.6%**
AVERAGE ARRIVAL DELAY **64 min**
ARRIVALS DELAYED **36.3%**

EWR
32 RATING

NEWARK
2007 DEPARTURES **151,102**
AVERAGE DEPARTURE DELAY **67.3 min**
DEPARTURES DELAYED **29.9%**
AVERAGE ARRIVAL DELAY **72.8 min**
ARRIVALS DELAYED **38.3%**

TRANSPORTATION. ¹TAMPA, CHICAGO MIDWAY, AND BALTIMORE RECEIVED THE SAME RATING. ¹¹SAN FRANCISCO AND ATLANTA RECEIVED THE SAME RATING.

JAN 2008 **0** **6** **5**

221

World of Rivers

This poster by *National Geographic* shows a digital compilation of the world's river channels and basins. It is based on a large geo-referenced dataset, HydroSHEDS, which was developed by the WWF and in turn draws on high-resolution elevation data gathered by NASA from space. With this global hydrological model, rivers and basins can be shown with unparalleled precision and estimates can be made as to how much water flows. Green shades on the map mark major wetlands, while red shades refer to arid areas.

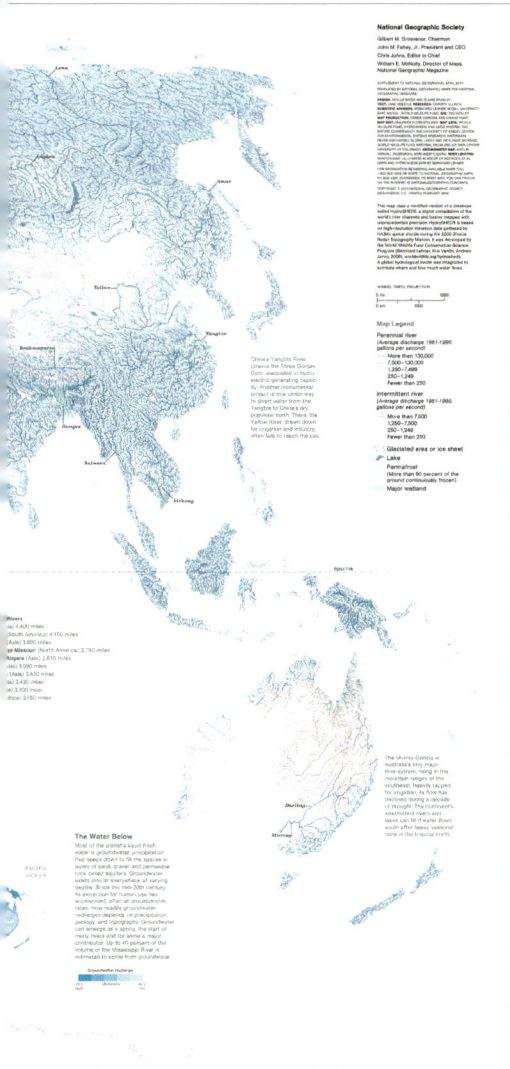

Project Info: *National Geographic*, poster, 2007, USA
Data Source: WWF; USGS; The Nature Conservancy; Center for Environmental Systems Research (University of Kassel); NSIDC; BGR / UNESCO; Shaochuang Liu (Chinese Academy of Sciences), WaterGAP2
Research: William McNulty, Kaitlin Yarnall, Jane Vessels, Christy Ullrich
Design: Mollie Bates, Elaine Bradley
Art Direction: William McNulty, Juan Velasco
Illustration: William McNulty

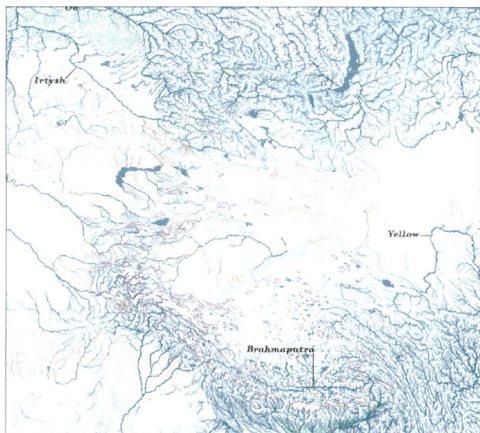

Time

224—343

"One significant difficulty is knowing,
given a set of data, how to glean
meaningful information from it."

Ben Fry

Time
Elements are organised against a timeline

The passage of time creates a fixed sequence. Time offers a simple organisational framework, because everyone knows how events unfold over the course of time. Timelines are the classic guides for the writing of history; they show how things have developed. Also, the arrangement of events in timelines permits one to create one's own version of history (*Andy Warhol – Chelsea Girls*, p.230) or even to predict the future (*The Afghan Conflict*, p.326).

Time series are pivotal tools for scientific or sociological analyses. Specific measurements are collected periodically for complex phenomena such as the weather or stock-market fluctuations. The graphic depiction of measurement series is the most intuitive method of analysis for this kind of data (*CNN.com Traffic Analysis*, p.308). Timelines serve to describe phenomena and make trends visible, but they do not explain their causes.

In Western cultures time is generally envisioned as being linear and moving towards the future. However, in its graphic representation a timeline is not necessarily a straight line; it can also be curved (*Motown's 191 Number One Hits*, p.295) or circular (*Cosmic 140 – Art for Geeks*, p.241).

Works that follow a strict sequence also belong in this chapter. The order of text in a novel is sequential and not randomly reversible, just as a play follows a set dramatic composition. This section also considers the kinds of data analyses that provide a graphic illustration of this type of predefined sequence (*TextArc*, p.320).

Flow charts are a different kind of time-based infographic. They describe the course of processes (*How Books are Made*, p.260), and in informatics they can also show the sequence of operations required to solve a problem. Unlike continuous timelines, flow charts can branch off in time and show sequences with several open outcomes. They can also be used to work through a difficult decision from start to finish (*So You Need a Typeface?*, p.306 and *Guess Who? Character Identification Chart*, p.264).

Visualising processes as a circle has its origins in biology and the life cycle of living organisms (*Swine Flu Life Cycle*, p.315). Lately this concept has also been applied to commercial products, especially in connection with aspects of sustainability. The entire life of a product from manufacture to disposal can be considered as a cycle (*Biofuel*, p.236).

"I do solemnly swear that I will faithfully execute the Office of President of the United States, and will to the best of my Ability, preserve, protect and defend the Constitution of the United States."

Legend

The Growth of the Republic: Population & Economy

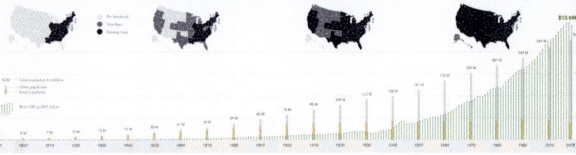

Visual Biographies of the Presidents

Presidential Transitions

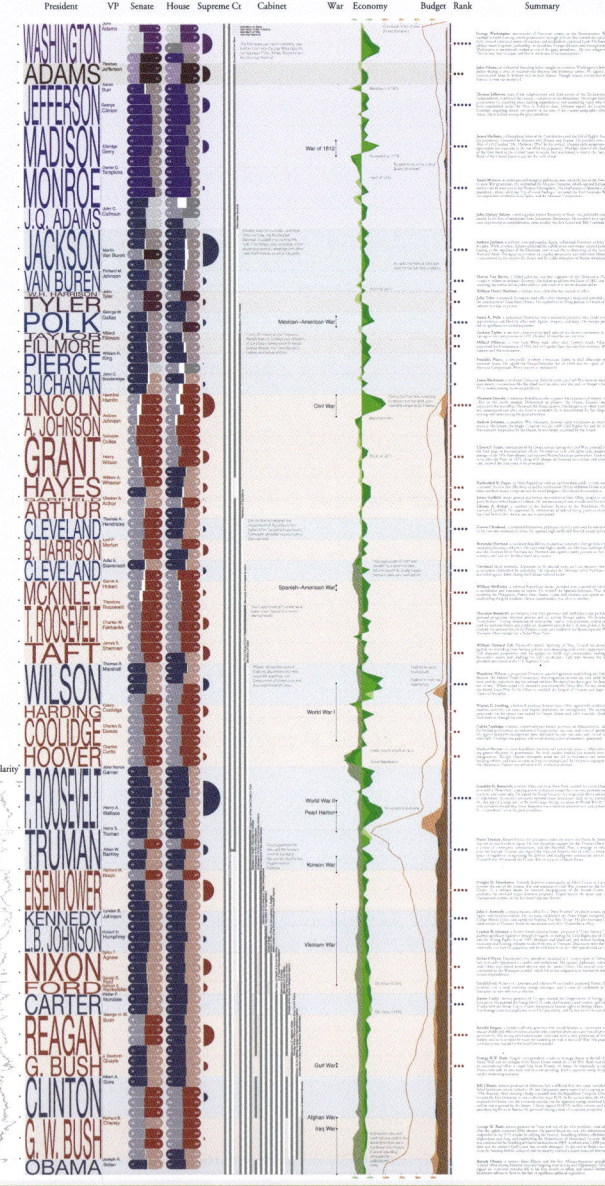

| President | VP | Senate | House | Supreme Ct | Cabinet | War | Economy | Budget | Rank | Summary |

WASHINGTON
ADAMS
JEFFERSON
MADISON
MONROE
J.Q. ADAMS
JACKSON
VAN BUREN
W.H. HARRISON
TYLER
POLK
FILLMORE
PIERCE
BUCHANAN
LINCOLN
A. JOHNSON
GRANT
HAYES
ARTHUR
CLEVELAND
B. HARRISON
CLEVELAND
McKINLEY
T. ROOSEVELT
TAFT
WILSON
HARDING
COOLIDGE
HOOVER
F. ROOSEVELT
TRUMAN
EISENHOWER
KENNEDY
L.B. JOHNSON
NIXON
FORD
CARTER
REAGAN
G. BUSH
CLINTON
G.W. BUSH
OBAMA

Popularity

-1789
-1792
-1796
-1800
-1804
-1808
-1812
-1816
-1820
-1824
-1828
-1832
-1836
-1840
-1844
-1848
-1852
-1856
-1860
-1864
-1868
-1872
-1876
-1880
-1884
-1888
-1892
-1896
-1900
-1904
-1908
-1912
-1916
-1920
-1924
-1928
-1932
-1936
-1940
-1944
-1948
-1952
-1956
-1960
-1964
-1968
-1972
-1976
-1980
-1984
-1988
-1992
-1996
-2000
-2004
-2008

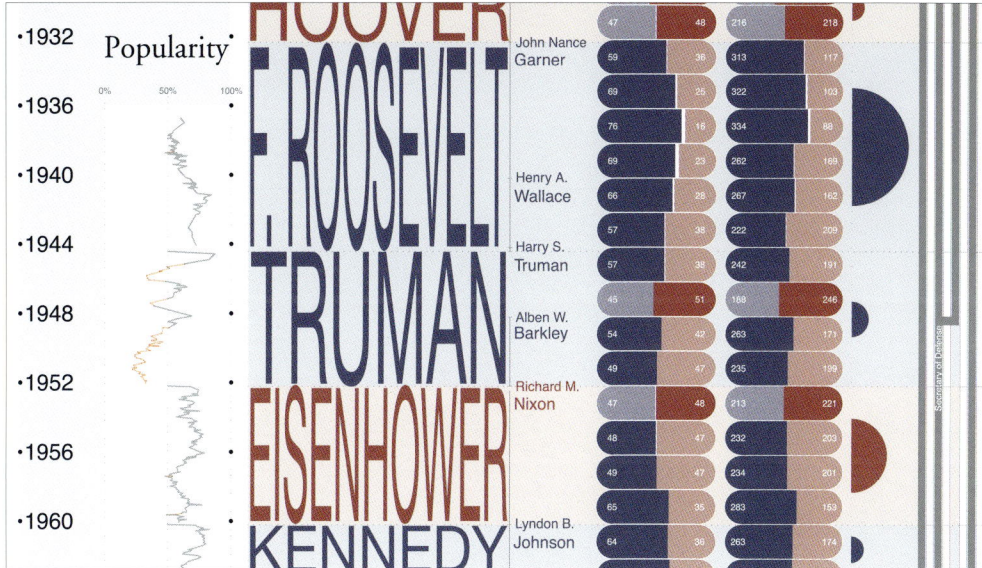

A Visual History of the American Presidency

This timeline covers 219 years of American presidency with a striking level of detail. In the centre, all the presidents since 1789 are named, with colour referring to the political party to which they were affiliated. Scaling indicates how long they were in office. The list is further enriched with data concerning majorities in Senate and Congress, the economy or the federal budget. The Presidential Transitions timeline on the left adds a narrative of larger political trends. The horizontal timeline in the top right gives contexts for how the United States grew over this period, geographically, economically (in terms of GDP) as well as in population numbers. Below, the "visual biographies" show what career experience each president brought to office when they began their term.

Project Info: Poster, 2010, USA
Research: Joe Williams, Eliza Keller, Abram Conrad
Design: Nathaniel Pearlman, Frank Hamilton (Timeplots)

Following spread

A Visual History of the United States Supreme Court

Finding new ways to communicate history: this large-scale time-plot covers the history of the United States Supreme Court over the more than 200 years of its history. The central time series features one line for each judicial seat, with the Chief Justice represented by the top line. The lines float up and down indicating how many justices have been appointed by each political force. Democrats are coded in blue towards the lower end, while Republican influence is coded in red towards the top. The central time-plot includes details of landmark cases, which are explained and classified along the bottom. Along the sides of the graphic, all justices are named along with biographical details as well as the appointing president and his vote results in the Senate.

Project Info: Poster, 2009, USA
Design: Nathaniel Pearlman, Frank Hamilton, Joe Williams (Timeplots).

A VISUAL HISTORY OF THE S

SEAL OF THE SUPREME COURT OF THE UNITED STATES

The Supreme Court of the United States is the final arbiter in the nation in all legal cases and controversies arising under the Constitution or the laws of the United States. The Supreme Court consists of one chief justice and a number of associate justices as set by Congress (currently eight). The president has the power to nominate justices, and their lifetime appointments are made with the advice and consent of the U. S. Senate. The ultimate responsibility of the Supreme Court, as illustrated by the words written above the main entrance to the Supreme Court Building, is "Equal Justice Under the Law."

How To Read This Timeplot

This Timeplot is a visual history of the Supreme Court of the United States from the original six justices in 1789 to the present-day nine-justice Court.

The central "river" represents a timeline of every justice's tenure. Each line is colored according to the party of the appointing president, as are the numbered circles at the start of each justice's tenure. The top line represents the chief justice's seat, and each successive line is an associate justice's tenure.

The "river" flows up and down according to the number of appointees by each party to the Court. In the modern era, the "river" flows up with more justices who are appointed by Republican presidents and down with more appointees of Democratic presidents. History is complicated, however; early presidents are non-partisan, Federalists, Democratic-Republicans and Whigs, and an occasional appointee is a special case: like William Brennan, Jr., a Democrat appointed by Republican President Eisenhower.

Each justice is numbered in successive order in columns on the far left and rig graphic. Here you can find his or her dates of tenure on the Court, years of birth religion, state, the appointing president and the confirmation vote in the Sen notes a chief justice and a ⊕ refers to justices of particular note.

- These symbols on the "river" represent each justice's vote on a landmark solid circle is a vote with the majority, a hollow circle represents a dissent, o circle occurs when a justice does not vote.

Follow the vertical line downward from those circles to the case's citation. Furt mation about each landmark case, including the citation, is in the lower left corn

JUSTICES TO 1900

John Jay (1789–1795)
John Rutledge (1790–1791)
William Cushing (1790–1810)
James Wilson (1789–1798)
John Blair, Jr. (1790–1796)
James Iredell (1790–1799)
Thomas Johnson (1791–1793)
William Paterson (1793–1806)
John Rutledge (1795–1795)
Samuel Chase (1796–1811)
Oliver Ellsworth (1796–1800)
Bushrod Washington (1798–1829)
Alfred Moore (1800–1804)
John Marshall (1801–1835)
William Johnson (1804–1834)
Henry Brockholst Livingston (1807–1823)
Thomas Todd (1807–1826)
Gabriel Duvall (1811–1835)
Joseph Story (1812–1845)
Smith Thompson (1823–1843)
Robert Trimble (1826–1828)
John McLean (1830–1861)
Henry Baldwin (1830–1844)
James Moore Wayne (1835–1867)
Roger Brooke Taney (1836–1864)
Philip Pendleton Barbour (1836–1841)
John Catron (1837–1865)
John McKinley (1838–1852)
Peter Vivian Daniel (1842–1860)
Samuel Nelson (1845–1872)
Levi Woodbury (1845–1851)
Robert Cooper Grier (1846–1870)
Benjamin Robbins Curtis (1851–1857)
John Archibald Campbell (1853–1861)
Nathan Clifford (1858–1881)
Noah Haynes Swayne (1862–1881)
Samuel Freeman Miller (1862–1890)
David Davis (1862–1877)
Stephen Johnson Field (1863–1897)
Salmon Portland Chase (1864–1873)
William Strong (1870–1880)
Joseph P. Bradley (1870–1892)
Ward Hunt (1873–1882)
Morrison Remick Waite (1874–1888)
John Marshall Harlan (1877–1911)
William Burnham Woods (1881–1887)
Stanley Matthews (1881–1889)
Horace Gray (1882–1902)
Samuel Blatchford (1882–1893)
Lucius Quintus Cincinnatus Lamar (1888–1893)
Melville Weston Fuller (1888–1910)
David Josiah Brewer (1891–1910)
Henry Billings Brown (1891–1906)
George Shiras, Jr. (1892–1903)
Howell Edmunds Jackson (1893–1895)
Edward Douglass White (1894–1910)
Rufus Wheeler Peckham (1896–1909)
Joseph McKenna (1898–1925)

President

Washington · J. Adams · Jefferson · Madison · Monroe · J. Q. Adams · Jackson · Van Buren · W. Harrison · Tyler · Polk · Taylor · Fillmore · Pierce · Buchanan · Lincoln · A. Johnson · Grant · Hayes · Garfield · Arthur · Cleveland

Solicitors General

Chief Justice

JAY / RUTLEDGE · ELLSWORTH · MARSHALL · TANEY · CHASE · WAITE

Framing the Republic · Expanding the Republic · Uniting the Republic

More Republican Appointees

More Democratic Appointees

Constitutional Amendments

I – X Bill of Rights (1791)
XI Suits against states (1795)
XII Election of president (1804)
XIII Abolish slavery (1865)
XIV Citizenship guarantees, privileges and immunities, due process and equal...
XV Right to vote unless regard to race (1870)

LANDMARK CASES

Chisholm v. Georgia (4–1)
Hylton v. United States (4–0)
Marbury v. Madison (4–0)
Fletcher v. Peck (3–1)
Martin v. Hunter's Lessee (6–0)
Gibbons v. Ogden (6–0)
McCulloch v. Maryland (7–0)
Slaughter-House Cases (5–4)
Dred Scott v. Sandford (7–2)
Ex parte Milligan (9–0)

...E COURT OF THE UNITED STATES

...tly beneath the "river" show the Court composition by party, ... it changes.

...tices to the Court for lifetime tenures. Above the "river" is a ..., each colored according to his political party. Semicircles are ... for estimating how much influence each president had on the ... of the semicircles reflect the total number of days each president's ... Court; current justices are shown as estimates.

...on is aligned with the modern-day party ...mocratic Party, up for the Republican ... taken with early nineteenth-century

On the graphic between the presidential timeline and the "river" are the solicitors general (sometimes referred to as the "10th justice"). The solicitors general represent the federal government in cases before the Court. For example, Kenneth Starr was solicitor general under President George Herbert Walker Bush.

At its best, the Court guards and interprets the Constitution. Through the Court's history reveals it, like all human institutions, to be imperfect, the Court is justly celebrated when it reflects and expresses the nation's highest ideals.

NOTABLE UNCONFIRMED NOMINATIONS
(chronological)

- 1795 John Rutledge (for chief) (Washington), Rejected (10-14)
- 1811 Alexander Wolcott (Madison), Rejected (9-24)
- 1828 Ebenezer R. Hoar (Grant), Rejected (24-33)
- 1894 William B. Hornblower (Cleveland), Rejected (24-30)
- 1930 John J. Parker (Hoover), Rejected (39-41)
- 1968 Abe Fortas (for chief) (Johnson), Withdrawn
- 1969 Clement F. Haynesworth, Jr. (Nixon), Rejected (45-55)
- 1970 G. Harrold Carswell (Nixon), Rejected (45-51)
- 1987 Robert H. Bork (Reagan), Rejected (42-58)
- 2005 Harriet E. Miers (G. W. Bush), Withdrawn

LONGEST-SERVING JUSTICES
(as of December 1, 2009)

- William Orville Douglas (1939–1975) 13,358 days
- Stephen Johnson Field (1863–1897) 12,614 days
- John Marshall (1801–1835) 12,570 days
- Hugo Lafayette Black (1937–1971) 12,447 days
- John Paul Stevens (1975–present) 12,401 days
- John Marshall Harlan (1877–1911) 12,360 days
- Joseph Story (1812–1845) 12,272 days
- James Moore Wayne (1835–1867) 11,860 days
- John McLean (1830–1861) 11,406 days

CURRENT CIRCUIT COURT ASSIGNMENTS

AFTER 1900 JUSTICES

- Oliver Wendell Holmes, Jr. (1902–1932)
- William Rufus Day (1903–1922)
- William Henry Moody (1906–1910)
- Horace Harmon Lurton (1910–1914)
- Charles Evans Hughes (1910–1916)
- Edward Douglass White (1910–1921)
- Willis Van Devanter (1911–1937)
- Joseph Rucker Lamar (1911–1916)
- Mahlon Pitney (1912–1922)
- James Clark McReynolds (1914–1941)
- Louis Dembitz Brandeis (1916–1939)
- John Hessin Clarke (1916–1922)
- William Howard Taft (1921–1930)
- George Sutherland (1922–1938)
- Pierce Butler (1923–1939)
- Edward Terry Sanford (1923–1930)
- Harlan Fiske Stone (1925–1941)
- Charles Evans Hughes (1930–1941)
- Owen Josephus Roberts (1930–1945)
- Hugo Lafayette Black (1937–1971)
- Benjamin Nathan Cardozo (1932–1938)
- Stanley Forman Reed (1938–1957)
- Felix Frankfurter (1939–1962)
- William Orville Douglas (1939–1975)
- Francis (Frank) William Murphy (1940–1949)
- Harlan Fiske Stone (1941–1946)
- James Francis Byrnes (1941–1942)
- Robert Houghwout Jackson (1941–1954)
- Wiley Blount Rutledge (1943–1949)
- Harold Hitz Burton (1945–1958)
- Fred Moore Vinson (1946–1953)
- Tom Campbell Clark (1949–1967)
- Sherman Minton (1949–1956)
- Earl Warren (1953–1969)
- William Joseph Brennan, Jr. (1956–1990)
- Charles Evans Whittaker (1957–1962)
- Potter Stewart (1958–1981)
- Byron Raymond White (1962–1993)
- Arthur Joseph Goldberg (1962–1965)
- Abe Fortas (1965–1969)
- Thurgood Marshall (1967–1991)
- Warren Earl Burger (1969–1986)
- Harry Andrew Blackmun (1970–1994)
- Lewis Franklin Powell, Jr. (1972–1987)
- William Hubbs Rehnquist (1972–1986)
- John Paul Stevens (1975–present)
- Sandra Day O'Connor (1981–2006)
- William Hubbs Rehnquist (1986–2005)
- Antonin Scalia (1986–present)
- Anthony McLeod Kennedy (1988–present)
- Clarence Thomas (1991–present)
- Ruth Bader Ginsburg (1993–present)
- Stephen G. Breyer (1994–present)
- John G. Roberts, Jr. (2005–present)
- Samuel A. Alito, Jr. (2006–present)
- Sonia Maria Sotomayor (2009–present)

Modernizing the Republic

| WHITE | TAFT | HUGHES | STONE | VINSON | WARREN | BURGER | REHNQUIST | ROBERTS |

Ideology Scores

Conservative — Median — Liberal

Supreme Court cases by topic

- Federalism
- Civil Rights
- Civil Liberties
- Property / Commerce
- Criminal Law

Andy Warhol – Chelsea Girls

Ward Shelley created this timeline about Andy Warhol and his work in film, and in particular about *Chelsea Girls*, with the film's poster making the centrepiece. The film is a collection of 12 scenes of ca. 30 minutes each, showed on a split screen. The yellow panel on the left of the poster lists all scenes in their order. The chart covers the 1960s and includes biographical facts about Warhol as well as some of the people who influenced him. All those involved with *Chelsea Girls* are named in coloured tags. Apart from this particular film nearly all the films produced in the Factory are mentioned, as well as the work of the band Velvet Underground and other related artists.

GOOD REVIEW IN NEWSWEEK
POSITIVE * IN NEW YORK TIMES
CROWDS BEGIN TO COME

1967

CHELSEA GIRLS
GOES UNDERGROUND TO MAINSTREAM

OPENS IN L.A.

LEFT FILM / NO PRESIDENT

WARHOL RETROSPECTIVE IN SWEDEN

CONTINUES TO PRODUCE OBSCURE AND ECCENTRIC PROJECTS — A HIGHLY INFLUENTIAL FIGURE, HE DIES FROM AIDS IN 1989

JACK SMITH
RON TAVEL
MARIO MONTEZ

CONTINUES CAREER IN THEATRE, ARTIST IN RESIDENCE AT YALE + CORNELL

FILMS BEING MADE MIDNIGHT COWBOY USING WARHOL'S 'REJECT' MATERIAL

ANDY SHOT

DIES SEVERAL OF THE NEW SUPERSTARS

FADES AWAY EXCEPT FOR RARE CAMEOS

JONAS MEKAS : STARTS ANTHOLOGY FILM ARCHIVES - - -

HANGS OUT WITH JOHN LENNON AND YOKO

JONAS IS ALIVE + WELL

MARIE MENKEN

MARIE DIES IN 1970, HER LIFE AND WORK BECOME SUBJECT OF DOCUMENTARY IN 2006

NEW SUPERSTARS COME (OLD ONES GO)

50 MORE FILMS

AFTER RECOVERY: ANDY WORKS ON INTERVIEW MAGAZINE + COMMISSIONED CELEBRITY PORTRAITS. HIRES A BUSINESS MANAGER.

PAUL MORRISSEY :

★★★★ (4 STARS) PM STARTS TO

PM IS RESPONSIBLE FOR MOST WARHOL FILMS FROM THIS POSITION.

THE LOVES OF ONDINE

A NOVEL IS PUBLISHED

LONESOME COWBOYS

BLUE MOVIE

SAN DIEGO SURF

DEPARTS MID 70'S TO DO HIS OWN PROJECTS. ALIVE + WELL

TRASH

FLESH

HEAT

ONDINE
ERIC EMERSON
BRIGID BERLIN
GERRARD MALANGA

BB IN ANDY'S FILMS UNTIL 1976. CLOSE FRIENDS, SHE IS "B" IN BOOK "ANDY WARHOL'S PHILOSOPHY, FROM A TO B". ALIVE AND WELL

ONDINE CLEANS UP AND "GETS BORING." WORKS IN POST OFFICE. DIES IN 1983 FROM LIVER DISEASE

INTERNATIONAL VELVET
INGRID SUPERSTAR

CONTINUES IN MORE WAR HOL FILMS AND GLAM ROCK BAND 'MAGIC TRAMPS' OVERDOSES IN 1975, AGE 3)

ACTUALLY MORRISSEY FIRES HIM

END OF SILVER FACTORY

14 MORE WARHOL FILMS. DISAPPEARS IN 1967 - PRESUMED DEAD - BODY NEVER FOUND

FIVE MORE FILMS WITH ANDY. HAS RELATIONSHIP WITH DESIGNER DAVID CROLAND. LEAVES THE FACTORY SOON AFTER. SUSAN BOTTOMLY LIVES IN HAWAII

CO-FOUNDS INTERVIEW MAGAZINE A YEAR LATER GERARD LEAVES WARHOL'S STUDIO TO WORK ON HIS OWN FILM AND POETRY PROJECTS. ALIVE + WELL

MARY WORONOV
ED HOOD
PATRICK FLEMING

ONE MORE FILM

ONE MORE FILM. IN 1978 HE IS STRANGLED BY A HUSTLER WHO COMMITS SUICIDE NEXT DAY

ANGELINA DAVIS
RONA PAGE

ONE MORE FILM

MARY SOON LEAVES WARHOL CIRCLE. ACTS IN B AND CULT MOVIES, E.G. ROCK-N-ROLL HIGH SCHOOL, EATING RAOUL (+10 MORE) EXHIBITS PAINTINGS, WROTE MEMOIR - ALIVE + WELL

FRIEND OF MEKAS WHO IS ABUSED BY ONDINE IN C-G. NO MORE INFO.

ED HOOD (THE MOVIE)

ARI IS OKAY

NICO CONTINUES TO RECORD + PERFORM. REMAINS ADDICTED IS HEROIN FOR 20 YEARS. FOUND NEXT TO HER BICYCLE IN 1988, SHE DIES OF A BRAIN HEMORRHAGE.

KISS THE BOOT

END OF E.P.I.

NICO RECORDS

NICO ALBUM 'CHELSEA GIRL'

POOR RICHARD'S - CHICAGO - BOSTON - MID WEST

VELVET UNDERGROUND EVENTUALLY SPLITS UP

LOU REED

JOHN CALE

BOTH HAVE CELEBRATED SOLO CAREERS

GREAT FILM PRESENCE V. U + NICO

OH FUCK ANDY + NICO

RECORD "WHITE LIGHT WHITE HEAT"

WL, WH RELEASED

GENE RICARD

FILM THE ANDY WARHOL STORY

UNAPPRECIATED

CIAO, MANHATTAN

EDIE GETS DEEPER INTO DRUGS AND DISAPPOINTMENT. SHE MARRIES, OVERDOSES IN 1971, AGE 28

GETS 20 SHOCK TREATMENTS

CHUCK WEIN

LAUNCHES CAREERS OF PAINTERS JULIAN SCHNABEL + JEAN-MICHEL BASQUIAT DIA FOUNDATION PUBLISHES HIS POETRY ALIVE + WELL

Chelsea Girls

1967   1968

Project Info: Painting, 2008, USA
Artist: Ward Shelley
Additional Info: Original size 147 cm x 77 cm; collection of Wendy and Peter Trevisani; Ward Shelley is represented by Pierogi Gallery

Recycling (paper, glass, alumimum, and plastic) is picked up together from your home on the same day in one bin.

1

21,000 tons of recycled material come through here every month (more than any other plant in the country)

Almost everything used to be sorted by hand.

Bob McCrann
Facility Manager

WASTE MANAGEMENT

3

The facility is ir
carrying all the
technology that
paper, glass an

Materials are baled and then sold (newspaper can bring in as much as $150/ton)

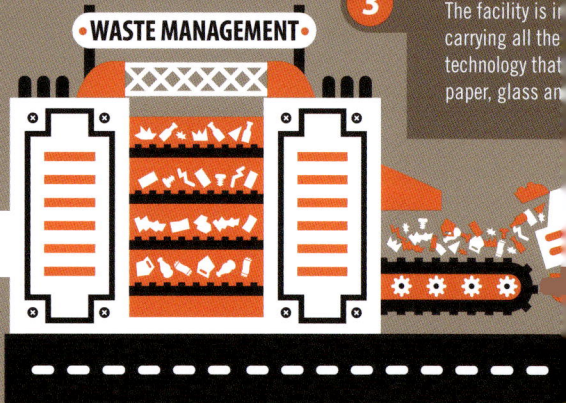

4

5

Bales of materials are sold to mills (paper, plastic, and aluminum mills and glass plants)... Many of these mills are in another country (60-70% of paper goes to China... But India, Mexico, and South America are also big markets)

6

At the mills, various things happen: paper mills turn old paper into pulp so it can be made into NEW paper; plastic mills melt most recycled plastic and turn it back into plastic although it CAN be made into other things like fiber for clothing and carpet; aluminum mills melt aluminum to make new cans; and glass is broken and melted to make new bottles

It is picked up and taken to a facility in Elkridge run by Waste Managvement Recycle America.

2

lled with moving ramps
d a computerized
ate it (by aluminum,

per can be turned around in as little as a
y! Aluminum or plastic can go from the
ridge facility back to a store shelf in about
o months!

Then they are sold to companies that use
them again for their products to be sold
back to consumers!

7

MARKET

OPEN

Baltimore Waste Management

This graphic explains the process of recycling waste using the example of a waste-management facility near Baltimore. Starting with the average household at the top left, the process is presented as single steps on a journey. The household's waste is picked up and delivered to the facility, then sorted and processed further by various companies. Each step is explained in little numbered boxes. As in certain children's illustrations, the picture space is flat, with no perspective.

Project Info: *Baltimore*, magazine article, 2010, USA
Design: Jan Kallwejt

Following spread

Best-Selling Books

Developed for Barcelona-based newspaper *La Vanguardia*, this piece is an unusual cross between a time series and a ranking, showing best-selling fiction books in Catalan between October 2007 and April 2008. Time runs from left to right and covers the period in 26 weekly steps. Within these, the graphic presents a succession of best-seller lists, showing evolutions and developments within the list. Catalan authors are shown with red dots, all others with blue. For certain titles, additional information is provided, like the number of pages (yellow circle attached) or a specially low price (tagged with a black circle). The continued presence of titles on the list is indicated using solid lines, while dotted lines show connections to ranks below the top ten.

Project Info: *La Vanguardia*,
newspaper article, 2008, Spain
Design: Lamosca

233

Los libros más vendidos
(antes de Sant Jordi)

Como contribución a la jornada de hoy, *Cultura/s* ha pedido a Lamosca que mostrara visualmente todas las implicaciones de un ranking de libros más vendidos. El fragmento analizado es el correspondiente a la literatura de ficción en catalán, entre octubre del 2007 y abril del 2008, tal como ha aparecido en este suplemento.

- ● Escritor/a catalán/a
- ● Escritor/a de otra procedencia
- ◉ Primera semana en lista
- ◉ Última semana en lista

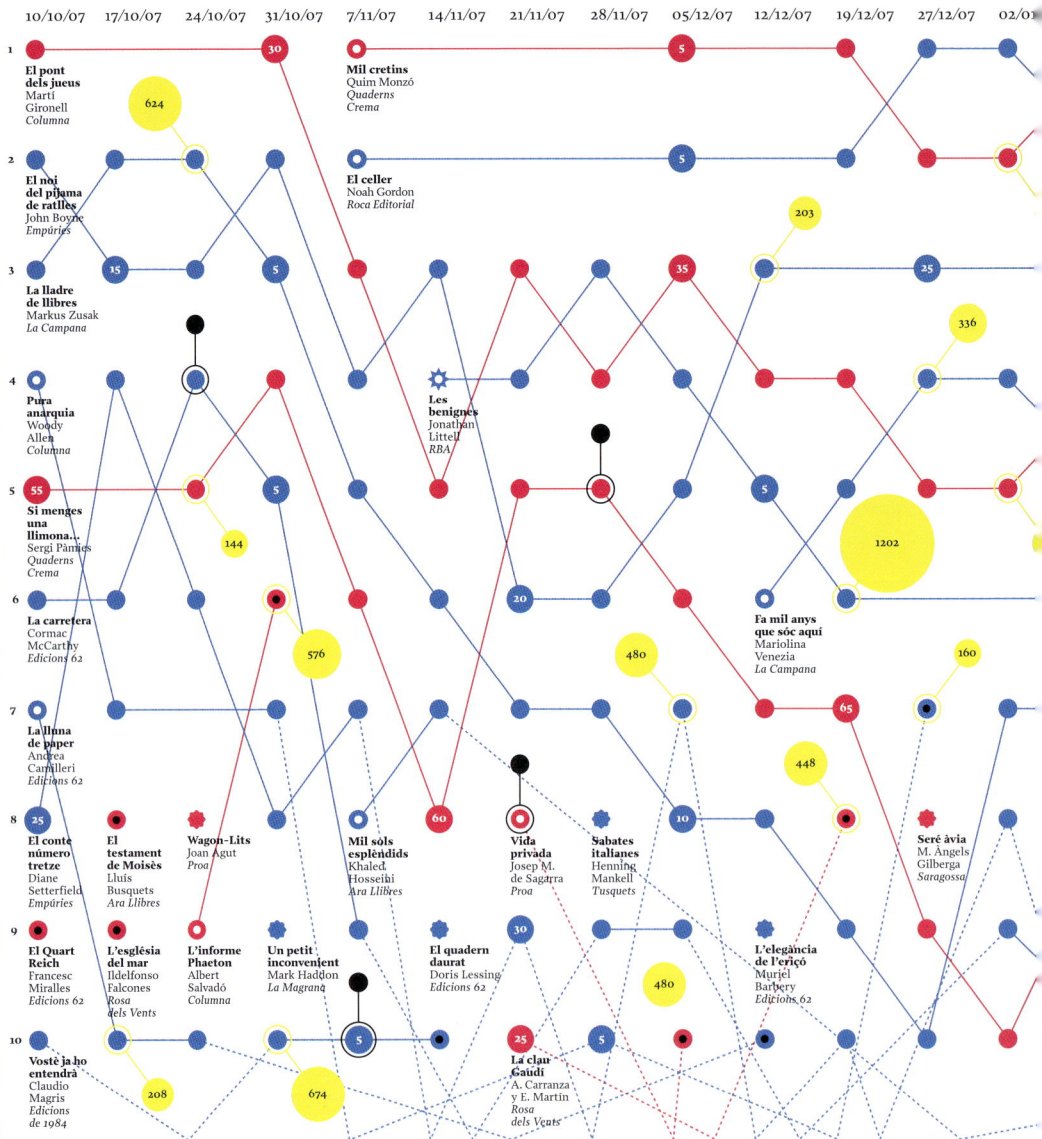

	10/10/07	17/10/07	24/10/07	31/10/07	7/11/07	14/11/07	21/11/07	28/11/07	05/12/07	12/12/07	19/12/07	27/12/07	02/0

1

El pont dels jueus
Martí Gironell
Columna

Mil cretins
Quim Monzó
Quaderns Crema

2

El noi del pijama de ratlles
John Boyne
Empúries

El celler
Noah Gordon
Roca Editorial

3

La lladre de llibres
Markus Zusak
La Campana

4

Pura anarquia
Woody Allen
Columna

Les benignes
Jonathan Littell
RBA

5

Si menges una llimona...
Sergi Pàmies
Quaderns Crema

6

La carretera
Cormac McCarthy
Edicions 62

Fa mil anys que sóc aquí
Mariolina Venezia
La Campana

7

La lluna de paper
Andrea Camilleri
Edicions 62

8

El conte número tretze
Diane Setterfield
Empúries

El testament de Moisès
Lluís Busquets
Ara Llibres

Wagon-Lits
Joan Agut
Proa

Mil sols esplèndids
Khaled Hosseini
Ara Llibres

Vida privada
Josep M. de Sagarra
Proa

Sabates italianes
Henning Mankell
Tusquets

Seré àvia
M. Àngels Gilberga
Saragossa

9

El Quart Reich
Francesc Miralles
Edicions 62

L'església del mar
Ildelfonso Falcones
Rosa dels Vents

L'informe Phaeton
Albert Salvadó
Columna

Un petit inconvenient
Mark Haddon
La Magrana

El quadern daurat
Doris Lessing
Edicions 62

L'elegància de l'eriçó
Muriel Barbery
Edicions 62

10

Vostè ja ho entendrà
Claudio Magris
Edicions de 1984

La clau Gaudí
A. Carranza y E. Martín
Rosa dels Vents

Una sola semana en lista

Portada en *Cultura/s*

Número de páginas

Continúan en lista

Libros que puedes adquirir por menos de 12 euros

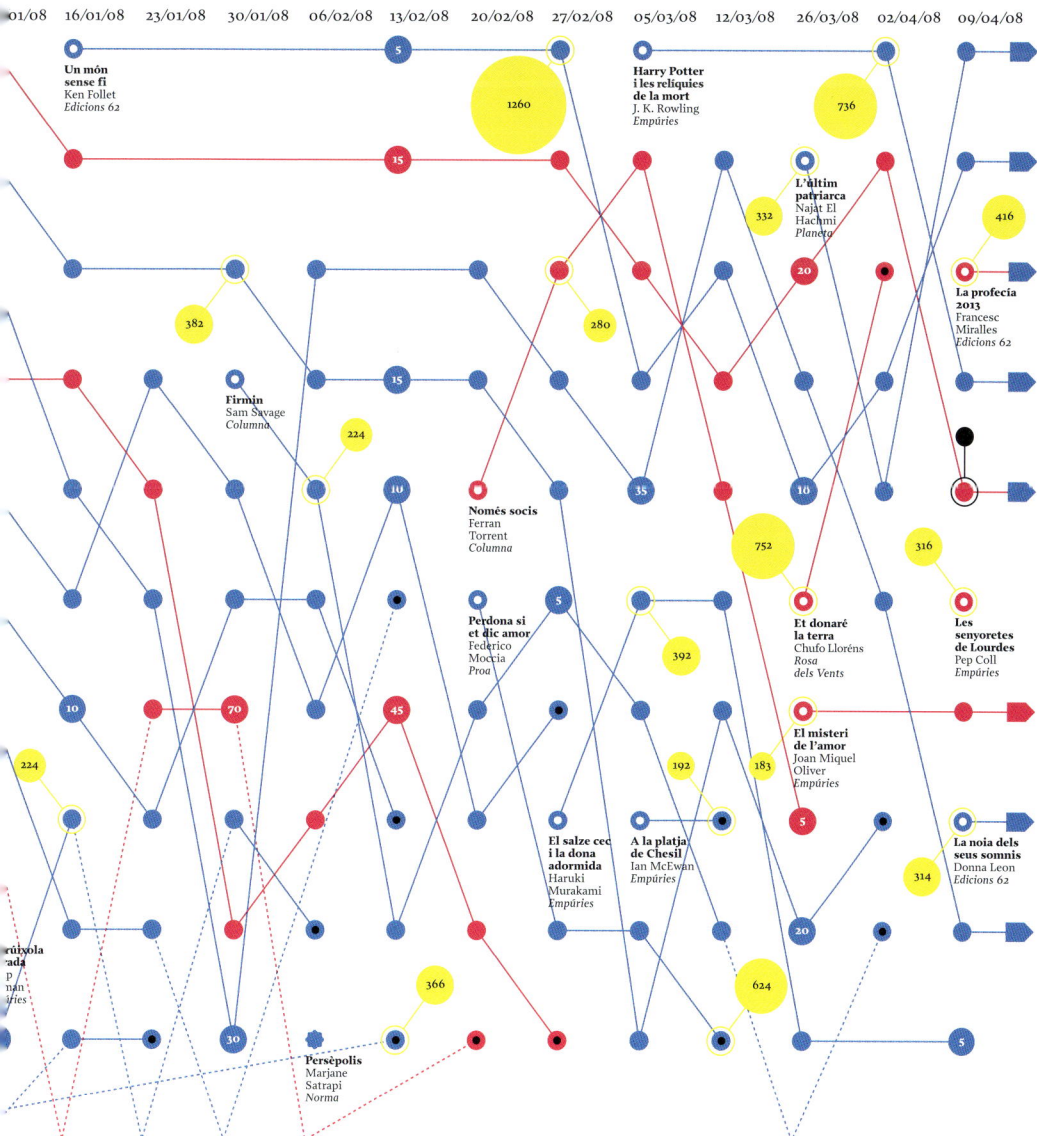

01/08 16/01/08 23/01/08 30/01/08 06/02/08 13/02/08 20/02/08 27/02/08 05/03/08 12/03/08 26/03/08 02/04/08 09/04/08

Un món sense fi
Ken Follet
Edicions 62

5

1260

Harry Potter i les relíquies de la mort
J. K. Rowling
Empúries

736

15

L'últim patriarca
Najat El Hachmi
Planeta

332

20

416

La profecia 2013
Francesc Miralles
Edicions 62

382

280

15

Firmin
Sam Savage
Columna

224

10

35

18

Només socis
Ferran Torrent
Columna

752

316

5

Perdona si et dic amor
Federico Moccia
Proa

Et donaré la terra
Chufo Lloréns
Rosa dels Vents

Les senyoretes de Lourdes
Pep Coll
Empúries

392

10

70

45

224

192

183

El misteri de l'amor
Joan Miquel Oliver
Empúries

5

El salze cec i la dona adormida
Haruki Murakami
Empúries

A la platja de Chesil
Ian McEwan
Empúries

La noia dels seus somnis
Donna Leon
Edicions 62

314

20

ruixola ada
p
nan
ries

30

366

624

5

Persèpolis
Marjane Satrapi
Norma

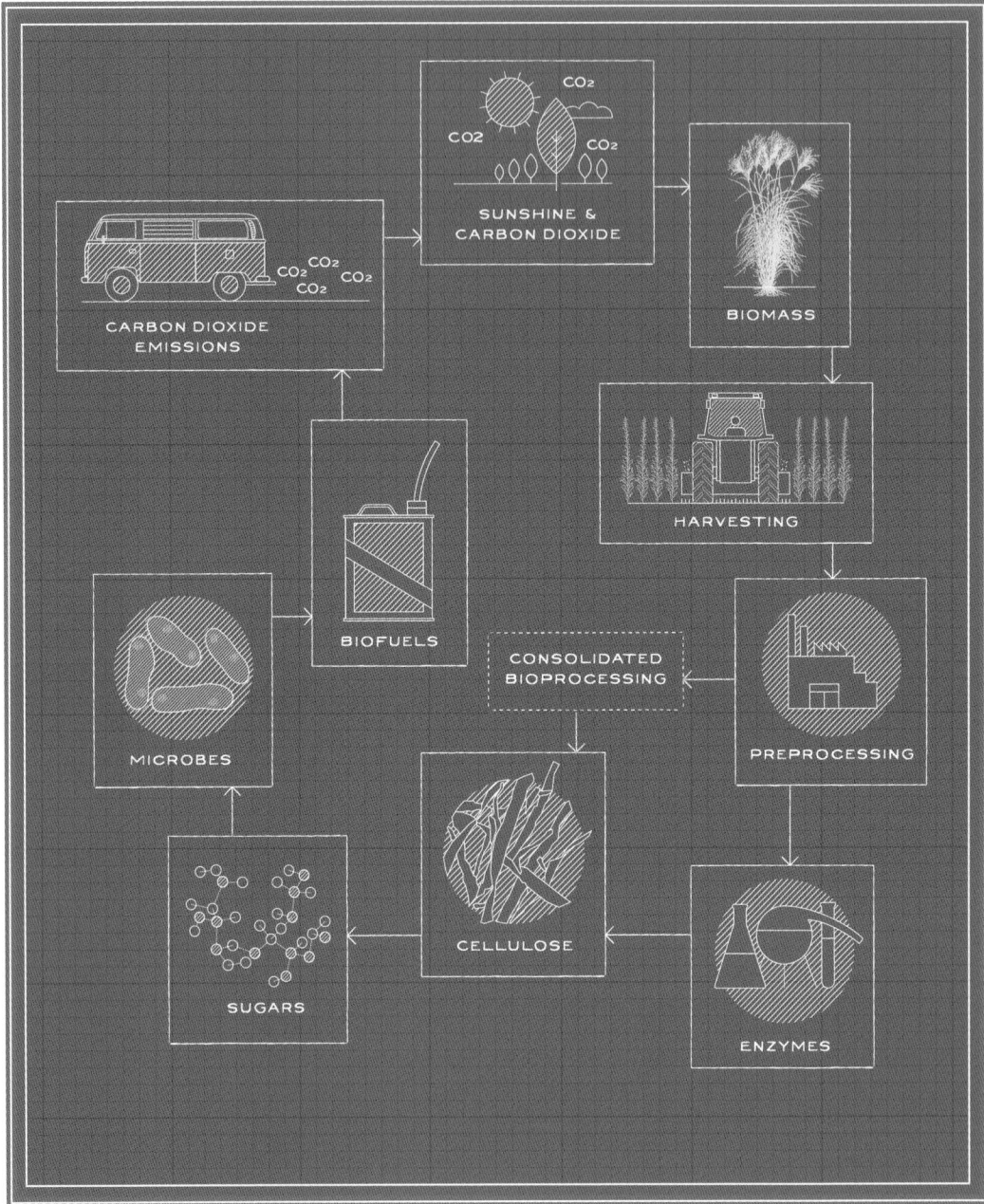

SUNSHINE &
CARBON DIOXIDE

BIOMASS

CARBON DIOXIDE
EMISSIONS

HARVESTING

BIOFUELS

CONSOLIDATED
BIOPROCESSING

PREPROCESSING

MICROBES

CELLULOSE

ENZYMES

SUGARS

Project Info: *Science News*, magazine article,
2009, USA
Design: Michael Newhouse (Newhouse Design)

Biofuel

This process diagram depicts the cycle of production and usage of biofuels. Icons represent each step in the cycle, from the growing and harvesting of plants for the biomass, via the various conversion steps to the canister of biofuel which allows the car to run. The connecting step at the top refers to the carbon balance of biofuels – upon combustion, they release only the amount of CO_2 which had previously been bound by the original plant from the atmosphere. However, the effects and the actual carbon balance are the subject of much discussion, with biofuels being a very recent technology.

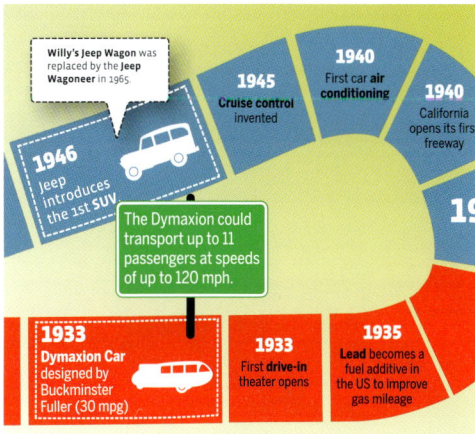

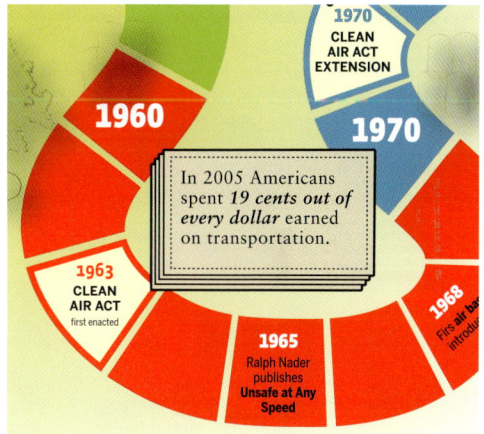

Willy's Jeep Wagon was replaced by the Jeep Wagoneer in 1965.

1946 Jeep introduces the 1st SUV

The Dymaxion could transport up to 11 passengers at speeds of up to 120 mph.

1945 Cruise control invented

1940 First car air conditioning

1940 California opens its first freeway

1933 Dymaxion Car designed by Buckminster Fuller (30 mpg)

1933 First drive-in theater opens

1935 Lead becomes a fuel additive in the US to improve gas mileage

1970 CLEAN AIR ACT EXTENSION

1960

1970

In 2005 Americans spent *19 cents out of every dollar* earned on transportation.

1963 CLEAN AIR ACT first enacted

1965 Ralph Nader publishes **Unsafe at Any Speed**

1968 First air bag introduced

Carland: A Century of Motoring in America

Driving in the United States: this is a history of the automobile in one image. Using the metaphor of a board game, the graphic follows the most important events and milestones in the first 100 years of cars. It shows some of the most prominent car models and the invention of such things as the car radio in 1930. History is thus conceived of as a path through a landscape, a timeline drawn into a fictional map.

Project Info: *GOOD*, magazine article, 2008, USA
Design: Colleen Corcoran, Joseph Prichard
Art Direction: Casey Caplowe

CARLAND

A Century of motoring in America.

START

1908
Ford **Model T** introduced (25 mpg)

1910
Traffic signals introduced

1911
First **Indy 500** race takes place on Memorial Day

= **1 Million barrels** of gasoline used per day in the United States.

Provides funding for states for the construction of two-lane interstate highways.

1920
Travel trailers are introduced as a predecessor to mobile homes

1920

1921
FEDERAL HIGHWAY ACT

1950

1955
James Dean dies in car accident in Los Angeles

1956
FEDERAL-AID HIGHWAY ACT
To ensure troop deployment in an emergency

Originally called a **Cigar Lighter Receptacle**, since it was intended to be used for cigars not cigarettes.

1926
Car **cigarette lighters** introduced

1948
Power windows invented

1948
In-N-Out opens the first drive thru

Willy's **Jeep Wagon** was replaced by the **Jeep Wagoneer** in 1965.

1945
Cruise control invented

1940
First car **air conditioning**

1940
California opens its first freeway

1946
Jeep introduces the 1st SUV

1940

1930

The **Motorola model 5T71**, originally sold for between $110 and $130

The Dymaxion could transport up to 11 passengers at speeds of up to 120 mph.

1930
First car **radio**

1932
First **parking meter**

1933
Dymaxion Car designed by Buckminster Fuller (30 mpg)

1933
First **drive-in** theater opens

1935
Lead becomes a fuel additive in the US to improve gas mileage

Automobile History

1984
MANDATORY SEAT BELT LAW

1984
Sammy Hagar releases **I Can't Drive 55**

1982
Knight Rider premiers on NBC

1981
De Lorean DMC12 is first sold

1980

1990

1990
CLEAN AIR ACT
Amended to reduce air pollution

The Clean Air Act requires the **EPA** to set limits on air pollutants emitted from the tailpipes of new motor vehicles. States with high air pollution must use oxygenated gasoline.

1992
First civilian version of the **Hummer** (15 mpg)

1996
LEADED GASOLINE BANNED

1997
Ford offers **EV1** electric car for lease

1975
Catalytic converter becomes standard to reduce car emissions

1974
Cadillac Ranch opens in Amarillo, TX

1973
Oil Crisis! Lose a turn.

2000

2000
Car **GPS** system patented

The first car phone weighed 90lbs and ran off a car battery.

First environmental law in the US to include a provision for citizen law suits

1956
first **car phone** released in Stockholm

1970
CLEAN AIR ACT EXTENSION

R.I.P.
Super Car

2001
Toyota Prius first sold in the US (55 mpg)

George Bush cancels federal program to design fuel efficent "super car" after **5 years** and more than **1 billion dollars** of federal money spent on research.

1960

1970

In 2005 Americans spent *19 cents out of every dollar* earned on transportation.

2003
Ford cancels all **EV1** leases

1963
CLEAN AIR ACT
first enacted

1968
First **air bag** introduced

1965
Ralph Nader publishes **Unsafe at Any Speed**

2005
Average fuel efficiency of a new car is **17.2 mpg**

2008

Los Angeles Times

FOOTBALL

COLLEGE & NFL PREVIEW

Saturday, September , 2007 , latimes.com/sports

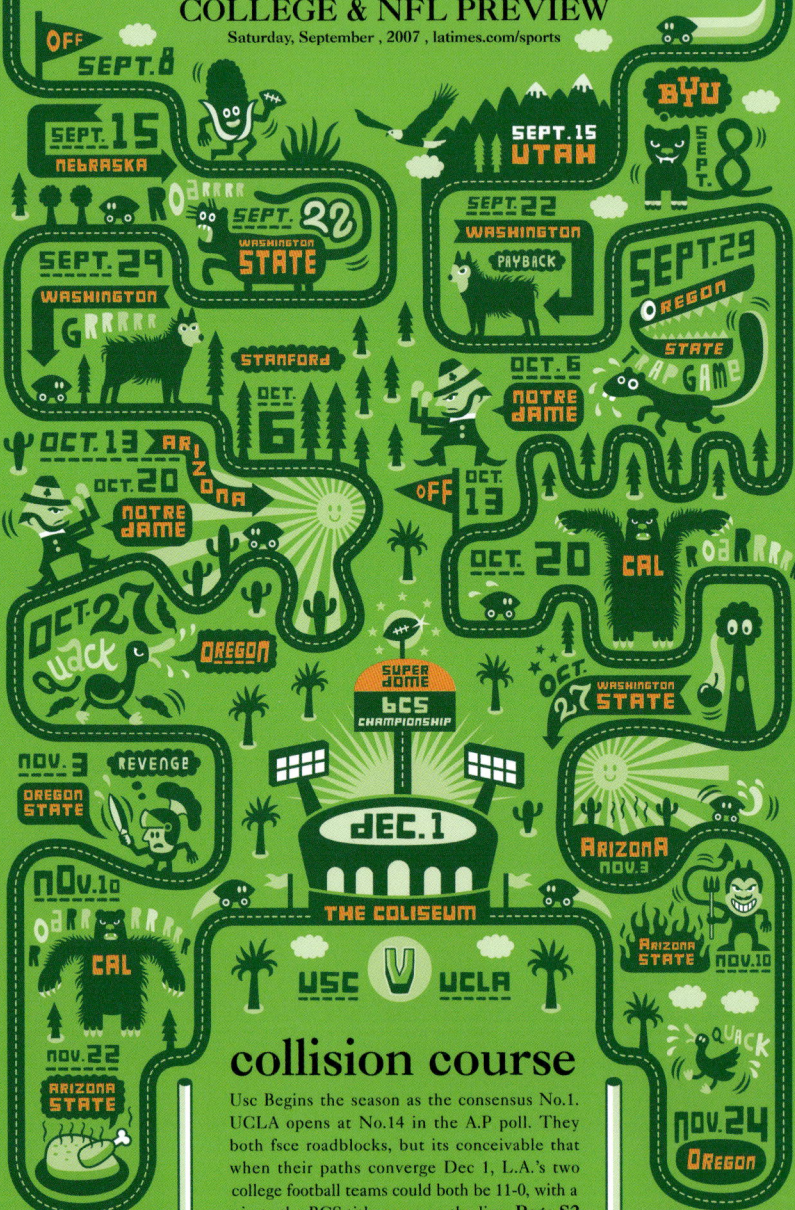

OFF SEPT. 8

SEPT. 15 NEBRASKA

SEPT. 22 WASHINGTON STATE

SEPT. 29 WASHINGTON GRRRRR

STANFORD OCT. 6

OCT. 13 ARIZONA

OCT. 20 NOTRE DAME

OCT. 27 Quack

OREGON

NOV. 3 OREGON STATE

REVENGE

NOV. 10 CAL

NOV. 22 ARIZONA STATE

SEPT. 15 UTAH

BYU SEPT. 8

SEPT. 22 WASHINGTON PAYBACK

SEPT. 29 OREGON STATE TRAP GAME

OCT. 6 NOTRE DAME

OFF OCT. 13

OCT. 20 CAL ROARRRR

OCT. 27 WASHINGTON STATE

SUPER DOME bCS CHAMPIONSHIP

DEC. 1

THE COLISEUM

ARIZONA NOV. 3

ARIZONA STATE NOV. 10

QUACK

NOV. 24 OREGON

USC V UCLA

collision course

Usc Begins the season as the consensus No.1. UCLA opens at No.14 in the A.P poll. They both fsce roadblocks, but its conceivable that when their paths converge Dec 1, L.A.'s two college football teams could both be 11-0, with a trip to the BCS title game on the line. **Page S2**

NFL PREVIEW INSIDE SEE PAGES 15-21

MORE COLLEGE FOOTBALL INSIDE SEE PAGES 2-14

Collision Course

The road to the future – this cover image sketches the course of the 2007 College Football Season for the two L.A. teams, USC Trojans and UCLA Bruins. Along the road, matches are lined up with dates and team names. Teams are represented by their animal mascots (e.g. BYU Cougars, Washington Huskies). Others are shown by symbols (sunshine for Arizona) or a football-playing corn cob for Nebraska. The team of the Catholic University of Notre Dame, Indiana is represented by an enraged little Irish mascot. Both roads end at the final game in the lower centre. The design is based solely on fixtures, but the visual arrangement plays with the notion that the two L.A. teams might be successful enough to be playing each other for the championship.

Project Info: Football College and NFL preview, *The Los Angeles Times*, newspaper article, 2007, USA
Design: Serge Seidlitz
Art Direction: Derek Simmons

Project Info: Poster, 2010, Japan / Switzerland
Data Source: Information Architects' Web Trend Engine; Max Planck Institute for Software Systems; Twitter Research Team
Research: Chris Luescher
Design: Oliver Reichenstein, Takeshi Tanka (Information Architects)
Additional Info: Original size A0

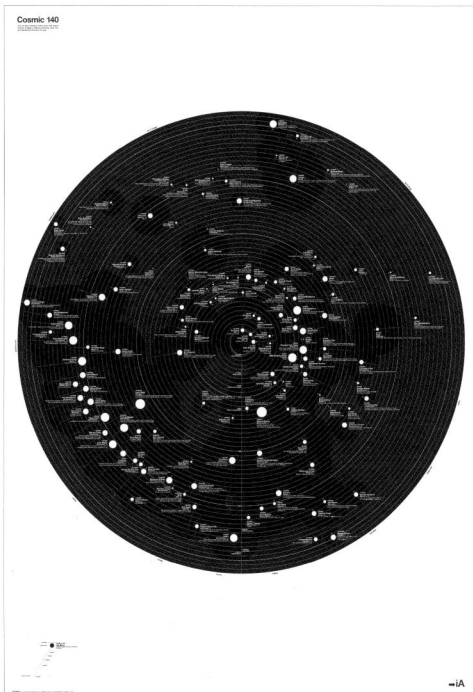

Cosmic 140

Cosmic 140 – Art for Geeks

Using the layout of star charts, this piece plots the 140 most influential Twitter users. Time runs from the centre outwards, with topics denominated around the outside, like directions on a map. Each of the selected users is marked with a dot, their distance from the centre indicating the time they began tweeting. Along with name and user name, the average number of daily tweets and the text of the first tweet are given. Black circles around each user indicate the number of their followers, while the full circle represents the total number of Twitter users. The piece thus locates the top Twitter users according to time and category (topics) and demonstrates their hierarchy by circle sizes.

88 | 11/4/2007
Jason Sweeney
@sween | 4.5
Lying on my side, spooning a cat, hoping Noel doe...

7/24/2008
Deepak Chopra
@DeepakChopra | 13 | 62
In Washington DC

135
3/3/2008
Paul Carr
@paulcarr | 13
Liveblogging (alljustwords.com) from GSP having just
signed up to Twitter against my better judgement.

7/11/2007
Marco Marcello Lupoi
@mlupoi | 2.9
Watching UN POSTO AL SOLE
episodes from last week, getting
ready for bed.

3/19/2007
Tina Roth Eisenberg | 113
@swissmiss | 2.9
Trying to get my ladies to twitter!

Doug Bow
@...
mellowing at the Driskill. my lore
a lot of people at sxsw

140

7/30/2008
Adam Savage 52
@donttrythis | 4.5
About to test the shinyness of mud.

89
5/24/2007
Jared M. Spool
@jmspool | 130
Signing up for twitter!

3/9/2007
Jason Kottke
@jkottke | 1.1
Finally caving to Twitter. Still no MySpace th

10/9/2008
Stephen Fry | 10
@stephenfry | 10 | 16
o fly to Africa for a new
eting whilst I'm filming.

5/24/2007
Warren Ellis
@warrenellis | 8.5
checking account validity

3/16/2007
Jason Santa Maria
@jasonsantamaria | 2.9 | 117
Trying to wake up.

12/12/2006
Jeffrey Zeldman
@zeldman | 7.1 | 100
scratching

4/26/2007
Paulo Coelho | 48
@paulocoelho | 4.7
...un regalo de un amigo y seguidor...
http://www.paulocoelhoblog.com/

Biz S
just setting up

3/15/2007
88 | **Major Nelson**
@majornelson | 9.2
Wondering why people want to know what I am doing.

110

2/13/2007
Joshua Allen
@fireland | 0.6
When I go into the office bathroom and someone is going #2
while I only have to go #1 ... I feel superior

59
11/21/2006
Veronica Belmont
@Veronica | 4.7
Gah! Will today never end?!

12/1/2008
Jonathan Ross
@Wossy | 22
Getting to know twitter

5/7/2008
Kevin Smith 29
@ThatKevinSmith | 11
Showing my flick to some fresh eyes,
backing up laptop.

34
3/14/2007
Wil Wheaton
@wilw | 7.9
Trying to figure out if I signed up with 'wilwheaton' to prevent
some jerk from stealing it, or if some jerk already stole it.

7

Start

1/26/2009
Demi Moore
mrskutcher | 8.8
trying to figure this twitter deal out!

Pul

1/28/2009
Rainn Wilson
@rainnwilson | 7.5
Rainn Wilson. Reporting for duty.

3/27/2008
Lady Gaga
@ladygaga | 0.4
op rehearsing for my video just dance and am now at wmc to perform
at the Armani and nervous records party. But I am no nervous record! ...

Obvious Co

4/30/2007
Natalie
@natalie_mu | 19
ダウンタウンの松本人志が監督・主演を務める話題の映画「大日
本人」の音楽をTOWA TEIが担当していることが明らかになった
http://natalie.mu/news/show/id/1564

1/22/2009
Perez Hilton
@PerezHilton | 48
17 | Hi! This is the real me bitches. I'm not on MySpace or
Facebook but I decided to start Twittering. Yee Haw!

86

24

Twitter domin

12/6/2008
Taylor Swift | 4
@taylorswift13 | 1.1
cat for being gone so long.

9/22/2008
Britney Spears
@britneyspears | 0.7
Welcome to Britney Spears' Twitter! Follow the latest in Britney
news and get updates straight from Britney and her entourage.

5/23/2007
116
Sascha Lobo
@saschalobo | 4
Prokrastinieren.

1/28/2009
Mariah Carey
@MariahCarey | 1.7 | 31
o Mariah's Official Twitter Page!
witter.com/MariahHBF and feel
to @MariahHBF about Miss M!

49

72

1/30/2009
John Mayer
@johncmayer | 7.5 | 11
The Perfect Fuzz Sound. If you do it right, the
reath swirling around in a saxophone. Cool.

8/19/2008
Trent Reznor
@trent_reznor | 0.9
hanging on the bus

4/29/2008
MC Hammer
@MCHammer | 12
boring night...my controller must have been broken...every channel had
some preacher name Rev. Wright...I think he's running for President??

21

12/19/2008
50 Cent

2

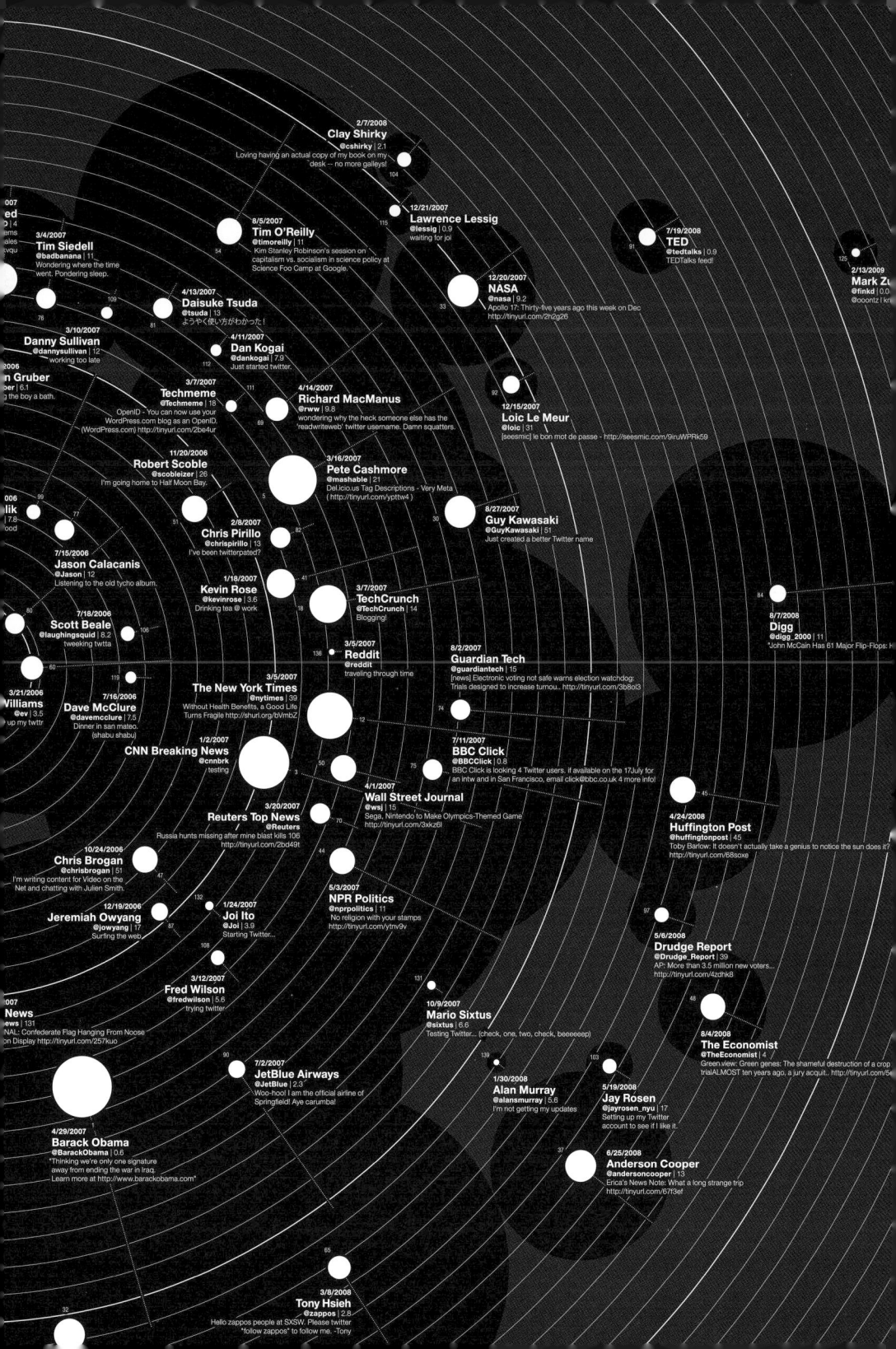

2/7/2008
Clay Shirky
@cshirky | 2.1
Loving having an actual copy of my book on my desk -- no more galleys!
104

12/21/2007
Lawrence Lessig
@lessig | 0.9
waiting for joi
115

8/5/2007
Tim O'Reilly | 11
@timoreilly | 11
Kim Stanley Robinson's session on capitalism vs. socialism in science policy at Science Foo Camp at Google.
54

7/19/2008
TED
@tedtalks | 0.9
TEDTalks feed!
91

2/13/2009
Mark Zu
@finkd | 0.0
@ooontz | kr
125

12/20/2007
NASA
@nasa | 9.2
Apollo 17: Thirty-five years ago this week on Dec
33

3/4/2007
Tim Siedell
@badbanana | 12
Wondering where the time went. Pondering sleep.
149

_07_
_ed_
ams
ales
_qu_

4/13/2007
Daisuke Tsuda
@tsuda | 13
ようやく使い方がわかった！
81

3/10/2007
Danny Sullivan
@dannysullivan | 12
working too late
78

4/11/2007
Dan Kogai
@dankogai | 7.9
Just started twitter.
122

3/7/2007
Techmeme
@Techmeme | 18
OpenID - You can now use your WordPress.com blog as an OpenID. (WordPress.com) http://tinyurl.com/2be4ur
111

4/14/2007
Richard MacManus
@rww | 9.8
wondering why the heck someone else has the 'readwriteweb' twitter username. Damn squatters.
69

12/15/2007
Loic Le Meur
@loic | 31
[seesmic] le bon mot de passe - http://seesmic.com/9iruWPRk59
92

_2006_
n Gruber | 6.1
g the boy a bath.

11/20/2006
Robert Scoble
@scobleizer | 26
I'm going home to Half Moon Bay.

3/16/2007
Pete Cashmore
@mashable | 21
Del.icio.us Tag Descriptions - Very Meta (http://tinyurl.com/ypttw4)

8/27/2007
Guy Kawasaki
@GuyKawasaki | 51
Just created a better Twitter name
36

_006_
lik
7.8
ood
99

77

91

2/8/2007
Chris Pirillo
@chrispirillo | 13
I've been twitterpated?

7/15/2006
Jason Calacanis
@Jason | 12
Listening to the old tycho album.

1/18/2007
Kevin Rose
@kevinrose | 3.6
Drinking tea @ work
41

3/7/2007
TechCrunch
@TechCrunch | 14
Blogging!

7/18/2006
Scott Beale
@laughingsquid | 8.2
tweeking twtta
108

80

3/5/2007
Reddit
@reddit
traveling through time
136

8/2/2007
Guardian Tech
@guardiantech | 15
[news] Electronic voting not safe warns election watchdog: Trials designed to increase turnou... http://tinyurl.com/3b8ol3

8/7/2008
Digg
@digg_2000 | 11
"John McCain Has 61 Major Flip-Flops: H
84

3/5/2007
The New York Times
@nytimes | 39
Without Health Benefits, a Good Life Turns Fragile http://shurl.org/bVmbZ
12

7/11/2007
BBC Click
@BBCClick | 0.8
BBC Click is looking 4 Twitter users. If available on the 17July for an intw and in San Francisco, email click@bbc.co.uk 4 more info!
74

4/24/2008
Huffington Post
@huffingtonpost | 45
Toby Barlow: It doesn't actually take a genius to notice the sun does it? http://tinyurl.com/68soxe
45

Williams
@ev | 3.5
up my twttr
60

7/16/2006
Dave McClure
@davemcclure | 7.5
Dinner in san mateo. (shabu shabu)
59

1/2/2007
CNN Breaking News
@cnnbrk
testing
3

4/1/2007
Wall Street Journal
@wsj | 12
Sega, Nintendo to Make Olympics-Themed Game http://tinyurl.com/3xkz6l
75

50

3/20/2007
Reuters Top News
@Reuters
Russia hunts missing after mine blast kills 106 http://tinyurl.com/2bd49t
70

5/3/2007
NPR Politics
@nprpolitics | 11
No religion with your stamps http://tinyurl.com/ytnv9v
44

10/24/2006
Chris Brogan
@chrisbrogan | 51
I'm writing content for Video on the Net and chatting with Julien Smith.
47

1/24/2007
Joi Ito
@Joi | 3.9
Starting Twitter...
87

132

3/21/2006
3.5

5/6/2008
Drudge Report
@Drudge_Report | 39
AP: More than 3.5 million new voters... http://tinyurl.com/4zdhk8
97

4/4/2008
The Economist
@TheEconomist | 4
Green.view: Green genes: The shameful destruction of a crop trialALMOST ten years ago, a jury. acquit. http://tinyurl.com/5
48

12/8/2006
Jeremiah Owyang
@jowyang | 17
Surfing the web

3/12/2007
Fred Wilson
@fredwilson | 5.6
trying twitter

10/9/2007
Mario Sixtus
@sixtus | 6.6
Testing Twitter... (check, one, two, check, beeeeeep)
131

1/30/2008
Alan Murray
@alansmurray | 5.6
I'm not getting my updates
139

5/19/2008
Jay Rosen
@jayrosen_nyu | 17
Setting up my Twitter account to see if I like it.
103

6/25/2008
Anderson Cooper
@andersoncooper | 13
Erica's News Note: What a long strange trip http://tinyurl.com/67f3ef
37

_007_
News
ews | 131
NAL: Confederate Flag Hanging From Noose on Display http://tinyurl.com/257kuo

7/2/2007
JetBlue Airways
@JetBlue | 2.3
Woo-hoo! I am the official airline of Springfield! Aye carumba!
90

4/29/2007
Barack Obama
@BarackObama | 0.6
"Thinking we're only one signature away from ending the war in Iraq. - Learn more at http://www.barackobama.com"

3/8/2008
Tony Hsieh
@zappos | 2.8
Hello zappos people at SXSW. Please twitter "follow zappos" to follow me. -Tony
65

32

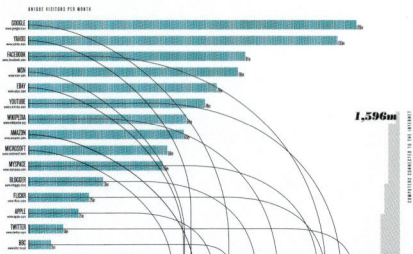

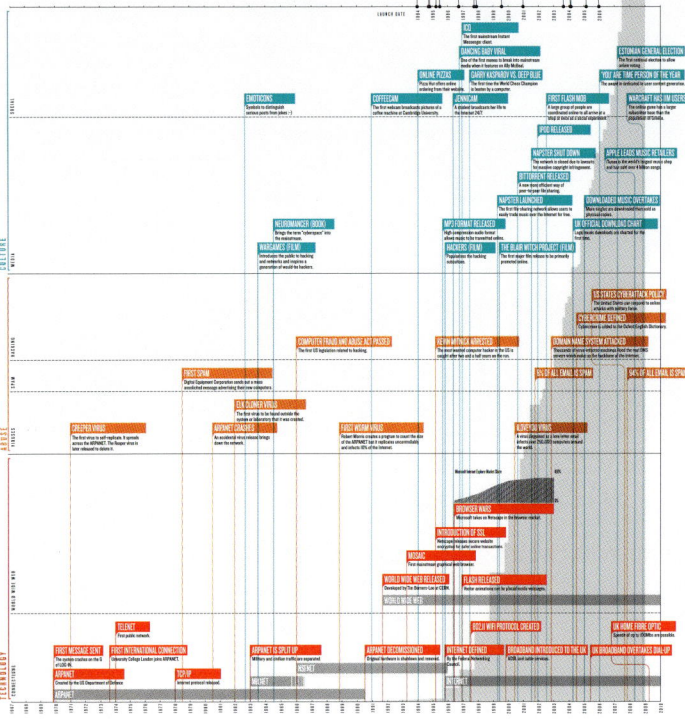

Project Info: Series of posters, 2009, UK
Design: Paul Butt (Section Design)

Digital Nostalgia

In this series, Paul Butt looks back at the rise of digital technologies in recent decades. The idea was not just to show the raw numbers but also the social ripples it has caused. Also, by demonstrating how quickly technological devices and data carriers have been developing, the posters indicate the emergence of nostalgic feelings for old and obsolete digital technology. Four posters use timelines to show the technological progress in the development of the Internet, audio & video formats, computer storage and mobile telephony.

AUDIO / VIDEO

The gramophone was the dominant recording format in the previous century and still carries on as a niche media to this day. The introduction of magnetic tape cassette allowed music to become much more portable whilst bring recording technology to the consumer market. The audio cassette became a cultural icon, allowing music and ideas to cross between political divides.

The invention of television requires its own type of media and the first major commercial video recording format was Ampex's two inch Quadruplex tape. This revolutionised television by allowing networks to record and re-broadcast shows much more practically than was possible before. It was Sony that were first to condense this technology to the home market with the CV-2000 video recorder although it was so expensive that it was out of reach of most consumers. Sony's Betamax was designed as a cheaper video format and regarded as technologically superior to VHS when it was first released but provided only half the recording time. Although this was increased to gain parity with the competing format, the perceived lack of recording time and extra cost of Betamax machines meant that VHS won the format war.

Analogue technology was replaced by digital as optical laser-read discs took over from magnetic tape. CDs could be copied again and again with no degradation in quality and had none of the previous drawbacks such as stretching and distortion. A major advance was the ability to easily skip between tracks giving consumers more choice on how they wanted to enjoy music or video.

The creation of high definition television required a new format capable of supporting the vastly increased data rate. Sony fought a fierce format war again with their Blu-Ray technology pitted against Toshiba's HD-DVD. Lack of content manufacturer and retailer support eventually caused the fall of HD-DVD and Sony's Blu-Ray was taken up as the standard format for high definition video.

VINYL LP

- NME magazine produces the first singles chart based on sales

COMPACT CASSETTE

8-TRACK

- First Sony Walkman on sale

COMPACT DISK

SONY MINIDISC

- MP3 compression format released

- Napster launched

APPLE IPOD

- Apple iTunes Store allows online music purchases
- Online music sales overtake physical copies in the UK
- It is estimated that half of all the cassettes sold in the UK are for police interview machines
- Apple becomes largest music retailer in the US

SONY CV-2000

SONY BETAMAX

VHS

LASERDISC

DIGITAL VERSATILE DISC

BLU-RAY

VIDEO RESOLUTION

DIGITAL DISTRIBUTION

The Internet has had a huge effect on the music and entertainment industry. The ability to buy music and video as 'downloads' removes most of the distribution costs of traditional media and allows smaller content producers to more easily reach their audience. Advances in computer storage and compression technology enable consumers to store an almost limitless amount of media when compared to tapes and optical discs, whilst playback devices become smaller and smaller.

86.6m

DOWNLOADS

COMPACT DISCS

CASSETTE TAPES

VINYL RECORDS

UK SINGLES SALES IN MILLIONS

2001 2002 2003 2004 2005 2006 2007

WEIGHT OF EQUIVALENT MEDIA

APPLE IPOD CLASSIC
120GB

3.5" HARD DISK DRIVE
500GB

INDIVIDUAL DOWNLOAD TIME
ON 5MB BROADBAND

245

DISK SPACE [3]

With the development of computers, the amount of data that could be processed rapidly expanded and methods of storing and transporting this amount of information had to be created. In the early years of personal computing, removable floppy disks were often the only storage format available as the hard disks of the time were large and expensive. Computers such as the Apple Macintosh ran completely off its 3.5″ floppy disk drive which contained the entire operating system. Fourteen years later Apple's iMac would be one of the first computers launched without a 3.5″ drive.

The slow speed and fragility of floppy disks led to the development of optical formats such as the CD-ROM, which was originally designed to be purely a medium for audio recordings. The development of user-writable CDs allowed a user to create perfect reproductions of music recordings every time. This created a feeling of unease amongst the American recording industry who imposed compulsory royalties on recordable drives and blank media. Later formats such as DVDs and Blu-ray would have increasingly complicated copy-protection systems which hackers would try to defeat in a constant game of cat and mouse.

The creation of high-compression audio formats such as MP3 further complicated the issue as users could compress audio tracks by up to 90%. With the rise of the Internet, these files could also be transferred and distributed to a worldwide audience, bypassing the need for removable storage completely.

With no moving parts to wear out as with floppy disks and less vulnerable to scratch damage as with optical discs, solid-state flash memory is the next generation of portable storage. these small cards are mostly used in small portable devices such as digital cameras and phones. The increasing development of integrated circuits has allowed these formats to grow in capacity exponentially, whilst retaining a level of backwards compatibility.

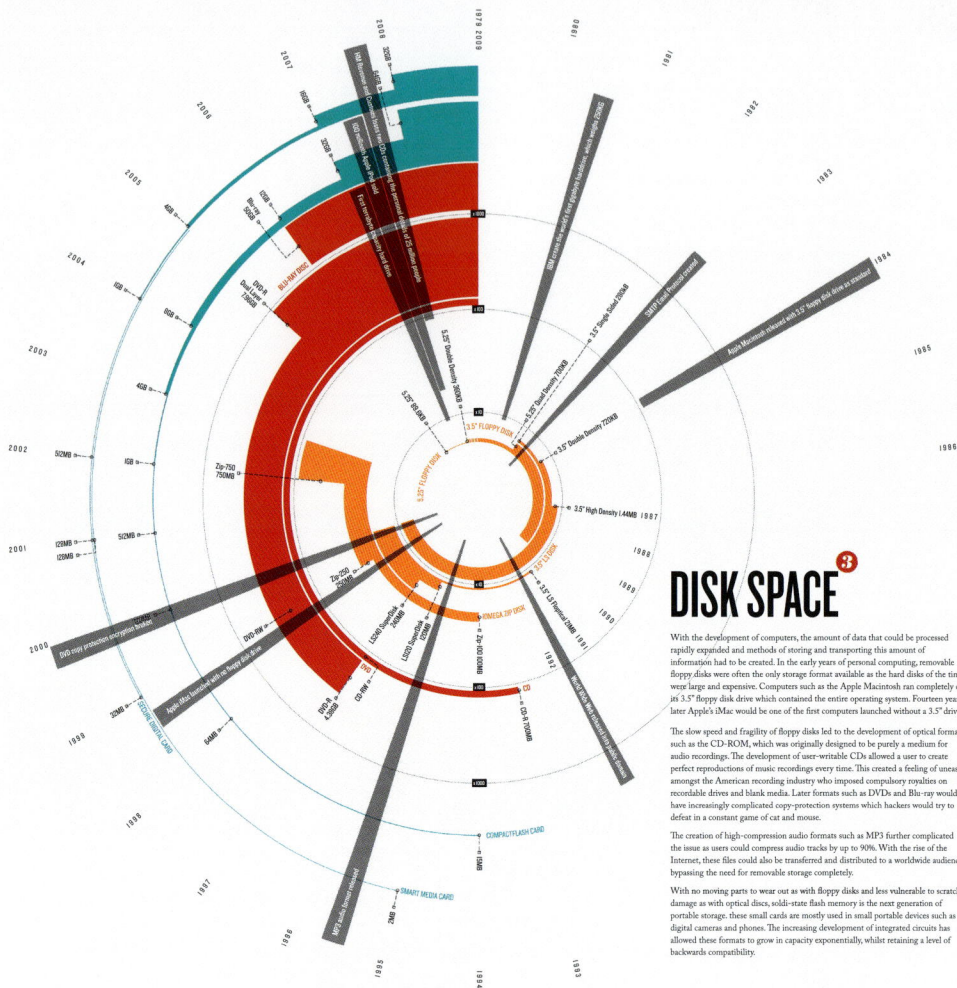

TRANSFER SPEEDS

○ Theoretical maximum read speed   ■ Time to transfer 3mb digital music file   ■ Time to transfer 1000mb digital video file

*Theoretical time due to capacity limitations.

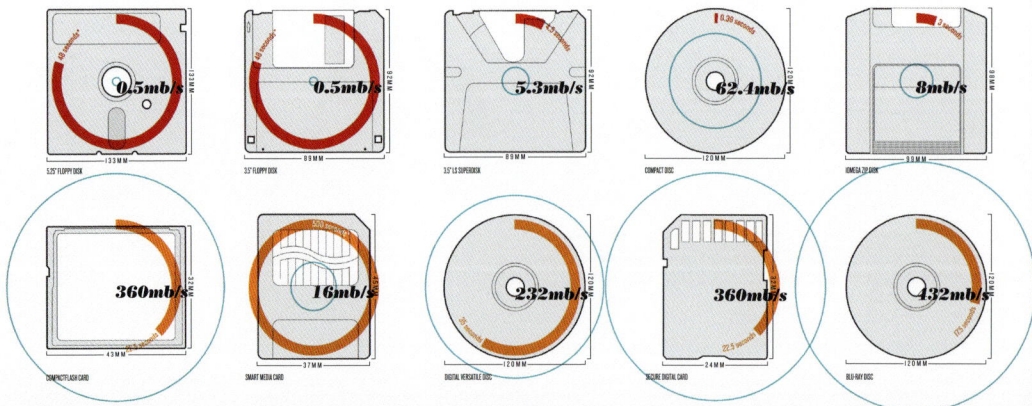

5.25″ FLOPPY DISK	3.5″ FLOPPY DISK	3.5″ LS SUPERDISK	COMPACT DISC	IOMEGA ZIP DRIVE
0.5mb/s	0.5mb/s	5.3mb/s	62.4mb/s	8mb/s

COMPACTFLASH CARD	SMART MEDIA CARD	DIGITAL VERSATILE DISC	SECURE DIGITAL CARD	BLU-RAY DISC
360mb/s	16mb/s	232mb/s	360mb/s	432mb/s

MOBILE EVOLUTION

Mobile phones originated from permanent vehicle mounted radio systems, as battery technology had not yet been refined to a portable enough size. A prototype of Motorola's DynaTAC was used to make the first phone call whilst walking the streets of New York in 1973, although it took another ten years for a commercial handheld device to be released. From then on mobile phones continued to decrease in size and weight and gain in technological features. Towards the end of the twentieth century, mobile phones changed from being luxury devices to a mainstream commodity - becoming the most rapidly adopted technology in human history. Now we are tethered to the rest of the world through this small device in our pockets and another person is only a few button presses away. For better or worse - the evolution of the mobile phone has changed the way we live our lives forever.

58.8bn

- 1 BILLION SMS SENT IN A MONTH (UK)
- COMMERCIAL SMS SERVICES LAUNCHED
- 214 MILLION TEXTS SENT ON NEW YEARS DAY (U...
- 5.4 MILLION MESSAGES SENT PER MONTH (UK)
- INTERCONNECT BETWEEN MAJOR UK PHONE PROVIDERS
  Users can now send messages to people on other networks.
- 1 BILLION SMS PER DAY SENT GLOBALLY
- FIRST TEXT MESSAGE SENT
  It reads 'Merry Christmas'.
- 70% OF UK MOBILE OWNERS USE SMS

TEXT MESSAGING
MOBILE PHONES

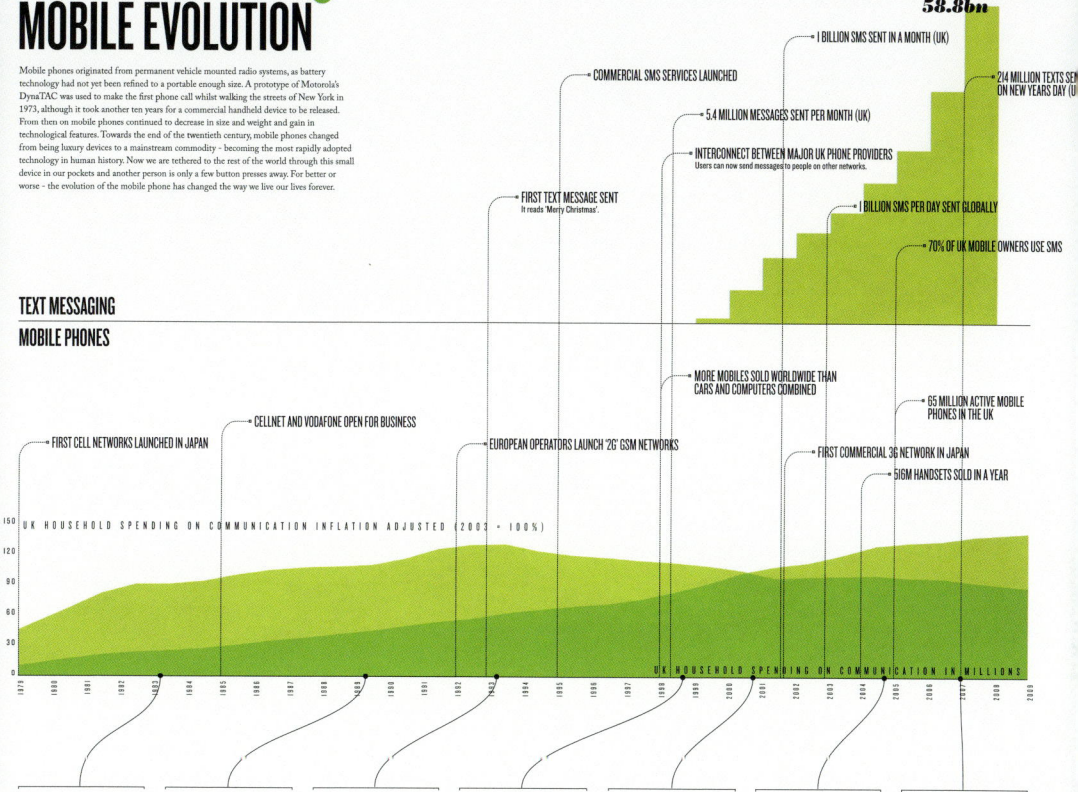

- MORE MOBILES SOLD WORLDWIDE THAN CARS AND COMPUTERS COMBINED
- 65 MILLION ACTIVE MOBILE PHONES IN THE UK
- FIRST CELL NETWORKS LAUNCHED IN JAPAN
- CELLNET AND VODAFONE OPEN FOR BUSINESS
- EUROPEAN OPERATORS LAUNCH '2G' GSM NETWORKS
- FIRST COMMERCIAL 3G NETWORK IN JAPAN
- 516M HANDSETS SOLD IN A YEAR

150 120 90 60 30 0 UK HOUSEHOLD SPENDING ON COMMUNICATION INFLATION ADJUSTED (2003 = 100%)

UK HOUSEHOLD SPENDING ON COMMUNICATION IN MILLIONS

1978 1980 1981 1982 1983 1984 1985 1986 1987 1988 1989 1990 1991 1992 1993 1994 1995 1996 1997 1998 1999 2000 2001 2002 2003 2004 2005 2006 2007 2008 2009

133g   95g   135g

MOTOROLA DYNATAC 8000X

MOTOROLA MICROTAC 9800X

NOKIA 2110

NOKIA 5110

NOKIA 3310

MOTOROLA RAZR V3

APPLE IPHONE

ACUMEN

The Tipsy Turvy Republic of Alcohol

ALCOHOL has triggered extreme cultural mood swings in American history, with periods of binge consumption alternating with periods of enforced abstinence. Enthusiastic tippling was the norm in the colonies and early republic, but in the 1840s a nation of hearty drinkers became zealous abstainers. A similar cycle occurred several decades later as a rise in consumption of alcohol at the turn of the century culminated in Prohibition.

DATAGRAPHIC BY NIGEL HOLMES
RESEARCH BY LORRAINE MOFFA

1770–2000
HOW MUCH WE DRANK

Americans in the late 1700s and early 1800s were awash in beer, wine and spirits—consuming 30-plus gallons a year per capita. On average, the amount of pure alcohol in those libations was 20 percent, a figure that has remained consistent until the modern day. Per capita consumption dropped by more than half in the mid-1800s and in recent years has hovered above 10 gallons a year.

Gallons of alcohol annually, per person (age 15+)

33 gallons
(5 bottles to a gallon)

1810
132 breweries produce 185,000 barrels of beer. (That's 61 million 12-oz. bottles; U.S. population was 7 million.)

1826
American Temperance Society forms in Boston. By 1829 it has 100,000 members.

1770–1830
WHY WE DRANK

In early America, gentry and common folk alike viewed alcohol as a source of energy, a palliative for disease and a necessary substitute for polluted water. Plus, a nip or two made folks a little happier. Rum fueled the slave trade and floated the colonial economy: 4.8 million gallons were distilled annually by 1770. When the Revolution cut off the rum makers' supply of Caribbean molasses, whiskey became the spirit of choice. Consumption of hard liquor increased as the early republic underwent the strains of an enormous population increase—from 4 million in 1790 to 13 million in 1830—and the beginnings of industrialization.

circa 1840
WHY WE STOPPED DRINKING SO MUCH

As consumption rose in the 1820s, so did the backlash against it. By 1835 temperance societies claimed 1.5 million converts to the cause of moral living. The temperance movement, which emerged amid a clamor for the abolition of slavery and other social reforms, at first condoned drinking in moderation but gradually adopted a zero-tolerance stance.

1787 Two days before completing their work, the 55 members of the Constitutional Convention adjourn to a Philadelphia tavern for a break. They consume:

- 54 bottles of Madeira
- 60 bottles of claret
- 8 bottles of whiskey
- 22 bottles of port
- 8 bottles of hard cider
- 7 bowls of punch so large that people say ducks could swim in them.

1794 U.S. navy ration includes "half-pint of distilled spirits."

1794 Near-tripling of excise tax on whiskey results in the Whiskey Rebellion. (The tax is repealed in 1802.)

1799 George Washington's stills, built at Mount Vernon after his presidency, produce 11,000 gallons of whiskey.

1809 James Madison tries to create a new Cabinet position: Secretary of Beer. He fails.

1849 Bartender in Martinez, Calif., invents the martini.

1862
Beer taxed $1 a barrel to help finance Civil War.

We the People HIC!

Data points: 33, 30.5, 29, 33, 35.5, 34, 35.5, 35.5, 15.5, 10.5, 9, 9.5, 9.5

Years: 1770 1785 1790 1800 1810 1820 1830 1840 1850 1860 1870 188[0]

SOURCES: LEDA at Harvard; *The Alcohol Republic: An American Tradition* by W.J. Rorabaugh; *The Control of Fuddle and Flash: A Sociological History of the Regulation of Alcohol and Opiates* by Jan-Willem Gerritsen; OECD 1989; U.S. Office of Management and Budget

1920–1933
PROHIBITION: WE KEPT ON DRINKING

The 1920 Volstead Act, which defined how Prohibition was carried out under the 18th Amendment, outlawed the manufacture, sale or transportation of "intoxicating liquor" and paved the way for organized crime to make a killing in the illegal booze trade during the next 13 years.

The Volstead Act was riddled with loopholes, including a lack of criminal penalties for possession and consumption of alcohol, so orders for sacramental wine spiked sharply, and doctors prescribed 1.8 million gallons of medicinal whiskey in 1927 alone. Another exception allowed households to produce 200 gallons of home-brewed cider or fruit juice a year that contained up to 0.5 percent alcohol.

By 1930, 70 percent of the public—fed up with corrupt enforcement officials, courts clogged with liquor cases and skyrocketing homicide rates—wanted to change the Volstead Act. Prohibition hit the federal pocketbook especially hard: The government lost $11 billion in liquor excise taxes.

The 21st Amendment repealed Prohibition in December 1933.

1792–2008
EXCISE TAX: WHAT THE GOVERNMENT COLLECTS
The percentage of federal revenue that is collected from taxes on alcohol

Alcohol excise taxes were an on-again-off-again source of federal revenue until Uncle Sam began to depend heavily on them during the Civil War. Personal income taxes became the main source of U.S. revenue after passage of the 16th Amendment in 1913 and now account for 45% of the federal budget while only about 3% comes from alcohol.

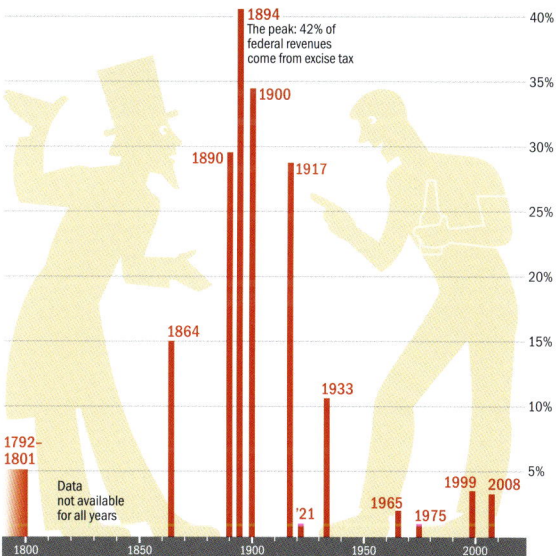

1894 The peak: 42% of federal revenues come from excise tax

Current taxes
Beer $18 barrel
Liquor $13.50 gallon
Wine $1.07 gallon

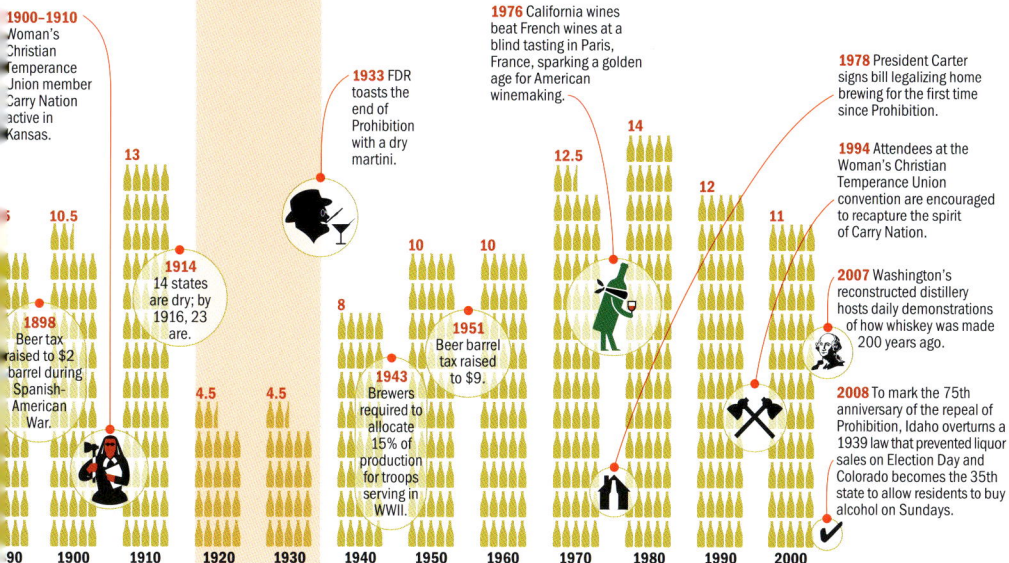

1900–1910 Woman's Christian Temperance Union member Carry Nation active in Kansas.

1898 Beer tax raised to $2 barrel during Spanish-American War.

1914 14 states are dry; by 1916, 23 are.

1933 FDR toasts the end of Prohibition with a dry martini.

1943 Brewers required to allocate 15% of production for troops serving in WWII.

1951 Beer barrel tax raised to $9.

1976 California wines beat French wines at a blind tasting in Paris, France, sparking a golden age for American winemaking.

1978 President Carter signs bill legalizing home brewing for the first time since Prohibition.

1994 Attendees at the Woman's Christian Temperance Union convention are encouraged to recapture the spirit of Carry Nation.

2007 Washington's reconstructed distillery hosts daily demonstrations of how whiskey was made 200 years ago.

2008 To mark the 75th anniversary of the repeal of Prohibition, Idaho overturns a 1939 law that prevented liquor sales on Election Day and Colorado becomes the 35th state to allow residents to buy alcohol on Sundays.

249

Previous spread

Drinking in the US

Casting a look into cultural history, this graphic demonstrates how drinking habits have changed in the US from 1770 to the present. This is shown as a bar chart, with the bars made up of rows of 5 bottles (there are 5 standard bottles to a gallon). The number of rows then indicates how many gallons of alcohol per capita were consumed annually. Text blocks address why the US drank so much, and why there was a backlash against drinking around 1840. The prohibition years are specially marked and are given an extended explanation. The bar chart at the top right shows the federal revenue the government collects from taxes on alcohol.

Project Info: "The Tipsy Turvy Republic of Alcohol", *American History*, magazine article, 2008, USA
Data Source: LEDA at Harvard; W.J. Rorabaugh: *The Alcohol Republic: An American Tradition*; Jan-Willem Gerritsen: *The Control of Fuddle and Flash: A social History of Alcohol and Opiates*; OECD 1989; US Office of Management and Budget
Research: Lorraine Moffa
Design: Nigel Holmes

Earthquakes and Wars

This drawing maps posited similarities between wars and earthquakes in the US, including data concerning their duration, location etc. It was created starting from both the top and bottom with thin vertical stripes for each event. The numerics of each particular year determine the length of the thin stripes in inches. From these, more irregularly shaped labels emerge, indicating further data for each event. Connecting the loose ends of these labels created a butterfly shape in the centre. John J. O'Connor emphasised this shape for its reference to the butterfly effect, a term from chaos theory. The piece is deceptive: instead of actually visualising information, the artist gets lost in the data in order to let it create its own visual shape.

Project Info: Drawing, 2003, USA
Artist: John J. O'Connor
Additional Info: John J. O'Connor is represented by Pierogi Gallery

MAJOR EARTHQUAKES IN CONTIGUOUS UNITED STATES

(En)tangled Word Bank

A visualisation of the textual development of *The Origin of Species*
by Charles Darwin, through six editions.

The Organism's Structure

Radiating outwards from the centre, the chapters divide
into subchapters, the subchapters divide into paragraphs,
and the paragraphs divide into sentences.

CHAPTERS   SUBCHAPTERS

PARAGRAPHS   SENTENCES

Close-up of a Chapter

The scale of the organism's different components is
determined by its number of words.

PARAGRAPH
LEAF   SENTENCE
                        LEAFLET

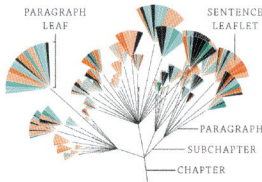

                        PARAGRAPH
                        SUBCHAPTER
                        CHAPTER

Basic Code of the Organism

The organism is encircled by the basic code of its information.

The location of a sentence leaflet
corresponds to its unique position
within the organism's basic code.

CHAPTERS
SUBCHAPTERS
PARAGRAPHS
SENTENCES

Colours

The sentence leaflets are coloured according to the rules below.

Text's age from insertion

TEXT WAS INSERTED

ONE   TWO   THREE   FOUR   FIVE   SIX

EDITION(S) AGO AND IS **SURVIVING**
TO THE NEXT EDITION

Text's age before deletion

TEXT HAS SURVIVED

ONE   TWO   THREE   FOUR   FIVE

EDITION(S) BEFORE BEING **DELETED**
IN THE NEXT EDITION

'Reading' the Colours

In the first edition, the colours are the lightest insertion/
deletion tone as all the text is new. In the sixth edition, a variety
of insertion colours are built up over the five previous editions,
with no deletion colours as this is the final edition.

LAST CHAPTER,   LAST CHAPTER,
FIRST EDITION   SIXTH EDITION

'Reading' the Organism

All information is read by starting from the top of the
organism and its basic code and moving clockwise.

Within the organism, 'reading'
begins with the text furthest to
the left of the section.

CHAPTERS
SUBCHAPTERS
PARAGRAPHS
SENTENCES

(En)tangled Word Bank

This project visualises the evolution of Darwin's *Origin of Species* through six editions. Data were gathered from a hierarchical structural analysis of every word in each edition. The resulting 'literary organism' is represented in circular form. From the centre, chapters branch out into sub-chapters, paragraphs and sentences. The outer circle repeats this structure in four lines. Colour quantifies the life-span of each entity, with saturation indicating how many editions back it was inserted. Orange elements are deleted in the next edition, while blue ones survive. Since the text is arranged clockwise, it can be seen how the final text grew to fill the complete circle in the sixth edition.

Project Info: Microsoft Research, website, 2009, UK
Data Source: The Complete Works of Charles Darwin Online
Design: Stefanie Posavec, Greg McInerny

PLATE 1

First Chapter

The Origin of Species
Charles Darwin
First Edition, 1859

Last Chapter

Complete Organism

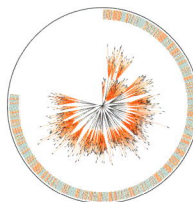

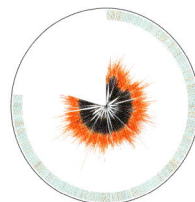

Chapters

Subchapters

Paragraphs

Sentences

(En)tangled Word Bank

Greg McInerny & Stefanie Posavec

253

PLATE 3

First Chapter

The Origin of Species
Charles Darwin
Third Edition, 1861

Last Chapter

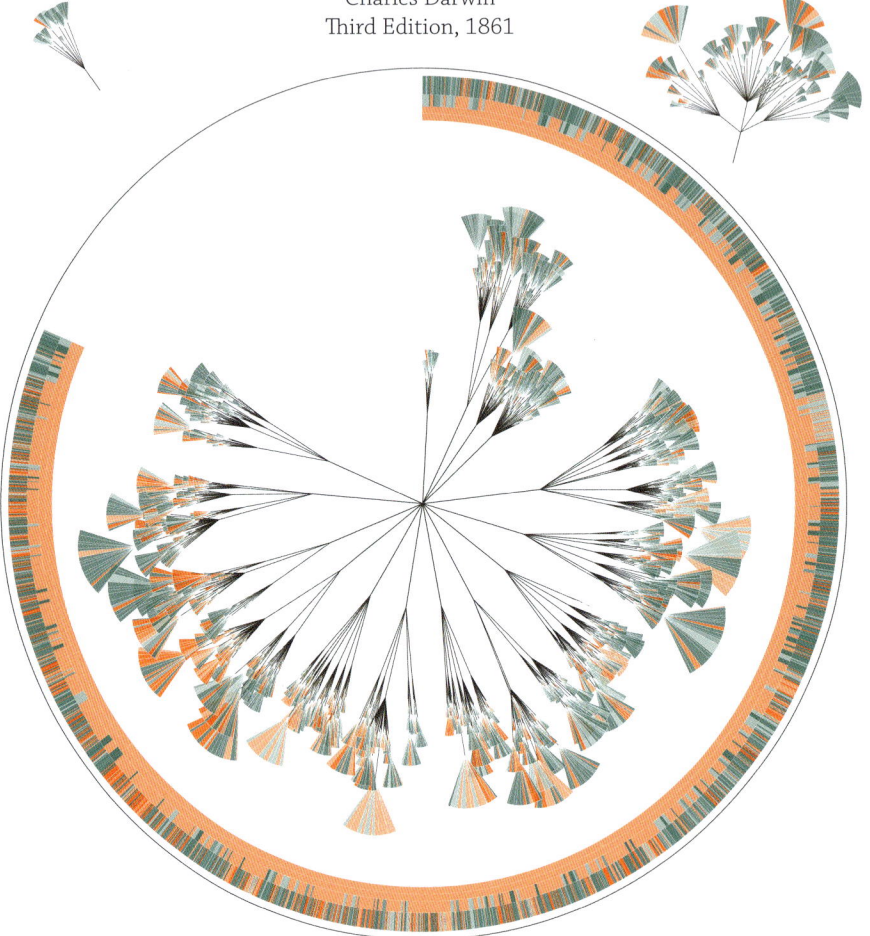

Complete Organism

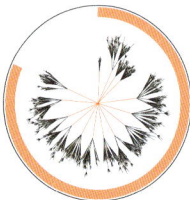

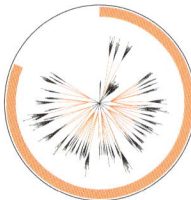

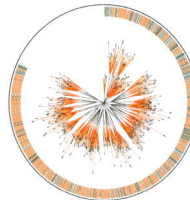

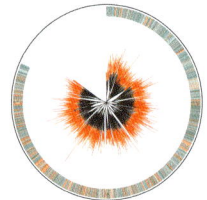

Chapters

Subchapters

Paragraphs

Sentences

(En)tangled Word Bank

Greg McInerny & Stefanie Posavec

PLATE 6

First Chapter

The Origin of Species
Charles Darwin
Sixth Edition, 1872

Last Chapter

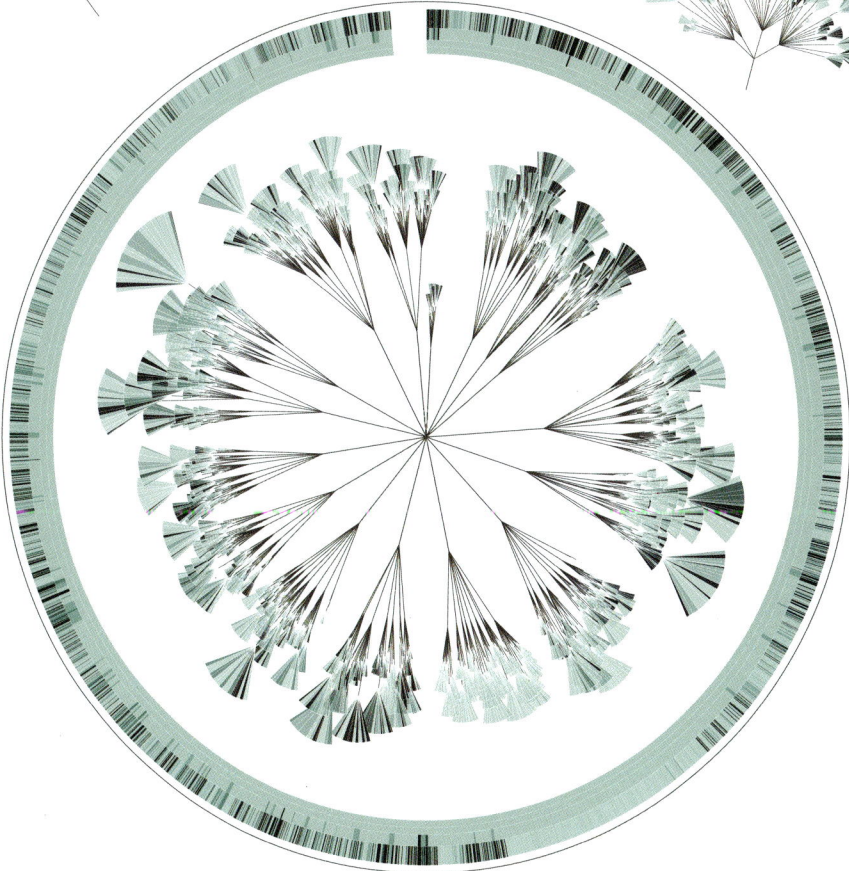

Complete Organism

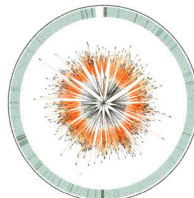

Chapters   *Subchapters*   *Paragraphs*   *Sentences*

(En)tangled Word Bank   Greg McInerny & Stefanie Posavec

Everyone Ever in the World

"Everyone Ever in the World" explores the recorded history of humankind: how many people in total have been born and how many of them were killed in wars? The total number of people ever born is an estimated 77.6 billion and is represented as the total poster area. The total number of people killed in conflicts is approximately 969 million or ca. 1.25 % of all the people ever to have lived. That number is represented by the die-cut circle in the centre. Around the centre, a time scale lists all recorded conflicts from 3200 BC to 2009 AD. The piece thus represents a rich set of historical data and discusses how militant human history actually is.

Project Info: Print, 2010, UK
Design: Peter Crnokrak (The Luxury of Protest)
Additional Info: Silkscreen print with transparent ink on matte plastic
Awards: NSF Science Visualization 2011

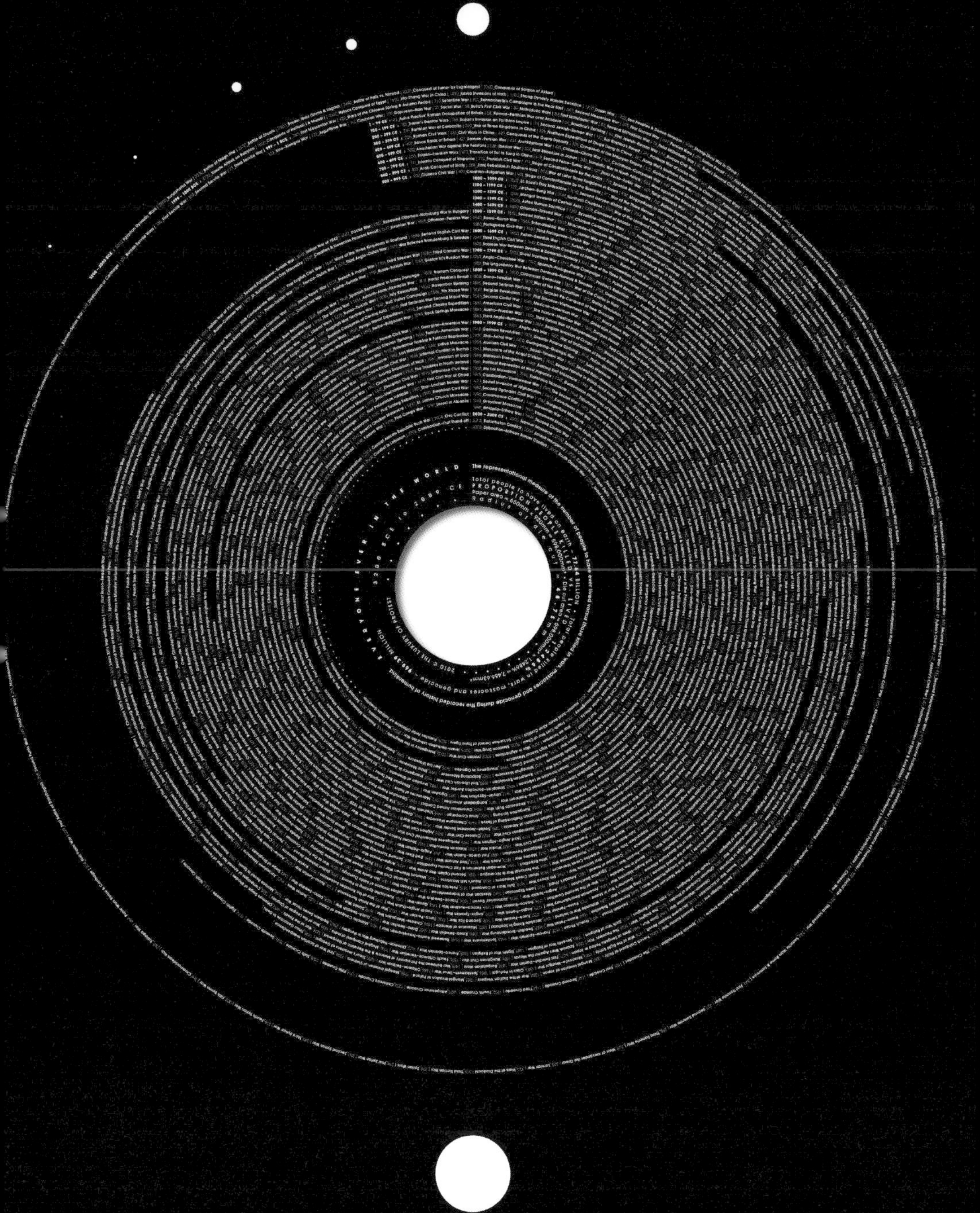

EVERYONE EVER IN THE WORLD

the representation...

total people...

PROPORTION

Paper dies...

EXPOSED TO D.&D. EARLY IN LIFE

RIP, GG & THX.

NO — YES

HANDMADE GANDALF COSTUME

WENT AS GANDALF SIX HALLOWEENS IN A ROW

STARTED BACKLASH AGAINST PETER JACKSON

SUN-LIGHT

ASIMOV — VIN DIESEL

SHORT-FICTION WRITER

INTENSE RELATIONSHIP WITH SCIENCE FICTION

NO

RENAISSANCE FAIRES

YES

NEUROMANCER

YES

PREFERRED PAINTING PEWTER FIGURES

WEB DESIGNER

YES

HARRY POTTER EARLY ADOPTER

INTENSE RELATIONSHIP WITH COMPUTERS

MOUNTAIN DEW

YES

LIFE CHANGED BY HARRY POTTER

WON'T SHUT UP ABOUT HARRY POTTER

YODA — C-3PO

WOULD TOTALLY MARRY HARRY POTTER

ATARI

TRS-80

TAUGHT YOURSELF PASCAL

REALLY PRETTY GREAT YODA IS

CASSETTE DRIVES

2600 Hz

I.T. DEPARTMENT

CTRL-ALT-DEL

EVEN IN CONTEMPLATING MARRIAGE, STILL REFERS TO BETROTHED BY FULL FIRST AND LAST NAME

NO

YES

"FOR DUMMIES" SERIES

NOW RE-READING *DUNE*

CAPTAIN CRUNCH

YES

HOT POCKETS

NO NO

CONS OF EVERY TYPE IMAGINABLE

NINTENDO

NO

L337

CHAT ROOMS

NO

YES

SEGA

THE WEB

GIRLS

NO

FUR CON

SWAG

M.M.O.R.P.G.'S

FANTASY BASEBALL

TECHNICALLY NOT THE SAME THING AS THE INTERNET

NO

GIRLS IN COSTUMES!

"THE ENEMY WITHIN"

PLAYSTATION — XBOX — WII

NO

NOT TOO CLOSE!

SECOND LIFE

BACK IN THE BASEMENT, BY YOURSELF, IN THE DARK

THE INTERNETS

YES

KHAAAN!!!

LOLCATS

NO

DOUBTING THE TECHNICAL ACCURACY OF THIS DIAGRAM

YES

PERL

GOOGLE

GOOGLE IS ALL ABOUT D.&D. AFTER ALL: PAGE RANK = CHARACTER LEVEL PAGE HITS = HIT POINTS INTERNET = DUNGEON

MICROSOFT OFFICE

THE GOOGLE EMAIL

BLOGGING ABOUT DIAGRAMS

THE OTHER GOOGLE STUFF

Exposed to Dungeons & Dragons Early in Life

This is a tribute to Gary Gygax, the co-creator of the role-playing game *Dungeons and Dragons* in 1974. With this famous table-top game, a fantasy world was created in which players actually assumed their characters' roles instead of just commanding faceless warriors. On the occasion of Gygax's death in 2008, Sam Potts created this graphic as a satirical but loving tribute to the world of fantasy-loving, geeky teenagers. Using the model of a flow chart, it plots the possible succession of life experiences following a boy's early exposure to the game. Admittedly, data input for this piece was partly derived from Potts' own life experience.

Project Info: "Geek Love", *The New York Times*, newspaper article, 2008, USA
Design: Sam Potts
Art Direction: Brian Rea
Article: Adam Rogers

Food Assistance

The food stamp program is a US federal government program to help low-income people buy food. This graphic looks at the increasing need for food stamps in the period from autumn 2008 to spring 2009. The consecutive months are shown in lines, with time running top down. Each line works as a bar to show the number of people who are using food stamps, showing the gradual increase towards the bottom. The bars themselves use small food icons to illustrate their subject.

Project Info: "The Growth of Food Stamps", *GOOD*, website, 2009, USA
Data Source: USDA
Design: Gavin Potenza
Art Direction: Morgan Clendaniel

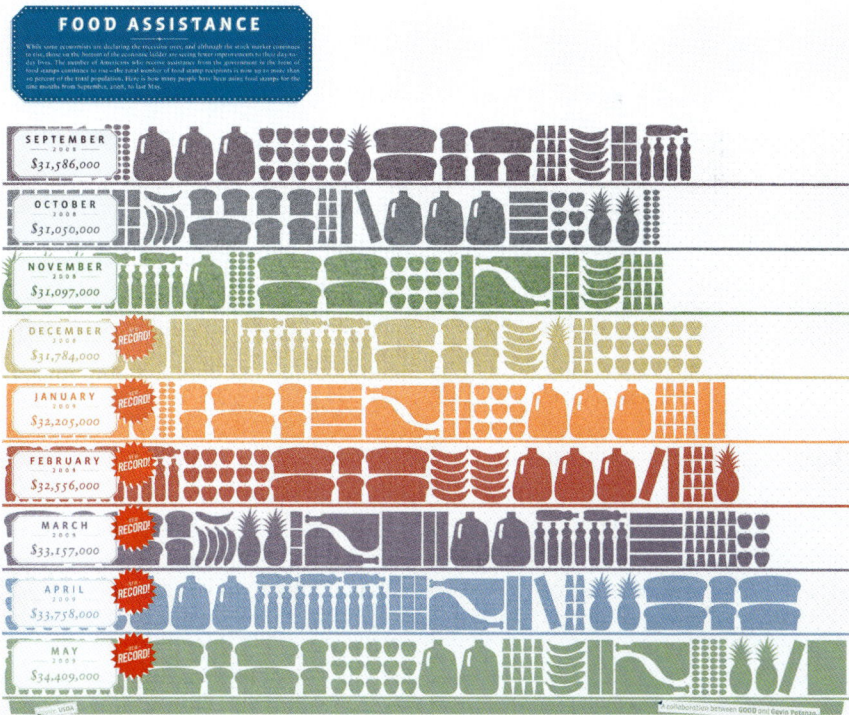

Project Info: Webcrafters, poster, 2005, USA
Design: Lin Wilson (Funnel Incorporated)

How Books are Made

When tasked to visualise what it takes to produce a book, Funnel Inc. developed a wide
panorama that is, at first sight, a model of a
printers' factory. Each step in the making of
a book is allocated to a specific workstation
within the factory, with little tags explaining
what is going on. The starting point is in the
top-left corner, and the production process
unfolds in a general reading direction towards
the lower right. With this piece, designer
Lin Wilson employed a somewhat cinematic
approach – mapping a developing process
on to a physical space which demands to be
traversed in order to access the information.

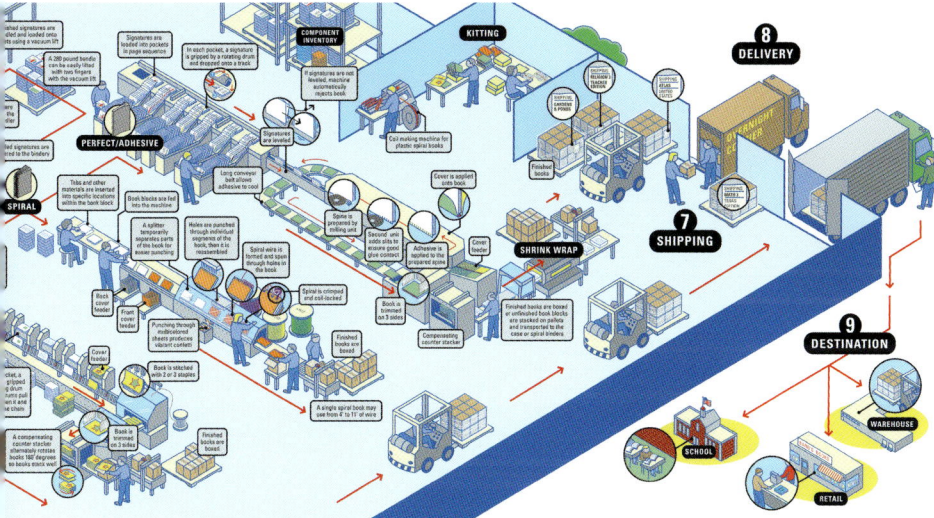

COMPONENT INVENTORY · **KITTING** · **8 DELIVERY** · **PERFECT/ADHESIVE** · **SPIRAL** · **SHRINK WRAP** · **7 SHIPPING** · **9 DESTINATION** · **WAREHOUSE** · **SCHOOL** · **RETAIL**

Signatures are loaded into pockets in page sequence

In each pocket, a signature is gripped by a rotating drum and dropped onto a track

If signatures are not leveled, machine automatically rejects book

Signatures are leveled

Coil making machine for plastic spiral books

Finished books

Cover is applied onto book

A 280 pound bundle can be easily lifted with two fingers with the vacuum lift

Tabs and other materials are inserted into specific locations within the book block

Book blocks are fed into the machine

Spine is prepared by milling unit

Second unit adds oils to ensure good glue contact

Cover feeder

A splitter temporarily separates parts of the book, then it is reassembled

Holes are punched through individual segments of the book

Adhesive is applied to the prepared spine

Long conveyer belt allows adhesive to cool

Spiral wire is formed and spun through holes in the book

Book is trimmed on 3 sides

Spiral is crimped and coil-locked

Finished books are boxed or unfinished book blocks are stacked on pallets and transported to the case or spiral binders

Back cover feeder

Front cover feeder

Punching through medicated sheets produces vibrant confetti

Finished books are boxed

Compensating counter stacker

Cover feeder

Book is stitched with 2 or 2 staples

A single spiral book may use from 4' to 11' of wire

A compensating counter stacker alternately rotates books 180 degree so books stack well

Back is trimmed on 3 sides

Finished blocks are boxed

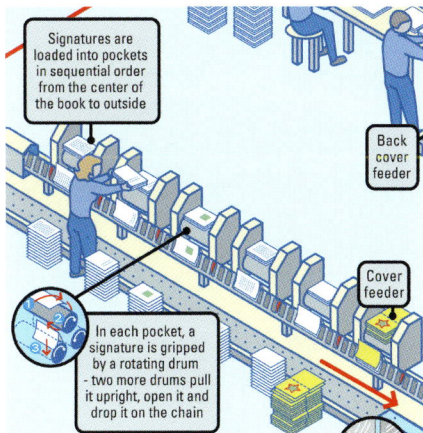

Signatures are loaded into pockets in sequential order from the center of the book to outside

Back cover feeder

Cover feeder

In each pocket, a signature is gripped by a rotating drum - two more drums pull it upright, open it and drop it on the chain

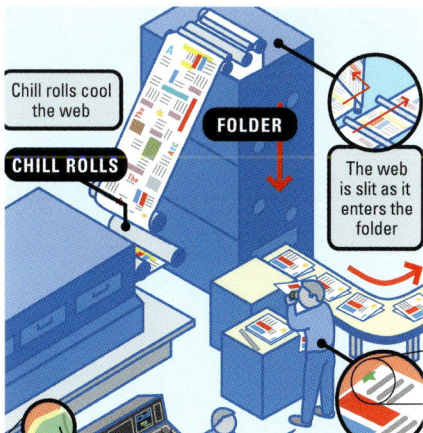

Chill rolls cool the web

FOLDER

CHILL ROLLS

The web is slit as it enters the folder

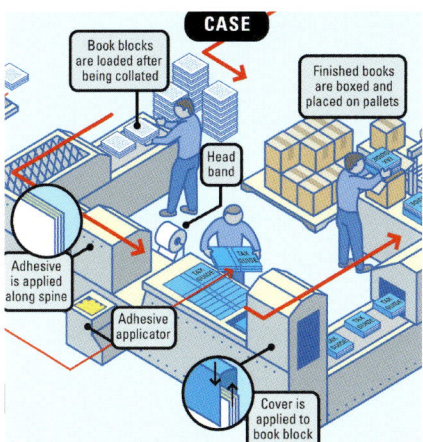

CASE

Book blocks are loaded after being collated

Finished books are boxed and placed on pallets

Head band

Adhesive is applied along spine

Adhesive applicator

Cover is applied to book block

SHIPPING
MATH 3
TEXAS
EDITION

7 SHIPPING

Project Info: *The New York Times*, blog, 2009, USA
Design: Christoph Niemann

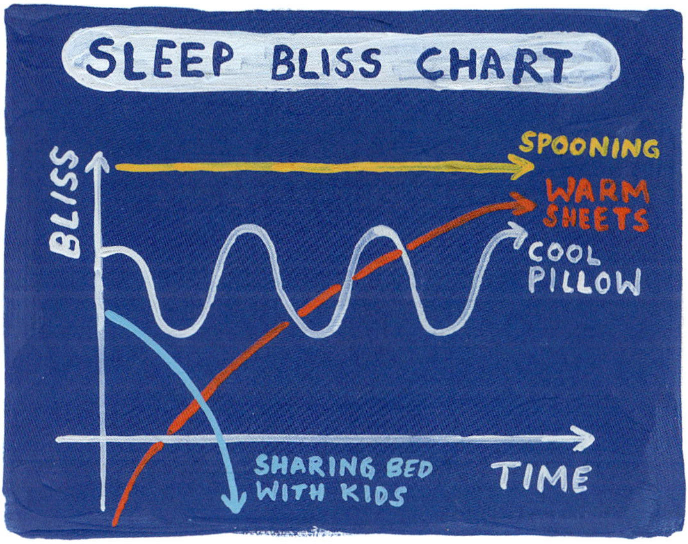

SLEEP BLISS CHART

SPOONING
WARM SHEETS
COOL PILLOW
SHARING BED WITH KIDS
BLISS
TIME

SLEEP AGONY CHART

STEPPING ON TOY WHILE CARRYING CHILD BACK TO OWN ROOM
HAVING TO PEE
MOSQUITO
A/C (SUMMER)
CLANKING HEATING PIPE (WINTER)
AGONY
TIME

Good Night and Tough Luck

In his blog *Abstract City* for the *New York Times*, German illustrator Christoph Niemann regularly comments on the mysteries of everyday urban life, developing a visual language for each individual series of images. In this series dating from September 2009, he uses hand-painted charts and infographics to explain the complications of a good night's sleep. The Sleep Agony Chart and its sibling, the Sleep Bliss Chart, mimic the classic format of a diagrammatic time series. The mosquito piece, in contrast, uses a hand-painted process chart to show the annoyance these little suckers are capable of causing on summer nights.

Project Info: Poster, 2009, UK
Design: Craig Ward (Words are Pictures)

Guess Who?
Character Identification Chart

This chart was inspired by "Guess Who?", a game for two players common in Great Britain and the United States during the 1980s. The game provided a range of characters, and players had to guess their opponent's current character by asking questions. By a process of elimination, players could eventually make a guess at which character was on their opponent's card. Beginning in the centre, the chart gives two starting points concerning the character's eyes. Further decisions are then made from there, with the questions leading up to the final character identification. Designed like a flow chart to provide help with complex decision processes, this piece is a happy homage to a childhood game.

Below and following spreads

Gulf of Maine – Sculptural Music Scores

Using a combination of basket-weaving techniques and information graphics, Boston-based artist Nathalie Miebach has transformed scientific data into representational sculptures. "Gulf of Maine" is a large body of work based on detailed weather data about storms, temperatures, winds or barometric pressure in the region. Information relating to marine life, such as whale sightings, was also taken into consideration. In the series shown here, Miebach introduced an additional dimension: she recorded the data as scores before turning them into sculptures. Besides weather data, these scores also recorded personal memories, which added to the perception of the weather. The results are playable music scores as well as the blueprint for constructing a sculpture.

Project Info: Series of sculptures and drawings, 2010–2011, USA
Data Source: Gulf of Maine Observation; National Oceanic Atmospheric Administration buoys; US Naval Observatory; Wunderground.com et al.
Artist: Nathalie Miebach
Awards: Visual Arts Sea Grant, Rhode Island

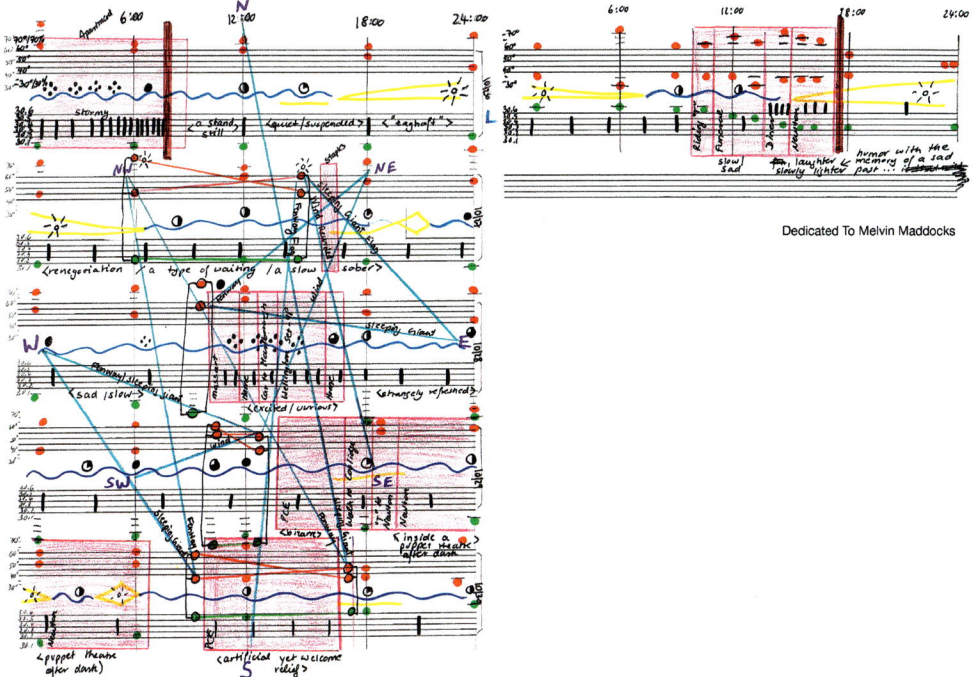

"Navigating Into A New Night"
Score for Sculptor and Musician

Dedicated To Melvin Maddocks

Navigating Into a New Night (above and previous page) translates weather data collected in Boston during autumn 2008. Interwoven with this are events from the artist's life (in pink) that dictate the mood of the musical interpretation. *Hurricane Noel* (right and next spread) presents a time series of the passing of a hurricane through the Gulf of Maine in 2007.

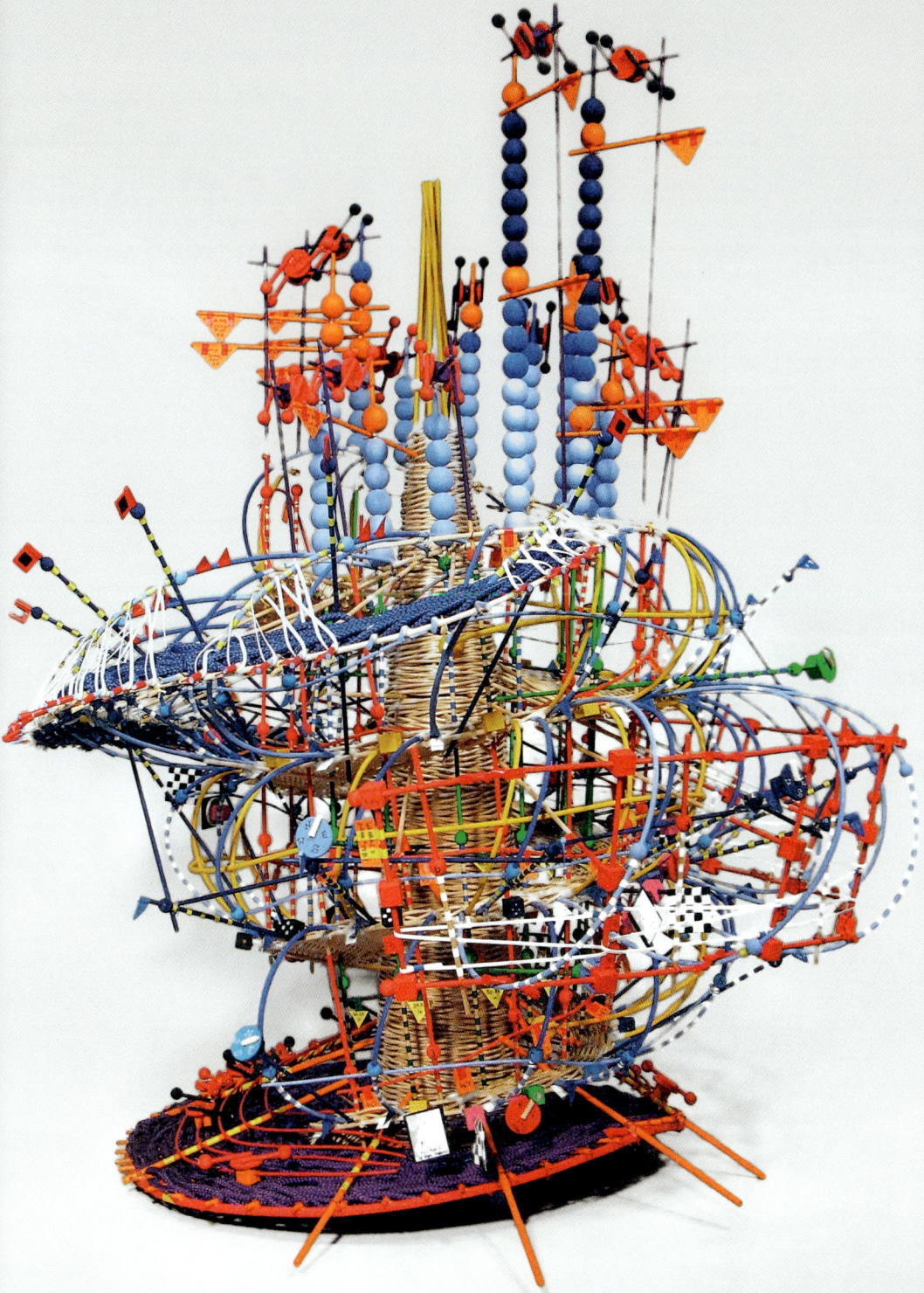

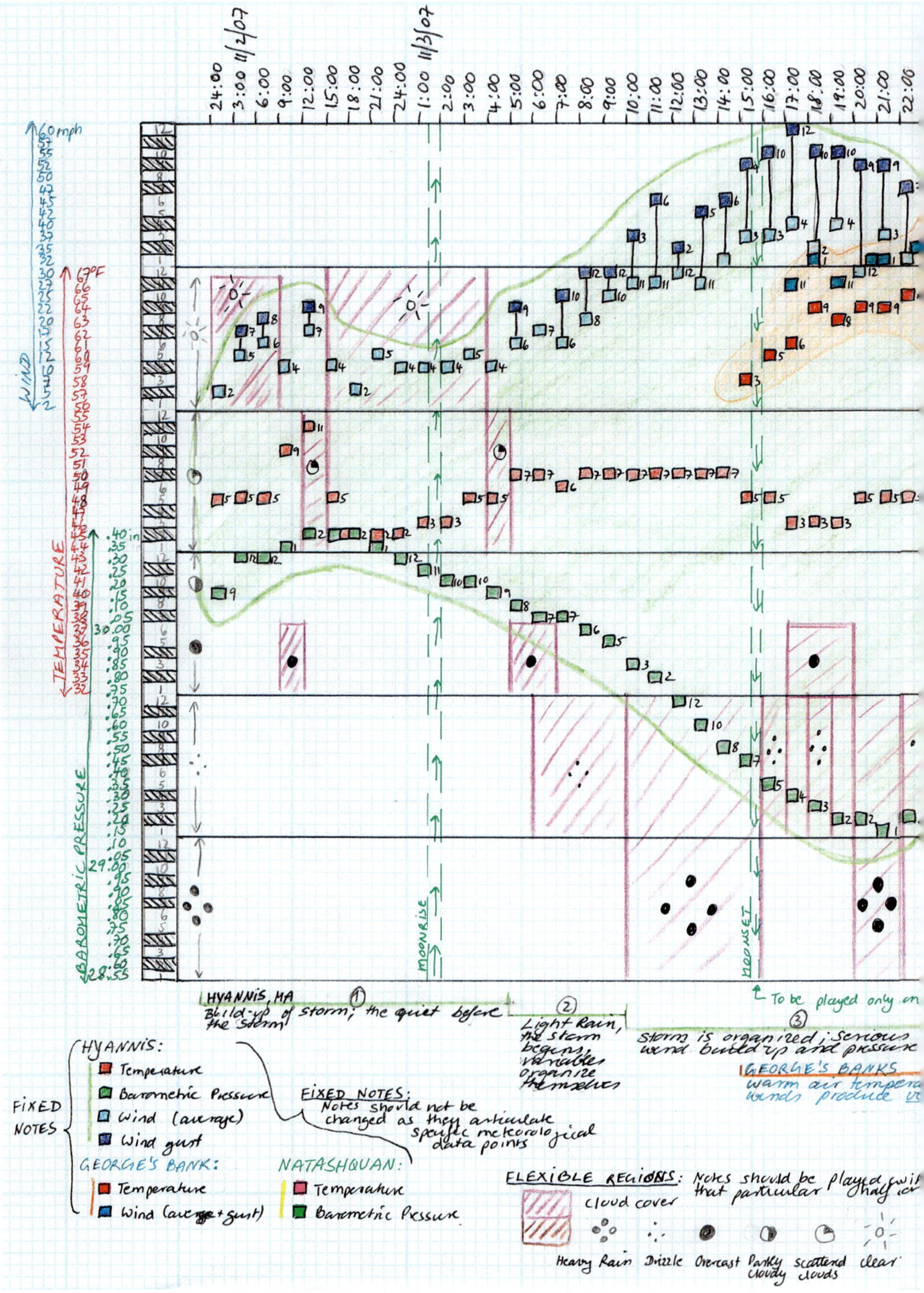

NOTES TO MUSICIANS:

This score follows the journey of Hurricane Noël as it entered the Gulf of Maine in early November 2007.

While it is written for a 6-octave piano keyboard, it can easily be arranged for other instruments.

The notes represent actual meteorological data from 3 weather stations. While it is a musical interpretation, these notes also reflect actual behavioral relationships of weather data. You hear music, but you also hear weather.

Some explanations:

• FIXED NOTES vs. FLEXIBLE REGIONS:

The score is made up of fixed notes, which represent actual numerical data. these should not be changed as they are weather. However, whether you play them as a cord or melody is up to you.

Flexible Regions indicate characteristics of weather not based on specific numbers. Within these regions, it is up to you to interpret them.

• Three:

The score is written in 3 parts (Hyannis, George's Bank and Natashquan). In addition, there are 3 main variables being translated: wind, temperature and barometric pressure.

• TEMPO, RHYTHM, SEQUENCE:

Tempo and rhythm are up to you. I have written some descriptions, but how you translate these into sound is yours. While the sequence of the storm should stay consistent, each part can be of different length.

keys; treat as "Flexible Region"

④

storm moves on and the ... find themselves again closer

...high
...cares
NATASHQUAN, QUEBEC
Noël makes landfall

HURRICANE NOEL

SCORE FOR MUSICIANS AND SCULPTOR

History of Current NFL Franchises

Whilst at first this looks like a bar chart showing the distribution of quantities, it is in fact a somewhat uncommon timeline, with time running top down. It describes the history of the 32 teams ("franchises") which currently form the US National Football League. Each team is represented by a bar, its height showing when the franchise was founded. Dotted lines through the bars indicate the renaming of a team, solid lines show when a franchise was relocated to another city. Colours show which league each team belonged to throughout its history. There is a clear mark in 1970, when the current structure was introduced with two conferences within the league: the American Football Conference (red) and the National Football Conference (blue).

NATIONAL FOOTBALL LEAGUE
HISTORY OF CURRENT FRANCHISES

CRAIG ROBINSON WWW.FLIPFLOPFLYBALL.COM

Following spread

History Flow

This project visualises the collaborative writing process of Wikipedia articles. The edit history (which is available for each article via a slider along the top) is turned into a timeline, and the example here shows the article on "Chocolate". Contributions are shown as coloured strips, with colours allotted to individual authors as listed on the left. The layers of colour reflect the structure of the text, which can be read on the very right in the version from July 27, 2003. The zigzag pattern that occurred during the month of July 2003 reveals an "edit-war": editors disagreed on whether or not to include a note on Surrealist chocolate sculptures. Developed at IBM Research in 2003, "History Flow" helped with understanding Wikipedia when it was very young.

Project Info: IBM Research, website, 2003, USA
Design: Fernanda Viegas, Martin Wattenberg

Pages 274/275

History of the Earth

This graphic covers the unimaginable period of 5 billion years. It is structured along a time-line at the bottom, which also distinguishes periods of development on Earth. The story unfolds in the direction of reading, starting top left and landing in the present on the lower right. At the same time, the unusual representation of the Earth plays with a fluctuating zoom. On the right, the flora and fauna of the past 300 million years is presented up front and is the richest and most detailed part of the picture. In contrast, the Big Bang, being the starting point to this story, is lost in the depths of remote space-time.

Project Info: *Superinteressante*, poster, 2002, Brazil
Research: Denis Russo Burgierman
Design: Rodrigo Maroja
Art Direction: Alceu Nunes
Illustration: Luiz Iria
Awards: Premio Abril de Jornalismo

Project Info: Website, 2009, UK
Design: Craig Robinson

Chocolate on Wikipedia

Authors
- Dmerrill
- Larry_Sanger
- Lee Daniel Crocker
- Conversion script
- Oliverkroll
- Brion VIBBER
- Bth
- Ortolan88
- Dachshund
- JakeVortex
- Olivier
- KF
- Vera Cruz
- Magnus Manske
- Zanimum
- Ellywa
- Youssefsan
- Wik
- Evercat
- Cyp
- Rmherman
- Daniel Quinlan

December 2001 Jan 2002 Feb Mar Apr Aug Sep Oct Nov Jan 2003 Feb May J

Chocolate

Chocolate is a common ingredient in many kinds of sweets -- one of the most popular in the world -- made from the fermented, roasted, and ground seeds of the tropical cacao tree Theobroma cacao. Dictionaries refer to this cacao substance as "chocolate," which is an intensely flavored bitter (not sweet) food, although this is legally defined as cocoa in many countries. This is usually sweetened with sugar and other ingredients and made into chocolate bars (the substance of which is also and commonly referred to as chocolate), or beverages (called cocoa or hot chocolate).

Extremely rarely, melted chocolate has been used to make a kind of surrealist sculpture called coulage.

Contents

Different kinds of chocolate

Chocolate is an extremely popular ingredient, available in many types, and great quantity. Different forms and flavors of chocolate are usually produced by varying the amount of the ingredients used to make the chocolate.
    Dark chocolate
    Milk chocolate
    Semisweet chocolate (used for cooking purposes)

The history of chocolate

The Aztecs associated chocolate with Xochiquetzal, the goddess of fertility. In the New World, chocolate was consumed in a drink called xocoatl, often seasoned with vanilla, chili pepper, and pimento. Xocoatl was believed to fight fatigue, a belief that is probably attributable to the caffeine content. The drink was said to be an acquired taste. Jose de Acosta, a Spanish Jesuit missionary who lived in Peru and then Mexico in the later 16th century, wrote:

Loathsome to such as are not acquainted with it, having a scum or froth that is very unpleasant to taste. Yet it is a drink very much esteemed among the Indians, where with they feast noble men who pass through their country. The Spaniards, both men and women, that are accustomed to the country, are very greedy of this Chocolate. They say they make diverse sorts of it, some hot, some cold, and some temperate, and put therein much of that "chili", yea, they make paste thereof, the which they say is good for the stomach and against the catarrh.

Christopher Columbus brought some cocoa beans to show Ferdinand and Isabella of Spain, but it remained for Hernando de Soto to introduce it to Europe more broadly.

The first recorded shipment of chocolate to the Old World for commercial purposes was in a shipment from Veracruz to Seville in 1585. It was still served as a beverage, but the Europeans added sugar to counteract the natural bitterness, and removed the chili pepper. By the 17th century it was a luxury item among the European nobility.

In 1828, Conrad J. van Houten patented a method for extracting the fat from cocoa beans and making powdered cocoa and cocoa butter. This made it possible to form the modern chocolate bar. It is believed that Joseph Fry made the first chocolate for eating in 1847.

Chocolate as a stimulant

Chocolate is very mildly psychoactive since it contains theobromine, small quantities of anandamide, an endogenous cannabinoid found in the brain, as well as caffeine and tryptophan.

Why chocolate tastes so good

Part of the enjoyability of the chocolate eating experience is ascribed to the fact that its melting point is slightly below human body temperature and so it melts in the mouth.

How chocolate is made

Chocolate in the media
        Charlie and the Chocolate Factory
        Chocolat
        The Poisoned Chocolates Case

See also: chocolate milk -- Kinder Egg -- Valentine's Day -- Christmas -- Easter

External Links
http://www.exploratorium.edu/exploring/exploring_chocolate/

SUPERNOVAS POSTER

LAR, DOCE LAR

A história da Terra

HÁ QUASE 5 BILHÕES DE ANOS, UMA ESTRELA EXPLODIU NA VIA LÁCTEA ESPALHANDO POEIRA PELO ESPAÇO. A GRAVIDADE JUNTOU OS GRÃOS EM PEDAÇOS MAIORES. ASSIM SURGIU O PLANETA TERRA.

células

Há 3,5 bilhões de anos, da massa de moléculas inanimadas de carbono surgiu a vida. Parece milagre, mas é pura química. O planeta, então, era freqüentemente bombardeado por meteoros, restos da explosão inicial.

3 bilhões

As células se espalham pela Terra. Mas o processo é lento, devido aos meteoros. O planeta ainda guarda o calor da explosão estelar e, por isso, seu interior vive vazando por vulcões. Outro problema são os tórridos raios solares.

2 bilhões

A agitação cósmica e geológica foi aos poucos diminuindo, enquanto o planeta esfriava. Forma-se a camada de ozônio, que torna os raios solares menos nocivos e permite o surgimento de formas de vida mais complexas.

1 bilhão

Aparecem células mais complicadas, as chamadas eucariontes, que possuem todas as organelas. A vida vai tomando o planeta, protegida do Sol pela camada de ozônio. Os meteoros são cada vez mais raros.

600 milhões

Surgem os primeiros organismos multicelulares – todos invertebrados. A variedade de vida aumenta de uma maneira impressionante. Os oceanos se povoam com os seres mais estranhos.

500

ERA ARQUEOZÓICA

ERA PROTEROZÓICA

Ao longo da história do planeta, os continentes navegaram sobre a rocha derretida.

TEXTO **DENIS RUSSO BURGIERMAN**
INFOGRÁFICO **LUIZ IRIA E RODRIGO MAROJA**

1 De tempos em tempos, a vida na Terra sofre um grande golpe e ocorre uma extinção em massa. Foi assim há meio bilhão de anos, quando boa parte dos seres sumiu de repente. Pouco se sabe sobre a tragédia – mas a prova de que ela aconteceu são as conchas fossilizadas de animais marinhos, cuja diversidade teve uma brusca redução.

2 Há 230 milhões de anos ocorreu outra grande extinção. Das espécies marinhas, 96% simplesmente sumiram. Algumas teorias especulam que grandes erupções vulcânicas provocaram isso. Essa extinção em massa, conhecida como a do fim do Permiano, foi muito pior do que a que acabou com os dinossauros.

3 A culpa pela extinção em massa que assolou o planeta há 65 milhões de anos, matando os dinossauros, geralmente é atribuída a um meteoro, embora ainda haja dúvidas. Paradoxalmente, o cataclismo foi um impulso para a vida: abriu espaço para que outras espécies se desenvolvessem. Fenômeno parecido aconteceu em outras extinções.

4 Vivemos hoje outra imensa extinção em massa, esta com uma causa bem diferente das outras: a ação humana. Centenas de espécies somem todos os dias por causa da perda de hábitats, principalmente nas florestas tropicais. O homem já é a maior força transformadora do planeta, superando tempestades, furacões e terremotos.

camada de ozônio

Aparecem os peixes primitivos – não muito diferentes dos atuais tubarões. São os primeiros vertebrados. A Terra fica mais interessante.

400 milhões
Há 350 milhões de anos, os vertebrados saem do mar – surgem os anfíbios. Todos os continentes estão unidos em um só grande bloco – a Pangéia, que começa a ser habitada por muitas plantas primitivas.

300 milhões
Os répteis aparecem há 300 milhões de anos e, em seguida, tomam o planeta. Os primeiros dinossauros passam a ser vistos em todos os continentes. Os insetos também se diversificam muito.

200 milhões
Surgem os mamíferos – então não muito mais que ratinhos com características de répteis. A Terra ainda é dos dinossauros. Outra inovação: as plantas ganham flores.

100 milhões
Com a extinção dos dinossauros, há 65 milhões de anos, sobra espaço para os mamíferos. Eles se tornam maiores e mais diversificados e herdam o trono do planeta. As aves também se espalham.

Hoje
Surge o homem – há apenas 100 mil anos, insignificantes para a história do planeta. A nova espécie altera a Terra como nenhuma antes.

ERA PALEOZÓICA   **ERA MESOZÓICA**   **ERA CENOZÓICA**

Hunting Whales

This maritime panorama explains how whales are hunted. Developed as two double spreads, it forms one continuous image. The left spread shows two harpoon boats in the process of killing a whale. Snippets of text explain each step, magnifying bubbles show details (like the tiny grenade at the tip of the harpoon, designed to kill the whale quickly with an explosion). The second spread takes the viewer aboard the accompanying factory ship. Here the whale is cut up, the meat and other parts are prepared for further processing. The box to the right adds information on the hunting of dolphins. The piece is striking in the way it uses an image to explain a process step by step.

Project Info: *Mundo Estranho*, magazine article, 2009, Brazil
Data Source: John Frizell, Greenpeace International Ocean Campaigner; Whale and Dolphin Conservation Society; American Cetacean Society
Research: Yuri Vasconscelos
Art Direction: Fabricio Miranda
Illustration: Sattu, Luiz Iria
Awards: Malofiej 2010

disparo do arpão

BARCO ARPOADOR

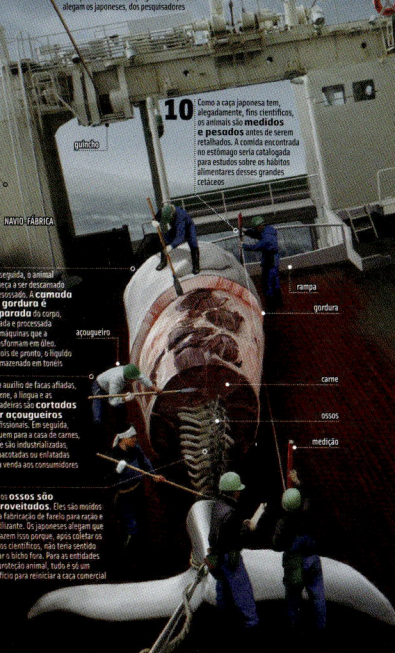

enquanto o sangue é derramado no mar, o **navio-fábrica**, líder da expedição, navega pelas redondezas, aguardando a chegada dos animais abatidos. No caso dos japoneses, esse navio é o *Nishin-maru*, uma baleineira de pesca que leva 112 tripulantes

9 À transferência das vítimas para o navio-fábrica rola por uma rampa na traseira do barco. O animal é preso a um cabo de aço e içado por um guincho. Quando chega ao convés, começa o trabalho dos açougueiros ou, como alegam os japoneses, dos pesquisadores

10 Como a caça japonesa tem, alegadamente, fins científicos, os animais são **medidos e pesados** antes de serem retalhados. À comida encontrada no estômago seria catalogada para estudos sobre os hábitos alimentares desses grandes cetáceos

Uma das "pesquisas" feitas pelos japoneses com os animais mortos foi a inseminação de vacas com o sêmen de baleias machos. Até hoje, não se sabe para quê...

NAVIO-FÁBRICA

guincho

rampa

gordura

11 Em seguida, o animal começa a ser descarnado e desossado. A **camada de gordura é separada** do corpo, fatiada e processada em máquinas que a transformam em óleo. Depois de pronto, o líquido é armazenado em tonéis

açougueiro

carne

12 Com auxílio de facas afiadas, a carne, a língua e as nadadeiras são **cortados por açougueiros** profissionais. Em seguida, seguem para a casa de carnes, onde são industrializadas, empacotadas ou enlatadas para venda aos consumidores

ossos

medição

13 Até os **ossos são aproveitados**. Eles são moídos para fabricação de farelo para ração e fertilizante. Os japoneses alegam que só fazem isso porque, após coletar os dados científicos, não teria sentido jogar o bicho fora. Para as entidades de proteção animal, tudo é só um artifício para reiniciar a caça comercial

YES, NÓS TEMOS BALEIA

De perseguidor, o Brasil hoje é um grande defensor do cetáceo

No passado, o litoral brasileiro também foi cenário para a cruenta caça a baleias. O porto de Cabedelo, na Paraíba, era um dos mais ativos e servia de sede para a empresa Copesbra, que, em seus 75 anos de atuação, matou milhares de baleias de várias espécies – o óleo retirado da gordura do bicho era usado para iluminação e preparo de tinta, entre outras coisas. Um decreto do governo proibiu a caça no país em 1986 e, hoje, o Brasil é uma das nações mais ativas na luta contra a caça aos cetáceos. Em 2007, por exemplo, o Brasil aderiu ao grande protesto diplomático em conjunto com outros 30 países contra a carnificina promovida pelo Japão.

BRUTALIDADE SEM FIM

Assim como suas "primas" baleias, os golfinhos também são barbaramente caçados

TRADIÇÃO MACABRA

Estima-se que mais de mil golfinhos-pilotos (*Globicephala melaena*) sejam barbaramente assassinados todos os anos apenas nas Ilhas Faroe (*veja no mapa*). A caçada é feita pelos moradores da própria comunidade, numa espécie de rito de passagem dos jovens para a idade adulta

Ilhas Faroe

A matança de golfinhos rola em três áreas: nas ilhas Faroe, território dinamarquês no Atlântico Norte; em Taiji, na costa do Japão; e nas ilhas Salomão, no oceano Pacífico

EUROPA

ENCURRALADOS

Logo que os golfinhos são avistados, os pescadores rumam em botes na direção dos animais, que são dóceis e pacíficos. Os caras então fazem um semicírculo com os botes para encurralar o bando, conduzindo os bichos para uma baía, de forma que não escapem

ATAQUE BRUTAL

Os jovens trucidam os animais com facas e arpões. Os animais se contorcem de dor e podem levar um tempão para morrer. Enquanto isso, os sobreviventes ficam juntos aos outros, sem esboçar qualquer reação agressiva nem tentar fugir

ÁGUA ESCARLATE

Enquanto os animais mortos são levados para praia ou colocados dentro dos barcos, a sanguaria vai tingindo o mar de vermelho. Infelizmente, a Comissão Baleeira Internacional não controla a matança de golfinhos, pois ela rola na costa dos países e não em águas internacionais, como no caso das baleias

277

IT'S THE ECONOMY, STUPID!

The dollar is weak. Food and oil prices are high. Our nation is spending well beyond its means and owes trillions of dollars in debt to foreign governments. What most of the gloom-and-doom reports don't provide, however, is perspective—a historical survey of an economy that's been through more than a few ups and downs in its day. Here's a farsighted view of how our temperamental economic machine works, and a close-up of how it stands today. 💰 KEY DEFINITIONS

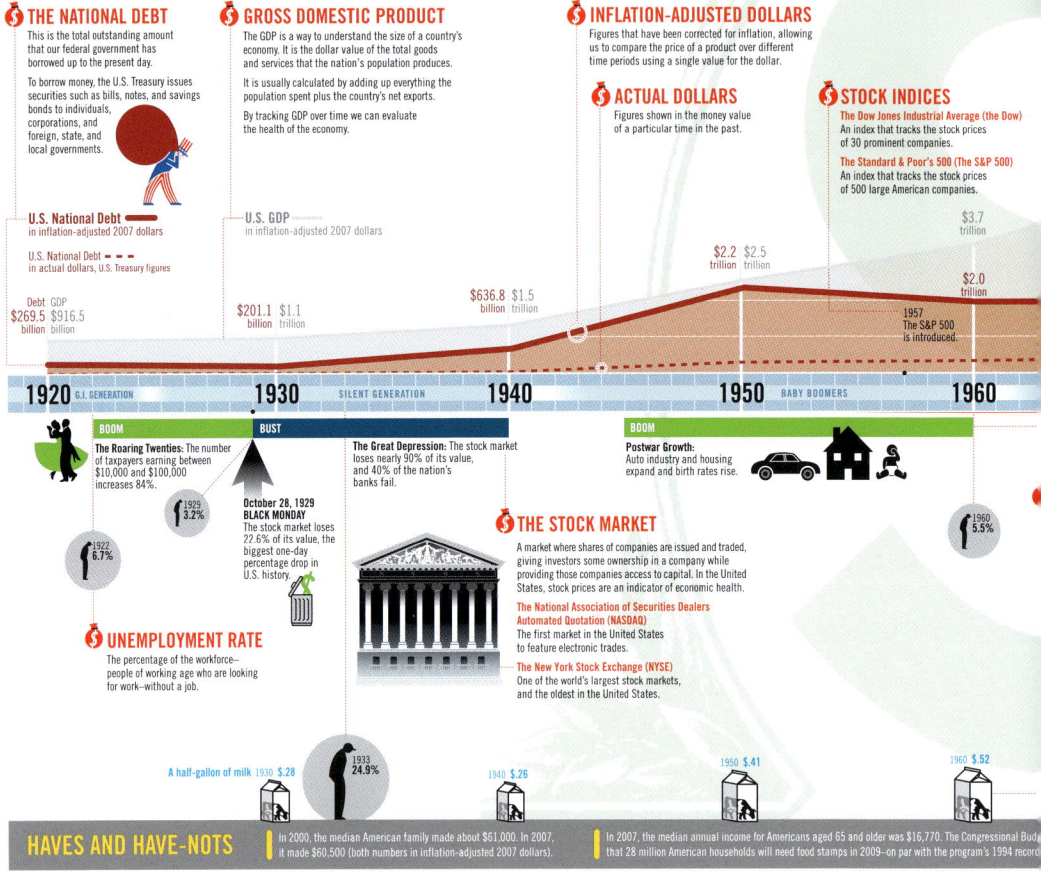

💰 **THE NATIONAL DEBT**
This is the total outstanding amount that our federal government has borrowed up to the present day.

To borrow money, the U.S. Treasury issues securities such as bills, notes, and savings bonds to individuals, corporations, and foreign, state, and local governments.

💰 **GROSS DOMESTIC PRODUCT**
The GDP is a way to understand the size of a country's economy. It is the dollar value of the total goods and services that the nation's population produces.

It is usually calculated by adding up everything the population spent plus the country's net exports.

By tracking GDP over time we can evaluate the health of the economy.

💰 **INFLATION-ADJUSTED DOLLARS**
Figures that have been corrected for inflation, allowing us to compare the price of a product over different time periods using a single value for the dollar.

💰 **ACTUAL DOLLARS**
Figures shown in the money value of a particular time in the past.

💰 **STOCK INDICES**
The Dow Jones Industrial Average (the Dow)
An index that tracks the stock prices of 30 prominent companies.

The Standard & Poor's 500 (The S&P 500)
An index that tracks the stock prices of 500 large American companies.

U.S. National Debt
in inflation-adjusted 2007 dollars

U.S. National Debt
in actual dollars, U.S. Treasury figures

U.S. GDP
in inflation-adjusted 2007 dollars

Debt	GDP
$269.5 billion	$916.5 billion

$201.1 billion $1.1 trillion

$636.8 billion $1.5 trillion

$2.2 trillion $2.5 trillion

$2.0 trillion

$3.7 trillion

1957
The S&P 500 is introduced.

1920 G.I. GENERATION	1930 SILENT GENERATION	1940	1950 BABY BOOMERS	1960

BOOM
The Roaring Twenties: The number of taxpayers earning between $10,000 and $100,000 increases 84%.

BUST

BOOM
Postwar Growth: Auto industry and housing expand and birth rates rise.

1929 3.2%

1922 6.7%

1960 5.5%

October 28, 1929 BLACK MONDAY
The stock market loses 22.6% of its value, the biggest one-day percentage drop in U.S. history.

The Great Depression: The stock market loses nearly 90% of its value, and 40% of the nation's banks fail.

💰 **THE STOCK MARKET**
A market where shares of companies are issued and traded, giving investors some ownership in a company while providing those companies access to capital. In the United States, stock prices are an indicator of economic health.

The National Association of Securities Dealers Automated Quotation (NASDAQ)
The first market in the United States to feature electronic trades.

The New York Stock Exchange (NYSE)
One of the world's largest stock markets, and the oldest in the United States.

💰 **UNEMPLOYMENT RATE**
The percentage of the workforce—people of working age who are looking for work—without a job.

1933 24.9%

A half-gallon of milk 1930 $.28

1940 $.26

1950 $.41

1960 $.52

HAVES AND HAVE-NOTS In 2000, the median American family made about $61,000. In 2007, it made $60,500 (both numbers in inflation-adjusted 2007 dollars). In 2007, the median annual income for Americans aged 65 and older was $16,770. The Congressional Budg... that 28 million American households will need food stamps in 2009—on par with the program's 1994 record...

It's the Economy, Stupid!

This timeline presents a history of the US economy, starting in 1920. Small red money-bags mark explanations of economic key concepts. Along the bottom, inflation is demonstrated by the changing price of a half-gallon of milk. Above the timeline, both the GDP and the national deficit increase massively. The measuring scale is given in trillions (white lines on red). Below the timeline, a red line starting in the Sixties indicates how the government started spending more than they earned and thus constantly increased the national debt. This deficit is shown to the same scale as the national debt above, and reaches 357 billion at the end of the line. The magnifying-glass shows this bigger, as it seems such a small amount when shown in the trillions scale.

WHO OWNS AMERICA?

A big chunk of the national debt—about 28%, or $2.6 trillion—is held by foreign governments.

Top five foreign holders of treasury securities from largest to smallest:
● Japan ● China ● the United Kingdom ● oil exporters* ● Brazil
*Ecuador, Venezuela, Indonesia, Bahrain, Iran, Iraq, Kuwait, Oman, Qatar, Saudi Arabia, the United Arab Emirates, Algeria, Gabon, Libya, and Nigeria

🔴 RECESSION

A recession, also called a "bust," is generally defined as two quarters of slow or negative GDP growth.

The technical definition, as set by the National Bureau of Economic Research, a private nonprofit research organization, is when economic factors such as GDP, income, employment, industrial production, manufacturing, and sales significantly decline over the course of more than several months.

SS CYCLE

f economic growth or
ST, or recession, is a long-term
raction. From 1854 to 1945, the
sted 21 months. Since World War II,
aged 50 months and contractions have

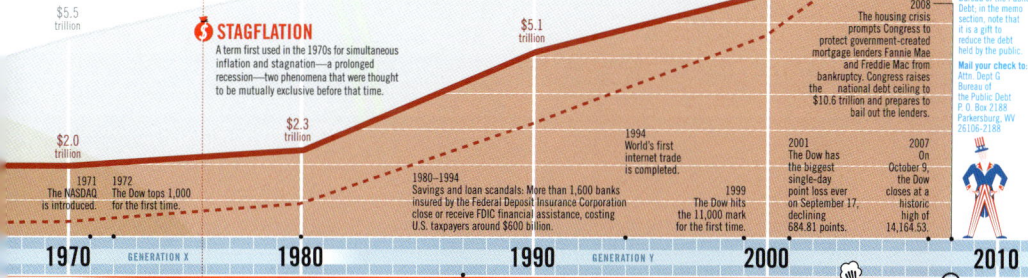

$11.8 trillion

$9.2 trillion

GDP $13.8 trillion (2007)

$7.0 trillion

The federal government doesn't follow the same accounting practices it requires corporations and state and local governments to follow. If it did, the national debt would actually be $59.1 trillion.

If U.S. citizens were to pay down the entire national debt today it would cost every household approximately $516,000.

$6.9 trillion

U.S. national debt $9.6 trillion (through summer 2008)

$5.5 trillion

🔴 STAGFLATION

A term first used in the 1970s for simultaneous inflation and stagnation—a prolonged recession—two phenomena that were thought to be mutually exclusive before that time.

$5.1 trillion

2008
The housing crisis prompts Congress to protect government-created mortgage lenders Fannie Mae and Freddie Mac from bankruptcy. Congress raises the national debt ceiling to $10.6 trillion and prepares to bail out the lenders.

$2.3 trillion

2007

Want to reduce the national debt? The government has a suggestion:

Send it a check payable to the Bureau of the Public Debt, on the memo section, note that it is a gift to reduce the debt held by the public.

Mail your check to:
Attn. Dept G
Bureau of
the Public Debt
P.O. Box 2188
Parkersburg, WV
26106-2188

$2.0 trillion

1971
The NASDAQ is introduced.

1972
The Dow tops 1,000 for the first time.

1980–1994
Savings and loan scandals: More than 1,600 banks insured by the Federal Deposit Insurance Corporation close or receive FDIC financial assistance, costing U.S. taxpayers around $600 billion.

1994
World's first internet trade is completed.

1999
The Dow hits the 11,000 mark for the first time.

2001
The Dow has the biggest single-day point loss ever on September 17, declining 684.81 points.

2007
On October 9, the Dow closes at a historic high of 14,164.53.

1970	1980	1990	2000	2010
GENERATION X		GENERATION Y		

BUST
GDP falls by 4.9% in inflation-adjusted dollars.

BUST
Business bankruptcies rise by 50% from 1981 to 1982.

BOOM
Tech revolution: Dotcom start-ups emerge; investments pour into information technology.

BUST
Dotcom bubble bursts and stocks on the tech-heavy NASDAQ exchange lose $5 trillion.

October 19, 1987
BLACK MONDAY
The largest one-day percentage drop of the Dow Jones index. The market declines 508.32 points (22.6%), losing $500 billion in one day.

1980
7.2%

🔴 THE NATIONAL DEFICIT

The national budget is financed by government income, i.e., what the government brings in through taxes and other fees for public services.

A budget deficit results when the federal government spends more than it brings in during a given year. A surplus is when more is brought in than spent.

When the government spends as much as it takes in, the budget is balanced. To cover a budget deficit the government borrows money; this borrowing then increases the national debt.

2008
5.2%
(est.)

2008
U.S. deficit
-$357 billion
(estimated)

-$100 billion
-$200
-$300
-$400
Scale enlarged for visibility

ods and services
as an oversupply
t or increasing
r corresponding
n's currency has

economy mostly
ctability—since
w when or how
consumers can
shock.

inflation:
of milk
ars

1970 $.66

1980 $1.05

1990 $1.39

Half-gallon price unavailable for 2000

2008 (1st q.) $2.40

43% of American households spend more than they earn annually.
44% of American employees said they live "paycheck to paycheck" in 2007, up from 37% in 2006.

The average American household has $8,565 in credit-card debt, which is 15% higher than it was in 2000.

Approximately 42% of American households lack enough liquid savings to support themselves for three months.

Project Info: GOOD, poster, 2008, USA
Data Source: American Farm Bureau Federation; Congressional Budget Office; The Economist; FDIC; Investopedia; PBS; US Bureau of Labor Statistics; US Census Bureau
Design: Nigel Holmes
Art Direction: Casey Caplowe (GOOD)

Jacko: éxito en negro, fracaso en blanco

Carrera artística

Vida personal

1958

Nace el 29 de agosto de 1958
Gary, Indiana, Estados Unidos

Es el séptimo de 9 hermanos.
Entre ellos el resto de los
Jackson Five, Janet y Latoya

Carrera

THE JACKSON FIVE

Ventas de álbumes en solitario
En millones de copias
No incluye reediciones

Debuta a los cinco años con
The Jackson Five — 1963

El padre de los
hermanos Jackson es
el mánager del grupo

Discográficas

MOTOWN

The Jackson Five
publica su primer sencillo
con la Motown **'I want you back'** — 1969

Conoce a Diana Ross

'ABC' primer número uno de con
The Jackson Five con sólo 12 años — 1970

SOLITARIO

Empieza su carrera en solitario
4,1 · **'Got to be there'** — 1972
4,4 · **'Ben'**

The Jackson Five abandona
la discográfica Motown — 1976

25

**EPIC
(SONY BMG)**

'Off the Wall'
producido por Quincy Jones
Primer grammy — 1979

109

'Thriller'
(8 premios grammy)
Su videoclip es un éxito mundial — 1982

Michael abandona The Jacksons — 1984

Participa en la grabación de
'We are the World' por África — 1985

**Aparece con la
piel blanqueada**

30

'Bad'
Se estrena la película 'Moonwalker' — 1987

— 1988

Publica su autobiografía
Protagoniza el primer anuncio
publicitario emitido en Rusia

32

'Dangerous'
y el single 'Black or White' — 1991

— 1993 Es acusado de pederastia

— 1994 Se casa con la hija de Elvis,
Lisa Marie Presley

18

'HIStory: Past, Present and Future'
Acompañado de una gran
campaña promocional — 1995

— 1996 Se divorcia y se casa con su dermatóloga

7

'Blood On The Dance Floor'
Album de remezclas — 1997

Nace su primer hijo, Prince Michael Jackson Jr.

— 1998 Nace su hija Paris Michael Katherine Jackson

— 1999 Se vuelve a divorciar

9

'Invencible'
Último álbum de estudio — 2001

— 2002 Nace su segundo hijo, Prince Michael II,
de madre desconocida

— 2003 Es acusado de abusar sexualmente
de un menor. Fue declarado inocente en 2005

— 2005 Se traslada a vivir a Bahrein.
Las autoridades ordenan el cierre de
su rancho 'Neverland'

En este periodo se especuló
con su vuelta al estudio
y se programó una gira que
empezaría este verano
en Londres — 2009

Fallece
25 de junio de 2009
Los Ángeles, Estados Unidos

Jacko: Success in Black, Failure in White

The day after Michael Jackson's death, Spanish newspaper *Público* published this timeline with important personal and professional landmarks in Jackson's life. With time running top down, the graphic shows his career on the left, and details of his personal life on the right. The strong contrast of black and white symbolises Jackson's ongoing quest for 'white' facial features and a lighter skin colour. The "white period" begins in the late 1980s, when his increasingly pale skin gained widespread media attention. The pink graph towards the left shows numbers of records sold, the bars to the very left indicate his affiliation with the Jackson Five vs. his solo career, and the labels on which he released his records.

Project Info: "Goodbye to the King of Pop", *Público*, newspaper article, 2009, Spain
Data Source: Billboard; IFPI; Sony Music; MichaelJackson.com
Design: Álvaro Valiño
Awards: Malofiej 2010, Silver

Jerry Garcia

Marian Bantjes designed this intriguing diagram for *Fader* magazine in 2007. It depicts the musical cosmos of Jerry Garcia and his legendary American rock band, The Grateful Dead. The history of music evolves top down in this diagram, starting with Garcia's roots in the American blues and rock'n'roll scene of the Fifties and Sixties. The central flower lists band members of The Grateful Dead, as well as many friends, contemporaries and collaborators Jerry Garcia was in touch with. At the bottom, influences are passed on to the next generations of younger musicians.

Project Info: *The Fader*, magazine article and poster, 2007, USA
Design: Marian Bantjes
Art Direction: Phil Bicker

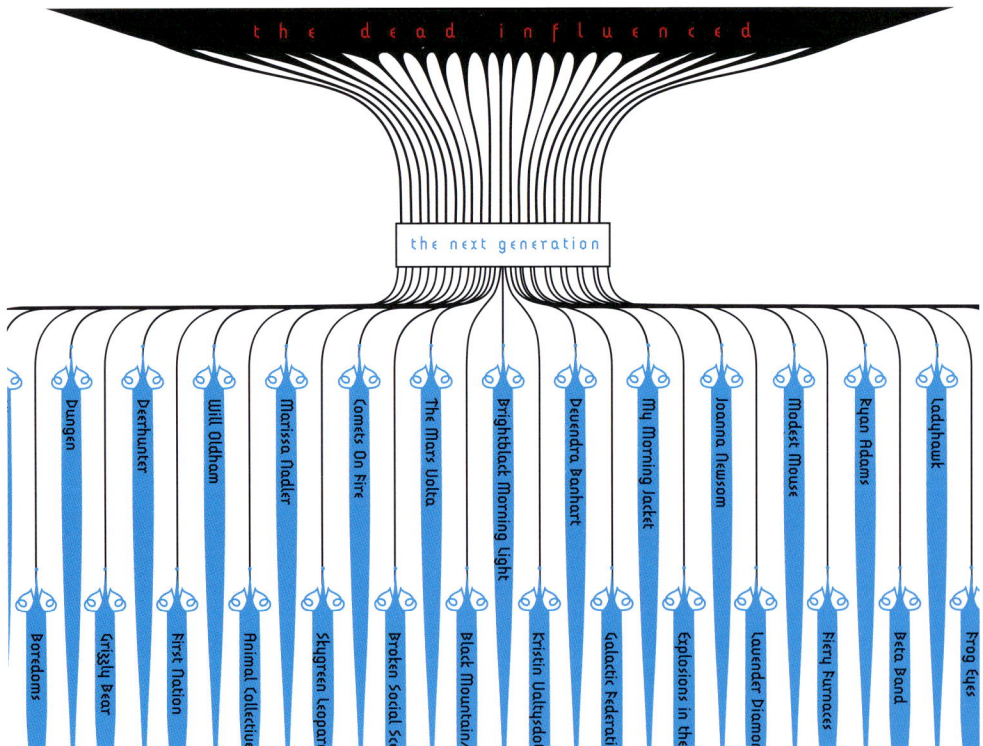

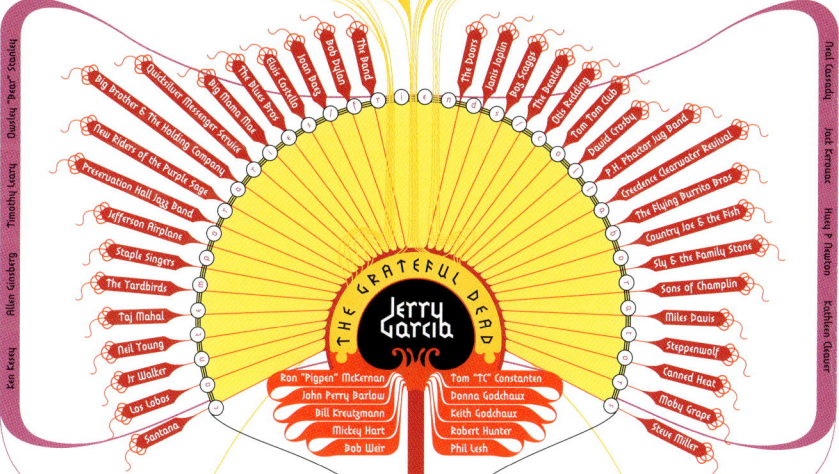

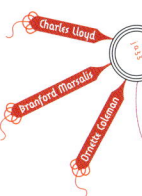

Project Info: Poster, 2010, USA
Design: Minh Anh Vo, Victor Schuft (Papercut)

RUI, MINH ANH, VICTOR & "SYLVIA" (THE CAR)

LA×NYC
ROAD TI
14 DAYS
4129 MI / 6645 KM / 7x LENGTH
11H ON THE PER DAY / 295 MI
ROAD 475 KM
WE DROVE 17 STATES / 94 POSTC
ACROSS

LA-NYC

For the visualisation of their road-trip through
the United States in 2009, French designers
Minh Anh Vo and Victor Schuft made the timeline their guiding principle. The days of their
trip are marked alternately in black and red.
Little flags above mark the states that were
crossed, while blue flashes show the mileage.
Below the timeline appear individual places
travelled through. In the upper part of the image, the red line follows their route on an invisible map of the US, with black tags indicating
the succession of days.

E /

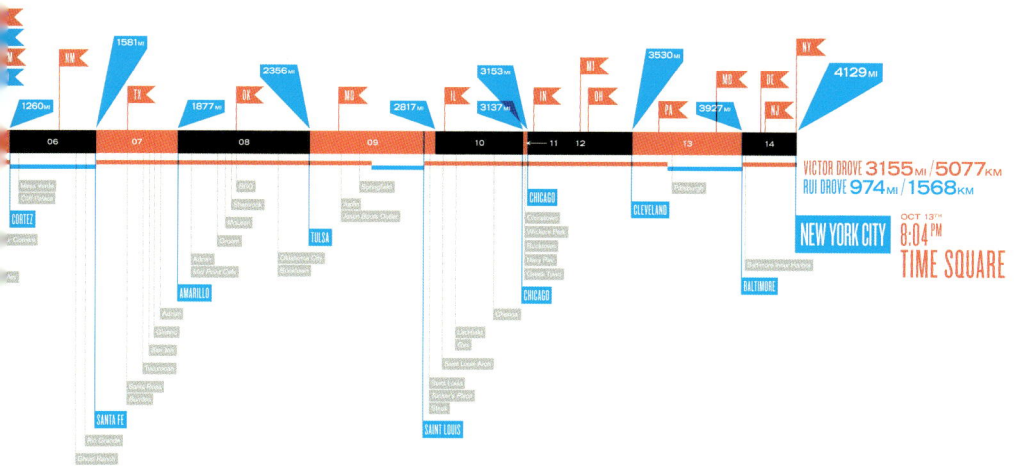

4129 MI
6645 KM

NEW YORK CITY, NY
ARRIVAL

CHICAGO IL
DAY #11, 12

CLEVELAND, OH
DAY #13

BALTIMORE, MD
DAY #14

SANTA FE, NM
DAY #7

TULSA, OK
DAY #9

SAINT LOUIS, MO
DAY #10

AMARILLO, TX
DAY #8

NM
NM
1581 MI
TX
1877 MI
OK
2356 MI
MO
2817 MI
IL
3153 KM
3137 MI
IN
OH
MI
3530 MI
PA
3927 MI
NJ
MD
DC
NY
4129 MI

1260 MI

| 06 | 07 | 08 | 09 | 10 | 11 | 12 | 13 | 14 |

Mesa Verde
Dennison
Cliff View
CORTEZ
El Comino
Aco
SANTA FE
Rio Grande
Great Depth

Aztec
Shiprock
Gallup
AMARILLO
Adrian
Glenrio
San Jon
Tucumcari
Santa Rosa
Albama

MEX
Shamrock
Waivewood
Adrian
Mid Point Cafe
Oklahoma City
Bricktown
TULSA

Birmingham
Martin
Hotel
Jesse Brooks Oudan
SAINT LOUIS
Saint Louis
Gateway Arch
Union
Chain

Chelsea
Llandale
Viso
West Louis Arch

Pleasanton
Childswood
City Hyde Park
Millenium Park
Hyde Park
Hyde Park
Mag Mile
Grate Tasty
CHICAGO
CHICAGO

Pittsburgh
CLEVELAND

Baltimore Inner Harbor
BALTIMORE

VICTOR DROVE 3155 MI / 5077 KM
RUI DROVE 974 MI / 1568 KM

NEW YORK CITY
OCT 13 TH
8:04 PM
TIME SQUARE

200 MI   400 KM

Life Map to Quarter-Life Crisis

Whilst diagrams have been constructed to chart statistical data or technical processes, and thus retain a reputation for belonging to the more boring and non-human things on Earth, designers are increasingly "using" them for charting emotional troubles or personal experiences. Corcoran's "Life Map to Quarter-Life Crisis" is a guide to the life experiences of an average youth in the US. Trying to make the step from adolescence to adulthood seems to entail the inevitable hardship of having to traverse a serious quarter-age crisis.

Project Info: Metro Design Studio, book, 2009, USA
Design: Colleen Corcoran

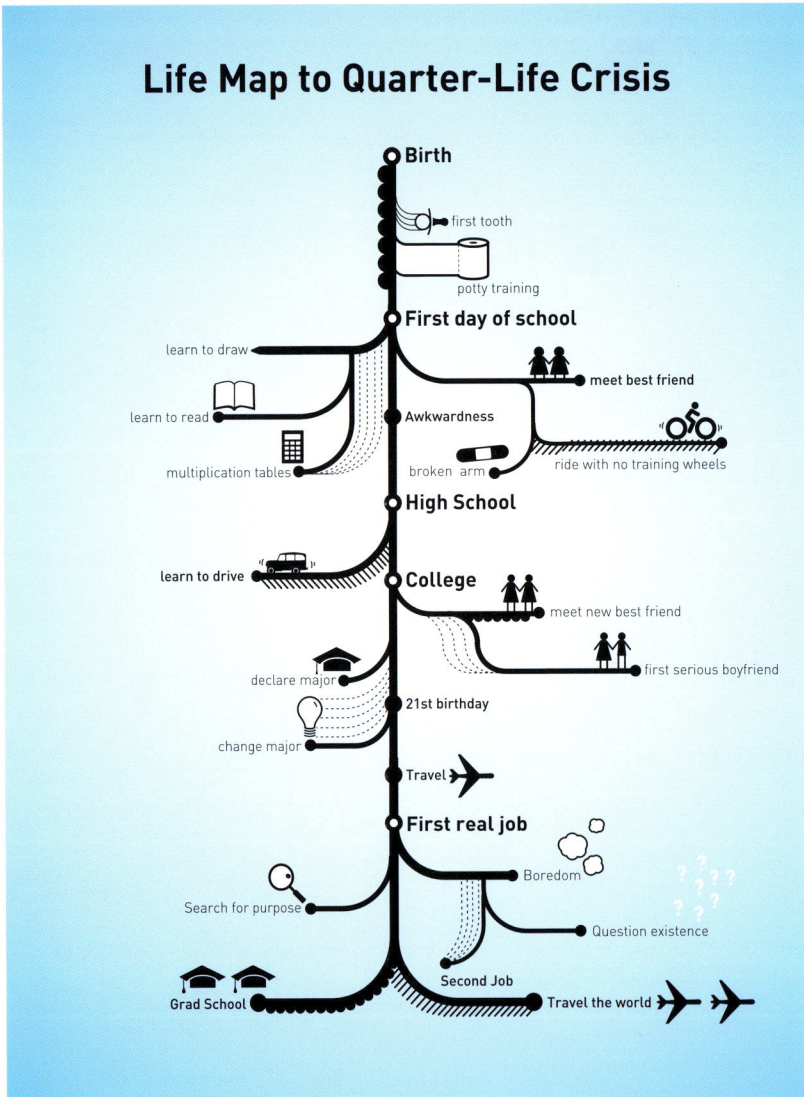

Life Map to Quarter-Life Crisis

Birth
first tooth
potty training
First day of school
learn to draw
meet best friend
learn to read
Awkwardness
multiplication tables
broken arm
ride with no training wheels
High School
learn to drive
College
meet new best friend
declare major
first serious boyfriend
21st birthday
change major
Travel
First real job
Boredom
Search for purpose
Question existence
Second Job
Grad School
Travel the world

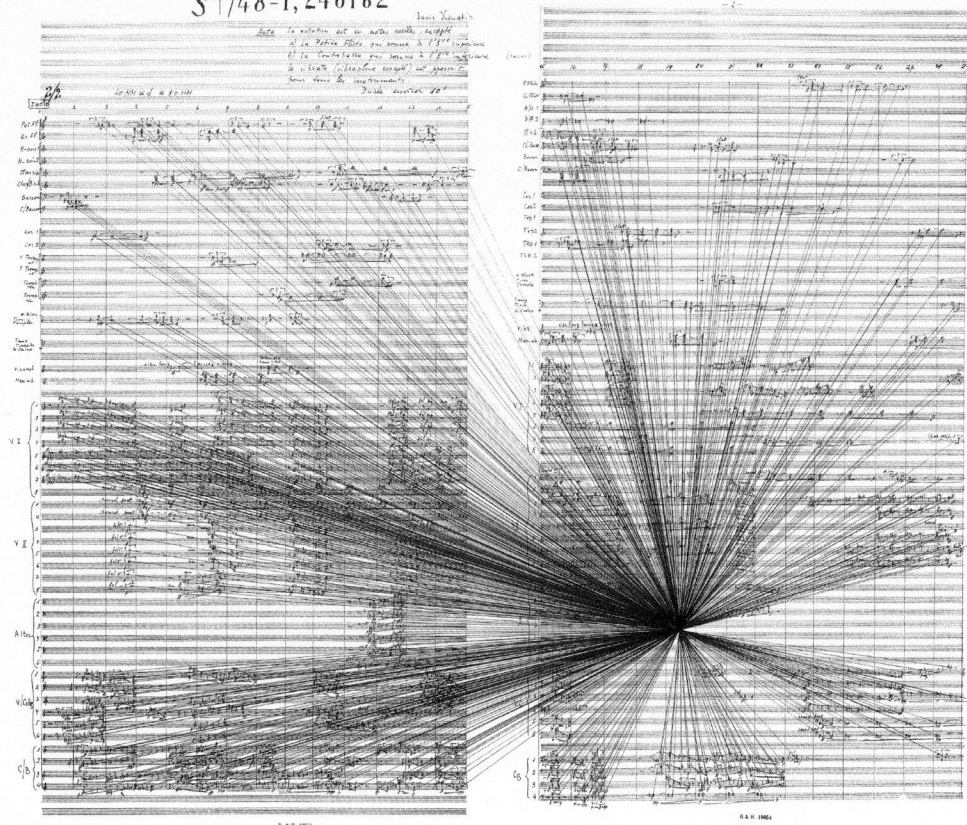

Mass Black Implosion

Australian visual and sound artist Marco Fusinato combines graphics and music in his "Mass Black Implosion" series. The drawings are based on the scores of post-war avant-garde or contemporary composers and on the only composition by painter Yves Klein. Fusinato connects all the notes of the individual pieces with fine lines to a freely chosen focal point – ignoring all other graphic notations in the scores. The many notes of a fast or polyphonic work result in density and

blackness, scores with fewer notes in more spread-out, calmer line drawings. By expanding the music notation, he creates a scheme to picture the style of each piece, and thus "makes visible the sound", or as the title suggests, the point where the music implodes.

Project Info: Series of drawings, 2007–2009, Australia
Artist: Marco Fusinato
Additional Info: Ink on archival facsimile of score; Marco Fusinato is represented by Anna Schwartz Gallery, Melbourne

Percy Grainger
FREE MUSIC No.1 (1937)

Composed for String Quartet,
arranged by the composer for four Theremins

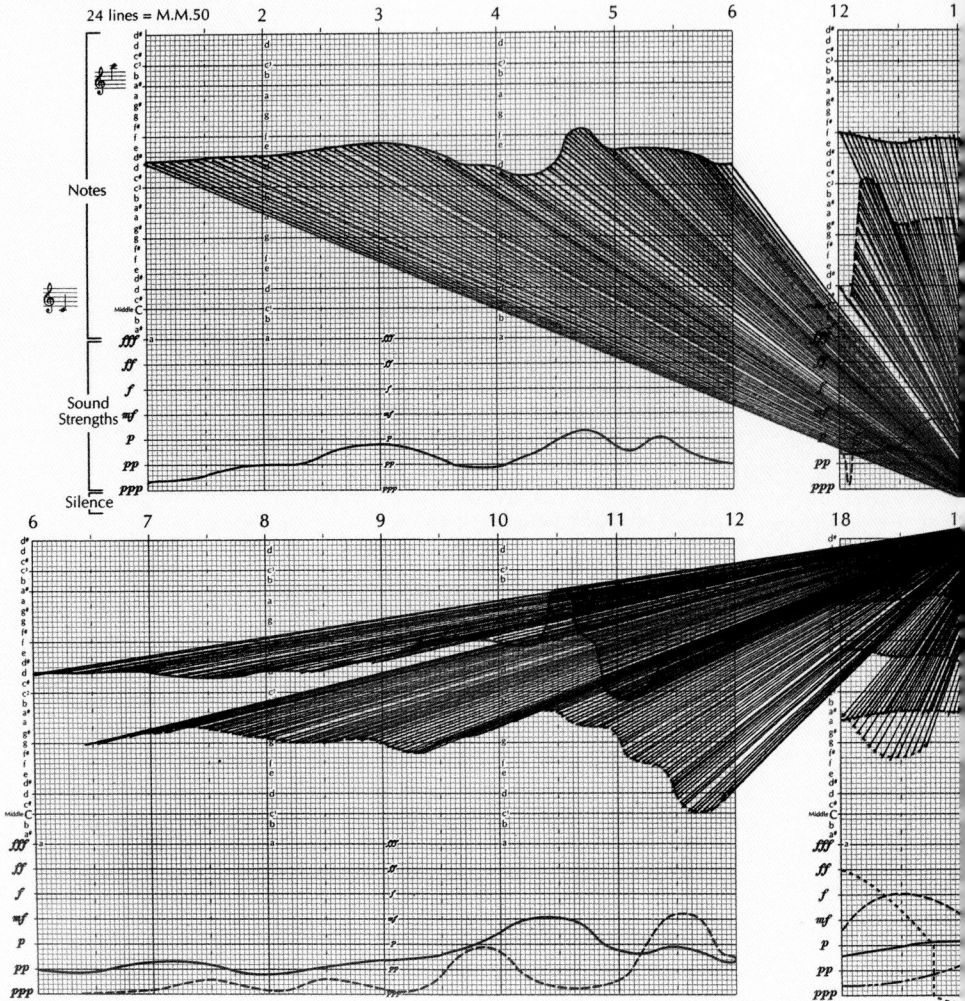

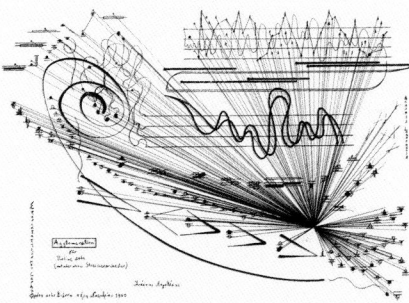

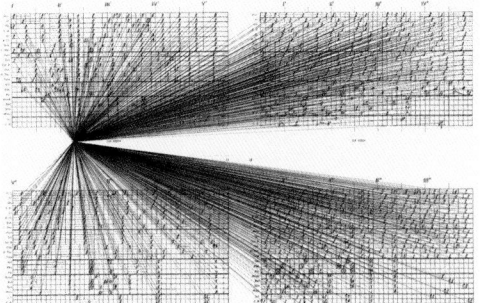

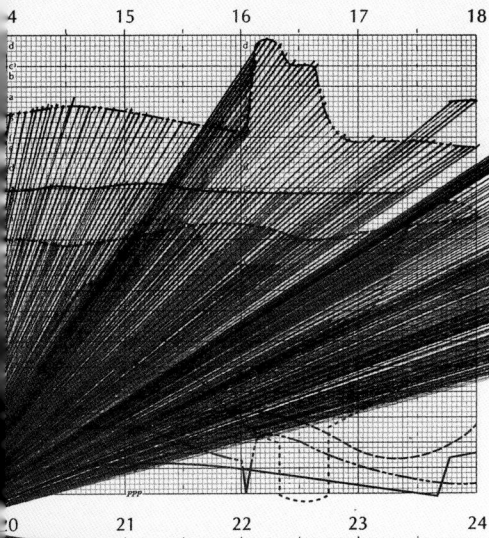

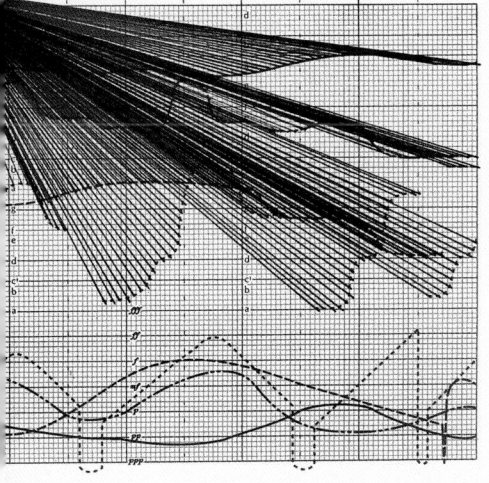

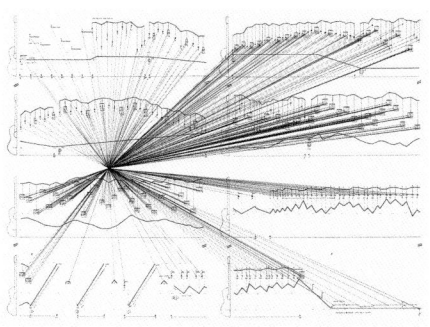

[READY, SET, GO]

MISSION(S) TO MARS

Though most missions TO THE RED PLANET HAVE FAILED, THE SUCCESS RATE IS DEFINITELY IMPROVING + + +

SOURCES: CORNELL UNIVERSITY, EUROPEAN SPACE AGENCY, NASA, RUSSIANSPACEWEB.COM

MISSION FAILURE
FLYBY
ORBITER
LANDER
ROVER

1960
MARSNIK 1
MARSNIK 2

1962
SPUTNIK 22
MARS 1
SPUTNIK 24

1963
KOSMOS 21

MARINER 3
MARINER 4
ZOND 2
ZOND 3 (PRIMARY MISSION NOT MARS)

1964

1965
MARINER 6
MARINER 7
MARS 1969A
MARS 1969B

1969
MARINER 8
KOSMOS 419
MARS 2
MARS 3
MARINER 9

1971
MARS 4
MARS 5
MARS 6
MARS 7

1973
VIKING 1
VIKING 2

1975

PHOBOS 1
PHOBOS 2

1988

MARS OBSERVER

1992

MARS GLOBAL SURVEYOR
MARS 96
MARS PATHFINDER

1996

NOZOMI
MARS CLIMATE ORBITER
MARS POLAR LANDER / DEEP SPACE 2 PROBES

1998

1999

MARS ODYSSEY

2001

MARS EXPRESS / BEAGLE 2
MARS EXPLORATION ROVER-SPIRIT
MARS EXPLORATION ROVER-OPPORTUNITY

2003

ROSETTA (PRIMARY MISSION NOT MARS)

2004

MARS RECONNAISSANCE ORBITER

2005

PHOENIX MARS LANDER
DAWN (PRIMARY MISSION NOT MARS)

2007

PHOBOS-GRUNT / YINGHUO-1 (2009)
MARS SCIENCE LABORATORY (2011)
MAVEN (2013)
EXOMARS (2016)

FUTURE

MARINER 4
Success. Returned 21 images. First successful flyby.

MARS 3
Partial success. Orbiter obtained eight months of data. Lander landed but gathered only 20 seconds of data. First successful landing on Mars.

MARS 5
Partial success. Returned 60 images but failed after only nine days.

MARS 6
Partial success. Lander produced data during descent but failed before landing.

PHOBOS 2
Partial success. Returned some data but lost contact before deploying lander.

MARS EXPRESS / BEAGLE 2
Partial success. Orbiter completed primary mission in November 2005 and is still in orbit on extended mission. Beagle 2 lander lost on arrival.

DAWN
On its way to proto-planets Vesta and Ceres. Completed Mars flyby in February 2009.

FUTURE
Phobos-Grunt/Yinghuo-1 will be a sample-return lander/orbiter, Mars Science Laboratory will be a rover, MAVEN will be an orbiter, and ExoMars will be an orbiter/lander/rover.

Legend:
- SOVIET UNION
- UNITED STATES
- RUSSIA
- JAPAN
- EUROPEAN SPACE AGENCY
- RUSSIA/CHINA

- ○ MISSION FAILURE
- ◐ FLYBY
- ◉ ORBITER
- ◍ LANDER
- ○ ROVER

BRYAN CHRISTIE DESIGN

Mission(s) to Mars

Our neighbouring planet Mars has been the destination of numerous space missions, with varying success. Bryan Christie Design developed this graphic for technology magazine *IEEE Spectrum* to show all the attempted missions to Mars, successful and unsuccessful. Traditionally this kind of information is often presented as a table, a simple list of entries, with additional information for each entry.

Here, the designers developed an image of Mars as the target destination for the various missions. The length of the bars shows the level of success and what type of mission it was, i.e. fly-by, orbiter, landing or rover. Colours represent the different countries that sent the missions; the missions themselves were then grouped by year.

Project Info: *IEEE Spectrum*, magazine article, 2009, USA
Data Source: Cornell University; European Space Agency;
NASA; RussianSpaceWeb.com
Design: Bryan Christie,Joe Lertola
Art Direction: Mark Montgomery, Michael Solita

Following spread

Mitsubishi Logistics Supply Chain

In this graphic developed for a Japanese logistics supplier, the company's portfolio is represented in a flow chart. Whilst the company focused on warehouse services after its founding in the late 19th century, it later branched out into transportation handling to and from Japan. This is reflected here in representing the full logistics chain in a process chart, from the production of goods through various transportation facilities down to storage and distribution to retailers. From the bottom left around the arc, motion is indicated by the direction in which vehicles move, while layers indicate the variety of services. The monochrome background recalls traditional ink drawings.

Project Info: Mitsubishi Logistics, booklet, 2011, Japan
Design: Kunihiko Nishiue (Dynamite Brothers Syndicate)
Illustration: Tokuma (Bowlgraphics)
Agency: Mainichi Communications Inc.

Supply Chain of Mitsubishi Logistics

グローバル化に対応した
国内外一体の
ロジスティクス事業

小さくて高価なモノや、
急いで運ばなければ
いけないモノは、
飛行機を手配して運ぶ。

ガントリークレーンによって
三菱倉庫が手配した
コンテナ船などに荷物が
積み込まれる。
国際輸送では船舶が
大きな割合を占める。

モノはいったん
三菱倉庫の倉庫に
集められる。
そこで、コンテナへの
積み込みなどが
行われる。

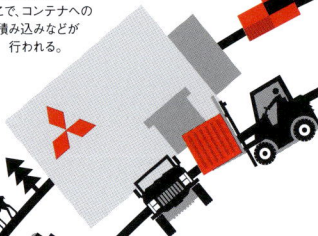

陸路では、トラックや鉄道を
手配してモノを運ぶ。
昨今は、環境対策として
モーダルシフト(トラックから、
よりCO₂排出量の少ない
鉄道へのシフト)も行われている。

扱う品目はコーヒー豆、
医薬品からジンベイザメ、
宇宙ステーションまで。
さまざまなモノが
最終目的地に向けて
出発する。

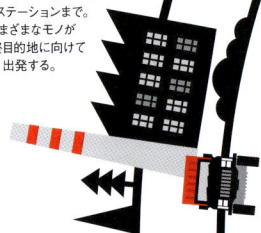

現在、三菱倉庫は、
「グローバル化に対応した
国内外一体のロジスティクス事業」を掲げ、
中国をはじめとしたアジアや、
ヨーロッパ、アメリカでも
日本と同様のロジスティクス事業を
展開できる環境を整備している。
上のイラストでいうと、
右側、左側がともに
日本にも外国にもなり得るということ。
三菱倉庫の拠点が世界各地にあり、
日本と同じように外国でも
その国の顧客に対して、物流プランを提案。
外国と日本、また、外国と外国との
力強いモノの流れを創り出すのだ。

三菱倉庫と聞くと、
「倉庫でモノを預かり、保管する」
という仕事を想像されるかもしれません。
確かにそれも当社の仕事です。
でも、それはあくまで三菱倉庫の
仕事の一部でしかありません。
このイラストは、モノが運ばれる際の
出発地から最終目的地までの
流れを示したもの。
実は、このすべての過程に
三菱倉庫がかかわっています。
モノの出発から到着まで、
すべてを三菱倉庫が設計し、
実際に取り扱っているのです。

港に隣接した
三菱倉庫の倉庫に
荷物を取り出し、
コンテナから荷物を取り出し、
トラックに積み込む。
海外の荷物を税関に申告し、
輸入許可を取る通関手続きも代行する。
ラベル付けなど簡単な加工を
行う場合もある。

スーパー、コンビニへ
卸業者や工場などへ
モノが運び込まれる。
工場に運んだモノは
加工後に、さらに
別の場所へ三菱倉庫が
運ぶこともある。

すべてが
三菱倉庫の
仕事です。

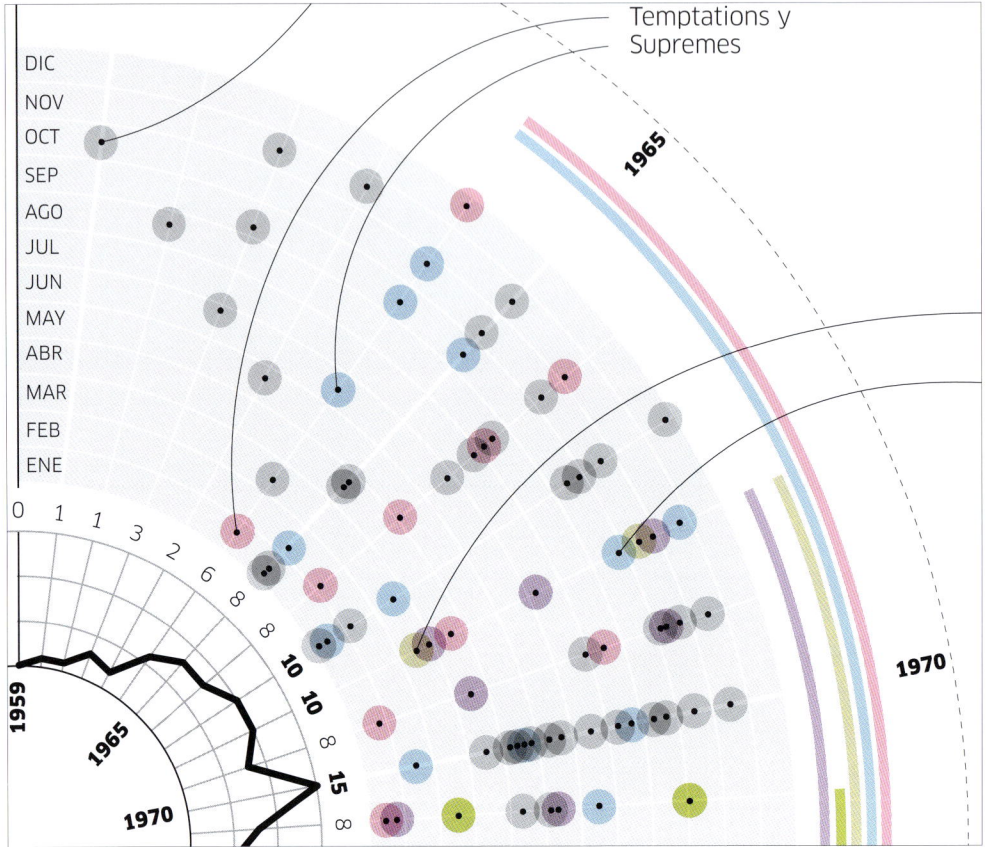

Temptations y
Supremes

DIC
NOV
OCT
SEP
AGO
JUL
JUN
MAY
ABR
MAR
FEB
ENE

1965

1970

1959
1965
1970

Project Info: "Motown, Half a Century of Churning Out Hits", *Público*, newspaper article, 2008, Spain
Data Source: Universal Music; Discogs.com; Rockhall.com; Top40-charts.com et al.
Design: Álvaro Valiño
Awards: Malofiej 2009, Silver

Motown's 191 Number One Hits

This circle timeline shows the history of legendary US record label Motown through its number one hits. With time running clockwise, the years are marked around the outside of the circle, while inner circle lines indicate the months. All 191 number ones in the history of the label are placed on the time-spot when they were released. Colour coding refers to the most successful artists and is explained by the legend down the right side. The timeline gives an impression at one glance of the label's history and when it had its most successful years. Text and icons along the bottom explain some of the principles label boss Berry Gordy followed in "creating" his musicians and their style.

Los 191 números uno de la Motown

Cincuenta años de la historia del sello negro a través de sus éxitos

Los artistas que lograron más números uno

The Temptations **16**

The Supremes y Diana Ross **22**

Marvin Gaye **10**

Stevie Wonder **20**

Jackson 5 y Michael Jackson **8**

The Commodores y Lionel Richie **21**

Boyz II Men **7**

- Cada círculo de la rueda temporal rempresenta un número uno. La ubicación en la rueda temporal responde a la fecha de lanzamiento del single

- THE TEMPTATIONS
- THE SUPREMES Y DIANA ROSS
- MARVIN GAYE
- STEVIE WONDER
- JACKSON 5 Y MICHAEL JACKSON
- THE COMMODORES & LIONEL RICHIE
- BOYZ II MEN
- OTROS

Berry Gordy crea Motown en un garage de Detroit con 800 dólares prestados por su familia

1960. El primer número uno de la Motown fue logrado por The Miracles

Su cantante, Smokey Robinson se convirtió en vicepresidente de la Motown

Debutan en el top one las 'franqui-cias' musicales Temptations y Supremes

El pequeño 'Little' Stevie Wonder se encarama al número uno con sólo 13 años

Diana Ross consigue su primer número uno en solitario

2000. Último número uno, logrado por Erykah Badu

23 años después, The Temptations logran un nuevo número uno con el single 'Stay'

Boyz II Men fue el último grupo superventas de la Motown

1989. Gordy vende la compañía a MCA por 61 millones de dólares

1972. Gordy traslada Motown a Los Ángeles

Michael Jackson debuta en solitario

The Commodores, de la mano de Lionel Richie, inician una nueva etapa para la Motown

1984. Muere Marvin Gaye

Primer número uno de la carrera en solitario de Lionel Richie, 'Truly'

Datos. EEUU: Billboard y Cash Box magazine. Internacionales: archivos de las respectivas listas de éxito de cada país (Reino Unido, Australia, Irlanda, Canadá, Italia, Suiza, Holanda, Austria, Alemania, Noruega y Nueva Zelanda)

Números 1 por mes — Números uno por año

La cadena de montaje

BANDAS DE CHICAS | SOLISTAS | BANDAS DE CHICOS
SUPREMES | STEVIE WONDER | TEMPTATIONS

1 Chico de la calle
Basándose en su experiencia como trabajador en una cadena de montaje de automóviles de Detroit, Gordy, estableció un ciclo de creación de estrellas musicales.

Un chico de la calle con talento salía de la factoría Motown convertido en una estrella rutilante

2 Creación de temas
Hasta que artistas como Stevie Wonder o Lionel Richie escribieron sus propios temas, grupos de profesionales se encargaba de componer los temas que cantaban las estrellas de la Motown.

Por ejemplo, el trío Holland-Dozier-Holland escribió la mayoría de los temas de las Supremes o Marvin Gaye

3 Música
Los músicos de sesión que tocaban en las grabaciones de la Motown raramente aparecían en los créditos de los discos.

Ejecutores de primera fila como los Funk Brothers grabaron temas como 'My Girl', 'I Heard It Through the Grapevine', 'Baby Love' o 'Papa Was a Rollin' Stone'

4 A brillar
Las nuevas estrellas de la Motown eran aleccionadas en todos los aspectos. Como una versión visionario de OT, bandas como The Temptations o The Supremes recibían clases de baile para que sus miembros coordinasen perfectamente los pasos de sus bailes

295

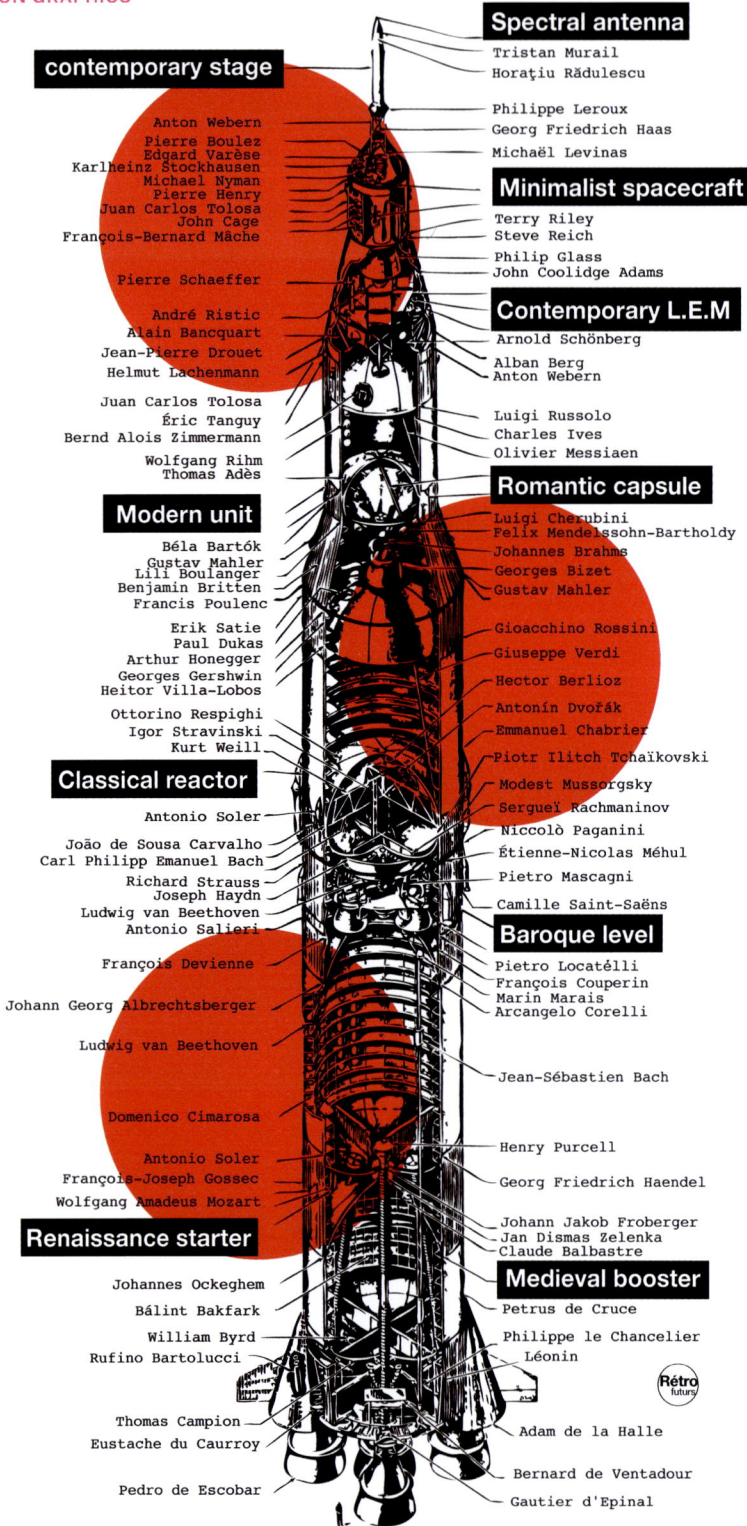

Spectral antenna

Tristan Murail
Horaţiu Rădulescu

Philippe Leroux
Georg Friedrich Haas
Michaël Levinas

contemporary stage

Anton Webern
Pierre Boulez
Edgard Varèse
Karlheinz Stockhausen
Michael Nyman
Pierre Henry
Juan Carlos Tolosa
John Cage
François-Bernard Mâche

Minimalist spacecraft

Terry Riley
Steve Reich

Philip Glass
John Coolidge Adams

Pierre Schaeffer

Contemporary L.E.M

André Ristic
Alain Bancquart
Jean-Pierre Drouet
Helmut Lachenmann

Arnold Schönberg

Alban Berg
Anton Webern

Juan Carlos Tolosa
Éric Tanguy
Bernd Alois Zimmermann

Luigi Russolo
Charles Ives
Olivier Messiaen

Wolfgang Rihm
Thomas Adès

Romantic capsule

Modern unit

Luigi Cherubini
Felix Mendelssohn-Bartholdy

Béla Bartók
Gustav Mahler
Lili Boulanger
Benjamin Britten
Francis Poulenc

Johannes Brahms
Georges Bizet
Gustav Mahler

Gioacchino Rossini

Erik Satie
Paul Dukas
Arthur Honegger
Georges Gershwin
Heitor Villa-Lobos

Giuseppe Verdi

Hector Berlioz

Antonín Dvořák

Ottorino Respighi
Igor Stravinski
Kurt Weill

Emmanuel Chabrier

Piotr Ilitch Tchaïkovski

Modest Mussorgsky

Classical reactor

Sergueï Rachmaninov

Antonio Soler

Niccolò Paganini
Étienne-Nicolas Méhul

João de Sousa Carvalho
Carl Philipp Emanuel Bach

Pietro Mascagni

Richard Strauss
Joseph Haydn
Ludwig van Beethoven
Antonio Salieri

Camille Saint-Saëns

Baroque level

François Devienne

Pietro Locatélli
François Couperin
Marin Marais
Arcangelo Corelli

Johann Georg Albrechtsberger

Ludwig van Beethoven

Jean-Sébastien Bach

Domenico Cimarosa

Henry Purcell

Antonio Soler
François-Joseph Gossec
Wolfgang Amadeus Mozart

Georg Friedrich Haendel

Johann Jakob Froberger
Jan Dismas Zelenka
Claude Balbastre

Renaissance starter

Medieval booster

Johannes Ockeghem

Petrus de Cruce

Bálint Bakfark

Philippe le Chancelier
Léonin

William Byrd
Rufino Bartolucci

Rétro
futurs

Thomas Campion
Eustache du Caurroy

Adam de la Halle

Pedro de Escobar

Bernard de Ventadour

Gautier d'Epinal

Music Evolution

This graphic uses an unusual metaphor for an evolution. Stéphane Massa-Bidal based it on an image of a Saturn V rocket, as used for space exploration from the late Sixties. It consists of three stages, two of which burn up and are disposed of in succession when carrying the vessel into space. Alongside the image of the rocket famous composers are listed, with time running bottom up. Composers are grouped into major periods of European classical music, shown on either side of the rocket, from the Middle Ages up to contemporary spectral music at the top of the spacecraft.

Project Info: *D'ici là* magazine, website, 2010, France
Design: Stéphane Massa-Bidal (Rétrofuturs)

Seismi

Seismi is an interactive visualisation for earthquakes. The data is plotted in five individual schemes, which are accessed through the navigation below left. NST shows the most recent events. MAP locates all earthquakes on a world map. DPT visualises at what depth activity occurred. LST subsumes all quakes as dots in a "list", with colour indicating the magnitude of each one. In the timeline (TML), all events are sorted chronologically. In all schemes, single events can be selected. The data band at the lower right then discloses information about this particular earthquake: time, depth, magnitude and location. By presenting the information in distinct schemes, the project allows people to draw various narratives from the dataset, both researchers and the general public.

Project Info: Website, 2010, Finland
Data Source: US Geological Survey; National Geophysical Data Center; The University of Texas Institute for Geophysics
Design: Niko Knappe, Gokce Taskan (Media Lab Helsinki)

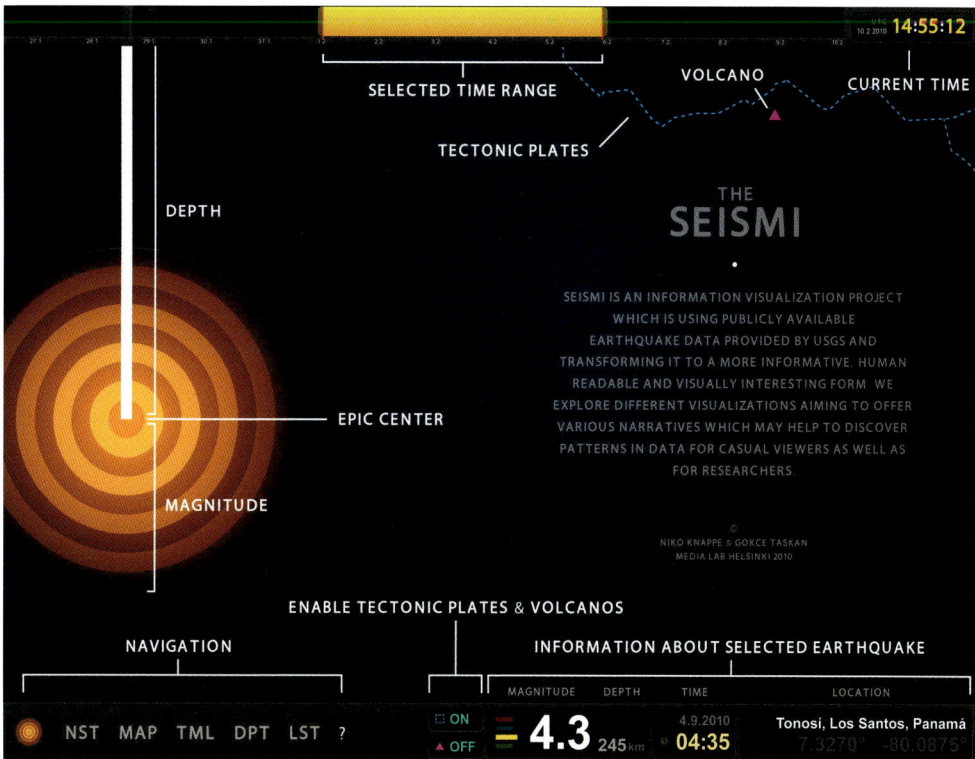

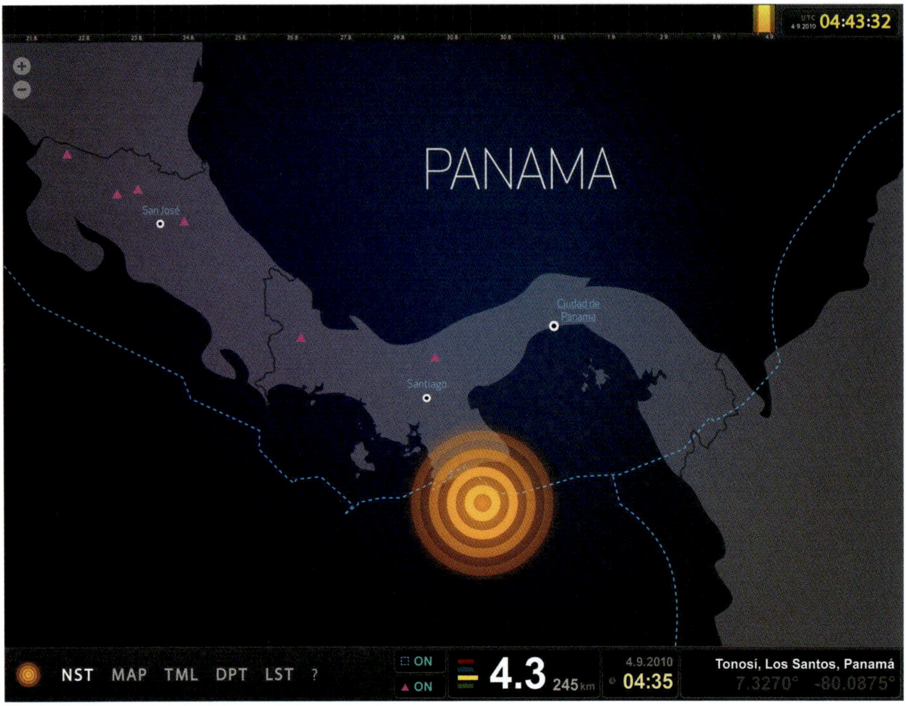
04:43:32
PANAMA
San José
Ciudad de Panamá
Santiago
NST
MAP
TML
DPT
LST
?
ON
ON
4.3
245 km
4.9.2010
04:35
Tonosí, Los Santos, Panamá
7.3270° -80.0875°

14:55:12
10
9
8
7
6
5
4
3
2
NST
MAP
TML
DPT
LST
?
OFF
OFF
3.2
413 km
4.2.2010
02:11
Sodankylä, Finland
67.4633° 26.5756°

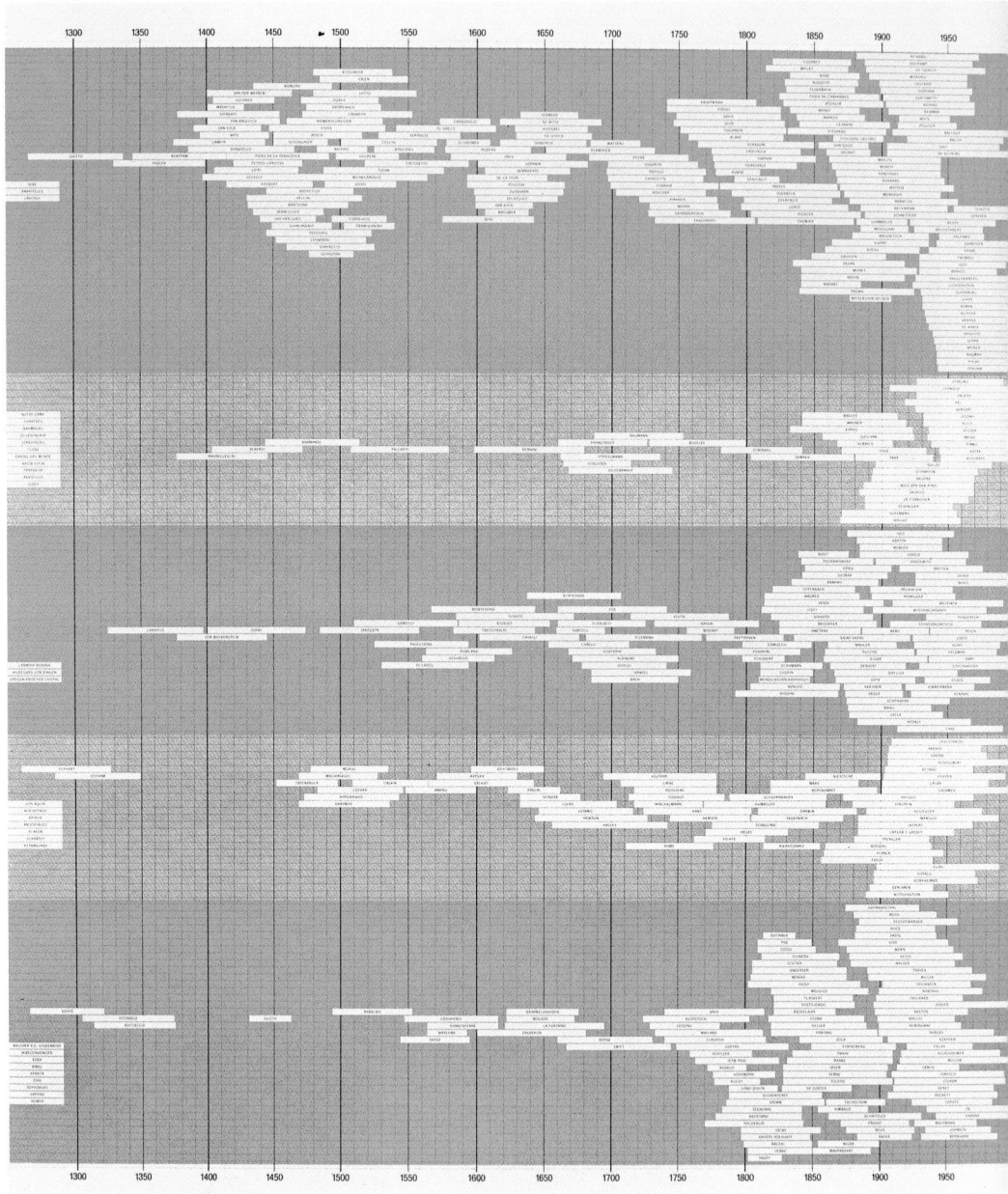

Project Info: Print, 1998, Germany
Artist: Gerhard Richter
Additional Info: Original size 82.8 cm x 68.2 cm;
published as Editions CR 93

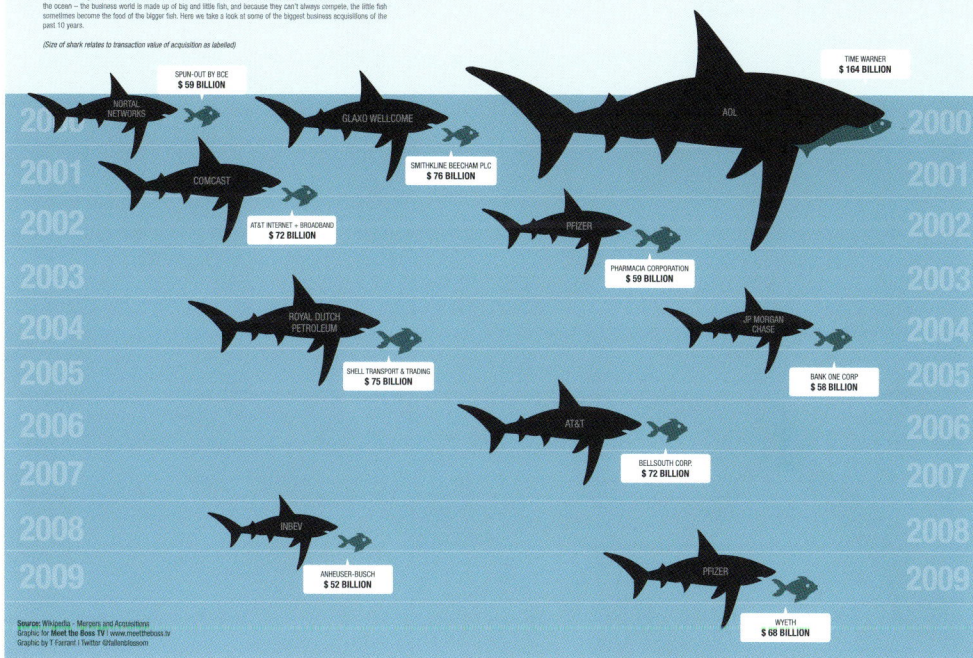

THE SHARKS OF BUSINESS

Meet The Boss™

As the Discovery Channel broadcasts its 23rd Shark Week, we ask: who are the sharks of the business world? Just like in the ocean – the business world is made up of big and little fish, and because they can't always compete, the little fish sometimes become the food of the bigger fish. Here we take a look at some of the biggest business acquisitions of the past 10 years.

(Size of shark relates to transaction value of acquisition as labelled)

SPUN-OUT BY BCE
$ 59 BILLION

TIME WARNER
$ 164 BILLION

NORTAL NETWORKS

GLAXO WELLCOME

AOL

2000

2001

COMCAST

SMITHKLINE BEECHAM PLC
$ 76 BILLION

2001

2002

AT&T INTERNET + BROADBAND
$ 72 BILLION

PFIZER

2002

2003

PHARMACIA CORPORATION
$ 59 BILLION

2003

2004

ROYAL DUTCH PETROLEUM

JP MORGAN CHASE

2004

2005

SHELL TRANSPORT & TRADING
$ 75 BILLION

BANK ONE CORP
$ 58 BILLION

2005

2006

AT&T

2006

2007

BELLSOUTH CORP.
$ 72 BILLION

2007

2008

INBEV

2008

2009

ANHEUSER-BUSCH
$ 52 BILLION

PFIZER

2009

WYETH
$ 68 BILLION

Source: Wikipedia - Merges and Acquisitions
Graphic for Meet the Boss TV | www.meettheboss.tv
Graphic by T Farrant | Twitter @tfallentblossom

Overview

Gerhard Richter is one of the most important of contemporary artists. In this editioned print, he has created a survey of Western cultural history which contains the names and dates of early works and important artists and thinkers from the Stone Age and Antiquity up to 2000. Time runs from left to right, with each vertical line marking a decade – except for the period before 1300 AD which is treated as one single unit. In the coloured sections, professional groups are categorised from top to bottom: painters, architects, composers, philosophers and authors. On simple white tags, only the family names are written, without any further comment. The checked background and bare typography recall administrative time-plans or clinical measurement diagrams.

Sharks of Business

This graphic takes a look at the biggest business acquisitions of the past 10 years. Each shark represents a company carrying out the acquiring, with the fish in front representing the company being acquired. The size of each shark indicates the transaction value of the acquisition. The depth of the water relates to a timeline, with the acquisition of Wyeth by Pfizer at the bottom being the most recent.

Project Info: Meet the Boss, for GDS International, website, 2010, UK
Data Source: Wikipedia, "Merges and Acquisitions"
Research and Design: Tiffany Farrant-Gonzalez

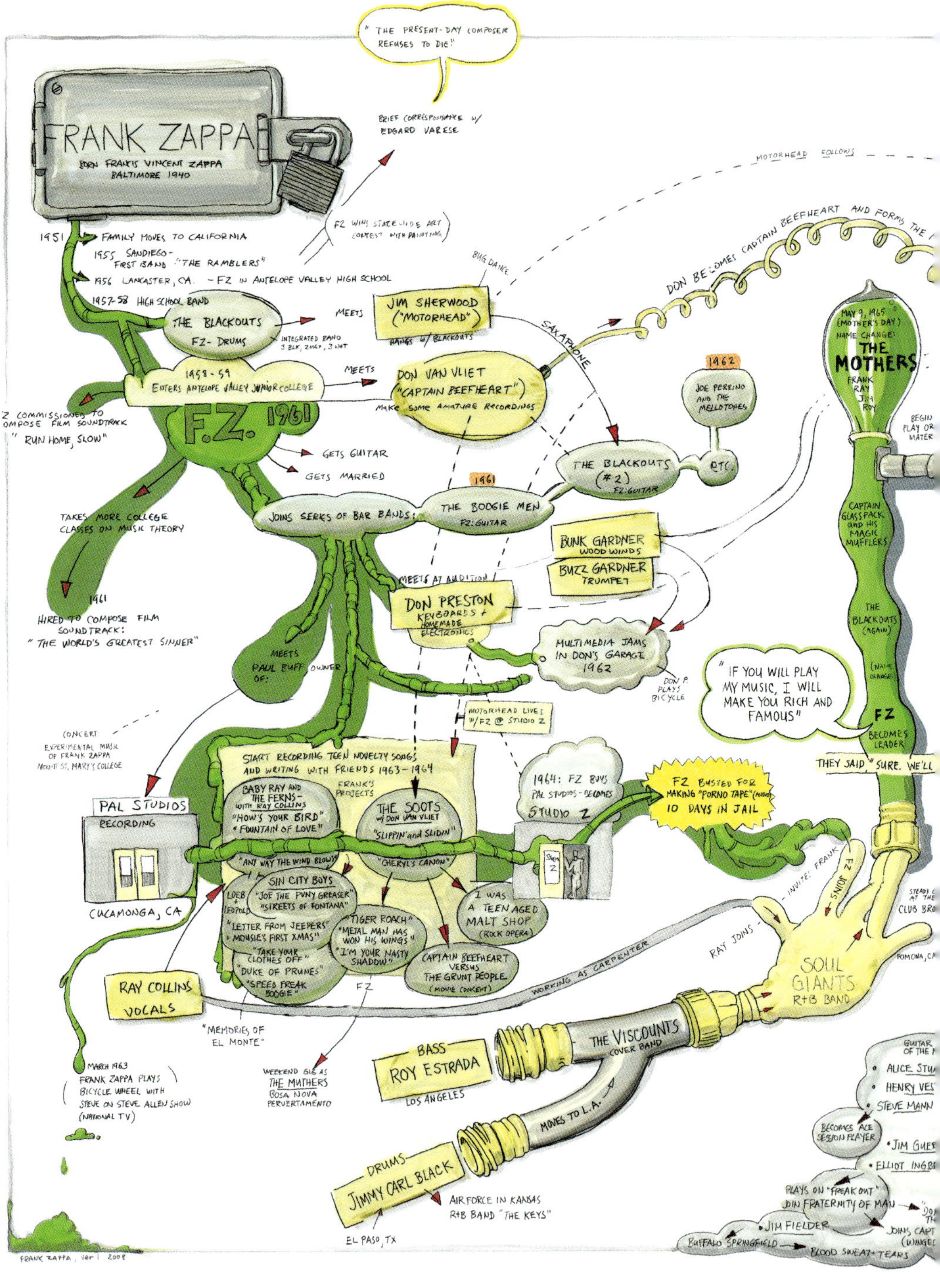

" THE PRESENT-DAY COMPOSER REFUSES TO DIE!"
FRANK ZAPPA
BORN FRANCIS VINCENT ZAPPA BALTIMORE 1940
BRIEF CORRESPONDANCE W/ EDGARD VARESE
FZ WINS STATEWIDE ART CONTEST WITH PAINTING
1951 FAMILY MOVES TO CALIFORNIA
1955 SANDIEGO- FIRST BAND "THE RAMBLERS"
1956 LANCASTER, CA. - FZ IN ANTELOPE VALLEY HIGH SCHOOL
1957-58 HIGH SCHOOL BAND
THE BLACKOUTS FZ- DRUMS
INTEGRATED BAND 3 BLK, 2 MEX, 3 WHT
MEETS
JIM SHERWOOD ("MOTORHEAD")
HANGS W/ BLACKOUTS
BUG DANCE
MOTORHEAD FOLLOWS
DON BECOMES CAPTAIN BEEFHEART AND FORMS THE
1958-59 ENTERS ANTELOPE VALLEY JUNIOR COLLEGE
MEETS
DON VAN VLIET ("CAPTAIN BEEFHEART")
MAKE SOME AMATURE RECORDINGS
SAXAPHONE
1962
JOE PERRINO AND THE MELLOTONES
Z COMMISSIONED TO COMPOSE FILM SOUNDTRACK " RUN HOME, SLOW"
F.Z. 1961
GETS GUITAR
GETS MARRIED
THE BLACKOUTS (#2) FZ: GUITAR
ETC.
1961
THE BOOGIE MEN FZ: GUITAR
JOINS SERIES OF BAR BANDS:
TAKES MORE COLLEGE CLASSES ON MUSIC THEORY
BUNK GARDNER WOOD WINDS
BUZZ GARDNER TRUMPET
MEETS AT AUDITION
DON PRESTON KEYBOARDS + HOMEMADE ELECTRONICS
1961 HIRED TO COMPOSE FILM SOUNDTRACK: " THE WORLD'S GREATEST SINNER"
MULTIMEDIA JAMS IN DON'S GARAGE 1962
DON P. PLAYS BICYCLE
MEETS PAUL BUFF OWNER OF:
MOTORHEAD LIVES W/FZ @ STUDIO Z
CONCERT: EXPERIMENTAL MUSIC OF FRANK ZAPPA MOUNT ST. MARY'S COLLEGE
START RECORDING TEEN NOVELTY SONGS AND WRITING WITH FRIENDS 1963-1964
FRANK'S PROJECTS
BABY RAY AND THE FERNS- WITH RAY COLLINS "HOW'S YOUR BIRD" "FOUNTAIN OF LOVE"
THE SOOTS W/ DON VAN VLIET "SLIPPIN' and SLIDIN'"
"ANY WAY THE WIND BLOWS"
"CHERYL'S CANON"
LOEB + LEOPOLD
SIN CITY BOYS "JOE THE PUNY GREASER" "STREETS OF FONTANA"
"LETTER FROM JEEPERS" "MOUSIE'S FIRST XMAS"
"TIGER ROACH" "METAL MAN HAS WON HIS WINGS" "I'M YOUR NASTY SHADOW"
"TAKE YOUR CLOTHES OFF" "DUKE OF PRUNES" "SPEED FREAK BOOGIE"
I WAS A TEEN AGED MALT SHOP (ROCK OPERA)
CAPTAIN BEEFHEART VERSUS THE GRUNT PEOPLE (MOVIE CONCEPT)
PAL STUDIOS RECORDING
CUCAMONGA, CA
1964: FZ BUYS PAL STUDIOS - BECOMES STUDIO Z
STUDIO Z
FZ BUSTED FOR MAKING "PORNO TAPE" (AUDIO) 10 DAYS IN JAIL
MAY 9, 1965 (MOTHER'S DAY) NAME CHANGE: THE MOTHERS
FRANK RAY JIM ROY
CAPTAIN GLASS PACK AND HIS MAGIC MUFFLERS
THE BLACKOUTS (AGAIN)
" IF YOU WILL PLAY MY MUSIC, I WILL MAKE YOU RICH AND FAMOUS"
FZ BECOMES LEADER
THEY SAID " SURE. WE'LL
INVITES FRANK
FZ JOINS
RAY JOINS
SOUL GIANTS R+B BAND
POMONA, CA
CLUB BRO
WORKING AS CARPENTER
RAY COLLINS VOCALS
"MEMORIES OF EL MONTE"
FZ
MARCH 1963 FRANK ZAPPA PLAYS BICYCLE WHEEL WITH STEVE ON STEVE ALLEN SHOW (NATIONAL TV)
WEEKEND GIG AS THE MUTHERS BOSA NOVA PERVERTAMENTO
BASS ROY ESTRADA LOS ANGELES
THE VISCOUNTS COVER BAND
MOVES TO L.A.
DRUMS JIMMY CARL BLACK
AIR FORCE IN KANSAS R+B BAND "THE KEYS"
EL PASO, TX
ALICE STU
HENRY VES
STEVE MANN
BECOMES ACE SESSION PLAYER
JIM GUER
ELLIOT INGB
PLAYS ON "FREAK OUT"
JOIN FRATERNITY OF MAN
JIM FIELDER
JOINS CAPT
BUFFALO SPRINGFIELD
BLOOD SWEAT + TEARS
FRANK ZAPPA, ver 1 2008

FZ POSITIONS THE MOTHERS AS THE CRITICAL OUTSIDERS.

SUZY CREAMCHEESE INTRODUCES FRANK TO GAIL SLOATMAN

FZ PRODUCES ERIC BURDON + ANIMALS FOR MGM

"IT WAS MY CAMPAIGN IN THOSE DAYS TO DO THINGS THAT WOULD SHAKE THEM OUT OF THEIR COMPLACENCY, OR THAT IGNORANCE, AND MAKE THEM QUESTION THINGS"

FZ MARRIES GAIL @ CITY HALL

1966

FIRST ALBUM:

FREAK OUT

FIRST ROCK DOUBLE ALBUM (SPECIAL PRICE)
FIRST ROCK CONCEPT ALBUM

1967

AMERICA DRINKS AND GOES HOME

BORN: MOON UNIT ZAPPA

EXPAND BAND

GUESTS INCLUDED: DR. JOHN, PAUL BUTTERFIELD, LES McCANN, MOTORHEAD PLUS THE GARDEN FREAKS

POOR (450% OVER BUDGET)

INCLUDES TEXTS AND GRAPHIC BY FZ "UNITED MUTATIONS" "NO COMMERCIAL POTENTIAL"

HERB COHEN

KIM FOWLEY

RAY FILLMORE SAN FRANCISCO WITH LENNY BRUCE

THE COMPLETE CLASSIC MOTHERS OF INVENTION
FRANK ZAPPA – GUITAR
RAY COLLINS – VOCAL
ROY ESTRADA – BASS
JIMMY CARL BLACK – DRUMS
DON PRESTON – KEYBOARDS
BUNK GARDNER – SAX
BILLY MUNDI – DRUMS
MOTORHEAD SHERWOOD – B.SAX

LENNY DIES

MOVES BAND TO NEW YORK CITY

ABSOLUTELY FREE

FZ OWNED IN MONKEES MOVIE "HEAD"

IAN UNDERWOOD JOINS

SATIRE ABOUT FLOW

"SERIOUS" STYLE COMPOSED WITH 52 PIECE ORCHESTRA
AVANT GARDE

DADA STYLE THEATER
GARRICK THEATER
GREENWICH VILLAGE

NAME CHANGED BY RECORD COMPANY
JOIN THE BAND

RENT PERCUSSION INSTRUMENTS

GIRL FRIENDS JONI MITCHEL

18 MONTHS

PIGS AND REPUGNANT REVIEW

FIRST EUROPEAN TOUR – PLAYS "LOUIE LOUIE" ON ROYAL ALBERT HALL ORGAN

BECOMES MOTHERS of INVENTION

"DISCOVERED" BY PRODUCER TOM WILSON
(BOB DYLAN, SIMON & GARFUNKLE, VELVET UNDERGROUND, JOHN CALTRANE...)

20 PC. ORCHESTRA

MGM RECORDS (VERVE)

FZ ADDS FREAKY FRIENDS

CAPTAIN BEEFHEART AND THE MAGIC BAND

RY COODER ASSISTS

ALBUM: "SAFE AS MILK"

ALBUM "STRICTLY PERSONAL"

FZ AS PRODUCER

1970

BURNT WEENY SANDWICH

LEFT OVER ORIGINAL MOTHERS ALBUMS:

JOIN NEW MOTHERS

THE BYRDS

LOVE

THE DOORS

THE SEEDS

BUFFALO SPRINGFIELD

THE MOTHERS PLAYING AT THE WHISKEY

THE L.A. BANDS

WHISKEY A GO GO

THE TRIP

PANDORA'S BOX

LONDON FOG

THE TURTLES

FRANK ZAPPA

FZ SOLO ALBUMS

JEAN-LUC PONTY ALBUM KING KONG PRODUCED BY FZ

SEAN & EDDIE

BIZARRE + STRAIGHT RECORDS

FLO + EDDIE

WILD MAN FISCHER

LORD BUCKLEY

ALICE COOPER

THE GTO's – GIRLS TOGETHER OUTRAGEOUSLY

TIM BUCKLEY

CAPTAIN BEEFHEART AND THE MAGIC BAND
TROUT MASK REPLICA

HOT RATS

STARTS FILM "UNCLE MEAT"

ALBUM FOR ZAPPA

BEEF LICK DECAL

CAPTAIN GETS DISGRUNTLE

MOVES TO ANOTHER

L.A. CLUB SCENE

THE TROUBADOUR

THE ACTION

MOTHERS CONNECT

FZ STARTS MAKING POSTERS, MAPS, AND PROMOTIONAL ITEMS OFTEN !?

THE L.A. FREE PRESS

BIZARRE RECORDS
"WE MAKE RECORDS THAT ARE A LITTLE DIFFERENT WE PRESENT MUSICAL AND SOCIOLOGICAL MATERIAL WHICH THE IMPORTANT RECORD COMPANIES WOULD PROBABLY NOT ALLOW YOU TO HEAR. JUST WHAT THE WORLD NEEDS... ANOTHER RECORD COMPANY"
FZ

IN HOME VERSION SHORT RUN IN L.A.

VERY BROKE AND HUNGRY

FILM: MONDO HOLLYWOOD

MOTHERS PLAY IN MOVIE

BECOMES MANAGER

FAMOUS FREAKS
CANTORS DELICATESSEN
VITO + SZOU
CARL FRANZONI
PAMELA ZARUBICA (SUZY CREAMCHEESE)

HERB COHEN

BUTCHIE
LINDA ROPP

KAREN YUM YUM
BEATLE BOB
ROXY FLYNN
EMERALD

FRANK AT HOME - (LA) IN WH

1972

1973

MOT

LAST VAUDEVILLE MOTHERS ALBUM

JUST ANOTHER BAND FROM L.A.

OVER NIG SENSATIC

SMALL STUDIO PROJECT

FRANK ZAPPA HOT RATS
WAKA JAWAKA

FORMS NEW MOTHERS

FZ BACK ON HIS FEET

BAND TOUR WORLD ALL YEA LONG

FZ MOVES INTO LA AND CONNECTS TO THE FREAK SCENE

STARTS TO GROW HIS HAIR

USED TO MANAGE CLUBS!
PURPLE ONION
THE UNICORN
AND RUN GUNS IN AFRICA

THE GRAND WAZOO

BIG BAND ALBUM

GOES ON 8 DATE TOUR

THE MOTHERS

FRANK EVENTUALLY BECOMES CONFIDENT ABOUT HIS OWN GUITAR PLAYING

ENTERING THE L.A. SCENE

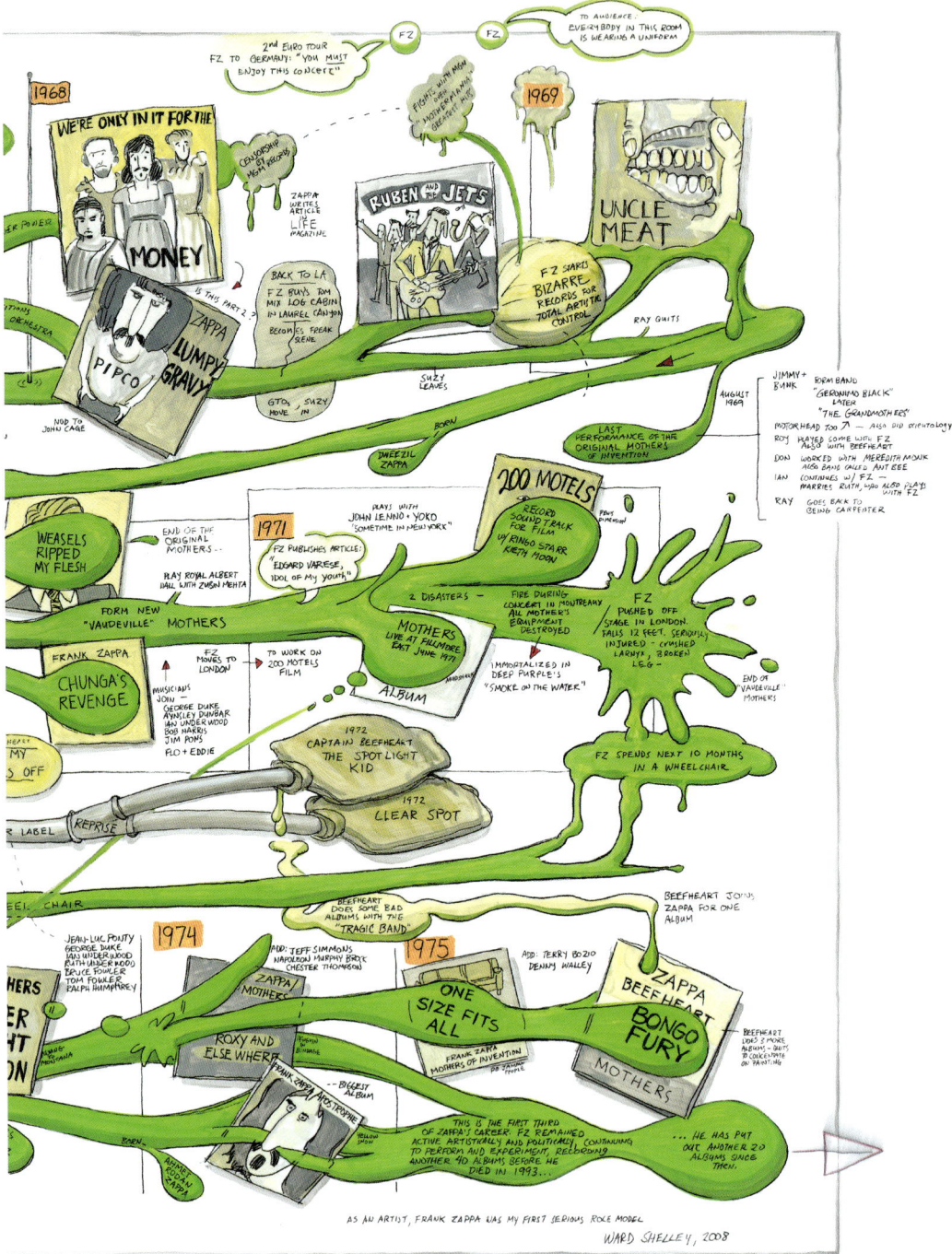

AS AN ARTIST, FRANK ZAPPA WAS MY FIRST SERIOUS ROLE MODEL.

WARD SHELLEY, 2008

Frank Zappa Chart

This is a graphic chronology, showing the life of musician and composer Frank Zappa. Data were drawn from a number of published biographies as well as fan websites. The visual look of the chart is a homage to the artist who created the artwork for many of Zappa's recordings, Cal Schenkel. The chart lists major events in Zappa's personal and artistic life, bands he was in, information about certain band members and a listing of major recorded works he made or produced. Rather than creating a conventional timeline, Ward Shelley devised a maze-like structure to capture the spirit of Zappa's non-conformity.

Project Info: Painting, 2008, USA
Artist: Ward Shelley
Additional Info: Original size 164 cm x 81 cm;
Ward Shelley is represented by Pierogi Gallery

Following spread

So You Need a Typeface?

This flow chart depicts a complex decision-making process with 40 possible results: choosing the right typeface for a design project. Starting in the middle, the first step in navigating the chart is to choose which kind of project you're working on. Then a carefully created sequence of questions directs you towards a typeface that will fit your practical and style requirements. While Julian Hansen originally aimed at developing a "serious" model for choosing a typeface, he soon realised most of the decisions that were to be made were closely related to personal taste. He therefore took things one step further and came up with a humorous piece on different typefaces and what people associate with them.

Project Info: Poster, 2010, Denmark
Data Source: FontShop ranking "Die 100 Besten Schriften"
Design: Julian Hansen

SO YOU NEED A TYPEFACE is a project by Julian Hansen. It's an alternative way on how to choose fonts (or just be inspired) for a specific project, not just by browsing through the pages of FontBook. The list is (very loosely) based on the top 50 of **Die 100 Besten Schriften** by Font Shop.
© 2010 Julian Hansen www.julianhansen.com

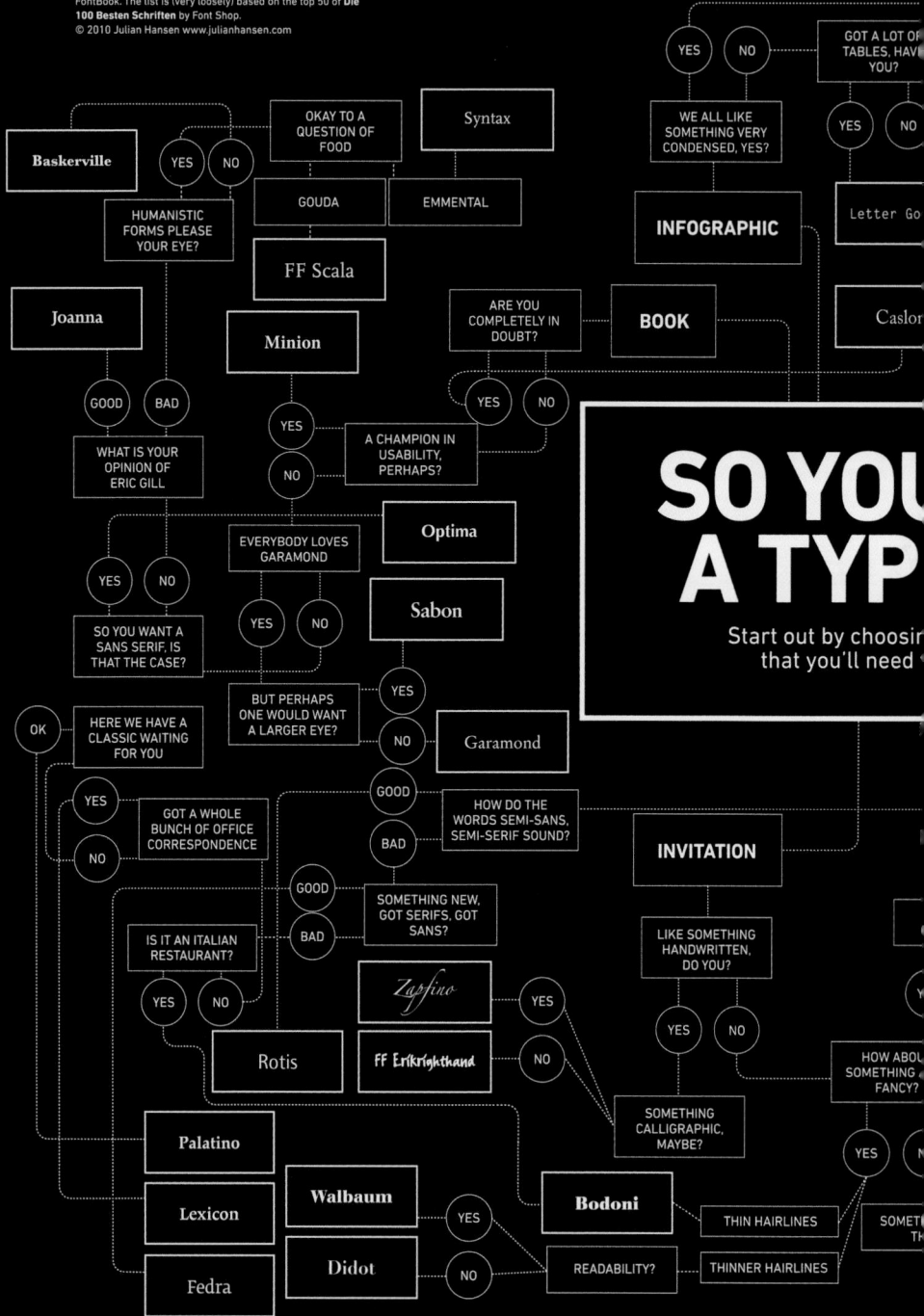

SO YOU
A TYP

Start out by choosir
that you'll need

Baskerville

YES NO

OKAY TO A QUESTION OF FOOD

Syntax

HUMANISTIC FORMS PLEASE YOUR EYE?

GOUDA EMMENTAL

FF Scala

Joanna

Minion

GOOD BAD

WHAT IS YOUR OPINION OF ERIC GILL

YES

NO

A CHAMPION IN USABILITY, PERHAPS?

EVERYBODY LOVES GARAMOND

Optima

YES NO

YES NO

Sabon

SO YOU WANT A SANS SERIF, IS THAT THE CASE?

BUT PERHAPS ONE WOULD WANT A LARGER EYE?

YES

NO

Garamond

OK

HERE WE HAVE A CLASSIC WAITING FOR YOU

GOOD

HOW DO THE WORDS SEMI-SANS, SEMI-SERIF SOUND?

YES

GOT A WHOLE BUNCH OF OFFICE CORRESPONDENCE

BAD

NO

GOOD

SOMETHING NEW, GOT SERIFS, GOT SANS?

IS IT AN ITALIAN RESTAURANT?

BAD

YES NO

Zapfino YES

Rotis

FF Erikrighthand NO

Palatino

SOMETHING CALLIGRAPHIC, MAYBE?

Lexicon

Walbaum

YES

Bodoni

THIN HAIRLINES

Fedra

Didot

NO

READABILITY?

THINNER HAIRLINES

YES NO

WE ALL LIKE SOMETHING VERY CONDENSED, YES?

GOT A LOT OF TABLES, HAV YOU?

YES NO

INFOGRAPHIC

Letter Go

BOOK

Caslor

ARE YOU COMPLETELY IN DOUBT?

YES NO

INVITATION

LIKE SOMETHING HANDWRITTEN, DO YOU?

YES NO

HOW ABOU SOMETHING FANCY?

YES N

SOMET TH

Univers

HOW ABOUT SOMETHING HEAVILY USED?

Times

YES   NO   YES   NO

Miller

U CRIED WHEN WATCHING TERMINATOR

YES

FF DIN

Proforma

GOOD

ES   NO

I MUST SAY THAT THIS FLOWCHART IS LOOKING HOT

DO PEOPLE CALL YOU BORING FROM TIME TO TIME?

HOW ABOUT SOMETHING AWARD WINNING?

BAD

OCR

TEXT FACE

COMBINATION

NEWSPAPER

DISPLAY

THINK MR. SPIEKERMANN IS MOSTLY RIGHT?

NEED FACE

DO YOU LIKE IT TRADITIONAL?

YES   NO

THE NETHERLANDS IS NICE, RIGHT?

YES

d of project eface for.

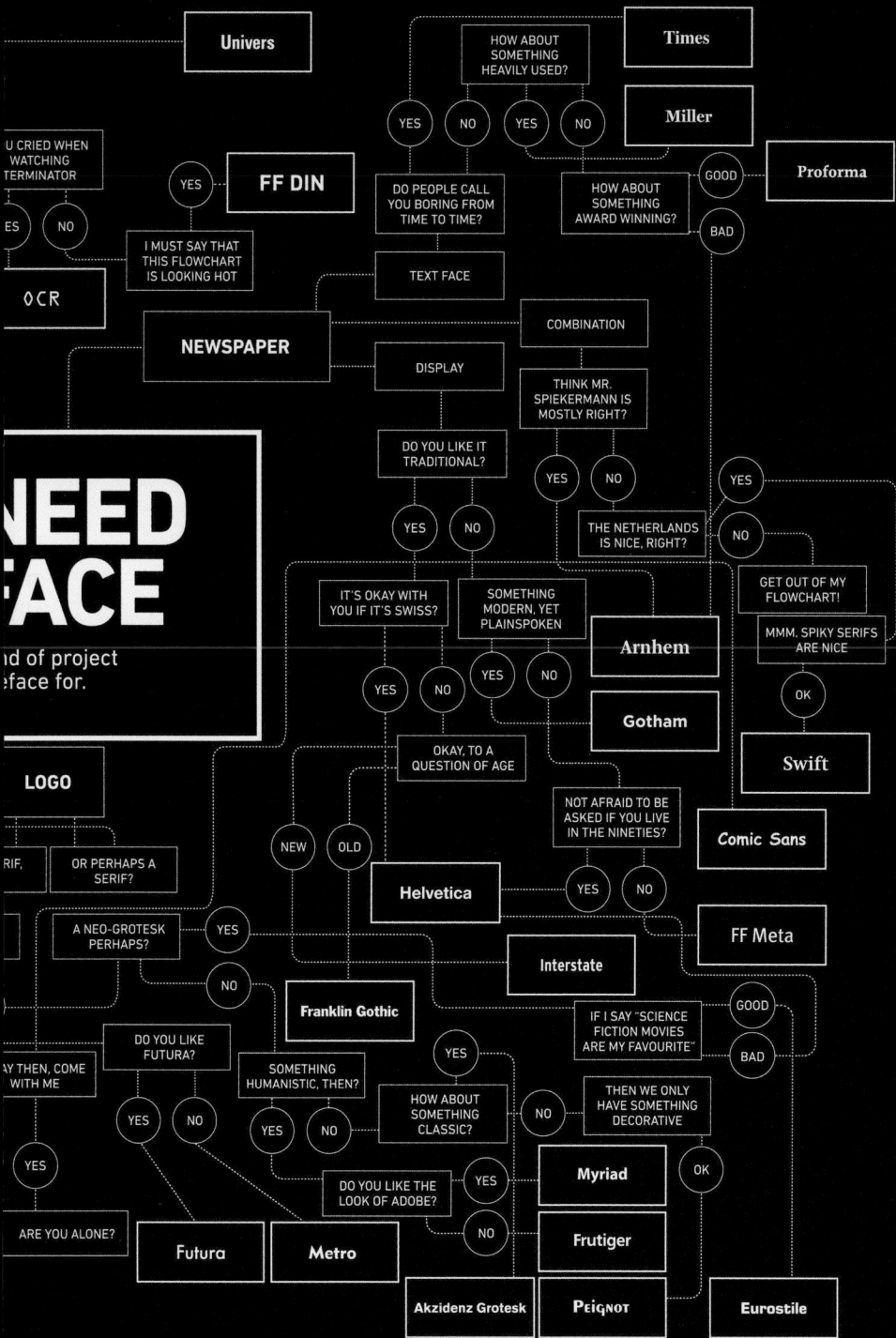

YES   NO

IT'S OKAY WITH YOU IF IT'S SWISS?

SOMETHING MODERN, YET PLAINSPOKEN

Arnhem

NO

GET OUT OF MY FLOWCHART!

MMM. SPIKY SERIFS ARE NICE

YES   NO   YES   NO

Gotham

OK

LOGO

OKAY, TO A QUESTION OF AGE

Swift

RIF,   OR PERHAPS A SERIF?

NEW   OLD

NOT AFRAID TO BE ASKED IF YOU LIVE IN THE NINETIES?

Comic Sans

A NEO-GROTESK PERHAPS?

YES

Helvetica

YES   NO

FF Meta

NO

Interstate

Franklin Gothic

IF I SAY "SCIENCE FICTION MOVIES ARE MY FAVOURITE"

GOOD

Y THEN, COME WITH ME

DO YOU LIKE FUTURA?

YES

BAD

SOMETHING HUMANISTIC, THEN?

HOW ABOUT SOMETHING CLASSIC?

NO

THEN WE ONLY HAVE SOMETHING DECORATIVE

YES   NO

YES   NO

Myriad

OK

YES

ARE YOU ALONE?

DO YOU LIKE THE LOOK OF ADOBE?

YES

Futura   Metro

NO

Frutiger

Akzidenz Grotesk   Peignot   Eurostile

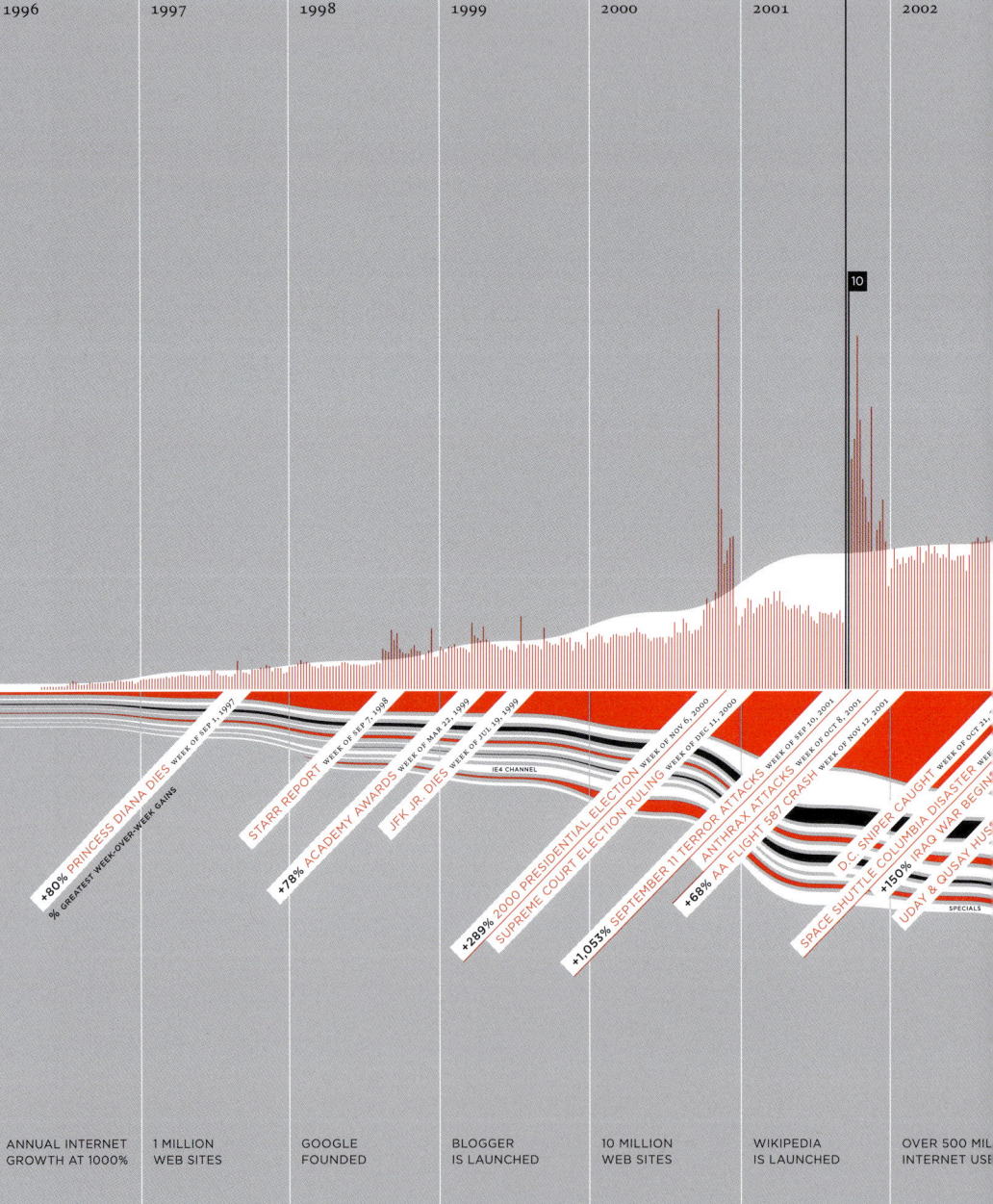

CNN.COM LAUNCHED AUGUST 30, 1995

PAGE VIEWS MAY 1, 1996 – SEP 30, 2009

121,853,965,311

DAY WITH MOST AVERAGE PAGE VIEWS

SEP. 12

DAY WITH LE.

DEC

1996	1997	1998	1999	2000	2001		2002

2

10

+80% PRINCESS DIANA DIES WEEK OF SEP 1, 1997

% GREATEST WEEK-OVER-WEEK GAINS

STARR REPORT WEEK OF SEP 7, 1998

+78% ACADEMY AWARDS WEEK OF MAR 22, 1998

JFK JR. DIES WEEK OF JUL 19, 1999

IE4 CHANNEL

+289% 2000 PRESIDENTIAL ELECTION WEEK OF NOV 6, 2000

SUPREME COURT ELECTION RULING WEEK OF DEC 11, 2000

+1,053% SEPTEMBER 11 TERROR ATTACKS WEEK OF SEP 10, 2001

ANTHRAX ATTACKS WEEK OF OCT 8, 2001

+68% AA FLIGHT 587 CRASH WEEK OF NOV 12, 2001

SPACE SHUTTLE COLUMBIA DISASTER

D.C. SNIPER CAUGHT WEEK OF OCT 21,

+150% IRAQ WAR BEGIN

UDAY & QUSAY HUS

SPECIALS

ANNUAL INTERNET
GROWTH AT 1000%

1 MILLION
WEB SITES

GOOGLE
FOUNDED

BLOGGER
IS LAUNCHED

10 MILLION
WEB SITES

WIKIPEDIA
IS LAUNCHED

OVER 500 MIL
INTERNET USE

SOURCES: WEBSTATS INTERNAL SERVER LOGS PRIOR TO AUG 2007, OMNITURE SITE CATALYST AUG 2007 FORWARD; TURNER RESEARCH FROM INTERNATIONAL TELECOMMUNICATIONS UNION (2009) FOR INTERNET USERS, UNITED NATIONS POPULATION DIVISION (2009) FOR POPULATION; AT&T LABS RESEARCH, NIELSEN ONLINE, AND GARNER RESEARCH

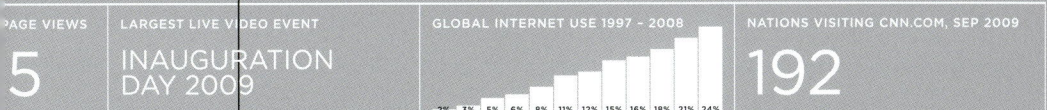

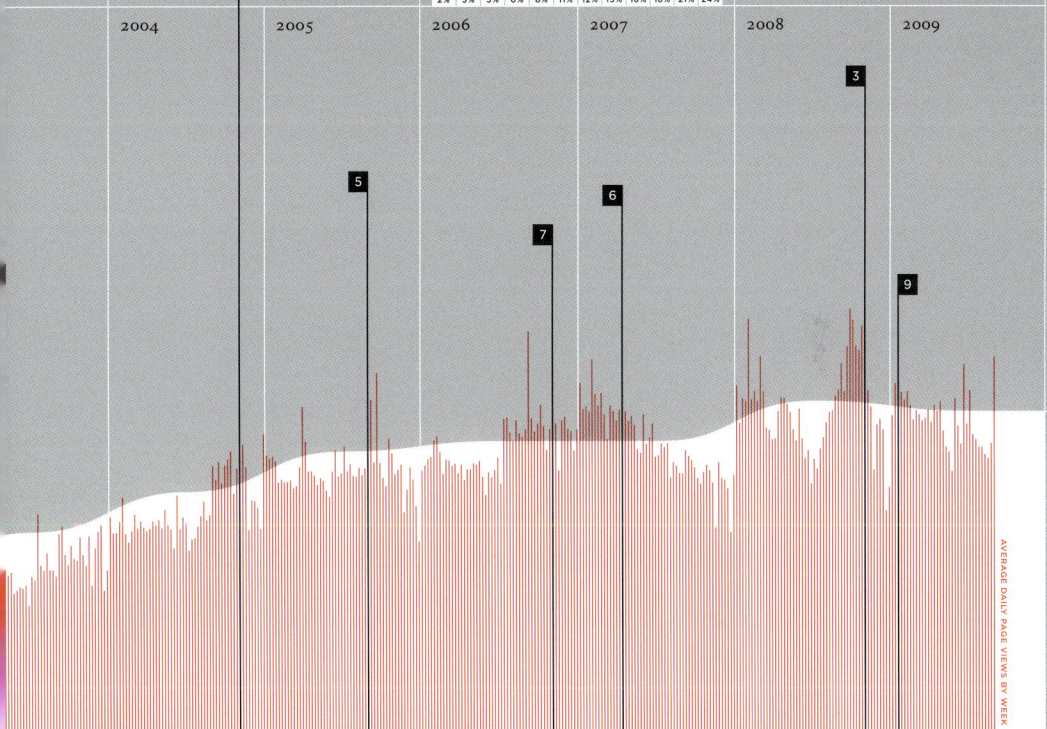

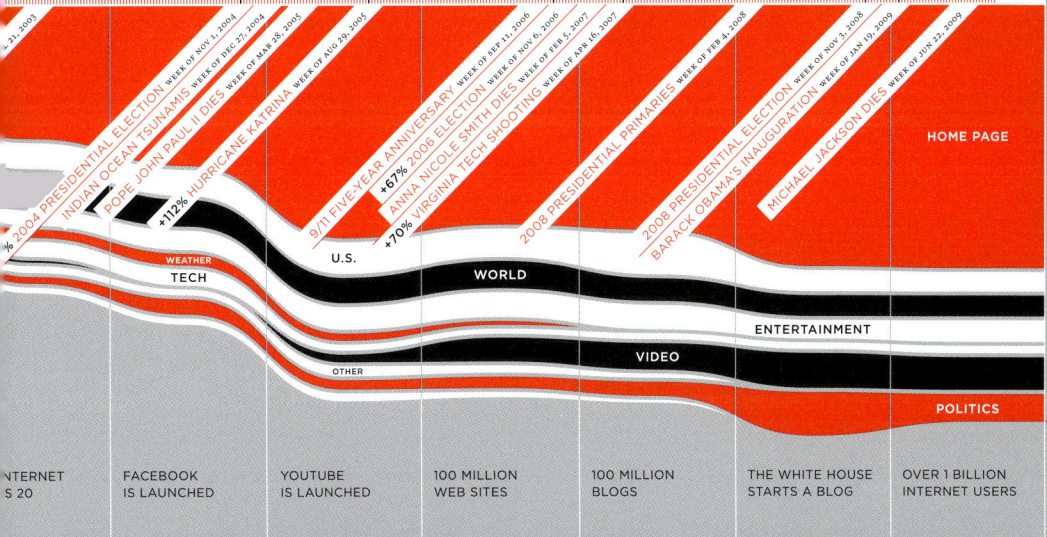

PAGE VIEWS | LARGEST LIVE VIDEO EVENT | GLOBAL INTERNET USE 1997 – 2008 | NATIONS VISITING CNN.COM, SEP 2009

5

INAUGURATION
DAY 2009

192

2% 3% 5% 6% 8% 11% 12% 15% 16% 18% 21% 24%

2004   2005   2006   2007   2008   2009

3

5

7

6

9

WEEKS WITH MOST AVERAGE PAGE VIEWS

ANNUAL WEEKLY AVERAGE

AVERAGE DAILY PAGE VIEWS BY WEEK

21, 2003
2004 PRESIDENTIAL ELECTION WEEK OF NOV. 1, 2004
INDIAN OCEAN TSUNAMIS WEEK OF DEC. 27, 2004
POPE JOHN PAUL II DIES WEEK OF MAR. 28, 2005
+112% HURRICANE KATRINA WEEK OF AUG. 29, 2005
9/11 FIVE-YEAR ANNIVERSARY WEEK OF SEP. 11, 2006
+67% 2006 ELECTION WEEK OF NOV. 6, 2006
ANNA NICOLE SMITH DIES WEEK OF FEB. 5, 2007
+70% VIRGINIA TECH SHOOTING WEEK OF APR. 16, 2007
2008 PRESIDENTIAL PRIMARIES WEEK OF FEB. 4, 2008
2008 PRESIDENTIAL ELECTION WEEK OF NOV. 3, 2008
BARACK OBAMA'S INAUGURATION WEEK OF JAN. 19, 2009
MICHAEL JACKSON DIES WEEK OF JUN. 22, 2009

HOME PAGE

WEATHER
TECH   U.S.   WORLD

ENTERTAINMENT

VIDEO

OTHER

POLITICS

SITE CATEGORY PAGE VIEWS

NTERNET
S 20

FACEBOOK
IS LAUNCHED

YOUTUBE
IS LAUNCHED

100 MILLION
WEB SITES

100 MILLION
BLOGS

THE WHITE HOUSE
STARTS A BLOG

OVER 1 BILLION
INTERNET USERS

Previous spread

CNN.com Traffic Analysis

In 2009, CNN cooperated with Nicholas Felton to create a visual history of its website since it was launched in 1996. The central spike chart demonstrates weekly page views over time. Black tags mark the ten busiest weeks, with specific events highlighted with white tags below the central axis. In the lower part, the growth of site categories is tracked. At the top of the chart, several unique metrics from the site's history are highlighted. To create a larger narrative, milestones in the history of the Internet were placed along the bottom. The piece is strong evidence of how CNN.com became accepted as a timely news source and more generally, how media habits have changed during this period.

Project Info: CNN, website, 2009, USA
Data Source: Webstats Internal Server Logs; Omniture SiteCatalyst; International Telecommunications Union; United Nations Population Division; AT&T Labs Research; Nielsen Online; Gartner Research
Design: Nicholas Felton

STAAT / Random I–XI

Using in-depth studies of natural phenomena as her starting point, Jorinde Voigt draws freely conceived motion sequences, visualising partly invisible occurrences. In large-format drawings, this series visualises the evolution of various phenomena, e.g. the flight of an eagle, temperature profiles, kissing, explosions, record charts etc., transferring them into rich graphic structures. There is no beginning or end to the series, since each phenomenon appears in all the drawings but each begins on a different sheet. The visualisation rules for each phenomenon vary from simple – "plus one" – to more complex patterns as with the Fibonacci numbers, changing too in the course of the series. In contrast to scientific data visualisations, Voigt's works remain open to interpretation.

Project Info: Series of drawings, 2008, Germany
Artist: Jorinde Voigt

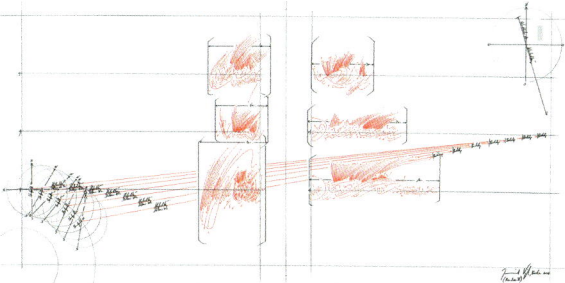

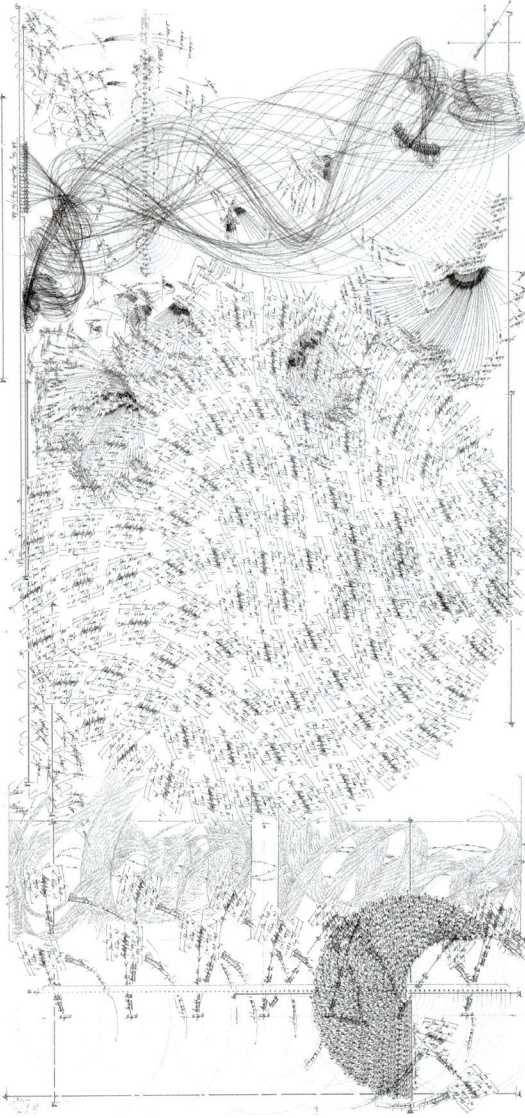

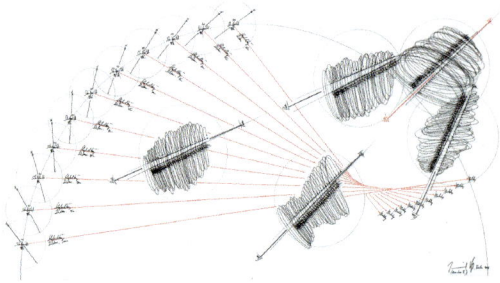

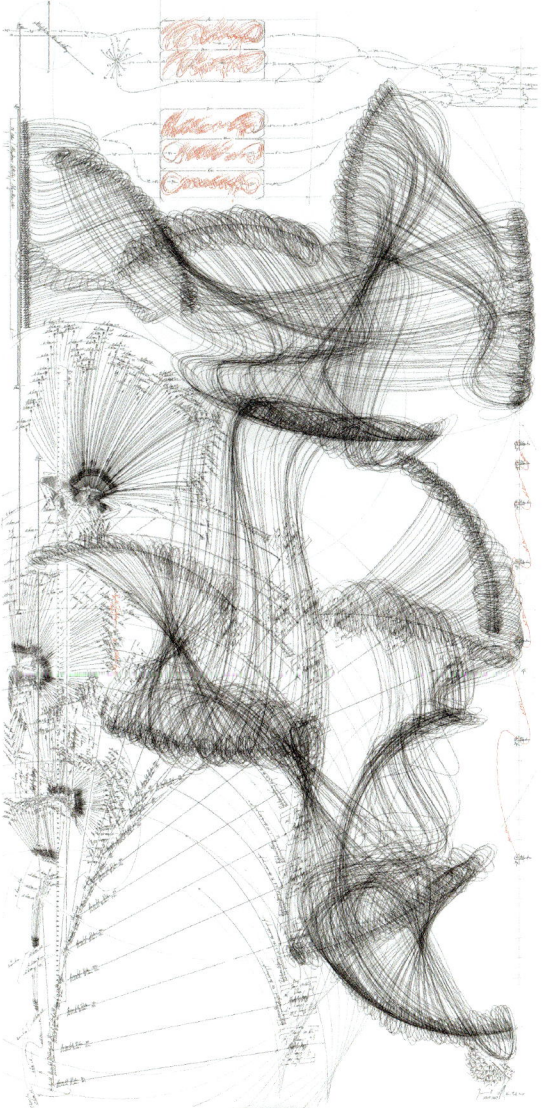
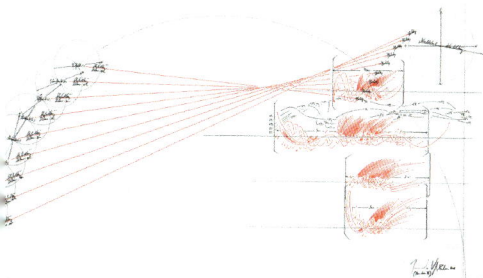
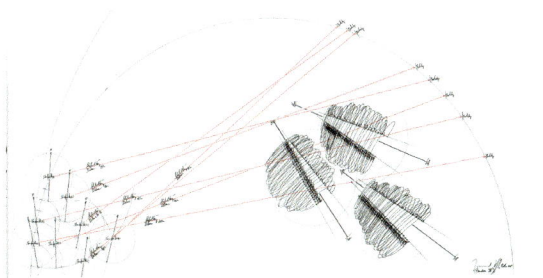

Swine Flu Life Cycle

In 2009 a new sub-type of the H1N1 virus, the so-called Swine Flu, appeared firstly in Mexico and caused the WHO to fear a major global influenza pandemic, similar to the Spanish Flu in 1918–1920. In the subsequent media frenzy, all coverage of the virus became rather sensational. In contrast, this graphic describes factually the process of how the virus proliferates by attacking human cells. The map beneath shows the number of reported deaths throughout the world by nation, which, compared with deaths caused by typical flu each year, are relatively insignificant.

Project Info: Blog, 2009, USA
Data Source: WHO; CDC; *Scientific American*
Research: Molly Frances
Design: Bryan Christie, Joe Lertola

Swine Flu Life Cycle

The current outbreak of swine flu is caused by a virus that is endemic in pigs. People who are in contact with pigs are at risk for the disease. Once the virus begins to spread from human to human there is a risk of a worldwide pandemic.

A Bryan Christie Design Information Graphic

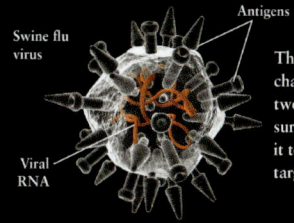

Antigens

Swine flu virus

Viral RNA

The virus is characterized by two antigens on its surface that allow it to attach to its target cells

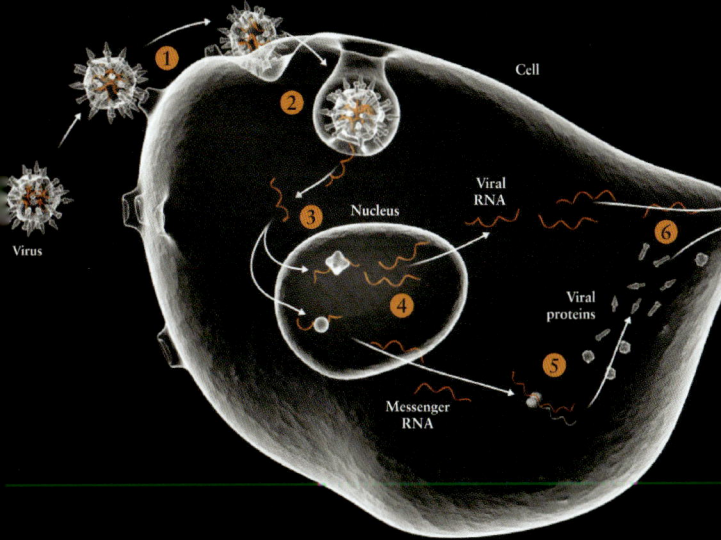

Cell

New virus

7

1

2

3

Nucleus

Viral RNA

6

4

Virus

Viral proteins

5

Messenger RNA

1 The virus uses its antigens to attach to the surface of cells in the nose, throat and lungs. 2 The cell engulfs the virus. 3 The virus is able to pierce the bubble of cell membrane that encloses it and release its RNA cargo into the cell. 4 In the nucleus copies of the viral RNA are made. 5 Viral messenger RNA causes the cell to make viral proteins. 6 These proteins and RNA migrate to the cell's surface where they are assembled into new virus particles. 7 New viruses start budding off from the cell surface.

Swine Flu Around The World

The human swine flu outbreak began in Mexico. Authorities in Mexico closed schools, museums, libraries and theaters in the capital on May 24th to try to contain an outbreak.

The disease has been detected in the U.S. and other countries. The World Health Organization has raised the level of influenza pandemic alert from the phase 4 to phase 5, indicating that human-to-human transmission of the virus is taking place in at least two countries.

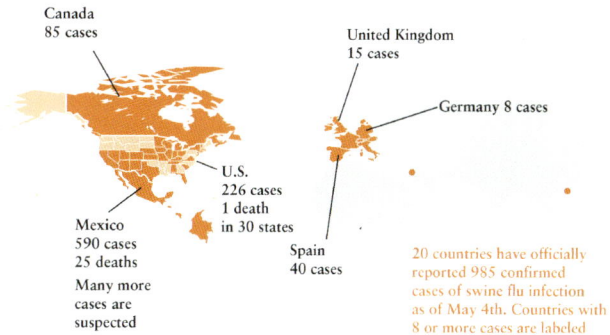

Canada 85 cases

United Kingdom 15 cases

Germany 8 cases

U.S. 226 cases 1 death in 30 states

Mexico 590 cases 25 deaths

Many more cases are suspected

Spain 40 cases

20 countries have officially reported 985 confirmed cases of swine flu infection as of May 4th. Countries with 8 or more cases are labeled

Sources: WHO, CDC, Scientific American
© 2009 Bryan Christie Design

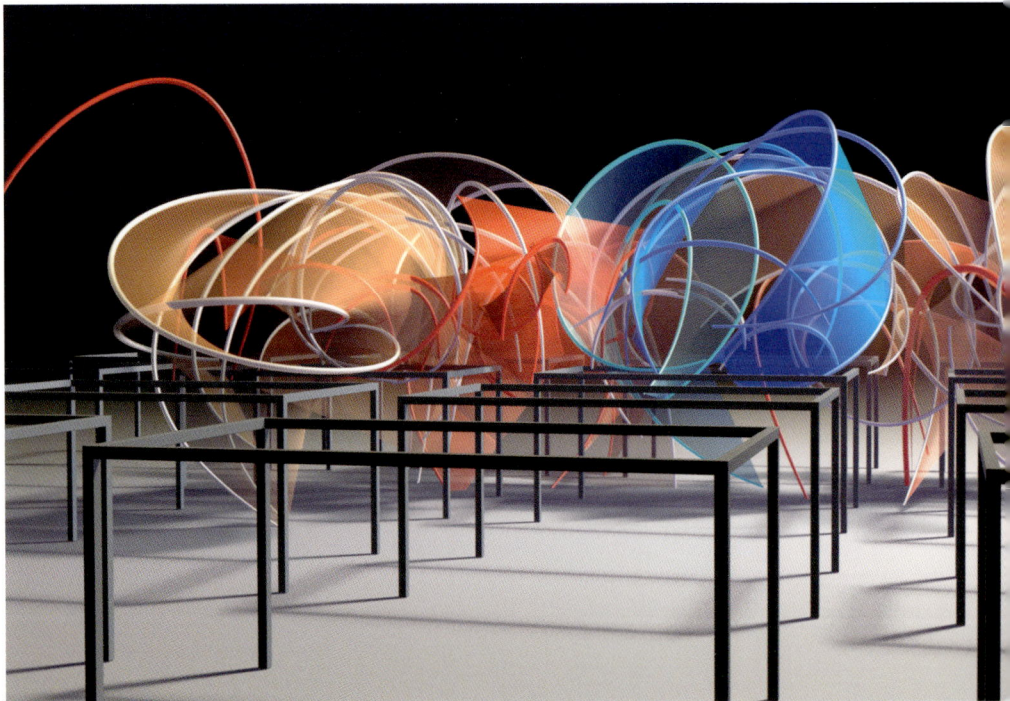

Synchronous Objects for
One Flat Thing, reproduced

William Forsythe is one of the most celebrated contemporary choreographers. His stage play *One Flat Thing, reproduced* is an arrangement for 17 dancers under and above a set of tables. The dance is generated from a set of motion themes, cues that dancers give each other and various instants when the movements of individual dancers are aligned. Forsythe worked with Ohio State University to develop a visualisation for this play. The research team collected two sets of data: spatial data indicating the position of each dancer at any given time, and qualitative data regarding the internal structure of the dance. These data were transformed into various visualisations of the play. *Form Flow* (top) shows how the movements of several dancers are aligned in one specific moment, while *3D Alignment* (bottom) traces the dancers' movements in space. *Cues and Themes* (following spread) is a graphic score of themes, cues and alignments over time.

Project Info: The Forsythe Company, interactive visualisation, 2009, Germany / USA
Research: Ohio State University; Forsythe Company; Amsterdam School of the Arts; University of California; University College London
Design: Matthew Lewis (ACCAD, Ohio State University)
Creative Direction: William Forsythe, Maria Palazzi, Norah Zuniga Shaw

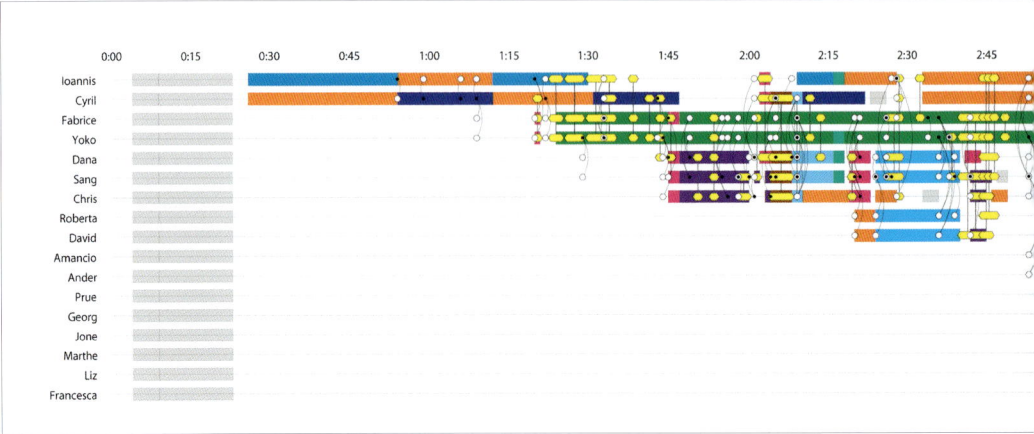

Full Score of Movement Material, Cues, and Sync-ups

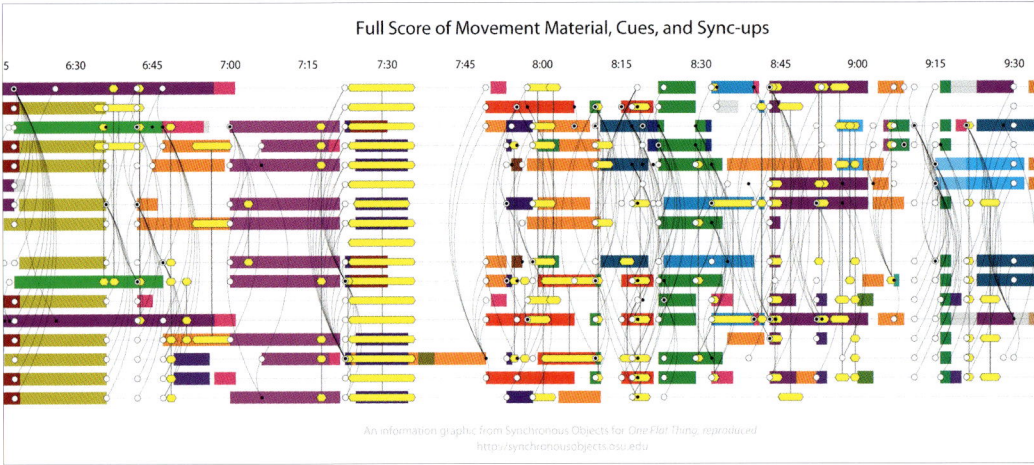

An information graphic from Synchronous Objects for *One Flat Thing, reproduced*
https://synchronousobjects.osu.edu

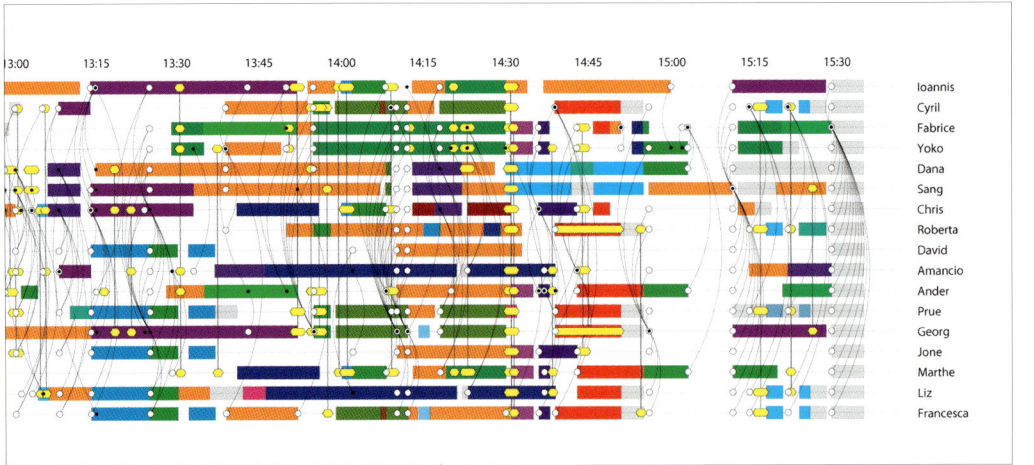

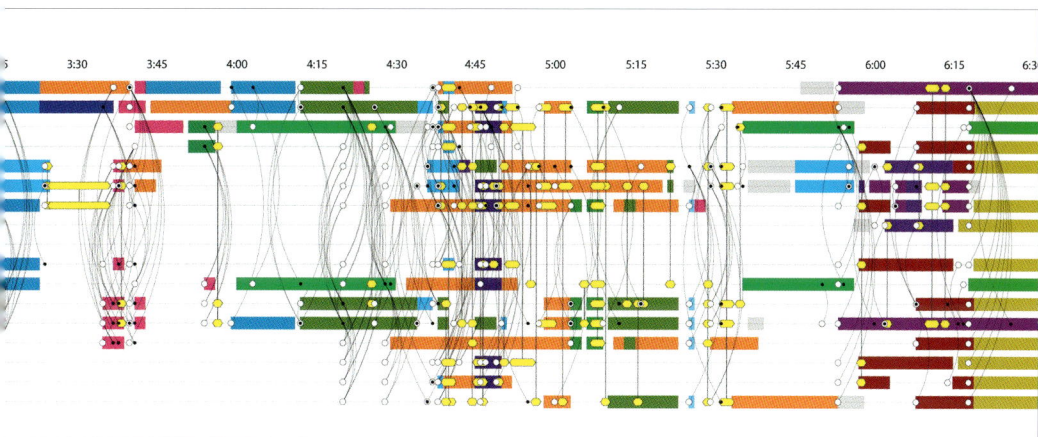

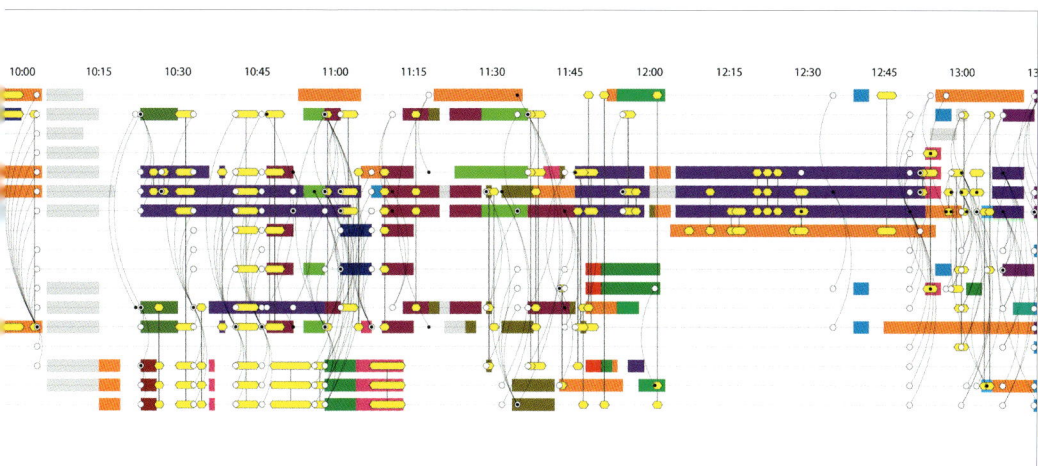

Project Info: The Forsythe Company, interactive visualisation, 2009, Germany / USA
Research: Ohio State University; Forsythe Company; Amsterdam School of the Arts; University of California; University College London
Design: Matthew Lewis (ACCAD, Ohio State University)
Creative Direction: William Forsythe, Maria Palazzi, Norah Zuniga Shaw

Project Info: Print, 2009, USA
Data Source: Project Gutenberg
Design: W. Bradford Paley
(Digital Image Design)

TextArc: Alice's Adventures in Wonderland

Bradford Paley created TextArc as a text-ana-lysing tool. In this example, all the text lines of *Alice in Wonderland* are arranged in sequence clockwise around a central area which is a map of all the words, placed near the lines in which they are used. Frequently used words thus appear towards the centre. Each word has a small distribution sign next to it, with tiny rays pointing towards all lines in which

the word is used. As an example, the Hatter, Dormouse and March Hare have similarly shaped distribution glyphs, indicating that they always appear together. In this enhanced version, Paley also employed spectral colour-ing. Chapters are coded in successive colours; key words are brighter, while peripheral words are darker and fade into the background.

Alice
Rabbit
White
King
Queen
Gryphon
Mock
Turtle
Hatter
Dormouse
Duchess
Cat
Majesty
jury
court
tarts
Lizard
guinea-pigs
Wonderland
dream
verses
paper
cupboards
brightened
mixed
simple
marked
bats
write
slates
knife
sister
written
shrill
passage
letter
trembling
sharply
explain
hastily
French
nonsense
begun
beautiful
porpoise
Quadrille
taught
cards
friend
pack
sea
sentence
Knave
Soup
exclaimed
school
Drawling
Uglification
Tortoise
crumbs
glad
added
creatures
beginning
rather
round
quite
talking
large
voice
nothing
hand
finished
course
curious
continued
different
surprised
began
great
CHAPTER
tone
day
please
right
certain
perhaps
minute
child
angrily
exactly
play
politely
story
ear
taken
pinched
introduce
flamingo
hedgehog
soldiers
ground
executioner
arches
players
moral
music
argument
game
fly
sighed
Hearts
sing
concert
checked
custody
choice
agree
way
moment
shoes
recovered
relief
regular
upset
bread-and-butter
rule
unfortunate
eager
ashamed
stupid
frowning
deep
learnt
pale
knee
sadly
assembled
fell
tea
whispered
rest
thoroughly
whether
shouted
lady
fun
otherwise
wide
watch
walked
face
piece
pleased

Being a TextArc of volumes I–IV of *A History Of Science* by Henry Smith Williams, M.D., LL.D.; assisted by Edward H. Williams, M.D.

A TextArc arranges an entire text in the form of a clock: first drawing every line of the text in a large arc, then drawing repeated words

at their average positions—as if rubber bands pulled toward every usage. A dark star next to a word tells when that word is used;

BOOK IV

MODERN DEVELOPMENT OF THE CHEMICAL AND BIOLOGICAL SCIENCES

As regards chronology, the epoch covered in the present volume is identical with that viewed in the preceding one. But now as regards subject matter we pass on to those diverse phases of the physical world which are the field of the chemist, and to those yet more intricate processes which force to do with living organisms. So radical are the changes here that we seem to be entering new worlds; and yet, here as before, there are intimations of the new discoveries away back in the Greek days. The solution of the problem of respiration will remind us that Anaxagoras had guessed the secret; and in these diversified studies which tell us of the Daltonian atom in its wonderful transmutations, we shall be reminded again of the Clazomenean philosopher and his successor Democritus.

Yet we should press the analogy much too far were we to intimate that the Greek of the older day or any thinker of a more recent period had penetrated, even in the vaguest way, all of the mysteries that the nineteenth century has revealed in the fields of chemistry and biology. At the very most the insight of those great Greeks and of the wonderful seventeenth-century philosophers who so often seemed on the verge of our later discoveries did no more than vaguely anticipate their successors of this later century. To gain an accurate, really specific knowledge of the properties of elementary bodies was reserved for the chemists of a recent epoch. The vague Greek guessings as to organic evolution were useful aside from the precise inductions of the Darwin. If the mediaeval Arabian endeavored to dull the knife of the surgeon with the use of drugs, his results hardly merit to be termed even an anticipation of modern anaesthesia. And when we speak of preventive medicine—of bacteriology in all its phases—we have to do with a marvellous field of which no previous generation of men had even the slightest inkling.

All in all, then, those that lie before us are perhaps the most wonderful and the most fascinating of all the fields of science. As the chapters of the preceding book carried us out into a macrocosm of inconceivable magnitude, our present studies are to reveal a microcosm of equally inconceivable smallness. As the studies of the physicist attempted to reveal the very nature of matter and of energy, we have now to seek the solution of the yet more inscrutable problems of life and of mind.

BOOK III

MODERN DEVELOPMENT OF THE PHYSICAL SCIENCES

With the present book we enter the field of the distinctively modern. There is no precise date at which we take up each of the successive stories, but the main sweep of development has to do in each case with the nineteenth century. We shall see at once that this is a time both of rapid progress and of great differentiation. We have heard almost nothing hitherto of such sciences as paleontology, geology, and meteorology, each of which now demands full attention. Meantime, astronomy and what the workers of the older day called natural philosophy become wonderfully diversified and present numerous strains that would have been startling enough to the star-gazers and philosophers of the earlier epoch.

Thus, for example, in the field of astronomy, Herschel is able, thanks to his perfected telescope, to discover a new planet and then to reach out into the depths of space and gain such knowledge of stars and nebulae as hitherto no one had more than dreamed of. Then, in rapid sequence, a whole science of hitherto unsuspected motor planets is discovered, while distances are measured, some members of the starry galaxy are timed in their flight, the direction of movement of the solar system itself is investigated, the spectroscope reveals the chemical composition even of suns that are unutterably distant, and a tangible theory is grasped of the universal cycle which includes the birth and death of worlds.

Similarly the new studies of the earth's surface reveal secrets of planetary formation hitherto quite inscrutable. It becomes known that the strata of the earth's surface have been forming throughout untold ages, and that successive populations offering utterly from one another have peopled the earth in different geological epochs. The entire point of view of thoughtful men becomes changed in contemplating the history of the world in which we live—albeit the newest thought harks back to some extent to those days when the inspired thinkers of early Greece dreamed out the wonderful theories with which our earlier chapters have made our readers familiar.

In the region of natural philosophy progress is no less pronounced and no less striking. It suffices here, however, by way of anticipation, simply to name the greatest generalization of the century in physical science—the doctrine of the conservation of energy.

ISTORY OF SCIENCE

white rays curve toward lines in which a word is mentioned. Words get larger and darker the more they are used. This particular TextArc has been enhanced to extract and enlarge historical context: numbers (mostly years) appear inside the arc, chapter headers & introductory paragraphs outside, book introductions in the corners. Typeset and drawn in November, 2005 by W. Bradford Paley; all rights reserved

BOOK I
THE BEGINNINGS OF SCIENCE

Should the story that is about to be unfolded be found to lack interest, the writers must stand convicted of unpardonable lack of art. Nothing but dulness in the telling could mar the story, for in itself it is the record of the growth of those ideas that have made our race and its civilization what they are; of ideas instinct with human interest, vital with meaning for our race; fundamental in their influence on human development; part and parcel of the mechanism of human thought on the one hand, and at practical civilization on the other. Such a phrase as 'fundamental principles' may seem at first thought a bad saying, but the idea it implies is less repellent than the phrase itself, for the fundamental principles in question are so closely linked with the present interests of every man, that they lie within the grasp of every average man and woman—nay, of every well-developed boy and girl. These principles are not merely the stepping-stones to culture, the prerequisites of knowledge—they are, in themselves, an essential part of the knowledge of every cultivated person.

It is our task, not merely to show what these principles are, but to point out how they have been discovered by our predecessors. We shall trace the growth of these ideas from their first vague beginnings. We shall see how sequences of thought gave way to precision; how a general truth, once grasped and formulated, was found to be a stepping-stone to other truths. We shall see that there are no isolated facts, no isolated principles, in nature; that each part of our story is linked by indissoluble bonds with that which goes before, and with that which comes after. For the most part the discovery of this principle or that is a given sequence is no accident; Galileo and Kepler must precede Newton. Cuvier and Lyell must come before Darwin.— Which, after all, is no more than saying that in our Temple of Science, as in any other piece of architecture, the foundation must precede the superstructure.

We shall best understand our story of the growth of science if we think of each new principle as a stepping-stone which must fit into its own particular niche; and if we reflect that the entire structure of modern civilization would be different from what it is, and less perfect than it is, had not that particular stepping-stone been found and shaped and placed in position. Taken as a whole, our stepping-stones lead to an end up towards the shining heights of an acropolis of knowledge, on which stands the Temple of Modern Science. The story of the building of this wonderful structure is in itself fascinating and beautiful.

BOOK II
THE BEGINNINGS OF MODERN SCIENCE

The studies of the present book cover the progress of science from the close of the Roman period in fifth century A.D. to about the middle of the eighteenth century. In tracing the course of events through so long a period, a difficulty becomes prominent which everywhere besets the historian to less degree—a difficulty due to the conflict between the strictly chronological and the topical method of treatment. We must hold as closely as possible to the actual sequence of events; since, as already pointed out, one discovery leads on to another. But, on the other hand, progressive steps are taken contemporaneously in the various fields of science, and if we were to attempt to introduce these in strict chronological order we should lose all sense of topical continuity.

Our method has been to adopt a compromise, following the course of a single science in each great epoch to a convenient stopping-point, and then turning back to bring forward the story of another science. Thus, for example, we tell the story of Copernicus and Galileo, bringing the record of cosmical and mechanical progress down to about the middle of the seventeenth century, before turning back to take up the physiological progress of the fifteenth and sixteenth centuries. Once the latter streams is entered, however, we follow it without interruption to the time of Harvey and his contemporaries in the middle of the seventeenth century, where we leave it to return to the field of mechanics as explained by the successors of Galileo, who were also the predecessors and contemporaries of Newton.

In general, it will aid the reader to recall that, so far as possible, we hold always to the same sequences of topical treatment at contemporary events, as a rule we must bear the constant, down the physical, then the biological sciences. The same order of treatment will be held to in succeeding volumes.

Several of the very greatest of scientific generalizations are developed in the period covered by the present book: for example, the Copernican theory of the solar system, the true doctrine of planetary emphasis; the laws of motion; the theory of the circulation of the blood, and the Newtonian theory of gravitation. The nature of the investigations of the early decades of the eighteenth century, terminating with Franklin's discovery of the nature of lightning and with the Linnaean classification of plants and animals, bring us to the close of our second great epoch; or, to put it otherwise, to the threshold of the modern period.

X. THE NEW SCIENCE OF ORIENTAL ARCHAEOLOGY

I. PREHISTORIC SCIENCE

HOW THE "RIDDLE OF THE SPHINX" WAS READ

Conspicuously placed in the great hall of Egyptian antiquities, the British Museum is a wonderful piece of sculpture known as the Rosetta Stone. I doubt if any object of the entire collection attracts so much attention from the casual visitor as this slab of black basalt on its telescope-shaped pedestal. The hall itself, despite its profusion of strange and wonderful objects, is always fairly crowded, but before this stone there are usually gathered one standing, gazing with much the same sort of interest at the strange characters that are graven on its surface. A glance at the glass-protected face. A glance is sufficient to show that three sets of inscriptions are there, the upper one occurring about one-fourth of the space, pictured scroll, made up of half-hundred serpents, hawks, lions, and other objects, as the learned initiate as hieroglyphics made of lines, angles, and other be a series of abbreviated or lower inscriptions is Greek screed above; also made of proving the text.

III. EGYPTIAN SCIENCE

To speak of a prehistoric science may seem like a contradiction of terms. The word prehistoric seems to imply barbarism, while science, clearly enough, seems the outgrowth of civilization; but rightly considered, there is no contradiction. For, on the one hand, man had ceased to be a barbarian long before what we call the historical period; and, on the other hand, science, of a kind, is no less a precursor and a cause of civilization than it is a consequent. To get this clearly in mind, we must ask ourselves: What, then, is science? The word is always ready enough upon the tongue of our everyday speech. But it is often, perhaps, that they who use it habitually ask themselves just what it means. Yet the answer is not difficult. A moment's attention will show that science, as the word is commonly used, implies these things: first, the gathering of knowledge through observation; second, the classification of such knowledge, and through this classification, the elaboration of ideas or principles. In the familiar definition of Herbert Spencer, science is organized knowledge.

In the previous chapter we have purposely refrained from referring to any particular tribe or race of historical man. The word, however, we are at the beginnings of national existence and consider the accomplishments of individual peoples. And at the same period, two or more races that occupy historical territory, but even now of a very general we shall be little individual scientists in the course of Egyptian culture. We are still, I must be understood in the elaboration of history, indeed we must bring the prehistoric before we may find ourselves at the line of march of historical science.

wolve smelalloyerries triownership
brain
language

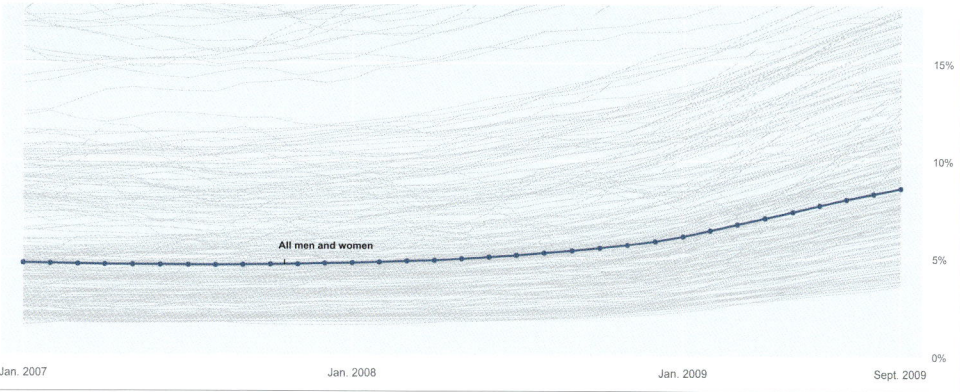

Published: November 6, 2009

The Jobless Rate for People Like You

Not all groups have felt the recession equally.

All races	Men and Women	All ages	All education levels
White	Men	Ages 15 to 24	Not a high school graduate
Black	Women	Ages 25 to 44	High school graduate
Hispanic		Age 45 and older	College graduate
All other races			

UNEMPLOYMENT RATE,
12 MONTH AVG. ENDING SEPT. '09

8.6%

For all men and women

All men and women

15%

10%

5%

0%

Jan. 2007   Jan. 2008   Jan. 2009   Sept. 2009

Previous spread and left

TextArc: Williams' History of Science

TextArc arranges a body of text clockwise, creating a visual index. Along the outer rim, text-lines are recorded in their order of appearance. Inside this, words are placed in their average position, in proximity to the individual lines around the circle in which they appear. This example covers four volumes of H. S. Williams' *History of Science*. The arc is formed by chapter titles and introductions. The first two volumes chronicle history until around 1800 (centre bottom). The third and fourth volumes cover the modern sciences. Concepts that are common to the sciences of all eras (like system, theory etc.) are drawn towards the centre, since they occur throughout the whole text. Others, being in use only in certain eras, float nearer specific edges.

Project Info: Print, 2005, USA
Data Source: Project Gutenberg: "A History Of Science" by Henry Smith Williams
Design: W. Bradford Paley (Digital Image Design)

The Jobless Rate for People Like You

This is an interactive time series covering US unemployment rates for the period from January 2007 to September 2009. It takes the general unemployment rate and breaks it down into specific population groups by gender, race, education and age. While most of the time unemployment rates in the western world are communi-cated in national average figures, this piece reveals the major social gaps behind these figures. Where the jobless rate is around 4% for white females with a college degree, it climbs to more than 30% for black mals who have never received further education.

Project Info: *The New York Times*, interactive visualisation, 2009, USA
Data Source: Bureau of Labor Statistics
Design: Shan Carter, Amanda Cox, Kevin Qualey
Art Direction: Steve Duenes

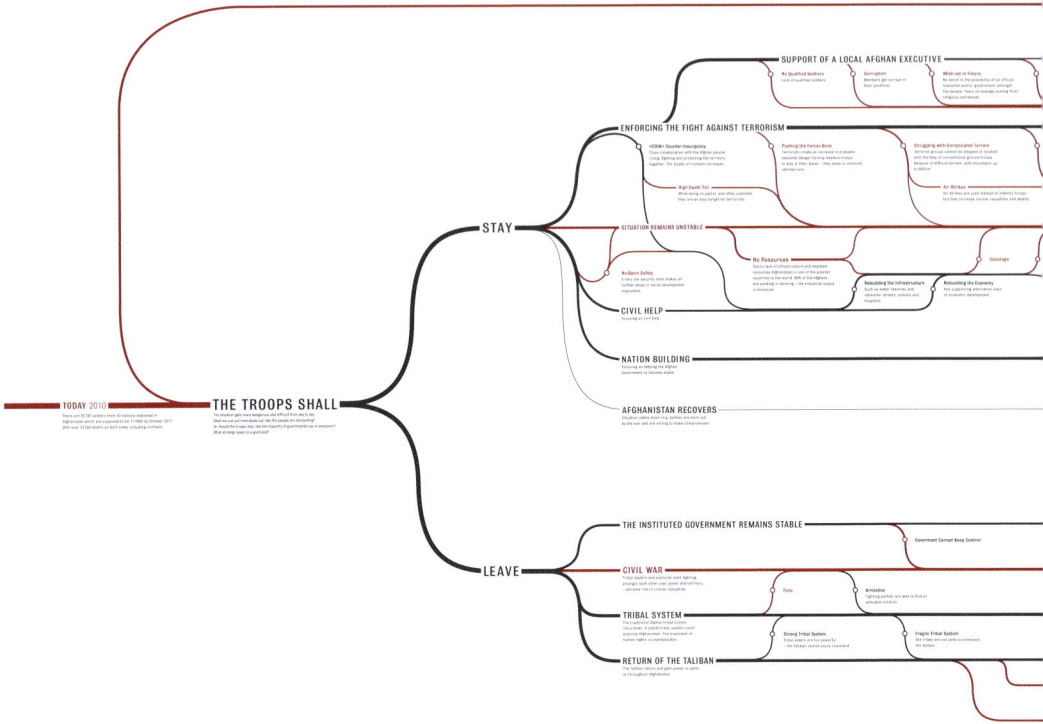

TODAY 2010
There are 30 185 soldiers from 43 nations stationed in Afghanistan which are supposed to be 111880 by October 2011. With over 10 000 deaths or both sides including civilians.

THE TROOPS SHALL
The situation gets more dangerous and difficult from day to day. Shall we just pull everybody out, like the people are demanding? Or should the troops stay like the majority of governments say is necessary? What strategy leads to a good end?

STAY

SUPPORT OF A LOCAL AFGHAN EXECUTIVE

No Qualified Seekers
Lack of qualified soldiers

Corruption
Members get corrupt in their positions

Mistrust in Future
No belief in the possibility of an official executive and/or government amongst the people. Years of revenge coming from religious extremists

ENFORCING THE FIGHT AGAINST TERRORISM

»COIN« Counter Insurgency
Close collaboration with the Afghan people. Living, fighting and protecting the territory together. The loyalty of civilians increases.

Pushing the Forces Back
Terrorists create an increase in probable assumed danger forcing soldiers troops to stay in their bases – they move in armored vehicles only

Struggling with Complicated Terrain
Terrorist groups cannot be stopped or located with the help of conventional ground troops because of difficult terrain, with mountains up to 4000 m

High South Toll
While being on patrol, and often unarmed, they are an easy target for terrorists

Air Strikes
Air strikes are used instead of infantry troops but this increases civilian casualties and deaths

SITUATION REMAINS UNSTABLE

No Resources
Due to lack of infrastructure and depleted resources Afghanistan is one of the poorest countries in the world. 50% of the Afghani are working in farming – the industrial output is minuscule

Sabotage

No Basic Safety
A very low security level makes all further steps in social development impossible

Rebuilding the Infrastructure
Build up water reserves and networks: streets, schools and hospitals

Rebuilding the Economy
Aid supporting alternative ways of economic development

CIVIL HELP
Focusing on civil help

NATION BUILDING
Focusing on helping the Afghan Government to become stable

AFGHANISTAN RECOVERS
Situation calms down e.g. parties are more out to the war and are willing to make compromises

LEAVE

THE INSTITUTED GOVERNMENT REMAINS STABLE

Government Cannot Keep Control

CIVIL WAR
Tribal leaders and warlords start fighting amongst each other over power and territory – someone rises in civilian casualties

Fails

Armistice
Fighting parties are able to find a peaceable solution

TRIBAL SYSTEM
The traditional Afghan tribal system reactivates. A stable tribal system could stabilize Afghanistan. The treatment of human rights is unpredictable.

Strong Tribal System
Tribal orders are too powerful – the Taliban cannot seize command

Fragile Tribal System
No tribes are not able to withstand the Taliban

RETURN OF THE TALIBAN
The Taliban return and gain power in parts or throughout Afghanistan

The Afghan Conflict
– A Map of Possible Scenarios

This is one of the rare examples where a time-line for the future is driven in order to compare and evaluate future options. In a synchronoptic timeline, the graphic displays various scenarios for the future in Afghanistan. The flow chart starts with a single point inthe present and follows two major options: the troops stay or leave. The scenarios developed consequently are based on wide media research and informed interviews with journalists, research think-tanks and political advisers. The synchronoptic format permits an overview of what political observers expect to happen, and thus makes it easier to evaluate differing political options.

Project Info: Poster, 2010, Germany
Data Source: Afghan Conflict Monitor; ZEIT-Stiftung; Heinrich Böll Foundation; Stiftung Wissenschaft und Politik; *The Guardian*; *The New York Times*
Research: Susanne Köbl (*Der Spiegel*); Can Merey (dpa); Hauke Friederichs (*Die Zeit*)
Design: Marc Tiedemann, Pierre la Baume, Karen Hentschel
Additional Info: Original size 164 cm x 70 cm; student project at University of Applied Sciences Potsdam, Germany

STABLE AFGHAN EXECUTIVE POWER
Afghan police and army can defend and protect their people

ARMY

ALLIED FORCES ASSERT CONTROL
Taliban cells (insurrection) weakened or wiped out of Afghanistan

Cultural Problems
The intruiging forces violate the private sphere the way it was defined to the local culture and turn hatred towards themselves.

Aid in Pakistan
Neighboring states allow territories to hide within their borders and deny western forces entry.

Pakistan Gains Control
Taliban cells severely weakened or completely wiped out.

Long and Enduring War
Terrorist forces gain power and support in tribal areas over the Afghan border.

Pakistan Focus on Taliban
Pakistan takes drastic measures in fighting the Taliban and terrorizing their influence especially in the tribal areas over the Afghan border.

No Effects
All efforts have no effect. And the Taliban stay as strong in Pakistan as before.

Riot in Pakistan
Areas like Taliban are strongly connected to the Pakistani citizens resources might cause as riot.

Pakistan Collapse
Taliban gains more influence in Pakistan because of the existing public support and some institutions – the existing system collapses.

...with the Taliban
...Taliban remain strong anti-resistance.

No Trust in Government

SITUATION REMAINS UNSTABLE

LEAVING ↓   LEAVING ↓   LEAVING ↓

The Taliban Take Over the System
New government based on Muslim or islamic law known as Sharia law be implemented. It would not conform to the human rights conventions. The body of law based on the Koran and the religion of Islam regulates civil and criminal justice system as well as individual conduct and personal choices – the religious laws and its interpretations will become the law.

Terrorism Eliminated
The terrorist forces seem to be destroyed but it is unsure if they will be able to regenerate and if a weak Afghanistan will be able to survive for a long time.

All Goals Fulfilled
A stable government restores the basic elements necessary for quality of life for the majority of the Afghan people and can protect them from any upcoming forces. Eventually the economy strengthens and cultural and social life recovers completely.

Fallback
Works runs out, and/or too many people are dying, which pressures the Allied forces including the UN to withdraw their troops, and leave Afghanistan in a disastrous situation, which will greatly affect the whole Middle Eastern area.

Tactif
No harder found, the election is rigged or swayed by corruption.

Integrate the Taliban
Establish as an official party or as part of other existing parties.

Staying with Karzai
A democratic election based on the existing constitution.

PUBLIC SUPPORT AND TRUST GOVERNMENT

Loya Jirga
Is a grand assembly of tribal elders who come together to discuss national, political or emergency matters.

QUALITY OF LIFE INCREASES

LEAVING ↓

THE PLACED GOVERNMENT REMAINS STABLE

CIVIL WAR
The country remains confused and at war with no single party – not even the Taliban, the tribe leaders or the warlords being able to gain power. It is very likely that the state will not be able to survive and relies by current turmoil.

No Terror Observation
Weak readiness for terror prevention or fighting against terrorist groups.

TRIBAL-SYSTEM

TALIBAN
Taliban gain power in parts or throughout Afghanistan.

...tured
...situation offers a breeding function.

Taliban Gain Power

Terrorism

Rising Taliban Power

Taliban Gain Power in Pakistan
With a good infrastructure and an increase of power in Afghanistan the insurgence Taliban infiltrates the Pakistani government. They might also get and use Pakistan's atomic bomb.

STAY

High Death-Toll
While being on patrol, and often unarmed, they are an easy target for terrorists.

SITUATION REMAINS UNSTABLE

No Resources
Due to lack of infrastructure and depleted resources Afghanistan is one of the poorest countries in the world. 80% of the Afghans are working in farming – the industrial output is miniscule.

No Basic Safety
A very low security level makes all further steps in social development impossible

CIVIL HELP
Focusing on civil help.

LEAVE

CIVIL WAR
Tribal leaders and warlords start fighting amongst each other over power and territory – extreme rise in civilian casualties.

Fails

TRIBAL SYSTEM
The traditional Afghan tribal system resurfaces. A stable tribal system could stabilize Afghanistan. The treatment of human rights is unpredictable.

Strong Tribal System
Tribal elders are too powerful – the Taliban cannot usurp command.

RETURN OF THE TALIBAN
The Taliban return and gain power in parts or throughout Afghanistan.

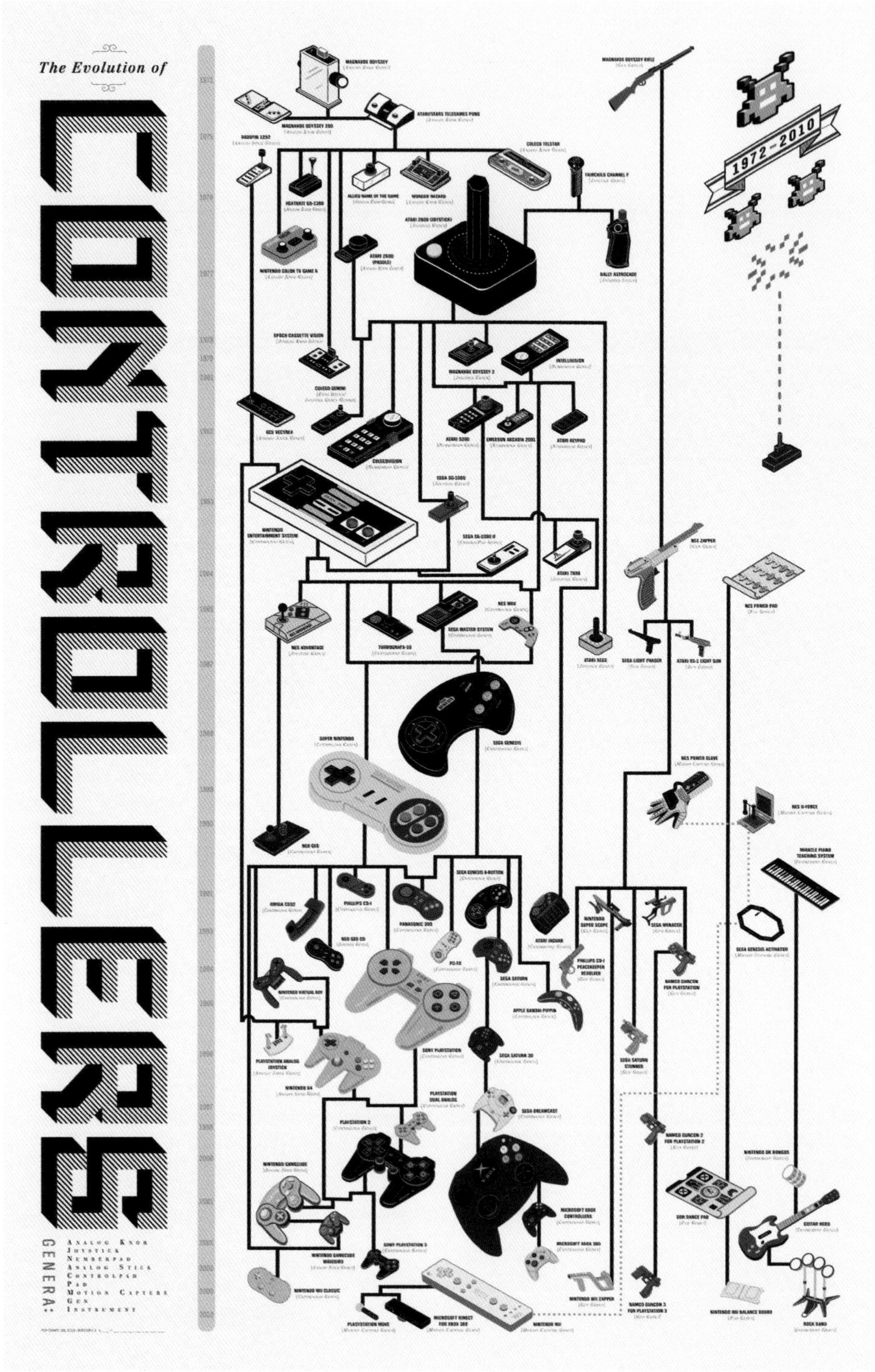

The Evolution of
CONTROLLERS

1972–2010

MAGNAVOX ODYSSEY
{*Analog Knob Genus*}

ATARI/SE
{*An*

MAGNAVOX ODYSSEY 200
{*Analog Knob Genus*}

RADOFIN 1292
{*Analog Stick Genus*}

HEATHKIT GD-1380
{*Analog Knob Genus*}

ALLIED NAME OF THE GAME
{*Analog Knob Genus*}

WONDER W
{*Analog Knob*}

NES ZAPPER
{*Gun Genus*}

ATARI 7800
{*Joystick Genus*}

NES PC
{*Pad*}

ATARI XEGS
{*Joystick Genus*}

SEGA LIGHT PHASER
{*Gun Genus*}

ATARI XG-1 LIGHT GUN
{*Gun Genus*}

DDR DANCE PAD
{*Pad Genus*}

GUITAR HERO
{*Instrument Genus*}

CO GUNCON 3
PLAYSTATION 3
{*Gun Genus*}

NINTENDO WII BALANCE BOARD
{*Pad Genus*}

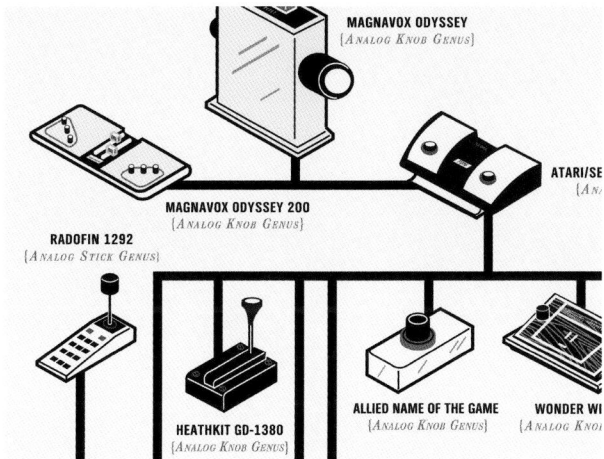

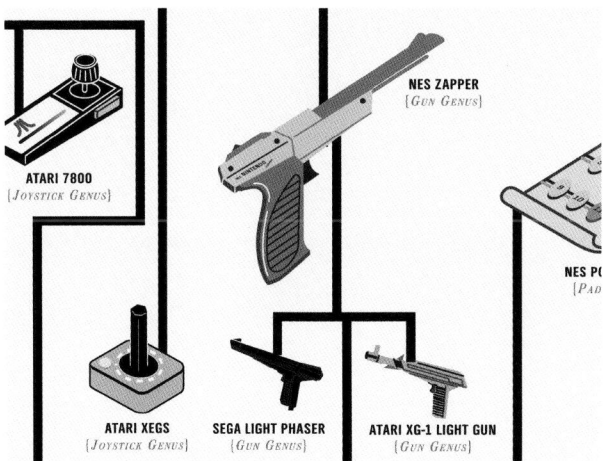

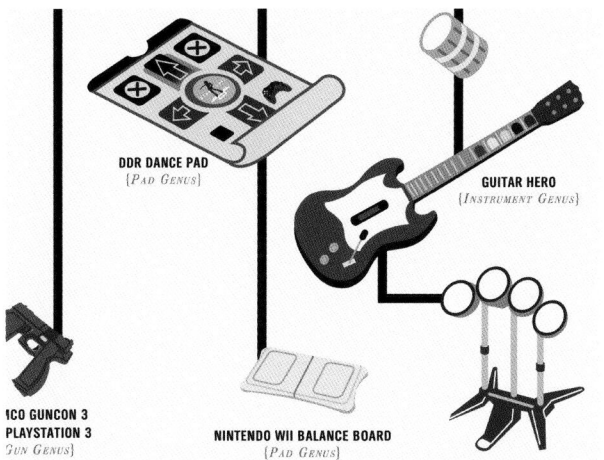

Project Info: Poster, 2010, USA
Design: Ben Gibson, Patrick Mulligan
(Pop Chart Lab)

5 Minute Increment

Wallet? Check. Phone? Check. T-shirt from show? Check. Dignity? Who needs that anyway? Okay maybe a little would've been nice but you can't have everything!

Ru-roh, that's an outgoing text to her at 4:43 a.m. on my phone. Worst. Dude. Ever.

Maybe I should quit my life and start over, cause something not awesome is definitely happening here.

Besides all the crippling darkness and self-loathing this actually feels regular. I mean, at least I feel SOMETHING, right? Please say yes.   hammock

Does hung-over instant messengering through the work day mean I'll never get that rooftop with the [   ] and Hummer-sized grill? Well, there're always scratch-lotto tickets!

Is apologizing buzzed via e-mail, about being an obnoxious lurker the night before, considered insincere? Wait! Did I just fall asleep with my eyes open!?

I've been doing this for 15 years. How bad could another night's (emotional) damage actually be? Not that bad.

Previous spread

The Evolution
of Video-Game Controllers

Much like a biological taxonomy, this piece presents the development of game controllers from the early days of 1972 up until 2010. The grey timeline next to the title works as the guide through the decades. Evolving top down, the graphic classifies 82 different "species" and 9 "genera", thus referring to two of the major ranks in biological classification. In the main chart, lines show family connections between devices, and along with the title of each one, its "genus "is named.

The First Two Hours of My Morning After

Andrew Kuo uses charts as a humorous medium for recording personal experiences and everyday confusion. His charts are single pieces, painted with acrylic on paper. Because of both this handmade look and the fact that his diagrams deal mostly with what's going on in Kuo's head, they mock the notion of the serious, fact-based communication that is associated with diagrams. This is a timeline of a morning after partying, charting the shame, loss of memory and the attempt to regain balance that typically occur with a major hangover. Each colour refers to one thought. Reading starts at the top left and goes back and forth along the lines. Each square equals five minutes, so that one line makes up half an hour.

Project Info: Painting, 2008, USA
Artist: Andrew Kuo
Additional Info: Original size 61 cm x 46 cm; Andrew Kuo is represented by Taxter & Spengemann, New York

The Soviet Union Olympic Medals Tally

Against a bright Communist-red background, this time series looks at how many medals were won by the Soviet Union and its successor states at Olympic Games in years after World War II. Along the bottom, the individual Games are labelled with their year. Purely yellow bars show the total number of medals won each year by the Soviet team. With the US boycott of the Moscow Olympics in 1980, this value peaked at almost 200 medals. The later bars show that, counted together, the individual teams of the successor states weren't doing any worse than in Soviet times. The white line shows the US medal count in comparison.

Project Info: Website, 2008, UK
Data Source: Olympic.org
Design: Craig Robinson

OLYMPIC MEDALS TALLY
SOVIET UNION & POST-SOVIET NATIONS

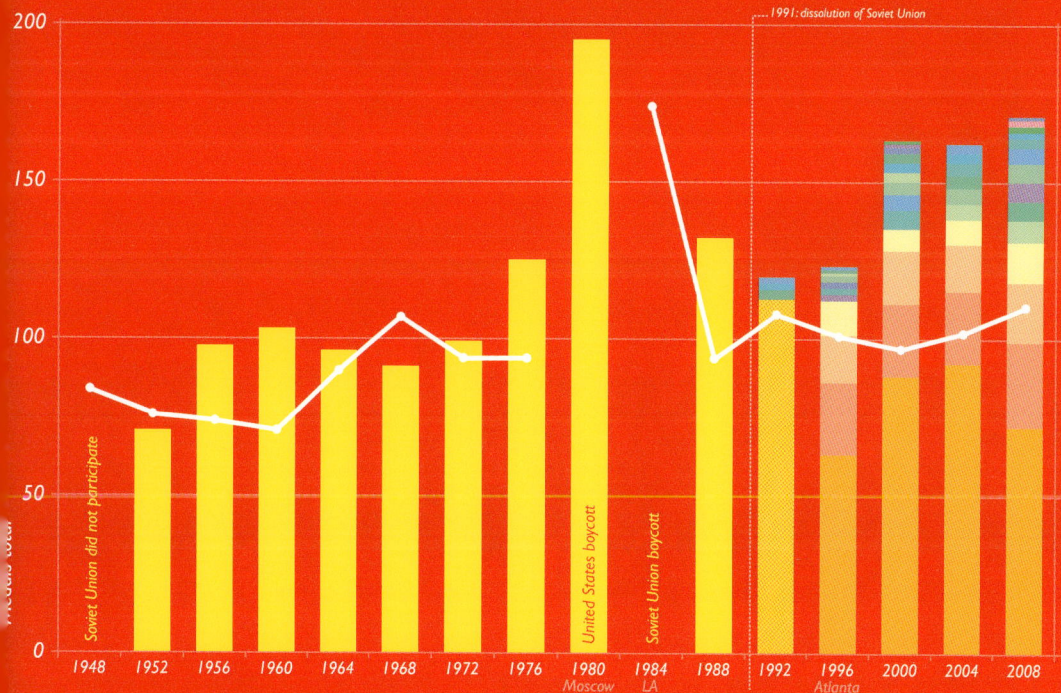

1991: dissolution of Soviet Union

Soviet Union did not participate

United States boycott

Soviet Union boycott

200

150

100

50

0

1948 | 1952 | 1956 | 1960 | 1964 | 1968 | 1972 | 1976 | 1980 *Moscow* | 1984 *LA* | 1988 | 1992 | 1996 *Atlanta* | 2000 | 2004 | 2008

Legend:

- USSR
- Unified Team*
- Armenia
- Azerbaijan
- Belarus
- Estonia
- Georgia
- Kazakhstan
- Kyrgyzstan
- Latvia
- Lithuania
- Moldova
- Russia
- Tajikistan
- Ukraine
- Uzbekistan
- USA

(Turkmenistan have yet to win medals)

* Joint team comprised of 12 of the 15 former Soviet republics: Armenia, Azerbaijan, Belarus, Georgia, Kazakhstan, Kyrgyzstan, Moldova, Russia, Tajikistan, Turkmenistan, Ukraine, and Uzbekistan

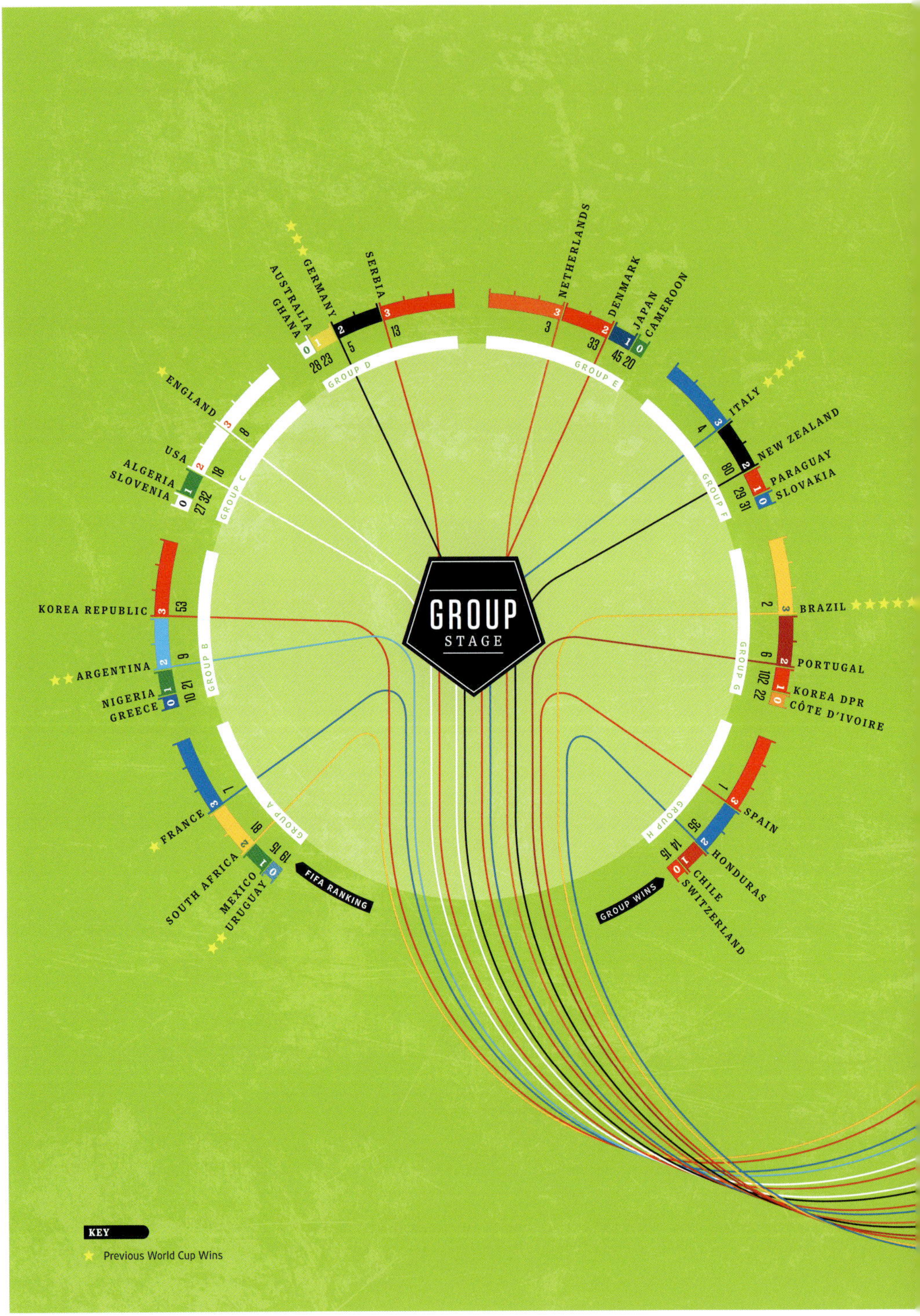

GROUP
STAGE

GERMANY
AUSTRALIA
GHANA
SERBIA
ENGLAND
USA
ALGERIA
SLOVENIA
NETHERLANDS
DENMARK
JAPAN
CAMEROON
ITALY
NEW ZEALAND
PARAGUAY
SLOVAKIA
KOREA REPUBLIC
ARGENTINA
NIGERIA
GREECE
BRAZIL
PORTUGAL
KOREA DPR
CÔTE D'IVOIRE
FRANCE
SOUTH AFRICA
MEXICO
URUGUAY
SPAIN
HONDURAS
CHILE
SWITZERLAND

FIFA RANKING
GROUP WINS

GROUP A
GROUP B
GROUP C
GROUP D
GROUP E
GROUP F
GROUP G
GROUP H

KEY
★ Previous World Cup Wins

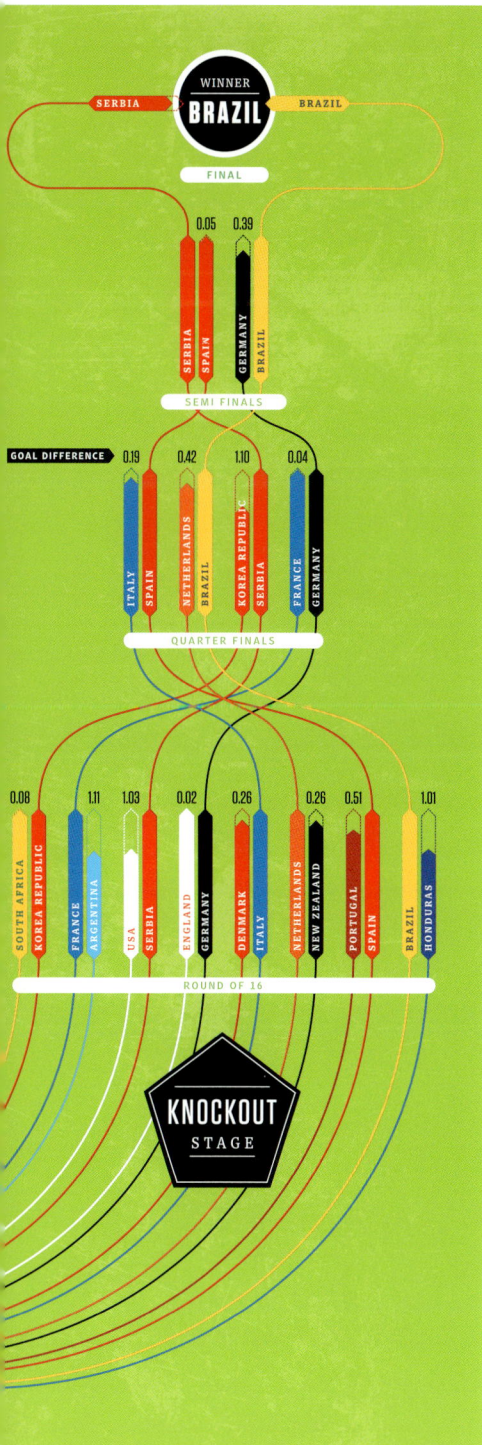

The World Cup Predicted

The intricate economics of football: this graphic draws on a formula developed by Simon Kuper and Stefan Szymanski to forecast international football results based on economic data. According to the model, a team's results are influenced by its country's GDP per capita, population size and experience in football. Here the model was used to forecast the results of the 2010 World Cup in South Africa, with, as it shows, somewhat deficient results. The left side illustrates the group stage with the teams that qualify then feeding into the knockout stage on the right, leading eventually to the final winner. Each team is represented by its national kit colour, the lines showing each team's progression through the tournament.

Project Info: *Wired*, magazine article, 2010, UK
Data Source: Simon Kuper, Stefan Szymanski: "Why England Lose", 2009
Design: Paul Butt (Section Design)

Understanding Shakespeare

Computer-based language-processing facilitates the analysis of large bodies of
literary text to an unprecedented level of
detail. The WordHoard database, provided
by Northwestern University in Illinois, offers
full text versions of Shakespeare's plays, with
detailed meta-data on how often each word
is used, by which character and what type of
word it is. This allows the texts to be looked
at in a somewhat mathematical manner.
Stephan Thiel has developed a series of visualisation patterns for these data. Each of his
approaches is governed by a different question
about what happens in each play. The visualisations were originally realised as large-scale
prints, featuring a large variety of sizes – from
large visual structures to very fine text details.

Project Info: Website, poster, 2010, Germany
Data Source: WordHoard (Northwestern University)
Design: Stephan Thiel
Additional Info: Student project at University
of Applied Sciences Potsdam, Germany

Act 3, Scene 1

Scene 2

Scene 3

Scene 4

Scene 5

guide time sceptre rebuke else always meet apart mongrel valour hail bear safe till nothing dog think grave
solemn go Banquo guest advice yet must
gripe slow notion rancour acquaint confess may catalogue absence dauntless speech
gift common life leave lineal sir fear keep attend close whereby station
Fleance weighty sundry place death cleanness adieu royalty seed come conclude yesterday near
strange wail nature deep alone soul supper Antony give advise consider write man back hour half good fate dark vessel far hound

malice Fleance shake prithee deed rouse black ring assailable rooky hold sleep shall marvel touch will bat face chuck Banquo note hum let tho
wood scotch treason thy danger piece oh wing heart jocund prey bad yawn present Duncan terrible eat go stream life mind safe drowse invisible come

slave revenge may give Fleance thou good ho fly will tonight light rain oh subject horse way glimmer well traveller bid

may attend majesty absence promise hide terrible air
good lord health lay well lord strange drink blood go face give use man may thou young sit keep yet breed
highness sit sir highness grace sight Fleance appetite time hearty brain sleep fee servant horrible Banquo baby pity bear good must
please reserve place sir rise company prithee mockery maw Macduff come dear
better night move please blame infirmity else host grace ear olden side best hardlook safe firm stool back fear perform encounter
royal upon deed nature

haste Hecate now will back come angry soon make scorn mortal riddle reason beldame draw wayward confusion death art son meet shall grace

Wybory prezydenckie 2010. Nareszcie możesz się zrewanżować. Jeśli nie wygrasz, wypadasz z gry.

26

27

28

Zarażasz ptasia gry
prezydenckiego p
to nie wystarcza , z
samolot. Musisz w
żeby pozostać w g

W co gra Tusk?

Niewinna z pozoru zabawa w kontrolera lotów może się skończyć dla Donalda tuska i PO katastrofą.

Andrzej Stankiewicz, Piotr Śmiłowicz, Joanna Kowalska-Iszkowska

16

15

WS

Odzyskujesz akt
Macierewicz dos
Oczko do przod

1

Macierewicz wywozi do prezydenta akta WSI. Cofasz się o jedno pole.

2

Wyrzuć "6". Wygrałeś wybory, możesz zagrać Tuska

4

3

PN i sam dostajesz
FA.
o 3 pola i przypalasz
owi cygaro

Stoczniom grozi upadek. Musisz negocjować z UE i postawić Jasińskiego przed Trybunałem Stanu. Czekasz dwie kolejki

21

24

23

22

Prezydent odmawia nominacji generalskich i ambasadorskich. Cofasz się o jedno pole.

Negocjacje w sprawie tarczy antyrakietowej. Jeśli znasz Rona Asmusa, cofasz się o 3 pola

20

17

18

19

Konflikt w Gruzji. Prezydent wychodzi na twardziela. Cofasz się o 6 pól

zydent wetuje ustawę
dialną. Musisz negocjować
apieralskim.
kasz jedną kolejkę

PiS traktat poparł ale prezydent go nie podpisal. Cofasz sie o dwa oczka.

Prezydent obiecuje ci, ze przekona PiS do poparcia Traktatu Lizbonskiego. Oczko do przodu.

11

14

12

13

10

Nominację dostałeś w bocznej salce. Trzy oczka do tyłu

9

6

7

8

zydent wręcza ci nominację
premiera. Dwa oczka do
odu.

Rada Gabinetowa o służbie zdrowia. Prezydent daje w kość tobie i ministrowi zdrowia. Cofasz się o jedno pole.

Previous spread

What's the Game, Tusk?

Made in 2009 for Poland's *Newsweek*, this info-graphic tackles the politics of Polish Prime Minister Donald Tusk. He has been in office since 2007, after unsuccessfully campaigning in the 2005 presidential elections. The piece starts with Tusk's portrait at the lower left. The reader plays Donald Tusk, jumping from field to field. Red fields represent political events during his mandate, such as the liquidation of the Polish Military Secret Service WSI (in nos. 3 and 15) or the Georgia Conflict in 2008 (in no. 20). No. 28 looks towards the 2010 presidential elections, suggesting a second chance for Tusk to run for president. However, in January 2010 Tusk decided not to campaign and remained as Prime Minister.

Project Info: *Newsweek*, magazine article, 2009, Poland
Research: Andrzej Stankiewicz, Piotr Śmiłowicz, Joanna Kowalska-Iszkowska
Design: Jan Kallwejt

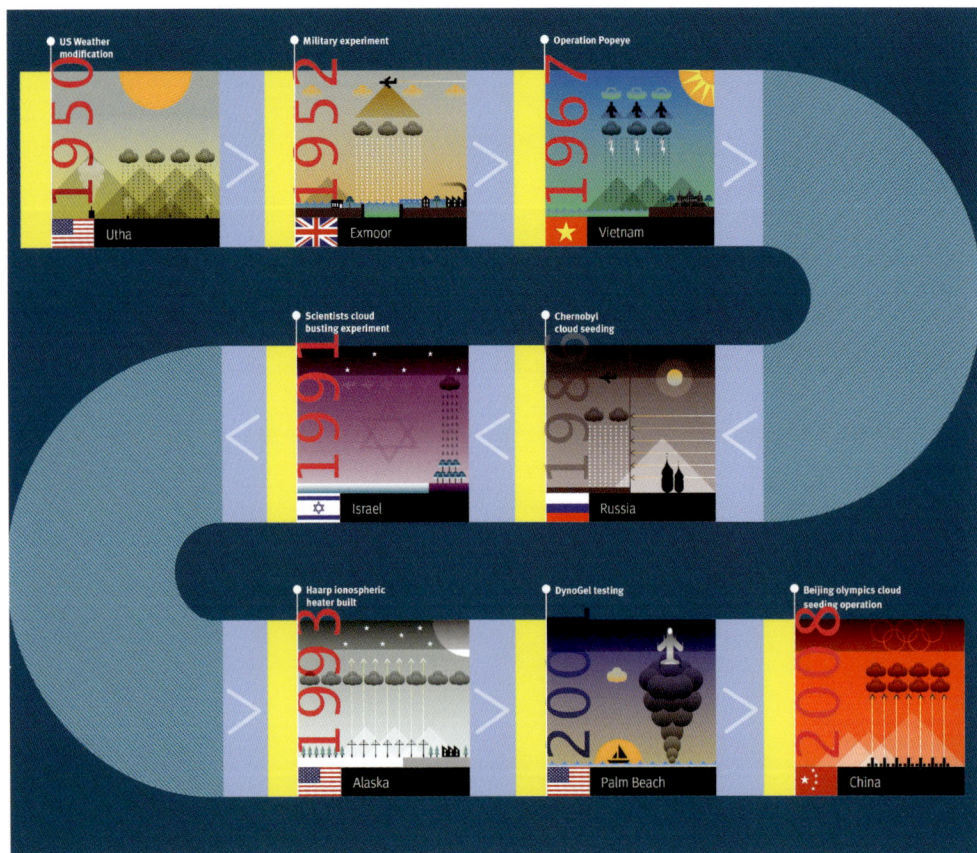

Project Info: *Audi* magazine, 2008, UK
Design: Infonauts

Wicked World Weather

Man has always been exposed to unpredictable weather conditions and always dreamed of controlling it. This double piece presents selected projects from around the world for influencing the weather. The blue timeline shows each event as a small vignette, indicating both the country as well as the occasion of each weather modification project. The second graphic (above) locates all projects on a light grey world map. Operation Popeye, for example, was a military operation during the Vietnam war – using cloud-seeding, the monsoon was intensified over the years in order to hinder the Vietnamese forces and their trucks from using the muddy roads. Other projects were launched in civil contexts, in the quest to control storms or to relieve drought.

Wired Anniversary

For the anniversary of *Wired* in 2008, Fernanda
Viégas and Martin Wattenberg created a
visual history of the magazine, referring to
the noted bold use of colour in its layout. The
circles depict every issue before June 2008 in
chronological order, with each circle displaying the colours used on the issue's cover. This
was done by an algorithm which extracts the
"peak" colours from an image. Circles are arranged in rows, each row being one year. As
the magazine began as a bi-monthly, the first
row is sparser. Overall circle sizes refer to the
magazine's circulation. *Wired* also created a
two-sided poster from this piece, showing the
circles on one side and the actual covers on
the other.

Project Info: *Wired*, magazine
article and poster, 2008, USA
Design: Fernanda Viégas,
Martin Wattenberg

Category
344—427

"In information visualisation it is often helpful to see data from a different angle and compare it with other information, update it, network it."

Joachim Sauter

Category
Elements are divided into classes

Categories create order. A confusing volume of information is easily structured by differentiating by type and by looking for shared characteristics. Key economic figures can be arranged by business sector or demographic group (*Economy Map*, p.356 and *2009: A Job Odyssey*, p.346). War may result in a large number of fatalities and the military powers involved need to know the groups to which the victims belonged (*Function*, p.363).

Distinguishing between types is a theoretical classification and often arbitrary. For instance, the immense number of books in a library could be categorised by size or colour, although it is customary to classify books by their subject matter. However, even sub-division by subject turns out to be so fuzzy that a range of different classification systems exist side by side (*Your Friend, The Library*, p.427).

In *Writing Without Words* (p.422) Stefanie Posavec works on the basis of subject matter when she analyses a novel by Jack Kerouac by dividing the entire text into central themes. *Influences of Edgar Allan Poe* (p.380) is concerned with a topic of a historical nature, namely Poe's place in the history of literature. However, the account's structure is only partially chronological; mostly it is arranged by the literary aspects of his work. On the other hand, what makes Jessica Hagy's blog *This is Indexed* (p.403) so appealing is the fact that she invents abstract categories for everyday problems and depicts them in simple diagrams.

This chapter also gathers together works that combine different aspects of a subject. Many infographics place several data records on an equal footing side by side, linked by a shared framework or central symbol (*Digital Dump*, p.354 and *Hamburgers: The Economy of America's Favorite Food*, p.367). The chapter also considers those series which unite a range of approaches. *Flocking Diplomats NYC* (p.358) creates a visual image of a comprehensive study of parking violations by diplomats in New York by combining a range of different layouts, from timelines and maps to individual graphs.

Mental maps have already been mentioned under Location. This chapter contains examples that no longer bear any reference to real places or images. For instance, when representing scientific disciplines, the position on the paper of mathematics or biology is less important than the relationships between the disciplines (*Relationships Among Scientific Paradigms*, p.390). The situation is similar with regard to modified subway maps where each line stands for a category (*Web Trend Map*, p.414).

Interactive visualisations make it possible to sort large data records into specific categories. Jonathan Harris, for example, collects personal statements from online dating sites (*I Want You To Want Me*, p.376). On-screen visualisation permits users to filter huge volumes of data by age, gender or other categories.

DEN—
SITY
GN+

LABORATORIO DI SINTESI FINALE
Politecnico di Milano | a.a. 2010-2011
M.Sc. Communication Design
Section c3

Paolo Ciuccarelli
Marco Maiocchi
Stefano Mandato
Tommaso Venturini
Salvatore Zingale

TEACHING ASSISTANTS
Giorgio Caviglia
Luca Masud
Azzurra Pini
Donato Ricci

2009:
A JOB ODYSSEY

The visualization illustrates, using official data exclusively, the Italian employment evolution from 2004 to 2010, comparing employed, unemployed and inactive population of the country, with the due subdivisions. The minimum and maximum peaks are underlined in order to faster understand the situation during the considered period of time. In the last part data from 2010 are compared to those of the other European countries. Moreover, we have realized a focus about the 15-34 years old population, analyzing the available data and reproducing, through the metaphor of the solar system, the actors system, the streams, the relationships through which each actor faces, in order to represent the dynamics against which they come up, through their journey from education conclusion or abandon to employment, with all the possibilities in-between and until the retirement moment. Observing the infographics in its entirety, it emerges that in italy the work force decreases, against the increase of the over-64 population, that needs the support of the welfare state.

PROJECT BY
Alessandro Dallafina
Francesco Faggiano
Stefano Greco
Marco La Mantia
Simone Paoli

ISTAT

2004 2005 2006 2007 2008 2009 2010

ITALY GERMANY FRANCE SPAIN U.K. SWEDEN

INACTIVE PEOPLE
58%
OF POPULATION
34.679 k

INACTIVES IN
WORKING AGE
25%
OF POPULATION
14.723 k

EMPLOYERS
BY AGE RANGE   BY GEOGRAPHICAL SHARING   BY EDUCATION DEGREE

42%
<15 YEARS OLD

58%
>64 YEARS OLD

INACTIVES IN
NON-WORKING AGE
33%
OF POPULATION
20.356 k

growing up (+15 y.o.)
growing old (+64 y.o.)

EDUCATION
SYSTEM

attends

57%
OTHER
INACTIVES

43%
YOUNG
INACTIVES

retirement
termination

pensions
€ 234.025 billions

UNIONS
bargains with
COMPANIES

SOCIAL SECURITY
INSTITUTIONS

ILLEGAL WORK
~ 2.600 k

looking for a job

pays
defends
joins
works for
pays
pays
improves
protests

71%
OTHER EMPLOYEES

29%
YOUNG EMPLOYEES

LIFELONG
LEARNING

"Hi! I'm Marco,
15-34 years old.
and I'm young"

transitions
relationships
money flows
human resources flows
unknown flows

FIRST JOB
CHANNELS

56%
YOUNG
UNEMPLOYED

44%
OTHER
UNEMPLOYED

UNEMPLOYED
3%
OF POPULATION
1.841 k

85.3% FRIENDS RELATIVES AND ACQUAINTANCES
18.8% DIRECT APPLICATION
6.0% WEB, PRESS AND MEDIA
5.2% SELF EMPLOYMENT
4% PREVIOUS WORK EXPERIENCES
3.8% SCHOOL AND EDUCATION
2.2% EMPLOYMENT AGENCIES
1.2% EMPLOYMENT EXCHANGES
2.2% OTHER CHANNELS

finds a job

EMPLOYEES
39%
OF POPULATION
23.203 k

ACTIVE PEOPLE
42%
OF POPULATION
25.044 k

<15 YEARS OLD	>64 YEARS OLD		YOUNG INACTIVES	OTHER INACTIVES		YOUNG EMPLOYEES	OTHER EMPLOYEES	
8.841 k	11.515 k		6.267 k	8.456 k		6.728 k	16.475 k	

YOUNG UNEMPLOYED   OTHER OTHER UNEMPLOYED
1.023 k   818 k

2009: A Job Odyssey

This is an overview of unemployment figures in Italy over a period of seven years. The population is categorised using colour coding, with orange representing people who are employed, yellow unemployed people and blue for people who are not in the workforce. The taller bars on the very right show comparative 2010 figures for selected European countries. In the lower part, developments in people's employment over the course of their lifetime is described, using the symbolism of a planetary system. The colour-coding compares with the upper part: blue represents people too young or too old to be in the workforce, the orange are the employed. Connecting lines between the planets indicate how people make the shift from one professional situation to another.

Project Info: Poster, 2010, Italy
Data Source: Institute for the Future, Palo Alto
Design: Alessandro Dallafina, Francesco Faggiano, Stefano Greco, Marco La Mantia, Simone Paoli (DensityDesign)

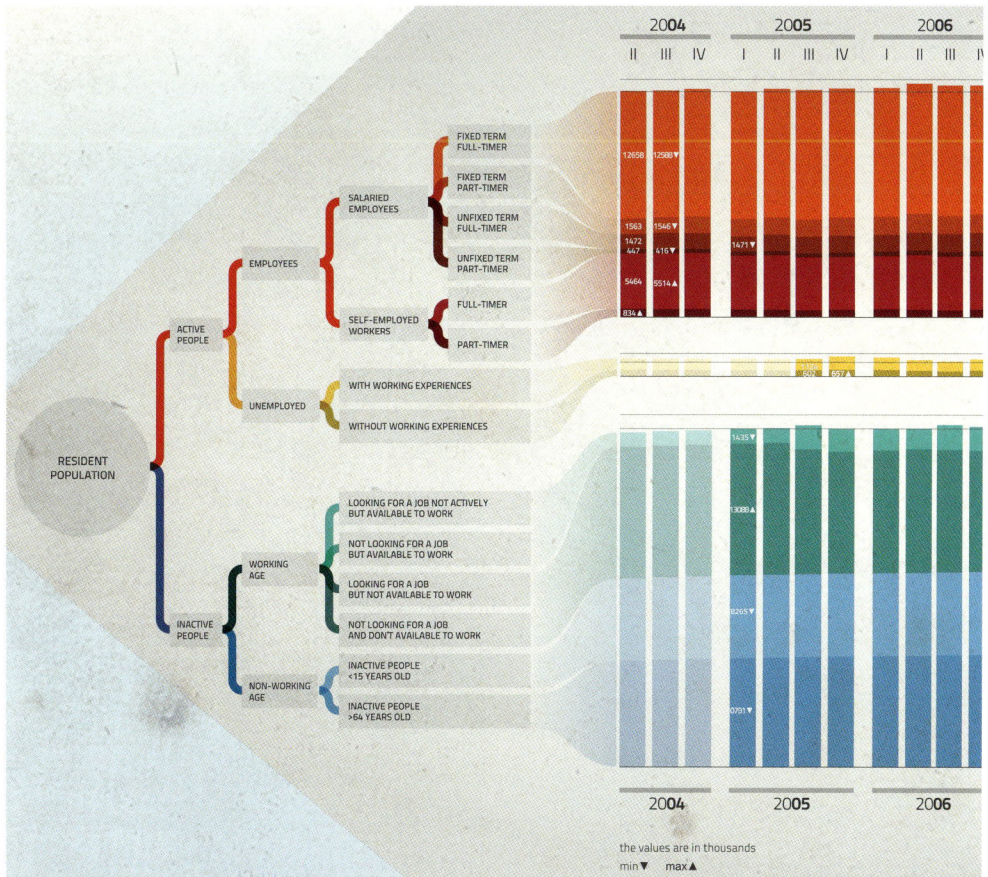

347

Annual Report Fira de Barcelona

Barcelona-based design studio Lamosca developed this series of infographics for the Barcelona Trade Fair, which has a great history in that city. In its annual report, the fair recounts activities during the last year and the economic impact the fair has had upon the city. In a series of individual graphics, significant figures derived from the report are shown either as single facts or in relation to each other. The clear and reduced design helps people grasp the facts and thus allows quick access to data covered in the report.

Project Info: Fira Barcelona, video, 2007, Spain
Design: Lamosca

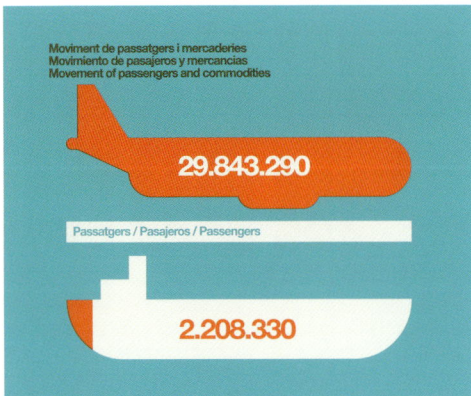

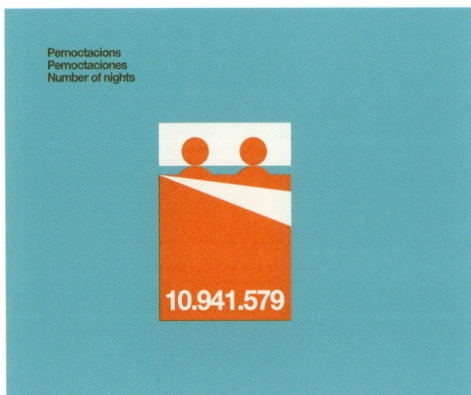

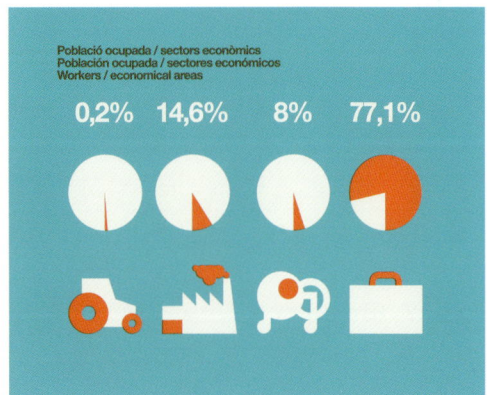

Moviment de passatgers i mercaderies
Movimiento de pasajeros y mercancías
Movement of passengers and commodities

29.843.290

Passatgers / Pasajeros / Passengers

2.208.330

Turistes
Turistas
Tourists

5.061.264

Pernoctacions
Pernoctaciones
Number of nights

10.941.579

Població ocupada / sectors econòmics
Población ocupada / sectores económicos
Workers / economical areas

0,2% 14,6% 8% 77,1%

Colours and Culture

In what looks like a wheel of fortune, David McCandless presents an overview of colour symbols among major cultures worldwide. The circle is chequered like a coordinate system: radial lines represent the categories of feelings or qualities numbered 1–84, such as anger or intelligence. Concentric lines around the circle represent international cultures labelled A–J, like Japanese or South American. In each of the coordinate squares, a colour field shows which colour represents the specific feeling or quality in that respective culture. Line 1 thus shows that red symbolises anger not only in American culture, but also in Japan, Eastern Europe and Africa, while Hindus use black to symbolise anger.

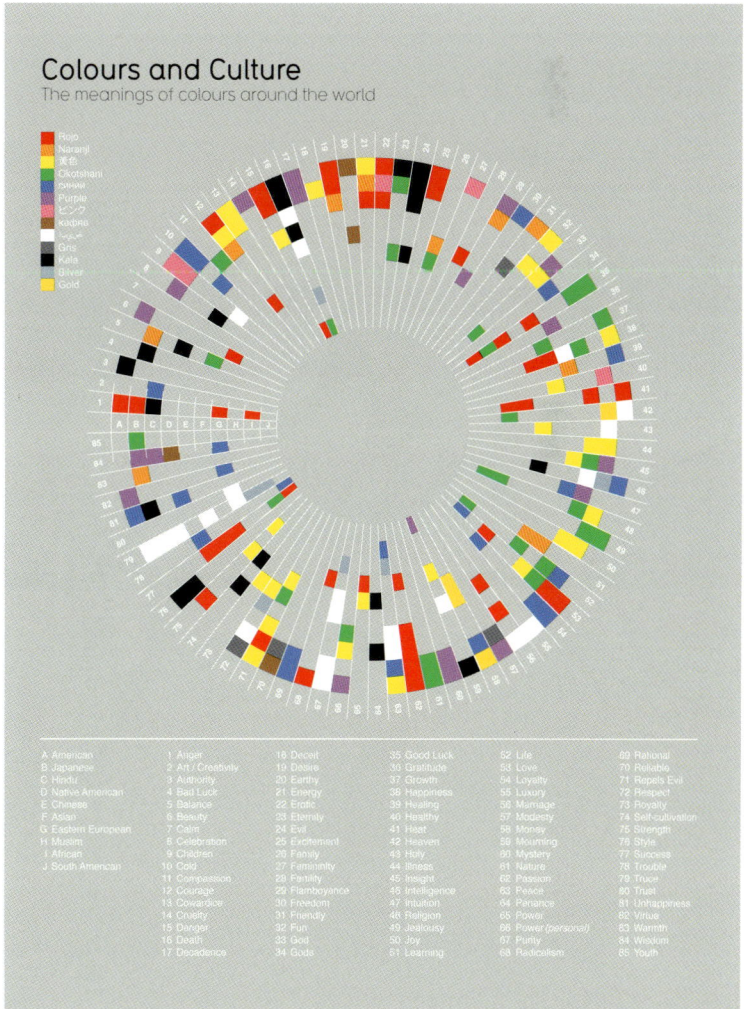

Colours and Culture
The meanings of colours around the world

Rojo
Naranji
黄色
Okotshani
ocre
Purple
ピンク
kadhra
ブルー
Gris
Kala
Silver
Gold

A American	1 Anger	18 Deceit	35 Good Luck	52 Life	69 Rational
B Japanese	2 Art / Creativity	19 Desire	36 Gratitude	53 Love	70 Reliable
C Hindu	3 Authority	20 Earthy	37 Growth	54 Loyalty	71 Repels Evil
D Native American	4 Bad Luck	21 Energy	38 Happiness	55 Luxury	72 Respect
E Chinese	5 Balance	22 Erotic	39 Healing	56 Marriage	73 Royalty
F Asian	6 Beauty	23 Eternity	40 Healthy	57 Modesty	74 Self-cultivation
G Eastern European	7 Calm	24 Evil	41 Heart	58 Money	75 Strength
H Muslim	8 Celebration	25 Excitement	42 Heaven	59 Mourning	76 Style
I African	9 Children	26 Family	43 Holy	60 Mystery	77 Success
J South American	10 Cold	27 Femininity	44 Illness	61 Nature	78 Trouble
	11 Compassion	28 Fertility	45 Insight	62 Passion	79 Truce
	12 Courage	29 Flamboyance	46 Intelligence	63 Peace	80 Trust
	13 Cowardice	30 Freedom	47 Intuition	64 Penance	81 Unhappiness
	14 Cruelty	31 Friendly	48 Religion	65 Power	82 Virtue
	15 Danger	32 Fun	49 Jealousy	66 Power (personal)	83 Warmth
	16 Death	33 God	50 Joy	67 Purity	84 Wisdom
	17 Decadence	34 Gods	51 Learning	68 Radicalism	85 Youth

Project Info: *Information is Beautiful*, book, 2009, UK
Design: David McCandless (Information is Beautiful); Always with Honor

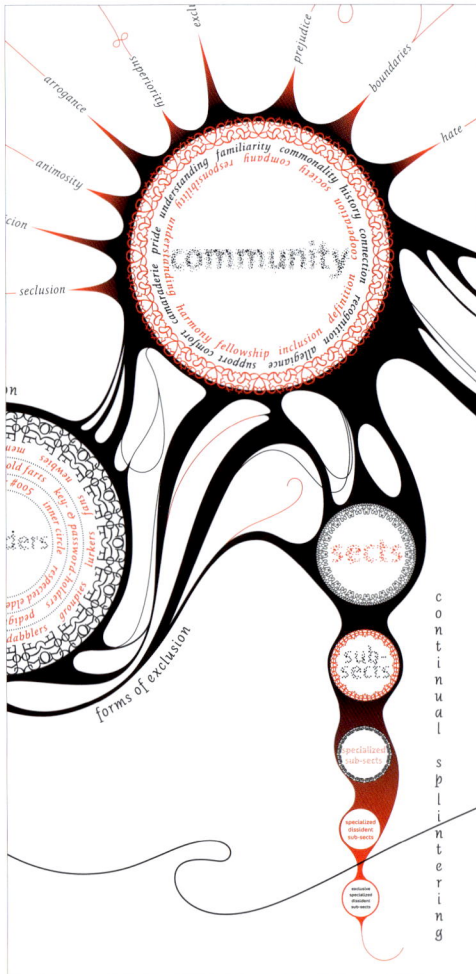

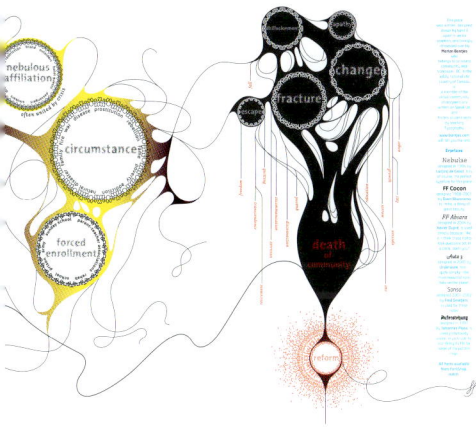

Community

Tasked with developing a piece on the notion of "community" by German font magazine *FontShop*, Marian Bantjes designed this graphic in an extreme horizontal format. Rather than visualising actual statistical data, Bantjes looks into how communities define themselves by defining who does not belong. Bantjes uses various clusters of circles as the most natural visual metaphor for symbolising a community, and with lines floating and growing from one circle to another she indicates how communities are never fixed phenomena, but keep changing constantly. With this piece, Bantjes delivers a striking example of how topics can be discussed by inscribing concepts into visual structures.

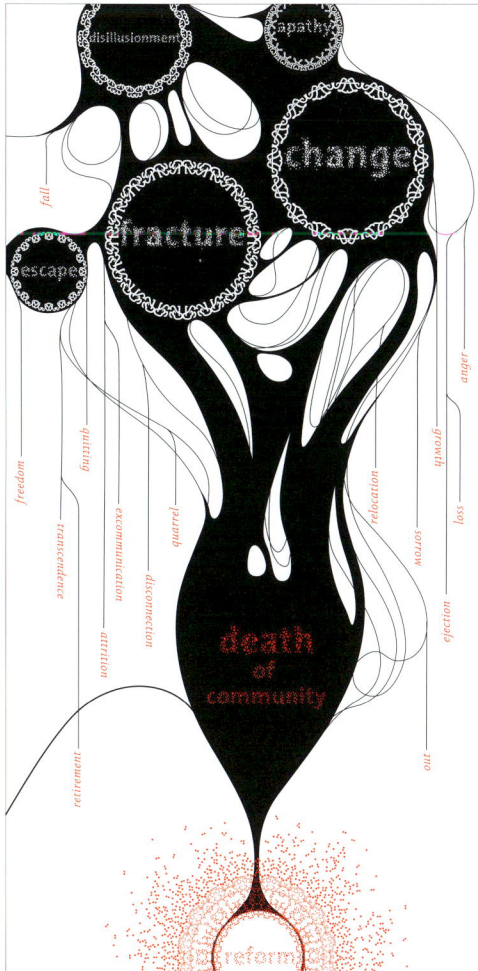

Project Info: *Font*, magazine article, FontShop, 2005, Germany
Design: Marian Bantjes

Data

This series appeared in the cultural supplement of Barcelona-based newspaper *La Vanguardia* in an extreme vertical format, as a weekly column lasting 152 weeks. The infographics drew on each supplement's specific theme and represented it in a meaningful dataset, or added extra information to the editorial story. Various sources, kinds of data and types of visualisations were used throughout the series. The overall design featured a minimalist graphic style.

Project Info: *La Vanguardia*, newspaper article, 2007–2010, Spain
Data Source: Recetario de Concepción Atienza; Boeing; POV: "Flagwars". Documentary 2003; Universitat Oberta de Catalunya; Leserglede.com, timesonline.co.uk; Lasker's Chess Primer; Jeffrey Kenworthy: "Traffic: Back to the Future? Urban Transport 2050"; Daylight and Architecture, 2009; otherpower.com; CollectorTimes.com; The Library of Iberian Resources Online; Cinemetrics.lv; metalyou.com; algalita.org; Friends of the Earth
Design: Lamosca

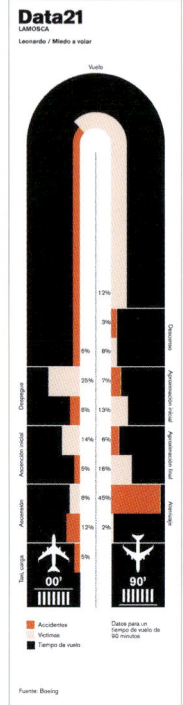

Following spread

Digital Dump

Technological devices have a rather short lifespan these days, but where do they go when they die? This graphic shows the amount of digital waste produced around the globe each year. Being the world's two biggest economies, China and the US are the top producers here. The graphic combines several elements to show different aspects of the problem. The trucks to the right demonstrate how little of this waste is actually being recycled. But how do people get rid of it then? The map beneath illustrates the alternative option: a lot of waste is being shipped to countries which have more space to dump it somewhere.

Project Info: "The Growing E-Waste Situation", *GOOD*, website, 2010, USA
Data Source: CBS News; ABI Research; US EPA; Basel Action Network; Silicon Valley Toxics Coalition
Research: Brian Wolford
Design: Andrew Effendy (Column Five Media)
Art Direction: Ross Crooks

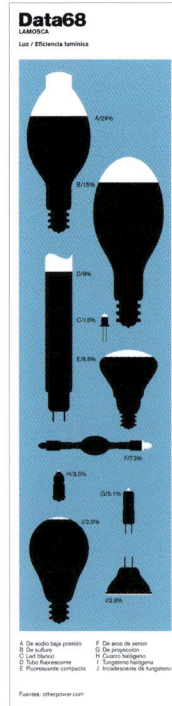

Data65
LAMOSCA

Fábricas de creación / Gentrificación

- Población original
- Artistas
- Profesionales liberales
- Centro de arte
- Precio renta
- Poder adquisitivo
- Edad media
- Equipamiento público

Fuente: pbs.org/pov/pov2003/lagwars/

Data86
LAMOSCA

Ferran Canyameres / Viajes de ida y vuelta

```
1899
1917
1921
1923
1930
1949
1954
1964
```

1.Terrassa. 2.París. 3.Londres. 4.Guadalajara. 5.Barcelona.

Fuente: uoc.edu

Data92
LAMOSCA

Lisbeth Salander / Exportaciones suecas

Ventas anuales de ABBA (actuales)

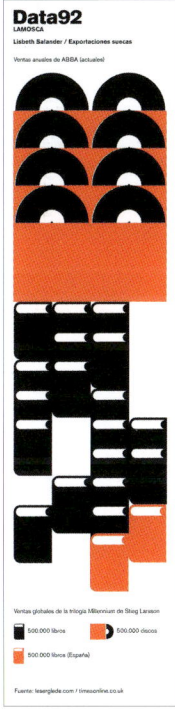

Ventas globales de la trilogía Millennium de Stieg Larsson

- 500.000 libros
- 500.000 discos
- 500.000 libros (España)

Fuente: laserglade.com / timesonline.co.uk

Data97
LAMOSCA

Ajedrez / Valor relativo

Valor relativo de las piezas de ajedrez

- El rey carece de valor relativo
- 9
- 5
- 3
- 1
- 3

Fuente: Lasker's Chess Primer

Data103
LAMOSCA

Cultura del coche / Aparcar está fatal

En Estados Unidos, por cada coche existen ocho plazas de aparcamiento en lugares separados (casa, trabajo, supermercado...). Ocupando una superficie equivalente a un campo y medio de tenis.

Fuente: Urban Transport 2050, Jeff Kenworthy

Data81
LAMOSCA

Geopolítica española / El increíble imperio menguante

- Pérdidas tras la Paz de Utrech
- Pérdidas tras las Guerras de Independencia americanas
- Pérdidas tras la Descolonización

Fuente: 9bro.uoc.edu

Data110
LAMOSCA

Marc Recha / Aguanta el plano

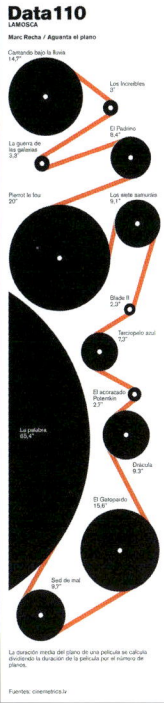

Cantando bajo la lluvia
14,7'

Los Increíbles
3'

El Padrino
6,4'

La guerra de las galaxias
3,3'

Pierrot le fou
20'

Los siete samuráis
9,1'

Blade II
2,8'

Terciopelo azul
7,3'

El acorazado Potemkin
2,7'

La palabra
65,4'

Drácula
9,3'

El Gatopardo
15,6'

Sed de mal
9,7'

La duración media del plano de una película se calcula dividiendo la duración de la película por el número de planos.

Fuentes: cinemetrics.lv

Data111
LAMOSCA

Música para la tortura/ ¡Súbelo al once!

My bloody valentine
130 dB

AC/DC

Rolling Stones

Motörhead

KISS

Iron Maiden
136 dB

Manowar

139 dB

Récord de volumen en concierto.
El umbral del dolor en humanos se sitúa en 120 dB.
Un reactor de aeroplano produce 150 dB.

Fuentes: metalyou.com

Data114
LAMOSCA

Tóxicos / La gran sopa de plástico

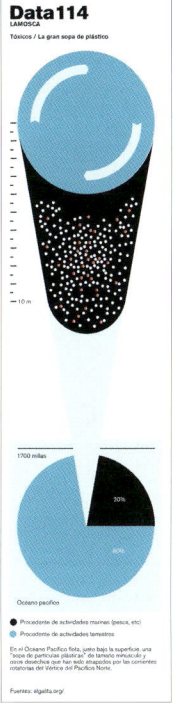

10 m

1700 millas

50%

40%

Océano pacífico

- Procedente de actividades marinas (pesca, etc)
- Procedente de actividades terrestres

En el Océano Pacífico flota, junto bajo la superficie, una "sopa de partículas plásticas" de tamaño minúsculo y cinco desechos que han sido atrapados por las corrientes rotatorias del Vértice del Pacífico Norte.

Fuente: algalita.org/

Data 125
LAMOSCA

Delta del Níger / A todo gas

Nigeria es la primera quemador mundial de gas asociado al petróleo. El 70% en gas natural asociado se quema sin haya explotando tonelada de CO_2 a la atmósfera.

- Gas asociado al petróleo
- Porción quemada

2.530.000.000m³
2.520.000.000m³

Fuente: www.fcs.co.uk/

THE DIGITAL DUMP

AS TECHNOLOGY ADVANCES AND WE BUILD MORE AND MORE DEVICES, THE NUMBER OF OBSOLETE ELECTRONICS
IN NEED OF DISPOSAL IS GROWING AS WELL. THE ISSUE OF GLOBAL E-WASTE IS A MOUNTING CONCERN.
AND AS THE PROBLEM PILES UP, MANY COUNTRIES ARE FINDING IT EASIEST TO JUST SHIP THEIR E-WASTE OVERSEAS.

EACH YEAR,
THE UNITED STATES TH

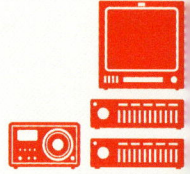

25 MILLION
TELEVISIONS

47.5 MIL
COMPUTERS

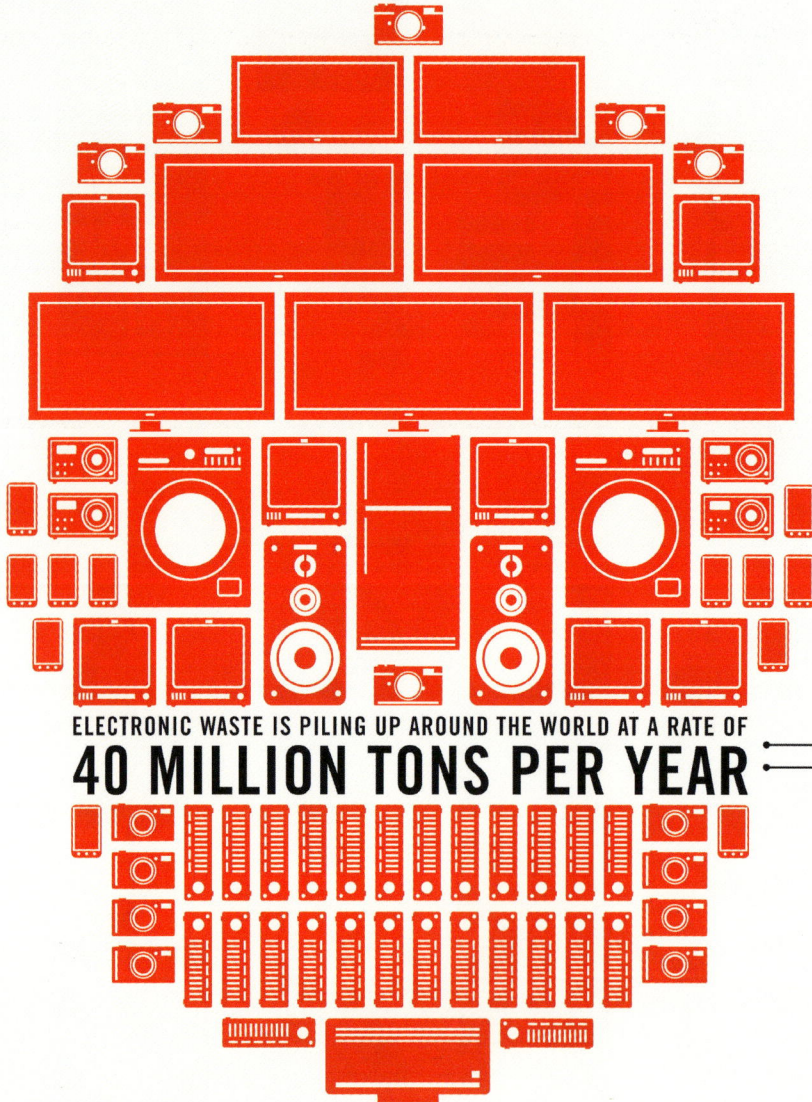

THE UNITED STATES
3.3 M

CHINA PRO
2

ELECTRONIC WASTE IS PILING UP AROUND THE WORLD AT A RATE OF
40 MILLION TONS PER YEAR

THE WORLDWIDE MARK
WILL GROW IN THE

2001

$5.7 BILLION

A COLLABORATION BETWEEN GOOD AND COLUMN FIVE

AVERAGE:

MILLION
ONES

ONS
STE IN A YEAR

ION TONS

STE
ARS

2014

$14.7 BILLION

RECYCLING VERSUS DISPOSAL ANNUALLY IN THE UNITED STATES

■ DISPOSED ■ RECYCLED

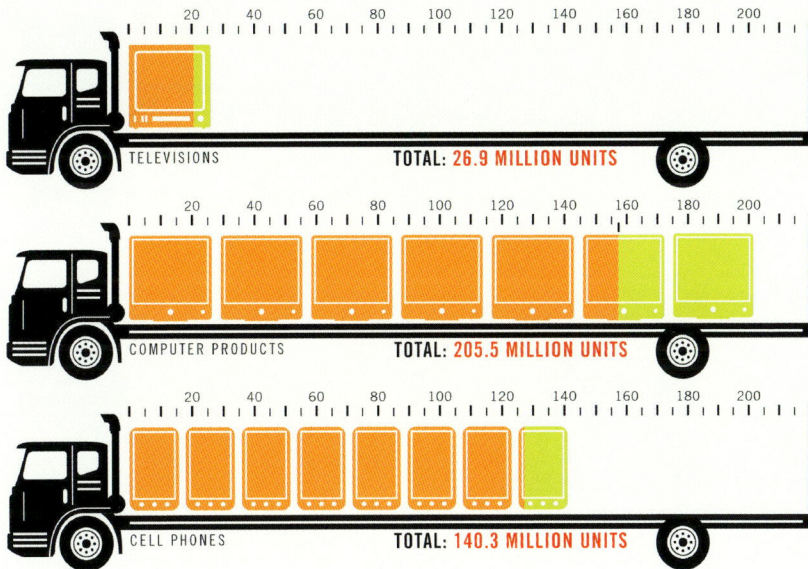

TELEVISIONS   **TOTAL: 26.9 MILLION UNITS**

COMPUTER PRODUCTS   **TOTAL: 205.5 MILLION UNITS**

CELL PHONES   **TOTAL: 140.3 MILLION UNITS**

— E-WASTE DESTINATIONS —

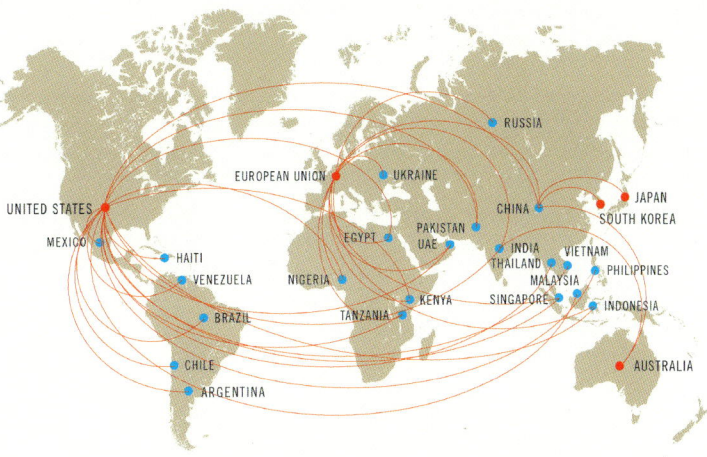

● KNOWN SOURCES   ● KNOWN AND SUSPECTED DESTINATIONS

cbsnews.com | abiresearch.com | epa.gov | ban.org | svtc.org

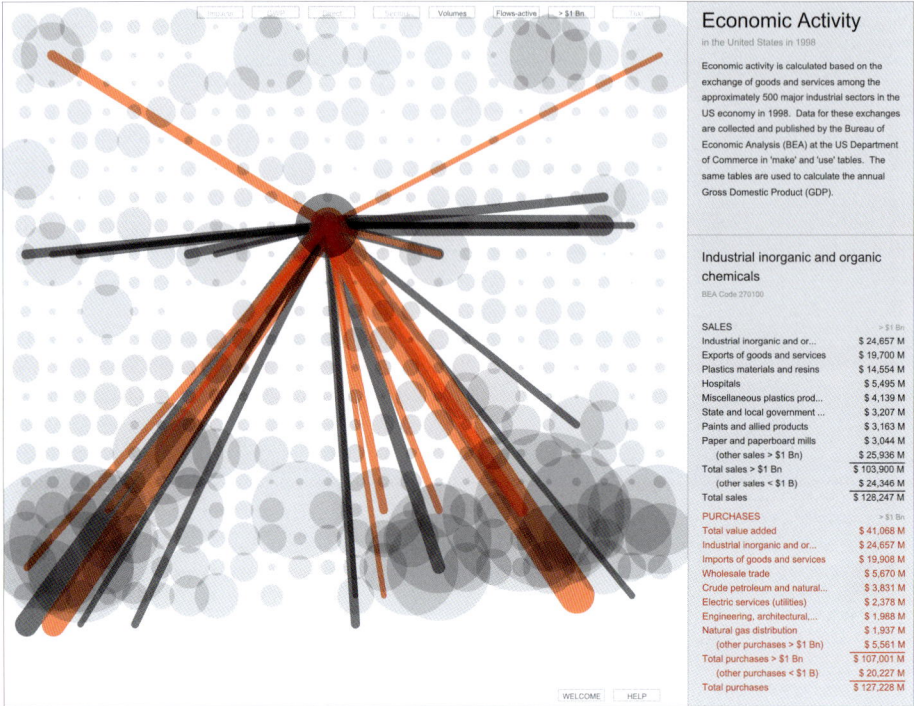

Economic Activity

in the United States in 1998

Economic activity is calculated based on the exchange of goods and services among the approximately 500 major industrial sectors in the US economy in 1998. Data for these exchanges are collected and published by the Bureau of Economic Analysis (BEA) at the US Department of Commerce in 'make' and 'use' tables. The same tables are used to calculate the annual Gross Domestic Product (GDP).

Industrial inorganic and organic chemicals

BEA Code 270100

SALES	> $1 Bn
Industrial inorganic and or...	$ 24,657 M
Exports of goods and services	$ 19,700 M
Plastics materials and resins	$ 14,554 M
Hospitals	$ 5,495 M
Miscellaneous plastics prod...	$ 4,139 M
State and local government ...	$ 3,207 M
Paints and allied products	$ 3,163 M
Paper and paperboard mills	$ 3,044 M
(other sales > $1 Bn)	$ 25,936 M
Total sales > $1 Bn	$ 103,900 M
(other sales < $1 B)	$ 24,346 M
Total sales	$ 128,247 M
PURCHASES	> $1 Bn
Total value added	$ 41,068 M
Industrial inorganic and or...	$ 24,657 M
Imports of goods and services	$ 19,908 M
Wholesale trade	$ 5,670 M
Crude petroleum and natural...	$ 3,831 M
Electric services (utilities)	$ 2,378 M
Engineering, architectural,...	$ 1,988 M
Natural gas distribution	$ 1,937 M
(other purchases > $1 Bn)	$ 5,561 M
Total purchases > $1 Bn	$ 107,001 M
(other purchases < $1 B)	$ 20,227 M
Total purchases	$ 127,228 M

WELCOME   HELP

Economy Map

"Economy Map" is an interactive visualisation of the US economy. The object is to provide an interface for exploring major industrial sectors, both in terms of economic activity and in regard to their ecological impact. Economy Map displays a grid of circles, each representing an industrial sector such as motor vehicles or retail trade. The grey version visualises economic flows between sectors. Here, circle size represents the sector's financial significance. In further visualisations, the project lists 13 different indicators for ecological impact, such as Land Use or Global Warming Potential. Circle size here represents the sector's ecological impact. Economy Map thus facilitates a synopsis of comprehensive financial and ecological data and allows the evaluation of individual sectors of the economy.

Project Info: Interactive visualisation, 2010, USA
Data Source: US Dept of Commerce;
US EPA: "Sustainable Materials Management:
The Road Ahead", 2009
Design: Jason Pearson (TRUTHstudio)

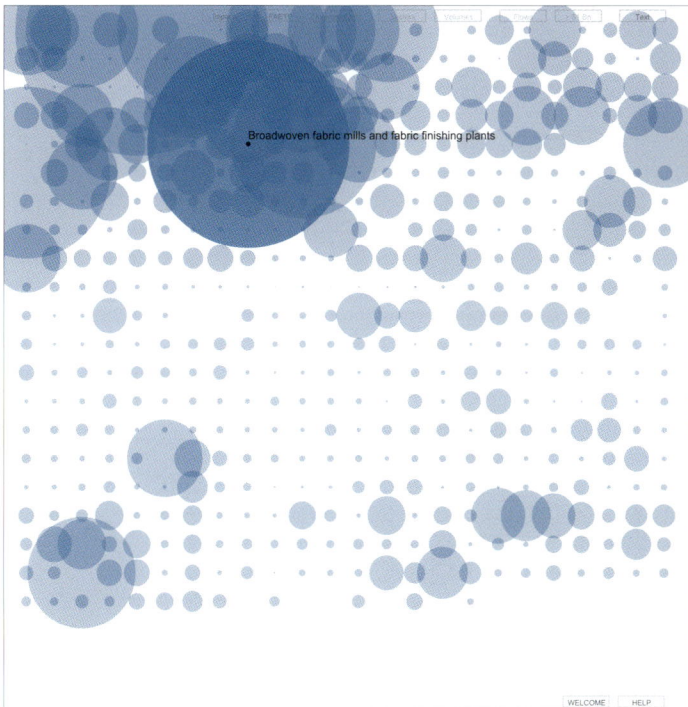

Freshwater Aquatic Ecotoxicity Potential

Fresh water aquatic ecotoxicity refers to the impact of toxic substances emitted to freshwater aquatic ecosystems.

Intermediate Impacts
(kg 1,4-dichlorobenzene eq.)

Intermediate impacts include a sector's direct impacts and the upstream impacts of its purchased goods/services. Sectors with high intermediate impacts offer opportunities for supply chain engagement.

Broadwoven fabric mills and fabric finishing plants

BEA Code 160100

IMPACTS by rank (% of total)	Direct	Intermed	Final
ADP		51 (00%)	199 (00%)
LUC		19 (00%)	77 (00%)
GWP	55 (00%)	43 (00%)	192 (00%)
ODP	234 (00%)	51 (00%)	205 (00%)
HTP	72 (00%)	46 (00%)	190 (00%)
FAETP	67 (00%)	2 (08%)	17 (01%)
MAETP	48 (00%)	44 (00%)	174 (00%)
TETP	68 (00%)	2 (07%)	18 (01%)
FSETP	56 (00%)	46 (00%)	178 (00%)
MSETP	51 (00%)	33 (00%)	168 (00%)
POCP	103 (00%)	62 (00%)	219 (00%)
AP	65 (00%)	47 (00%)	201 (00%)
EP	84 (00%)	6 (02%)	58 (00%)

WELCOME   HELP

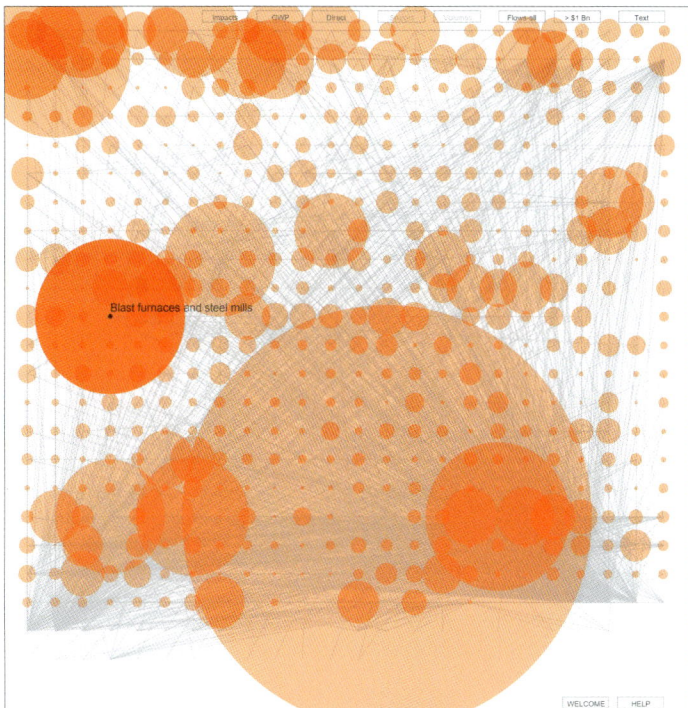

Global Warming Potential

Global Warming Potential ('greenhouse effect') is the impact of human emissions on the heat absorption of the atmosphere, which may have adverse impacts on ecosystem health, human health, and material welfare.

Direct Impacts
(kg CO2 eq.)

Direct impacts are those generated directly by the activities of a sector. Sectors with high direct impacts offer opportunities for direct regulation by government to encourage technology improvement or substitution.

Top 20 Sectors

contributing direct impacts to Global Warming Potential in 1998:

1.	Electric services (utilities)	35.01 %
2.	Crude petroleum and natural...	4.81 %
3.	Blast furnaces and steel mills	4.71 %
4.	Sanitary services, steam su...	4.33 %
5.	Air transportation	2.74 %
6.	Petroleum refining	2.60 %
7.	Trucking and courier servic...	2.55 %
8.	Feed grains	1.78 %
9.	Meat animals	1.77 %
10.	Coal	1.28 %
11.	Land Subdividers and Develop...	1.25 %
12.	New residential 1 unit stru...	1.25 %
13.	Industrial inorganic and or...	1.10 %
14.	Paper and paperboard mills	1.01 %
15.	Fruits	0.84 %
16.	New office, industrial and ...	0.80 %
17.	Vegetables	0.72 %
18.	Cement, hydraulic	0.70 %
19.	Water transportation	0.69 %
20.	Poultry and eggs	0.67 %

WELCOME   HELP

357

Flocking Diplomats NYC

This project is based on a study which documented parking violations by international diplomats in New York City between 1998 and 2003. In a series of six posters Daniel Gross and Joris Maltha explore different ways to show patterns in the large dataset. Visualisation thus becomes a tool for analysing mass behaviour and showing recurrent trends. FD1 is a time series for every day between 1999 and 2002. FD6 charts violations on an invisible Manhattan map with the UN headquarters placed at the centre. FD3 is a polar graph which charts addresses, days of the week and time of day, displaying the most frequent combination of these variables. Meanwhile, FD2 traces the frequency of the top 20 diplomats and their accumulated parking violations. Whenever their violation frequency rises or decreases, the graph takes a left or a right turn.

Project Info: Series of posters, 2007 / 2008, Netherlands
Data Source: Ray Fisman, Edward Miguel: "Corruption, Norms and Legal Enforcement: Evidence from Diplomatic Parking Tickets", Journal of Political Economy, 2007; NYC Department of Finance; NASA; Google Answers (Question-ID 782886); US Naval Observatory / Astronomical Applications Department
Design: Daniel Gross, Joris Maltha (Catalogtree)
Additional Info: Original print size 70 cm x 100 cm, part of the permanent collection of the Cooper-Hewitt Design Museum
Awards: Dutch Design Award 2008

99

00

01

02

FLOCKING
DIPLOMATS NYC
1999–2002

// VIOLATIONS/HOUR

Parking Violations by Diplomats / Hour in 1999 to
2002 in New York City. The violations are plotted in
relation to the sun-position as seen from Central
Park (LATITUDE 40° 47' N / LONGITUDE 73° 58' W).

ANNUAL TOTALS (YEAR: TOTAL (MAX / DATE)

1999: 42.542 (65 / 09–24) -- Security Council /
Fifty-fourth Year, 4048th Meeting, Small Arms.
Friday, 24 September 1999, 9.30 a.m.

2000: 38.338 (62 / 02–24) -- Security Council /
Fifty-fifth Year, 4104th Meeting, The situation
concerning the Democratic Republic of the Congo.
Thursday, 24 February 2000, 11.30 a.m.

2001: 25.390 (56 / 02–12) -- Security Council /
Fifty-sixth Year, 4276th Meeting, The situation
along the borders of Guinea, Liberia, Sierra Leone.
Monday, 12 February 2001, 3 p.m.

2002: 12.703 (33 / 04–23) -- Security Council /
Fifty-seventh year, 4517th Meeting, The situation
in Angola. Tuesday, 23 April 2002, 10.30 a.m.

SOURCES

-- Based on data from: Ray Fisman and Edward Miguel,
   "Corruption, Norms and Legal Enforcement: Evidence
   from Diplomatic Parking Tickets", forthcoming,
   December 2007, Journal of Political Economy.
-- Daylight Saving Time: http://sunearth.gsfc.nasa.gov/
   eclipse/SEhelp/daylightsaving.html
-- Sun-position (method of calculation): http://answers.
   google.com/answers/threadview?id=782886 (L. Flores)
-- Time of sunrise and dawn: http://aa.usno.navy.mil/
   data/docs/RS_OneYear.php
-- New York City Department of Finance

DATA MINING / SCRIPTING / DESIGN

Catalogtree, january 2008

printed at Plaatsmaken, Arnhem

FD-2

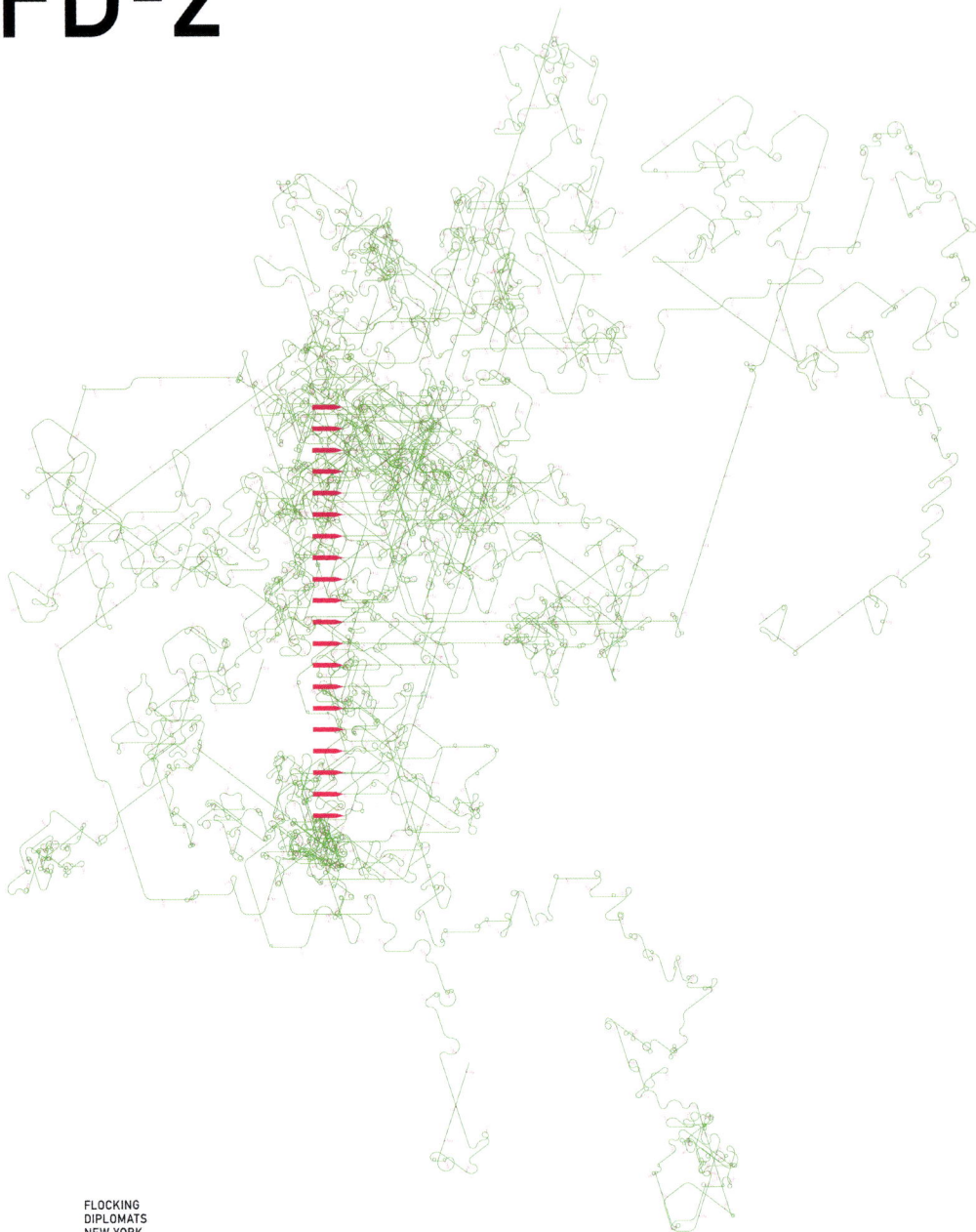

**FLOCKING
DIPLOMATS
NEW YORK**

INDIVIDUAL FREQUENCY TRACES 1999
The diagram shows the development of violation-
frequency of the 20 most violating diplomats in
1999. Accumulated violations are shown per week.
Frequency in- and decrease is shown as left and
right curves.

SOURCES
Raymond Fisman and Edward Miguel, Cultures of
Corruption: Evidence from Diplomatic Parking
Tickets / New York City Department of Finance

THANKS TO
Edward Miguel (raw data), Plaatsmaken (printing)

DESIGN / SCRIPTING
Catalogtree, december 2007

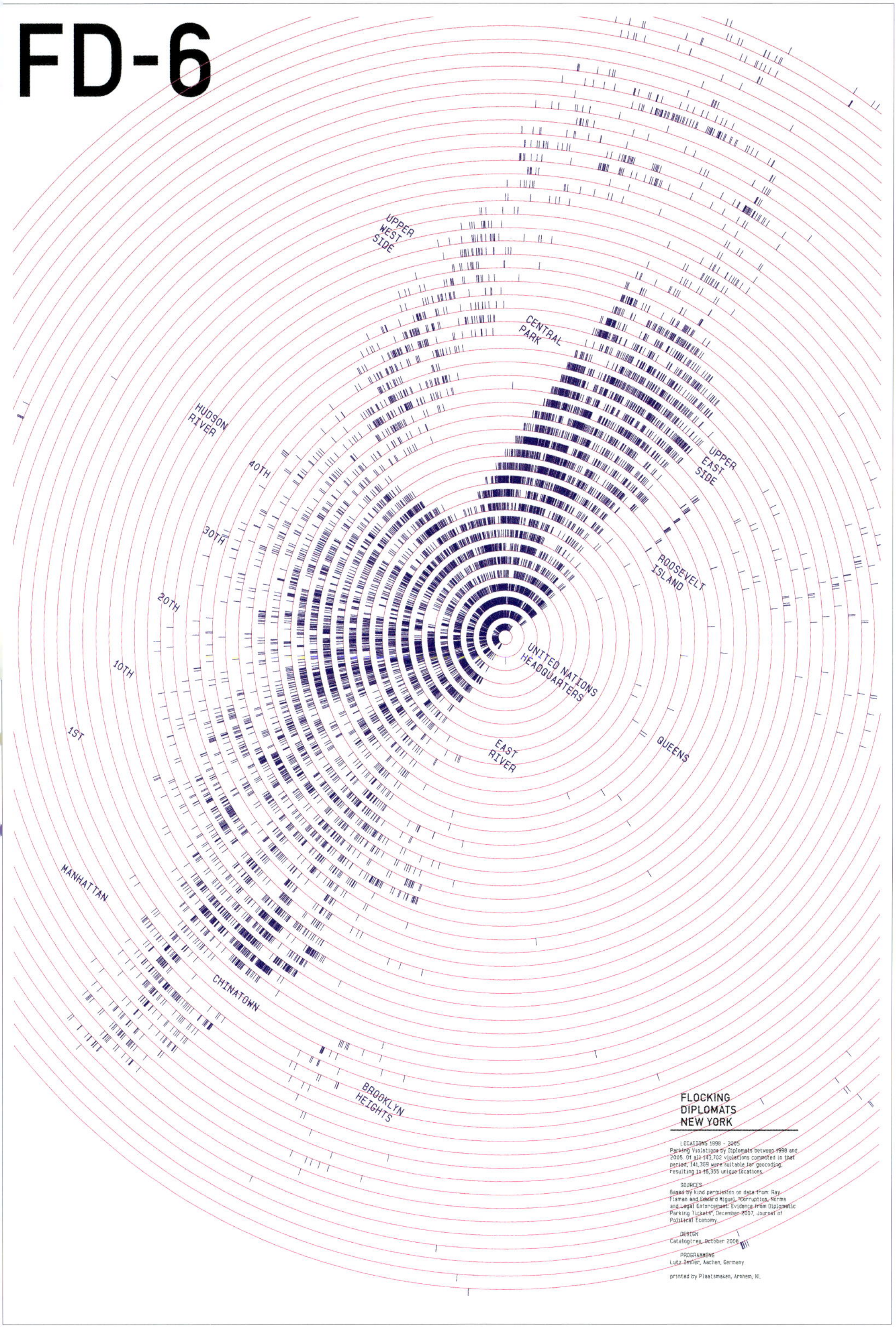

FD-6

UPPER
WEST
SIDE

CENTRAL
PARK

HUDSON
RIVER

40TH

30TH

20TH

UPPER
EAST
SIDE

ROOSEVELT
ISLAND

10TH

1ST

UNITED NATIONS
HEADQUARTERS

EAST
RIVER

QUEENS

MANHATTAN

CHINATOWN

BROOKLYN
HEIGHTS

**FLOCKING
DIPLOMATS
NEW YORK**

LOCATIONS 1998 - 2005
Parking violations by Diplomats between 1998 and
2005 of all 143,702 violations committed in that
period, 141,359 were suitable for geocoding,
resulting in 15,355 unique locations.

SOURCES
Based by kind persuasion on data from: Ray
Fisman and Edward Miguel, "Corruption, Norms
and Legal Enforcement: Evidence from Diplomatic
Parking Tickets", December 2007, Journal of
Political Economy.

DESIGN
Catalogtree, October 2009

PROGRAMMING
Lutz Zeidler, Aachen, Germany

printed by Plaatsmaken, Arnhem, NL.

FRAUD: THE REAL SECURITY ISSUE

Meet The Boss ™

A new report released this week revealed that more than 15,000 people in the UK have become victims of fraud in the first six months of 2010. Recent figures also state that in 2009 total fraud losses on plastic cards was over £440 million, fraud losses on cheques reached almost £30 million and online banking fraud losses increased by 14% to £59.7 million.

£620 BILLION IN TRANSACTIONS
- 143.7 million cards in issue
- 11 billion transactions

53% OF INTERNET USERS BANK ONLINE
That's 24 million adults in 2009

CHEQUE USE HAS DECREASED, HOWEVER
- 3.5 million cheques issued each day, 2009
- 11 million cheques issued each day, 1990

EVERY 60 SECONDS IN 2009...
- £56 was lost in cheque fraud
- £113 was lost in online banking fraud
- £837 was lost in plastic card fraud

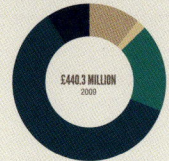

£188.4 MILLION
1999

£440.3 MILLION
2009

CARD FRAUD LOSSES BY TYPE
- Lost / stolen
- Mail non-receipt
- Counterfeit
- Card-not-present (phone, internet etc)
- Card ID theft

UK CARD FRAUD ABROAD
- £54.2 million in 1999
- £122.7 million in 2009

FORMS OF CHEQUE FRAUD
Counterfeit Cheques £4.7 million
Forged Cheques £15.7 million
Fraudulently Altered Cheques £9.3 million

PHISHING WEBSITES TARGETING UK BANKS
- 1,700 in 2005
- 51,161 in 2009

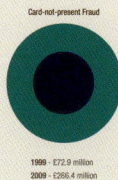

THE RISE OF FRAUD IN THE UK
- 1999
- 2009

Plastic Card Fraud
1999 - £188.4 million
2009 - £440.3 million

Card-not-present Fraud
1999 - £72.9 million
2009 - £266.4 million

Lost and Stolen Fraud
1999 - £79.7 million
2009 - £47.9 million

ID Theft
1999 - £14.4 million
2009 - £38.2 million

At UK Retailers
1999 - £93 million
2009 - £72.1 million

At Cash Machines
1999 - £12.2 million
2009 - £36.7 million

Internet / E-Commerce Fraud
2000 - £3.8 million
2009 - £153.2 million

Graphic for **Meet The Boss TV** | www.meettheboss.tv

Source: Financial Fraud Action UK - Fraud the Facts UK Report, all figures for the UK from 2009 unless otherwise stated

Graphic by T Farrant | Twitter @fallenblossom

Σ

t

Fraud: The Real Security Issue

This infographic takes a look at fraud in the UK and how cases of fraud have substantially increased. The piece lists various types of fraud and compares figures from 1999 and 2009. The colour coding and sizes vary for the different types of fraud. The graphic gives an overview of how the shift to online banking has facilitated a growth in fraud cases.

Project Info: Meet the Boss, website, for GDS International, 2010, UK
Data Source: Financial Fraud Action UK: "Fraud. The Facts"
Design: Tiffany Farrant-Gonzalez

Function

At first, these images do not appear to be diagrams, but resemble modernist artworks. Only when the four colours are further explained do they reveal their discomforting information and charged subject: they are pixellated representations of deaths in Iraq, as recorded in the WikiLeaks War Logs from 2004 to 2009. Each pixel represents one victim. The colour code refers to how victims have been categorised. Blue = "friendly" (allied forces) casualties, green = "host nation" (Iraqi government) forces, orange = civilians, grey = enemies (insurgents). The graphic on the left shows all victims by category, the other is a time plot, representing all victims in chronological order. The categories, employed in the US army reports, blur one simple fact: that "host nation" victims, civilians and enemies are all mostly Iraqis.

Project Info: Website, 2010, Canada
Data Source: Wikileaks Iraq War Logs
(analysed version from *The Guardian* Datastore)
Design: Kamel Makhloufi

Each week the Guardian's Leo Hickman and award-winning information design agency Grundy Northedge collaborate on a unique in-depth graphic providing an instant briefing on one of the issues of the week

Pets

The 103rd Crufts show gets under way on Thursday – probably Britain's biggest pet love-in of the year. But just how many dogs, cats guines pigs and goldfish do we keep? And how much do they really cost?

The g2 graphic

1 | What kind of pets do we keep?

● In 2003, 52.7% of UK households owned a pet – of these households, 24.4% owned a cat, 20.9% owned a dog and 8.6% owned goldfish

Pet population in the UK, 2002

Pet	Population
Dogs	6.1m
Cats	7.5m
Budgerigars	0.75m
Rabbits	1.1m
Goldfish	14.7m
Tropical fish	9.3m
Marine fish	0.7m
Guinea pigs	0.73m
Hamsters	0.86m
Canaries	0.26m
Other birds	1.06m
Reptiles	0.14m

Total number of pets 44.26m

Cats and dogs

Least and most popular regions to own a cat and dog in UK, 2003

Adults who own a dog		Adults who own a cat	
30%	18%	21%	35%
Scotland	South east	Scotland	South east

Population of domestic cats and dogs, 1992-2002

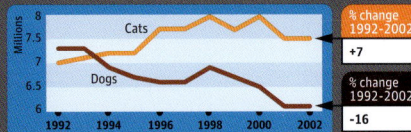

Cats — % change 1992-2002 **+7**

Dogs — % change 1992-2002 **-16**

(Millions, 1992 1994 1996 1998 2000 2002)

2 | How much do we spend on pets?

Pedigree pets
Percentage of dogs and cats that are non-pedigree

Dog

24.7%

Cat

92%

Average lifetime costs for dogs and cats, RSPCA estimate, 2004

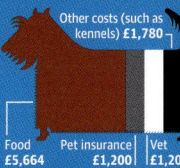

Dog (12 yrs) — **Total £9,844**

Other costs (such as kennels) **£1,780**

| Food £5,664 | Pet insurance £1,200 | Vet £1,200 |

Cat (14 yrs) — **Total £9,459**

| Food £5,664 | Vet £1,300 |

| Pet insurance £1,050 | Cat litter £2,184 |

Other costs (such as cattery) **£1,276**

NB A Great Dane can cost up to £33,000 over its average 10-year life, according to Churchill Insurance

● The world's oldest cat is "Creme Puff" of Texas who turned **37** in 2004, according to the Guinness World Records

● In 2003, 27% of women in the UK owned a cat, compared to **20%** of men

3

What do we buy our pets?

Total household spending on pets in 2003

Total £3,640

Pet purchase and accessories £832m | Pet food £1,872m | Veterinary and other services £936m

● The total market for dog and cat food was valued at an estimated £1.55bn in 2003

● In 2005, 34% of dogs and 21% of cats were insured. The pet insurance market was worth £265m in 2005 – a 157% increase since 1996

● On average, each pet-owning household spent £2.90 a week on pets in 2002/03

Most popular breeds of pedigree cats and dogs in UK, 2002

Pet accessories, by sector, 2003

Grooming/ toilet equipment £32.4m | Other £4m | Toys £61.0m

Collars and leads £39.0m

Baskets, bedding and carriers £41.0m

Cat litter £50.8m

Pet healthcare sales, 2003

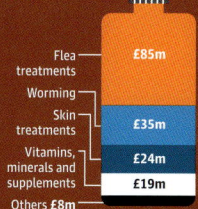

Flea treatments — £85m
Worming
Skin treatments — £35m
Vitamins, minerals and supplements — £24m
— £19m
Others £8m

Typical cost of puppy

£300–£500 Labrador retriever
£400–£600 Cocker spaniel
£300–£600 English springer spaniel

Typical cost of kitten

£250–£500 British short haired
£250–£350 Siamese
£250–£400 Persian

4 | How many pets are poorly treated?

● In 2004, the RSPCA removed 157,482 animals from danger or abuse. It rehomed 69,787 animals, mostly through its network of 175 branches

Dogs	18,334
Farm animals	16,174
Small domestic	7,630
Cats	7,349
Equines	5,884

Top five dog breeds involved in RSCPA prosecution cases, 2004

Non-pedigree	268
German shepherd	106
Staffordshire bull terrier	80
Rottweiler	43
Jack Russell	39

Number of reptiles that passed through the animal reception centre at Heathrow Airport

2001 **67,000** | 2002 **100,000**

The RSPCA estimates that up to 15% of reptiles kept as pets are undernourished

● In 2003, the average initial vet consultation fee in London was £18.72. In Scotland, it was **£11.92**

● In 2003, Masterfoods (includes Cesar, Sheba and Whiskas) and Nestlé Purina (includes Bakers Complete, Winalot, Arthur's and Felix) between them controlled 79% of the cat food market and **68%** of the dog food market

● In 1999, "single-serve" foods accounted for 16% of the cat food market. In 2005, they accounted for **54%**

● The largest ever litter of puppies is **24**, born to "Tia", a Neopolitan mastiff, in Cambridgeshire in 2004

Additional research by Lucy Clouting and Saleem Vaillancourt. Sources: 1) Mintel Report: Cat and Dog Food, May 2004; 2) Royal Society for the Prevention of Cruelty ro Animals, Kennel Club, Churchill Insurance; 3) Mintel, Pet Food Manufacturers' Association; 4) RSPCA, International Fund for Animal Welfare: also, Guinness World of Records

The Guardian 07.03.06 **17**

Previous spread

G2 Information Spreads

In 2005/2006, Tilly Northedge and Peter Grundy designed a weekly series of rich information spreads for *The Guardian*'s supplement G2. Each week, one topic was chosen and structured into several bite-size parts, each of which was numbered and given a concise question as a heading. The central image always presented a symbol of the general topic and provided spaces for presenting the individual statistics, using as few words as possible. The briefings were usually confined to the actual words that would be printed, making it a creative challenge to conceptualise each piece.

Project Info: *The Guardian*, newspaper article, 2005–2006, UK
Data Source: Mintel Report; Royal Society for the Prevention of Cruelty to Animals; Kennel Club; Churchill Insurance; PFMA; RSPCA; IFAW; Guinness World of Records
Research: Lucy Clouting, Saleem Vaillancourt
Design: Peter Grundy, Tilly Northedge (Grundini)

Hamburgers: The Economics of America's Favorite Food

There is hardly any food that's more American than the hamburger. Many industries capitalise on the burger, including fast-food restaurants, cattle farmers, ketchup and mustard producers. This infographic dissects a typical hamburger, researching into the economics of America's favourite dish. The graphic is categorised by the ingredients. Attached to the ingredients are three types of data: a few statistics as to which ingredients Americans most prefer; absolute numbers of how much of each ingredient is consumed per capita in the US annually; and lastly, the annual production and value of each ingredient in the US.

Project Info: Mint.com, website, 2010, USA
Data Source: Agricultural Marketing Resource Center; USDA Economic Research Service; USDA-ESMIS; Blog "A Hamburger Today"
Research: Brian Wolford
Design: Jarred Romley, Andrew Effendy (Column Five Media)
Art Direction: Ross Crooks
Photography: Jimmy Pham

HAMBURGERS

THE ECONOMICS OF AMERICA'S FAVORITE FOOD

mint.com

● **WHAT ARE AMERICANS SAYING** ABOUT THEIR FAVORITE BURGER?

■ **HOW MUCH OF EACH INGREDIENT** IS CONSUMED ANNUALLY?

★ **U.S. PRODUCTION AND VALUE** FOR EACH INGREDIENT ANNUALY

FAVORITE TYPE OF MUSTARD ●

YELLOW: 55%
BROWN: 20%
DIJON: 19%
OTHER: 4%
SWEET: 2%

41.3 MILLION POUNDS ★
OF MUSTARD VALUED AT
$18.0 MILLION

20.0 POUNDS ■
PER PERSON

7.4 BILLION POUNDS ★
OF ONIONS VALUED AT
$843 MILLION

28.0 POUNDS ■
PER PERSON

9 BILLION POUNDS ★
OF LETTUCE VALUED AT
$2.2 BILLION

FAVORITE BURGER SIZE ●

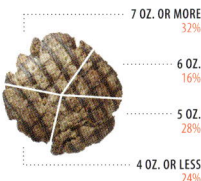

7 OZ. OR MORE
32%

6 OZ.
16%

5 OZ.
28%

4 OZ. OR LESS
24%

61.2 POUNDS ■
PER PERSON
IN 2009, THE U.S. CONSUMED
26.9 BILLION LBS. OF BEEF

26.1 BILLION POUNDS ★
OF BEEF PRODUCED VALUED AT
$2.2 BILLION
AMERICANS SPEND $270 PER
PERSON ON BEEF EACH YEAR.

FAVORITE BURGER BUN ●

POTATO ROLL
31%
SESAME SEEDS
23%
WHITE
16%
KAISER ROLL
10%
BRIOCHE
9%
OTHER
5%
CIABATTA
3%
ENGLISH MUFFIN
3%

■ 134.6 POUNDS PER PERSON

★ ONE BILLION BUSHELS
USED FOR FLOUR VALUED AT
$6.64 BILLION

■ 71 POUNDS
PER PERSON

★ 12 MILLION TONS
OF KETCHUP VALUED AT
$901 MILLION

■ 20.3 POUNDS
PER PERSON

★ 14 MILLION TONS
OF TOMATOES VALUED AT
$1.2 BILLION

FAVORITE CHEESE ●

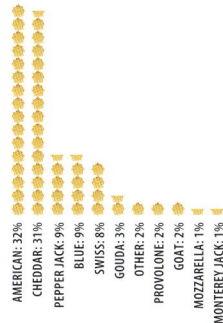

AMERICAN: 32%
CHEDDAR: 31%
PEPPER JACK: 9%
BLUE: 9%
SWISS: 8%
GOUDA: 3%
OTHER: 2%
PROVOLONE: 2%
GOAT: 2%
MOZZARELLA: 1%
MONTEREY JACK: 1%

■ 32.4 POUNDS
PER PERSON

★ 10.1 BILLION POUNDS
OF CHEESE VALUED AT
$14 BILLION

SOURCES: AHT.SERIOUSEATS.COM ● AGMRC.ORG ■ ERS.USDA.GOV ★ USDA.MANNLIB.CORNELL.EDU   PHOTO: JIMMY PHAM

Map of the Future

In this collaborative work, DensityDesign in Milan visualised future scenarios developed by the Institute for the Future, in Palo Alto. Like an elaborate mind map, this piece combines a collage landscape in the background with a map of interrelated ideas. Along the top, five areas of activity are labelled, from politics to society. Associated with these aspects are ideas about how people will live together in the future and how advances in knowledge will change life on Earth. Each idea is shown in a colour-coded circle: green circles show ideas about how people will create new networks in the future; red relates to future scientific knowledge and understanding; yellow represents changing political and social habits.

Project Info: *Wired*, magazine article, 2009, Italy
Data Source: Institute for the Future, Palo Alto
Design: Luca Masud, Mario Porpora, Gaia Scagnetti (DensityDesign)
Art Direction: Donato Ricci
Illustration: Michele Graffieti

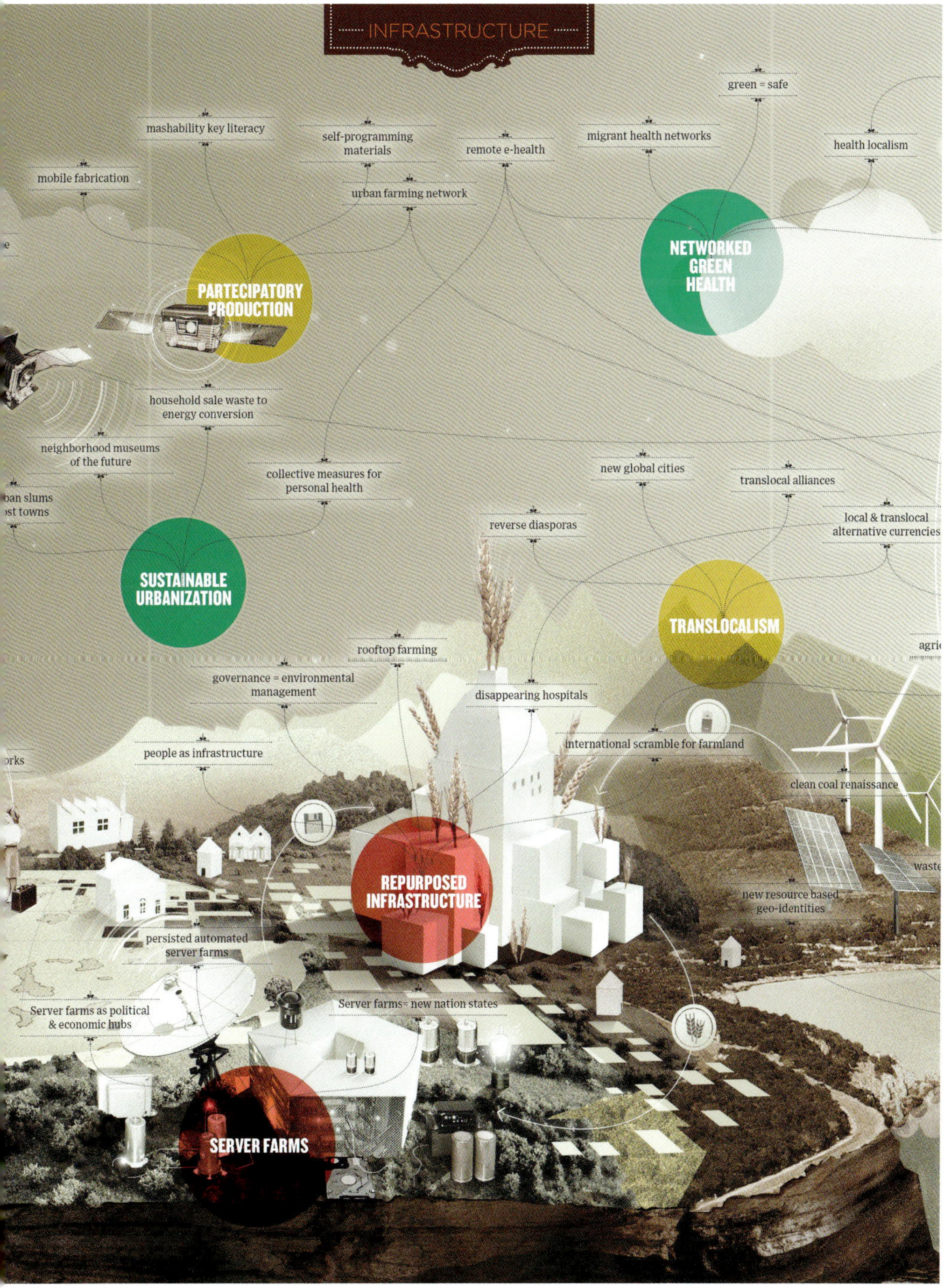

INFRASTRUCTURE

mashability key literacy

self-programming materials

remote e-health

migrant health networks

green = safe

health localism

mobile fabrication

urban farming network

PARTECIPATORY PRODUCTION

NETWORKED GREEN HEALTH

household sale waste to energy conversion

neighborhood museums of the future

collective measures for personal health

new global cities

translocal alliances

ban slums
st towns

local & translocal alternative currencies

reverse diasporas

SUSTAINABLE URBANIZATION

rooftop farming

TRANSLOCALISM

agric

governance = environmental management

disappearing hospitals

people as infrastructure

international scramble for farmland

clean coal renaissance

orks

waste

REPURPOSED INFRASTRUCTURE

new resource based geo-identities

persisted automated server farms

Server farms as political & economic hubs

Server farms = new nation states

SERVER FARMS

369

ENVIRONMENT

ECONOMICS

C

O

tp health management

space as market

orbital debris

ubiquitous cubesats

digital labeling and packaging

open food

SPACE:
THE NETWORKED
FRONTIER

urgency filters on drugs

social networking tools for gift
economie

open

CO_2

new search engines: multimedia,
social, "human flesh"

Google

sulphate injection
of stratosphere

FILTERS
AS BRANDS

amazon

academic recognition/
reward crisis

al waste sequestration

non zero sum currencies

carbon accounting

global conflict over climate
goals and impacts

ocean iron fertilization

SOLIDARITY
NETWORKS

ities

mobile phone minutes as
currency

Medea Hypothesis

GEOENGINEERING

social stock exchange

ALTERNATIVE
CURRENCIES

Fe

Fe

Fe

micro-philantropy networks

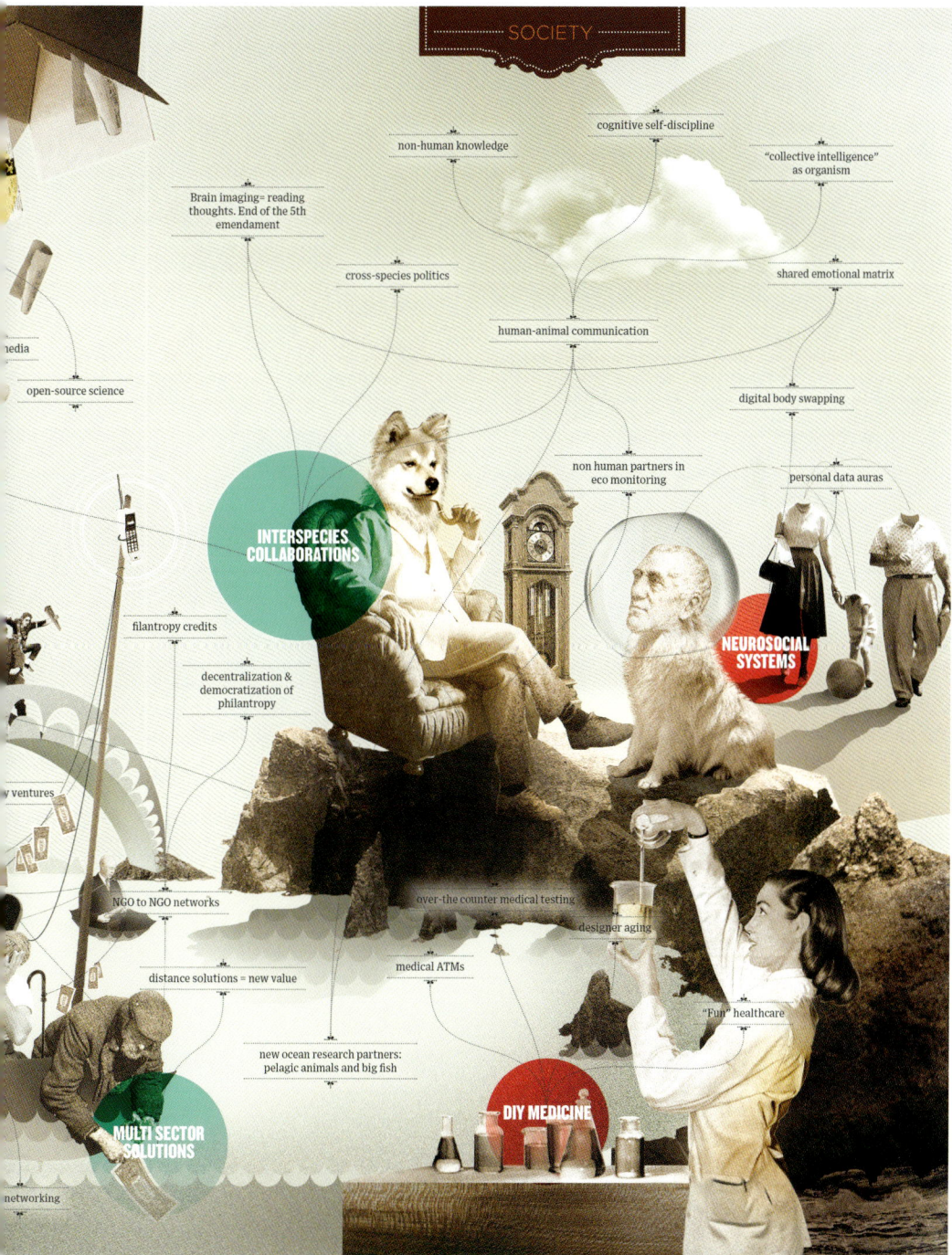

SOCIETY

cognitive self-discipline

non-human knowledge

"collective intelligence"
as organism

Brain imaging= reading
thoughts. End of the 5th
emendation

cross-species politics

shared emotional matrix

...edia

human-animal communication

open-source science

digital body swapping

INTERSPECIES
COLLABORATIONS

non human partners in
eco monitoring

personal data auras

filantropy credits

NEUROSOCIAL
SYSTEMS

decentralization &
democratization of
philanthropy

...w ventures

over-the counter medical testing

NGO to NGO networks

designer aging

distance solutions = new value

medical ATMs

"Fun" healthcare

new ocean research partners:
pelagic animals and big fish

DIY MEDICINE

MULTI SECTOR
SOLUTIONS

...networking

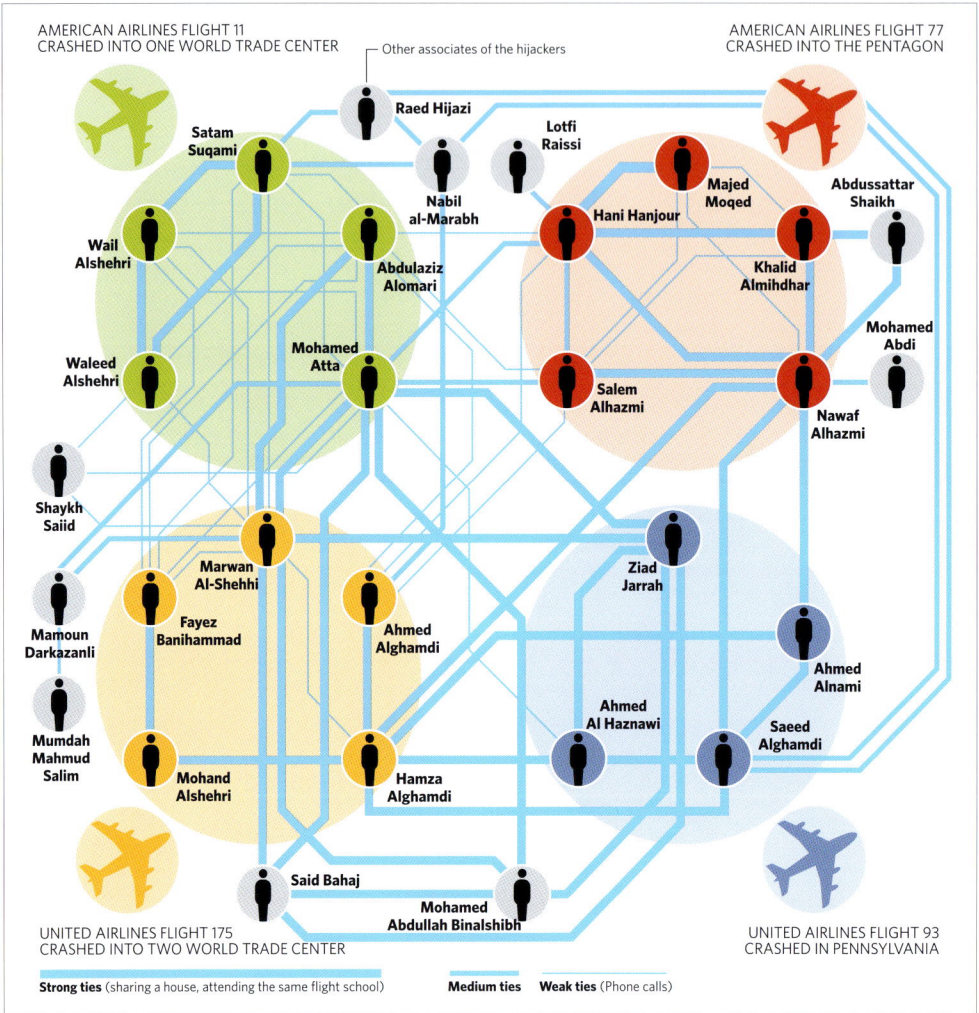

AMERICAN AIRLINES FLIGHT 11
CRASHED INTO ONE WORLD TRADE CENTER

Other associates of the hijackers

AMERICAN AIRLINES FLIGHT 77
CRASHED INTO THE PENTAGON

Raed Hijazi

Satam Suqami

Lotfi Raissi

Majed Moqed

Abdussattar Shaikh

Nabil al-Marabh

Hani Hanjour

Wail Alshehri

Abdulaziz Alomari

Khalid Almihdhar

Mohamed Abdi

Waleed Alshehri

Mohamed Atta

Salem Alhazmi

Nawaf Alhazmi

Shaykh Saiid

Ziad Jarrah

Marwan Al-Shehhi

Mamoun Darkazanli

Fayez Banihammad

Ahmed Alghamdi

Ahmed Alnami

Mumdah Mahmud Salim

Ahmed Al Haznawi

Saeed Alghamdi

Mohand Alshehri

Hamza Alghamdi

Said Bahaj

Mohamed Abdullah Binalshibh

UNITED AIRLINES FLIGHT 175
CRASHED INTO TWO WORLD TRADE CENTER

UNITED AIRLINES FLIGHT 93
CRASHED IN PENNSYLVANIA

Strong ties (sharing a house, attending the same flight school)   **Medium ties**   **Weak ties** (Phone calls)

Hijacker Connections, 9/11

This network map shows the relationships between the 19 hijackers who attacked the US in four planes on September 11th, 2001, and with other associates of the hijackers. The four planes and the hijackers who flew on them are colour coded. Blue lines show the connections between the men involved, with line thickness indicating how close the association was. With the four flights structuring the map, Nigel Holmes created a very plausible frame for visualising the complex net of associations.

Project Info: *Business 2.0*, magazine article, 2001, USA
Data Source: Valdis Krebs (Orgnet)
Design: Nigel Holmes
Art Direction: Susan Scandrett

Infinite Jest Diagram

The sheer abundance of characters is a significant feature of the novel *Infinite Jest*. The setting presents a future vision, with Northern America forming one state. The diagram here connects characters and places. Two circles represent locations: the "Enfield Tennis Academy" and the "Ennet House Drug and Alcohol Recovery House". The third represents the "Wheelchair Assassins", a separatist group from Quebec. The "Great Concavity/Great Convexity" map to the lower left shows a waste dump in the area of the northern US/southern Canada. The map below shows the setting of "Eschaton", a computer-aided war game, which is played every year on November 8 at the Tennis Acad emy. Students are organised in militaristic groups ("AMNAT" etc.) and are located virtually around the globe.

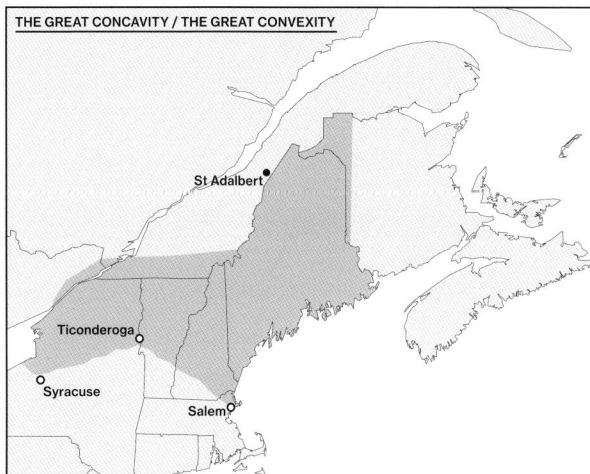

THE GREAT CONCAVITY / THE GREAT CONVEXITY

St Adalbert

Ticonderoga

Syracuse

Salem

Project Info: Poster, 2010, USA
Data Source: David Foster Wallace: "Infinite Jest", 1996
Design: Sam Potts

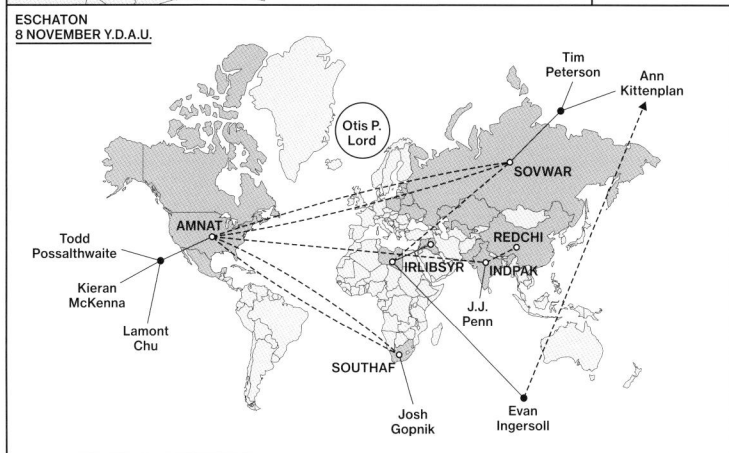

ESCHATON
8 NOVEMBER Y.D.A.U.

Tim Peterson

Ann Kittenplan

Otis P. Lord

SOVWAR

Todd Possalthwaite

AMNAT

REDCHI

Kieran McKenna

IRLIBSYR

INDPAK

Lamont Chu

J.J. Penn

SOUTHAF

Josh Gopnik

Evan Ingersoll

OUS

AFR

OUS

AFR

Marathe

Sharyn Vaught
Caryn Vaught
Ann Kittenplan
Jennie Bash
Shoshana Abrams
Carol Spodek
Amy Wingo
Frances L. Unwin
Gretchen Holt
Felicity Zweig
Zoltan Csikzentmihalyi
Jeff Wax
Stephen Wagenknecht
Chip Sweeny
Todd "Postal Weight" Possalthwaite
Otis P. Lord
Coach Kirk White
Dean of Admissions
Director of Composition
Dean of Athletic Affairs
Dean of Academic Affairs
University of Arizona
Thierry Poutrincourt
Rik Dunkel
Mary Esther Thode
Ruth
Erica Siress
Lori Clow
Tine Echt
Jolene Criess
Bernard Makulic
Graham "Yard-Guard" Rader
Anton "Booger" Doucette
Miles Penn
Esteban Reyes
Guglielmo Redondo
Petropolis Kahn
Jeffrey Joseph Penn
Elxit Kornspen
Tim "Sleepy TP" Peterson
Kieran McKenna
Brian van Vleck
Lamont Chu
Cisne
Younger players
Ortho "The Darkness" Stice
Kent Blott
Lyle
Barry Loach
Therese Loach
"U.S.S." Millicant Kent
Players
Gerhardt Schtitt
Militant Grammarians of Massachusetts
"Lateral" Alice Moore
Audern Tallat-Kelpsa
Philip Traub
Josh Gopnik
Virgilio
Peter Beak
Evan Ingersoll
Idris "Id" Arslanian
Tunnel Club
Elizabeth Tavis
Trevor "Axhandle" Axford
Diane Prins
Bernadette Longley
Kyle D. Coyle
Keith B. "The Viking" Freer
Dymphna
Mario Incandenza
Avril "The Moms" Mondragon Tavis Incandenza
John "N.R." Wayne
WETA
James Albrecht Lockley Struck Jr.
Hugh Pemberton
Bridget C. Boone
Harold James "Hal" Incandenza
Orin James Incandenza
James Orin "Himself" Incandenza Jr.
James Orin Incandenza Sr.
Eric Clipperton
Ross Reat
Mario Sr.
Tall Paul Shaw
Tenuate
Seniors (tbs)
B.U.
Dwight Flechette
Nickerson
"Jethro Bodina"
Jim Troeltsch
Michael Pemulis
sister
at ETA
Smothergill
Jim
Harv
Inner Infant Group
Kevin Bain
Marlon K. Bain
Bain parents
Glockner
Stockhausen
Ted Schacht
van Slack
Saprogenic Greetings
"Moment" magazine
Acmé Inc.
Thomas M. Flatto
Dick Willis
Miriam Hoyne
Henri F. Hoyne
M. Hugh "Helen P." Steeply
Muminsky
father
Mo Cheery
Rémy Marathe
Gertraud
Nell in Spin
Dick Desai
Input/Output
Broullîme
Bernard Wayne
Noreen Lace-Forché
InterLace
Johnny Gentle, F.C.
Clean U.S. Party
Office of Unspecified Services
father
St. Adalbert, L'Islet Province, Québec
American Council of Disseminators of Cable
Albertan mogul
Organization of North American Nations
Mexican President
Vienna VA Szechuan Steakhouse
Lurie Perec
R. Ossowiecke
Balbalis
Beausoleil
Tassigny
Desjardins
Heart in purse
Maureen Hooley
Nunhagen Aspirin
Canadian P.M.
Other Members
Joubet
LipoVac UnItd.
Fond du Lac NoCoat Inc.
P. Tom Veals
Rodney "The God" Tine Sr.
Fortier
Rodney Tine Jr.
Fully Functional Phil
Virey & Veals
Carl E. "Buster" Yee
Glad
Jeu Du Prochain Train
Brandeis
Guillaume Duplessis
Sheraton Commander
Sto "Dark Mol
Lola
Bridg Tender
Susa Chee
LES ASSASSINS DES FAUTEUILS ROLLENTS

Le Bloc Québécois
Calgarian Pro-Canada Phalanx
Séparatisteurs Québécois
Antitoi Entertainment
Les Fils de Montcalm
Le Parti Québécois
Bertrand
Le Culte de Baiser Sans Fin
Les Fils de Papineau
Le Front de la Libération de Québec
Lucien
Test Subjects
Da
Matty Pemulis

THE GREAT CONCAVITY / THE GREAT CONVEXITY

St Adalbert
Ticonderoga
Syracuse
Salem

ESCHATON
8 NOVEMBER Y.D.A.U.

Otis P. Lord
Tim Peterson
Ann Kittenplan
Todd Possalthwaite
AMNAT
SOVWAR
REDCHI
Kieran McKenna
Lamont Chu
RUSBSYR
INDPAK
J.J. Penn
SOUTHAF
Josh Gopnik
Evan Ingersoll

OUS
AFR
OUS
AFR
Marathe

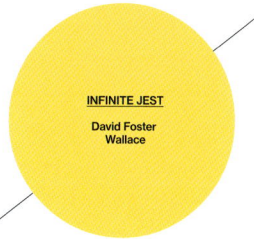

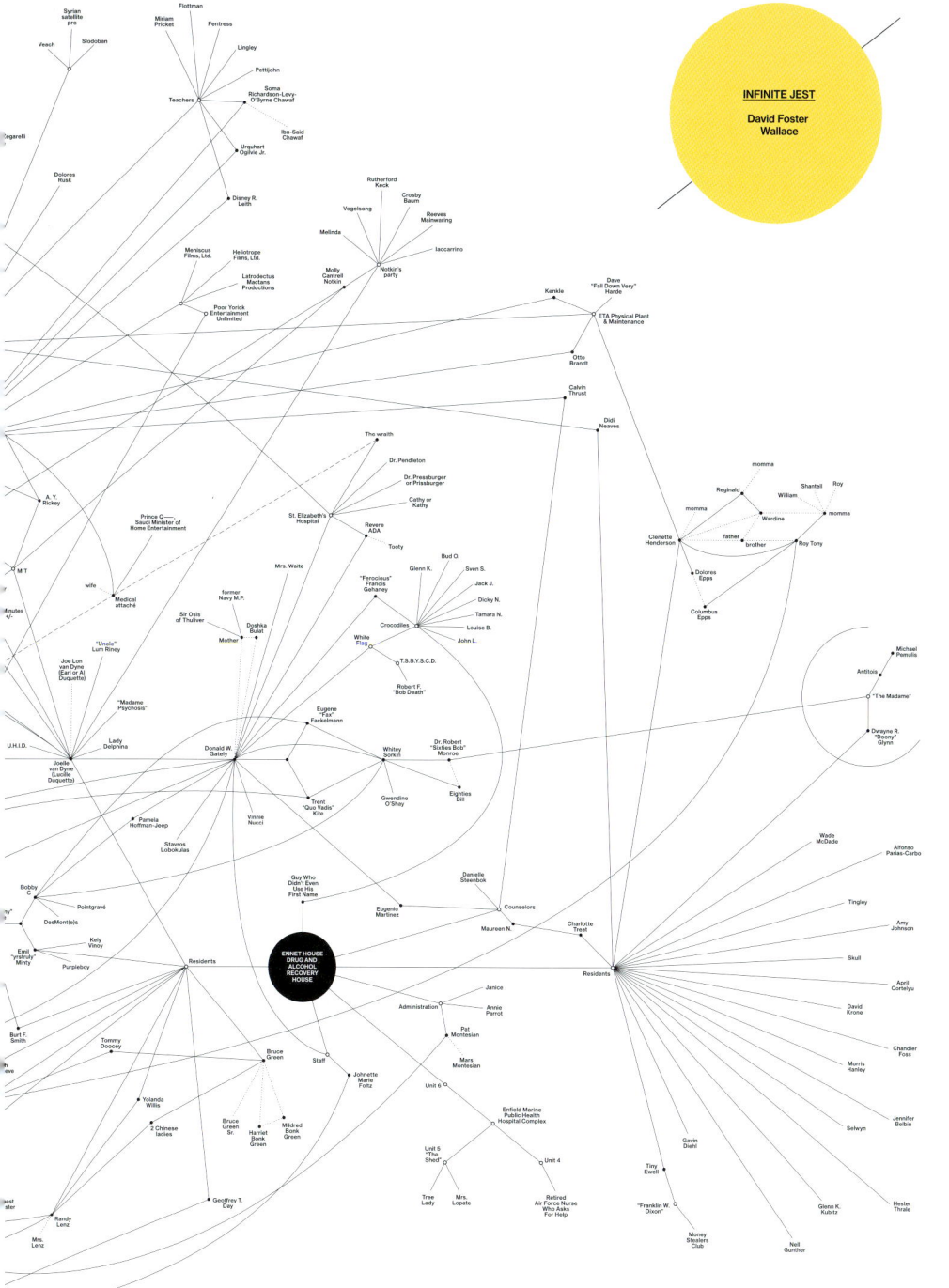

INFINITE JEST

David Foster Wallace

Syrian satellite pro
Veach
Slododan
Iagarelli
Miriam Pricket
Flottman
Fentress
Lingley
Pettijohn
Soma Richardson-Levy-O'Byrne Chawaf
Ibn-Said Chawaf
Urquhart Ogilvie Jr.
Teachers
Dolores Rusk
Disney R. Leith

Rutherford Keck
Crosby Baum
Reeves Mainwaring
Vogelsong
Melinda
Iaccarrino
Molly Cantrell Notkin
Notkin's party
Kenkle
Dave "Fall Down Very" Harde
ETA Physical Plant & Maintenance

Meniscus Films, Ltd.
Heliotrope Films, Ltd.
Latrodectus Mactans Productions
Poor Yorick Entertainment Unlimited

Otto Brandt
Calvin Thrust
Didi Neaves

The wraith
Dr. Pendleton
Dr. Pressburger or Prissburger
Cathy or Kathy
A. Y. Rickey
Prince Q—Saudi Minister of Home Entertainment
St. Elizabeth's Hospital
Revere ADA
Toofy
wife
MIT
Medical attaché
Minutes +/-

momma
Reginald
William
Shantell
Roy
momma
Wardine
momma
father
brother
Roy Tony
Clenette Henderson
Dolores Epps
Columbus Epps

Mrs. Waite
former Navy M.P.
Sir Osis of Thuliver
Doshka Bulat
Mother
"Uncle" Lum Riney
Joe Lon van Dyne (Earl or Al Duquette)
"Madame Psychosis"
U.H.I.D.
Joelle van Dyne (Lucille Duquette)
Lady Delphina

"Ferocious" Francis Gehaney
Glenn K.
Bud O.
Sven S.
Jack J.
Dicky N.
Tamara N.
Louise B.
John L.
Crocodiles
White Flag
T.S.B.Y.S.C.D.
Robert F. "Bob Death"

Michael Pemulis
Antitois
"The Madame"
Dwayne R. "Doony" Glynt

Eugene "Fax" Fackelmann
Whitey Sorkin
Dr. Robert "Sixties Bob" Monroe
Donald W. Gately
Trent "Quo Vadis" Kite
Gwendine O'Shay
Eighties Bill
Vinnie Nucci
Pamela Hoffman-Jeep
Stavros Lobokulas

Bobby C
Pointgravé
DesMont(e)s
Emil "yrstruly" Minty
Kely Vinoy
Purpleboy
Residents

Guy Who Didn't Even Use His First Name
Eugenio Martinez
Danielle Steenbok
Counselors
Maureen N.
Charlotte Treat
Residents

ENNET HOUSE DRUG AND ALCOHOL RECOVERY HOUSE

Wade McDade
Alfonso Parias-Carbo
Tingley
Amy Johnson
Skull
April Cortelyu
David Krone
Chandler Foss
Morris Hanley
Jennifer Belbin
Selwyn
Hexter Thrale

Administration
Janice
Annie Parrot
Pat Montesian
Mars Montesian
Unit 6
Burt F. Smith
Tommy Doocey
Bruce Green
Staff
Johnette Maria Foltz
Yolanda Willis
2 Chinese ladies
Bruce Green Sr.
Harriet Bonk Green
Mildred Bonk Green
Geoffrey T. Day
Randy Lenz
Mrs. Lenz

Enfield Marine Public Health Hospital Complex
Unit 5 "The Shed"
Unit 4
Tree Lady
Mrs. Lopate
Retired Air Force Nurse Who Asks For Help

Gavin Diehl
Tiny Ewell
"Franklin W. Dixon"
Money Stealers Club
Nell Gunther
Glenn K. Kubitz

ORGANIZATION OF NORTH AMERICAN NATIONS' REVENUE-ENHANCING SUBSIDIZED TIME™

Whopper → Tucks Medicated Pad → Trial-Size Dove Bar → Perdue Wonderchicken → Whisper-Quiet Maytag Dishmaster → Yushityu 2007 MRCVMETIUFI/ITPSFH(O)OM (s) → Dairy Products from the American Heartland → Depend Adult Undergarment → Glad

375

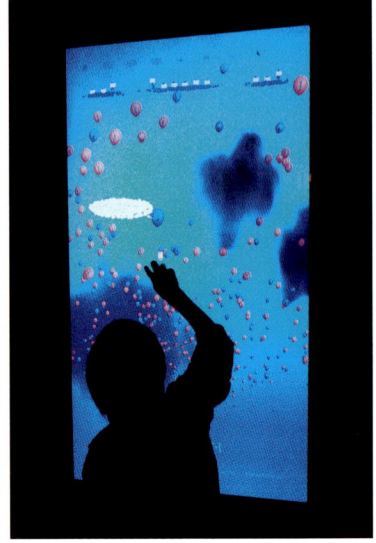

Project Info: Interactive installation,
Museum of Modern Art, 2008, USA
Design: Jonathan Harris, Sep Kamvar

I Want You To Want Me

This interactive installation takes a look into contemporary online dating, visualising people's self-descriptions and desires. Every few hours, data from dating profiles on various websites are collected. Against a background of a large area of sky, each profile is shown as a balloon containing a tiny silhouette, offering a little glimpse of a private life. Male profiles are blue, female profiles are shown in pink, with colour intensity corresponding to age – brighter balloons belong to younger people. Icons along the top allow control of the weather. Figures on the clouds provide filters pertaining to gender and age. Statements are classified in five major "movements", which are accessed using the navigation along the bottom. *Matchmaker* algorithmically pairs people based on their self-descriptions. *Snippets* displays specific lines from dating profiles, like subject lines or openers. *What I Want* presents sentences beginning with the phrase "I am looking for" as balloons which together form the shape of a pulsing heart. *Who I Am* displays sentences beginning with "I am". *Breakdowns* reveals the most popular turn-ons, first dates, desires and commonest self-descriptions.

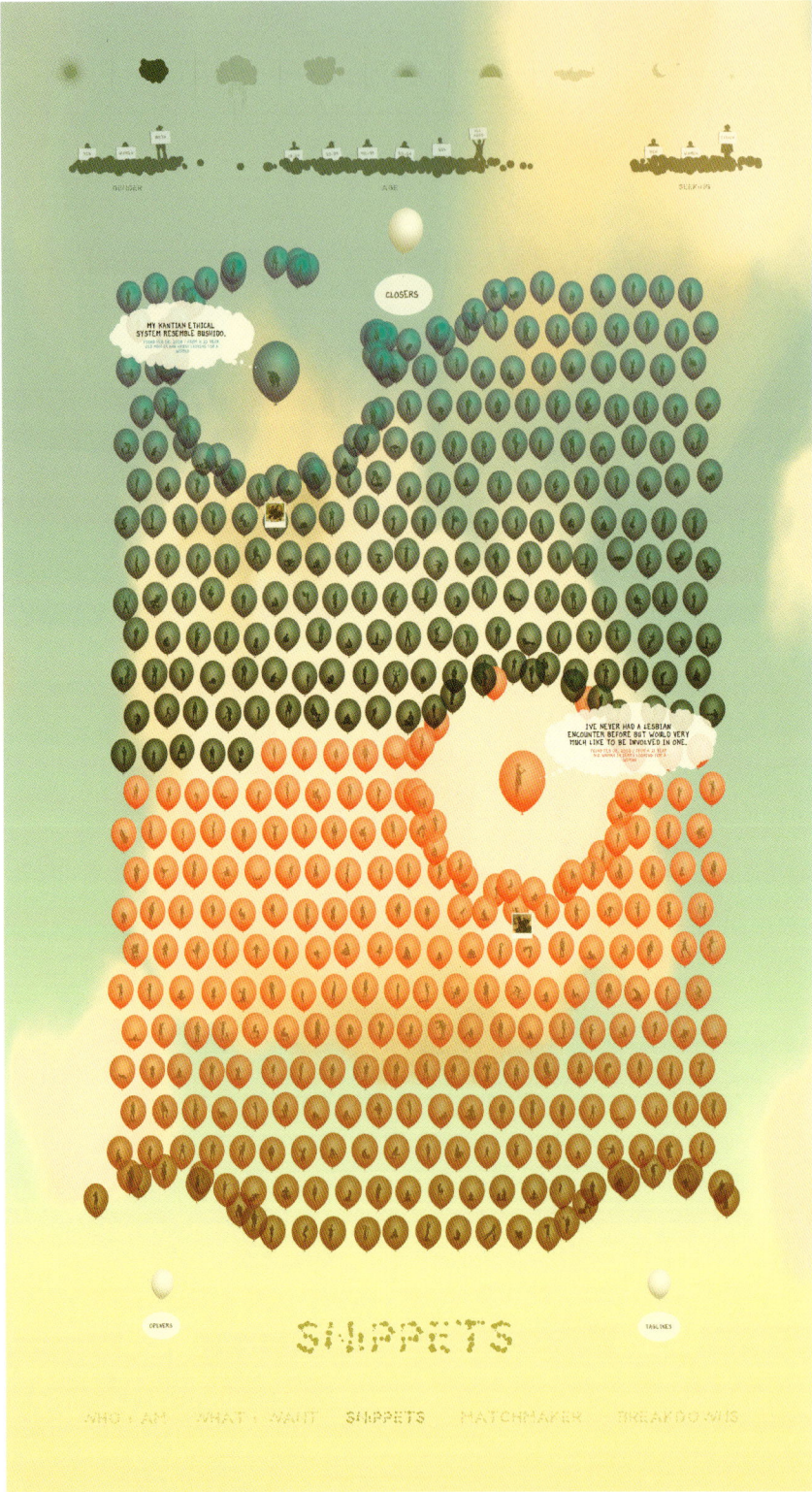

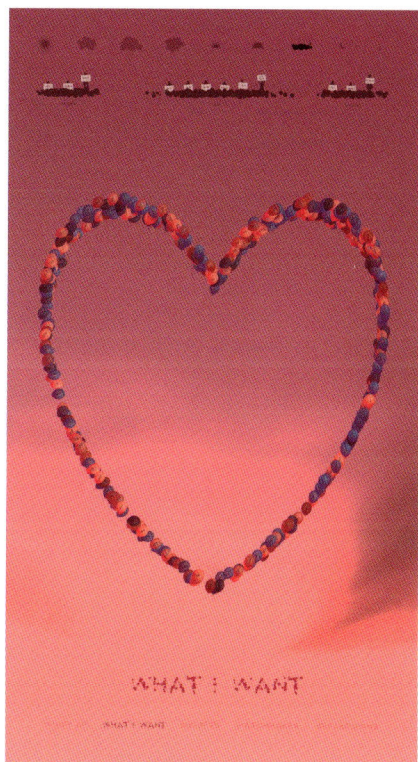

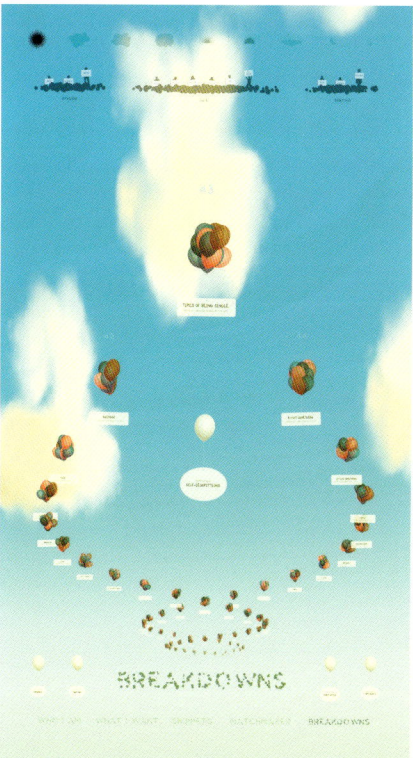

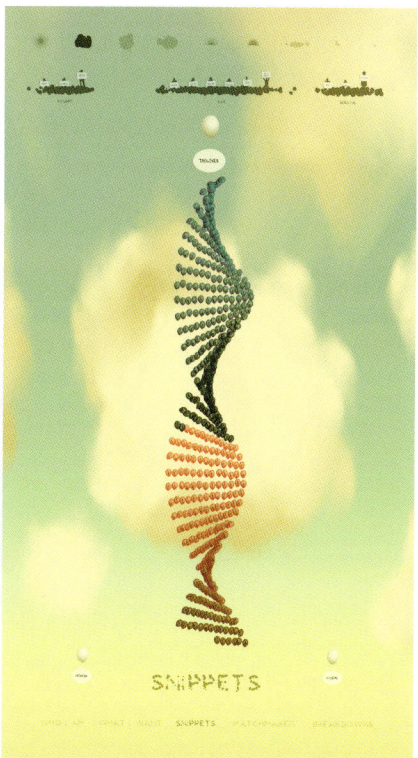

Influences of Edgar Allan Poe

Designed on the occasion of Edgar Allan Poe's 200th birthday, this infographic explains his literary cosmos. The circle diagram places Poe in the centre. Forerunners are shown in blue, while contemporaries with whom he exchanged inspirations are coded in purple. Later writers, who drew upon various aspects of Poe's work, are shown in pink. Individual aspects of Poe's writing are listed around the inner circles of the diagram, and refer to style, main topics and genres. An axis connects Poe with each author, with dots marking the aspects the author shares with Poe. It is interesting how this piece is mainly structured by the categories of literary writing, whereas the historical succession is elegantly integrated into a closed circle.

INFLUENCIAN A POE

CONTEMPORÁNEOS

DANTE ALIGHIERI
1265-1321

WILLIAM BLAKE
1757-1827

LORD BYRON
1788-1824

GUSTAVO ADOLFO BÉCQUER
1836-1870

GUY DE MAUPASSANT
1850-1893

ARTHUR CONAN DOYLE
1859-1930

G. K. CHESTERTON
1874-1936

H.P. LOVECRAFT
1890-1937

RAY BRADBURY
1920

STEPHEN KING
1945

JORGE LUIS BORGES
1899-1986

FRANZ KAFKA
1883-1924

ANTÓN CHEJOV
1860-1904

OSCAR WILDE
1854-1900

AMBROSE BIERCE
1842-1914

CHARLES BAUDELAIRE
1821-1867

SHERIDAN LE FANU
1814-1873

CHARLES DICKENS
1812-1980

MARY SHELLEY
1797-1851

POESÍA
SIMBOLISMO
ROMANTICISMO
TERROR
SOBRENATURAL
RELATO
CUENTISTAS
POLICÍACA
PERIODISMO
AVENTURAS
MODERNO

INFLUIDOS POR POE

Project Info: *Público*, newspaper article, 2009, Spain
Research: Jesús Rocamora
Design: Álvaro Valiño

ИТОГО РАСХОДОВ: 665 ТЫС. РУБ

ИТОГО ДОХОДОВ: 700 ТЫС. РУБ

Методические пособия
20 тыс. руб

Обслуживающий персонал
100 тыс. руб

Приходящие специалисты
(логопед, музыкальный работник и т. д.)
40 тыс. руб

Налоги и бухгалтерское обслуживание
35 тыс. руб

Доходы
600 тыс. руб

Аренда
150 тыс. руб

Бытовые расходы
(туалетная бумага, лампочки и т.д.)
20 тыс. руб

ПРИХОДИТЕ
К НАМ

Госдотации
100 тыс. руб

Реклама
50 тыс. руб

Воспитатели (4 чел.)
120 тыс. руб

Питание
90 тыс. руб

Компенсация за простой
в летние месяцы 40 тыс. руб

Аренда
150 тыс. руб

Реклама
50 тыс. руб

ПРИХОДИТЕ
К НАМ

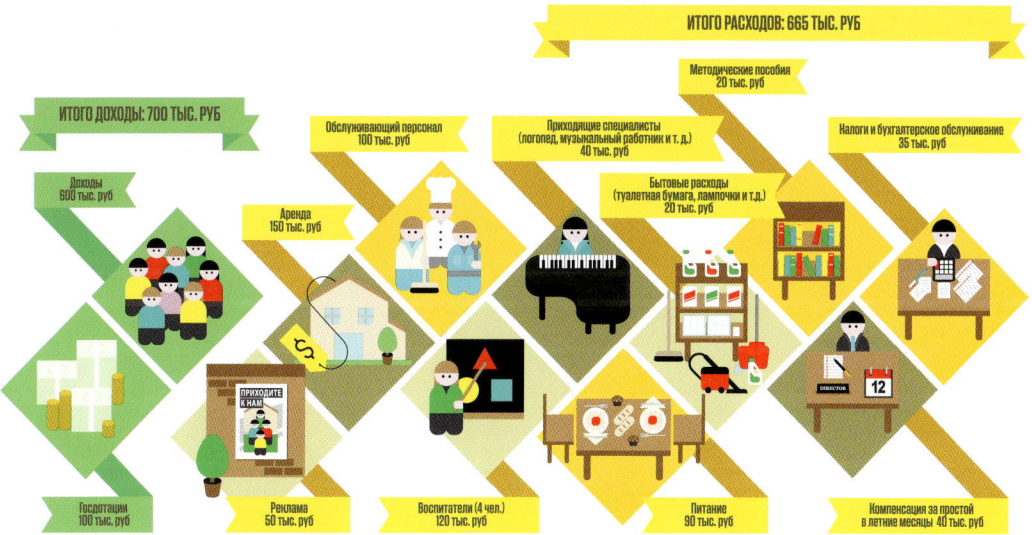

Kindergarten

This infographic, developed for Russian business magazine *Sekret Firmy*, tackles the economic aspects of running a kindergarten. It shows the data for an average kindergarten in Russia, with the budget indicated in the green boxes on the left, differentiated between regular income and state subsidies. The yellow boxes show the various types of expenses: rent for the premises, teachers' earnings, expenses for service staff, external professionals like music teachers, advertisements or food. Numbers are given in thousands of rubles.

Project Info: *Sekret Firmy*,
magazine article, 2010, Russia
Design: Alberto Antoniazzi

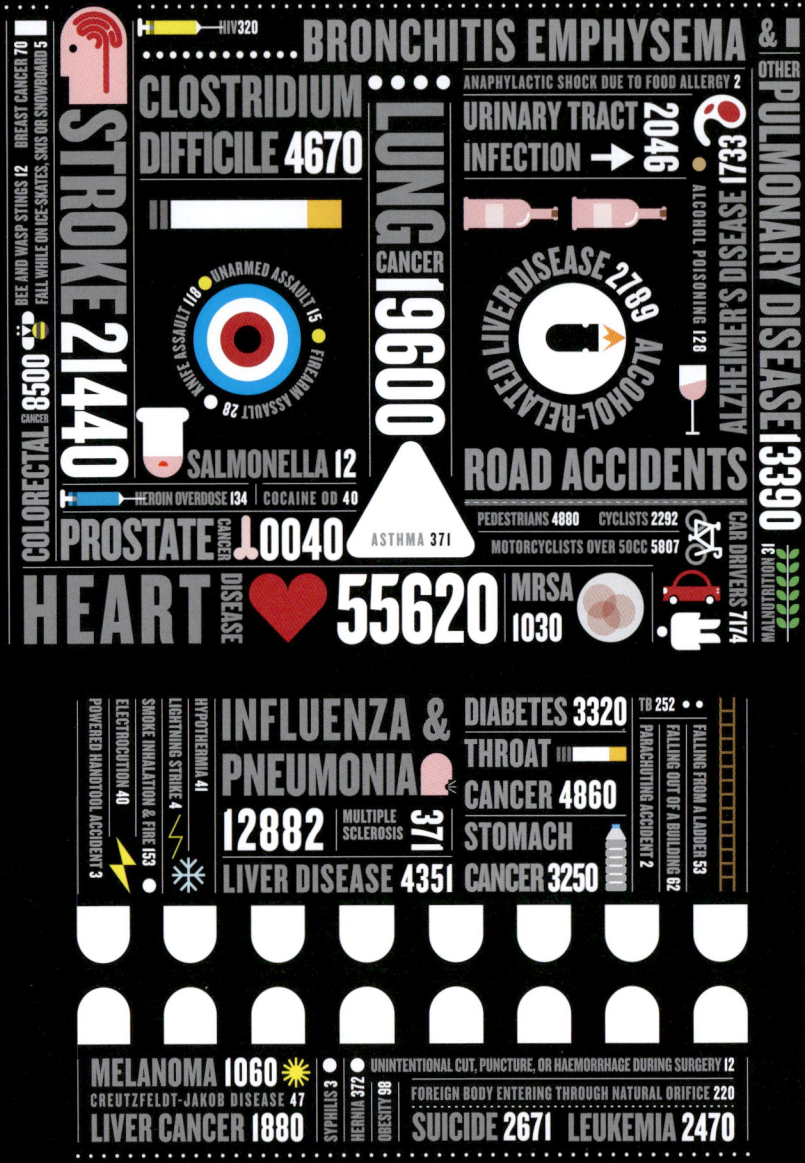

HIV 320

BREAST CANCER 70

FALL WHILE ON ICE-SKATES, SKIS OR SNOWBOARD 5

BEE AND WASP STINGS 12

BRONCHITIS EMPHYSEMA & OTHER PULMONARY DISEASE 13390

CLOSTRIDIUM DIFFICILE 4670

ANAPHYLACTIC SHOCK DUE TO FOOD ALLERGY 2

URINARY TRACT INFECTION 2046

ALCOHOL POISONING 128

ALZHEIMER'S DISEASE 1733

STROKE 21440

LUNG CANCER 19600

ALCOHOL-RELATED LIVER DISEASE 2789

KNIFE ASSAULT 119

UNARMED ASSAULT 15

FIREARM ASSAULT 28

CANCER 8500

COLORECTAL

SALMONELLA 12

HEROIN OVERDOSE 134 | COCAINE OD 40

PROSTATE CANCER 10040

ASTHMA 371

ROAD ACCIDENTS

PEDESTRIANS 4880 | CYCLISTS 2292
MOTORCYCLISTS OVER 50CC 5807

CAR DRIVERS 7174

MALNUTRITION 31

HEART DISEASE 55620

MRSA 1030

INFLUENZA & PNEUMONIA 12882

MULTIPLE SCLEROSIS 371

LIVER DISEASE 4351

DIABETES 3320

THROAT CANCER 4860

STOMACH CANCER 3250

TB 252

PARACHUTING ACCIDENT 2

FALLING OUT OF A BUILDING 53

FALLING FROM A LADDER 62

POWERED HANDTOOL ACCIDENT 3

ELECTROCUTION 40

SMOKE INHALATION & FIRE 153

LIGHTNING STRIKE 4

HYPOTHERMIA 41

MELANOMA 1060

CREUTZFELDT-JAKOB DISEASE 47

LIVER CANCER 1880

SYPHILIS 3

HERNIA 372

OBESITY 98

UNINTENTIONAL CUT, PUNCTURE, OR HAEMORRHAGE DURING SURGERY 12

FOREIGN BODY ENTERING THROUGH NATURAL ORIFICE 220

SUICIDE 2671   LEUKEMIA 2470

Life and Death

Peter Grundy designed this piece for the UK edition of *Men's Health*. As he had been tasked to visualise death rates for a health-oriented magazine, he opted for a humorous approach and assembled the letters and figures to create a skull, as a general symbol of death. UK death rates are categorised by cause of death.

Project Info: *Men's Health*, magazine article, 2008, UK
Design: Peter Grundy (Grundini)
Art Direction: Kerem Shefik
Awards: AOI Images 2009

Little Book of Shocking Global Facts: Deforestation

The Little Book of Shocking Global Facts by Jonathan Barnbrook reports political and economic data in a startling variety of designs. In its quest to establish a visual argument, the book challenged widely accepted principles for reporting information, such as that design should be clear and not take a stand of its own. Barnbrook deliberately questioned whether this neutrality was either possible or desirable.The critical reaction the book has given rise to attests to a clash of cultures within graphic design in regard to these basic tenets. The book is divided into topics, ranging from trade via human rights to drugs. The example below shows how much forest has been gained or lost on each continent. The word "China" is highlighted and linked to other facts elsewhere in the book.

Project Info: Fiell Publishing, book, 2010, UK
Data Source: UN Food and Agriculture Organization; FAO Global Forest Resources Assessment et al.
Design: Jonathan Abbott, Jonathan Barnbrook (Barnbrook)

CHANGE IN FOREST AREA 1990—2005

The primary source of greenhouse gas emissions is not the burning of fossil fuels, but deforestation. In fact 25% of greenhouse gases released each year – 1.6 billion tonnes – are caused by the felling or burning of trees.

Deforestation occurs at a rate of 13 million hectares per year, and is mainly caused by converting forests into agricultural land. The main areas of deforestation occur in the tropics of Africa and South America. Deforestation also occurs at a high rate in Asia, but total figures are distorted by large scale afforestation reported by China. The only continent to report a positive change in forest area during the period 1990 – 2005 was Europe.

25% OF GREENHOUSE GASES ARE CAUSED BY DEFORESTATION

If every passenger car in the U.S. (all 135,399,945 of them[1]) were a MINI Cooper, we would ...

▶ free up 94,000 miles of lanes[***]

A real **MINI Cooper** is 223 times larger than the MINIs pictured below.

That's still almost 25% smaller than the average sedan in the U.S.[***]

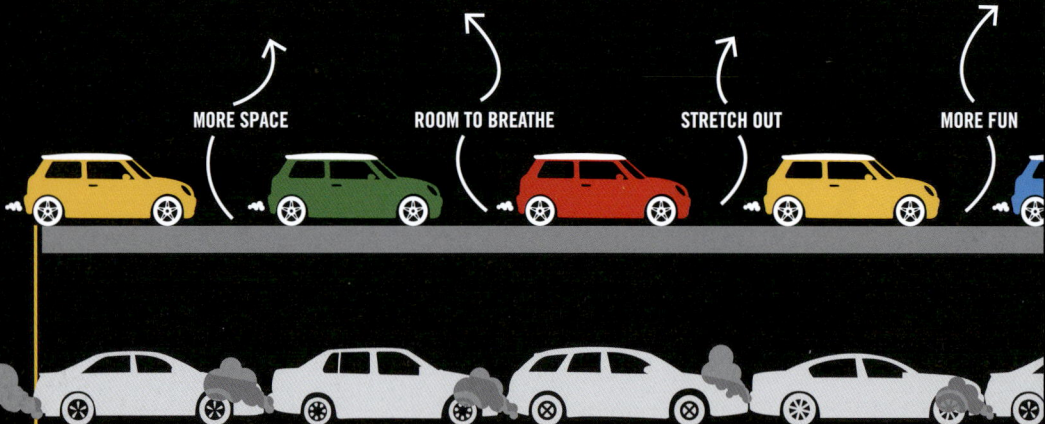

MORE SPACE   ROOM TO BREATHE   STRETCH OUT   MORE FUN

If 135 million U.S. sedans were sitting bumper to bumper, they would make a line that stretched 400,000 miles....

1 INCH = 44,300 MILES · EACH CAR ABOVE = 15 MILLION REAL CARS

1. U.S. Bureau of Transit Statistics
2. Fuelgagereport.com (premium gas, 7/30/08)
3. Federal Highway Administration
4. Source data from Edmunds.com; **5.** EPA

* 37 hwy/28 city MPG MINI Cooper Hardtop with manual transmission. EPA estimate. Actual mileage will vary with options, driving conditions, driving habits and vehicle operation.

save $61 billion in gas $/yr

	MINI Cooper	Avg. U.S. sedan	
	12000	12000	AVG MILES DRIVEN / YEAR
	÷ 37	÷ 27.8	HWY MPG
	× 4.21[9]	× 4.21[9]	AVG PRICE / GALLON GAS[2]
	= $1368	= $1821	TOTAL $ SPENT / YEAR

$453 saved gas $/yr per car

MINI Cooper: 37 MPG*

Avg. U.S. sedan: 27.8 MPG**

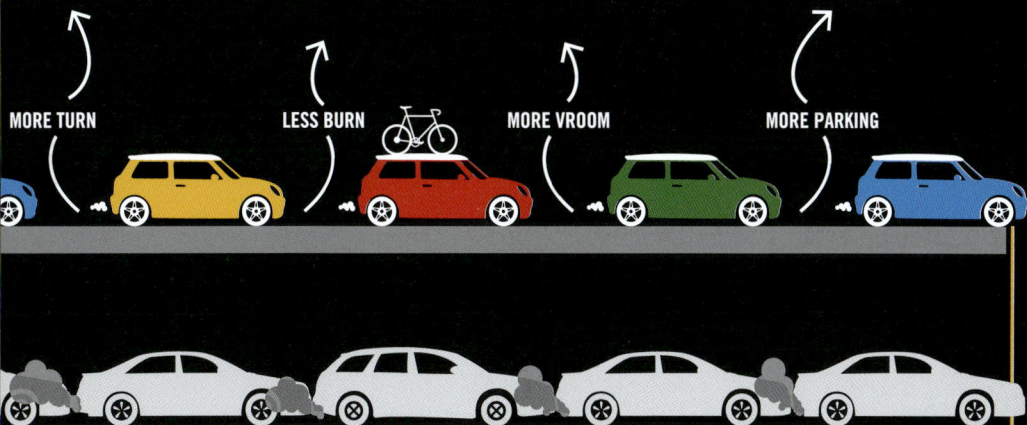

MORE TURN   LESS BURN   MORE VROOM   MORE PARKING

... If every one of those became a MINI Cooper, we'd save the equivalent of more than twice the length of the entire National Highway system.***

Learn more about MINI at **CarfunFootprint.com**

** 27.8 highway MPG, is the weighted average of 2007 small, medium, and large-sized cars and wagons according to EPA estimates.

*** Based on the length of the MINI Cooper Hardtop (145.6") and the length of the average U.S. sedan (189.6")[4] and 46,837 total miles of National Higthway System[3]

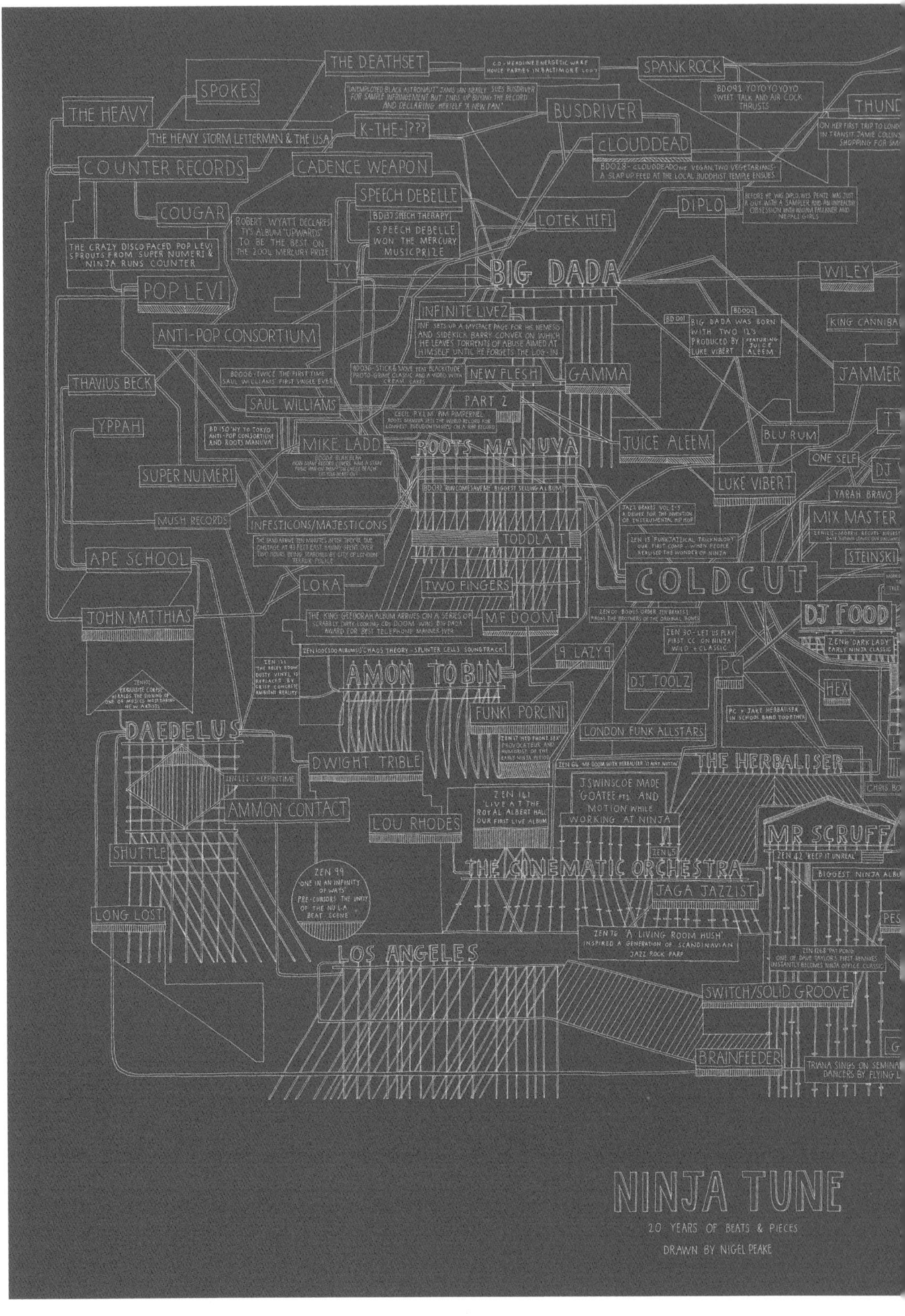
THE DEATHSET
SPANK ROCK
SPOKES
THE HEAVY
BUSDRIVER
K-THE-I???
THE HEAVY STORM LETTERMAN & THE USA
CLOUDDEAD
COUNTER RECORDS
CADENCE WEAPON
SPEECH DEBELLE
COUGAR
DIPLO
LOTEK HIFI
BIG DADA
POP LEVI
ANTI-POP CONSORTIUM
INFINITE LIVEZ
THAVIUS BECK
SAUL WILLIAMS
NEW FLESH
GAMMA
YPPAH
MIKE LADD
ROOTS MANUVA
JUICE ALEEM
SUPER NUMERI
LUKE VIBERT
MUSH RECORDS
INFESTICONS/MAJESTICONS
TODDLA T
APE SCHOOL
COLDCUT
LOKA
TWO FINGERS
DJ FOOD
JOHN MATTHIAS
MF DOOM
9 LAZY 9
AMON TOBIN
DJ TOOLZ
FUNKI PORCINI
LONDON FUNK ALLSTARS
DAEDELUS
DWIGHT TRIBLE
THE HERBALISER
AMMON CONTACT
LOU RHODES
MR SCRUFF
SHUTTLE
THE CINEMATIC ORCHESTRA
JAGA JAZZIST
LONG LOST
LOS ANGELES
SWITCH/SOLID GROOVE
BRAINFEEDER
NINJA TUNE
20 YEARS OF BEATS & PIECES
DRAWN BY NIGEL PEAKE

Previous spread

Mini Cooper

This graphic by Fogelson-Lubliner appeared in *Mini Zine*, a miniature issue of *GOOD* magazine. The piece makes clear two major benefits to driving a smaller and more fuel-efficient car like the Mini Cooper. The road lanes along the bottom demonstrate how small cars take less road space. The billboard display (top right) explains how the fuel-efficient car saves gas costs.

Project Info: *GOOD*, magazine article, 2008, USA
Data Source: US Bureau of Transit Statistics; Daily Fuel Gauge Report; US EPA; Federal Highway Administration; Edmunds Car Buying Guide
Design: Gary Fogelson, Phil Lubliner (Fogelson-Lubliner)

Ninja Tune – Family Tree

This drawing charts the history of London-based record label Ninja Tune, on the occasion of its 20th anniversary in 2010. Despite the title, the piece is not a strict historical genealogy. Rather, the piece unfolds a sort of mental map of the Ninja Tune cosmos, with the founding DJ team Coldcut at the heart. The individual artists are shown, mentioning their most important projects and collaborations. The piece was originally produced as a poster in two colour versions. As a map, it is a variation on Nigel Peake's distorted maps of real and fictional places.

Project Info: Poster, 2010, UK
Design: Nigel Peake
Art Direction: Peter Quicke, Kevin Foakes

PERIODIC TABLE OF METAPHORS

(I) THE CLASSICS — Steadfast and reliable, they are an illustrators best companion.

(II) THE TRICKIES — Beware of this mean little bunch. They look so promising, but as soon as I try to twist them, they fall apart.

(IV) THE EDITOR'S FAVS — I have empirical proof that editors just L-O-V-E these, though I have not the slightest clue why.

(V) THE ZOMBIES — They should be long dead, but keep crawling out of their graves and there is nothing I can do.

(VI) THE TOXICS — Use at your own peril.

(VII) THE NO WAYS — Don't even think about it. Ever.

HOW TO MAKE A CONCEPTUAL ILLUSTRATION

A lot of conceptual illustrations are simply a graphic combination of two metaphors.
Let's take for example the following assignment:
Make an illustration for an Article with the headlline

"SEARCHING FOR AN EXIT STRATEGY."

Step I:
Consult the Table of Metaphors and find appropriate symbols for A:"Searching" and B:"Exit."

Step II:
Mix Metaphors

Step III:
TA-DAH...

Project Info: *Print*, magazine article, 2004, USA
Design: Christoph Niemann

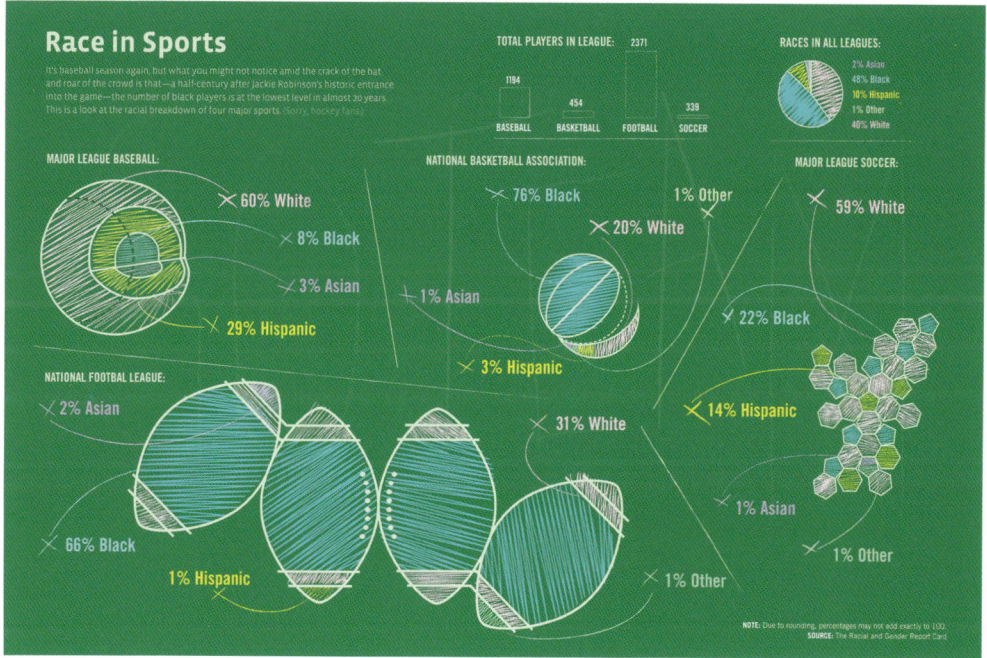

Race in Sports

It's baseball season again, but what you might not notice amid the crack of the bat and roar of the crowd is that—a half-century after Jackie Robinson's historic entrance into the game—the number of black players is at the lowest level in almost 20 years. This is a look at the racial breakdown of four major sports. (Sorry, hockey fans.)

TOTAL PLAYERS IN LEAGUE: 2371

1184

454

338

BASEBALL   BASKETBALL   FOOTBALL   SOCCER

RACES IN ALL LEAGUES:

2% Asian
48% Black
10% Hispanic
1% Other
40% White

MAJOR LEAGUE BASEBALL:

60% White
8% Black
3% Asian
29% Hispanic

NATIONAL BASKETBALL ASSOCIATION:

76% Black
1% Other
20% White
1% Asian
3% Hispanic

MAJOR LEAGUE SOCCER:

59% White
22% Black
14% Hispanic
1% Asian
1% Other

NATIONAL FOOTBALL LEAGUE:

2% Asian
66% Black
1% Hispanic
31% White
1% Other

NOTE: Due to rounding, percentages may not add exactly to 100.
SOURCE: The Racial and Gender Report Card

Project Info: "Who Is Playing Sports?",
GOOD, online article, 2009, USA
Data Source: The Institute for Diversity and Ethics in Sport: "The Racial and Gender Report Card"

Research: Morgan Clendaniel
Design: Joshua Covarrubias (Kiss Me I'm Polish)
Art Direction: Agnieszka Gasparska (Kiss Me I'm Polish)

Periodic Table of Metaphors

Christoph Niemann created a series for *Print* magazine in 2004, humorously unveiling the secrets of his life as an illustrator. The series tackled all aspects of an illustrator's working life, including communication troubles with editors, the challenges of working on a chaotic desk or the dilemma posed by the blank piece of paper each job starts with. In this piece, Niemann drew on one of the most famous scientific visualisation patterns, the periodic table of the elements, in order to display and categorise a tool-kit of metaphors, which illustrators can use to create illustrations on any current topic in a journalistic context. The diagram below explains how to create an illustration by mixing two metaphors together.

Race in Sports

Developed for *GOOD* magazine, this graphic looks at the racial breakdown in the US's four most popular sports: baseball, football, basketball and soccer. Each sport is represented by its own particular ball. The football and the soccer ball are shown like sewing patterns, with their component parts spread out against a flat background. The baseball to the left is cut open, showing the composition of the ball in layers. Colours indicate the racial distribution in each sport, indicating that football and basketball are predominantly played by African Americans, while baseball is a mostly "white" sport.

Project Info: Poster, 2006, USA
Data Source: Thompson ISI
Research: Kevin Boyack, Dick Klavans
Design: W. Bradford Paley (Digital
Image Design)

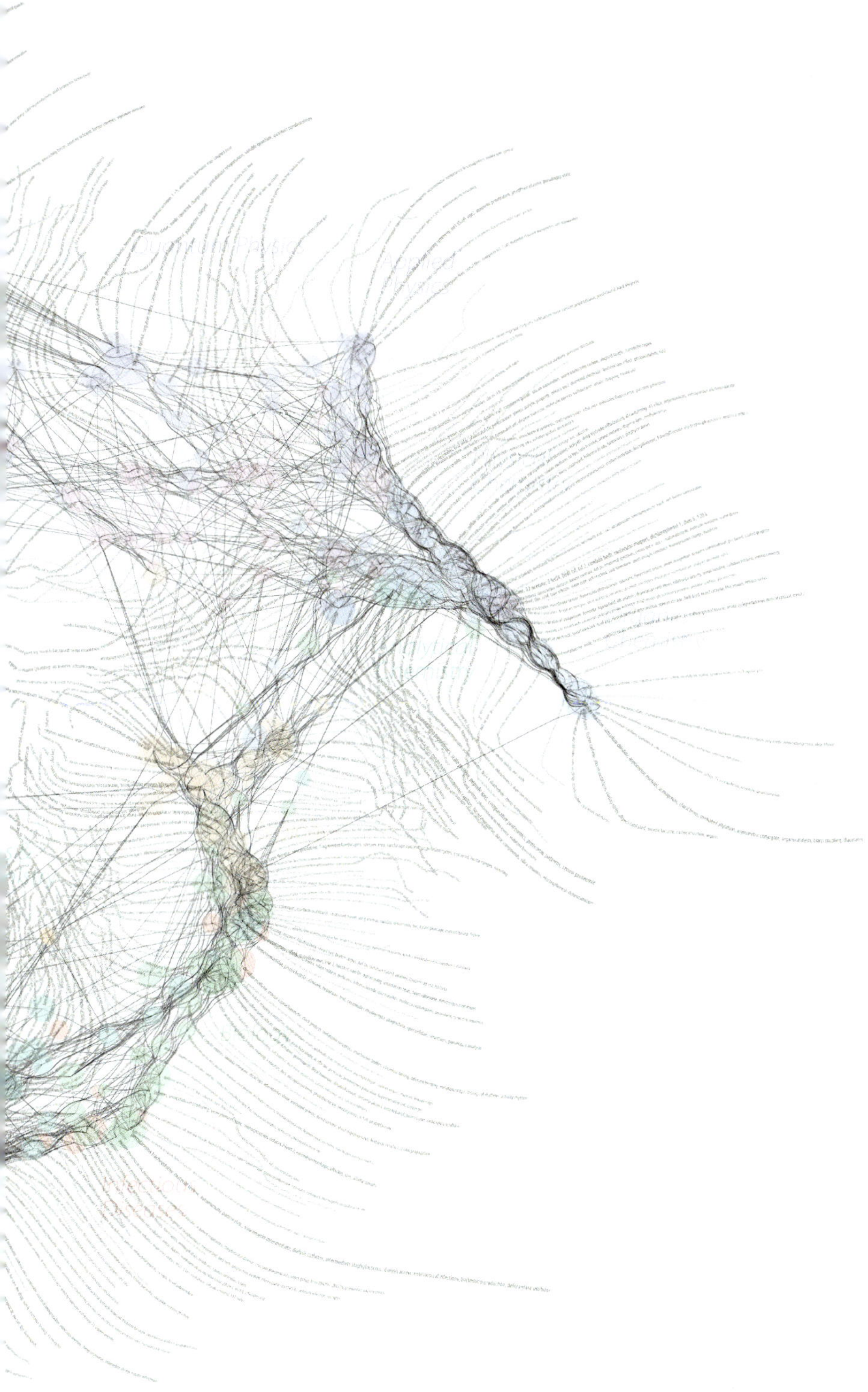

Previous spread and below

Relationships Among
Scientific Paradigms

This is a very special "map" – it categorises scientific paradigms. Bradford Paley sorted 800,000 research papers published in 2003 into 776 distinct paradigms based on how often the papers were cited together by authors of other papers. Paradigms are depicted as pale, colour-coded circles: orange for social sciences, pink for medicine, green for biology, etc.

All connections between paradigms, based on quotes in other papers, are visualised by thin hairlines. The spatial layout forces all paradigms to repel each other, while the hairline connections work as rubber-bands keeping similar paradigms connected. The map thus shows relations between paradigms by proximity.

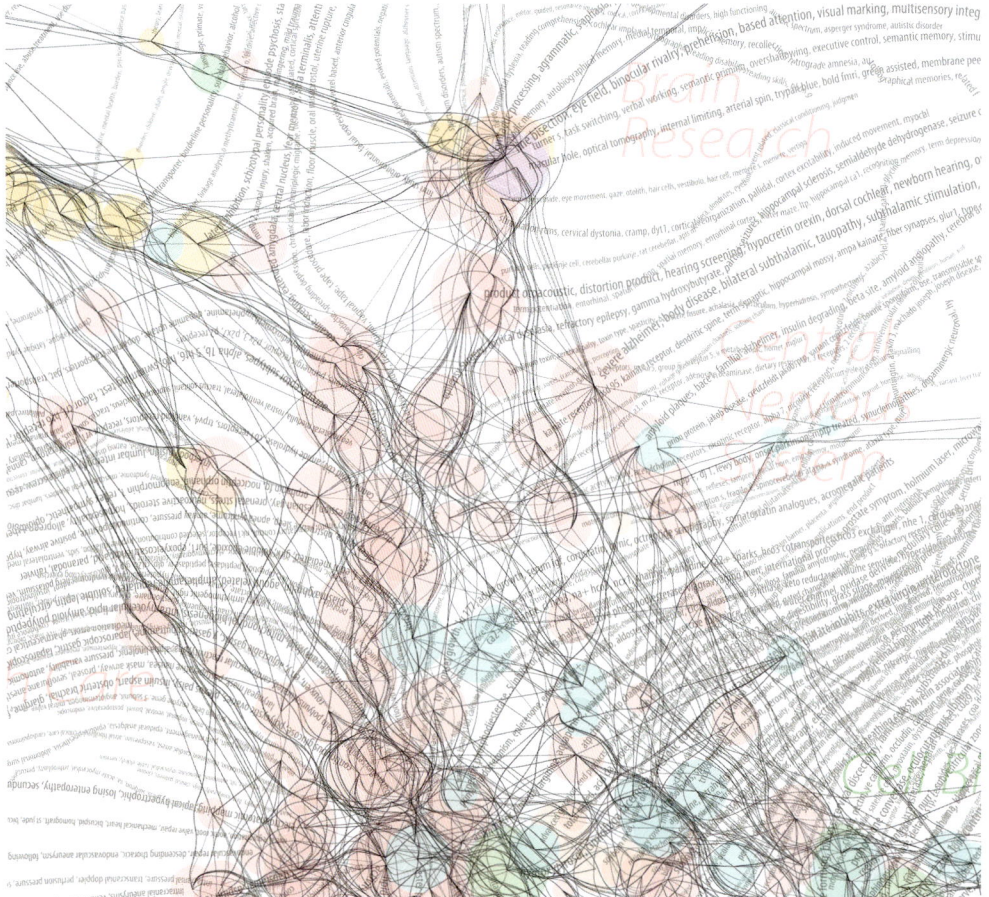

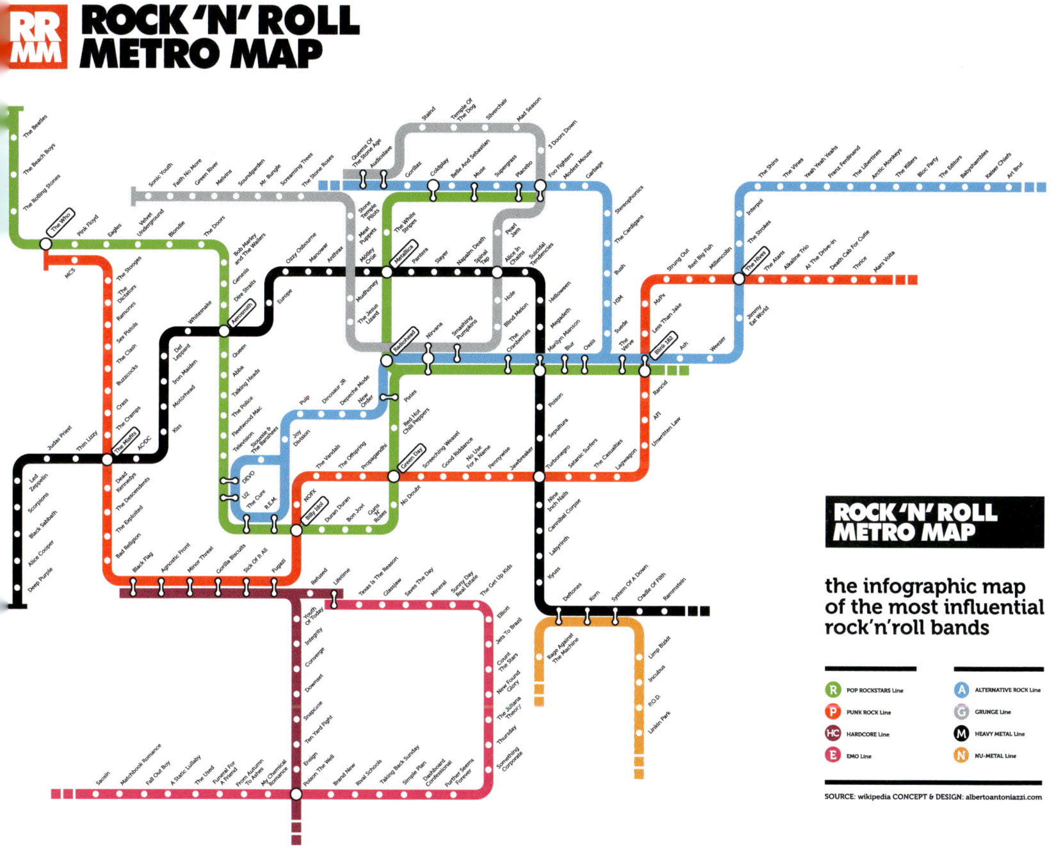

ROCK 'N' ROLL METRO MAP

ROCK 'N' ROLL METRO MAP

the infographic map of the most influential rock'n'roll bands

- **R** POP ROCKSTARS Line
- **P** PUNK ROCK Line
- **HC** HARDCORE Line
- **E** EMO Line
- **A** ALTERNATIVE ROCK Line
- **G** GRUNGE Line
- **M** HEAVY METAL Line
- **N** NU-METAL Line

SOURCE: wikipedia CONCEPT & DESIGN: albertoantoniazzi.com

Rock 'n' Roll Metro Map

This graphic is based on the idea of representing the various genres of rock music as separate lines of a subway system. The abstract tube-map here is used to describe categories of rock music: by ascribing a category to each line, the graphic creates a virtual rock-music landscape. Bands are depicted as individual stations, sometimes marking the intersection of two distinct lines. The graphic considers only bands and not single artists and defines "rock 'n' roll" as music played with drums, bass, guitar(s) and singing voice. Including more than 200 bands, the piece is Alberto Antoniazzi's personal vision of music history since the 1960s.

Project Info: Poster, 2010, Italy
Data Source: Wikipedia
Design: Alberto Antoniazzi

The Roman Alphabet

Morse Code

Binary Code

Sea Mail: We are still transmitting information via underwater cables.

··· · ·—

—— ·—· ·· ·—··

01010011 01100101 01100001
00100000 01001101 01100001
01101001 01101100

THE WORLD'S UNDERWATER CABLE:

1901
2009

SUBMARINE TELEGRAPH CABLE   SUBMARINE COMMUNICATIONS CABLE

HOW MUCH DO WE HAVE?
1 SPOOL = 40,000 MILES

25×
AROUND
THE WORLD

65×
AROUND
THE WORLD

1901   2009

Re: Then & Now

How much does it cost?

Telegram

ACCOUNTING FOR INFLATION
ONE DOLLAR IN 1901
WOULD EQUAL 25 DOLLARS IN 2009

Date 3-2-1901   No. of Words 13   Cost $13

*inter*net

MONTHLY BILL
AVERAGE TIME SPENT ONLINE: 13 HOURS

TOTAL DUE: $39 (U.S. avg)   ¢4/minute

How fast is it?

Submarine Communications Cable:
7.1 terabits/second, or:

712,118,930
IMs/sec

430,185
websites/sec

2,274,876
emails/sec

15,604
videos/sec

Transatlantic Telegraph Cable
80 to 90 words/minute, or:

TELEGRAM RECE
1.5 words/sec

IVED

Sea Mail

Already in 1901 telegrams were being transmitted globally through underwater cables. Today, underwater cables transport digital signals and assure access to data available on the Internet. The graphic compares this submarine dataflow now and in the beginning according to capacities, cable infrastructure and transmission speeds. This has been visualised by using a map chart, cable spools, service receipts and cable cross-sections.

Project Info: "Where Does the Internet Come From?", *GOOD*, magazine article, 2009, USA
Data Source: Atlantic-cable.com; Da Vinci Institute; Encyclopedia Americana; Naomi S. Baron: "Instant Messaging by American College Students"; Nielsen Company
Design: Gary Fogelson, Phil Lubliner (Fogelson-Lubliner)

The Corporate Vermin that Rules America

With an unusual political emphasis, this piece takes a stand. Produced in 2003, it shows how closely the George W. Bush administration was interwoven with major industries and business. The then president is shown in the centre as a money-driven monkey, while members of his administration are shown as cockroaches, weevils and flies all surrounding him. For the named politicians, current connections or earlier engagements with major companies are listed, with selected companies explained at the sides. The piece thus strongly suggests how political decisions in the Bush era were driven by corporate interests.

Project Info: Poster, 2003, UK
Data Source: AlterNet; Stop Esso campaign; CleanUpGE.org; Disinfopedia.org; Multinational Monitor; World Policy Institutes et al.
Design: Jonathan Barnbrook, Pedro Inoue (Barnbrook)

the corporate vermin

LOCKHEED MARTIN
$17 BILLION DEFENCE CONTRACT WITH THE U.S. GOVERNMENT

ChevronTexaco
THE SECOND-LARGEST U.S. OIL COMPANY

ExxonMobil
THE WORLD'S BIGGEST TRADED OIL COMPANY

Raytheon
$7 BILLION DEFENCE CONTRACT WITH THE U.S. GOVERNMENT

BOEING
$16.6 BILLION DEFENCE CONTRACT WITH THE U.S. GOVERNMENT

BECHTEL

NORTHROP GRUMMAN
$7 BILLION DEFENCE CONTRACT WITH THE U.S. GOVERNMENT

HALLIBURTON

KBR KELLOGG, BROWN & ROOT

SECRETARY OF THE AIR FORCE
JAMES ROCHE

CHIEF OF STAFF
ANDREW H. CARD JR.

DEFENCE SECRETARY
DONALD RUMSFELD

DEPUTY SECRETARY OF DEFENCE
PAUL WOLFOWITZ

HEALTH AND HUMAN SERVICES SECRETARY
TOMMY G. THOMPSON

INTERIOR SECRETARY
GALE NORTON

AGRICULTURE SECRETARY
ANN M. VENEMAN

TREASURY SECRETARY
PAUL O'NEILL

ENERGY SECRETARY
SPENCER ABRAHMS

DEPARTMENT OF HOMELAND SECURITY
DEPUTY SECRETARY
GORDON ENGLAND

FORMER SECRETARY OF STATE
GEORGE SCHULTZ

U.S. AMBASSADOR TO THE UNITED NATIONS
JOHN NEGROPONTE

GEORGE
PR...

DONALD L. E...

rules america

THE ENRON SCANDAL IS THE LARGEST BANKRUPTCY IN U.S. HISTORY. ENRON WAS AN ENERGY COMPANY BASED IN HOUSTON, TEXAS, WHICH BECAME ONE OF THE LARGEST U.S. COMPANIES IN ONLY 15 YEARS. WHAT WAS NOT KNOWN WAS THAT THE WHOLE COMPANY SUCCESS WAS BASED ON ARTIFICIALLY INFLATED PROFITS, ILLEGAL ACCOUNTING PRACTICES AND FRAUD. ENRON USED TO STUDY IRREGULAR AND FEDERAL REGULATIONS ABOUT THE REAL COMPANY'S FINANCIAL SITUATION AND ARTIFICIALLY BOOSTED ENRON FUND ACCOUNTS. PARTNERS OF THE COMPANY. BEFORE COLLAPSING, PARTNERS OF THE COMPANY SOLD OFF $1 BILLION IN STOCKS WHILE PREVENTING ENRON EMPLOYEES TO DO THE SAME. 75% OF THE EMPLOYEES SHARES WERE INVESTMENTS IN RETIREMENT PLANS.

WHEN THE COMPANY REVEALED ITS FINANCIAL SITUATION THE PRICE OF THE SHARES DROPPED TO 61 CENTS. ORIGINALLY $90. LEAVING EMPLOYEES WITH NOTHING. SINCE 1990 IT MADE CAMPAIGN CONTRIBUTIONS OF $5.8 MILLION. THREE QUARTERS OF IT TO REPUBLICANS. ENRON SPENT BETWEEN $2.4 MILLION AND $3.5 MILLION TO INFLUENCE TEXAS OFFICIALS IN THE LAST TWO ELECTION CYCLES. ENRON WAS ONE OF THE BIGGEST DONORS TO GEORGE BUSH GIVING HIM $113.8, 2000 FROM 1993–2000. JOHN ASHCROFT, BUSH GENERAL ATTORNEY, WAS RESISTED MORE THAN $57,000 IN CAMPAIGN CONTRIBUTIONS FROM ENRON. HE EXCLUDED HIMSELF FROM THE ENRON SCANDAL INVESTIGATION. THEY HAVE BOTH ACCUSED OF CORPORATE COMPLICITY OF HUMAN RIGHTS VIOLATIONS IN INDIA, WHERE THE COMPANY WAS DEALING WITH POWER GENERATION INDUSTRIES.

GENERAL DYNAMICS
64.9 BILLION DEFENCE CONTRACT WITH THE U.S. GOVERNMENT

GM
GENERAL MOTORS IS THE LARGEST U.S. AUTOMAKER

GE

Microsoft
COMPUTER WORLD WIDE GIANT

PHARMACIA MONSANTO
PIONEER OF GENETIC MODIFIER BIOTECHNOLOGY

CARGILL
INTERNATIONAL FOOD AND AGRICULTURAL COMPANY

Ford
SECOND LARGEST U.S. AUTOMAKER

DaimlerChrysler
THIRD LARGEST U.S. AUTOMAKER

KRAFT Altria
ALTRIA (FORMERLY PHILLIP MORRIS) CIGARETTE MANUFACTURERS

PAUL COOPER

RICHARD PERLE — FORMER CHAIR OF PENTAGON DEFENCE BOARD

KARL ROVE — SENIOR ADVISER TO GEORGE BUSH

JN POWELL — SECRETARY OF STATE

JOHN ASHCROFT — ATTORNEY GENERAL

KENNETH LAY — SENIOR ADVISER TO GEORGE BUSH

CONDOLEEZZA RICE — NATIONAL SECURITY ADVISER

BUSH

DICK CHENEY — VICE-PRESIDENT — CEO OF HALLIBURTON KBR

MRS. CHENEY — WIFE OF VICE-PRESIDENT

ELAINE CHAO — LABOUR SECRETARY

ANTHONY PRINCIPI — VETERANS AFFAIRS SECRETARY

NORMAN Y. MINETA — TRANSPORTATION SECRETARY

NELSON GIBBS — ASSISTANT SECRETARY OF THE AIR FORCE FOR INSTALLATIONS & ENVIRONMENT

RICHARD ARMITAGE — DEPARTMENT OF STATE DEPUTY SECRETARY OF STATE

PETER TEETS — DEPARTMENT OF DEFENCE UNDER SECRETARY OF THE AIR FORCE

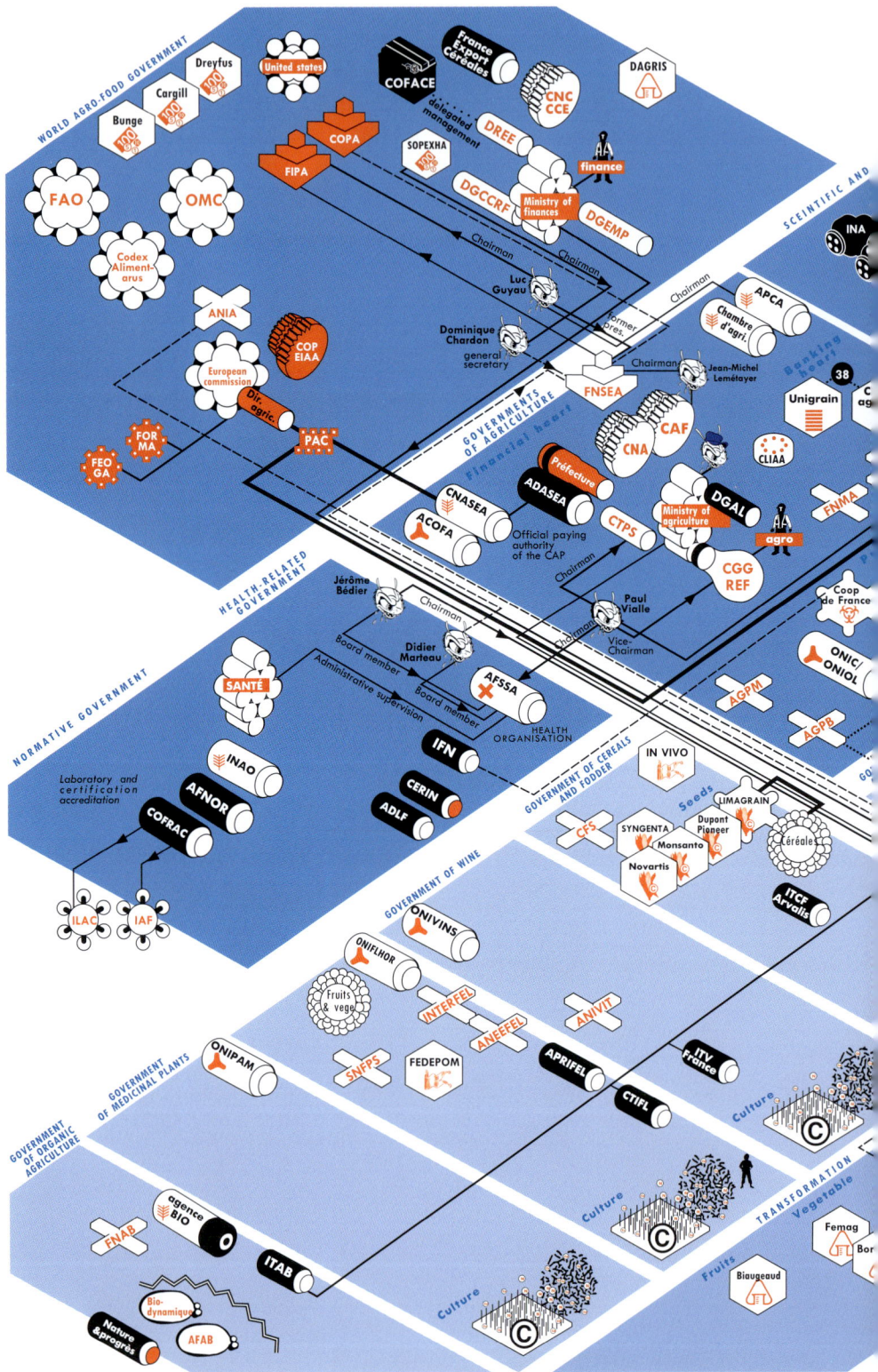

WORLD AGRO-FOOD GOVERNMENT

Dreyfus
100%
Cargill
100%
Bunge
100%

United States

COFACE

France Export Céréales

CNC CCE

DAGRIS

delegated management

DREE

SOPEXHA

finance

FAO

OMC

Codex Alimentarus

COPA

FIPA

DGCCRF

Ministry of finances

DGEMP

SCEINTIFIC AND

INA

ANIA

COP EIAA

European commission

Dir. agric.

Dominique Chardon
general secretary

Luc Guyau

Chairman

Chairman

former pres.

Chairman

APCA

Chambre d'agri.

Jean-Michel Lemétayer

Banking board

38

Unigrain

C agro

FOR MA

FEO GA

PAC

FNSEA

Chairman

CAF

CNA

CLIAA

FNMA

GOVERNMENTS OF AGRICULTURE

Financial heart

HEALTH-RELATED GOVERNMENT

CNASEA

ACOFA

ADASEA

Préfecture

Official paying authority of the CAP

CTPS

Chairman

Ministry of agriculture

agro

DGAL

CGG REF

P

Jérôme Bédier

Chairman

Didier Marteau

Board member

Administrative supervision

Board member

AFSSA

Paul Vialle

Chairman

Vice-Chairman

Coop de France

NORMATIVE GOVERNMENT

SANTÉ

INAO

AFNOR

Laboratory and certification accreditation

COFRAC

IFN

CERIN

ADLF

HEALTH ORGANISATION

GOVERNMENT OF CEREALS AND FODDER

IN VIVO

Seeds

ONIC/ ONIOL

AGPM

AGPB

GO

ILAC

IAF

CFS

SYNGENTA

Monsanto

Novartis

Dupont Pioneer

LIMAGRAIN

Céréales

ITCF Arvalis

GOVERNMENT OF WINE

ONIVINS

ONIFLHOR

Fruits & vege

INTERFEL

ANEFEL

ANIVIT

SNFPS

FEDEPOM

APRIFEL

CTIFL

ITV France

GOVERNMENT OF MEDICINAL PLANTS

ONIPAM

Culture

Culture

GOVERNMENT OF ORGANIC AGRICULTURE

agence BIO

FNAB

ITAB

Culture

TRANSFORMATION

Vegetable

Femag

Bor

Bio-dynamique

Nature &progrès

AFAB

Biaugeaud

Fruits

Culture

Government of the Agro-Food System

Bureau d'études, 2006

Institut Kepler

CNEAP

CIRAD

ANIMAL FODDER AND FERTILISER

Fertilizer

Grande Paroisse

EMC

TECA LIMAN

ERNMENT
agricultural studies

ANRT

ANVAR

Institut de l'élevage

ADAR

ACTA

Research

CEMAGREF

INRA

general director

GOVERNMENT OF POULTRY F ARMING AND FISH FARMING

IFOP

OFIMER

IFREMER

ONILAIT

GOVERNMENT OF DAIRY PRODUCTS

OCMV

FNPL

CNIEL

SEA

POULTRY

FIA

ITAVI

FACCO

Feeding

CT ICS

GOVERNMENT OF MEAT PRODUCTS

Organisation of markets

Interbev

FNB

FNPV

OFIVAL

SODIAAL

NESTLÉ

DANONE

Livestock breeding

Breeding

Viandes

ITP

Cheese

Roquefort CIGC

BEL

CIF

CGB

Financing

Financing

GOVERNMENT OF SUGAR BEET PRODUCTION

FIRS

NOUS LANTS

FOP CNIPT

ITB

ARTB

ITPT

CETIOM

SNDA

PMAF

FAI

Abattoir

CARUE

SARIA

Caillaud

OABA

SOPARIND

Fleury Michon

Unilever

Alliance végétarienne

GCIRC

Saint Louis Sucre

Sugar

KELLOGG

CNF

AFF

Flour

Grands Moulins de Paris

Kronenbourg

FCD

Pôle DISTRIB

INC

MDC

UFC que choisir

LARGE-SCALE RETAILING CHAINS

LUCIE

CARREFOUR

AUCHAN

SEMMARIS

CNC

Joint-venture initiative

MASS CONSUMPTION

CNAFAL

CNAFC

CSF

FR

ALLDC

ASSECO CFDT

Pictographic Grammar

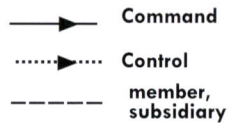

Command →

Control ·····►·····

member, subsidiary ‒ ‒ ‒ ‒

1 — dominant human organisations

Inernational organizations

ÉTATS-UNIS — State

Commission européenne / Dir agric — Regional governmental organisation

ITU — International organisation

W3C — International Non Governmental Organisation (NGO)

Central Administration

Defense États-Unis / MAAPAR — **MINISTRY** With a nine-branch ministerial structure

Outer European Or European — national

COGIC / DDAF — Ministerial management

Crisis management group

LNCR — Associated service or laboratory

CGG REF — Expert advisory body

FNLON / Institut de l'élevage — semi-public association

public service "avatar" or "sock puppet" of the administration

GI EC / DU SA — Strategic-control body

Outer European Or European — national

GI EC / GN IS — Regulatory or steering body

IA Independent authority

Outer European Or European — national

AF TN / CNE — Inspection and accreditation body

Outer European Or European — national

Préfecture — Préfecture

SIB FCE — National domain section

Establishments and organisations

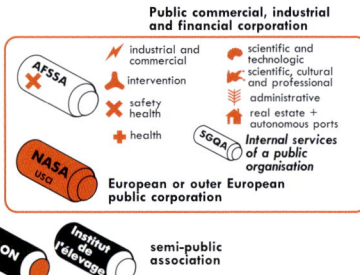

Public commercial, industrial and financial corporation

AFSSA

⚙ industrial and commercial
🛠 intervention
✖ safety health
✚ health

✖ scientific and technologic
✖ scientific, cultural and professional
administrative
real estate + autonomous ports

SGQA — *Internal services of a public organisation*

NASA usa — **European or outer European public corporation**

Grignon — **Educational and training establishments**
SUP *Higher education and research*

COFACE — **Export credit bureaus**
ECBs provide loans, guarantees and insurance to export businesses and commercial banks based in their home countries, protecting them against the risks of foreign buyers or debtors failing to respect contracts for political or commercial reasons.

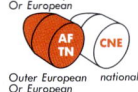

CNR ACL — **Public social security, pension and health corporation**

geno plante / ESA — **Public / private group**
Consortium
Scientific interest group SIG
Commercial interests group CIG
Public interests group PIG

Outer European Or European

2 — Human organisation in conflict with the state complex or in a minority position

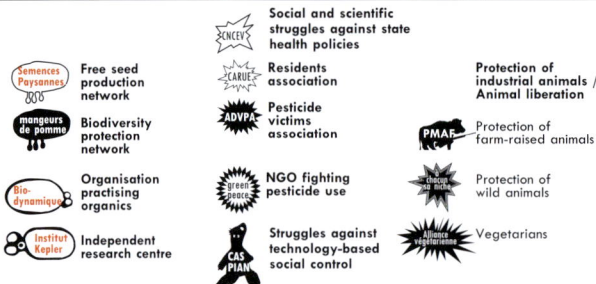

Semences Paysannes — Free seed production network

mangeurs de pomme — Biodiversity protection network

Bio-dynamique — Organisation practising organics

Institut Kepler — Independent research centre

CNCEV — Social and scientific struggles against state health policies

CARUE — Residents association

ADVPA — Pesticide victims association

green peace — NGO fighting pesticide use

CAS PIAN — Struggles against technology-based social control

PMAF — Protection of farm-raised animals

chacun sa niche — Protection of wild animals

Alliance végétarienne — Vegetarians

Protection of industrial animals / Animal liberation

3 — Technical an

Social and economic organisati

Social organisations

CFS — Interest group / National professional association

ISTA — International professional federation

COPA — Confederation of labour organisations

Production organisati

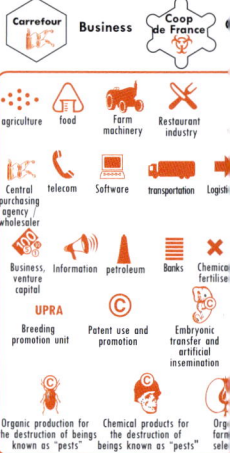

Carrefour — Business — Coop de France

agriculture / food / Farm machinery / Restaurant industry

Central purchasing agency wholesaler / telecom / Software / transportation / Logisti

Business, venture capital / Information / petroleum / Banks / Chemical fertilise

UPRA — Breeding promotion unit

© Patent use and promotion

Embryonic transfer and artificial insemination

© Organic production for the destruction of beings known as "pests"

© Chemical products for the destruction of beings known as "pests"

Org farm sele

5 — Human being

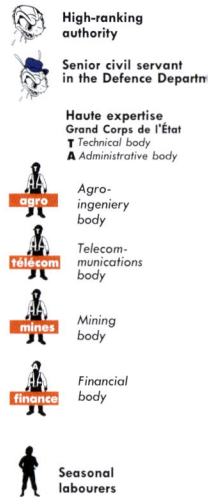

High-ranking authority

Senior civil servant in the Defence Departm

Haute expertise
Grand Corps de l'État
T Technical body
A Administrative body

agro — Agro-ingeniery body

télécom — Telecom-munications body

mines — Mining body

finance — Financial body

Seasonal labourers

.... **Management delegation**

----- **Co-operation**

2,2 → y **Percentage of property:**
x holds 2,2% of y

⋀⋀⋀ **Line of struggle between antagonistic forces**

olic systems

Large-scale technical systems

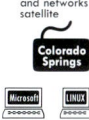

Transportation network
Information transportation
S satellite
W Internet (network of networks)

European satellite and networks of satellite

RA radar

Physical transportation
R Highways
F Railways

American satellite and networks of satellite

Colorado Springs

Calculation centre

Microsoft **LINUX** **Operating system used in the information system**

National pressure group (lobby)

International pressure group (lobby)

Think tank

Labour organisation

AGRI STAT **Information processing system**

WGS 84 **Geodesic referencing system**
■ National or european
■ American

STICS **Simulation device**

Satellite captor

NAC **Electronic identification**

Large-scale symbolic systems

| Legal-administrative systems | Financial system |

PAC **HA CCP** **Programme, plan or project**
non-european or european

ADPIC **Contract, accord, treaty, law, decree code...**
non-european or european

CIE **DAB** **Identity card or certificate**

NFV01-005 **Norm**

FAC **Fund**

FEO GA **Income tax, other taxes, allocations, lotteries**
non european or european

Research

Resa path **Laboratory animalery**

High security Laboratory (pathogens class 2, 3, 4)

Agro pôle **Research network**

Competitiveness pole

electronics

nuclear

Aerospace industry

Vaccine producers and animal medicine

Meat sector abattoirs

4 — Waste products

Sludge

Manure

Collective sludge
Annually in France: 900.000 tonnes sludge from sewage, 600.000 tonnes from the dredging of ditches, rivers and canals; 300.000 tonnes of animal slurry. Animal waste represents 94 % of all agricultural manuring.

✝ **Individual sludge**
15 to 20 kg per person per year of sludge (dry matter). 60% of the tonnage of dry matter is used in farm manuring.

Nutriments

(N) **Nitrogen**
Nitrogen (periodic symbol N) changes its chemical composition very easily, through association with oxygen or hydrogen molecules. Nitrogen and hydrogen form ammonia (NH4). Nitrogen, by consuming oxygen, forms nitrates (NO2 or NO3).

(P) **Phosphorus**
Nitrogen and phosphorus are the basic ingredients of fertilisers.

(A) **Ammonia**
95% of ammonia emissions come from agriculture, of which 80% come from livestock farming.

Micro-pollutants

(Cd) **Cadmium**
89% of cadmium contamination of French soil is caused by fertilisers.

(Zn) **Zinc**
69% of zinc contamination of French soil is caused by pig manure.

(Cu) **Copper**
92% of copper contamination of French soil is caused by pesticides.

6 — Non-human beings

Plant life

Plants reproduced by humans for eating

(C) **Licensed or certified seeds of plant clones**

Unlicensed plant seeds

Cultivated fields with licensed seeds

Freely reproducing plants considered detrimental

Thistles
Plant able to accumulated large quantities of nitrates.

Nettles

Couch grass
Considered one of the most undesirable weeds because of the fact that it has invaded 37 different crops in 65 countries. Certain natural chemical substances extracted from couch grass have shown insecticidal properties against mosquito larvae and molluscs, particularly slugs.

Animals

Animals reproduced by humans for eating

(C) **Horses**

(C) **Cattle**
4,15 million dairy cows. 4,3 million suckling calves.

(C) **Goats**
5,2 million milk ewes. 1,4 million suckling kids. 800 000 goats.

(C) **Poultry**

(C) **Pigs**
15 million head

(C) **Fish**

Insects and micro-organisms reproduced for biological struggle

(C) **Bacillus thuringiensis**
Beauveria bassiana
Trichogram

Freely reproducing animals considered pests

Mouse **moths** **aphids**

Fieldmice

moles **slugs** **spiders**

Genetic capital

Genetic databanks

FNR **Breeding databanks**

CCV EGC **Catalogue of licensed plant clones**

CCV EGC **Plant databank**

Conservatory of plant varieties

Intensification devices

SNAG **Breeding improvement scheme**

IBOVAL **Animal selection criteria**

DHS **Plant selection criteria**

Previous spreads

The French Agro-Food System

French artist group Bureau d'études conducts conceptual research into social and economic systems. The results of their findings are conveyed in complex diagrams. The artists conceive of their diagrams as a compass through a given economico-political system. This piece is a series of four diagrams on economic and political interrelations in French agriculture, with an accompanying legend, the *Pictographic Grammar* (p.400–401). The diagrams are based on elements that symbolise institutions, groups, laws etc., which are explained in the *Pictographic Grammar*. The allocation of the symbols on a virtual map shows certain invisible relations between different players in the field, whilst interlinking lines further explain these relations.

Project Info: Series of diagrams, Le Bon Accueil Contemporary Art Space, 2006, France
Artists: Bureau d'études

This is Indexed

In her blog, *This is Indexed*, Jessica Hagy uses little hand-drawn infographics "to make fun of some things and sense of others without resorting to doing actual math". Started in August 2006, she has published one piece every week-day. Index cards, the analogue data-carrier for little bits of information, afford the background to her reflecting by charting. Over time, certain formats have evolved as Hagy's favourites: 1. the set diagram of overlapping circles showing as-yet-undetected intersections between things; 2. the simple two-axis diagram showing an X in relation to a Y; 3. the polygon made of lines, representing multiple connections in a problematic chaos.

Project Info: *This is Indexed* blog, since 2006, USA
Design: Jessica Hagy

Diagram 1 (Venn): high school | A = doing what others want | B = the office

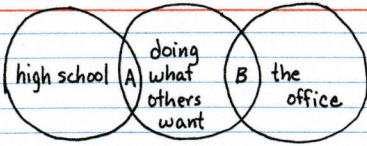

A = Giving in to peer pressure

B = Being a team player

Diagram 2 (graph): Prestige & Money vs. Time

A
C
B

A = Your intended career path

B = Your actual career path

C = Why you drink

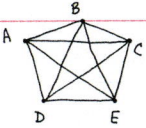

Diagram 3 (pentagon network A B C D E):

A = Suppliers
B = New Entrants
C = Rivalry
D = Substitutes
E = Customers

$\overline{AB}$ = People smugglers
$\overline{AC}$ = ESPN
$\overline{AD}$ = Asking for wooden toys for Xmas
$\overline{AE}$ = Swap meet
$\overline{BC}$ = Baby brother
$\overline{BD}$ = Trading the convertible for a van
$\overline{BE}$ = Tweens
$\overline{CD}$ = Cola wars
$\overline{CE}$ = Cat fight at the sample sale
$\overline{DE}$ = Winning the lottery

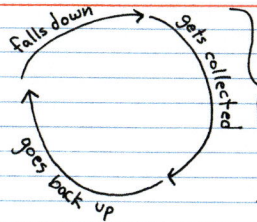

Diagram 4 (water cycle):

falls down — gets collected — goes back up

The Water Cycle
-or-
Persistence

Diagram 5 (equations):

(A > B) = Stagnation

(A = B) = Implementation

(A < B) = Imagination

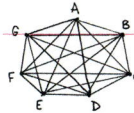

A = Reality

B = Ideas

Diagram 6 (network A B C D E F G):

A = Chastity
B = Generosity
C = Moderation
D = Diligence
E = Kindness
F = Patience
G = Modesty

$\overline{AB}$ = Hand job
$\overline{AC}$ = Tease
$\overline{AD}$ = Thinking about baseball
$\overline{AE}$ = Pity date
$\overline{AF}$ = After Prom
$\overline{AG}$ = Granny panties
$\overline{BC}$ = Buying gifts on sale
$\overline{BD}$ = Kissing up to your boss
$\overline{BE}$ = Complimenting bad art
$\overline{BF}$ = Waiting for your rich aunt to die
$\overline{BG}$ = Lending the stripper your coat
$\overline{CD}$ = Procrastination
$\overline{CE}$ = 15% Tip
$\overline{CF}$ = Occasional Outbursts
$\overline{CG}$ = Just a little cleavage
$\overline{DE}$ = Forced Smiles
$\overline{DF}$ = Making license plates in prison
$\overline{DG}$ = Always wearing your eye-patch
$\overline{EF}$ = Your friend's Pampered Chef party
$\overline{EG}$ = Keep the door closed, Mom.
$\overline{FG}$ = Holding in a toot

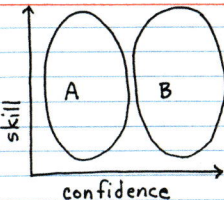

Diagram 7 (graph skill vs confidence):

A = wannabe
B = rock star

Diagram 8 (Venn): Economic Trouble | A | Willingness to take Risks | Optimism about Love

Diagram 9 (Venn): Unwilling to take risks | B | Economic Advantage | Pessimism about Love

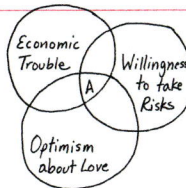

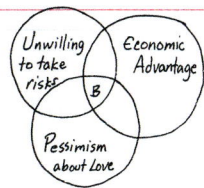

A = Mail Order Bride

B = Who she's going to marry

Two Mindsets

Dr. Carol Dweck is a psychology professor at Stanford University. According to her there are two major views on where ability comes from – while some people believe their abilities can be improved by working hard, others believe that success comes from innate abilities. Both mindsets can be recognised by how they deal with failures and setbacks. Nigel Holmes' graphic is a great example of how a visualisation can have the power to allow quick access to a complex theory. Both mindsets are set opposite each other, and in a series of steps the piece explains how someone with a fixed mindset will constantly find his deterministic world-view confirmed by not using opportunities to grow.

Project Info: *Stanford*, magazine article, 2007, USA
Data Source: Carol Dweck: "Mindset: The New Psychology of Success", 2006
Design: Nigel Holmes

Following spread

Tree World

This graphic originally appeared as a sequence of two double spreads in the Brazilian magazine *Superinteressante*. It explains how a rainforest tree is home to numerous species and an ecosystem of its own. The large tree is imagined and shown from top to bottom, with some animals and plants just named, others accompanied by brief texts. The bubbles work like magnifying lenses, showing the animals in detail. While each animal is shown in relation to the part of the tree where it lives, the image is not meant to be an accurate map. Rather, the tree is the background for presenting individual animals that live together and sometimes depend on each other in a confined natural space.

Project Info: *Superinteressante*, poster, 2007, Brazil
Research: Yuri Vasconscelos, Sergio Gwercman
Art Direction: Adriano Sambugaro
Illustration: Eber Evangelista, Luiz Iria
Awards: Malofiej 2008; Premio Abril de Jornalismo 2008

TWO MINDSETS

CAROL S. DWECK, Ph.D.

Graphic by
Nigel Holmes

Fixed Mindset
Intelligence is static

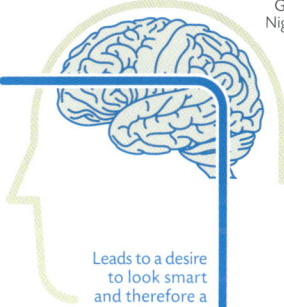

Growth Mindset
Intelligence can be developed

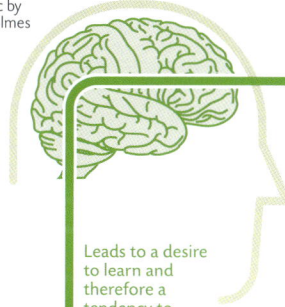

Leads to a desire
to look smart
and therefore a
tendency to...

Leads to a desire
to learn and
therefore a
tendency to...

CHALLENGES

...avoid
challenges

...embrace
challenges

OBSTACLES

...give up
easily

...persist in the
face of setbacks

EFFORT

...see effort as
fruitless or worse

...see effort as
the path to mastery

CRITICISM

...ignore useful
negative feedback

...learn from
criticism

SUCCESS OF OTHERS

...feel threatened
by the success
of others

...find lessons and
inspiration in the
success of others

As a result, they may plateau early
and achieve less than their full potential.

As a result, they reach ever-higher levels of achievement.

All this confirms a **deterministic view of the world.**

All this gives them a **greater sense of free will.**

405

MUNDO ÁRVORE

UMA ÚNICA ÁRVORE PODE ABRIGAR UM ECOSSISTEMA COMPLEXO – DAS DEZENAS DE SERES VIVOS QUE HABITAM A ÁGUA ACUMULADA NAS BROMÉLIAS AOS TUCANOS QUE FAZEM DO CAULE SEU NINHO DE AMOR. ABAIXO, SELECIONAMOS COMO MORADA UMA ESPÉCIE FICTÍCIA DA MATA ATLÂNTICA E APRESENTAMOS OS ANIMAIS E AS PLANTAS QUE DEPENDEM DELA PARA SOBREVIVER.

TEXTO YURI VANCONCELOS INFOGRAFIA LUIZ IRIA E ÉBER EVANGELISTA DESIGN ADRIANO SAMBUGARO EDIÇÃO SÉRGIO GWERCMAN (sgwercman@abril.com.br)

ABELHA-CACHORRO
Não morde ninguém: é desprovida de ferrão. Constrói na copa das árvores ninhos de barro e cera parecidos com cupinzeiros e se alimenta da seiva das plantas.

seiva
ninho da abelha-cachorro

MORCEGO-DE-FRUTAS
A vida passa pelo intestino do morcego: ele come frutas, voa e defeca as sementes. Das fezes, nascerá uma nova árvore.

FORMIGA CAÇAREMA
Milhares de espécies de formigas vivem em árvores. A caçarema se alimenta de gotículas de néctar eliminadas pelos ramos. Em troca, protege a planta de pragas como pulgões e cochonilhas.

cochonilhas

SABIÁ-CICA
Costuma ser visto na parte superior da copa. Mas, na hora de fazer o ninho, prefere buracos no tronco. Lá encontra suas comidas prediletas: sementes, insetos e larvas.

tiê-sangue

MOSCA ANASTREPHA FRATERCULUS
As larvas começam a vida nos frutos. Quando crescem, não mudam de bairro: voam sempre ao redor das árvores da vizinhança.

larvas
fruta

GATO-MARACAJÁ
O mais arborícola dos felinos gasta as manhãs dormindo nos galhos. À noite, vai tocar a vida: come passarinhos, roedores e acasala. Mas a vida pode trazer surpresas: há sempre o risco de um ataque dos temíveis saguís.

CUÍCA
Parente do gamba, esse pequeno marsupial costuma ser encontrado na copa das árvores, onde caça os insetos que gosta de comer. Raramente desce ao chão.

VESPA
Também chamada de marimbondo, poliniza as flores das orquídeas e usa os galhos para pendurar seu ninho.

dormideira

IGUANA-VERDE
Quando filhote, ela tira dos galhos os insetos que come. Adulta, torna-se vegetariana: passa a se alimentar apenas de folhas.

BICHO-PREGUIÇA-DE-COLEIRA
As folhas alimentam e protegem: quando não estão na boca, ajudam a preguiça a se camuflar de predadores como a harpia e o gavião.

COBRA-DE-VEADO
Também conhecida como suaçubóia, vive enrolada em galhos. Lagartos, aves e roedores que aparecem quando bate a fome são mortos por constrição.

orquídeas
saguis
bromélia
ninho de vespas
lagarto-papa-vento

PERERECA MARSUPIAL
A fêmea carrega os ovos nas costas até que os girinos estejam prestes a nascer. Então ela os transfere para a água nas bromélias. E fica por lá para comer: o lugar é ótimo para caçar insetos.

TUCANO-DE-PAPO-AMARELO
Os tucanos fazem do tronco seu ninho de amor. É lá que eles se encontram. Ali o macho oferece um fruto. Se a corte é aceita, eles realizam a cópula. Tudo dura alguns segundos.

ARANHA ARANEUS
Faz belíssimas teias geométricas na folhagem. E se aproveita da diversidade que habita as árvores para capturar suas presas.

RÃ-BUGIO
Esta perereca esverdeada usa os galhos para acasalar. A fêmea coloca os ovos nas folhas, que depois são dobradas em forma de tubo para proteger os futuros filhotes.

bromélia
girinos

ovos

SAGÜI-DA-SERRA
Na hora das refeições, raspa o tronco com os dentes para se alimentar da seiva. Costuma viver em grupos de 5 a 15 animais.

seiva

MONO-CARVOEIRO
Também chamado de muriqui, é encontrado somente na mata Atlântica. Chega a 15 kg – é o maior primata do continente americano.

BESOURO
Com cerca de 6 cm, vive na mata e sobe nas árvores para se alimentar. Come a resina que escorre de cortes no tronco ou frutas em decomposição.

resina

MICO-LEÃO-DE-CARA-DOURADA
Vive trepado nas árvores e se alimenta de insetos e frutos. À noite, para se manter protegido de seus predadores, procura abrigo em buracos dos troncos.

CIPÓS
Crescem no solo e se agarram às árvores ainda pequenas. Quando elas crescem, os cipós pegam carona. Lá do alto, ajudam animais a se locomover entre as copas.

PICA-PAU-REI
Considerado o maior pica-pau do Brasil, com 36 cm e 200 g, faz seu ninho em ocos nos troncos. Na hora das refeições, martela o tronco com força, perfura a casca e captura insetos com a língua pegajosa de ponta afiada.

ARANHA-CARANGUEJEIRA
As caranguejeiras do gênero *Lasiodora* são as mais comuns na mata Atlântica. Fazem seus ninhos no pé das árvores, sob folhas secas.

LACRAIA
Dá expediente na casca do tronco, onde caça pequenos insetos. Chega a medir 7 cm.

CUPINS
Suas colônias abrigam milhares de indivíduos de paladar duvidoso: comem tanto a árvore viva quanto troncos mortos sobre o solo.

BROMÉLIA
É a comunidade hippie da árvore: na água entre as folhas se reúnem insetos, larvas e qualquer um que queira compartilhar a bebida.

BORBOLETA
Tem asas tão verdes que se confundem com as folhas da mata. Frutas fermentadas servem como fonte de néctar que ela utiliza como alimento.

MUSGO
Um centro de gosmas: o tapete verde sobre o tronco serve de alimento e abrigo para sapos, lesmas e caracóis. Mas pelo menos o efeito visual é bonito.

orelha-de-pau

CIGARRAS
Quando as ninfas nascem, ficam enterradas no solo e se alimentam da seiva da raiz. Adultas, sobem na vida: costumam ser vistas na copa.

ovos

ninfa

seiva

MACACO-PREGO-DE-PEITO-AMARELO
Faz o tipo caseiro: raramente sai das árvores. Ele come, reproduz e descansa nos galhos. Só vai ao chão para beber.

MINHOCA
Seu deslocamento cria galerias que ajudam a drenagem do solo. Assim, a água penetra na terra e alimenta a raiz.

Fontes: Adriano Paglia, Afrânio Augusto Guimarães, Carlos Brisola Marcondes, Carlos Campaner, Carlos Eniicker Lamas, Dante Pavan, Eduardo Wienskoski, Eliana Marques Cancello, Felipe Toledo, Flávio Gandara, Helenice Mercier, Jaime Aparecido Bertolucci, Luís Fábio Silveira, Odair Correa Bueno, Osmar Malaspina, Raquel Lima da Silveira, Rogélio Dosouto, Rosângela Branchini, Sandra Regina Visnadi, Tasso Leo Krugner.

Are mammograms important?

average size of breast tumor
at diagnosis in early 1980s
when only 13% of women were
getting regular mammograms

average size of breast tumor
at diagnosis in late 1990s
when 60% of women were
getting regular mammograms

Source: American Cancer Society

Understanding Healthcare

In *Understanding Healthcare*, Richard Saul Wurman created a visual encyclopedia of healthcare in the US. Like his earlier books, it is driven by the quest to structure all relevant information and statistics in a way that allows the reader to understand the complex topic without any further prerequisites. Every double spread tackles one specific question. The book is divided into three chapters. "Understanding Yourself" covers the human body. "Understanding Them" introduces the professionals involved with healthcare. The third chapter is a practical guide to the US healthcare system. All graphics were developed in cooperation between Wurman and a range of graphic designers, creating an individual look for each chapter.

Project Info: *Understanding Healthcare*, book, 2004, USA
Data Source: UNDP Human Development Report, 2002; National Vital Statistics Report, 2002; US Bureau of Census; American Cancer Society; Centers for Disease Control adn Prevention, 2003; *To Err is Human: Building a Safer Health System*, National Academy Press, 1999; Archives of Family Medicine
Research: Loren Appel
Concept / Art Direction: Richard Saul Wurman
Design: Various designers. Examples shown here by Nigel Holmes, Richard Saul Wurman

Life expectancy in the United States...

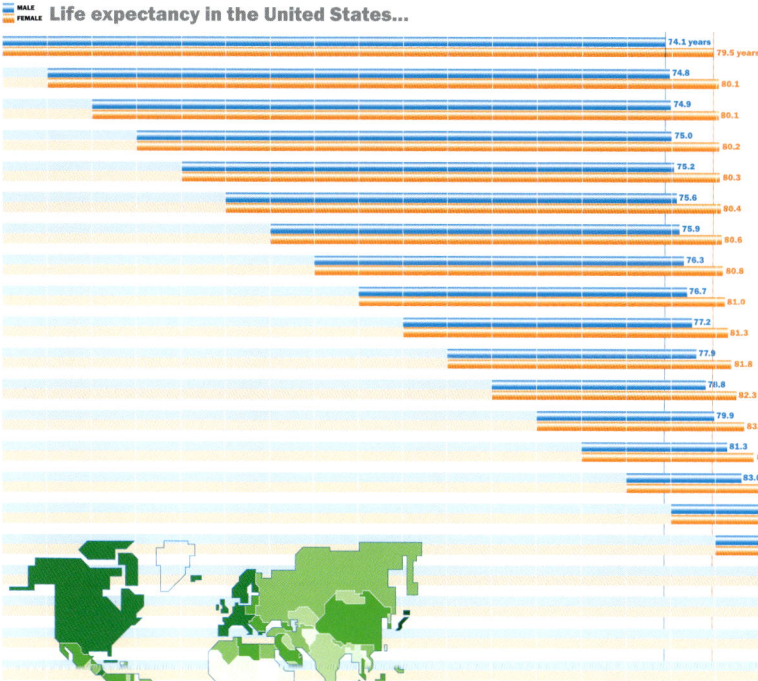

▬ MALE
▬ FEMALE

Age	Male	Female
at birth	74.1 years	79.5 years
5 yrs	74.8	80.1
10	74.9	80.1
15	75.0	80.2
20	75.2	80.3
25	75.6	80.4
30	75.9	80.6
35	76.3	80.8
40	76.7	81.0
45	77.2	81.3
50	77.9	81.8
55	78.8	82.3
60	79.9	83.1
65	81.3	84.2
70	83.0	85.5
75	85.2	87.1
80	87.6	89.1
85	90.6	92.7
90	94.2	94.8
95	98.1	99.5
100	101.4	102.7

How long can we live?

Horace Deets, former Executive Director of the AARP, was often how long we can live. His answer was: **121 years.** When asked how he knew this, he replied that a Frenchwoman, Jeanne Calment, had lived to that age.

THE 100 CLUB
Projected number of centenarians in the US

Year	Number
2000	72,000
2010	131,000
2020	214,000
2030	324,000
2040	447,000
2050	834,000

Source: U.S. Bureau of the Census

...and in the rest of the world

Source: UNDP Human Development Report, 2002

KEY Years of life expectancy, at birth

Representative countries:
- 80–85 Japan
- 75–80 N. America, W.Europe
- 70–75 China
- 65–70 Russia
- 60–65 India
- 55–60
- under 55 Most of Africa
- n/a

Men, at birth: **74.1 years**
Women, at birth: **79.5 years**

Source for main chart: National Vital Statistics Report, 2002. Numbers are for 2000, all races, both sexes.

Top 10 causes of death in the US, by

① ② ③ ④

age	1	2	3	4
1 – 4	accidents	congenital defects	cancer	homicide
	deaths 1,826	495	420	356
5 – 14	accidents	cancer	congenital defects	homicide
	2,979	1,014	399	371
15 – 24	accidents	homicide	suicide	cancer
	14,113	4,939	4,646	1,713
25 – 44	accidents	cancer	heart disease	suicide
	27,182	20,436	16,139	11,354
45 – 64	cancer	heart disease	accidents	cerebro-vascular diseases
	137,039	98,879	19,783	15,967
65 – 74	cancer	heart disease	lower respiratory diseases	cerebro-vascular diseases
	150,131	122,405	31,157	23,649
75	heart disease	cancer	cerebro-vascular diseases	lower respiratory diseases
	471,302	242,235	124,396	75,218

National Vital Statistics Report, 2002.
...are for 2000, all races, both sexes.

6	**7**	**8**	**9**	**10**	age
...monia and 'flu	septicemia	prenatal conditions	benign neoplasms	lower respiratory diseases	**1** ↕ **4**
...03	99	79	53	51	
...art ...ease	lower respiratory diseases	benign neoplasms	pneumonia and 'flu	cerebrovascular diseases	**5** ↕ **14**
...71	139	99	87	76	
...enital ...ects	cerebrovascular diseases	pneumonia and flu	diabetes mellitus	human immuno-deficiency virus	**15** ↕ **24**
...71	199	189	162	144	
...icide	chronic liver disease	cerebrovascular diseases	diabetes mellitus	pneumonia and 'flu	**25** ↕ **44**
...383	3,786	3,201	2,549	1,068	
...ic liver ...ease	lower respiratory diseases	suicide	human immuno-deficiency virus	nephritis	**45** ↕ **64**
...428	13,990	8,336	4,142	3,100	
...dents	pneumonia and flu	nephritis	septicemia	chronic liver disease	**65** ↕ **74**
...698	7,189	6,990	5,704	5,482	
...eimer's	diabetes mellitus	nephritis	accidents	septicemia	**75** ↕
...462	35,740	24,235	23,353	19,082	

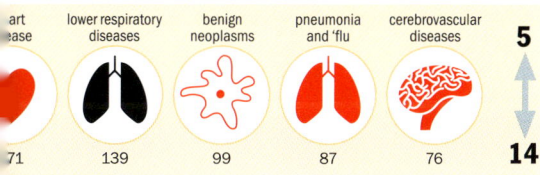

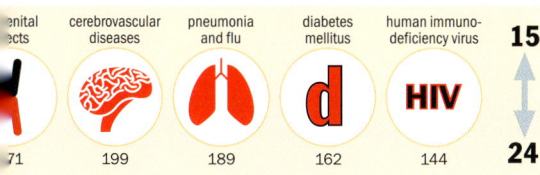

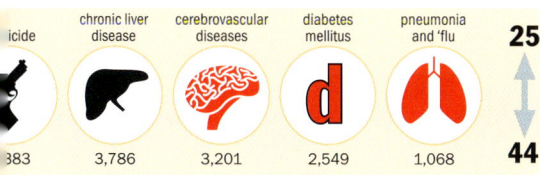

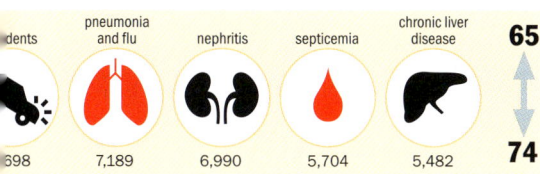

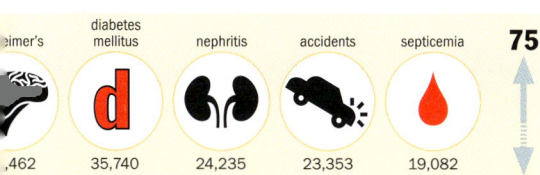

What are the leading causes of death?

Overall, they are:

①
heart disease
710,760 deaths; 29.6% of total deaths

②
cancer
553,091; 23.0%

③
cerebro-vascular diseases
167,661; 7.0%

④
lower respiratory diseases
122,009; 5.1%

⑤
accidents
97,900; 4.1%

⑥
diabetes mellitus
69,301; 2.9%

⑦
pneumonia and 'flu
65,313; 2.7%

⑧
Alzheimer's
49,558; 2.1%

⑨
nephritis
37,251; 1.3%

⑩
septicemia
31,224; 1.3%

The diseases people fear most are not necessarily the ones most likely to kill them.
For instance, in a survey of women aged 25 or older, these were what they perceived to be their greatest health problems:

BREAST CANCER	34%
STROKE	1%
HEART DISEASE	7%

…but, at the time of the survey, the actual number of deaths from these causes were:

BREAST CANCER	43,000
STROKE	97,500
HEART DISEASE	234,000

Source: *Archives of Family Medicine.*

We Feel Fine

For this interactive project, blogs around the world are searched for the phrases "I feel" and "I am feeling". When these words occur, the full sentence is recorded. Where possible, the age, gender and geographical location of the author are also extracted, as well as the local weather. This rich database is visualised in six modes, available by way of the navigation lower left. The colour of each dot corresponds to a particular type of feeling, and the diameter indicates the length of the sentence inside. *Madness* shows a swirl of particles, while *Murmurs* simply lists feelings. *Montage* shows entries that include an image. The pink bar at the top opens a panel which allows the feelings on display to be filtered at any time.

Project Info: Interactive visualisation, 2005, USA
Design: Jonathan Harris, Sep Kamvar

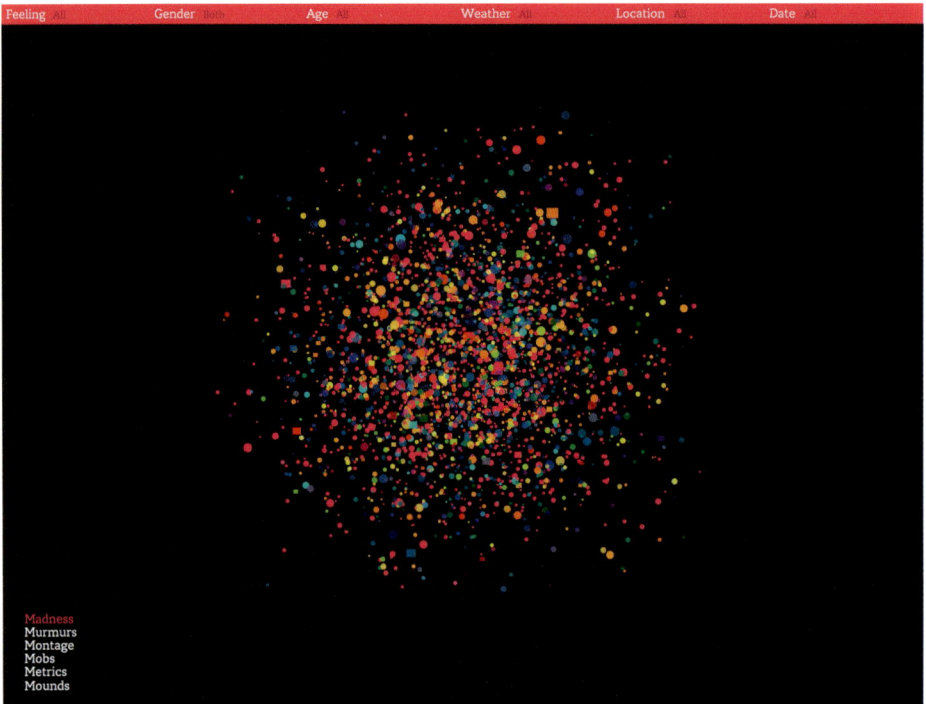

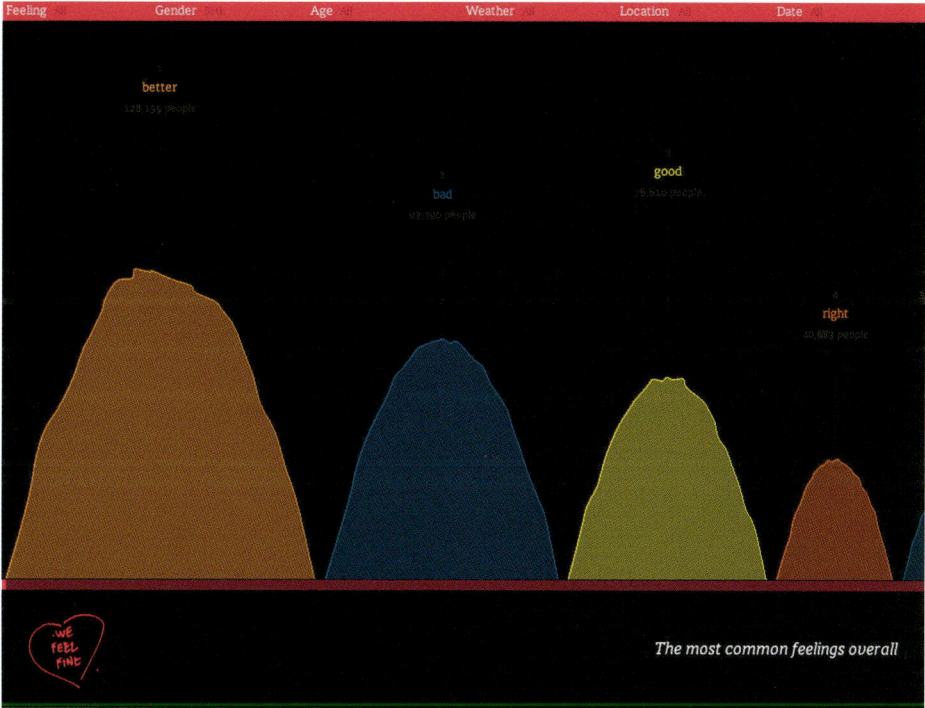

The most common feelings overall

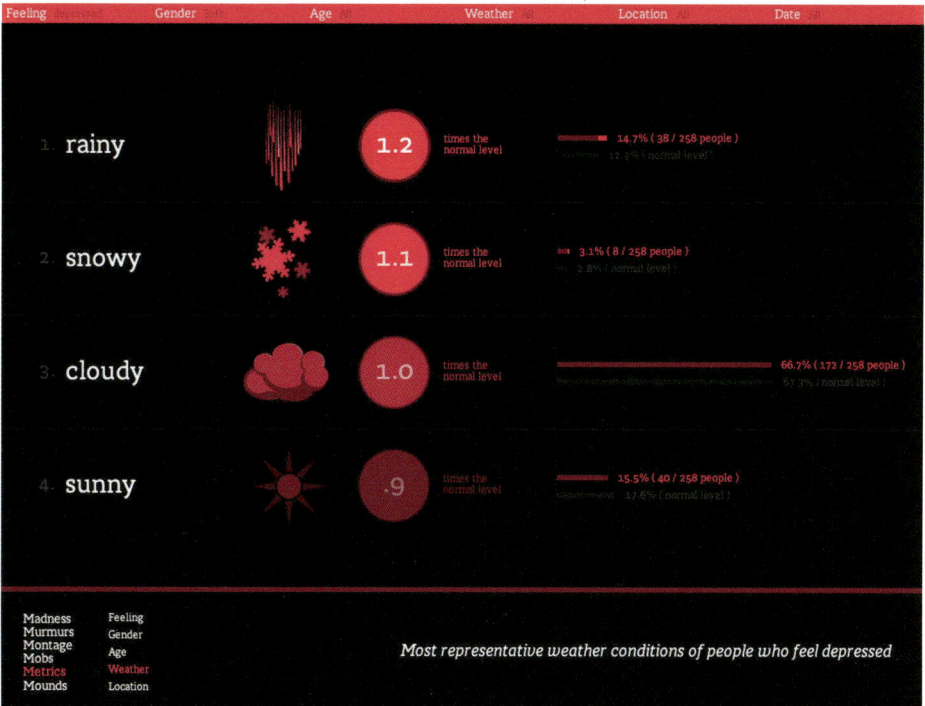

Most representative weather conditions of people who feel depressed

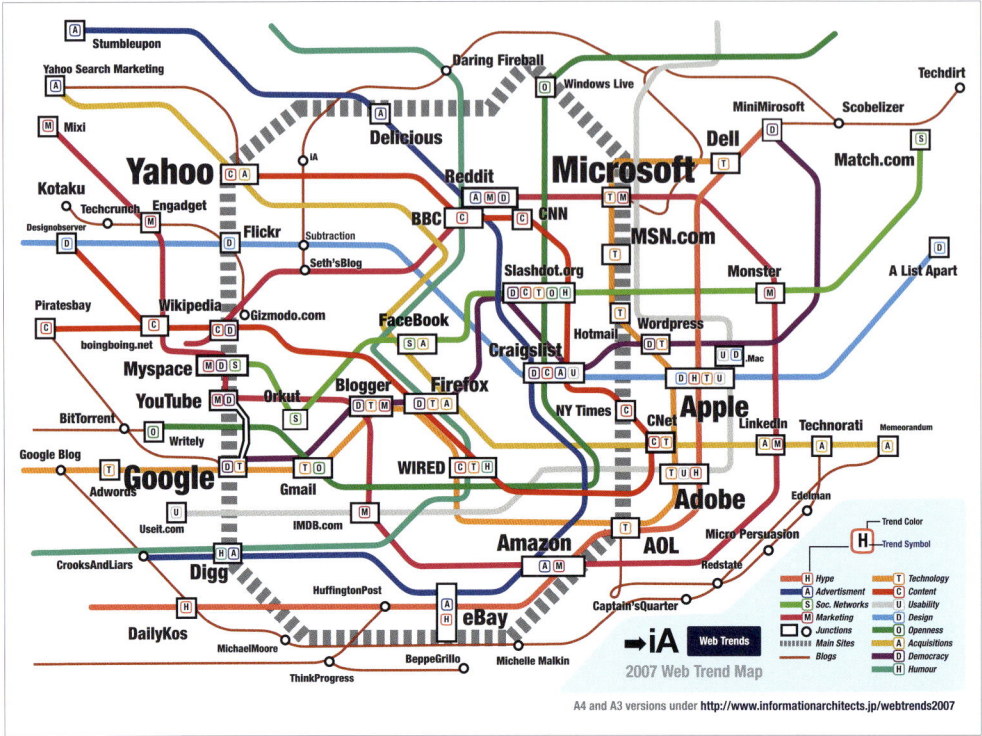

Web Trend Map

Tokyo-based Information Architects developed this piece in 2006 and since then have updated it annually. It categorises online services according to type of business. Categories are shown as subway lines, with each domain being one tube station, with the station symbol showing both the stability (width) and degree of success (height) of each service. Stations are arranged according to popularity (distance from the centre). While the earlier versions were largely based on the actual Tokyo subway map, the 2010 version employs an individual isometric design. Despite being called a map, it does not allocate information to specific places. Rather, domains are categorised using the metaphor of subway lines. The ranking along the bottom adds a hierarchy for some of the domains above.

Project Info: Series of posters, website, 2006–2010, Japan / Switzerland
Data Source: Alexa; Compete; comScore; Crowdsourcing; Nielsen NetRatings
Research: Chris Luescher
Design: Oliver Reichenstein, Takeshi Tanka, Matt Gerber (Information Architects)

Web Trend Map

→iA

WHAT IT IS

iA's Web Trend Map plots the leading Internet names onto the Tokyo Metro system.

The domains and personalities are carefully selected through dialogue with map enthusiasts. Each domain is evaluated based on traffic, revenue, age, owner and character.

Paying attention to the intersections, we grouped associated websites and ensured every domain is on a line that suits it. As a result, the map produces a web of associations: some provocative, some curious, others ironically accurate.

As a few examples: Twitter is located in Shibuya, the train station with the biggest buzz. Google and its network are placed around Shinjuku, the most highly trafficked station in the world. The New York Times is located in Sugamo, the shopping paradise for Tokyo's grandmothers.

Why Tokyo Metro? Because it works.

HOW IT'S USED

You can evaluate a domain based on its station's height, width and position.

The height represents the domain's success according to traffic, revenue and media attention.

The width illustrates the stability of the domain as a business entity. Yet not every heavyweight property has a large building. Unless it has proven itself as a significant online component, its station remains thin.

The position on the map—whether inside, on, or outside the main line—indicates if it belongs to the tech establishment, the major traffic hubs or the online suburbs.

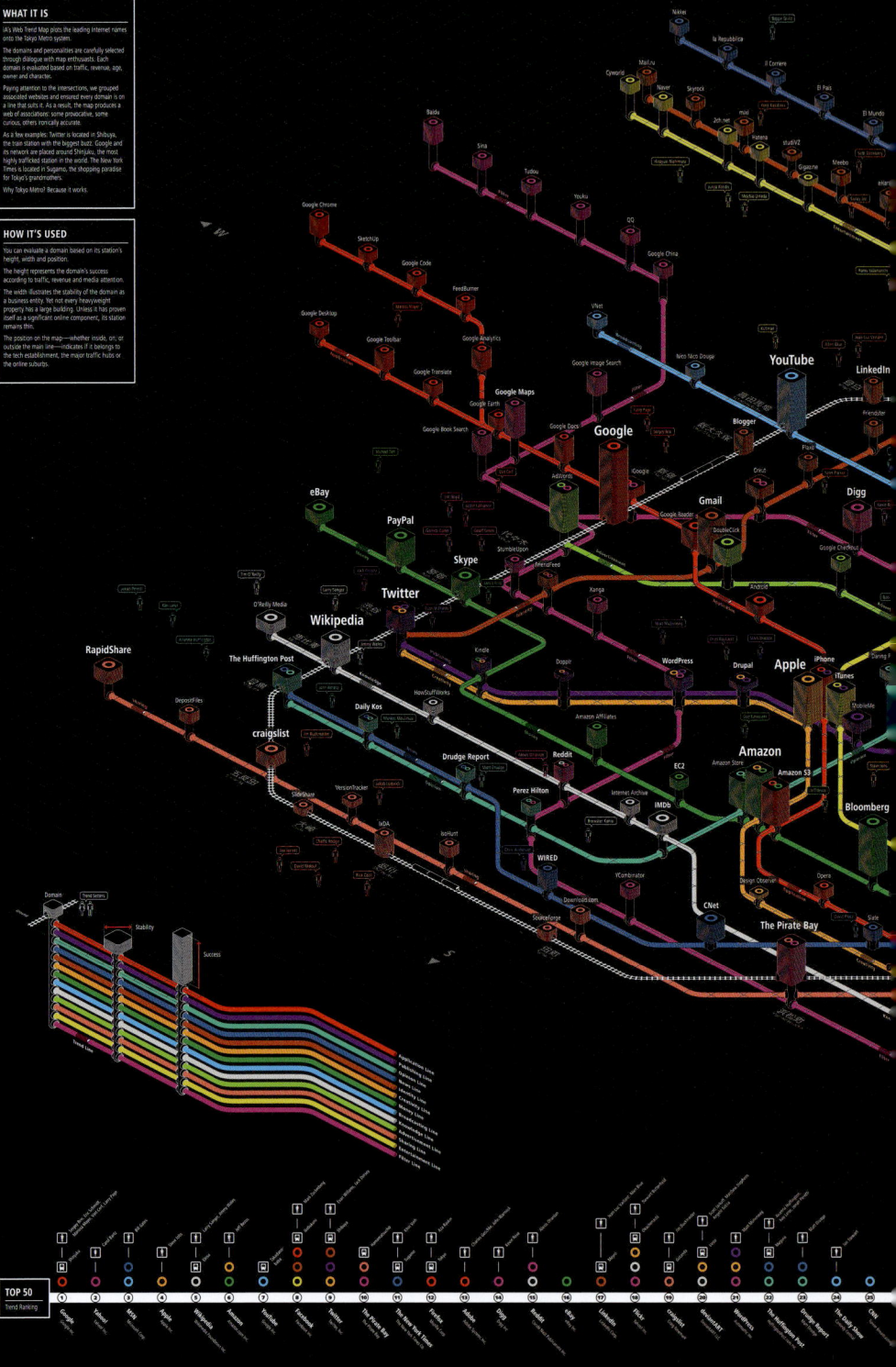

YouTube · LinkedIn · Google · Blogger · Digg · Gmail · Apple · iPhone · iTunes · Amazon · Bloomberg · eBay · PayPal · Skype · Twitter · Wikipedia · RapidShare · The Huffington Post · craigslist · Daily Kos · Drudge Report · Reddit · Perez Hilton · IMDb · WIRED · CNet · The Pirate Bay

Google Chrome · SketchUp · Google Code · FeedBurner · Google Desktop · Google Toolbar · Google Analytics · Google Translate · Google Maps · Google Earth · Google Book Search · Google Docs · AdWords · Google Reader · DoubleClick · WordPress · Drupal · Amazon Affiliates · EC2 · Amazon Store · Amazon S3 · Internet Archive

Domain · Stability · Success · Trend Setters · Trend Line

Application Line · Advertising Line · Blog Line · News Line · Sharing Line · Creativity Line · Broadcasting Line · Knowledge Line · Social Networking Line · Commerce Line · Peer Line

WEB TREND MAP 4

The State of the Web Mapped onto Tokyo's Metro System

newsnetz
ZEIT Online
Heise
Mashable
Techdirt
Ars Technica
ReadWriteWeb
Der Spiegel
Globe
BBC
kotaku
Blizzard
The New York Times
About
Gizmodo
Basecamp
Guardian
The Onion
USA Today
TechCrunch
Delicious
ESPN
The Guardian
Engadget
Expedia
Disney
Yahoo!
Valleywag
MetaFilter
Yahoo! Answers
Yahoo! Mail
Yahoo! News
Monster
ABC
moo
FontShop
HBO
Getty Images
Metacafe
The Economist
Hotmail
Yahoo! Japan
Adaptive Path
UIE
snatt.com
Newsvine
MSN Messenger
deviantART
Alibaba
MSNBC
Flickr
Swissmiss
Live Search
Office Live
TED
A List Apart
MSN Microsoft
DZone
I Love Typography
Internet Explorer
Federated Media
Wikileaks
W3C
Xbox LIVE
Coudal Partners
Doodle
The Deck
Projector
Firefox
Smashing Magazine
Seth's Blog
Something Awful
Linux
MySpace
AdBrite
Bloglines
Joblet
Rakuten
Vimeo
Photobucket
Adobe
Adobe Flash
Fotolog
jQuery
Bigpoint
Netvibes
livedoor
Netlog
CyberAgent
QRY
W3Schools
hulu
Gutenberg
1UP.com
OVGuide
Vox
AOL
Six Apart
Ask.com
ExpressionEngine
Boing Boing
Mixisip
Crunchyroll
TV.com
Machine
GameFAQs
last.fm
Pandora
Netflix
Dailymotion
GameSpot
→iA

What are Infovis and Datavis About?

Using the metaphor of a tree, the infographic aims to describe the field of Information Visualisation. Roots sketch out the individual skills that are involved in creating complex visualisations. The dark-green strand demonstrates how datasets must be thoroughly analysed. Light blue alludes to visual skills for developing a clear design. The designing of interaction patterns is coded light green.

The dark-blue strand shows how it is necessary to keep up with software development, as this enables ever newer visualisation techniques and broader user interaction. At the top, the tree shows the two main applications: statistical graphics and thematic mapping. The piece illustrates the complexity of the field, and how it is difficult to represent the components as distinct and strict categories.

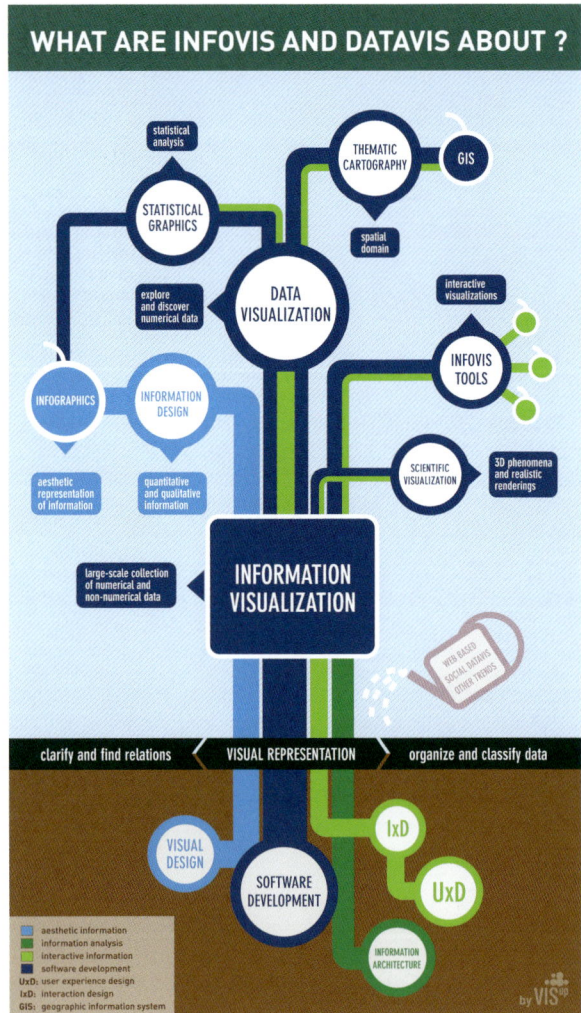

Project Info: Website, 2010, Italy
Design: Eloisa Paola Fontana (VISup)

World Government

Founded in 2000, artist duo Bureau d'études develop research-based diagrams of complex economic or social systems. *World Government* is a piece that analyses the interconnections between political institutions and economic powers, indicating how political decision structures may be distorted by the influence of big money. The legend in the top-left corner explains the various symbols used. Three major complexes are depicted: the political complex (bottom left), various major business sectors (bottom right) and the financial sector (top right). Some extra space is devoted to the "intelligence complex" (top centre).

Project Info: Poster, 2005, France
Artists: Bureau d'études

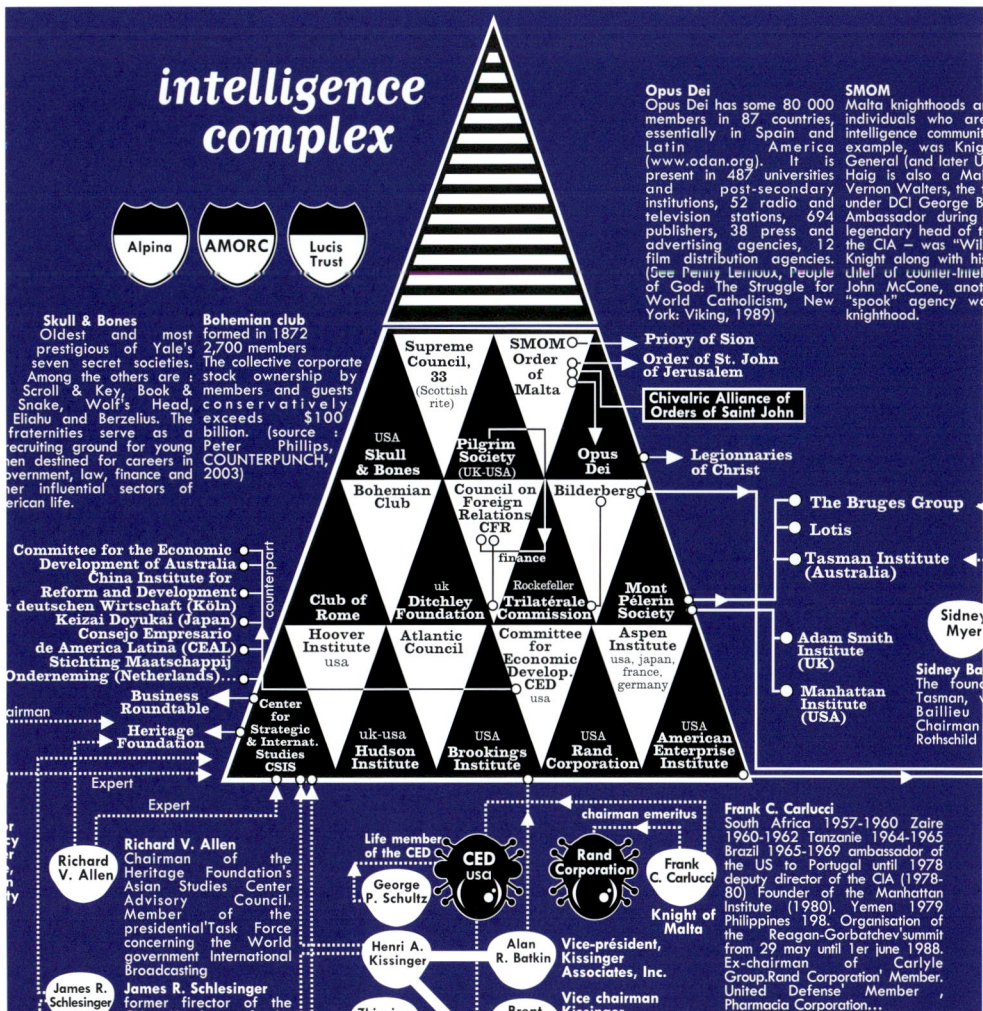

The World Government

financial heart
Vatican
Bush Clan
Rothschild Clan
Rockefeller Clan
Windsor Clan
Al Saud Clan
Bin Laden Clan
Li family
Soong family
Mitsubishi Clan
Mitsui Clan
Sumitomo Clan
Matsushita Clan
Hitotsubashi Clan
Fitch
Moody's
Standard & Poor's
Fimalac
Dakevoise
Skadden, Arps
Banco Santander
Carlyle Group
MDM Financial Group
NIKoil Financial Corporation
Groupe Bolloré
Vincent Bolloré
Michel Roussin
Rothschild Group
George Soros
Schiff family
Warburg Dillon Read
Warburg family
Lazard LLC
Michel David-Weill
Antoine Bernheim
Anglo American Corporation
Sir Chips Keswick
De Beers
Nicky Oppenheimer
J. P. Morgan Chase
Milbank
Rockefeller Group
ABN Amro Holding NV
MMC Marsh & McLennan
Lehman Brothers
Fidelity
State Street Corp.
mellon financial corp
Merrill Lynch
John Deutch
citigroup inc.
Goldman Sachs
Mitsubishi Corporation
Bank of Tokyo-Mitsubishi
Sumitomo Kichizaemon
Mizuho Financial Group
ITOCHU corp.
Seibu Group
Kikkoman corporation
LG Group
Keizai Doyukai
Hutchison Whampoa
Li Ka-shing
Citic pacific
Henry Fok
China Life
China Resources Enterprise (CRE)
Power Corporation
Pargesa Holdings
Wheelock Co. Ltd.
Jardine Fleming Unit Trusts
El-Baraka
Dar el-Mal
National Commercial Bank
UBS
Crédit Suisse First Boston
Pictet & cie
Lombard Odier
Union Bancaire Privée
Investor AB
Barclays Plc
HSBC
Nova Scotia
Royal Bank of Canada
Lloyds
King & Spalding
Clifford Chance
Royal Bank of Scotland
NatWest
Sir Iain Vallance
deutsche bank
Société Générale
Crédit Agricole
BNP Paribas
Michel Pébereau
Allianz
AXA
Claude Bébéar
Bank of Japan
European Bank
Bank of England
Bundesbank
Banque de France
World Bank
International Monetary Fund
CLUB DE PARIS
Bank for International Settlements (BIS)
Basel Committee on Banking Supervision
TABD
ERT
Davos Economic Forum
Klaus Schwab
psychological complex (medias)
Comcast
abril
Disney Corp.
News Corporation
Rupert Murdoch
FOX
B SKY B
Metro Goldwyn Mayer
Kirk Kerkorian
Viacom
CBS
MTV
Sony
Telemundo
Liberty Media
Bertelsmann
Lagardère SCA
Hachette
Cisneros Group
Reuters
AFP
BBC
RAI
Rete 4
Berlusconi
Voice of America
FCC
MPA
USIA
OSI
Rendon Group
agro-business cartel
Tradax
Cargill
ContiGroup
Bunge & Born
ConAgra
Walmart
Louis Dreyfus
Nestlé
Kraft Food
Unilever
grain cartel
meat cartel
food cartel
petroleum cartel
Exxon
BP
Royal Dutch Shell
Chevron Texaco
Total
Rio Tinto
Rockefeller
Bush
Queen Beatrix (Netherlands)
Desmarais
Albert Frère
WCC
World Council of Churches
Thai State
Indian state
Tata Sons

Writing Without Words

This is an exploration into how to visualise literature. Stefanie Posavec focused her project on Jack Kerouac's *On the Road* and went through the text by hand, marking each word according to a colour code which discerns the themes most prevalent in the book. She developed various visualisations for this body of data. The *Sentence Drawing* (p.424) follows the course of each sentence. The length of a line indicates the number of words in a sentence. Starting in the top-right corner, the line turns right with the beginning of every new sentence, thus re-writing the whole novel. In *Rhythm Textures* (p.425), Posavec analysed the inner structure of single sentences and visualised them in circle diagrams. Irregular structures indicate variations in the punctuation of a particular sentence.

Project Info: Series of posters, 2006, UK
Design: Stefanie Posavec
Additional Info: MA project at Central Saint Martins College

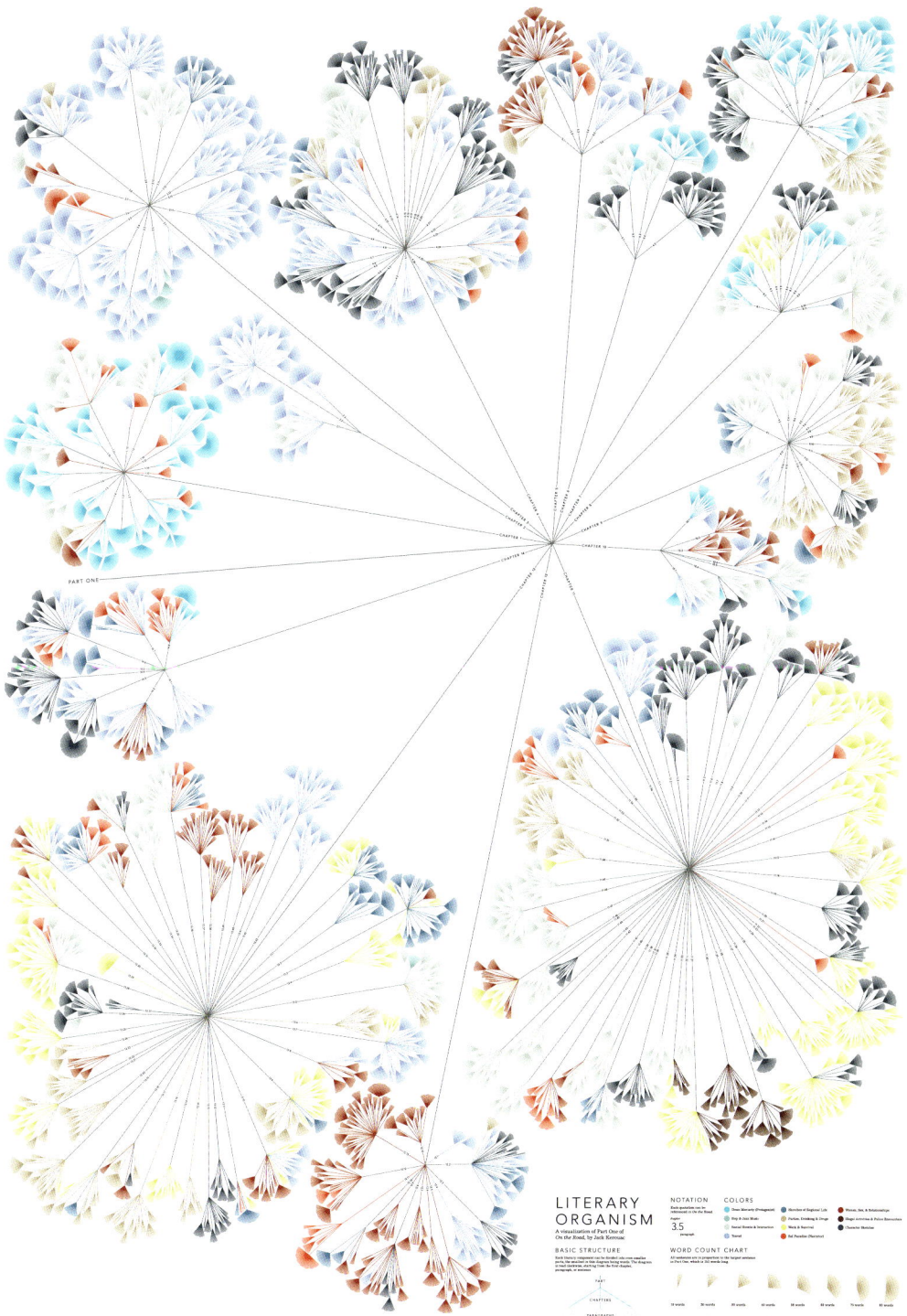

LITERARY ORGANISM

A visualisation of Part One of
On the Road, by Jack Kerouac

BASIC STRUCTURE

NOTATION

COLORS

WORD COUNT CHART

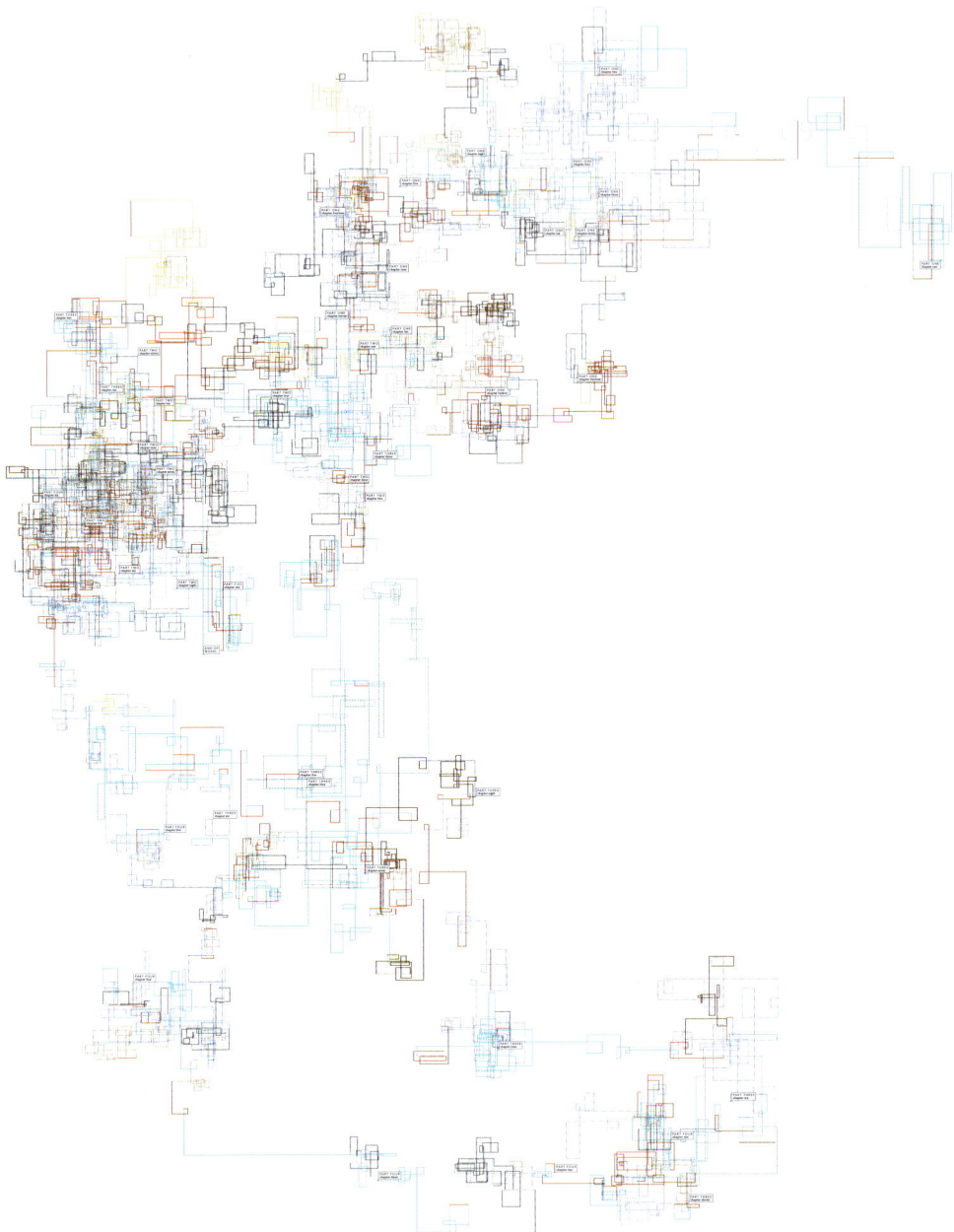

SENTENCE
DRAWINGS
The entirety of *On the Road*,
by Jack Kerouac

WORD COUNT
One word equals 40 mm

1 word
5 words
10 words

100 words

BASIC STRUCTURE
After each sentence, the line turns right, creating the drawing

COLORS

Inner Maturity (Protagonist)
Bop & Jazz Music
Social Events & Interaction
Travel
Sketches of Regional Life
Parties, Drinking & Drugs
Work & Survival
Sal Paradise (Narrator)
Women, Sex, & Relationships
Illegal Activities & Encounters with Police
Character Sketches

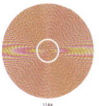
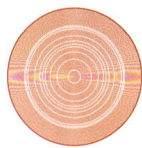
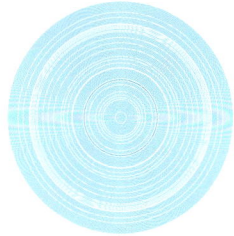

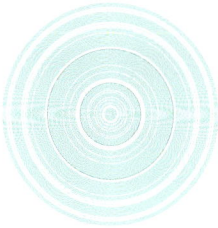

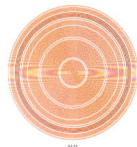
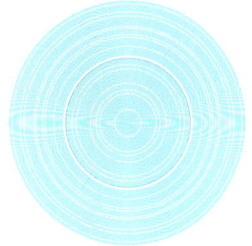

RHYTHM TEXTURES

Selected Quotes from *On the Road*,
by Jack Kerouac

BASIC STRUCTURE

DIAGRAM ONE

DIAGRAM TWO

DIAGRAM ONE

DIAGRAM TWO

NOTATION

Each quotation can be referenced to
On the Road.

COLORS

- Time Warmerly (Portuguese)
- Bop & Jazz Music
- Travel
- Hardships of Regional Life
- Parties, Drinking & Drugs
- Work & Survival
- Sel Paradise (Narrator)
- Women, Sex, & Relationships
- Illegal Activities & Encounters with Police
- Character Sketches

QUOTATIONS

Your Friend, the Library

Using the metaphor of a set of bookshelves, this is a comparison of two library classification systems. The Dewey Decimal System, shown in green, is based on ten main classes of themes, like psychology, religion or general arts. They are named on the spines of individual books, starting on the lowest shelf. These main classes are further divided into sub-topics and referred to by three-digit numbers. The Library of Congress classification, on the other hand, is based on letters to classify the main categories. In order to compare both approaches, books of similar topics are placed on neighbouring shelves. The comparison shows that the classification labels of both systems are not interchangeable just like that.

Project Info: *Rough*, Dallas Society of Visual Communications, magazine article, 2007, USA
Design: Michael Newhouse (Newhouse Design)

DEWEY LIBRARY

770 Photography

710 PHOTOGRAPHY · 780 MUSIC · 790 RECREATION · 800 LITERATURE · POETRY · FICTION BY COUNTRY · FICTION BY AUTHOR · COVERS BY CHIP KIDD · 900 HISTORY · GEOGRAPHY / BIOGRAPHY

730 SCULPTURE · 740 DECORATIVE ARTS

741.2 Drawing
741.5 Cartooning
741.6 Graphic Design, Posters, Showcards & Labels
745 Decoration

750 PAINTING · 760 GRAPHIC ARTS

749 Furniture
760 Engraving
769 Postcards, Stamps, Paper Money Bookplates & Ephemera

WHEN IN DOUBT, WANDER AROUND TO SEE WHAT'S NEARBY

600 APPLIED SCIENCES · TECHNOLOGY / MEDICINE

646 Fashion
655 Graphic Arts
676 Wallpaper
686 Design History, Book Design, Alphabets & Printer's Ornaments

700 GENERAL ARTS · 710 CIVIC & LANDSCAPE ART · 720 ARCHITECTURE

000 REFERENCE WORKS · ENCYCLOPEDIAS / MAGAZINES · 100 PSYCHOLOGY & BEHAVIORAL · 200 RELIGION · 300 SOCIAL SCIENCES · LAW / EDUCATION · 400 LANGUAGES · 500 BASIC SCIENCES · MATHEMATICS / CHEMISTRY

THE KID'S SECTION USUALLY HAS PICTURE BOOKS IN ALL THESE SUBJECTS

DEWEY LIBRARY

CONVERTING BETWEEN THESE CLASSIFICATION SYSTEMS IS TRICKY ✦ DON'T TRY THIS AT HOME ✦ CONSULT THE PROFESSIONALS! ✦

LIBRARY OF CONGRESS

P LANGUAGES / LITERATURE · SPEECH / DRAMA · Q R SCIENCE / MEDICINE · COMPUTER SCIENCE · S AGRICULTURE · T TECHNOLOGY · COMPUTER SOFTWARE · A PHOTOGRAPHY

TR624 Photography

TRY THE FILMS, DVDs, BOOKS ON TAPE & MUSIC CDs, ESPECIALLY THE OLDER STUFF

U V W X Y MILITARY SCIENCE · Z LIBRARY SCIENCE

ILLUSTRATION · ND PAINTING · NE PRINT MEDIA

NK1150 Decoration & Ornament
NK1775 Design History
NK1700 Interior Design
NK2200 Furniture
NK3375 Wallpaper

REFERENCE BOOKS CAN'T BE CHECKED OUT, SO FIND A QUIET PLACE AND SETTLE IN FOR THE AFTERNOON

NK DECORATIVE ARTS · NX ARTS IN GENERAL

J K POLITICS / LAW · L EDUCATION · M MUSIC · N VISUAL ARTS · NA ARCHITECTURE · NB SCULPTURE · NC DRAWING · DESIGN

NC950 Drawing & Illustration
NC997 Advertising & Commercial Art
NC1280 Ephemera
NC1800 Posters
NC1860 Postcards & Book Jackets

A GENERAL WORKS · B PHILOSOPHY / PSYCHOLOGY · RELIGION / THEATER · C HISTORY OF CIVILIZATION · A BIOGRAPHY · D WORLD HISTORY · E F HISTORY OF THE AMERICAS · G GEOGRAPHY / ANTHROPOLOGY · SPORTS · H I SOCIAL SCIENCES / FINANCE · ACCOUNTING / CRIMINOLOGY

LIBRARY OF CONGRESS

SOME SCHOOLS WILL GIVE CARDS TO NON-STUDENT CITY RESIDENTS

MEANWHILE, HIDDEN DEEP WITHIN THE BOWELS OF THE LIBRARY, THERE ARE TREASURES UNTOLD...

- EPHEMERA & PHOTO MORGUES
- RARE BOOK COLLECTIONS & ART EXHIBITS
- COOL OLD BOOKS FOR SALE CHEAP
- CHANGE MACHINE IF YOU'RE LUCKY
- PAPERS & MAGAZINES BEYOND BELIEF
- EVERY SOFTWARE MANUAL EVER MADE
- YOUR TAX DOLLARS AT WORK
- AND OH, THOSE REFERENCE MATERIALS!

A True Story About Libraries. Books are taken off the shelves if they are "not used enough." Older books sitting dormant will vanish into remote storage and are nearly impossible to get to. Check 'em out, or at least move them around each time you visit - do you really want to lose the Japanese Art Director's Annual from 1964 – even if it hasn't been checked out since 1987? City libraries are the worst about this, as they aren't really into archiving, but they also have the best used book sales. In school libraries, put them in the Book Return Slot so they get circulated.

Hierarchy
428 — 509

Hierarchy
Elements are ranked in order of priority

Hierarchies are vertical arrangements. Elements are sorted in order of rank, from largest to smallest, highest to lowest, and so on. In a linear hierarchy, e.g. a ranking, there is for each element a superior and a subordinate element, and the rank order results in a continuous sequence. *Fast Faust* (p.454) is a list of all the words in Goethe's *Faust*, arranged according to the frequency with which they appear in the text. *Super Vision Chart* (p.480) paces out at regular mathematical intervals the units of length that occur in the universe, from the smallest subatomic units to the very largest.

Hierarchies are created when ratios are visualised, as in the classic pie chart in which quantities are depicted as a proportion of the area of a circle. The prevalence of these charts in the worlds of business and science has provoked numerous wry comments (*Faces Diagrams*, p.448). Nevertheless, the transmission of data in scaled colour fields remains one of the most effective means by which infographics can clarify proportions. *Billion Dollar Gram* (p.436) shows the international movement of money through various channels as a series of colour fields that provide a visual display of the order of rank between large and small.

Ramified hierarchies split from the highest element into numerous sub-elements. The tree provides a classic way of portraying ramified hierarchies: starting at the root, elements are divided into increasing numbers of sub-groups. This image was frequently used to describe the evolution of species; family trees are another traditional example. In *Natural Selections* (p.465) the tree image is used to group animal and plant logos used by American publishers.

Taxonomies, on the other hand, deal with self-contained fields of knowledge by depicting continuous organisation from largest to smallest in hierarchical diagrams. Hence *A Taxonomy of Complete World Knowledge* (p.434) arranges all of the (imaginary) world knowledge from top to bottom in a tree structure. *Taxonomy of Team Names* (p.482) depicts the shared root at the centre, while the sub-species branch out into a circle around it. In the taxonomy of types of beer, "beer" as the most general category is placed at the centre and forms the starting point from which the various sub-groups of beer are classified (*The Very Many Varieties of Beer*, p.497).

Websites are also organised hierarchically; the site map of an Internet site contains all its individual pages within a tree structure. In the case of a major Internet platform like Facebook this hierarchy of pages is vast and confusing, making it harder to find individual pages. *A Nightmare on Privacy Street* (p.430) illustrates how the website's complicated hierarchic structure conceals privacy settings and makes them very difficult for users to find.

1.
Settings

2.
Account Settings

a nightmare
on privacy stre

62
checkboxes

6
links

9
"edit settings" links

2
"manage" link

28
drop down menus

7
tabs

1
"desactivate" link

2
"edit settings" buttons

1
"buy more" link

9
"profile" links

3.
Privacy Settings

4.
Application Settings

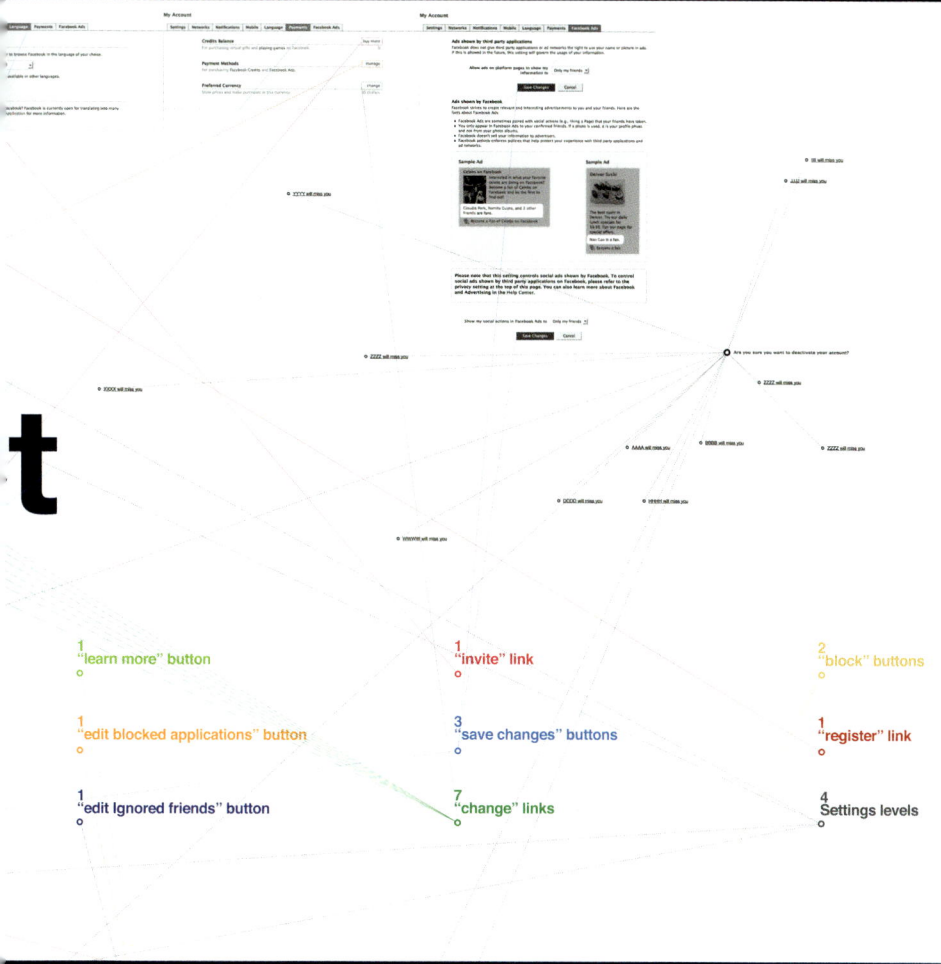

t

1
"learn more" button

1
"invite" link

2
"block" buttons

1
"edit blocked applications" button

3
"save changes" buttons

1
"register" link

1
"edit Ignored friends" button

7
"change" links

4
Settings levels

3.
Privacy Settings

Privacy Settings

Privacy Settings ▸ Personal Information and Posts

◂ Back to Privacy

Personal Information and Posts
Control who can see your photos and videos, and who can post to your wall

Bio
Bio refers to the Bio description in the About Me section of your profile

🔒 Eve

Contact Information
Control who can contact you on Facebook and see your contact information and email

Birthday
Birth date and Year

🔒 Fri

Friends, Tags and Connections
Control whether your friends, tags and connections display on your profile

Interested In and Looking For

🔒 Eve

Applications and Websites
Control what information is available to Facebook-enhanced applications and websites

Religious and Political Views

🔒 Fri

Search
Control who can see your search result on Facebook and in search engines

Photo Albums

Edit S

Block List
Control who can interact with you on Facebook

Posts by Me
Default setting for Status Updates, Links, Notes, Photos, and Videos you post

🔒 Eve

Allow friends to post on my Wall

☑ Frie

Posts by Friends
Control who can see posts by your friends on your profile

🔒 Fri

Comments on Posts
Control who can comment on posts you create

🔒 On

To edit settings for Groups and other applications, visit the Application Settings Page .

4.
Application Settings

Application Settings - Recently Used

A Nightmare on Privacy Street

Since the social network Facebook invites all kinds of personal expressions by its very nature, users have developed an increasing awareness as regards their privacy. In this piece, Florent Guerlain and Samuel Degrémont show the interface structure for users to regulate their individual privacy settings (as of May 2010). Listed from the top down are all four navigation levels in which settings can be regulated. From left to right, all the interface windows per level are represented. Coloured figures in the middle show the type and absolute numbers of interaction buttons involved. By visually combining all these elements in one graphic, the authors provided strong evidence that the interface for privacy settings is actually counterintuitive.

Project Info: Website, 2010, France
Research: Samuel Degrémont
Design: Florent Guerlain

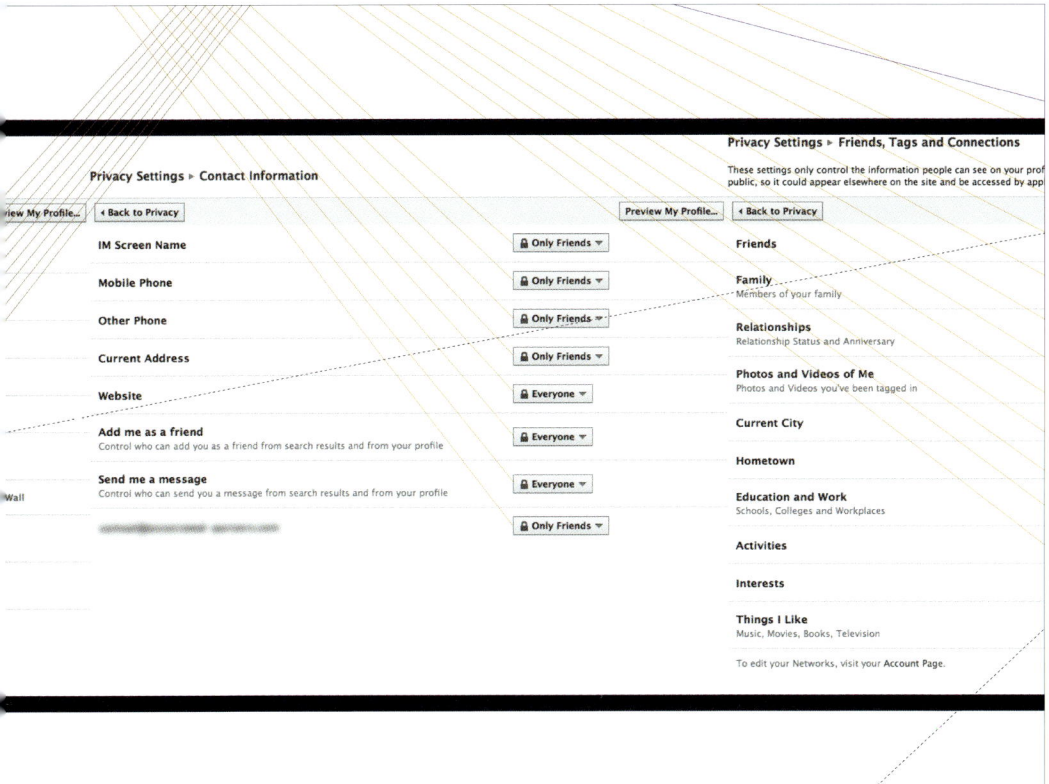

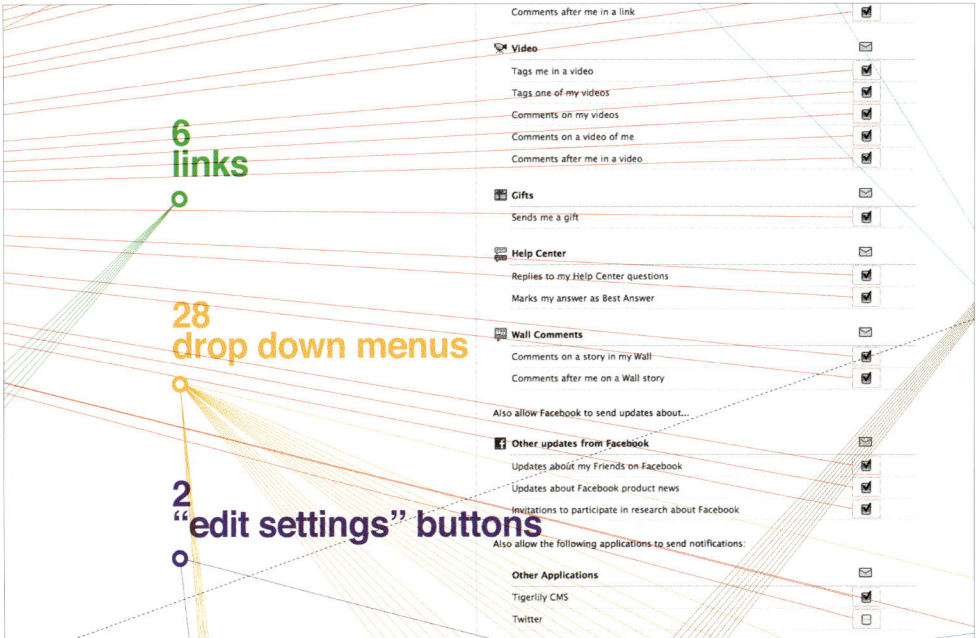

Project Info: *More Information Than You Require*, Dutton Books, book jacket, 2008, USA
Design: Sam Potts
Text: John Hodgman

A TAXONOMY *of* COMPI

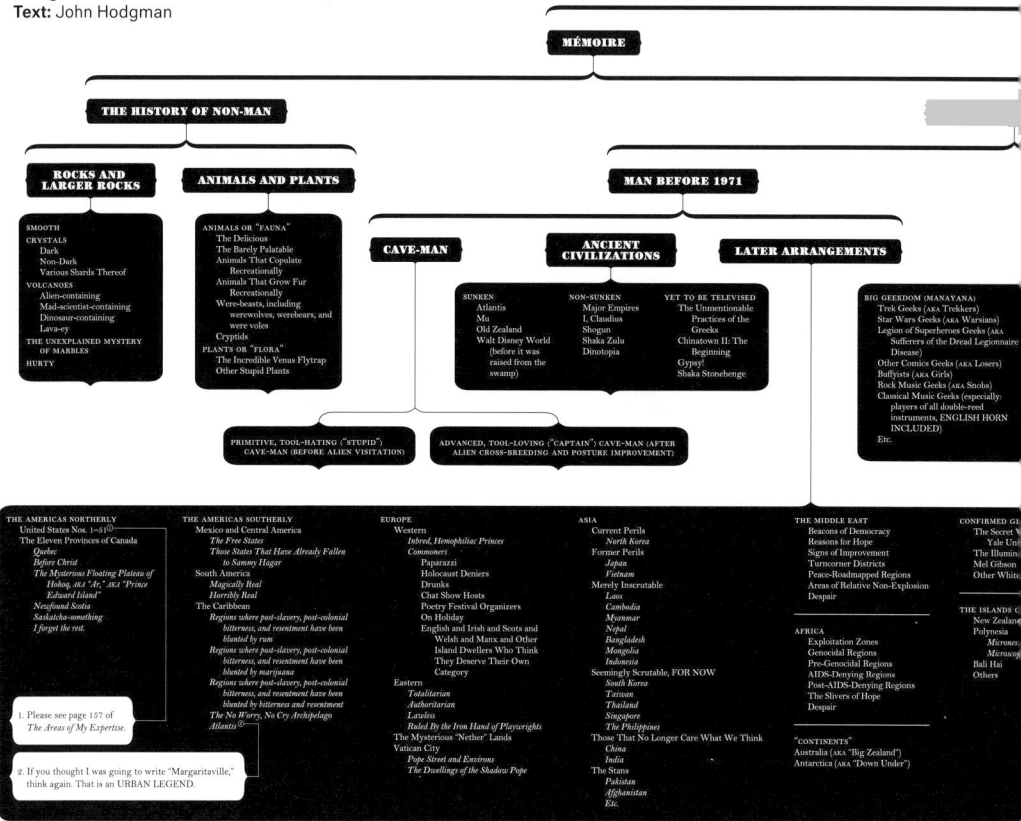

MÉMOIRE

THE HISTORY OF NON-MAN

ROCKS AND LARGER ROCKS

SMOOTH
CRYSTALS
Dark
Non-Dark
Various Shards Thereof
VOLCANOES
Alien-containing
Mad-scientist-containing
Dinosaur-containing
Lava-ey
THE UNEXPLAINED MYSTERY
OF MARBLES
HURTY

ANIMALS AND PLANTS

ANIMALS OR "FAUNA"
The Delicious
The Barely Palatable
Animals That Copulate
Recreationally
Animals That Grow Fur
Recreationally
Were-beasts, including
werewolves, werebears, and
were voles
Cryptids
PLANTS OR "FLORA"
The Incredible Venus Flytrap
Other Stupid Plants

MAN BEFORE 1971

CAVE-MAN

ANCIENT CIVILIZATIONS

SUNKEN
Atlantis
Mu
Old Zealand
Walt Disney World
(before it was
raised from the
swamp)

NON-SUNKEN
Major Empires
I, Claudius
Shogun
Shaka Zulu
Dinotopia

YET TO BE TELEVISED
The Unmentionable
Practices of the
Greeks
Chinatown II: The
Beginning
Gypsy!
Shaka Stonehenge

LATER ARRANGEMENTS

BIG GEEKDOM (MANAYANA)
Trek Geeks (AKA Trekkers)
Star Wars Geeks (AKA Warsians)
Legion of Superheroes Geeks (AKA
Sufferers of the Dread Legionnaire
Disease)
Other Comics Geeks (AKA Losers)
Buffyists (AKA Girls)
Rock Music Geeks (AKA Snobs)
Classical Music Geeks (especially:
players of all double-reed
instruments, ENGLISH HORN
INCLUDED)
Etc.

PRIMITIVE, TOOL-HATING ("STUPID")
CAVE-MAN (BEFORE ALIEN VISITATION)

ADVANCED, TOOL-LOVING ("CAPTAIN") CAVE-MAN (AFTER
ALIEN CROSS-BREEDING AND POSTURE IMPROVEMENT)

THE AMERICAS NORTHERLY
United States Nos. 1–51
The Eleven Provinces of Canada
Quebec
Before Christ
The Mysterious Floating Plateau of
Hoboq, AKA "Ar," AKA "Prince
Edward Island"
Newfound Scotia
Saskatcha-something
I forget the rest.

1. Please see page 157 of
The Areas of My Expertise.

2. If you thought I was going to write "Margaritaville,"
think again. That is an URBAN LEGEND.

THE AMERICAS SOUTHERLY
Mexico and Central America
The Free States
Those States That Have Already Fallen
to Sammy Hagar
South America
The Caribbean
Regions where post-slavery, post-colonial
bitterness, and resentment have been
blunted by rum
Regions where post-slavery, post-colonial
bitterness, and resentment have been
blunted by marijuana
Regions where post-slavery, post-colonial
bitterness, and resentment have been
blunted by bitterness and resentment
The No Worry, No Cry Archipelago
Atlantis

EUROPE
Western
Inbred, Hemophiliac Princes
Commoners
Paparazzi
Holocaust Deniers
Drunks
Chat Show Hosts
Poetry Festival Organizers
On Holiday
English and Irish and Scots and
Welsh and Manx and Other
Island Dwellers Who Think
They Deserve Their Own
Category
Eastern
Totalitarian
Authoritarian
Lawless
Ruled By the Iron Hand of Playwrights
The Mysterious "Nether" Lands
Vatican City
Pope Street and Environs
The Dwellings of the Shadow Pope

ASIA
Current Perils
North Korea
Former Perils
Japan
Vietnam
Merely Inscrutable
Laos
Cambodia
Myanmar
Nepal
Bangladesh
Mongolia
Indonesia
Seemingly Scrutable, FOR NOW
South Korea
Taiwan
Thailand
Singapore
The Philippines
Those That No Longer Care What We Think
China
India
The Stans
Pakistan
Afghanistan
Etc.

THE MIDDLE EAST
Beacons of Democracy
Reasons for Hope
Signs of Improvement
Turncorner Districts
Peace-Roadmapped Regions
Areas of Relative Non-Explosion
Despair

AFRICA
Exploitation Zones
Genocidal Regions
Pre-Genocidal Regions
AIDS-Denying Regions
Post-AIDS-Denying Regions
The Slivers of Hope
Despair

"CONTINENTS"
Australia (AKA "Big Zealand")
Antarctica (AKA "Down Under")

CONFIRMED GI
The Secret V
Yale Uni
The Illumin
Mel Gibson
Other White

THE ISLANDS C
New Zealand
Polynesia
Micrones
Microco
Bali Hai
Others

A Taxonomy of Complete World Knowledge

This is a hierarchy of everything, as described by American writer and expert-on-all-things, John Hodgman. The general division into Memory, Reason and Imagination refers to the system of knowledge Denis Diderot created for his *Encyclopedia* in the 18th century. However, with the absurd classification which unfolds beneath, Hodgman creates an ironic account of the world and mocks the traditional scientific taxonomy. Memory is divided into "The History of Non-Man" and "The History of Man", the latter being divided into "Man before 1971" and "Man since 1971". The complete list of continents, countries and regions of the world is filed under "Later Arrangements" and jolts all the geopolitical knowledge ever taught. The strict black and white design by Sam Potts emphasises the extreme variations in size among the individual categories.

WORLD KNOWLEDGE

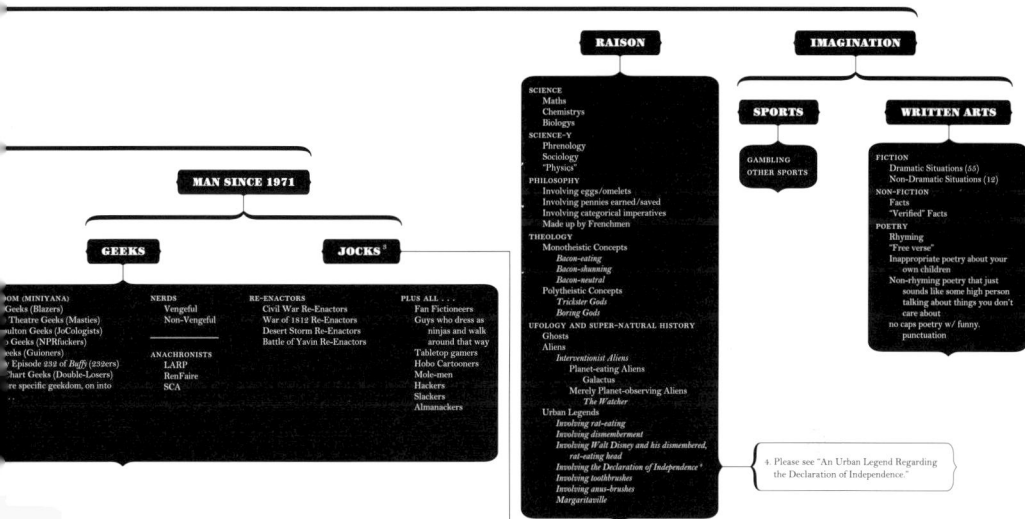

RAISON

IMAGINATION

SCIENCE
   Maths
   Chemistrys
   Biologys
SCIENCE-Y
   Phrenology
   Sociology
   "Physics"
PHILOSOPHY
   Involving eggs/omelets
   Involving pennies earned/saved
   Involving categorical imperatives
   Made up by Frenchmen
THEOLOGY
   Monotheistic Concepts
     Bacon-eating
     Bacon-shunning
     Bacon-neutral
   Polytheistic Concepts
     Trickster Gods
     Boring Gods
UFOLOGY AND SUPER-NATURAL HISTORY
   Ghosts
   Aliens
     Interventionist Aliens
       Planet-eating Aliens
         Galactus
     Merely Planet-observing Aliens
       The Watcher
   Urban Legends
     Involving rat-eating
     Involving dismemberment
     Involving Walt Disney and his dismembered,
       rat-eating head
     Involving the Declaration of Independence [4]
     Involving toothbrushes
     Involving anus-brushes
     Margaritaville

SPORTS

GAMBLING
OTHER SPORTS

WRITTEN ARTS

FICTION
   Dramatic Situations (55)
   Non-Dramatic Situations (12)
NON-FICTION
   Facts
   "Verified" Facts
POETRY
   Rhyming
   "Free verse"
   Inappropriate poetry about your
     own children
   Non-rhyming poetry that just
     sounds like some high person
     talking about things you don't
     care about
   no caps poetry w/ funny.
     punctuation

MAN SINCE 1971

GEEKS

JOCKS [3]

DOM (MINIYANA):
Geeks (Blazers)
Theatre Geeks (Masties)
ulton Geeks (JoCologists)
Geeks (NPRfuckers)
eeks (Guioners)
Episode 232 of *Buffy* (232ers)
hart Geeks (Double-Losers)
re specific geekdom, on into

NERDS
Vengeful
Non-Vengeful

ANACHRONISTS
LARP
RenFaire
SCA

RE-ENACTORS
Civil War Re-Enactors
War of 1812 Re-Enactors
Desert Storm Re-Enactors
Battle of Yavin Re-Enactors

PLUS ALL . . .
Fan Fictioneers
Guys who dress as
   ninjas and walk
   around that way
Tabletop gamers
Hobo Cartooners
Mole-men
Hackers
Slackers
Almanackers

> 4. Please see "An Urban Legend Regarding
> the Declaration of Independence."

ADDITIONALLY . . .
Cities Kept in Bottles
   Kandor
   Baghdad
Nomadic Civilizations
   The Romans
   The Bedouins
   The Irish Travelers
   The Australian Backpackers
   The Chicagoans
Hoboes and Their Ilk
   The Hoboes
   The Stevedores
   The Safecrackers
   The Cat Burglars
   The Scrimshanders
   The Clamdiggers
   The Child Pickpockets
   The A Cappellists
   The Chain Restaurant Waiters
   The Objectivist Bridge Players
   And other esoteric subcultures that shall
     never be mentioned again.

3. Actual, professional athletes are not included in this group. While it is possible that such persons may be as essentially fear-filled and contemptuous as actual jocks, successful athletes tend to be so insulated by thick layers of money, privilege, and actual achievement that they stride across the earth like giants, occasionally stopping to be on TV, pick up a check, or murder their wives. But largely, athletes are untroubled by the battle raging below them between those who WISH ABOVE ALL ELSE TO BECOME THEM (jocks) and those who wish merely NOT TO BE CRUSHED by them (geeks).

    Indeed, an affinity for sports or physical culture has very little to do with jockism. All martial arts practitioners and rugby players, for example, are in fact geeks, affined always to the esoteric. By the same token, for his preoccupation with minutiae, the fantasy baseballist has more in common with the man who dresses up like an orc on weekends than the man who dons the fringed cape and goggles of an actual baseballer.

    Meanwhile, all "hipsters" are actually jocks who want to be geeks but are afraid to admit it. This interior struggle manifests itself outwardly in the adoption of a different kind of uniform (though one that is as carefully regulated as the length of a baseballer's cape) and distinguished by the jockist's endemic, cringing cynicism. As currently incarnated, this uniform may include an "ironic," "joke" T-shirt, sarcastic jeans, cynical tube socks, derisive sneakers, and a morose belt.

    I could go on and on about such subtle differences.

    (For example, "foodies" are geeks, often of the most hateful kind, but Rachael Ray is a jock, because her cowboy steaks and yum-o cheeseburger soup-piles are merely the thirty-minute paving upon the path of her insatiable ambition. Also, she will punch you. ((Similarly, I am a geek at birth simply by virtue of my asthma, but my unreasoning, snobby contempt for jockism is itself, paradoxically, jockish. (((Oh, and one final example: Anyone who invokes the "original intent" of the framers of the Constitution is unquestionably a jock insofar as a) he hates hippies; and b) he ignores the fact that the Constitution is perhaps one of the most geeky documents ever committed to parchment—essentially it is our nation's FAQs. He also ignores that the framers themselves were moneyed, sickly, book-mad, bifocal-wearers who believed God did not interfere in man's fate, but served instead as a distant, uncaring Dungeon Master, which is to say: Geeks. ((((The Magna Carta, on the other hand, is jock all the way: a jock-ument, if you will.))))))))

    But such endless, obsessive parenthesizing over fine-grain distinctions is an eminently geekish trait, ill-suited and offensive to jocks, who may be simply and purely broken down into two groups:

        1) Bitter failures
           and
        2) Bitter successes

Following page

Billion Dollar Gram

This piece establishes a direct visual hierarchy. Large sums of money in media reports are hard to comprehend, and remain mostly abstract figures and unrelated to each other. David McCandless works with simple colour fields in order to give an impression of the relative rate of individual money flow in international politics and business. The colour code refers to what happens with this individual money flow – blue is for business-related revenues, while military spending is coded in purple and illegal money flows are shown in grey.

The Billion Dollar Gram

Billions spent on this. Billions spent on that. It's all relative right?

■ spending ■ earning ■ giving ■ fighting ■ losing ■ illin'

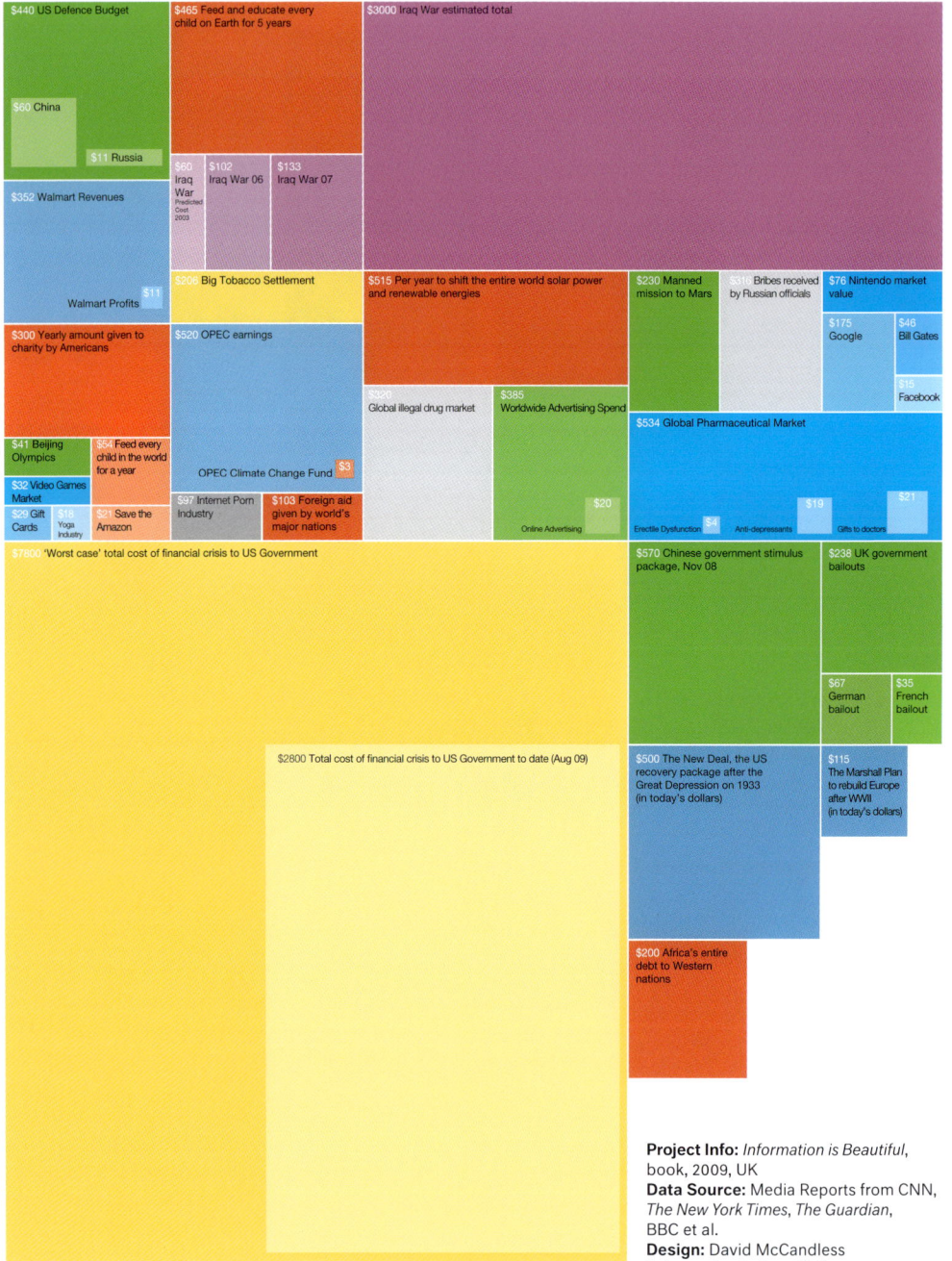

$440 US Defence Budget

$60 China

$11 Russia

$352 Walmart Revenues

Walmart Profits $11

$300 Yearly amount given to charity by Americans

$43 Beijing Olympics

$55 Feed every child in the world for a year

$32 Video Games Market

$20 Gift Cards

$18 Yoga Industry

$11 Save the Amazon

$465 Feed and educate every child on Earth for 5 years

$60 Iraq War Predicted Cost 2003

$102 Iraq War 06

$133 Iraq War 07

$206 Big Tobacco Settlement

$520 OPEC earnings

OPEC Climate Change Fund $3

$97 Internet Porn Industry

$103 Foreign aid given by world's major nations

$3000 Iraq War estimated total

$515 Per year to shift the entire world solar power and renewable energies

$320 Global illegal drug market

$385 Worldwide Advertising Spend

$20 Online Advertising

$230 Manned mission to Mars

$316 Bribes received by Russian officials

$76 Nintendo market value

$175 Google

$46 Bill Gates

$15 Facebook

$534 Global Pharmaceutical Market

Erectile Dysfunction

$4 Anti-depressants

$19

Gifts to doctors

$21

$7800 'Worst case' total cost of financial crisis to US Government

$2800 Total cost of financial crisis to US Government to date (Aug 09)

$570 Chinese government stimulus package, Nov 08

$238 UK government bailouts

$67 German bailout

$35 French bailout

$500 The New Deal, the US recovery package after the Great Depression on 1933 (in today's dollars)

$115 The Marshall Plan to rebuild Europe after WWII (in today's dollars)

$200 Africa's entire debt to Western nations

Project Info: *Information is Beautiful*, book, 2009, UK
Data Source: Media Reports from CNN, *The New York Times*, *The Guardian*, BBC et al.
Design: David McCandless (Information is Beautiful)

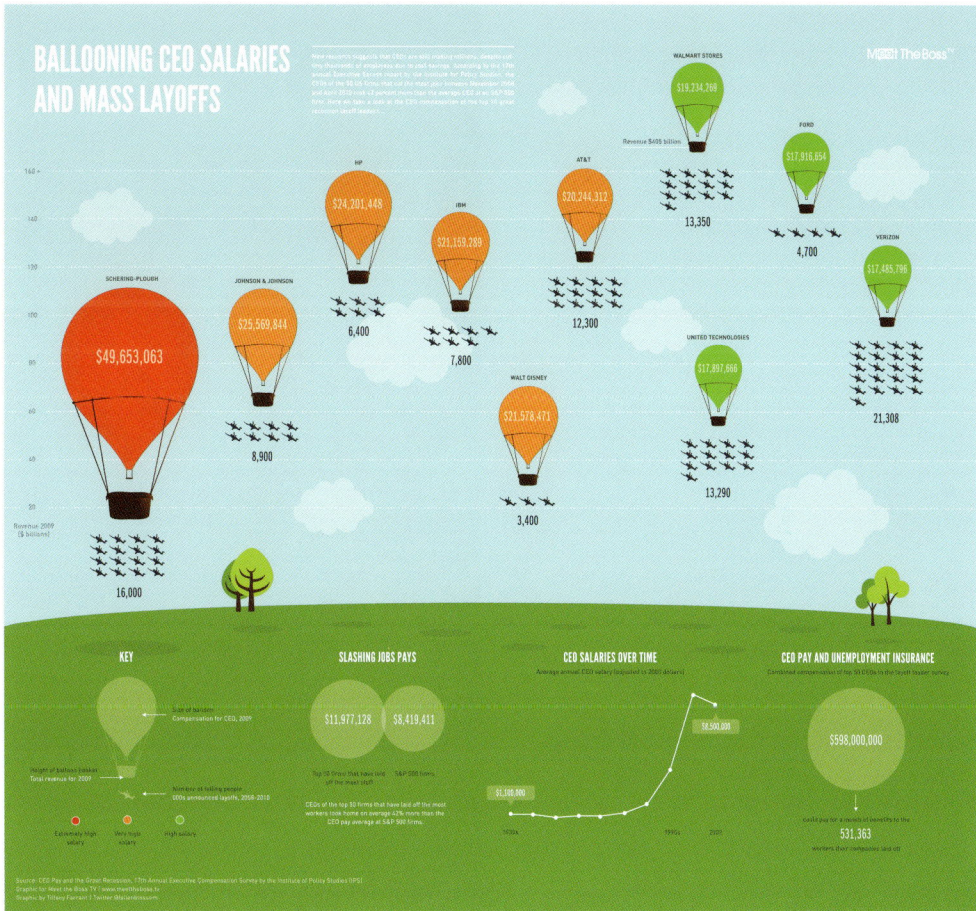

Ballooning CEO Salaries and Mass Layoffs

The Institute for Policy Studies, a think-tank based in Washington, D.C., researched into CEO salaries during the recession of 2008-2010. Results of this study show that those CEOs who have cut the most jobs received 42% more compensation than CEOs on the US average. The graphic takes a look at the top 10 recession lay-off leaders and how much the CEO received compared to how many people were laid off. The balloon size shows the amount of CEO compensation, the height it floats at indicates the company's revenue, whilst the little silhouettes falling overboard correspond to the number of jobs cut.

Project Info: Meet the Boss, for GDS International, website, 2010, UK
Data Source: Institute of Policy Studies: "CEO Pay and the Great Recession, 17th Annual Executive Compensation Survey"
Design: Tiffany Farrant-Gonzalez

Deadly Genomes

This diagram charts diseases according to mortality (y-axis) and incident rates (x-axis). While leprosy is both rare and shows a low mortality (below left), AIDS occurs relatively frequently and is still 100 % fatal (top right). Although media coverage often focuses on more fatal but rarer diseases such as avian flu, this chart shows how many more people are affected by less relatively fatal diseases like malaria. Each disease is symbolised by the genome of its agent virus or bacteria. Introducing a new concept, genomic sequence is represented as a continuous line. The genome size is reflected in the line's length, colour refers to guanine-cytosine content in the sequence

Project Info: Poster, National Science Foundation Visualization Challenge, 2010, Canada
Data Source: World Health Organization; National Center for Biotechnology Information Genbank
Research: Ian Bosdet (BC Cancer Agency), Cydney Nielsen (Genome Sciences Center)
Design: Martin Krzywinski
Illustration: Jonathan Corum

Following spread

Death and Taxes

"Death and Taxes" is a large representational graph of the federal US budget and how it is spent. The total amount of the budget is represented by the central circle, while arranged around it are over 500 programs and federal institutions which receive their funding from this budget. All item circles are proportional in size to the amount of their funding, for visual comparison. The scaling shows a priority on military- and security-related spending. The exceptionally large circle shown by the dollar bills below the centre visual gives a hint of the enormous size of the US national debt. Jess Bachmann has been producing this piece since 2007 and updates it annually.

Project Info: Poster, 2010, USA
Data Source: US Office of Management and Budget
Design: Jess Bachmann

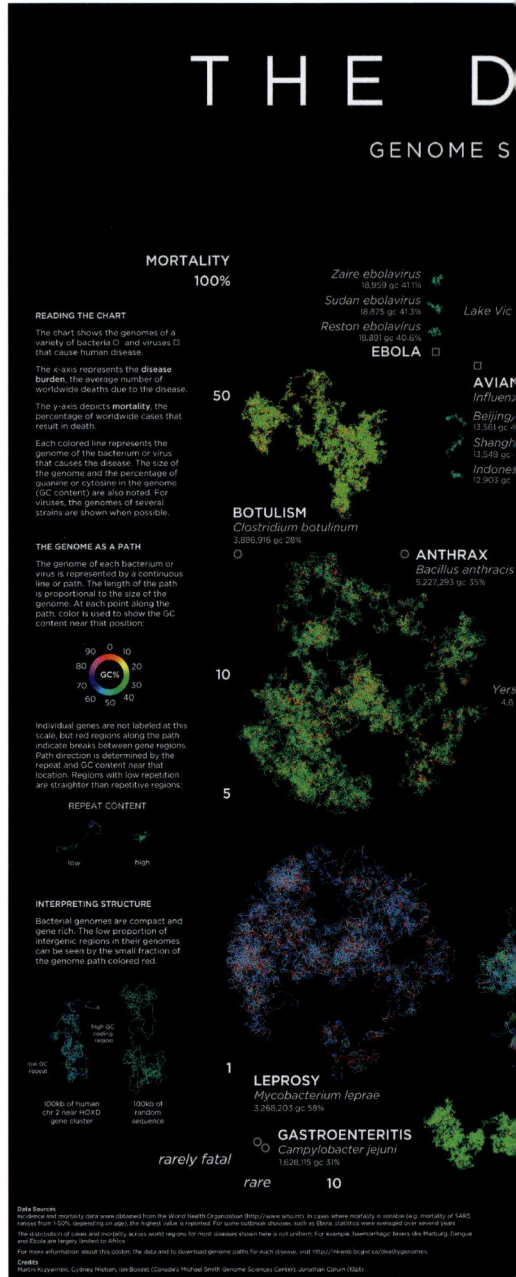

ADLY GENOMES

RE AND SIZE OF HARMFUL BACTERIA AND VIRUSES

WORLDWIDE ANNUAL CASES

1,000   10,000   100,000   1,000,000   10,000,000

AIDS
HIV virus
US 1982
9,747 gc 42.5%
Senegal 1995
8,777 gc 41.5%
Spain 2008
8,471 gc 41.3%

SARS
SARS coronavirus TOR2
29,751 gc 41%

LISTERIOSIS
Listeria monocytogenes
2,905,187 gc 38%

MRSA
Staphylococcus aureus 252
2,902,619 gc 33%

TUBERCULOSIS
tobacterium tuberculosis
4,411,532 gc 66%

YELLOW FEVER
Yellow fever virus
10,862 gc 49.7%
17DD   17D-213

100,000,000

MENINGITIS
Neisseria meningitidis
2,272,360 gc 52%

SYPHILIS
Treponema pallidum
1,134,371 gc 53%

DENGUE FEVER
Dengue virus
Type 1
10,735 gc 46.7%
Type 2, FJ-10
10,723 gc 45.8%
Type 3, 80-2
10,695 gc 46.6%

TYPHOID
Salmonella typhi
4,809,037 gc 52%

CHOLERA
Vibrio cholerae
2,959,609 gc 48%

PNEUMONIA
Streptococcus pneumoniae
2,160,842 gc 40%

C35
3,221 gc 48.9%
GU1214
3,072 gc 48.3%
A1_50115
2,853 gc 49.2%

POISONING
ichia coli O157
5,405,525 gc 50%

SWINE FLU
Influenza A H1N1
Wisconsin/629-D00015
13,272 gc 43.5%
Thailand/CU-B5
13,611 gc 43.4%
Taiwan/115/200915
13,255 gc 43.4%

HEPATITIS B
Hepatitis B virus

MALARIA
Plasmodium falciparum
23,020,762 gc 19%

1,000   10,000   100,000   1,000,000   10,000,000

WORLDWIDE ANNUAL DEATHS

Death & Taxes

How to read the data
Each item is packed with data. This is how it works.

How much does this cost YOU?
The average tax payer will pay $5 per billion on discretionary spending. To figure out how much the items on this poster will cost you, simply multiply the numeral by 5 or your corresponding cost per billion figure.

Income	Cost per billion
$1,000,000	$230
$500,000	$108
$250,000	$47
$100,000	$15
$50,000	$6
$43,650	$5
$30,000	$3
$10,000	$.75

$1 $5 $20 $50 $100

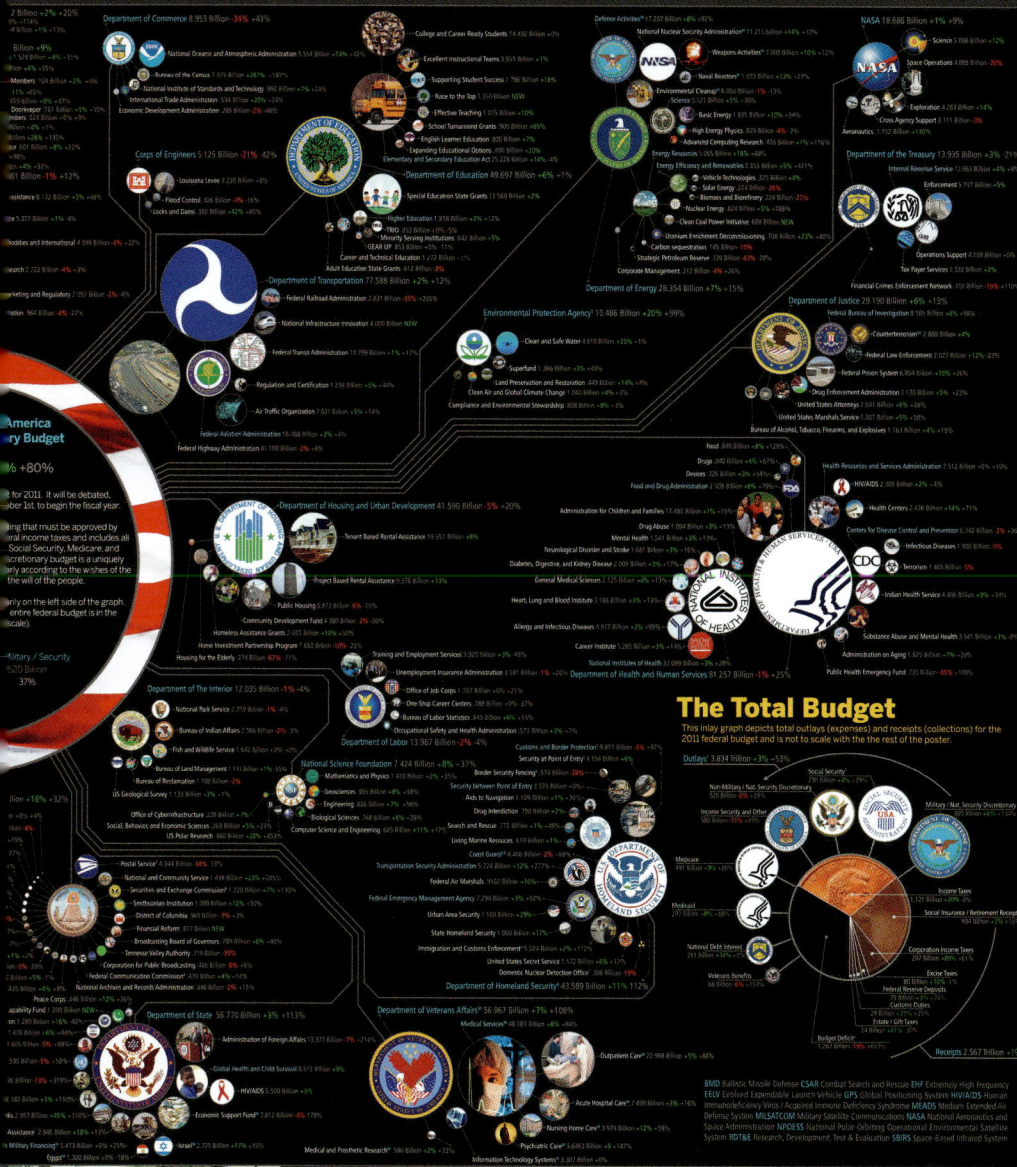

A VISUAL GUIDE TO WHERE YOUR
FEDERAL TAX DOLLARS GO

The Total Budget

This inlay graph depicts total outlays (expenses) and receipts (collections) for the 2011 federal budget and is not to scale with the rest of the poster.

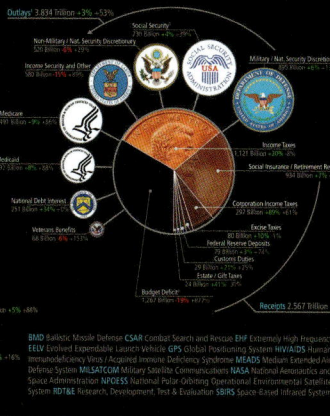

DeathandTaxesPoster.com

Where your money goes: the defin

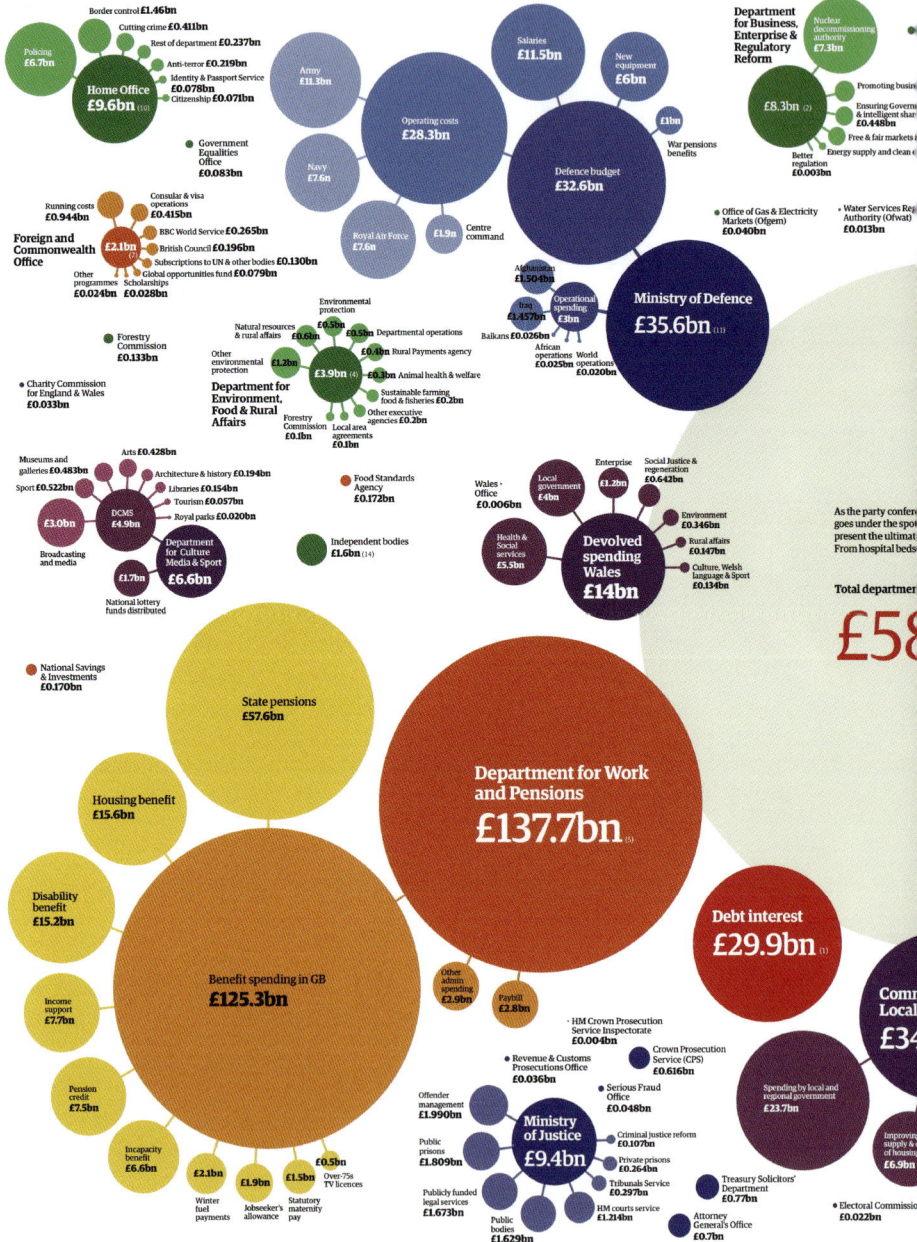

Home Office £9.6bn (10)
- Border control £1.46bn
- Cutting crime £0.411bn
- Rest of department £0.237bn
- Anti-terror £0.219bn
- Identity & Passport Service £0.078bn
- Citizenship £0.071bn
- Policing £6.7bn

Government Equalities Office £0.083bn

Foreign and Commonwealth Office £2.1bn (7)
- Running costs £0.944bn
- Consular & visa operations £0.415bn
- BBC World Service £0.265bn
- British Council £0.196bn
- Subscriptions to UN & other bodies £0.130bn
- Global opportunities fund £0.079bn
- Other programmes £0.024bn
- Scholarships £0.028bn

Forestry Commission £0.133bn

Charity Commission for England & Wales £0.033bn

Army £11.3bn
Navy £7.6bn
Royal Air Force £7.6bn
Operating costs £28.3bn
£1.9n Centre command
Salaries £11.5bn
New equipment £6bn
War pensions benefits £1bn
Defence budget £32.6bn

Ministry of Defence £35.6bn (11)
- Afghanistan £1.504bn
- Iraq £1.457bn
- Operational spending £3bn
- Balkans £0.026bn
- African operations £0.025bn
- World operations £0.020bn

Department for Business, Enterprise & Regulatory Reform £8.3bn (2)
- Nuclear decommissioning authority £7.3bn
- Better regulation £0.448bn
- Promoting busin...
- Ensuring Governm... & intelligent shar...
- Free & fair markets...
- Energy supply and clean... £0.003bn

Office of Gas & Electricity Markets (Ofgem) £0.040bn

Water Services Reg... Authority (Ofwat) £0.013bn

Department for Environment, Food & Rural Affairs £3.9bn (4)
- Environmental protection £0.5bn
- Natural resources & rural affairs £0.6bn
- Other environmental protection £1.2bn
- Departmental operations £0.5bn
- Rural Payments agency £0.4bn
- Animal health & welfare £0.3bn
- Sustainable farming food & fisheries £0.2bn
- Other executive agencies £0.2bn
- Forestry Commission £0.1bn
- Local area agreements £0.1bn

Food Standards Agency £0.172bn

Independent bodies £1.6bn (14)

Department for Culture Media & Sport £6.6bn
- Museums and galleries £0.483bn
- Arts £0.428bn
- Architecture & history £0.194bn
- Sport £0.522bn
- Libraries £0.154bn
- Tourism £0.057bn
- Royal parks £0.020bn
- DCMS £4.9bn
- Broadcasting and media £3.0bn
- National lottery funds distributed £1.7bn

Devolved spending Wales £14bn
- Wales Office £0.006bn
- Local government £4bn
- Enterprise £1.2bn
- Social Justice & regeneration £0.642bn
- Environment £0.346bn
- Rural affairs £0.147bn
- Culture, Welsh language & Sport £0.134bn
- Health & Social services £5.5bn

As the party confere...
goes under the spo...
present the ultimat...
From hospital beds...

Total departmer

£58

National Savings & Investments £0.170bn

Department for Work and Pensions £137.7bn (5)
- State pensions £57.6bn
- Housing benefit £15.6bn
- Disability benefit £15.2bn
- Income support £7.7bn
- Pension credit £7.5bn
- Incapacity benefit £6.6bn
- Winter fuel payments £2.1bn
- Jobseeker's allowance £1.9bn
- Statutory maternity pay £1.5bn
- Over-75s TV licences £0.5bn
- Benefit spending in GB £125.3bn
- Other admin spending £2.9bn
- Paybill £2.8bn

Debt interest £29.9bn (1)

Ministry of Justice £9.4bn
- Offender management £1.990bn
- Public prisons £1.809bn
- Publicly funded legal services £1.673bn
- Public bodies £1.629bn
- HM Crown Prosecution Service Inspectorate £0.004bn
- Crown Prosecution Service (CPS) £0.616bn
- Revenue & Customs Prosecutions Office £0.036bn
- Serious Fraud Office £0.048bn
- Criminal justice reform £0.107bn
- Private prisons £0.264bn
- Tribunals Service £0.297bn
- HM courts service £1.214bn
- Treasury Solicitors' Department £0.77bn
- Attorney General's Office £0.7bn
- Electoral Commissio... £0.022bn

Comm... Local... £34...
- Spending by local and regional government £23.7bn
- Improving supply &... of housing... £6.9bn

NOTES

The figures give a picture of major expenditure but exclude local government spending not controlled by central government. It also excludes government departments who are predominantly financed by their income, such as the Crown Estate or the Export Credits Guarantee Department. The totals here add up to more

than the total budget, because some of the smaller government departments are funded via the larger ones, such as the Parliamentary Counsel Office, funded via the Cabinet Office.
(1) Interest paid on the public debt.
(2) Total spending on energy liabilities is actually £6.8bn, less

than that spent on the NDA. This is because the department makes money back with efficiency savings
(5) SureStart spending includes childcare and nursery funding
(4) Animal health includes disease prevention, dealing with BSE etc. The Rural Payments Agency is the body that distributes CAP

payments – these payments are large but covered by transfers from EU so do not show up as net spending here
(5) benefit spending excludes child benefit, guardians' allowance, widow's pensions; statutory paternity pay, statutory adoption pay - these paid by HMRC, MoD, DBERR respectively

(10) Hospital and community health services spending is estimated – figures to be published December 2008. Estimate based on previous annual spending. Excludes spending on fam... health services and GP prescriptions. Wages are also estimated based on previous year's figures

atlas of UK government spending

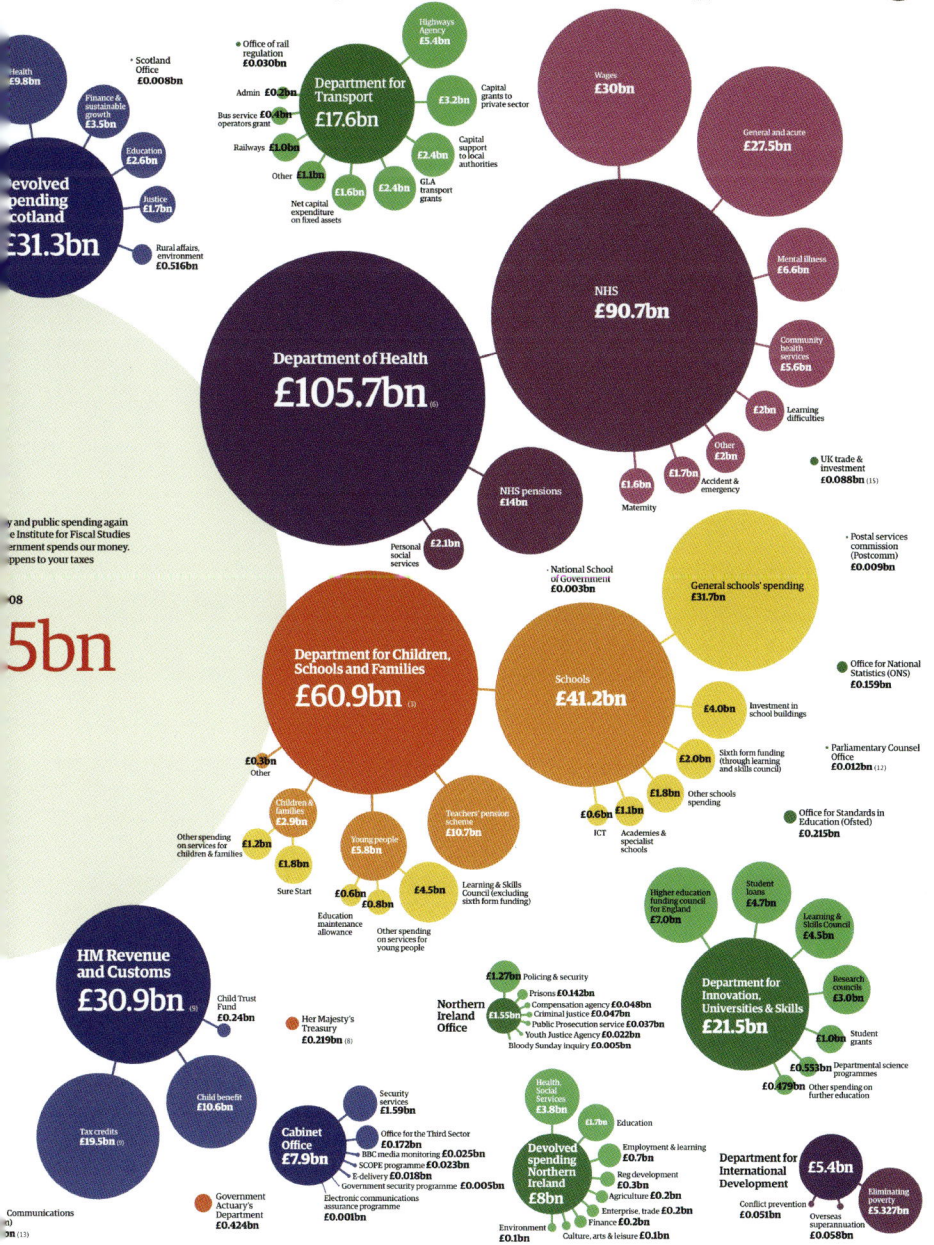

Health £9.8bn

Scotland Office £0.008bn

Finance & sustainable growth £3.5bn

Education £2.6bn

Devolved spending Scotland £31.3bn

Justice £1.7bn

Rural affairs, environment £0.516bn

Office of rail regulation £0.030bn

Highways Agency £5.4bn

Department for Transport £17.6bn

Admin £0.2bn

Bus service operators grant £0.4bn

Railways £1.0bn

Other £1.1bn

£3.2bn

Capital grants to private sector

£2.4bn

Capital support to local authorities

£2.4bn

GLA transport grants

£1.6bn

Net capital expenditure on fixed assets

Wages **£30bn**

General and acute **£27.5bn**

NHS £90.7bn

Mental illness £6.6bn

Community health services £5.6bn

£2bn Learning difficulties

Other £2bn

£1.7bn

£1.6bn

Accident & emergency

Maternity

UK trade & investment £0.088bn (15)

Department of Health £105.7bn (6)

NHS pensions £14bn

Personal social services £2.1bn

National School of Government £0.003bn

Postal services commission (Postcomm) £0.009bn

General schools' spending **£31.7bn**

Office for National Statistics (ONS) £0.159bn

and public spending again
e Institute for Fiscal Studies
ernment spends our money.
ppens to your taxes

08

5bn

Department for Children, Schools and Families £60.9bn (3)

Schools £41.2bn

£4.0bn Investment in school buildings

£2.0bn Sixth form funding (through learning and skills council)

Parliamentary Counsel Office £0.012bn (12)

£1.8bn Other schools spending

£0.6bn £1.1bn

ICT Academies & specialist schools

Office for Standards in Education (Ofsted) £0.215bn

£0.3bn Other

Children & families £2.9bn

Other spending on services for children & families £1.2bn

Teachers' pension scheme £10.7bn

Young people £5.8bn

£1.8bn

Sure Start

£0.6bn £0.8bn

Education maintenance allowance

Other spending on services for young people

£4.5bn Learning & Skills Council (excluding sixth form funding)

Higher education funding council for England £7.0bn

Student loans £4.7bn

Learning & Skills Council £4.5bn

Department for Innovation, Universities & Skills £21.5bn

Research councils £3.0bn

£1.0bn Student grants

£0.553bn Departmental science programmes

£0.479bn Other spending on further education

£1.27bn Policing & security

Prisons £0.142bn

Compensation agency £0.048bn

£1.55bn Criminal justice £0.047bn

Public Prosecution service £0.037bn

Youth Justice Agency £0.022bn

Bloody Sunday inquiry £0.005bn

Northern Ireland Office £1.55bn (8)

HM Revenue and Customs £30.9bn (5)

Child Trust Fund £0.24bn

Her Majesty's Treasury £0.219bn (8)

Child benefit £10.6bn

Tax credits £19.5bn (9)

Security services £1.59bn

Cabinet Office £7.9bn

Office for the Third Sector £0.172bn

BBC media monitoring £0.025bn

SCOPE programme £0.023bn

E-delivery £0.018bn

Government security programme £0.005bn

Electronic communications assurance programme £0.001bn

Government Actuary's Department £0.424bn

Health, Social Services £3.8bn

£1.7bn Education

Devolved spending Northern Ireland £8bn

Employment & learning £0.7bn

Reg development £0.3bn

Agriculture £0.2bn

Enterprise, trade £0.2bn

Finance £0.2bn

Department for International Development £5.4bn

Conflict prevention £0.051bn

Eliminating poverty £5.327bn

Overseas superannuation £0.058bn

Environment £0.1bn

Culture, arts & leisure £0.1bn

Communications
n)
n (13)

Running costs includes salaries, hospitality budgets, home
overseas accommodation costs. Administration and
gramme amounts combined here
Excludes Northern Rock, 2008-09 spending of at least
bn

(6) Spending on Child Benefits and Tax Credits etc does not come out of the departmental expenditure pot
(10) Rest of policing funding includes funding of bodies related to policing, such as the Police Complaints Authority and the National Crime Intelligence Service

(11) Includes £1bn extra above budget from Treasury reserves to cover operations. The total amounts may not sum as there are overlapping amounts, ie between salaries and running costs
(12) Now part of the Cabinet Office
(13) The amount of government funding from DBERR and

DCMS, rest from licence fees from broadcasters and media organisations
(14) Includes: House of Commons, House of Lords and National Audit Office
(15) Split between Parliament direct, the FCO and DBERR

SOURCES: DEPARTMENTAL REPORTS, INSTITUTE FOR FISCAL STUDIES, PUBLIC EXPENDITURE STATISTICAL ANALYSES (PESA)

RESEARCH: SIMON ROGERS, GEMMA TETLOW, MAX OFFRAY

GRAPHIC: JENNY RIDLEY, MICHAEL ROBINSON

Previous spread

Definitive Atlas
of UK Government Spending

Large amounts of money are difficult to imagine and therefore difficult to compare. This graphic, developed as a double spread for *The Guardian*, shows UK spending by each government department, with each circle sized by the amount spent. The pale circle in the middle represents total governmental spending in 2007/2008, while the coloured circles show the distribution of the budget to various departments. The data is not centrally supplied by the government but gathered from individual departmental reports. Since its first launch in 2008, the piece has been updated regularly.

Project Info: "Where Your Money Goes",
The Guardian, newspaper article, 2008, UK
Research: Simon Rogers, Gemma Tetlow,
Max Opray
Design: Jenny Ridley
Art Direction: Michael Robinson

Essentials of Sociology

This series of infographics was developed for a student textbook, *Essentials of Sociology*, published in 2010. As an introduction to the subject, the book is organised around themes of globalisation and everyday life. The infographics were developed to help make the abstract data more concrete and accessible for students. A selection of sociological surveys is represented in various diagrams, using colour coding and size relations as the main visual tools.

Project Info: *Essentials of Sociology*, book,
W. W. Norton & Company, 2010, USA
Data Source: The World Bank; UNDP;
US Census Bureau; Edward Laumann
et al.: *The Social Organization of Sexuality*; Gapminder.com
Design: Louise Ma (Kiss Me I'm Polish)
Art Direction: Agnieszka Gasparska
(Kiss Me I'm Polish)

Figure 8.1

GLOBAL INEQUALITY

Comparing Quality of Life Among Countries

	LOW INCOME COUNTRIES	MEDIUM INCOME COUNTRIES	HIGH INCOME COUNTRIES	WORLD
GROSS NATIONAL INCOME PER CAPITA (Current U.S. $)	$524	$3,260	$39,345	$8,613
TOTAL POPULATION	973 million	4,651 million	1,069 million	6,692 million
ANNUAL POPULATION GROWTH	+ 2.1%	+ 1.1%	+ 0.7%	+ 1.2%
LIFE EXPECTANCY AT BIRTH	59 years	69 years	79 years	69 years
FERTILITY RATE	4 Births per woman	2.4 Births per woman	1.8 Births per woman	2.5 Births per woman
MORTALITY RATE	120 Per 1,000	58 Per 1,000	7 Per 1,000	68 Per 1,000

Source: World Bank 2009b.

Figure 9.4

GENDER EMPOWERMENT AROUND THE WORLD

Ten Countries Ranked by Gender Empowerment Measure

% of seats in parliament

% of legislators, senior officials, & managers

% of professional and technical workers

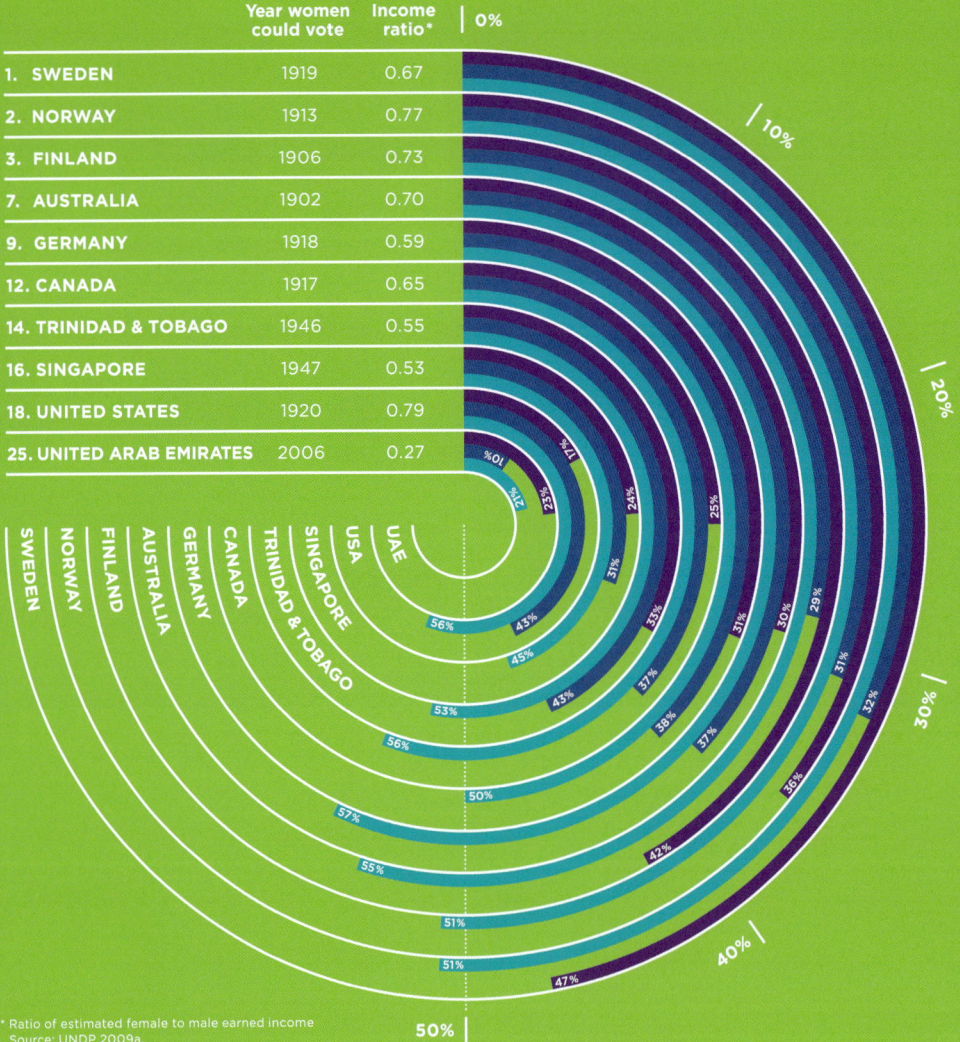

	Year women could vote	Income ratio*
1. SWEDEN	1919	0.67
2. NORWAY	1913	0.77
3. FINLAND	1906	0.73
7. AUSTRALIA	1902	0.70
9. GERMANY	1918	0.59
12. CANADA	1917	0.65
14. TRINIDAD & TOBAGO	1946	0.55
16. SINGAPORE	1947	0.53
18. UNITED STATES	1920	0.79
25. UNITED ARAB EMIRATES	2006	0.27

0%

10%

20%

30%

40%

50%

SWEDEN NORWAY FINLAND AUSTRALIA GERMANY CANADA TRINIDAD & TOBAGO SINGAPORE USA UAE

10% 23% 22%

11% 24% 25%

31% 33% 31% 30% 29% 31% 32%

56% 43% 45% 43% 37% 38% 37% 36%

53% 56% 50% 42% 47%

57% 55% 51% 51%

* Ratio of estimated female to male earned income
Source: UNDP 2009a.

Figure 16.3

THE WIDENING GAP

Between Richer and Poorer Countries, 1800 to 2008

GDP PER CAPITA*	1800	2008
USA	$1,343	$42,922
GERMANY	$1,643	$32,637
JAPAN	$896	$31,824
REPUBLIC OF KOREA	$740	$23,845
BRAZIL	$509	$9,633
SOUTH AFRICA	$759	$9,360
EGYPT	$748	$5,678
CHINA	$992	$5,520
PAKISTAN	$665	$2,671
DEM. REP. OF CONGO	$394	$370

* 2008 U.S. $

Note: GDP for South Africa from 1911; 1900 data not available.

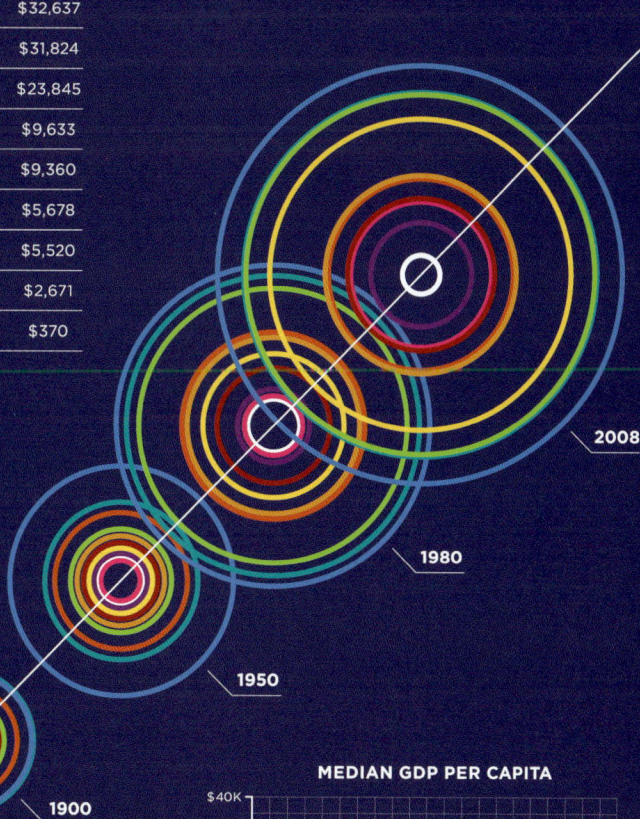

Source: Gapminder.com 2009.

2008

1980

1950

1900

1800

MEDIAN GDP PER CAPITA

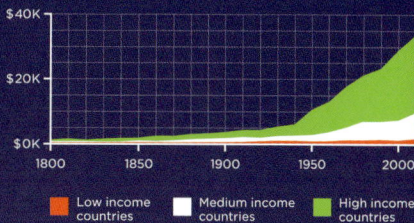

$40K
$20K
$0K
1800 1850 1900 1950 2000

Low income countries
Medium income countries
High income countries

THE THINGS I ENJOY LISTENING TO MAKE ME FEEL LIKE

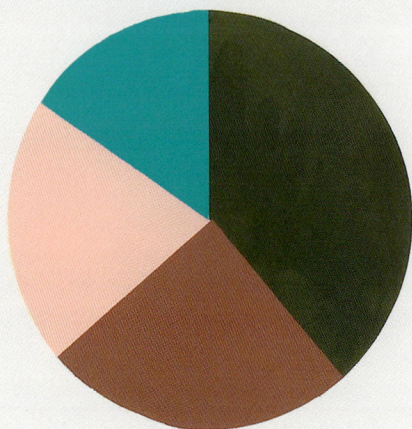

THE THINGS I HATE LISTENING TO MAKE ME FEEL LIKE

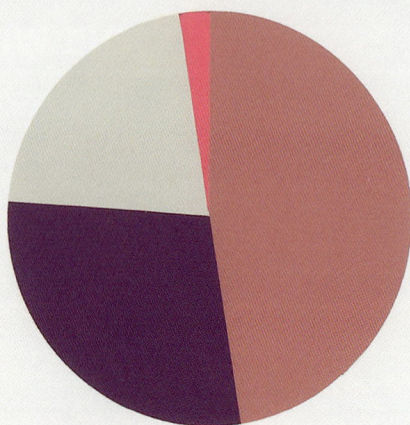

- I'm 19 again [the good part with all the wonder and no bitterness].
- I need to throw a chair through a window [in a triumphant way].
- Call everyone I know and convince them of good it is. how
- I will never make anything that good if I tried!

- I really don't understand shit about people in general.
- With things like this who needs things?
- I'm turning into someone who's weird. "Turning."
- I'm about to get beat up.

GIVE UP THE ABILITY TO LISTEN TO MUSIC OR ANY OF THESE EIGHT THINGS?

TERRIFIED! Take my ears instead!

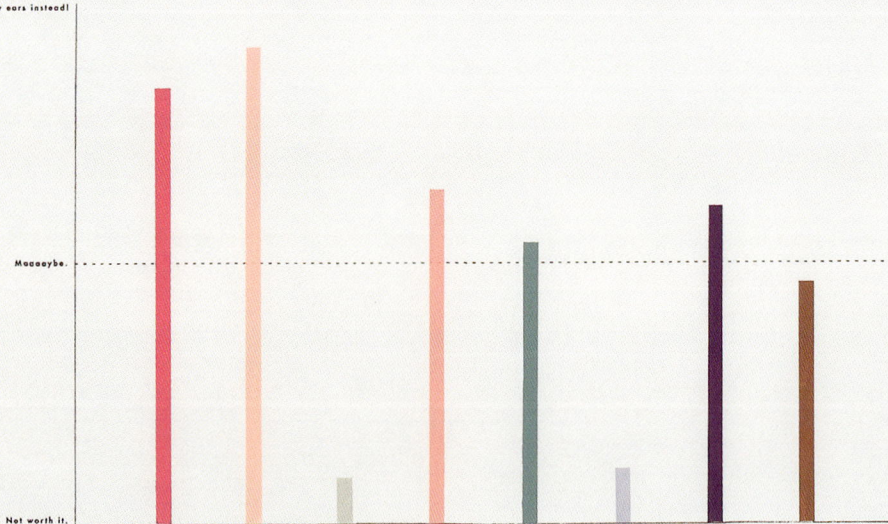

Maaaaybe.

Not worth it.

- Not doing or trying the things I want to do or try.
- Making a mistake that I'll regret for the rest of my life.
- Fast-forward 20 years from now and I'm still at the bar.
- Not having anyone to call.

- Being insanely poor and not being able to do anything about it.
- Moving away from New York City to anywhere except LA .
- House arrest. No visitors. Five years.
- Internet blackout for life.

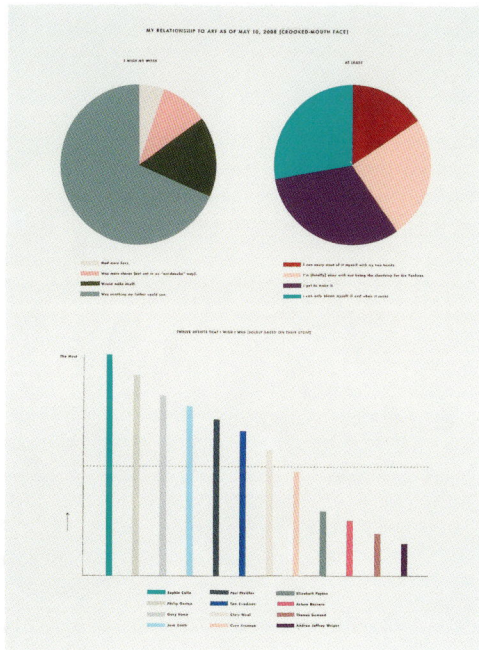

Faces Diagrams

Andrew Kuo has turned diagrams into his personal means to assess things happening in his life. For some time he has used diagrams to report on his blog how he liked the recent concert of this or that band. In 2008 he developed a series of hand-painted diagrams that portrayed a wider record of what inspired him. The two examples here chart his relation to fine arts and music, respectively. Both feature two pie-charts at the top and a bar chart along the bottom, mimicking faces. They gain their individual traits depending on which personal feelings and thoughts Kuo decides to evaluate and the subjective order in which he places them.

Project Info: Series of paintings, 2008, USA
Artist: Andrew Kuo
Additional Info: Andrew Kuo is represented by Taxter & Spengemann, New York

Following spread

One Nation, Under God

The US has a wide diversity of religious beliefs, but the number of Americans who consider themselves atheists is rising. This infographic uses a photograph to show the percentage of the population and actual number of people claiming to belong to big Christian, Jewish or Muslim communities. The image plays with hiding the people's faces, but shows some of them in half profile or in the mirror behind the bar. The female bartender on the other hand, facing the group heavily tattooed and seemingly uninterested, is clearly associated with the atheist figures to the very right of the image by the colour of her shirt.

Project Info: *GOOD*, magazine and online article, 2009, USA
Data Source: The 2009 American Religious Identification Survey
Design: Chris Korbey
Editors: Morgan Clendaniel, Atley Kasky

ONE NATION, UNDER GOD

America has always been a religious country. But a recent study finds that might be changing; The percent of the country who considers themselves atheists is rising rapidly. While they still make up a small minority in comparison to the major religions, the current trends indicate that we may not be one nation, under God, forever. Here is a look at what we believe.

PERCENTAGE OF POPULATION

POPULATION IN MILLIONS

BAPTIST

19.3%
15.8%
34.0
36.2

1990 2008 1990 2008

JEWISH

1.8%
1.2%
3.1
2.7

1990 2008 1990 2008

CATHOLIC

26.2%
25.1%
46.0
57.2

1990 2008 1990 2008

A COLLABORATION BETWEEN
GOOD AND CHRIS KORBEY

SOURCE: The 2009 American Religious Identification Survey

34.2

15.0%

8.2%   14.3

1990   2008   1990   2008

NO RELIGION

14.8% 14.2%   32.4
              26.0

1990   2008   1990   2008

GENERIC CHRISTIAN

0.3% 0.6%   0.5   1.4

1990 2008   1990 2008

MUSLIM

18.7%   32.8   29.4
      12.9%

1990   2008   1990   2008

MAINLINE CHRISTIAN

CHIVAS

GENERIC CHRISTIAN: Born Again, Evangelical, Non-denominational, Unspecified
MAINLINE CHRISTIAN: Episcopalian, Lutheran, Methodist, Presbyterian, United Church of Christ

Gapminder World Map

Health *Life expectancy at birth (years)*

Money *GDP per person in US dollars (purcha.*

2010

Japan
France
Sweden
Germany
Hong Kong
Iceland
Andorra
Italy
Switzerland
Spain
Australia Singa-
Israel
Finland
pore
Norway
New Zealand
Liechten-
Malta
South
2
UK
stein
Korea
Bel-
Lux-
gium
embourg
Greece
Slovenia
USA
Denmark
Cuba
Costa
Rica
Chile
Puerto
Rico
Portugal
Kuwait
Taiwan
UAE
Brunei
Mexico
Barbados
Albania
Croatia
Czech Rep.
Belize
Uruguay
Oman
Qatar
Panama
Poland
Grenada
Argen-
Slovakia
Dominica
tina
Bahrain
Macedonia
Venezuela
Serbia
Malaysia
Antigua & Barbuda
Ecuador
Colo-5
Libya
Hungary
Bahamas
Tunisia
mbia
4
Algeria
Jordan
Bulgaria
Estonia
Saudi Arabia
Peru
Brazil
St Kitts & N.
Romania
Seychelles
DR
Lithuania
Tonga
Samoa
Lebanon
Leba-
El
6
non
Salvador
Jamaica
Mauritius
rocco
Palau
Iran
Turkey
uate-
a
Azerbaijan
Egypt
Trinidad &
Suriname
Belarus
Tobago
kraine
Thailand
Guyana
Russia
Bhutan
a
Nauru
Kazakhstan
Turkmenistan
Kiribati
Namibia
Gabon

Colour by region:

Size by population:

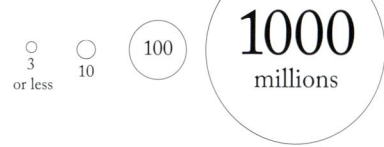

100

1000
millions

3
or less
10

Botswana

p.

South Africa

Equatorial Guinea

Data are for 2009 for all 192 UN member states and the other
5 countries and territories with more than 1 million people
(Hong Kong, Taiwan, Palestine, Puerto Rico and Kosovo).
Free to copy, share and remix but attribute Gapminder.
For sources see:

www.gapminder.org
http://www.gapminder.org/worldmap

Angola
Swaziland

1. San Marino
2. Monaco
3. Cyprus
4. Montenegro
5. Saint Lucia
6. St Vincent &
   Grenadines

00
10 000
20 000
50 000

ower adjusted) (log scale)

UND ICH DIE DER
NICHT DAS EIN ZU IST DU
IN SIE ES SO MEPHISTOPHELES
DEN MIT FAUST SICH IHR MIR
MICH ER WAS WIE AUF DEM NUR
VON DOCH AN EUCH WENN IM DICH DA WIR
DASS MAN ALS AUCH MEIN DIR HIER UNS NUN DES
NOCH NACH SCHON MARGARETE AUS WIRD SIND IHN
WOHL HAT VOR FÜR BIN UM KANN EINEN DENN EINE AM SOLL
WAR ZUM SEIN WILL DURCH ACH WER GEIST MUSS WELT GLEICH GAR
ALLE DANN BEI NICHTS O IHM EINEM WO ALLEIN ALLES MARTHE GUT RECHT
JA MEINE MANN SELBST IMMER VOM GEHN HERR LEBEN LASS HAB VIEL WIEDER
MAG MEHR TEUFEL GERN GRETCHEN BIST GOTT HAST ÜBER FORT MEINEM ZUR HERZ INS
TAG NIE NACHT FROSCH ERST GANZ ZEIT KEIN MENSCHEN KOMMT DIESER GEHT SEI IST'S DEIN
STEHT WEISS WEH DEINE MUTTER HABEN HERRN MACHT KOMM BALD SEID AB KIND DIESEM SEH SAGEN
ALLEN ABER HIN LANGE HERZEN EINMAL SEHR WÄR HAUS SCHÜLER SONST FREUND HABT BRUST NEIN MEINER
MEINEN LIEBE SIEBEL DORT EINER WAGNER ALTMAYER HIMMEL BUSEN GEWISS LÄSST BLUT DEINEN DIESEN HEXE
DAVON KRAFT WEIT ERDE DIESE SIEHT ANDERN SEINE DEINEM HAND NATUR GESCHEHN SCHÖNE EBEN SEHN HÖREN
SCHÖNEN LIEB DIES JEDER HER BRANDER JETZT BEIM TRITT FREI EWIG GETAN WARUM KEINE AUGEN DRUM SCHÖN CHOR IHRE
UNTER WEG LIEGT KOPF DARF MUSST GENUG SAGT ENDE SINGT MACHEN LANG ODER GLÜCK SEHT WENIG FRAU TUT GANZE
KEINEN SEELE JEDEM HEREIN FASST GROSS STIMME KÖNNT OFT WEIN LUFT GANZEN SINN WERDEN DAMIT OHNE NIEDER HINAUS HEUTE
MÄDCHEN DRAN SIEH IHREN FREUDE KANNST DRÄNGT HEUT ETWAS SIEHST LUST HABE TAUSEND FEUER SEINEM GEBEN SEINER ALTE HINEIN DEINER
SCHRITT WEIB TAGE LIESCHEN WELCH GIBT WORT GROSSEN HERREN OBEN MEER ZWAR BLICK LEICHT WOLLEN ANDRE KOMMEN SAG HÖLLE SINNEN
ALTEN SCHWER ALLER WOLLT ZURÜCK KUNST MÜSSEN SCHEINT LIEBT ERSTE HERAN GLAS MENGE FÜHL GEHEN GUTEN TOD NEUEN FÜSSEN RUH WILLST
WELCHE BIS HEISST FÜHREN HÄLT NOT FENSTER HÖRT ZEITEN LIED ERSTEN KREIS TIERE SOLLT VALENTIN LICHT MORGEN TIER HÖR VATER GESCHWIND LOS GEISTER
SEINEN TRANK HALB HÄTT SCHAUEN MIR'S OB ZWEI GEBT ARM LEIB SCHMUCK ZIEHT ACHT BUCH LIEBEN HÄTTE IHREM BESTEN MÖCHTE ARMEN SITZT DAZU LEIBE
GUTE MENSCH DIESES LASSEN SAH ICH'S STEHN LEBT LÄSST KAUM TOT EINS NAH EI KURZ PUDEL MANCHE JEDES BÖSER PLATZ STEIGT ANDERS GEFÜHL WEIL ZEICHEN FEST
VORBEI HATT ORT KEINER WIRST WERD LEISE HATTE ALLEIN KLEIN FLAMME VOLL HINTER SOLLST GIB TRÄGT VIELLEICHT MÖCHT EUREM JUNGE LEBENS WEITER ENGEL BLEIBT JE DOKTOR
DICHTER WIRD'S BESSER HERAUS FÜHRE TUN GEWALT SINNE FASSE BRINGT GESELLSCHAFT GLÜT WORTE JENEM BEREIT BÖSEN MACH ARME FIND HILFT SCHAFFEN EURE HEUTE DABEI
JENEM ELEND TRAGEN WISSEN ART DREI GESELLEN HERUM STERNE GENIESSEN JUCHHE HERRLICH EINES DIESMAL GLAUB LESEN HINAUF WÜRDE SCHAFFT GING GUTER DRINGT FREILICH
FÜHLT TOR JEDEN BESTE SCHÄTZEN HEXEN STETS ALTER JAHR MANCHEN SACHEN HERVOR VOLK GROSSE VORÜBER LAUF SCHMERZ WARD FRISCH NIEMAND BISSCHEN GESANG JAMMER
REGT VERGEBENS LIESCHEN RECHTE KLEINE LACHEN RECHTEN SCHLECHT SOHN GEDANKEN HALT TRETEN SITZEN SCHLAGE FRÜH AUGENBLICK NENNEN RINGS GEGEREN EURER FEHLT HERBEI INDEM
HERAUF SCHLÄGT UNTEN FÜHLE SAGE ÜBERALL WORTEN STREBEN KLEINEN BRÜDER WEISE BRAUCH FÄNGT NIMMT VERZEIHT JAHRE NEBEL FLUCH HOFFNUNG UMHER FERNE BRICHT GEWESEN INDESSEN
KESSEL FROH WERDE HALTEN IHRER SCHAU STUNDEN NASE TIEF BRINGEN UNSRE DU'S KONNTE ALL HERZLICH LETZTE DARUM TEIL SCHEIN GESICHT SCHWELLE VERLIEREN FAST DREIN STILLEN WASSER AUFS
TRAUM KERL WAHRHEIT LAND RETTE NEU TIEFE TUN WOLLTE WIRKT WUNDER BEHAGEN SCHWEBEN FRAGEN KNECHT DENNEN FINDEN SEIN TRÄNEN SPRINGT GEGENWART NAMEN ERGETZEN LAMPE GRAD
VERSCHWINDET KLANG LEID FELD STUNDE HOHEN GEISTERN HEILGEN DING MAGST DAHIN FLIEGEN FRAUEN WIDER STAND WANN WESEN ERDEN MUT HÖRE GLAUBEN DURCHS HERAB ARMER SOLCH STELLT
KAM FINDE GABEN KÖNIG CHRIST FÜHLEN EH STADT SCHLOSS FLAMMEN KLUG JUGEND SCHÖNER FÜRWAHR DIR'S TATEN FREUNDLICH BRENNT HOFF ZIEHEN BITTE HEINRICH GENUSS SEHEN GRAB STEHEN
SINGEN SPASS VERFLUCHT RIEGEL EDLEN WAHRLICH FÄLLT KOMMST VIELEN MÜSST GEBRACHT NEUE WIE'S ERSCHEINT SCHADEN GLIEDER SPIEGEL SONNE SOLLTE PEIN HAUSE RAUM TRINKT SCHREIN
GROSSER BEWEGT GIFT ENGEN FASSEN REICH EHRE FINDET WERT JUNGEN BERG BEIDEN BLEIBEN PLAGEN SEITE TÖNEN SPIEL JUNG SELIG DARFST WEIBER WOHNE NEHMEN LIEGEN WISSENSCHAFT VERLOREN
SELBER HEIT LIEBER REISE STEIN GRUSS KRONE GEWINNEN DAFÜR DRANG RAT NEHMT KALT WAREN STOCK FRAGT CHORUS TRINKEN WEINE EINST BAND WALD WEDER GEISTES MANCHER TRIEB SCHAFF SOLCHE ER'S SATT BREIT SEINE
TU BITT KÄSTCHEN GARTEN KATER LAUT TRUG GELD GUNST HUND VERNUNFT GRUND ANFANG SASS SOLCHEN NIMMERMEHR NÄHER TÖNT LANGEN ORDNUNG KONNT MUND SCHNELL WAGEN OFFEN IRRLICHT BUNTEN IHR'S BEQUEMEN GEN
SCHAUER DROBEN MENSCHHEIT UNSER GEWÖHNLICH FELSEN WÜNSCHTE GEFALLEN ZUGRUNDE TAT SCHELM FAHREN DENKT SCHÖNES HEILGEN TANZ WILDE EUER NACHBARIN STROH RECHTS GESCHRIEBEN GENAU KOMME SPRECHEN
WILLEN BREITEN LEBENDIG SPUR TREIBT EIGNER FREIHEIT STELLE DIRNE REGEN GENUNG VERDERBEN BLUMEN SICH'S ENDLICH BOCK TIEFER KÖNNEN SOGLEICH RUFT LUSTIGE GIBT'S KLINGT SCHATZ GABST IHNEN DIREKTOR SPRICHT

Previous spread

Gapminder World Map

This diagram shows life expectancy in relation to a country's income. Countries are shown as circles, sized according to their population. The piece originated with the Gapminder Foundation, based in Stockholm, and founded by Hans Rosling, a professor of International Health and an ardent ambassador for educating the public about global population and health trends. Rosling has campaigned for a more engaging use of statistics in general and higher education. His talks are famous for his humorous way of recounting "deadly serious" global trends. The Gapminder Foundation continues to promote this sophisticated worldview by providing global statistics in animated and interactive presentations. This material is made available for free.

Project Info: Poster, 2010, Sweden
Design: Anna Rosling Rönnlund, Ola Rosling, Daniel Lapidus (Gapminder)

Fast Faust

Fast Faust is a straight hierarchy. It contains all the words Johann Wolfgang von Goethe used in the first part of his famous tragedy *Faust*, sorted and scaled by the frequency of their use throughout the play. The most frequent word "und" (and) occurs 918 times. Since this is classical German literature, the most frequent nouns are "Geist" (mind) and "Welt" (world). Developed in 2000, the piece anticipated the principle of tag clouds, which later became a prominent feature of web 2.0. As it was hardly possible to translate the frequency of words into exact point sizes for the letters, Boris Müller used logarithmic scaling to show the relative frequency of each word.

Project Info: Poster, 2000, Germany
Design: Boris Müller

Following spread

Food Poisoning

This piece shows cases of food poisoning in the US since 1990, as caused by foods like vegetables, milk and cheese, seafood or eggs. In a pleasant dinner-setting, which doesn't fail to suggest images of the Last Supper, each of the foods is shown on a table with a glass of liquid behind it. Quantities on the plates and in the glasses refer to the number of outbreaks and the number of cases.

Project Info: *GOOD*, website, 2010, USA
Data Source: The Center for Science in the Public Interest
Design: Chris Korbey
Editors: Morgan Clendaniel, Atley Kasky

CASES *of* ILLNESS (1000) / NUMBER *of* OUTBREAKS

BERRIES	SPROUTS	TOMATOES	CHEESE	ICE CREAM	POTATOES
339.7	201.2	329.2	259.4	276.1	365.9
25	31	31	74	83	108

A COLLABORATION BETWEEN GOOD AND CHRIS KORBEY

UNTIL RECENTLY, *food-borne illness was most often associated with contaminated meat. But after last year's tomato scare, illness from more innocuous-seeming foods has become more acknowledged. With the exception of meat, which falls under the purview of the U.S. Department of Agriculture, most of America's food sources are overseen by the Food and Drug Administration. Some argue that the FDA isn't empowered to do enough to enforce food-safety regulations, and legislation is currently before Congress to give it more power. Right now, these are the FDA-regulated foods that have made the most people sick since 1990.*

132

268

352

362

OYSTERS

TUNA

EGGS

LEAFY GREENS

SOURCE: The Center for Science in the Public Interest

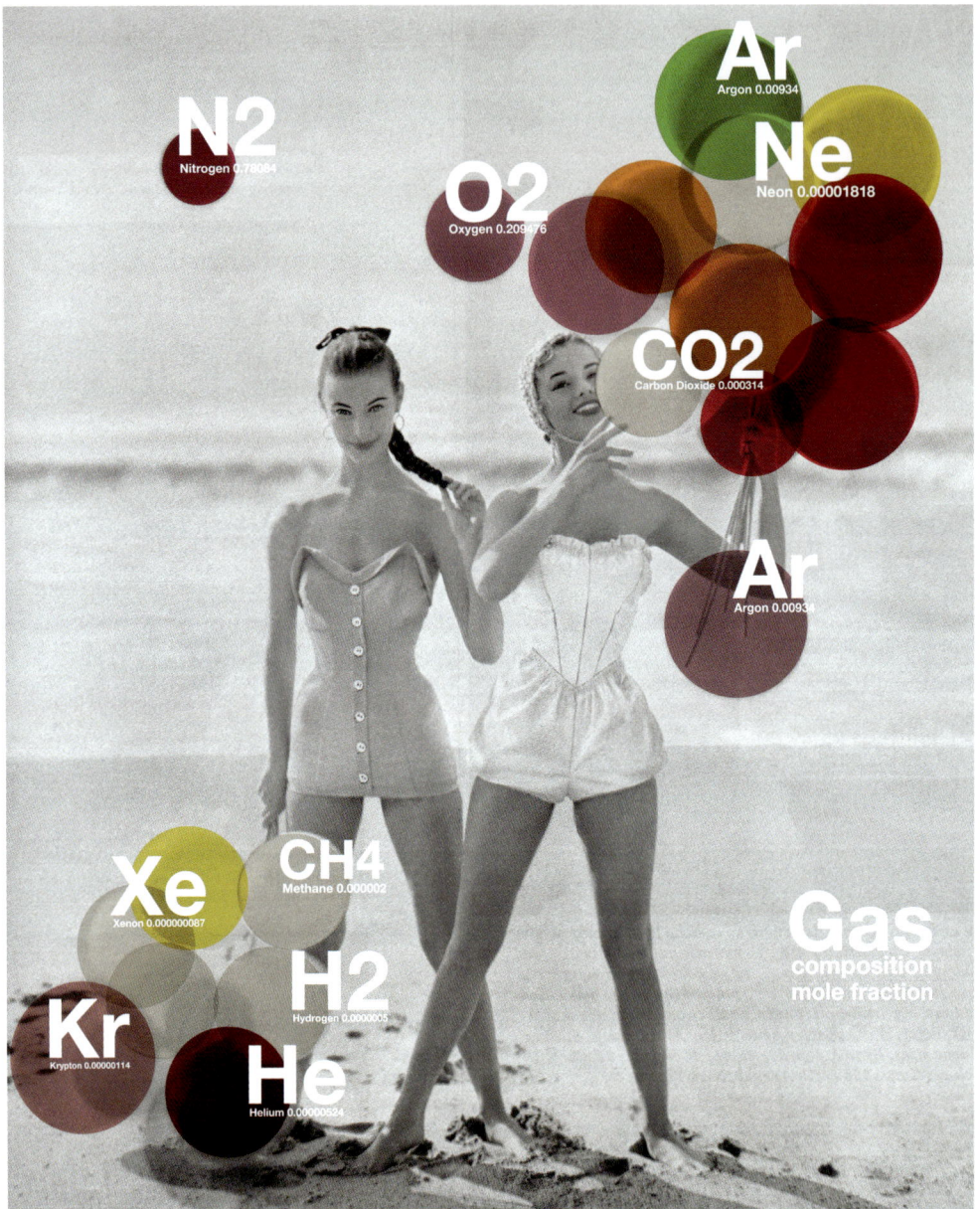

Gas Composition

Like the encounter of a nostalgic postcard with the periodic table of elements: this piece lists the composition of gases in the Earth's atmosphere. The black and white image shows two young ladies holding a bouquet of balloons. Coloured circles float through the image like bubbles of gas, whilst typographic information provides data about the constituent gases in normal air and the percentage of their concentration. The piece works like a display board to assist with memorising the composition of the atmosphere.

Project Info: Website, 2009, France
Design: Stéphane Massa-Bidal (Retrofuturs)

How Do We Achieve Harmony?

In their 2009 project "How Do We Achieve Harmony?", *GOOD* magazine looked at a range of global issues pertaining to sustainability and participation. The pieces shown here were contributed by Fogelsen-Lubliner. "The Cell Phone Revolution" looks at how mobile phones became widely available in various countries around the world. The distribution in percentage is compared between 2002 and 2007, with the pattern allowing comparison at a glance. "War, What Is It Good For?" gives a hierarchy of countries, according to how many armed conflicts they were involved in since the end of World War II, with France leading the list at 25. Each conflict is represented by a drawing of a torn-out headline from a local newspaper.

Project Info: *GOOD*, website, 2009, USA
Data Source: International Telecommunication Union; United Nations Statistics Division; International Peace Research Institute
Design: Gary Fogelson, Phil Lubliner (Fogelson-Lubliner)

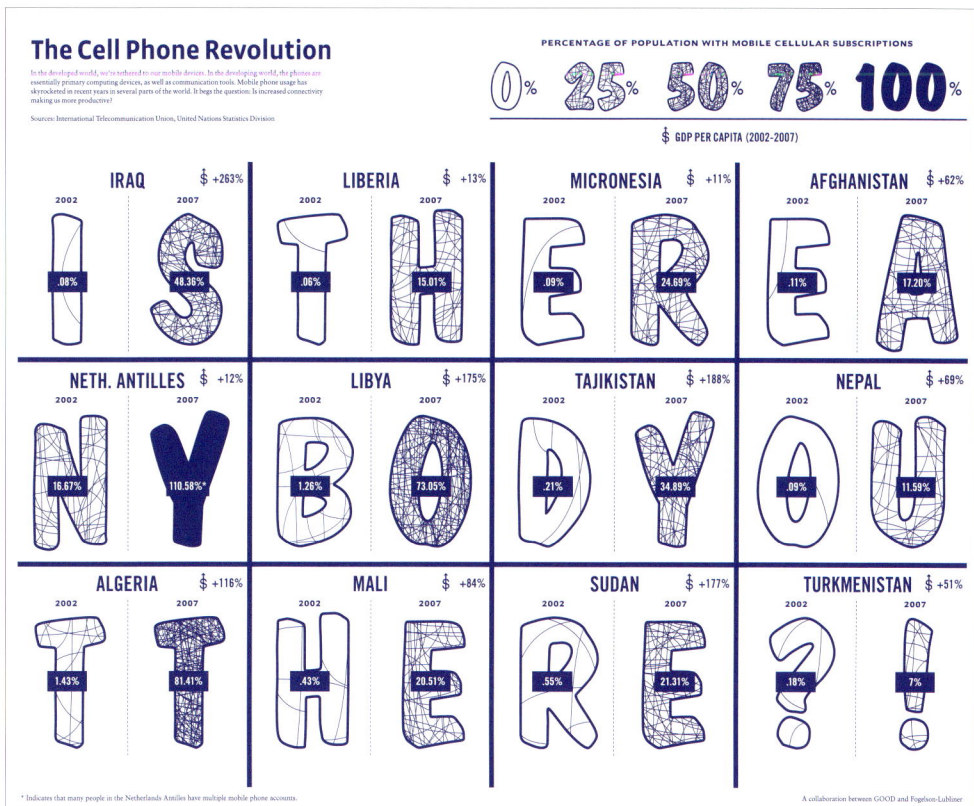

The Cell Phone Revolution

War, What Is It Good For?

Sharing is part of coexisting—and that means fairly distributing land and resources, but also respecting rights and freedoms. Armed conflicts worldwide are down from a peak in the early-1990s, but we're still not enjoying an era of peace. Below are the countries involved in the most skirmishes (both internal and international) since the end of World War II.

FRANCE 25

UNITED KINGDOM 23

RUSSIA 18

UNITED STATES

INDEX OF MAJOR POST-WWII INTERN

A	1946-1949	**INDONESIAN NATIONAL REVOLUTION**
B	1946-1954	**FIRST INDOCHINA WAR**
C	1949-1953	**KOREAN WAR**
D	1956	**SUEZ CRISIS**
E	1962 & 1967	**SINO-INDIAN WAR**

A collaboration between GOOD and Fogelson-Lubliner

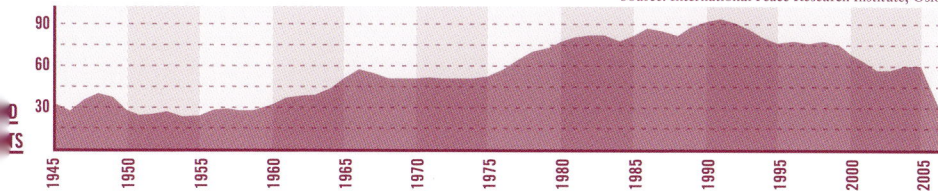

90
60
30

1945 1950 1955 1960 1965 1970 1975 1980 1985 1990 1995 2000 2005

DIA
14

ETHIOPIA
10

BURMA
10

CHINA
9

STRALIA
8

NETHERLANDS
8

SPAIN
8

INDONESIA
8

L CONFLICTS

1963-1966	INDONESIA-MALAYSIA CONFRONTATION	K	1991	GULF WAR
1965-1974	VIETNAM WAR	L	1998	KOSOVO WAR
1969	SINO-SOVIET BORDER CONFLICT	M	2001-2008	WAR ON TERROR
1975 -1990	LEBANESE CIVIL WAR	N	2003	IRAQ WAR
1978-2008	WAR IN AFGHANISTAN	O	2004-PRES.	IRAQ OCCUPATION/INSURGENCY

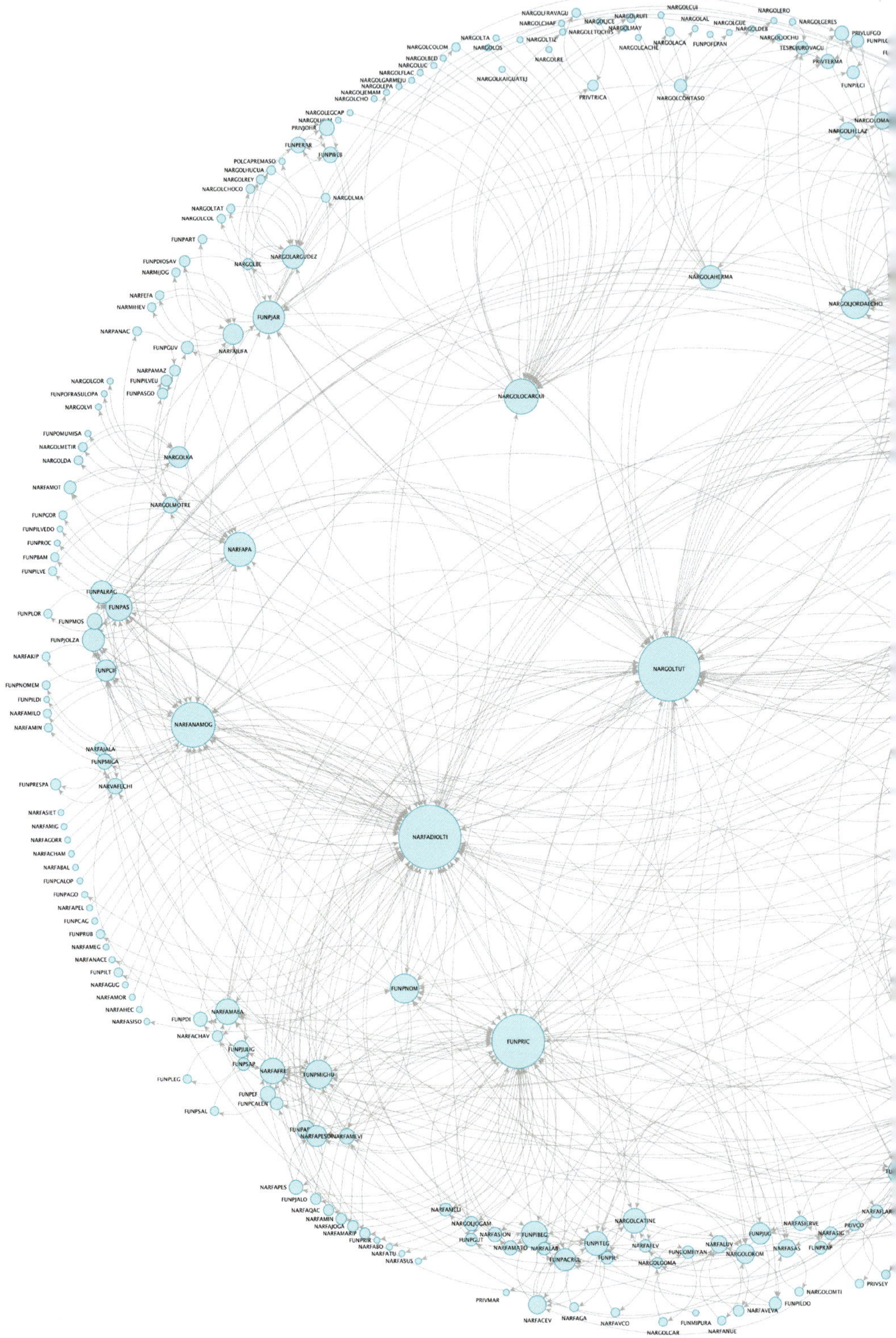
NARFADIOLTI
NARGOLTUT
FUNPRIC
NARFANAMOG
NARGOLOCARCUI
NARFAPA
FUNPJAR
NARGOLARGUDEZ
NARGOLAHERMA
NARGOLJORDALCHO
FUNPNOM
FUNPMIGHU
NARFAFRE
NARFAMARA
FUNPAS
FUNPALRAG
FUNPJOLZA
FUNPCII
NARGOLKA
NARGOLMOTRE
NARFAJUFA
FUNPGUV
NARGOLCATINE
FUNPIBEG
FUNPITEG
FUNPACRUL
NARGOLOKOM
FUNPJUG
NARFASAS
NARFACEV
NARGOLCONTASO
PRIVTRICA
NARGOLMA
FUNPERAR
FUNPWEB
PRIVJOHR
NARFAMOT
NARFAKIP
FUNPRESPA
NARVAFUCHI
FUNPMIGA
NARFAJALA
FUNPLEG
FUNPSAL
NARFAPES
NARFAMELI
NARGOLJOGAM
PRIVMAR
NARFAGA
NARFAVCO
NARGOLCAR
FUNMIPURA
NARFANUE
NARFAVEVA
FUNPILDO
NARGOLOMTI
PRIVSEY
NARGOLERO
NARGOLGERES
PRIVLUFGO
PRIVTERMA
FUNPILCI
NARGOLHLLAZ
NARGOLKAIGUATEJ
NARGOLRE
NARGOLTA
NARGOLOS
NARGOLCOLOM
NARGOLFRAVAGU
NARGOLCHAF
NARGOLCUI
FUNPOFEPAN
NARGOLACA
NARGOLCACHE
POLCAPREMASO
NARGOLHUCUA
NARGOLREY
NARGOLCHOCO
NARGOLTAT
NARGOLCOL
FUNPART
FUNPDIOSAV
NARMIJOG
NARFEFA
NARMIHEV
NARPANAC
NARPAMAZ
FUNPILVEU
FUNPASGO
NARGOLGOR
FUNPOFRASULOPA
NARGOLVI
FUNPOMUMISA
NARGOLMETIR
NARGOLDA
FUNPGOR
FUNPILVEDO
FUNPROC
FUNPBAM
FUNPILVE
FUNPLOR
FUNPMOS
FUNPNOMEM
FUNPILDI
NARFAMILO
NARFAMIN
NARFASIET
NARFAMIG
NARFAGORR
NARFACHAM
NARFABAL
FUNPCALOP
FUNPAGO
NARFAPEL
FUNPCAG
FUNPRUB
NARFAMEG
NARFANACE
FUNPILT
NARFAGUG
NARFAMOR
NARFAHEC
NARFASISO
FUNPDI
NARFACHAV
FUNPJULIG
FUNPSAP
FUNPEF
FUNPCALEN
NARFAPESO
NARFAMEVI
FUNPJALO
NARFAQAC
NARFAJOGA
NARFAMARIP
FUNPRIR
NARFABO
NARFATU
NARFASUS
NARFASION
NARFAMATO
NARFALAB
FUNPCUT
NARFAFEV
FUNCOMEIYAN
NARGOLOOMA
NARFALUV
NARFASIERVE
NARFASIG
FUNPRAF
PRIVCO

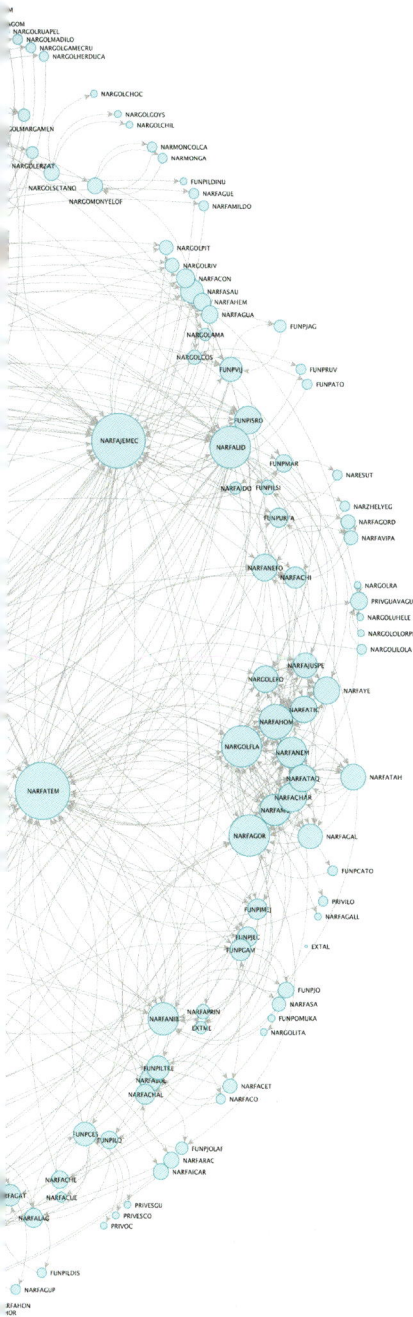

Mexican Drug Cartel "La Familia Michoacana"

"La Familia Michoacana" is a drug cartel based in the Mexican state of Michoacán, controlling the production and distribution of drugs in the area. This network graph reveals relationships within the organisation. A relational matrix of 284 individuals was enriched with qualitative information from judicial files, based on testimonies from members of the organisation. Lines show individual connections. Nodes represent individuals: drug traffickers ("NAR") and public servants ("FUN"). The graph also shows the hierarchy: the bigger and more central a node, the more influential the person is. The graph is a result of the research project "The Effects of Drug Trafficking and Corruption on Democratic Institutions in Mexico, Colombia and Guatemala", supported by the Foundation Open Society Institute.

Project Info: Website, 2010, UK
Design: Eduardo Salcedo-Albarán
Additional Info: Exhibited during the Map Marathon 2010 at the Serpentine Gallery, London

Monkeys and Typewriters

This is a variation on the so-called "Infinite Monkey Theorem". As a thought experiment, the theorem is used to establish the conceivability of infinity through an image: a monkey randomly hitting keys on a typewriter for an infinite amount of time will – at some point – type any given text, such as the complete works of Shakespeare. Østring humorously refers to this theorem and makes up events which could also happen, but which are never mentioned: the monkey could be interrupted or he might eat the manuscript. The probability of these events is charted in percentages around the centre. The bar diagram at the very bottom plays with the notion of parallel universes.

Project Info: Website, 2009, Norway
Design: Ole Østring

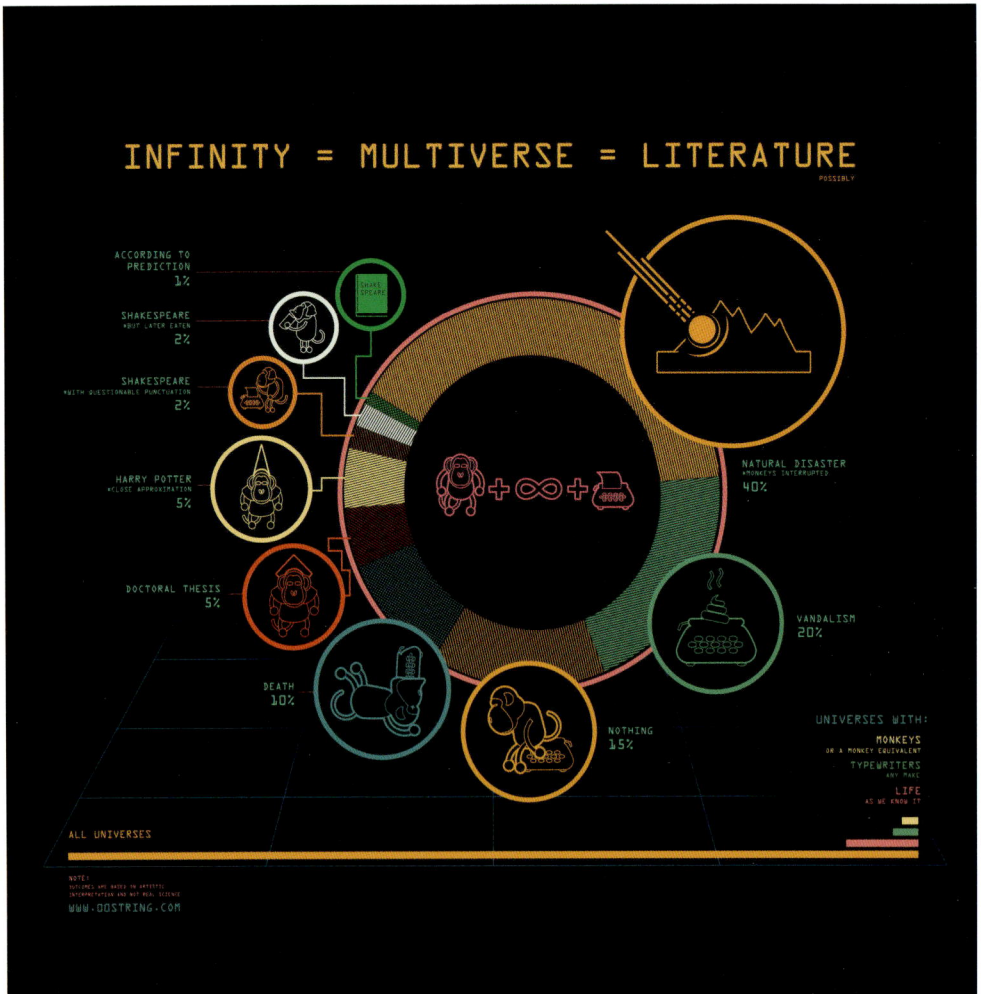

BANTAM

PENGUIN

HARVILL SECKER

PIMLICO

PHILOMEL

BLACK SWAN

PUFFIN

MARGARET K. McELDERRY

ALLEN LANE

RAZORBILL

CROCODILES AND BIRDS

SNAKES AND LIZARDS

MAMMALS

CORGI

YEARLING

HUTCHINSON

POCKET

SIMON SPOTLIGHT

DOUBLEDAY

WATERBROOK

IMAGE

LITTLE SIMON

EVERYMAN'S LIBRARY

ALFRED A. KNOPF

SEAL

THE DIAL

LIBROS PARA NIÑOS

ORION

ROBOTS

ANGRY ROBOT

AMNIOTES

TETRAPODS

BONY FISH

CRUSTACEANS

CHELICERATES

INSECTS AND MYRIAPODS

GRASSET-JEUNESSE

TURTLES

AMPHIBIANS

CARTILAGINOUS FISH

VERTEBRATES

ECHINODERMS

ARTHROPODS

LADYBIRD

MOLLUSKS

LAUREL-LEAF

NAN A. TALESE

ORCHARD

ROTIFERS

ROUNDWORMS

LOPHOPHORATES

SEGMENTED WORMS

GREENWILLOW

DUTTON CHILDREN'S

WELLNESS CENTRAL

SPONGES

FLATWORMS

IVY

LAROUSSE

FERNS AND FERN ALLIES

CNIDARIANS

VIRGIN

HAMISH HAMILTON

ÉDITIONS DU CHÊNE

POPPY

MOSSES AND ALLIES

GREEN ALGAE

ANIMALS

FUNGI AND LICHENS

FLOWERING SEED PLANTS

NON-FLOWERING SEED PLANTS

PROTOCTISTS

VINTAGE

FIREBIRD

RANDOM HOUSE

HARPERCOLLINS

SIMON & SCHUSTER

PENGUIN GROUP

HACHETTE

PLANTS

ARCHAEBACTERIA

EUKARYOTES

TRUE BACTERIA

CLARKSON POTTER

GODSFIELD

SALVAT

LIFE

MYTHOLOGY

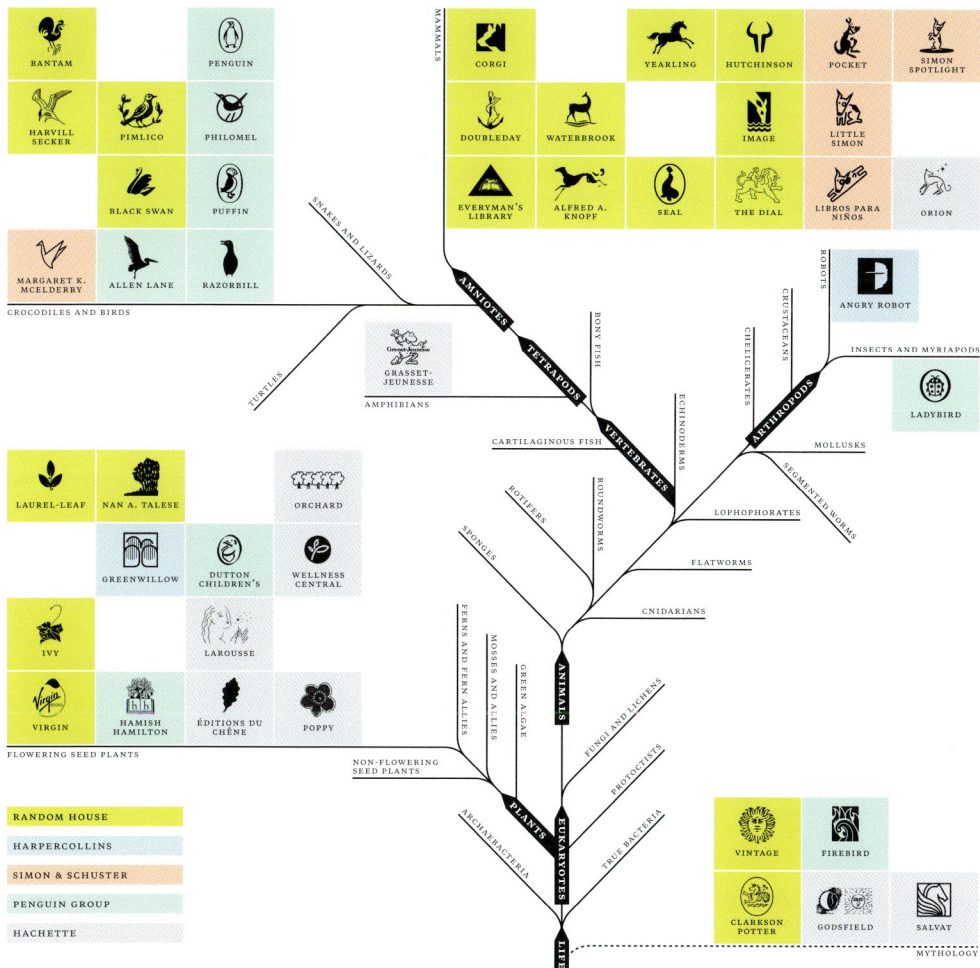

Natural Selections

The tree has been a powerful model for explaining how various species have sprung from a common background in the course of evolution. In this piece for the *New York Times*, Nicholas Felton used this model to explain a different phenomenon: the abundant use of animals and plants in logos of the publishing industry. Starting from the base and passing by the small "Mythology" family in the lower right, it can be seen that mammals are the most popular of the logo animals, followed closely by flowering seed-plants. Animals like flatworms and sponges, on the other hand, don't seem to make an appropriate mascot for a publishing business. Colour coding indicates to which publishing group the mentioned imprints belong.

Project Info: *The New York Times*, newspaper and online article, 2009, USA
Design: Nicholas Felton

Near Earth Objects

Near-Earth objects are asteroids, comets and meteoroids, which come into close proximity to the Earth when orbiting the Sun. These objects are observed by astronomers for the potential danger of a collision with Earth. The unit for measuring the proximity of such an object is an "astronomic unit", which equals the distance between Sun and Earth. The graphic shows those near-Earth objects which are bigger than 1000 m in diameter and which have, or will approach closest to us. Sorted according to their distance from Earth, asteroid 1999 AN 10 is listed as the closest to approach, set for August 2027. Each object's size is listed by diameter, whilst below, the same objects are listed with the exact date of their closest approach.

Project Info: Website, 2010, USA
Data Source: National Space Science Data Center; National Aeronautics and Space Administration
Design: Zachary Vabolis

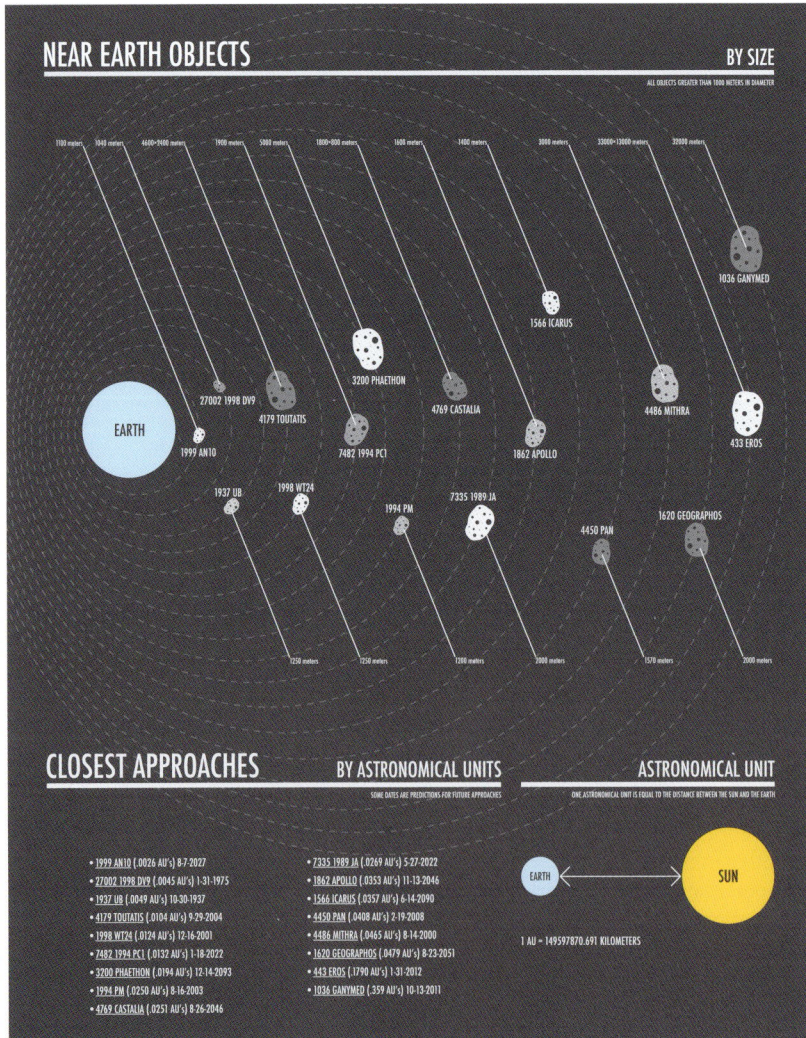

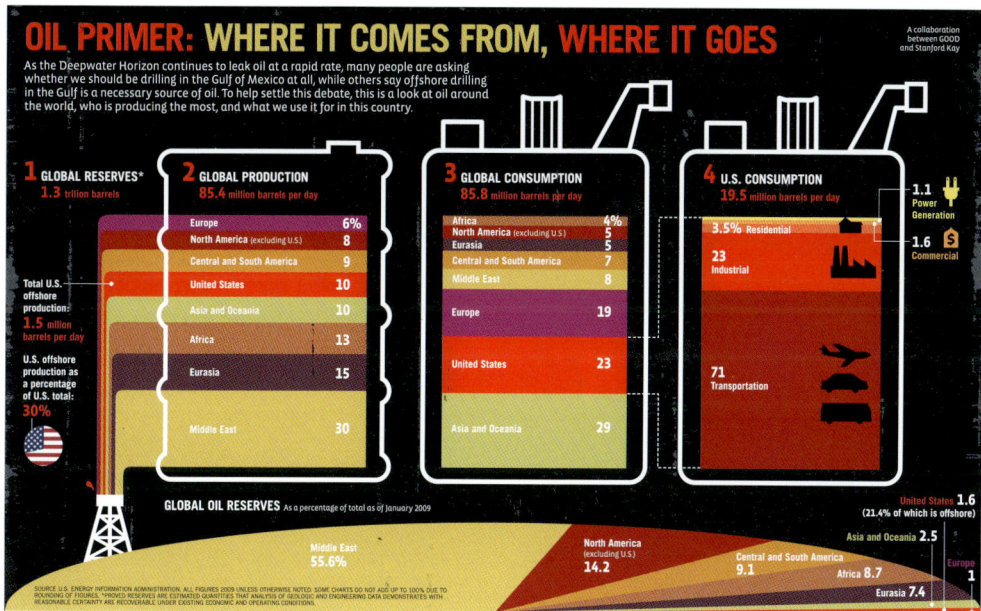

OIL PRIMER: WHERE IT COMES FROM, WHERE IT GOES

A collaboration between GOOD and Stanford Kay

As the Deepwater Horizon continues to leak oil at a rapid rate, many people are asking whether we should be drilling in the Gulf of Mexico at all, while others say offshore drilling in the Gulf is a necessary source of oil. To help settle this debate, this is a look at oil around the world, who is producing the most, and what we use it for in this country.

1 GLOBAL RESERVES*
1.3 trillion barrels

Total U.S. offshore production: 1.5 million barrels per day

U.S. offshore production as a percentage of U.S. total: 30%

2 GLOBAL PRODUCTION
85.4 million barrels per day

Europe	6%
North America (excluding U.S.)	8
Central and South America	9
United States	10
Asia and Oceania	10
Africa	13
Eurasia	15
Middle East	30

3 GLOBAL CONSUMPTION
85.8 million barrels per day

Africa	4%
North America (excluding U.S.)	5
Eurasia	5
Central and South America	7
Middle East	8
Europe	19
United States	23
Asia and Oceania	29

4 U.S. CONSUMPTION
19.5 million barrels per day

3.5% Residential
23 Industrial
71 Transportation

1.1 Power Generation
1.6 Commercial

GLOBAL OIL RESERVES As a percentage of total as of January 2009

Middle East 55.6%
North America (excluding U.S.) 14.2
Central and South America 9.1
Africa 8.7
Eurasia 7.4
Europe 1

United States 1.6 (21.4% of which is offshore)
Asia and Oceania 2.5

SOURCE: U.S. ENERGY INFORMATION ADMINISTRATION. ALL FIGURES 2009 UNLESS OTHERWISE NOTED. SOME CHARTS DO NOT ADD UP TO 100% DUE TO ROUNDING OF FIGURES. *PROVED RESERVES ARE ESTIMATED QUANTITIES THAT ANALYSIS OF GEOLOGIC AND ENGINEERING DATA DEMONSTRATES WITH REASONABLE CERTAINTY ARE RECOVERABLE UNDER EXISTING ECONOMIC AND OPERATING CONDITIONS.

Oil Primer: Where it Comes From, Where it Goes

In a series of four hierarchical sets of statistics, this graphic looks at oil resources and consumption around the world. Statistic number one is a distorted pie chart at the bottom, showing the distribution of global reserves in percentages for individual world regions. The silhouettes of an oil barrel and jerry cans provide the outline for stats number two to four. Global production and global consumption are shown in percentages for individual world regions. The last part on the right indicates what oil is used for in the US, and how transportation accounts for 71 % of the total US consumption. With its muddy, dark grey colour, the background evokes the consistency of the "black gold".

Project Info: "How Much Oil Do We Get From Offshore Drilling?", GOOD, website, 2010, USA
Data Source: US Energy Information Administration
Research: Morgan Clendaniel
Design: Stanford Kay

Following spread
On Hold
Hold On

The relationship between the rise of skyscrapers and economic prosperity is a much-discussed topic in the history of modern architecture. This piece takes a look at skyscraper construction projects around the world which have been put on hold because of the world financial crisis in 2008 / 2009. The collage scales the towers according to their projected height, the chart at the bottom listing them all with their names and allocating them to continents. In his text, Theo Deutinger indicates an additional information layer not visualised in the image: an estimate of how many jobs have been lost from putting all these projects on hold.

Project Info: Mark, magazine article, 2009, Netherlands
Data Source: SkyscraperPage.com;
Emporis.com; Oobject.com; BBC News
Design: Theo Deutinger, Barbara Weingartner

On Hold
Hold On

42,1 km of skyscrapers 'On Hold' (198 buildings > 100 meter)

'On hold' is probably the most-heard phrase in the past several months in architecture offices around the world. What might sound at first like a slight delay has had an effect similar to stepping on an active garden hose: either the stoppage is brief and the project jumps into realization, or the hose bursts – end of project.

According to Emporis and Skyscraperpage, two major high-rise building survey websites, there are currently 198 skyscrapers (>100 m) 'on hold', amounting to 10% (Skyscraperpage) or 11% (Emporis) of the skyscraper projects around the world. Among the skyscrapers on hold are superlatives like the Nakheel Tower (1,050 m), the most promising aspirant for the label 'world's next tallest building', as well as contenders in Europe, North America, South America and Africa.

In total there are 42.1 km of high-rise buildings on hold, with Asia home to more than one third (16.1 km) of the accumulated height. The impact on employment is severe. For example, delay of South America's proposed tallest building, Gran Torre Costanera (300 m), has resulted in 2,000 jobs on hold, according to local unions. Extrapolating this metres-to-jobs ratio to all 198 skyscraper projects on hold, the niche product 'skyscraper' would be good for about 280,000 job losses worldwide.

So please hold on, or get off the hose.

Text and Collage Theo Deutinger, Barbara Weingartner

600m

500m

400m

300m

200m

100m

TD©
www.theodeutinger.eu

sources:
skyscraperpage.com
emporis.com
www.oobject.com
news.bbc.co.uk

Middle East 10.9km   North America 6.9km   Europe 3.5km   Latin America   Australia   Africa

Piemonte: worldwide visits

A barcode infographic about worldwide flows of people moving to Piemonte's provinces in 2008.

This infographic shows the amount of visits to the Italian region of Piemonte and their provenance.
The flow has been divided in three main categories:
EU - European states;
EX - Extra-European states;
ITA - Italian regions.

Each category has been respectively divided in the following groups:
EU: Northern, Southern, Eastern, Central Europe, other european states;
EX: North America, South America, Asia, Africa, Oceania, other countries;
ITA: all regions are shown.

The aim of this visualization is to quickly highlight the number and the provenance of each flow of visits towards each specific Piemonte province, and most of all to put these data in proportion, also summing up the top countries. Each flow has been visualized through the metaphore of barcodes, for obtaining a "chromatic worldwide barcode" identifying a sort of "Piemonte DNA".

The source of the information is the site http://www.dati.piemonte.it, an Open Data initiative launched by the Region itself.

4.033.122
from Europe

547.154
from the Rest of the World

Top 5

Germania	968.398
Paesi Bassi	526.992
Regno Unito	455.156
Francia	385.412
Svizzera	272.452

Province	
Torino	692.177 / 814.851 / 4.365.630
Verbano Cusio Ossola	1.764.948 / 142.082 / 577.521
Cuneo	745.057 / 46.530 / 923.563
Novara	479.808 / 90.961 / 621.098
Alessandria	157.078 / 46.665 / 410.806
Vercelli	38.894 / 48.413 / 522.951
Biella	44.413 / 21.065 / 279.308
Asti	84.758 / 46.860 / 137.113

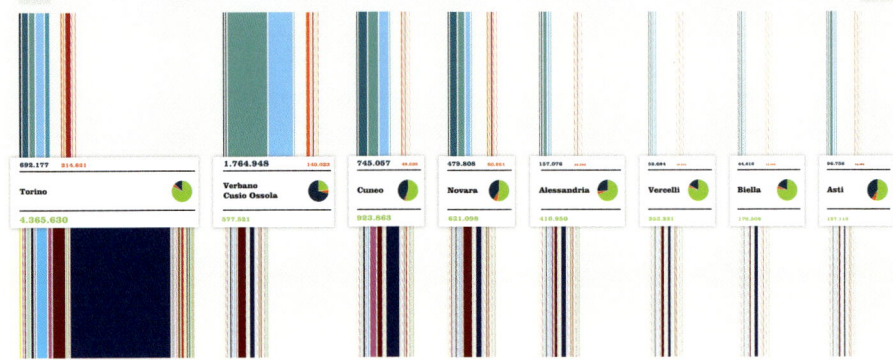

7.473.297
people coming from Italy to Piemonte

How to read this infographic

Barcodes

Pie charts

Piemonte: Worldwide Visits

This piece shows visitor traffic to the Italian
region of Piemonte. Boxes in the centre list
all Piemonte provinces. Line diagrams classify visitor groups: line thickness indicates the
relative numbers and colour shows the visitors'
origin. Above the centre, visitors from outside
Italy are shown: blue colours refer to European
tourists, while reddish colours are visitors from
elsewhere. Line diagrams below the boxes
group visitors from Italy. Separate bars indicate visitor numbers for all of Piemonte. This
combined visualisation quickly highlights
specific trends. Each flow has been visualised
using the metaphor of bar codes, to obtain a
"chromatic worldwide bar-code" identifying
a sort of "Piemonte Visitor DNA".

Project Info: Website, 2010, Italy
Data Source: Dati.Piemonte.it
Design: Manuela Ciancilla, Davide Genco (VISup)

692.177   214.621

Torino

4.365.630

1.764.948   140.023

**Verbano
Cusio Ossola**

577.521

Poetry on the Road

Since 2002, Boris Müller has created the visual theme for an annual German poetry festival. Based on software, he visualises selected poems, using a new set of rules each year. The visual for 2008 lists poems in lines (right page). Words are sorted (left to right) and scaled hierarchically according to their frequency in the poem. Words appearing in several poems are connected by vertical lines.

Project Info: Poetry on the Road Literature Festival, series of visuals and posters, since 2002, Germany
Design: Boris Müller , Friederike Lambers, Florian Pfeffer, Matthias Woerle (one / one)
Awards: 100 beste Plakate 2002; TDC New York 2002: Certificate of Typographic Excellence

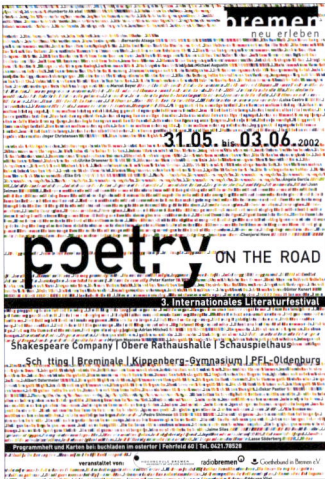

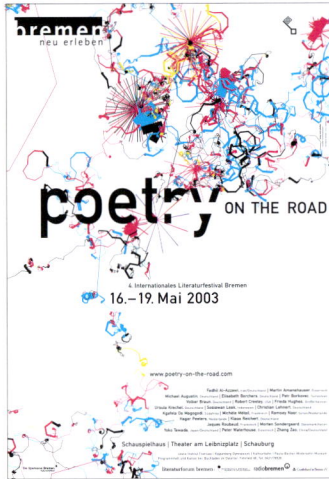

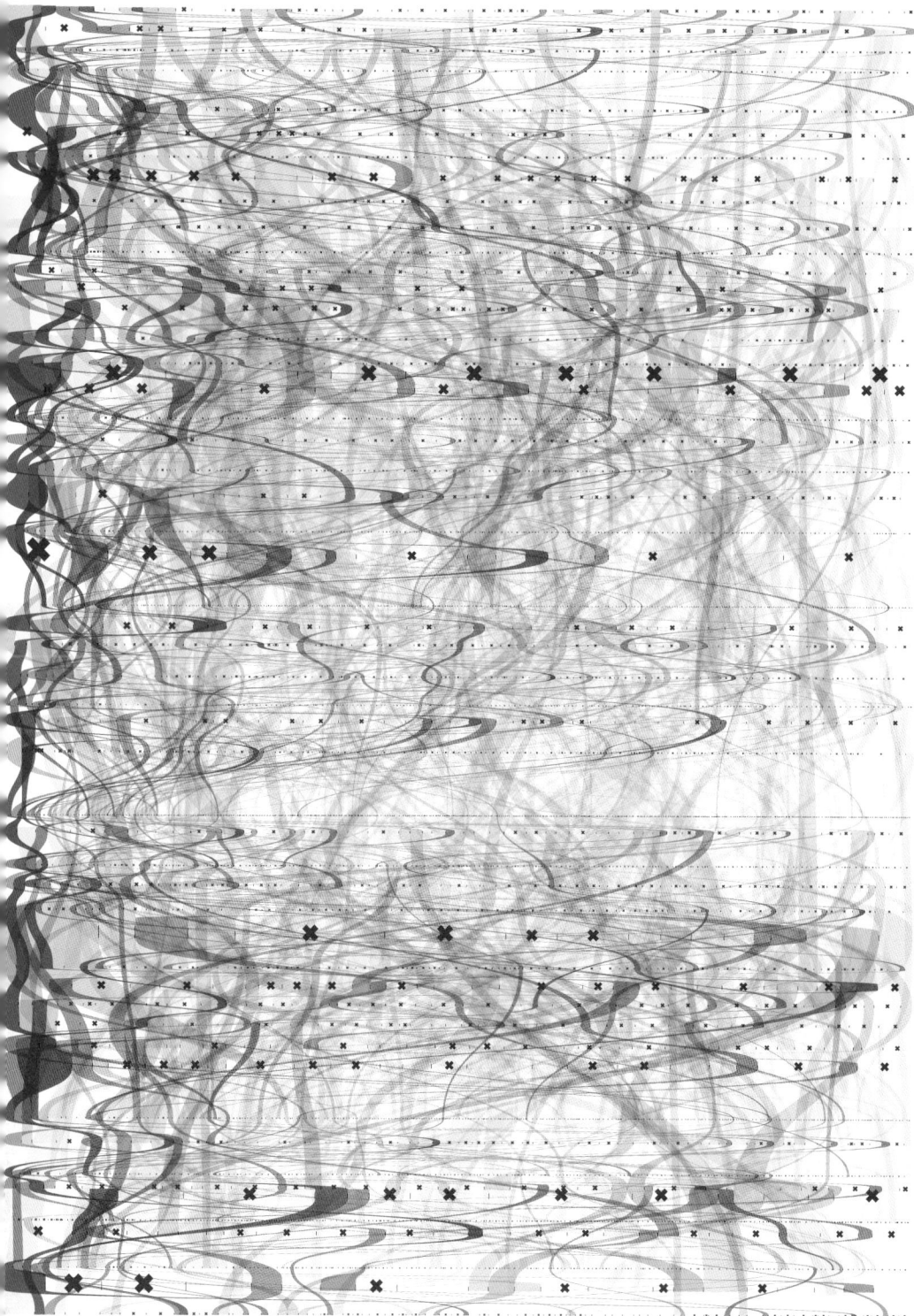

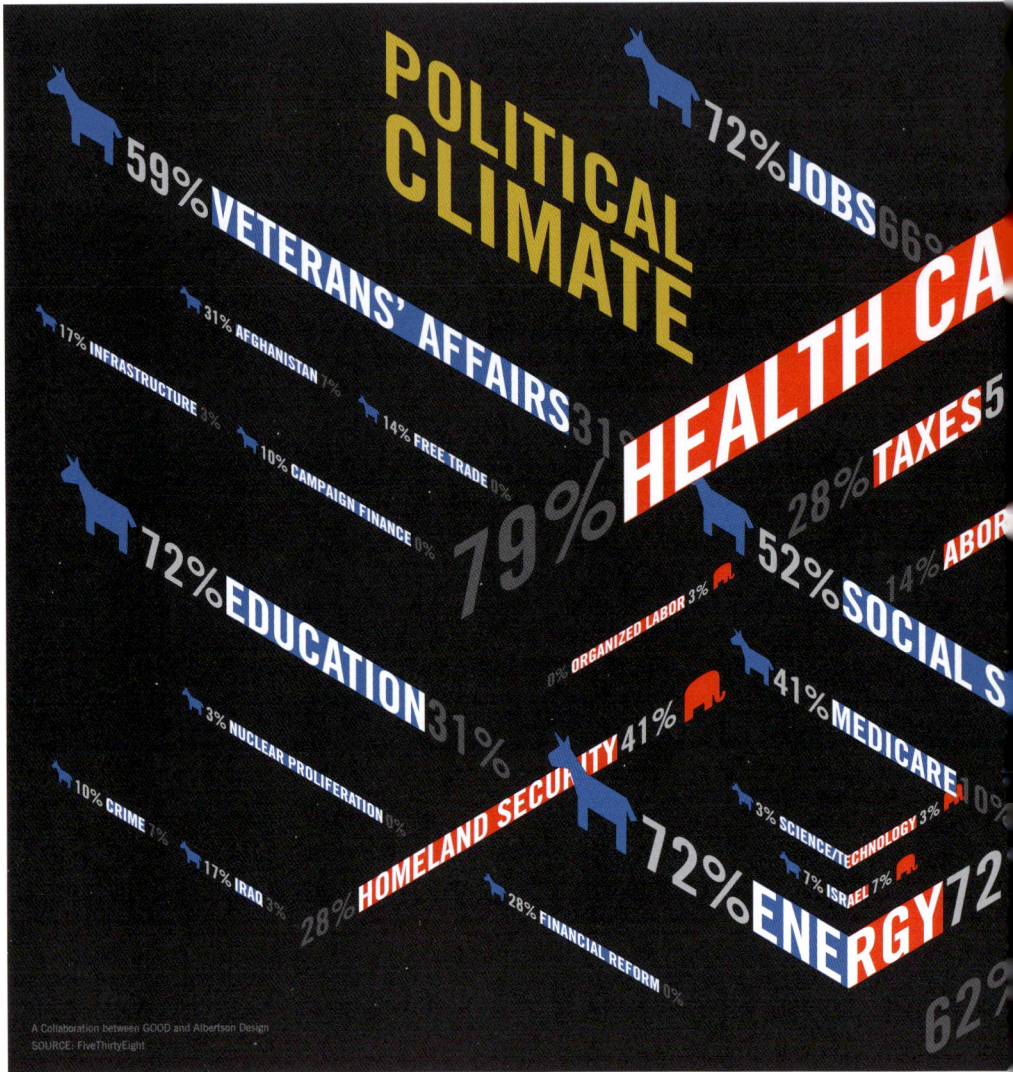

Political Climate

The US mid-term elections of November 2010 resulted in a landslide victory for Republicans. This graphic for *GOOD* magazine visualises which issues were discussed by the parties' candidates in the run-up to the elections. The websites of 29 Democratic and 29 Republican candidates were analysed for the number of times they mentioned the political issues, showing how consistent their messages were.

Political issues dominated by Republicans are shown in red, whereas Democrats' messages are given in blue. Clearly, the Republicans were better at speaking as a party and winning votes by focusing on healthcare and the national debt.

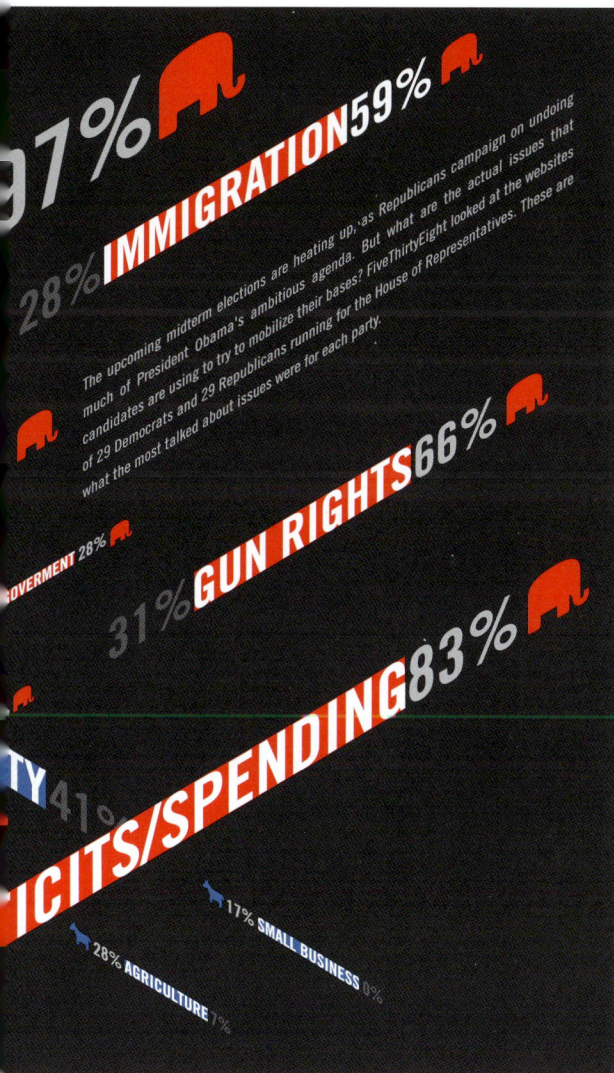

Project Info: *GOOD*, website, 2010, USA
Data Source: *Five Thirty Eight* blog
(*The New York Times*)
Design: David Albertson,
 Paul Torres (Albertson Design)

Following spread

Self Economy

Paris-based conceptual artist group Bureau d'études uses complex diagrams as a tool to conduct and visualise social and economical analyses. This piece is a study on how an individual's identity is formed. The centre is taken up by individual decisions and perceptions in the mind, whilst the second ring lists various perspectives which can be used to define the individual: economical, psychological, biological etc. The outermost white sphere is occupied by the "Other", beings and forces which don't relate to the concept of the self. Positioning oneself within society thus becomes a complex game of decisiontaking and freedom of choice.

Project Info: Poster, 2009, France
Artist: Bureau d'études

Complex of the self

METAPHYSICAL alterity

- Gods
- Devils
- Angels
- Nature
- Forces
- Hazard

There is a world outside of myself

Universe is not my creation

Human behavior simulation system

Human behavior simulation system simulate me

USER PROFILE

Media-industrial complex

- Vodafone
- Lagardère
- AOL
- Microsoft
- News corp.
- Bertelsmann

Personality profile
- Introversion
- Extraversion
- Tendency to risk behavior
- Tendency to neuroticism

Emotional profile
- Skin Galvanic Response Module
- Systolic Blood Pressure Module
- Diastolic Blood Pressure Module
- EEG Module
- Muscular Tonus Module
- Respiratory Frequency Module

Cognitive profile

Cognitive functions
- Perception
- Interpretation
- Planning and Execution
Cognitive processes
- Memory/Knowledge Base
- Allocation of Resources

"I" is a spirit

A part of me is unconscious

I am conscious of myself

Television enters in my private space

I dream

I watch Television

PSYCHOLOGICAL double

I learn language

I accept to learn

I think with my brain

METAPHYSICAL double

"I" is an illusion

Universe is me

I feel myself

I feel a world

The world feels me

I feel

TC/TP

"I" is a function in an information system

"I" is a linguistic fiction

NAME

SEMIOTIC double

I move my body

I refuse to use some car

Lockheed Martin
Rockwell
TRW
SAIC

RoyalDutchShell
BP
EXXON
TOTAL

the petroleum industries use my car

I finance the weapons industries

I finance the petroleum oligarchs

I provoke some wars for oil

I use oil for transportation

I refuse to travel by legs

I travel by car

I learn to drive

I buy a car

I receive some money for my work

Bureau d'études, 2009

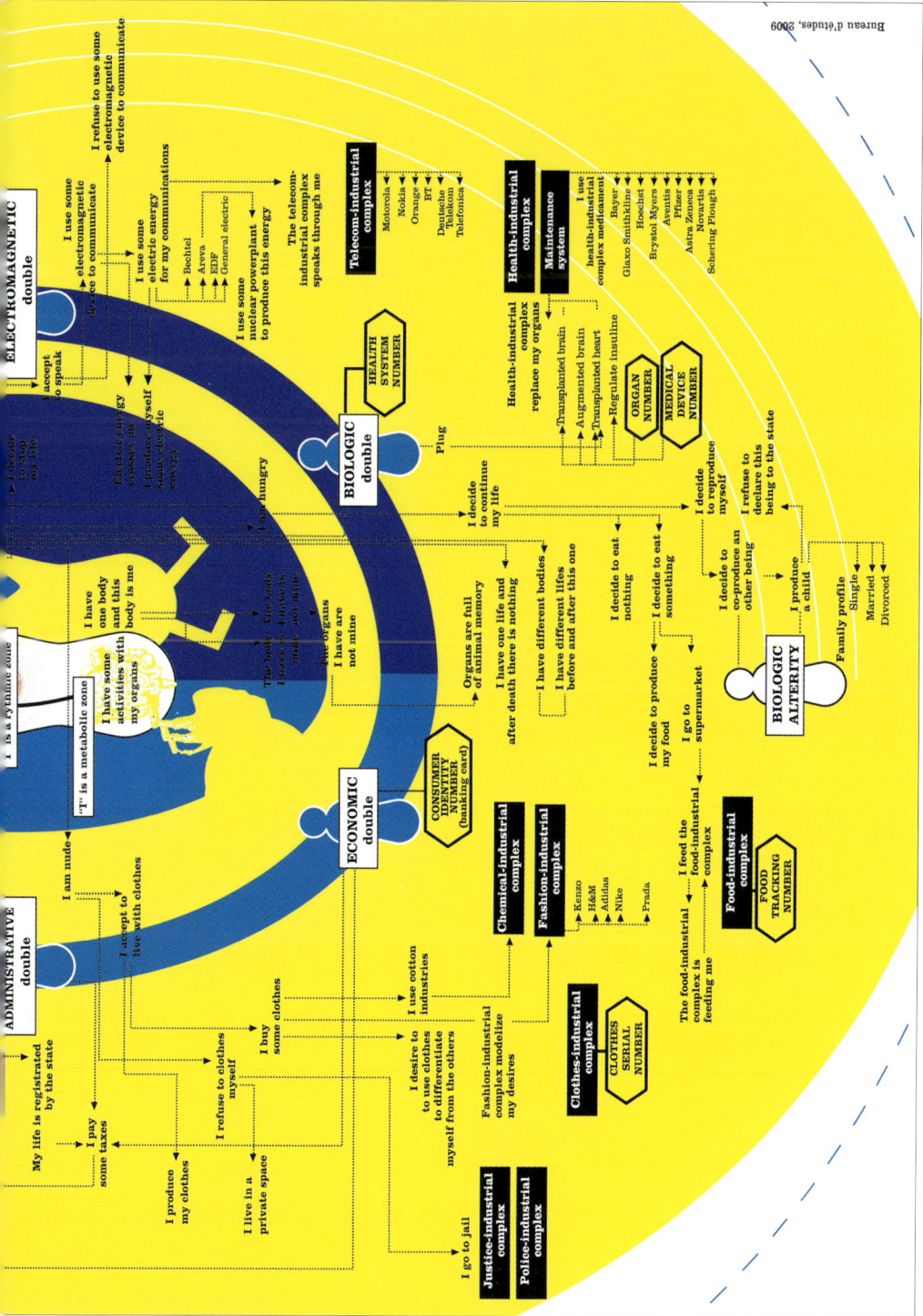

ELECTROMAGNETIC double

I refuse to use some electromagnetic device to communicate

I use some electromagnetic device to communicate

I use some electric energy for my communications

The telecom-industrial complex speaks through me

Telecom-industrial complex
- Motorola
- Nokia
- Orange
- BT
- Deutsche Telekom
- Telefonica

I accept to speak

I use some nuclear powerplant to produce this energy

- Bechtel
- Areva
- EDF
- General electric

Electric energy passes me

I produce myself some electric energy

I decide to stop my life

BIOLOGIC double

HEALTH SYSTEM NUMBER

Plug

I decide to continue my life

Health-industrial complex

Maintenance system

I use some health-industrial complex medicament
- Bayer
- Glaxo Smithkline
- Hoechst
- Bristol Myers
- Aventis
- Pfizer
- Astra Zeneca
- Novartis
- Schering Plough

Health-industrial complex replace my organs
- Transplanted brain
- Augmented brain
- Transplanted heart
- Regulate insuline

ORGAN NUMBER

MEDICAL DEVICE NUMBER

I decide to reproduce myself

I refuse to declare this being to the state

ADMINISTRATIVE double

I am nude

"I" is a metabolic zone

I have some activities with my organs

I have one body and this body is me

I am hungry

The organs I have are not mine

The body, the dead I have, I have is mine and not mine

Organs are full of animal memory

I have one life and after death there is nothing

I have different bodies

I have different lifes before and after this one

I decide to eat nothing

I decide to eat something

I decide to produce my food

I go to supermarket

I decide to co-produce an other being

I produce a child

BIOLOGIC ALTERITY

Family profile
- Single
- Married
- Divorced

I accept to live with clothes

I refuse to live with clothes

ECONOMIC double

CONSUMER IDENTITY NUMBER (banking card)

Chemical-industrial complex

Fashion-industrial complex
- Kenzo
- H&M
- Adidas
- Nike
- Prada

I buy some clothes

I desire to use clothes to differentiate myself from the others

I use cotton industries

Fashion-industrial complex modelize my desires

Clothes-industrial complex

CLOTHES SERIAL NUMBER

The food-industrial complex is feeding me

I feed the food-industrial complex

Food-industrial complex

FOOD TRACKING NUMBER

My life is registered by the state

I pay some taxes

I produce my clothes

I buy some clothes

I live in a private space

I refuse to clothes myself

I go to jail

Justice-industrial complex

Police-industrial complex

Satellites

United Kingdom 1

Italy 2

Europe 36

France 28 | 16

United Kingdom 15 | 10

Netherlands 0 | 5

Canada 2

Luxemburg 13 | 2

Italy 9 | 5

United States[1] 3258

Spain 4 | 5

Portugal 0 | 1

Europe[1] 30 | 12

NATO 5 | 3

Canada 14 | 11

United States 683 | 453

Mexico 4 | 3

Colombia 1 | 0

Chile 1 | 0

Brazil 5 | 7

Argentina 4 | 6

China & Brazil 60

China & Brazil 0 | 3

International[2] 60 | 49

International 3

Australia 5 | 6

Mauritius 0 | 1

South Africa 1 | 0

Nigeria 0 | 2

Morocco 0 | 1

Algeria 0 | 1

Egy

Australia 2

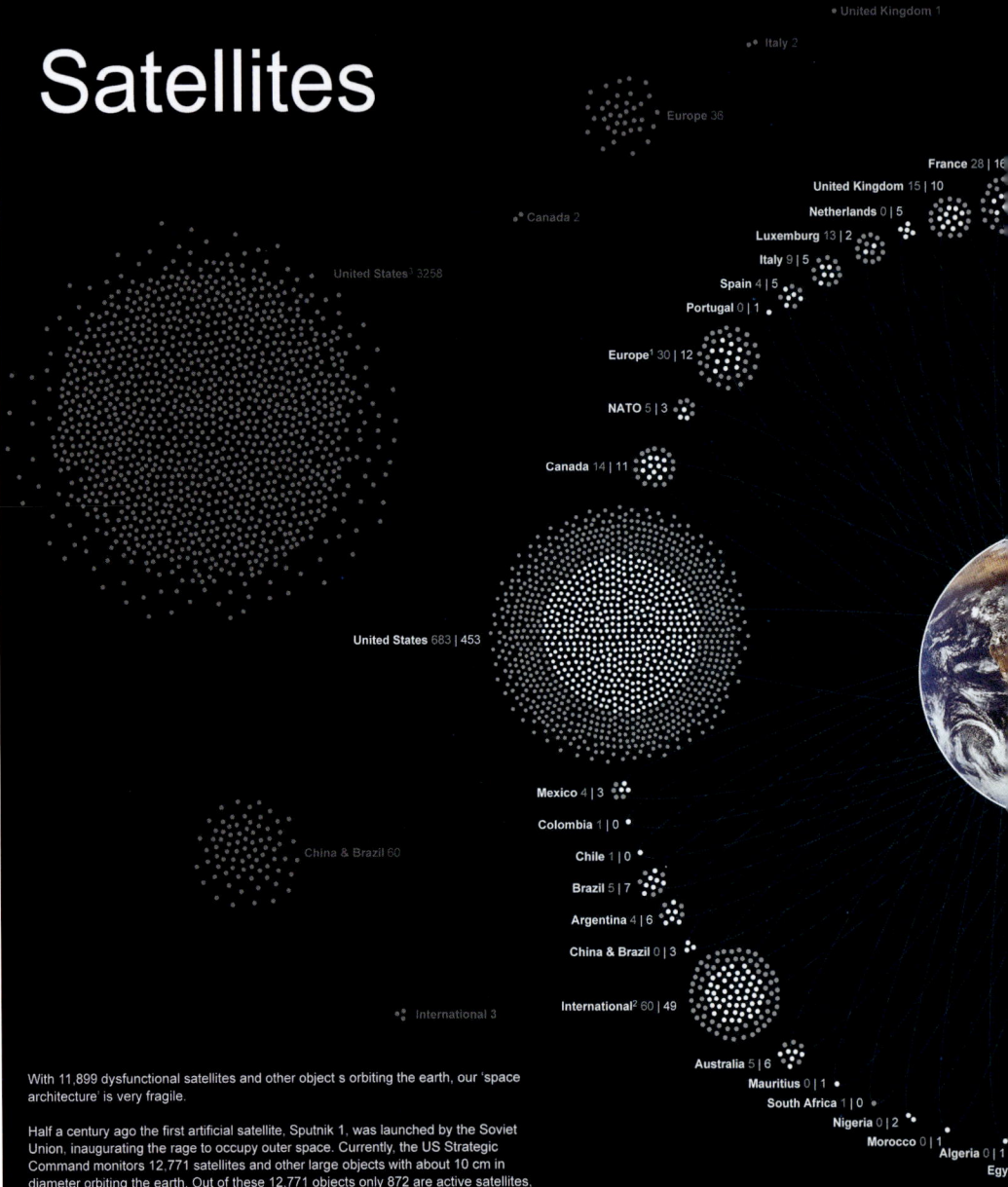

With 11,899 dysfunctional satellites and other object s orbiting the earth, our 'space architecture' is very fragile.

Half a century ago the first artificial satellite, Sputnik 1, was launched by the Soviet Union, inaugurating the rage to occupy outer space. Currently, the US Strategic Command monitors 12,771 satellites and other large objects with about 10 cm in diameter orbiting the earth. Out of these 12,771 objects only 872 are active satellites, while most of the remaining 11,899 monitored pieces are dysfunctional and considered 'space debris'. Together with millions of other smaller pieces of debris generated by spacecraft explosions or by collisions between satellites, they form a rapidly growing dangerous nebula, causing a major threat for damage on satellites and spacecrafts. The power released by a 1 cm piece of space debris is equivalent to a hand grenade. While our lives on earth depend more and more on GPS satellite support, the space they are imbedded in becomes more and more threatened. As an American general put it in The Economist in January this year: 'Our space architecture is very fragile.'

Text and Graphics Theo Deutinger

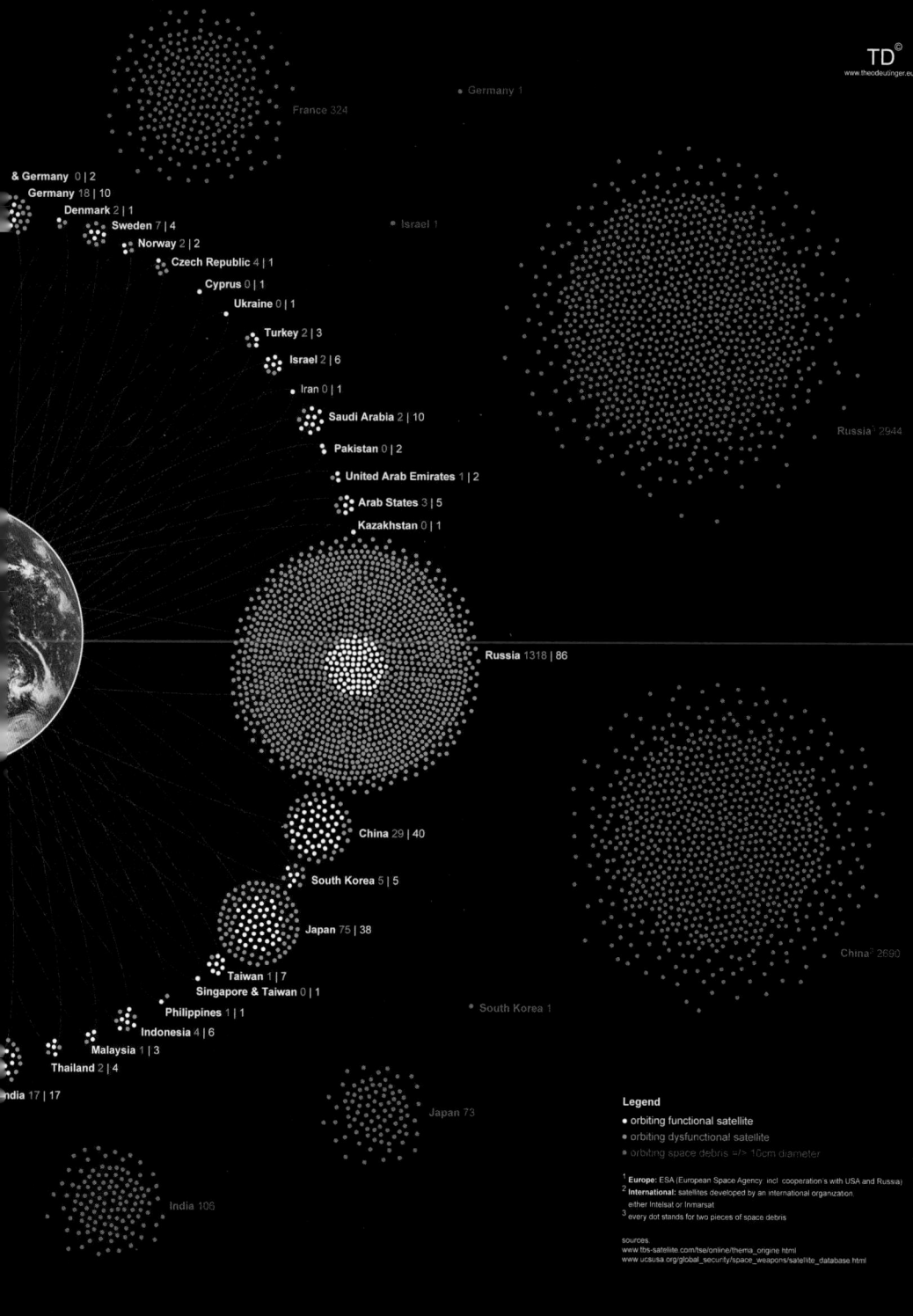

France 324

Germany 1

& Germany 0 | 2
Germany 18 | 10
Denmark 2 | 1
Sweden 7 | 4
Norway 2 | 2
Czech Republic 4 | 1
Cyprus 0 | 1
Ukraine 0 | 1
Turkey 2 | 3
Israel 2 | 6
Iran 0 | 1
Saudi Arabia 2 | 10
Pakistan 0 | 2
United Arab Emirates 1 | 2
Arab States 3 | 5
Kazakhstan 0 | 1

Israel 1

Russia¹ 2944

Russia 1318 | 86

China 29 | 40

South Korea 5 | 5

Japan 75 | 38

Taiwan 1 | 7
Singapore & Taiwan 0 | 1
Philippines 1 | 1
Indonesia 4 | 6
Malaysia 1 | 3
Thailand 2 | 4

ndia 17 | 17

South Korea 1

China² 2690

Japan 73

India 106

Legend

● orbiting functional satellite
● orbiting dysfunctional satellite
● orbiting space debris =/> 10cm diameter

¹ **Europe:** ESA (European Space Agency: incl. cooperation's with USA and Russia)
² **International:** satellites developed by an international organization.
  either Intelsat or Inmarsat
³ every dot stands for two pieces of space debris

sources:
www.tbs-satelite.com/tse/online/thema_ongine.html
www.ucsusa.org/global_security/space_weapons/satellite_database.html

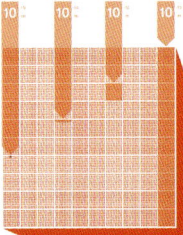
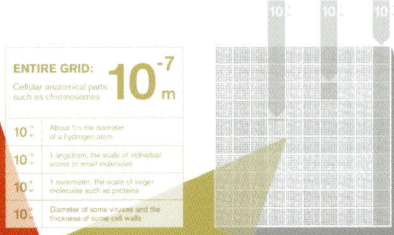
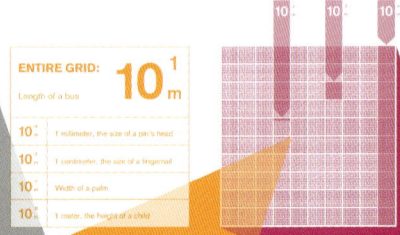

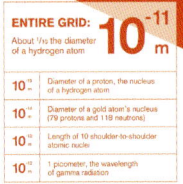
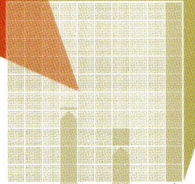

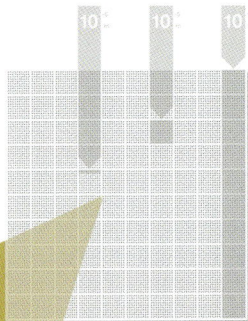

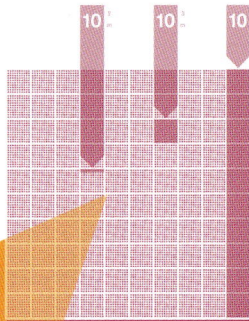

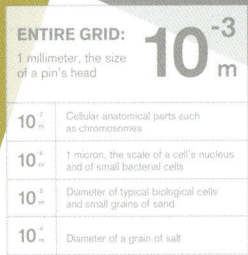
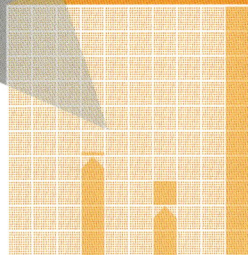
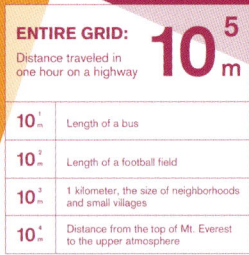

$10^9 \, \text{m}$

ENTIRE GRID: $10^{17} \, \text{m}$
Distance to the star Sirius

$10^?$ Distance light travels in half a day
$10^?$ Distance light travels in one week
$10^?$ Distance light travels in several months
$10^?$ Just over 1 light year = 9.46 x 10^{15} m

ENTIRE GRID: $10^{25} \, \text{m}$
Distance to quasars

$10^?$ Diameter of the Milky Way Galaxy
$10^?$ Distance to the Andromeda Galaxy
$10^?$ Sum of galactic clusters, each at our own Local Group
$10^?$ Distance light travels in 100 million years

ENTIRE GRID: $10^{13} \, \text{m}$
Distance light travels in half a day

$10^?$ Diameter of the Sun
$10^?$ Average distance of Mercury to the Sun
$10^?$ Average distance of Saturn to the Sun
$10^?$ Mean distance of Pluto to the Sun; the scale of the Solar System

ENTIRE GRID: $10^{21} \, \text{m}$
Diameter of the Milky Way Galaxy

$10^?$ Distance to the star Sirius
$10^?$ Thickness of the Milky Way
$10^?$ Distance to the Horsehead Nebula
$10^?$ Distance from Earth to the center of the Milky Way

$10^{26} \, \text{m}$
The largest structural scales of the known universe, about 13.7 billion light years

10^9_m — $10^9_m - 10^{13}_m$ — $10^{13}_m - 10^{17}_m$ — $10^{17}_m - 10^{21}_m$ — $10^{21}_m - 10^{25}_m$ — 10^{26}_m

Previous spread

Satellites

Austrian architect Theo Deutinger, based in Rotterdam, uses visualisations as a tool for the analysis of social and environmental phenomena. In this piece, he creates a visual impression of how technological progress in satellite deployment produces increasing amounts of space debris. Active and obsolete satellites are visualised as clouds of dots and collated to their nation of origin. The US and Russia can be quickly identified as the two major sources of space debris to date. Although the Earth sits at the centre of the graphic, the piece is not a map. Instead, it is a chart showing the distribution of quantities of space debris among different nations.

Project Info: "Space Architecture", *Mark*, magazine article, 2008, Netherlands
Data Source: The Satellite Encyclopedia; Union of Concerned Scientists: Satellite Database
Design: Theo Deutinger

Super Vision Chart

This chart was designed for the book *Super Vision: A New View of Nature* in 2003. The book shows scientific images that span the world of phenomena from subatomic particles to the biggest structures in the universe and explains the technology necessary to perceive and represent these structures. The chart helps illustrate the relative sizes of the objects documented in the book. Size dimensions are represented as sequential powers of 10 m, shown in order from smallest to largest, broken down into colour-coded groups. For each group of powers, a quadratic grid indicates the full scale of the group's biggest size in order to demonstrate the neighbouring smaller sizes.

Project Info: *Super Vision: A New View of Nature*, book, Harry N. Abrams, 2003, USA
Design: Agnieszka Gasparska (Kiss Me I'm Polish)
Creative Direction: Michael Walsh, Harry N. Abrams
Book Design: Helene Silverman

Taxonomy of Team Names in the Major Professional Sports Leagues of the United States

ANIMALS

ABSTRACTS

OBJECTS

PEOPLES

Animals

birds
Arizona Cardinals · Atlanta Hawks · Baltimore Ravens · Philadelphia Eagles · Seattle Seahawks · Atlanta Hawks · Toronto Blue Jays · Baltimore Orioles · St. Louis Cardinals · Anaheim Ducks · Atlanta Thrashers · Pittsburgh Penguins

cats
Carolina Panthers · Cincinnati Bengals · Detroit Lions · Jacksonville Jaguars · Detroit Tigers · Charlotte Bobcats · Florida Panthers · Nashville Predators

fish
Miami Dolphins · San Jose Sharks · Florida Marlins · Tampa Bay Rays

hooved
Denver Broncos · Indianapolis Colts · Saint Louis Rams · San Diego Chargers · Chicago Bulls · Milwaukee Bucks · Detroit Pistons

reptiles
Arizona Diamondbacks · Toronto Raptors

bears
Chicago Bears · Chicago Cubs · Memphis Grizzlies · Boston Bruins

insects
New Orleans Hornets

wolves
Minnesota Timberwolves · Phoenix Coyotes

Abstracts

culture
Utah Jazz · Saint Louis Blues

nature
Colorado Rockies · Denver Nuggets · Miami Heat · Oklahoma Thunder · Orlando Magic · Phoenix Suns · Calgary Flames · Carolina Hurricanes · Colorado Avalanche · Dallas Stars · Minnesota Wild · Tampa Bay Lightning · Toronto Maple Leafs

unknown
Minnesota Twins · Philadelphia Phillies · Detroit Red Wings · Philadelphia Flyers

Objects

technology
New York Jets · Houston Astros · San Antonio Spurs · Houston Rockets · Indiana Pacers · Los Angeles Clippers

gear
Cleveland Browns · New Jersey Nets · New York Knicks · Boston Red Sox · Chicago White Sox · Cincinnati Reds

Peoples

locals
Houston Texans · Los Angeles Dodgers · New York Mets · New York Yankees · Oakland Athletics · Washington Nationals · Montreal Canadiens · New York Islanders · Vancouver Canucks · Washington Capitals · Boston Celtics · Los Angeles Lakers

myths
New Orleans Saints · New York Giants · Tennessee Titans · New Jersey Devils · Los Angeles Kings · Kansas City Royals · Los Angeles Angels · San Francisco Giants · Sacramento Kings · Washington Wizards

workers
Green Bay Packers · Pittsburgh Steelers · Edmonton Oilers · Milwaukee Brewers · San Diego Padres · Ottawa Senators

adventurers
Buffalo Bills · Dallas Cowboys · Texas Rangers · Dallas Mavericks · Portland Trailblazers · New York Rangers

militia
New England Patriots · Oakland Raiders · Buffalo Sabres · Columbus Blue Jackets · Cleveland Cavaliers · Golden State Warriors · Philadelphia 76ers

seamen
Minnesota Vikings · Tampa Bay Buccaneers · Pittsburgh Pirates · Seattle Mariners

Indians
Kansas City Chiefs · Washington Redskins · Chicago Blackhawks · Atlanta Braves · Cleveland Indians

---

The one hundred and twenty-two professional teams in the major sports leagues have been named after everything from a poem (the Baltimore Ravens) to a movie (the Mighty Ducks of Anaheim) and anything in between. Some cities have chosen common themes to name their teams around (Atlanta's locker rooms might as well be an aviary), while the vast majority have little or nothing in common.

The origins of the team names are as varied as the names themselves. Some are named after local mascots, organizations, or even landmarks, while other owners opted to pursue more exotic identities. Local competitions and elections have become team names here also been a popular method for selecting mascots.

When attempting to categorize the names into a distinct taxonomy, countless difficulties arise. Team identities have changed over the years, origin stories have been lost, and a select few have a team name that is totally unknown in its meaning. For the purposes of this graphic, the best possible fit has been selected for each team. While certainly a lot than scientific approach (some on, everyone knows dolphins are mammals, not fish), this graphic comprises of our best effort to sort through the bestiary of team names.

LEAGUE BREAKDOWNS

animals · objects · abstracts · peoples

NATIONAL FOOTBALL LEAGUE · MAJOR LEAGUE BASEBALL · NATIONAL BASKETBALL ASSOCIATION · NATIONAL HOCKEY LEAGUE

CHAMPIONSHIPS WON

★ Super Bowl/NFL Champ · ★ World Series · ★ NBA Finals/ABA Finals · ★ Stanley Cup

reptiles · fish · seamen · cats · technology · militia · indians · adventurers · bears · hooved · myths · unknown · nature · gear · workers · birds · locals

The art of sports statistics.
infojocks SPORTS GRAPHICS
http://www.infojocks.com
http://www.infojocks.com/shop
http://www.twitter.com/infojocks
FIRST EDITION · PRESSED IN 2011 · of 500
Copyright Infojocks © 2011

Taxonomy of Team Names

This poster classifies the team names of 122 sports teams in the major US professional leagues. Even though it forms a taxonomy it is not visualised as a tree. Instead, the four types are arranged in four directions, with the sub-types forming a halo around the centre. Each sub-type is represented by a character recalling 19th-century book illustrations. Teams are listed by origin and name. Colours and icons refer to the sport being illustrated: football, baseball, basketball and hockey. In the lower part, sub-types are broken down by "success". The pie charts show the distribution of types among the team names of each individual league. The bar chart shows how many championships were won according to sub-type.

Project Info: Poster, 2009, USA
Design: Jeremy Yingling (Infojocks Sports Graphics)

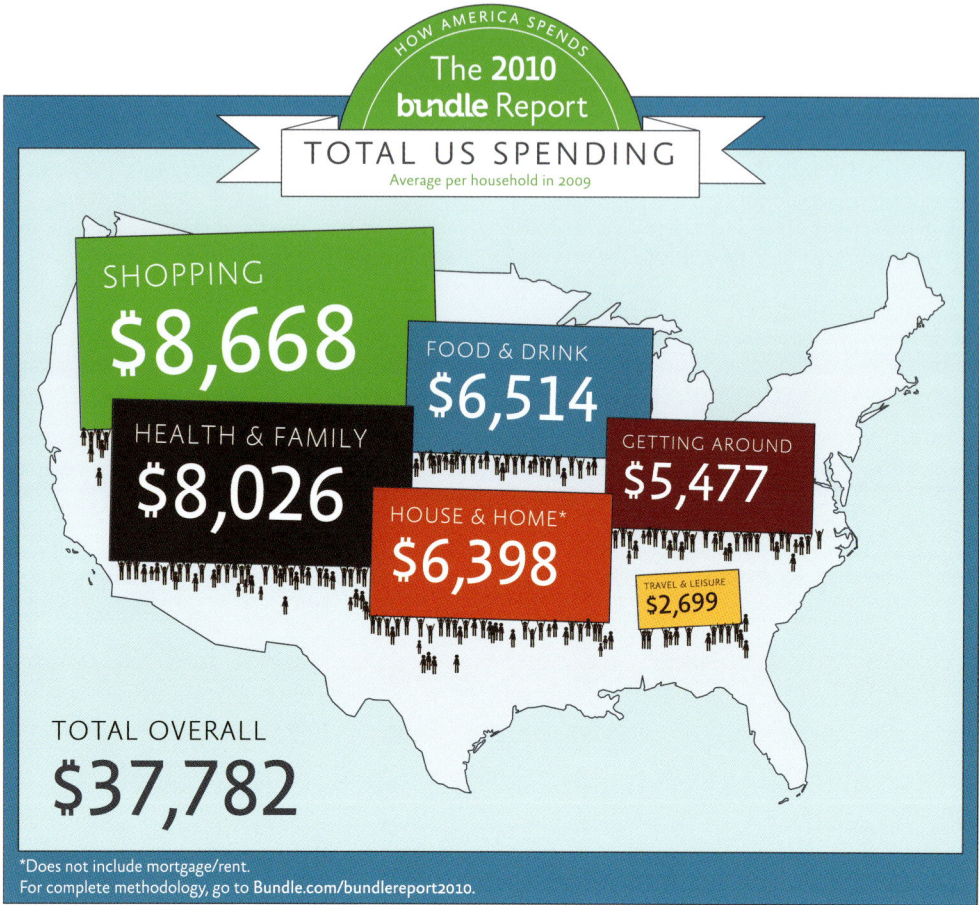

HOW AMERICA SPENDS

The **2010**
bundle Report

TOTAL US SPENDING
Average per household in 2009

SHOPPING
$8,668

FOOD & DRINK
$6,514

HEALTH & FAMILY
$8,026

GETTING AROUND
$5,477

HOUSE & HOME*
$6,398

TRAVEL & LEISURE
$2,699

TOTAL OVERALL
$37,782

*Does not include mortgage/rent.
For complete methodology, go to Bundle.com/bundlereport2010.

The 2010 Bundle Report

Bundle.com offers an interactive tool which allows people to control their private money flows. The website collaborated with Stefanie Posavec to create a report about private spending in the US in 2009. Private expenses are broken down into five different graphics to make values comparable: by age, type of household, by US state and by city, whilst a US map lists the major expenses in private spending and gives average national figures.

Project Info: Website, Bundle, 2010, USA
Design: Stefanie Posavec

The 2010 bundle Report — SPENDING BY HOUSEHOLD
Average annual spending in 2009

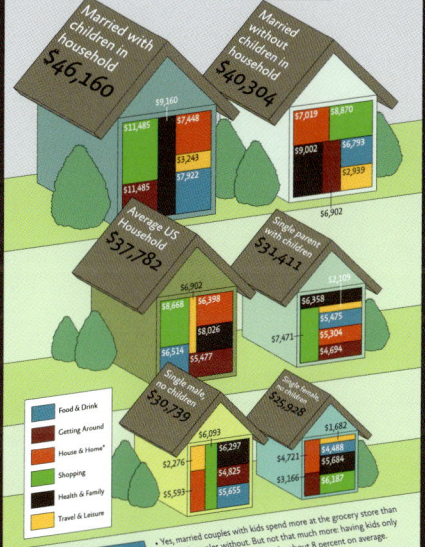

- Married with children in household **$46,160** — $9,160 · $11,485 · $7,448 · $3,243 · $11,485 · $7,922
- Married without children in household **$40,304** — $7,019 · $8,870 · $9,002 · $6,793 · $2,939 · $6,902
- Average US Household **$37,782** — $6,902 · $8,668 · $6,398 · $8,026 · $5,477
- Single parent with children **$31,411** — $2,109 · $6,358 · $5,475 · $7,471 · $5,304 · $4,694
- Single male, no children **$30,739** — $6,093 · $2,276 · $6,297 · $4,825 · $5,593 · $5,655
- Single female with children **$25,938** — $3,682 · $4,721 · $4,488 · $3,166 · $5,684 · $6,187

Legend: Food & Drink · Getting Around · House & Home* · Shopping · Health & Family · Travel & Leisure

DON'T BLAME THE KIDS:
- Yes, married couples with kids spend more at the grocery store than married couples without. But not that much more: having kids only boosts annual grocery spending by about 8 percent, on average.
- Young parents with kids spend less on restaurants than young marrieds without; after age 36, the trend reverses.
- On what do married people without kids consistently outspend married parents? Pets and pet care.

*Does not include mortgage/rent. For complete methodology, go to Bundle.com/bundlereport2010.

The 2010 bundle Report — SPENDING BY CITY
Average per household in 2009

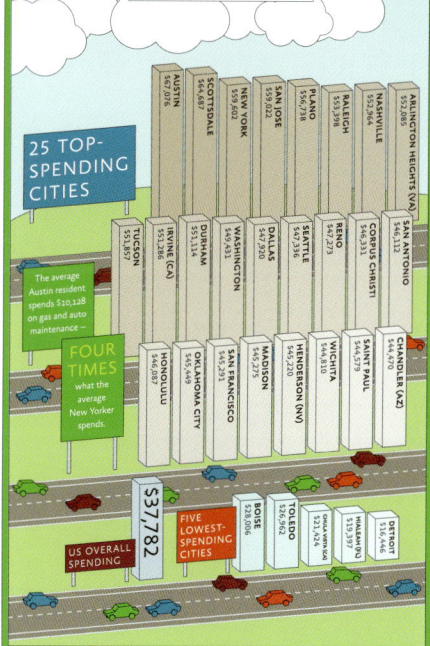

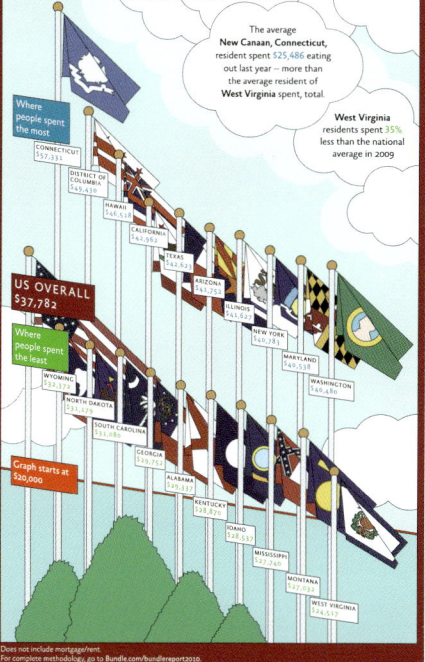

25 TOP-SPENDING CITIES
- AUSTIN $47,076
- SCOTTSDALE $64,457
- NEW YORK $59,602
- SAN JOSE $56,738
- PLANO $56,922
- RALEIGH $53,398
- NASHVILLE $52,364
- ARLINGTON HEIGHTS (VA) $52,085
- TUCSON $51,857
- IRVINE (CA) $51,286
- DURHAM $51,114
- WASHINGTON $48,641
- DALLAS $47,320
- SEATTLE $47,316
- MADISON $47,275
- RENO $47,351
- CORPUS CHRISTI $44,331
- SAINT PAUL $44,579
- SAN ANTONIO $43,112
- CHANDLER (AZ) $44,470
- HENDERSON (NV) $45,220
- WICHITA $44,910
- HONOLULU $46,087
- OKLAHOMA CITY $45,449
- SAN FRANCISCO $45,291

The average Austin resident spends $10,128 on gas and auto maintenance — FOUR TIMES what the average New Yorker spends.

US OVERALL SPENDING $37,782

FIVE LOWEST-SPENDING CITIES
- BOISE $28,006
- TOLEDO $26,762
- CHULA VISTA (CA) $23,424
- HIALEAH (FL) $19,397
- DETROIT $16,446

Does not include mortgage/rent. For complete methodology, go to Bundle.com/bundlereport2010.

The 2010 bundle Report — SPENDING BY STATE
Average per household in 2009

The average New Canaan, Connecticut, resident spent $25,486 eating out last year — more than the average resident of West Virginia spent, total.

West Virginia residents spent 35% less than the national average in 2009

Where people spent the most
- CONNECTICUT $57,331
- DISTRICT OF COLUMBIA $45,439
- HAWAII $44,118
- CALIFORNIA $42,992
- TEXAS $42,543
- ARIZONA $41,757
- ILLINOIS $41,537
- NEW YORK $40,981
- MARYLAND $40,538
- WASHINGTON $40,480

US OVERALL $37,782

Where people spent the least
- WYOMING $32,372
- NORTH DAKOTA $21,378
- SOUTH CAROLINA $21,685
- GEORGIA $20,765
- ALABAMA $20,517
- KENTUCKY $28,820
- IDAHO $28,537
- MISSISSIPPI $27,760
- MONTANA $27,033
- WEST VIRGINIA $24,519

Graph starts at $20,000

Does not include mortgage/rent. For complete methodology, go to Bundle.com/bundlereport2010.

The 2010 bundle Report — SPENDING BY AGE
Average annual spending per household in 2009

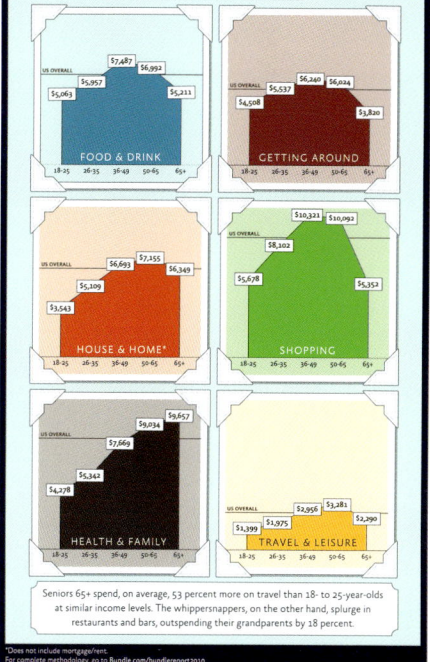

Age groups: 18-25, 26-35, 36-49, 50-65, 65+

- **FOOD & DRINK** — US OVERALL $5,957; $7,487; $6,992; $5,063; $5,211
- **GETTING AROUND** — US OVERALL $5,537; $6,240; $6,024; $4,508; $3,820
- **HOUSE & HOME*** — US OVERALL $5,109; $6,693; $7,155; $6,349; $3,543
- **SHOPPING** — US OVERALL $8,102; $10,321; $10,092; $5,678; $5,352
- **HEALTH & FAMILY** — US OVERALL $7,669; $9,034; $9,657; $5,342; $4,278
- **TRAVEL & LEISURE** — US OVERALL $1,975; $2,956; $3,281; $2,290; $1,399

Seniors 65+ spend, on average, 53 percent more on travel than 18- to 25-year-olds at similar income levels. The whippersnappers, on the other hand, splurge in restaurants and bars, outspending their grandparents by 18 percent.

*Does not include mortgage/rent. For complete methodology, go to Bundle.com/bundlereport2010.

OF POVERTY
AND THE UNEQUAL
DISTRIBUTION OF WEALTH
AS SEEN IN WASHINGTON D.C.

BY LUCA MASUD

POVERTY
(% on total)

40%
35%
30%
25%
20%
15%
10%
5%
0%

0   20   40   60   80   100   120   140   **GDP PER CAPITA**
(thousands of USD)

37% POVERTY PEAK
(MISSISSIPI &
WASHINGTON D.C.
CHILDREN)

23% CHILDREN 0-18 AVG

17% ALL AVG
15% ADULTS 19-64 AVG
13% ELDERLY 65+ AVG

TENDENCY

Mississippi, West Virginia, Arkansas, Montana, Oklahoma, South Carolina, Alabama, Kentucky, Maine, Idaho, New Mexico, Utah, Louisiana, Missouri, Arizona, Michigan, Florida, Indiana, Kansas, Tennessee, North Dakota, Vermont, Ohio, Pennsylvania, Georgia, Wisconsin, Iowa, South Dakota, Rhode Island, Nebraska, North Carolina, Texas, Oregon, New Hampshire, Hawaii, Wyoming, Maryland, Illinois, Washington, Minnesota, Nevada, California, Virginia, Colorado, Alaska, New Jersey, New York, Massachusetts, Connecticut, Delaware, District of Columbia

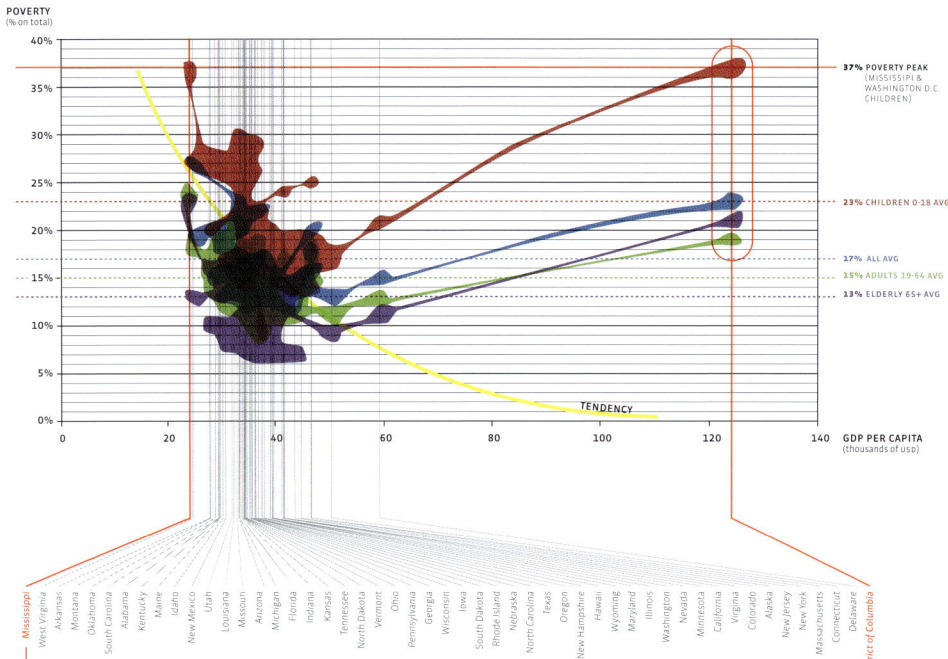

USA poorest state based on GDP

USA richest state based on GDP

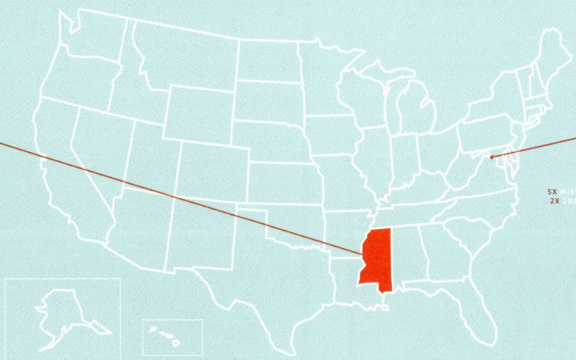

**WASHINGTON D.C.
GDP PER CAPITA**
124363 USD
5X MISSISSIPPI'S GDP
2X 2ND HIGHEST GDP

**WASHINGTON D.C.
POVERTY RANKING**
2nd total
1st children
6th adults
2nd elderly

Washington D.C. despite being the highest GDP per capita state in the confederation, suffers the highest children's poverty rate and one of the highest total average poverty rates, making it the state with the most unequal distribution of wealth.

Unequal Distribution of Wealth

This diagram looks at poverty by age in the US. The x-axis shows the GDP per capita, with all states listed below according to their wealth. While many states are rather close to each other, Washington D.C. more than doubles the GDP of the second richest listed, Delaware. The y-axis represents the percentage of population who live in poverty. Age groups are colour coded: red are children, green are adults etc. The dotted lines show national median values, indicating, for instance, that compared with the national average, 23 % of children are living in poverty. Washington D.C. as the wealthiest state by far exceeds this with 37 % of children living in poverty.

Project Info: Website, 2009, Italy
Data Source: Kaiser State Health Facts
Design: Luca Masud (DensityDesign)

Following spread

The Real US National Debt

Lorraine Moffa and Nigel Holmes demonstrate the enormous national debt the United States owed to various lenders in 2009. They also explain how the government does not include two major programs, Social Security and Medicare / Medicaid, when publishing figures about the national debt. The graphic is all about making this unimaginable amount of money conceivable. First, the total 2009 figures are summed up and compared to the figures for 2000. Second, all the big lenders are named. In the next three steps, this enormous debt is compared to an average household to give a relative impression of the amount. A small timeline on the lower left shows how the national debt has grown exponentially over the past 30 years.

Project Info: "How Much Do We Really Owe?",
American History, magazine article, 2009, USA
Data Source: Congressional Budget Office; Jess Bachmann (WallStats.com); Federal Reserve; Patrick Creadon, Christine O'Malley, Addison Wiggin: "I.O.U.S.A."; US Treasury
Research: Lorraine Moffa
Design: Nigel Holmes

How Much Do We REALLY Owe?

DATAGRAPHIC
BY NIGEL HOLMES
RESEARCH BY
LORRAINE MOFFA

1

The **$11 trillion national debt** equals the sum of all the outstanding loans the federal government has incurred since the founding of the country. Not included is the projected cost of funding entitlement programs like Social Security and Medicare/Medicaid.

When those are added, the national debt is:

$53 trillion

National debt
$11 trillion

Social Security
$7 trillion

Medicare/
Medicaid
$34 trillion

Misc.
$1 trillion

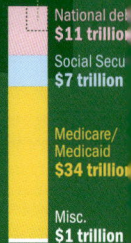

In **2000**, the numbers were:

$19 trillion

$6 trillion
$3.8 trillion
$9.2 trillion

$11 trillion
$10
$9
$8
$7
$6
$5
$4
$3
$2
$1 trillion

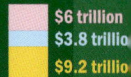

HOW THE NATIONAL DEBT HAS GROWN

It took the U.S. 191 years to run up the first trillion. The second and third trillion were both reached in 4 years. Between 2000 and 2008, the nation's debt went from $5.7 trillion to $10.6 trillion.

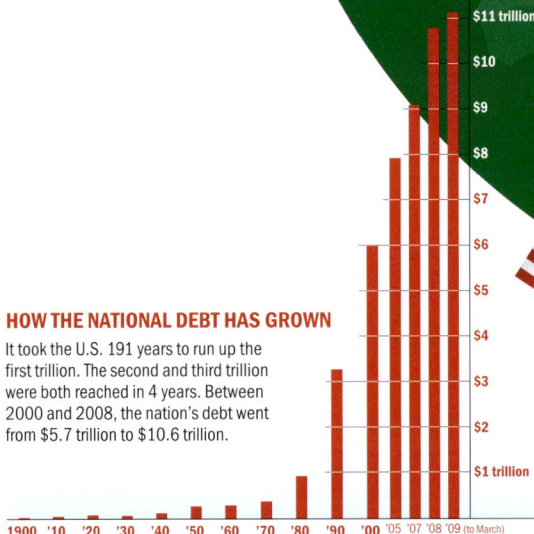

1900 '10 '20 '30 '40 '50 '60 '70 '80 '90 '00 '05 '07 '08 '09 (to March)

Sources: Congressional Budget Office; Jess Brachman, WallStats.com; Federal Reserve Flow of Funds Report; Federal Reserve Survey of Consumer Finance; 2000 & 2007 Financial Report of the U.S. Government; *I.O.U.S.A.*, by Patrick Creadon, Christine O' Malley and Addison Wiggin; treasurydirect.gov; U.S. Treasury

2

BIG LENDERS
Just over a
quarter of the
national debt
is owned by
foreign banks:

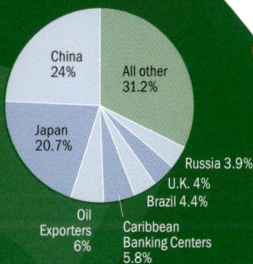

China 24%

All other 31.2%

Japan 20.7%

Russia 3.9%
U.K. 4%
Brazil 4.4%

Oil Exporters 6%

Caribbean Banking Centers 5.8%

The remaining national debt is owned by:

Depository institutions	1.2%
Insurance companies	1.3%
State and local government pensions	1.8%
U.S. Savings Bonds	2.1%
Private pensions	2.4%
Other investors	3.8%
Mutual funds	4.8%
State and local government	5.5%
Federal Reserve and Intragovernmental Holdings	49.4%

3

It is hard
to comprehend the
size of these numbers.
To give them an everyday
context, let's scale
the U.S. economy …

The government takes in about $3 trillion a year from taxes, etc.

… down to the
size of one
U.S.
house-
hold

(Median household income is $47,300)

Each household
would have
$189,200
of annual debt, if it
borrowed as much
money as the
government.

5

The United States
also spends more
than it earns.
Much more.
If each household
borrowed like the
government, the
picture would look
like this:

$
S
P
E
N
D
I
N
G

$
I
N
C
O
M
E

To make
up the
difference
between
income and
spending, most
households
take out loans
(mainly credit
cards). Average
household
debt is
$23,500.
(Does not
include
mortgages.)

$
S
P
E
N
D
I
N
G

$
I
N
C
O
M
E

4

Many
households
spend more
than they earn.

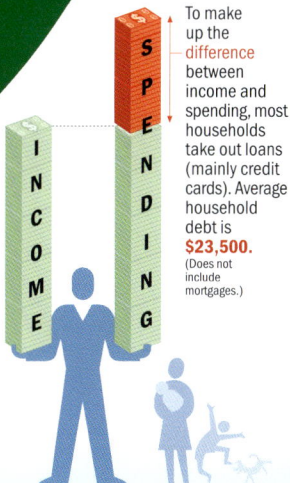

489

2010

Puma

Algerien,
Elfenbeinküste,
Ghana, Italien,
Kamerun,
Schweiz,
Uruguay

Australien,
Brasilien,
Neuseeland,
Niederlande,
Portugal, Serbien,
Slowenien,
Südkorea,
USA

Nike

Chile

Brooks

Argentinien,
Dänemark, Deutschland,
Frankreich, Griechen-
land, Japan, Mexiko,
Nigeria, Paraguay,
Slowakei, Spanien,
Südafrika

Adidas

Eng-
land

Umbro

Hon-
duras,
Nord-
korea

Joma

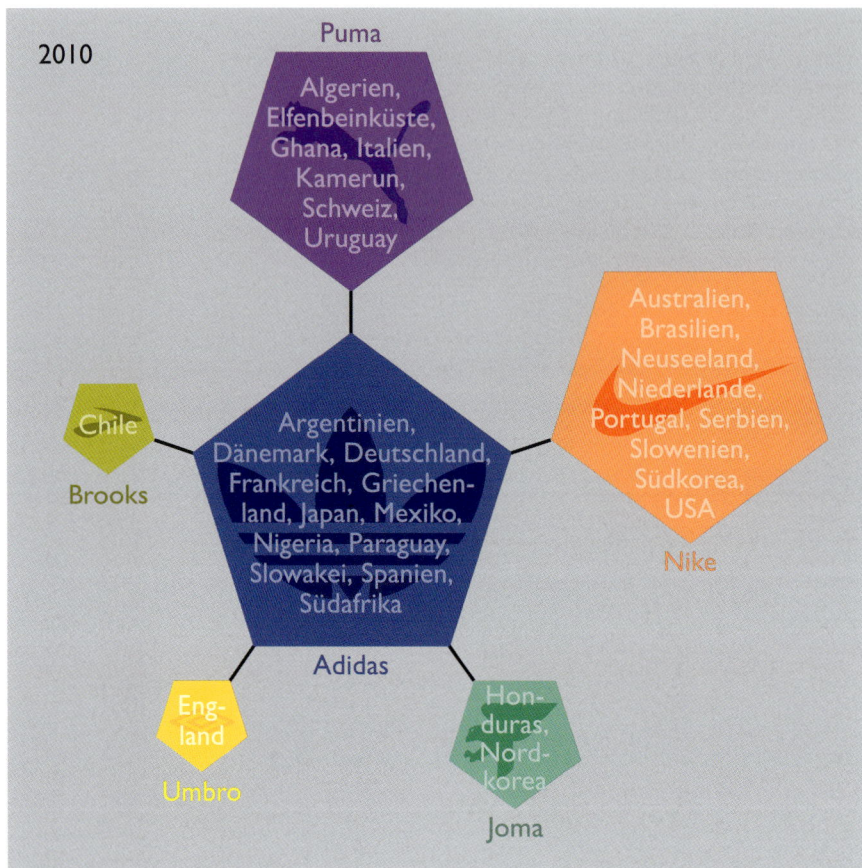

Footballistics

On the occasion of the FIFA World Cup in 2010, the German magazine *Die Zeit* created two double spreads to cover the magic with a collection of infographics. Individual topics ranged from how collecting Panini stickers really works through to a timeline with the most significant footballer hairstyles from 3 decades. The hierarchy of little Subbuteo-type figures shows teams ranked from the most expensive according to the market value of individual players. A tree chart divides into groups the mascots of earlier tournaments. The white figure shows German icon Michael Ballack and lists his injuries, which prevented him from joining the tournament. Blue boxes in various sizes indicate selected German players' popularity on Facebook.

Project Info: *ZEITmagazin*, 2010, Germany
Data Source: Transfermarkt.de; Andreas Binzenhöfer (University of Würzburg); Statistisches Bundesamt Deutschland; Deutscher Fussball-Bund; FIFA
Research: Matthias Stolz (*Die Zeit*), Enrique García de la Garza, Friederike Milbradt
Design: Ole Häntzschel

MICHAEL BALLACKS VERLETZUNGEN

(seit Juni 2006)

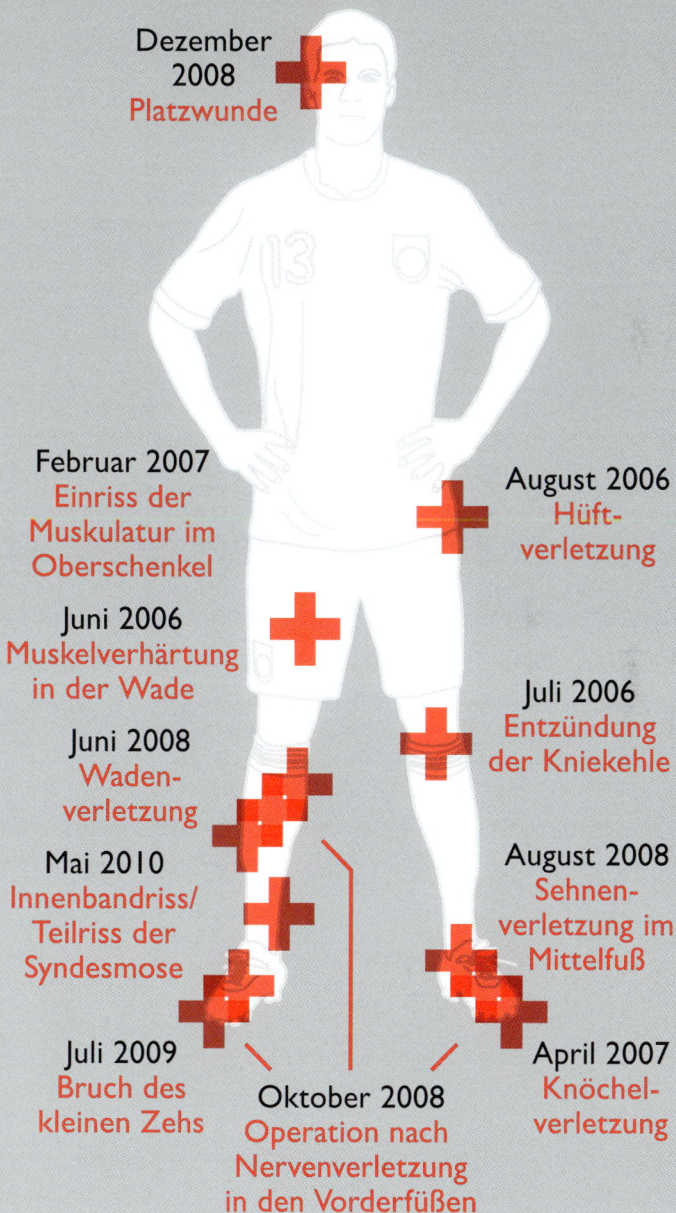

Dezember 2008
Platzwunde

Februar 2007
Einriss der Muskulatur im Oberschenkel

August 2006
Hüftverletzung

Juni 2006
Muskelverhärtung in der Wade

Juli 2006
Entzündung der Kniekehle

Juni 2008
Wadenverletzung

Mai 2010
Innenbandriss/ Teilriss der Syndesmose

August 2008
Sehnenverletzung im Mittelfuß

Juli 2009
Bruch des kleinen Zehs

Oktober 2008
Operation nach Nervenverletzung in den Vorderfüßen

April 2007
Knöchelverletzung

FUSSBALLISTIK

DIE MAGIE DER WELTMEISTERSCHAFT, ENTSCHLÜSSELT IN VIERZEHN INFOGRAFIKEN

Von
MATTHIAS STOLZ

Infografiken
OLE HÄNTZSCHEL

PANINI-BILDER
der Weltmeisterschaften seit 1970

Anzahl der Päckchen, die man
kaufen muss, damit das Album
mit mehr als 90-prozentiger
Wahrscheinlichkeit komplett wird

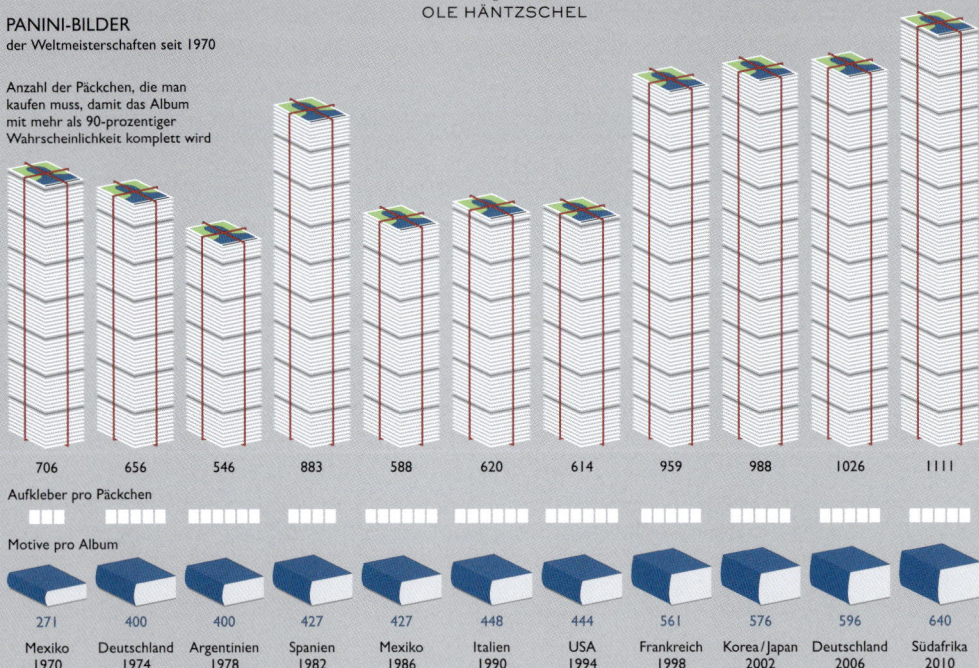

| 706 | 656 | 546 | 883 | 588 | 620 | 614 | 959 | 988 | 1026 | 1111 |

Aufkleber pro Päckchen

Motive pro Album

271	400	400	427	427	448	444	561	576	596	640
Mexiko 1970	Deutschland 1974	Argentinien 1978	Spanien 1982	Mexiko 1986	Italien 1990	USA 1994	Frankreich 1998	Korea/Japan 2002	Deutschland 2006	Südafrika 2010

DIE TEUERSTEN MANNSCHAFTEN
Durchschnittlicher Marktwert pro Spieler in Millionen Euro (Schätzwerte)

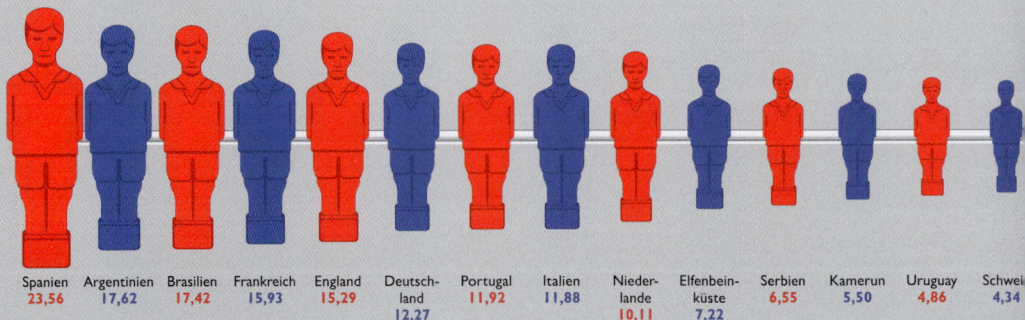

Spanien	Argentinien	Brasilien	Frankreich	England	Deutschland	Portugal	Italien	Niederlande	Elfenbeinküste	Serbien	Kamerun	Uruguay	Schwei
23,56	17,62	17,42	15,93	15,29	12,27	11,92	11,88	10,11	7,22	6,55	5,50	4,86	4,34

RECHERCHE ENRIQUE GARCÍA DE LA GARZA; FRIEDERIKE MILBRADT

GATTUNGEN DER MASKOTTCHEN

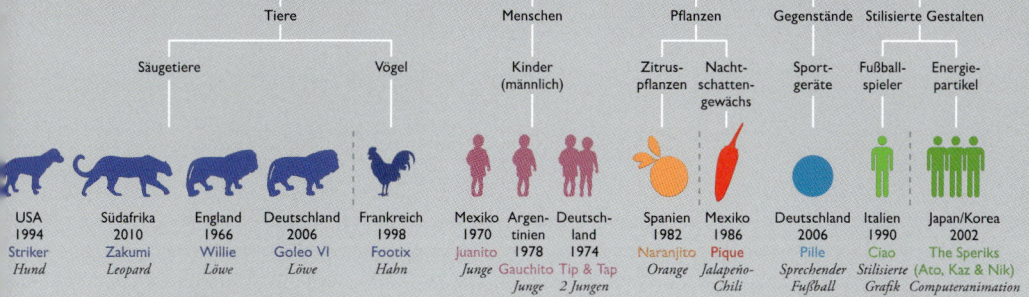

Tiere
- Säugetiere
- Vögel

Menschen
- Kinder (männlich)

Pflanzen
- Zitruspflanzen
- Nachtschattengewächs

Gegenstände
- Sportgeräte

Stilisierte Gestalten
- Fußballspieler
- Energiepartikel

USA 1994	Südafrika 2010	England 1966	Deutschland 2006	Frankreich 1998	Mexiko 1970	Argentinien 1978	Deutschland 1974	Spanien 1982	Mexiko 1986	Deutschland 2006	Italien 1990	Japan/Korea 2002
Striker	Zakumi	Willie	Goleo VI	Footix	Juanito	Gauchito	Tip & Tap	Naranjito	Pique	Pille	Ciao	The Speriks (Ato, Kaz & Nik)
Hund	*Leopard*	*Löwe*	*Löwe*	*Hahn*	*Junge*	*Junge*	*2 Jungen*	*Orange*	*Jalapeño-Chili*	*Sprechender Fußball*	*Stilisierte Grafik*	*Computeranimation*

WM-BABYS
Wie veränderte die WM die Geburtenquote in Deutschland?

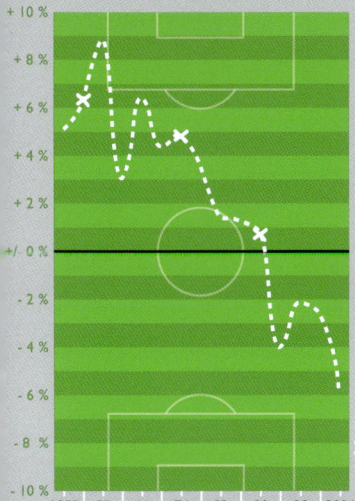

Änderung der Geburtenrate neun Monate nach der WM (im Vergleich zum jeweiligen Jahresdurchschnitt)

✕ Deutschland Weltmeister

+ 10 % · + 8 % · + 6 % · + 4 % · + 2 % · +/- 0 % · - 2 % · - 4 % · - 6 % · - 8 % · - 10 %

1950 54 58 62 66 70 74 78 82 86 90 94 98 02 2006

BLONDINENQUOTE DER SPIELERFRAUEN DER DEUTSCHEN NATIONALMANNSCHAFT

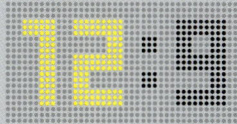

12:6

blonde Spielerfrau — nicht blonde Spielerfrau

Die restlichen sechs Spieler des Kaders sind entweder nicht liiert oder die Haarfarbe ihrer Partnerin ist nicht bekannt
Stand: 18.5.2010

BIERKONSUM

6%

... mehr Bier wurde im WM-Sommer 2006 in Deutschland im Vergleich zum Sommer 2005 getrunken

MICHAEL BALLACKS VERLETZUNGEN
(seit Juni 2006)

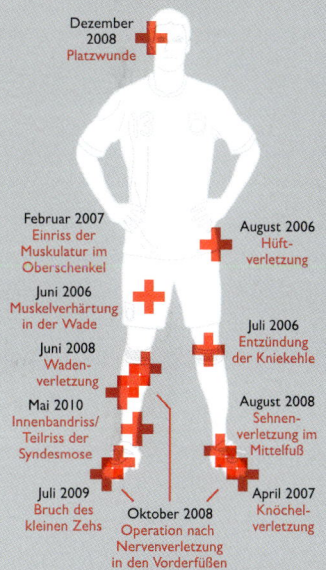

- Dezember 2008 Platzwunde
- Februar 2007 Einriss der Muskulatur im Oberschenkel
- Juni 2006 Muskelverhärtung in der Wade
- Juni 2008 Wadenverletzung
- Mai 2010 Innenbandriss/ Teilriss der Syndesmose
- Juli 2009 Bruch des kleinen Zehs
- August 2006 Hüftverletzung
- Juli 2006 Entzündung der Kniekehle
- August 2008 Sehnenverletzung im Mittelfuß
- April 2007 Knöchelverletzung
- Oktober 2008 Operation nach Nervenverletzung in den Vorderfüßen

DAS DURCHSCHNITTSALTER DER FIFA-PRÄSIDENTEN bei Amtsantritt im Vergleich

US-Präsidenten	UN-Generalsekretäre	IOC-Präsidenten	Bundeskanzler	FIFA-Präsidenten	Päpste
54,7	55,1	56,8	58,5	60,9	66,2

Päpste und US-Präsidenten seit Beginn des vorigen Jahrhunderts

Nigeria	Mexiko	Griechenland	Ghana	Dänemark	Chile	Japan	Slowakei	Paraguay	Algerien	Südkorea	Slowenien	Australien	Honduras	Südafrika	USA	Neuseeland	Nordkorea
4,22	3,79	3,58	3,36	3,31	3,23	2,82	2,50	2,22	2,17	1,94	1,71	1,66	1,39	1,30	1,22	0,57	0,43

DIE BAYERN-QUOTE

Anteil der FC-Bayern-München-Spieler am Kader der (west-)deutschen Nationalmannschaft

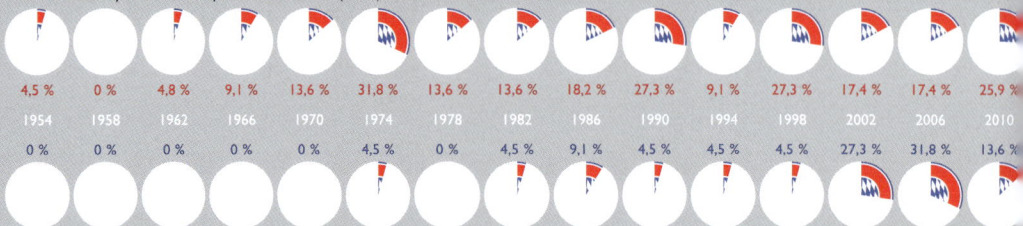

4,5 %	0 %	4,8 %	9,1 %	13,6 %	31,8 %	13,6 %	13,6 %	18,2 %	27,3 %	9,1 %	27,3 %	17,4 %	17,4 %	25,9 %
1954	1958	1962	1966	1970	1974	1978	1982	1986	1990	1994	1998	2002	2006	2010
0 %	0 %	0 %	0 %	0 %	4,5 %	0 %	4,5 %	9,1 %	4,5 %	4,5 %	4,5 %	27,3 %	31,8 %	13,6 %

Anteil der FC-Bayern-München-Spieler, die für andere Nationen an der WM teilnahmen

ZWEITFARBEN
Auf welche Trikots können die 32 WM-Nationen ausweichen, wenn sonst zwei Gegner dieselbe Farbe tragen würden?

Kamerun
Ghana
England
Südafrika
Slowenien
Elfenbeinküste
Algerien
Neuseeland
Mexiko
Deutschland
Australien
USA
Spanien
Slowakei
Honduras
Griechenland
Brasilien
Argentinien
Portugal
Uruguay
Südkorea
Serbien
Schweiz
Paraguay
Nordkorea
Nigeria
Niederlande
Japan
Italien
Frankreich
Dänemark
Chile

ANZAHL DER FACEBOOK-FANS VON SPIELERN DES DEUTSCHEN WM-KADERS

Stand: 18.5.2010

marko marin
2 584

mario gomez
7 279

toni kroos
2 724

tim wiese
1 065

heiko westermann
404

arne friedrich
1 294

mesut özil
10 972

andreas beck
443

manuel neuer
4 611

jérôme boateng
106

hans-jörg butt
2 653

per mertesacker
2 204

philipp lahm
9 992

michael ballack
49 458

EINIGE STILPRÄGENDE FRISUREN VON WM-SPIELERN

1954	1966	1974			1986		
Fritz Walter	Bobby Charlton	Günter Netzer	Norbert Nigbur	Paul Breitner	Diego Maradona	Chris Waddle	Carlos Valderrama

Brasilien China Europa Indien
Japan Korea USA Südafrika
Vereinigte Arabische Emirate

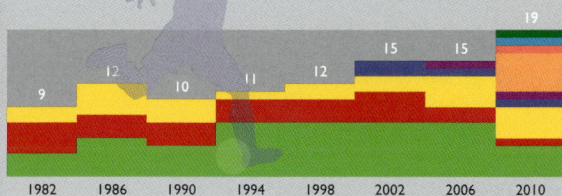

9 — 1982
12 — 1986
10 — 1990
11 — 1994
12 — 1998
15 — 2002
15 — 2006
19 — 2010

DIE HERSTELLER DER TRIKOTS 1974, 1990 UND 2010

1974

Argentinien, Australien, Bulgarien, Chile, DDR, Haiti, Italien, Jugoslawien, Niederlande, Polen, Schweden, Zaire

Brasilien — Athleta

Adidas

Schottland — Umbro

Deutschland — Erima

Der Hersteller der Trikots von Uruguay ist dem Verband nicht bekannt

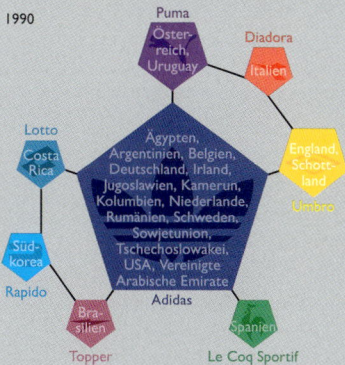

1990

Puma

Österreich, Uruguay

Diadora — Italien

Lotto — Costa Rica

Ägypten, Argentinien, Belgien, Deutschland, Irland, Jugoslawien, Kamerun, Kolumbien, Niederlande, Rumänien, Schweden, Sowjetunion, Tschechoslowakei, USA, Vereinigte Arabische Emirate

England, Schottland — Umbro

Südkorea — Rapido

Brasilien — Topper

Adidas

Spanien — Le Coq Sportif

bastian schweinsteiger
46 390

marcell jansen
558

marcell jansen
558

=

christian träsch
19

lukas podolski
11 723

holger badstuber
2 991

dennis aogo
802

dennis aogo
802

piotr trochowski
2 279

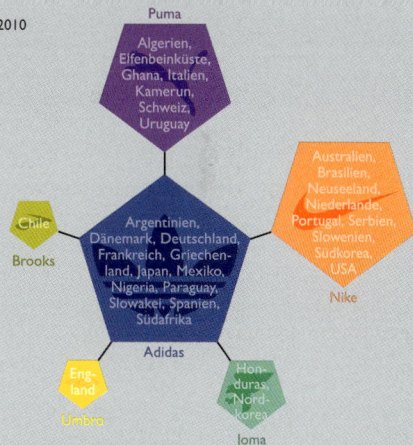

2010

Puma

Algerien, Elfenbeinküste, Ghana, Italien, Kamerun, Schweiz, Uruguay

miroslav klose
23 427

serdar tasci
757

serdar tasci
757

Chile — Brooks

Argentinien, Dänemark, Deutschland, Frankreich, Griechenland, Japan, Mexiko, Nigeria, Paraguay, Slowakei, Spanien, Südafrika

Australien, Brasilien, Neuseeland, Niederlande, Portugal, Serbien, Slowenien, Südkorea, USA — Nike

cacau
3 342

Adidas

England — Umbro

Honduras, Nordkorea — Joma

thomas müller
4 432

sami khedira
93

stefan kießling
992

1990
René Higuita — Rudi Völler — Alexi Lalas — 1994 Claudio Caniggia — Stefan Effenberg — 2002 Ronaldinho — David Beckham — 2006 Bastian Schweinsteiger — Cristiano Ronaldo

QUELLEN EIGENE RECHERCHEN; TRANSFERMARKT.DE; PANINI UND ANDREAS BINZENHÖFER / UNI WÜRZBURG; STATISTISCHES BUNDESAMT; DFB; FIFA; FACEBOOK

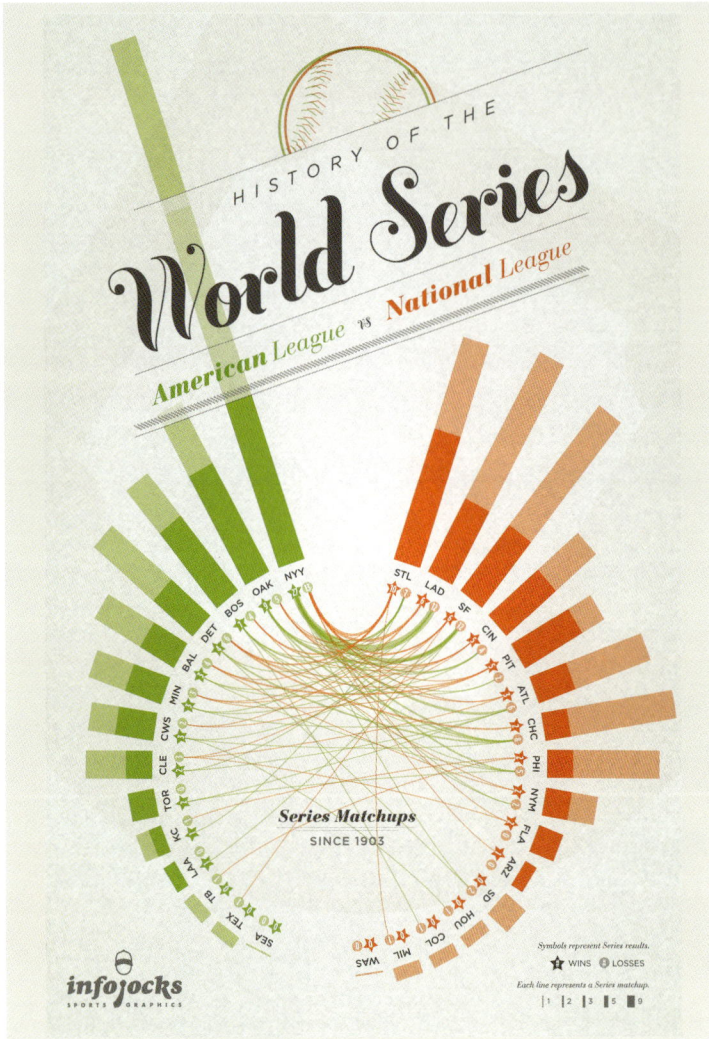

History of the World Series

The World Series is the annual championship in US Major League Baseball, played between the two winning clubs of the American League and the National League since 1903. Despite its title, this isn't a historical timeline. Instead, the circular diagram shows all match-ups between teams and compares victories and defeats. The bars show how many matches a team played in the World Series and how many of these were won. Teams are arranged by success rate. The not very successful Milwaukee Brewers (MIL, below right) used to belong to the American League but switched to the National League in 1998. This explains the seemingly irregular inner-league match-up with the St. Louis Cardinals (STL, top right), which occurred in 1982.

Project Info: Poster, 2009, USA
Data Source:
Baseball-reference.com
Design: Jeremy Yingling (Infojocks Sports Graphics)

The Very Many Varieties of BEER

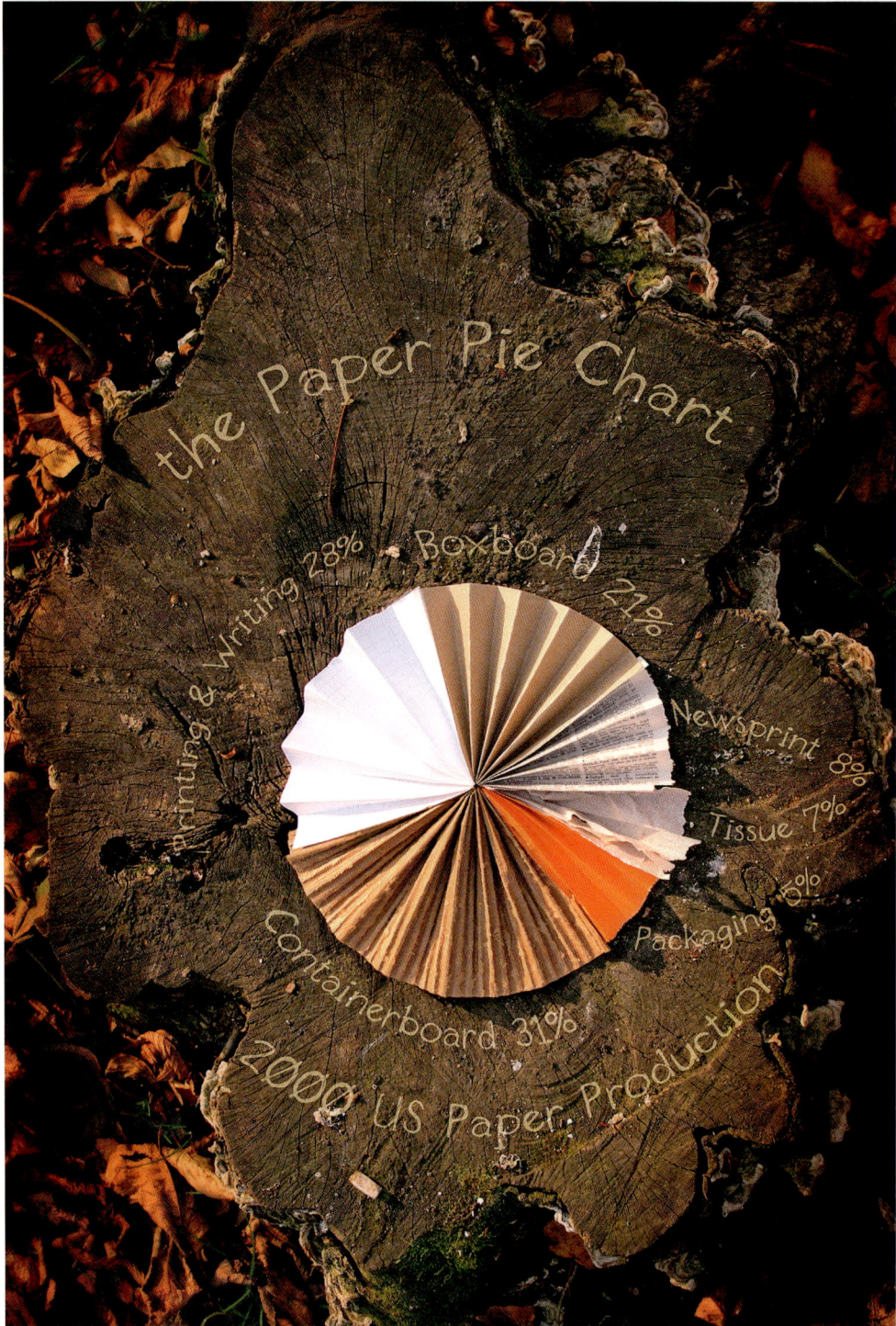

Page 497

The Very Many Varieties of Beer

Beer belongs amongst the most popular drinks on Earth, and there seem to be a million philosophies as to how to brew it. Team Pop Chart Lab employ the rather dull scientific scheme of a taxonomy and turn it into a chart of great use in everyday life: a taxonomy of beer types. While presenting a hierarchy, the types are not arranged in a tree. Instead, the most general type, "beer", is placed in the middle, and the sub-types branch out from there. All types and sub-types are presented in a circle, whilst specific examples for each type are named in simple lettering.

Project Info: Poster, 2010, USA
Design: Ben Gibson, Patrick Mulligan (Pop Chart Lab)

The Paper Pie Chart

The pie chart as physical object: this piece shows annual US paper production in total and the percentage in which various types of paper have been produced, by being literally made from those types of paper. The graphic thus not only refers to the statistics by means of an abstract diagram, but the elements of the diagram actually show what they are.

Project Info: Poster, 2010, Romania
Data Source: American Forest and Paper Association
Design: Alexandra Muresan

Following spread

Tracking Carbon Emissions

This graphic shows CO_2 emissions for some 200 nations worldwide. Relative quantities are represented by bubble size. The bubbles on the left show the absolute quantity of emissions per nation, with China and the US being the number one emission sources. The graphic on the right relates emissions to the number of inhabitants, which presents a different picture. Tiny nations like Gibraltar or the Virgin Islands top this second list as they need to have a lot of goods shipped in, which increases relative emissions per capita. The "footprint" refers to the concept of the ecological footprint, which allows people to quantify the environmental impact of their own lifestyle.

Project Info: Miller-McCune, magazine and online article, 2010, USA
Data Source: US Energy Information Administration
Design: Stanford Kay

Tracking Carbon Emissions

A footprint comparison of total carbon dioxide emissions by nation and per capita shows there's plenty of room for smaller countries to reduce their carbon footprints.

By Stanford Kay

Total Carbon Emissions by Nation

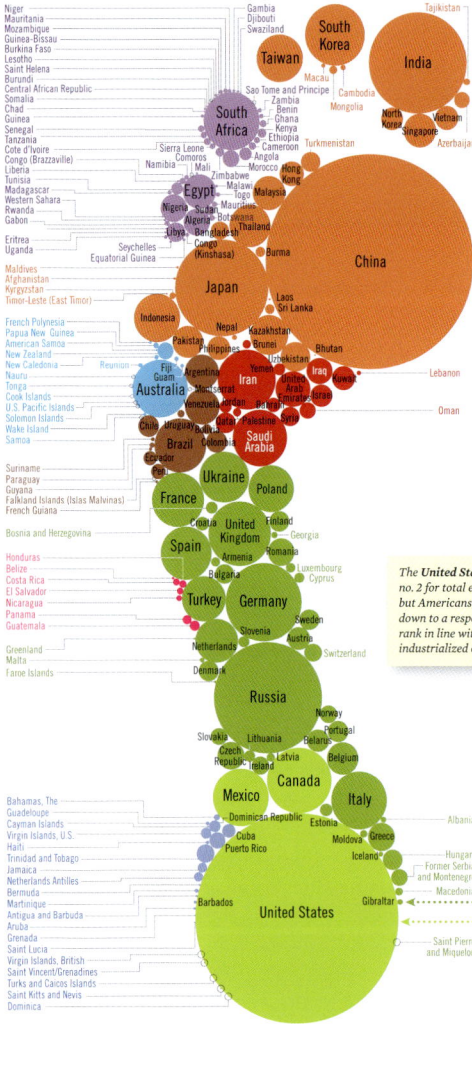

Total Carbon Emissions Per Capita

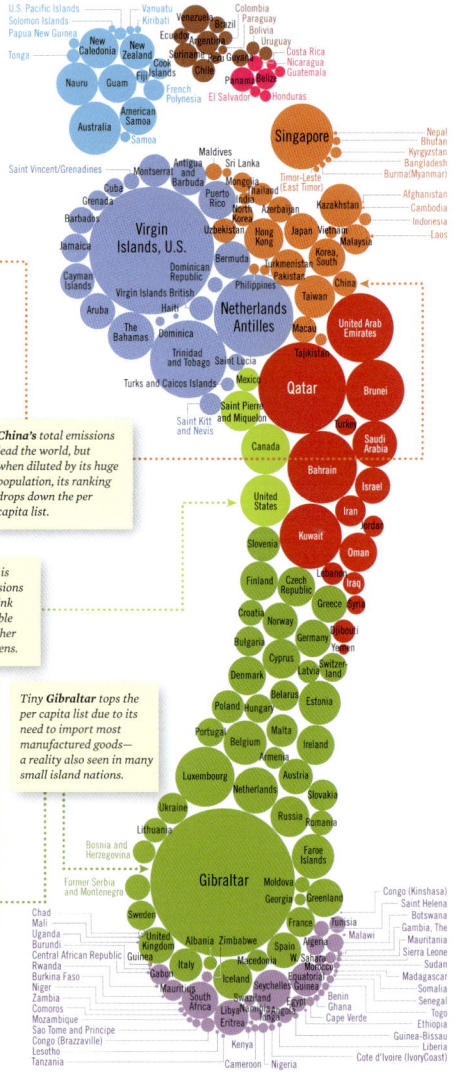

China's total emissions lead the world, but when diluted by its huge population, its ranking drops down the per capita list.

The **United States** is no. 2 for total emissions but Americans shrink down to a respectable rank in line with other industrialized citizens.

Tiny **Gibraltar** tops the per capita list due to its need to import most manufactured goods—a reality also seen in many small island nations.

KEY

● AFRICA ● ASIA ● MIDDLE EAST ● CARIBBEAN ● CENTRAL AMERICA ● EUROPE ● NORTH AMERICA ● OCEANIA ● SOUTH AMERICA

DESIGN: STANFORD KAY STUDIO

NOTE: BASED ON 2007 DATA. SOURCES: U.S. ENERGY INFORMATION ADMINISTRATION

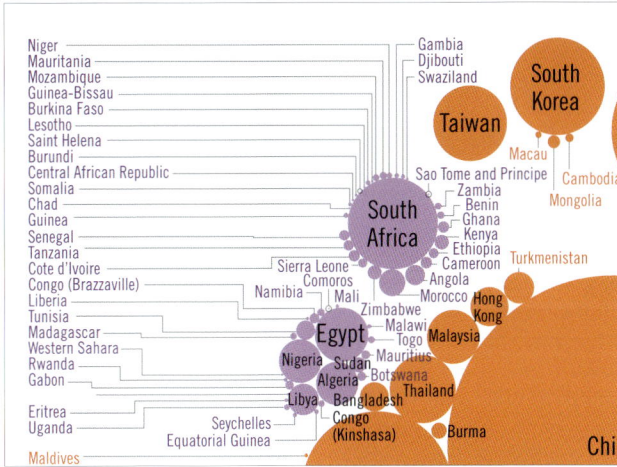

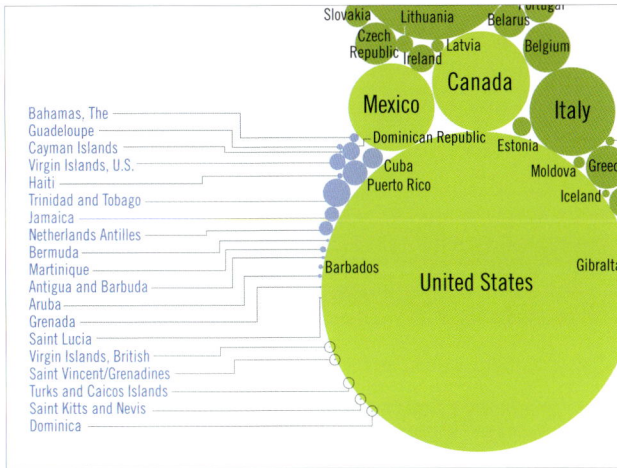

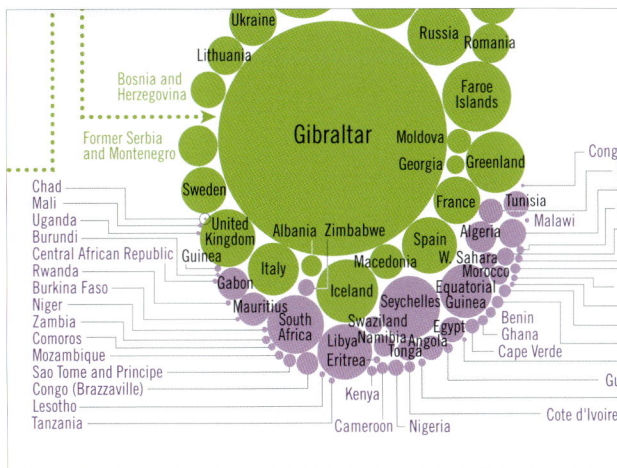

Upswing with Risks and Side Effects

As a forecast of global and national business developments in 2010, Golden Section Graphics created a series of works in an extreme vertical format for German newspaper *Handelsblatt*. One piece ranks the top world economies according to their contribution to global GDP in 2000 and 2010. Another graphic presents several economic key figures for four countries by way of a toppled diagram. The countries are listed vertically, with the rise and fall of figures shown by right or left movements in the graph. A third piece ranks Germany's most innovative companies in order. Bubble sizes indicate the business volume of each company, whilst the smaller bubble to the right indicates how much money has been spent on research and development.

Project Info: *Handelsblatt*, newspaper article, 2009, Germany
Data Source: Economist Intelligence Unit; OECD
Research: Susanne Wesch
Design: Paul Blickle, Jan Schwochow (Golden Section Graphics)
Art Direction: Nils Werner

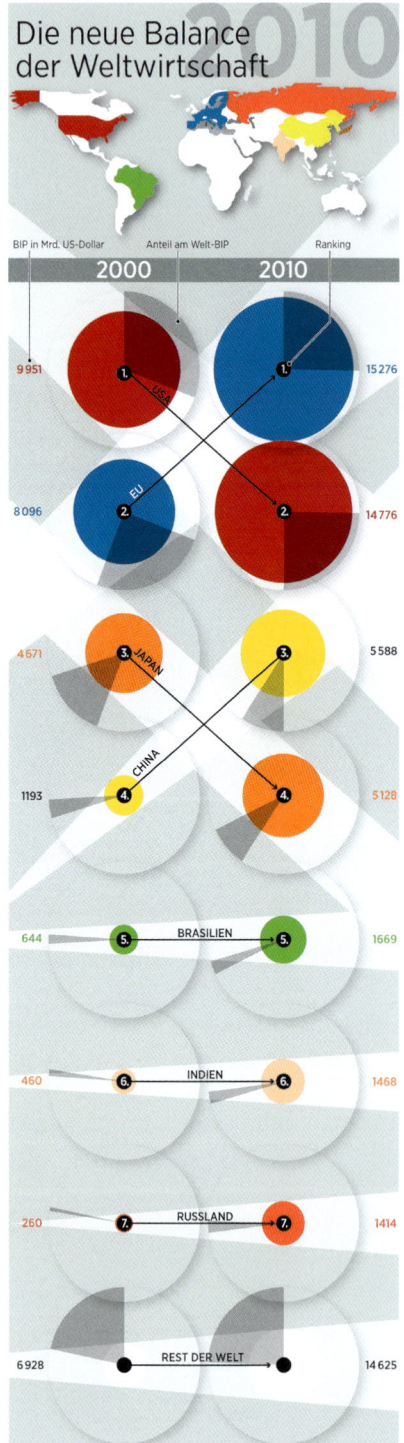

Die neue Balance der Weltwirtschaft 2010

BIP in Mrd. US-Dollar	Anteil am Welt-BIP	Ranking
	2000	2010	

9 951 — 1. USA — 1. — 15 276
8 096 — 2. EU — 2. — 14 776
4 671 — 3. JAPAN — 3. — 5 588
1 193 — 4. CHINA — 4. — 5 128
644 — 5. BRASILIEN — 5. — 1 669
460 — 6. INDIEN — 6. — 1 468
260 — 7. RUSSLAND — 7. — 1 414
6 928 — REST DER WELT — 14 625

2010
Auf der Suche nach neuen Wachstumsmodellen

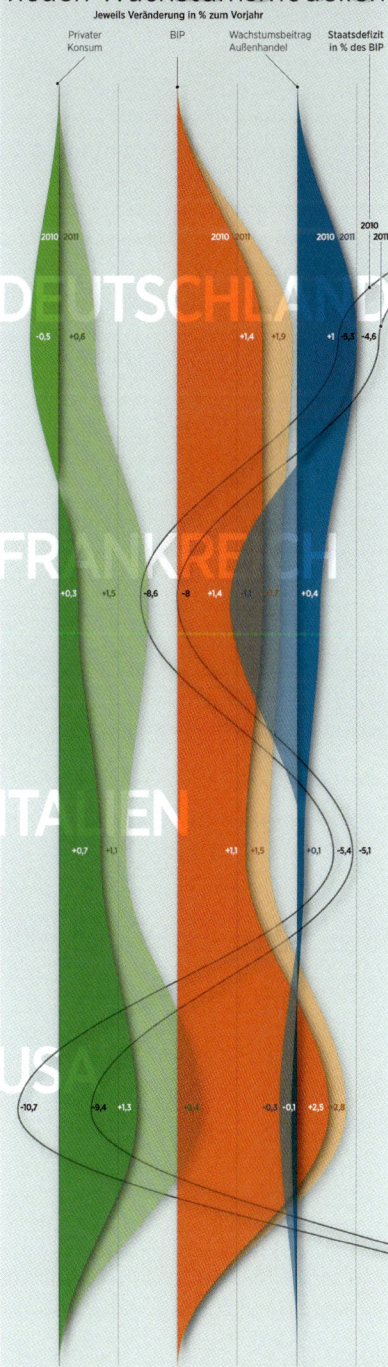

Jeweils Veränderung in % zum Vorjahr

| Privater Konsum | BIP | Wachstumsbeitrag Außenhandel | Staatsdefizit in % des BIP |

DEUTSCHLAND

| 2010 | 2011 | | 2010 | 2011 | | 2010 | 2011 | 2010 | 2011 |

-0,5 +0,6 | +1,4 +1,9 | +1 -5,5 -4,6

FRANKREICH

+0,3 +1,5 | -8,6 -8 +1,4 | -1,1 -0,2 +0,4

ITALIEN

+0,7 +1,1 | +1,1 +1,5 | +0,1 -5,4 -5,1

USA

-10,7 -9,4 +1,3 | +9,4 | -0,1 -0,1 +2,5 +2,8

2010
Deutschlands innovativste Unternehmen

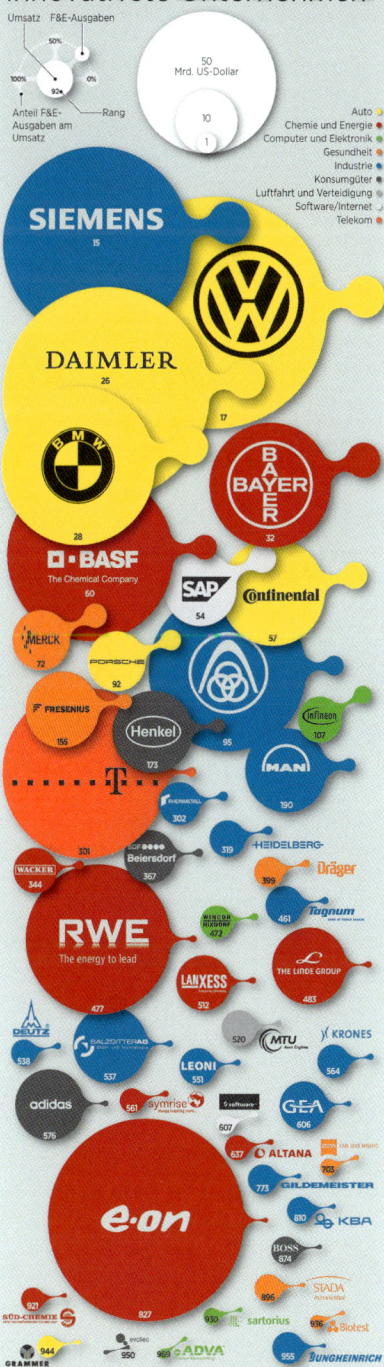

Umsatz · F&E-Ausgaben

50%

100% 0%

94%

Anteil F&E-Ausgaben am Umsatz — Rang

50 Mrd. US-Dollar

10

1

- Auto
- Chemie und Energie
- Computer und Elektronik
- Gesundheit
- Industrie
- Konsumgüter
- Luftfahrt und Verteidigung
- Software/Internet
- Telekom

SIEMENS 15

VW

DAIMLER 26

17

BMW 28

BAYER 32

BASF 60
The Chemical Company

SAP 54

Continental 57

MERCK 72

PORSCHE 92

FRESENIUS 155

Henkel 173

infineon 107

MAN 190

95

T 301

THYSSENKRUPP 302

HEIDELBERG 319

KSB Beiersdorf 367

Dräger 399

WACKER 344

WINCOR NIXDORF 472

Tognum 461

RWE 477
The energy to lead

THE LINDE GROUP 483

LANXESS 512

DEUTZ 538

SALZGITTER AG 537

520

MTU Aero Engines

KRONES 564

LEONI 551

adidas 576

561 symrise

507 softwareag

GEA 606

e·on 827

637 ALTANA

703

GILDEMEISTER 773

810 KBA

BOSS 874

SÜD-CHEMIE 921

896

STADA 936

930 sartorius

936 Biotest

944 GRAMMER

950 erotec

969 ADVA

955 Jungheinrich

503

Wine Consumption Chart

Developed for a Brazilian wine exporter, this double piece compares worldwide consumption and the global production of red wine in 2006. Shaped as a bunch of grapes, the countries are represented as circles scaled according to their average total consumption of red wine. This shows that red wine is very popular in France, Italy and tiny Luxemburg, whereas Brazileiros have yet to introduce red wine as part of their daily habits. The second sheet refers to production quantities, with absolute numbers showing France as the biggest producer worldwide. Quantities in both pieces are structured hierarchically.

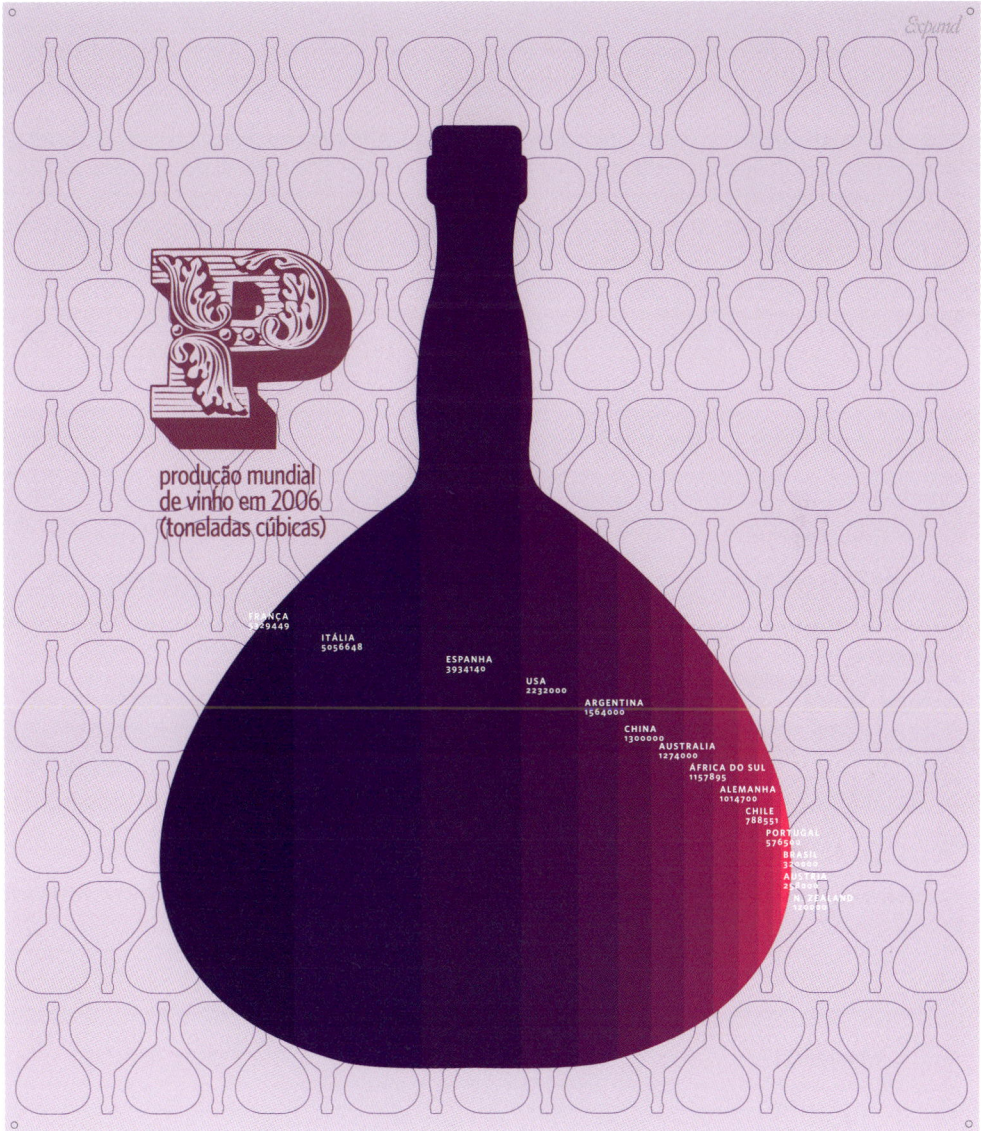

Project Info: Expand Wine Importers,
poster and magazine article,
2007, Brazil
Design: Alexandre Suannes

World of 100

This series refers to the popular concept of imagining the world as a village of 100 people. It allows global population statistics to be presented scaled down to a total population of 100 people. The image seems to appeal to people's imagination and breaks unimaginable global figures down to a human scale. Toby Ng translated the statistical information into a series of posters, each explaining one fact. One major topic is the composition of global population in terms of age or gender or religion. Another strand addresses access to material and non-material goods such as education, clean air, water, computers etc. Each diagram is centred around an icon symbolising the respective topic.

Project Info: Series of posters, 2008, China
Data Source: *If the World Were a Village*, David J. Smith, Kids Can Press

Design: Toby Ng
Awards: Red Dot Award 2009; GDC 09 Awards; International Design Awards 2009; HOW 2010 International Design Awards

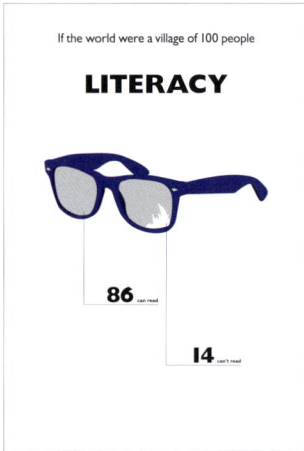

If the world were a village of 100 people

LITERACY

86 can read

14 can't read

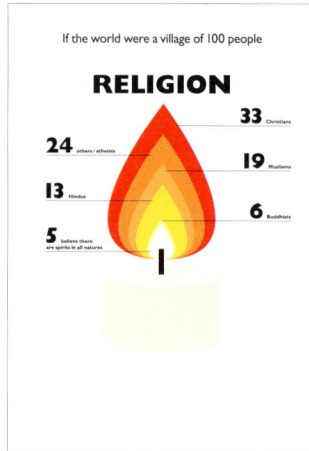

If the world were a village of 100 people

RELIGION

33 Christians
24 others / atheists
19 Muslims
13 Hindus
6 Buddhists
5 believe there are spirits in all natures
1

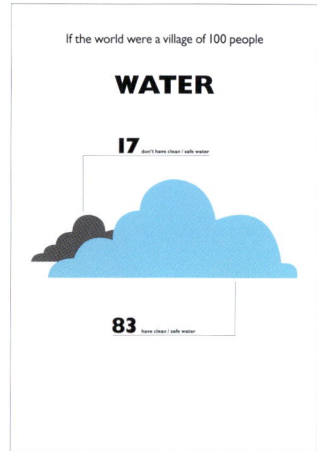

If the world were a village of 100 people

WATER

17 don't have clean / safe water

83 have clean / safe water

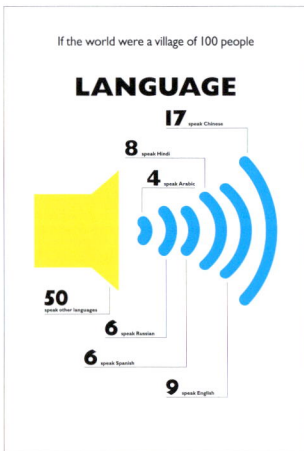

If the world were a village of 100 people

LANGUAGE

17 speak Chinese
8 speak Hindi
4 speak Arabic
50 speak other languages
6 speak Russian
6 speak Spanish
9 speak English

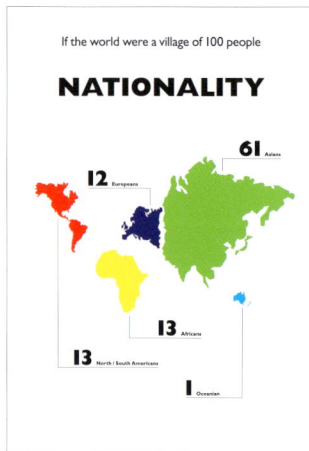

If the world were a village of 100 people

NATIONALITY

61 Asians
12 Europeans
13 Africans
13 North / South Americans
1 Oceanian

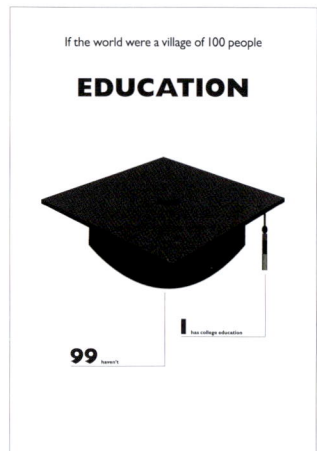

If the world were a village of 100 people

EDUCATION

1 has college education

99 haven't

If the world were a village of 100 people

FEAR

20 live in fear of death by bombardment armed attack, landmines, or of rape or kidnapping by armed groups

80 don't

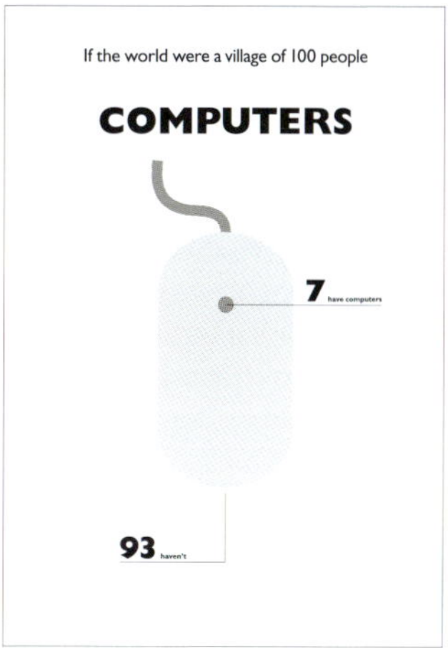

If the world were a village of 100 people

COMPUTERS

7 have computers

93 haven't

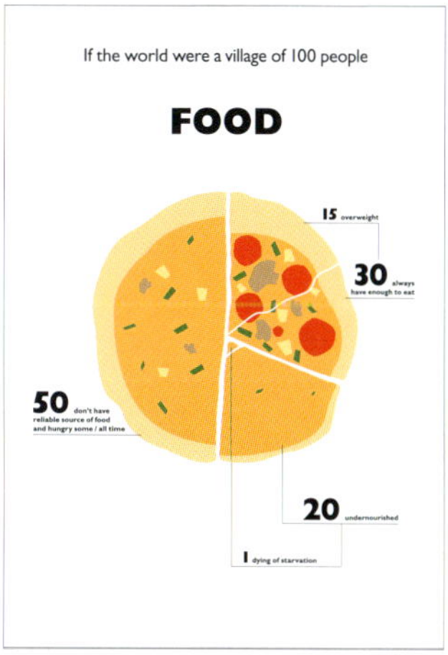

If the world were a village of 100 people

FOOD

15 overweight

30 always have enough to eat

50 don't have reliable source of food and hungry some / all time

20 undernourished

1 dying of starvation

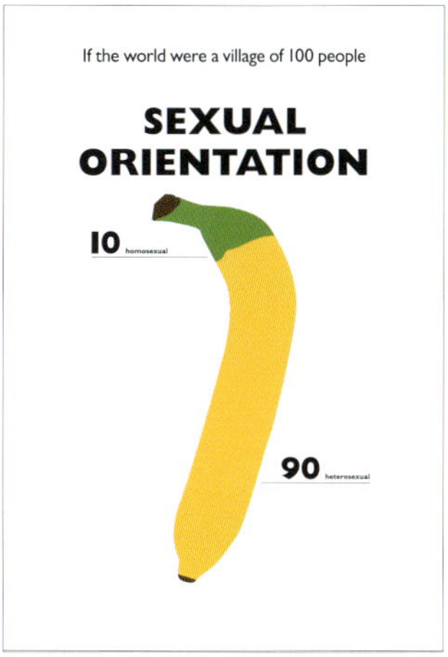

If the world were a village of 100 people

SEXUAL ORIENTATION

10 homosexual

90 heterosexual

If the world were a village of 100 people

FREEDOM

48 can't speak, act according to their faith and conscience due to harassment, imprisonment, torture or death

52 can

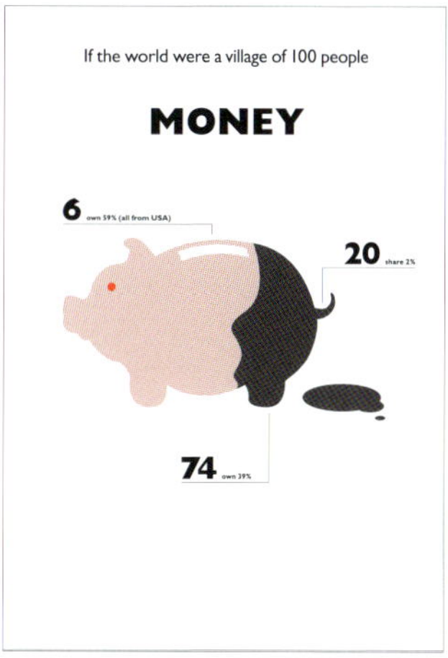

If the world were a village of 100 people

MONEY

6 own 59% (all from USA)

20 share 2%

74 own 39%

507

The Wheel O' Happiness

The volvelle or wheel chart is a paper construction with rotating parts, used for simple calculations or looking up information before the age of computers. Michael Newhouse uses this type of chart for his guide to career satisfaction. The wheel shows a list of college majors and indicates what percentage of people are satisfied with their job after graduating in each one. The wheel employs two different ways of structuring this list: from the top down on the right, majors are listed alphabetically, from the top down on the left, majors are listed by satisfaction level, starting with the radically unhappy nutritionists.

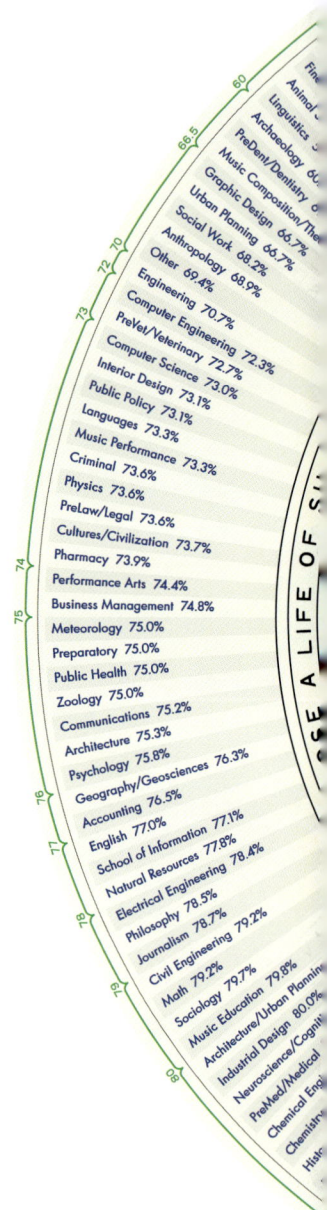

Fine
Animal
Linguistics
Archaeology &
PreDent/Dentistry o
Music Composition/The
Graphic Design 66.7%
Urban Planning 66.7%
Social Work 68.2%
Anthropology 68.9%
Other 69.4%
Engineering 70.7%
Computer Engineering 72.3%
PreVet/Veterinary 72.3%
Computer Science 72.7%
Interior Design 73.0%
Public Policy 73.1%
Languages 73.3%
Music Performance 73.3%
Criminal 73.6%
Physics 73.6%
PreLaw/Legal 73.6%
Cultures/Civilization 73.7%
Pharmacy 73.9%
Performance Arts 74.4%
Business Management 74.8%
Meteorology 75.0%
Preparatory 75.0%
Public Health 75.0%
Zoology 75.0%
Communications 75.2%
Architecture 75.3%
Psychology 75.8%
Geography/Geosciences 76.3%
Accounting 76.5%
English 77.0%
School of Information 77.1%
Natural Resources 77.8%
Electrical Engineering 78.4%
Philosophy 78.5%
Journalism 78.7%
Civil Engineering 79.2%
Math 79.2%
Sociology 79.7%
Music Education 79.8%
Architecture/Urban Planning
Industrial Design 80.0%
Neuroscience/Cogniti
PreMed/Medical
Chemical Eng
Chemistry
His

SE A LIFE OF S

Project Info: "A Guide to Career Satisfaction by Major", website, 2009, USA
Data Source: CollegeDegrees.com; StudentsReview
Design: Michael Newhouse (Newhouse Design)

THE WHEEL O' HAPPINESS

THE COLLEGEDEGREES.COM GUIDE to CAREER SATISFACTION by MAJOR

YOU CAN'T HAVE IT BOTH WAYS, SON

THIS CHART SHOWS PERCENTAGES OF PEOPLE WHO ARE SATISFIED WITH THEIR JOB AFTER GRADUATING IN EACH MAJOR

SOURCE
www.studentsreview.com/satisfaction_by_major.php3

DESIGN BY
NEWHOUSE DESIGN
Bozeman Montana

CAN'T PICK A DEGREE?

ARE YOU LAZY ▼ OR JUST CONFUSED?

YOUR CAREER HERE

You can predict your Future Now!

Why waste years of your Life?

IT'S UP TO YOU * CHOOSE A LIFE OF HAPPINESS OR MISERY * CHOOSE A LIFE OF FULFILLMENT OR FRUSTRA...
ADEQUACY *

OR, CHOOSE YOUR MAJOR

BETTER FACE IT NOW

You will be doing this Job until you die.

GOOD LUCK!

SPIN WISELY MY FRIEND

▼ ALPHABETICAL

Accounting 76.5%
Aerospace Engineering 82.8%
Agriculture/Horticulture 54.3%
Animal Studies 58.3%
Anthropology 68.9%
Archaeology 60.0%
Architecture 75.3%
Architecture/Urban Planning 80.0%
Art & Design 57.8%
Astronomy 87.5%
Athletics/Training 55.0%
Biology 83.6%
Automotive Engineering 72.3%
Business Management 74.8%
Chemical Engineering 81.9%
Chemistry 79.2%
Civil Engineering 72.3%
Computer Engineering 73.0%
Computer Science 73.6%
Criminal 73.7%
Cultures/Civilization 84.1%
Economics 82.8%
Education 78.4%
Electrical Engineering 70.7%
Engineering 77.0%
English 84.1%
Finance 84.1%
Fine Arts 57.8%
Genetics 50.0%
Geography/Geosciences 76.3%
Graphic Design 66.7%
History 82.4%
Industrial Design 80.0%
Industrial Operations 82.6%
Interior Design 73.1%
Journalism 78.7%
Languages 73.3%
Linguistics 58.3%
Math 79.2%
Mechanical Engineering 82.8%
Meteorology 75.0%
Music Composition/Theory 64.4%
Music Performance 73.3%
Music Education 79.8%
Natural Resources 77.8%
Naval Engineering 90.9%
Neuroscience/Cognitive 80.0%
Nuclear Engineering 50.0%
Nursing 82.8%
Other 14.3%
Performance Arts 69.4%
Pharmacy 74.4%
Philosophy 73.9%
Physical Therapy 78.5%
Physics 73.6%
Political Science 45.5%
PreDent/Dentistry 84.4%
PreLaw/Legal 61.5%
PreMed/Medical 80.9%
PreVet/Veterinary 75.0%
Psychology 72.7%
Public Health 75.8%
Public Policy 73.1%
Radiology 44.4%
Religion 77.1%
School of Information 84.6%
Social Work 68.7%
Sociology 79.70
Telecommunications 84.4%
Undecided 66.7%
Urban Planning 57.3%
Video/Media 43.8%
Zoology 75.0%

▼ NUMERICAL
Nutrition 14.3%
Video/Media 43.8%
Radiology 44.4%
Physical Therapy/Exercise 45.8%
Automotive Engineering 50.0%
...Engineering 50.0%
...Culture 54.3%

...logy 82.8%
...8%
...ology 83.0%
Economics 84.1%
Finance 84.1%
Political Science 84.4%
Telecommunications 84.4%
Religion 84.9%
Astronomy 87.5%
Kinesiology 88.0%
Naval Engineering 90.9%

40 14

06

509

Essay Image Credits

New York / Scala, Florence; © VG Bild-Kunst, Bonn 2025
p.96 Mark Lombardi, *World Finance Corporation and Associates, ca. 1970–84: Miami, Ajman, and Bogota-Caracas*, 1999 © Courtesy of Pierogi Gallery
p.97 Ad Reinhardt, 1955 © VG Bild-Kunst, Bonn 2025, photograph by

Al Mozell, Courtesy The Pace Gallery
p.98 Jacques Bertin, Paris, 1967 La Haye, Mouton, Gauthiers-Villars
p.99 © Getty Images / Science & Society Picture Library
p.100 *Periodic Table of Swearing*, 2010 © Jon Link & Mick Bunnage / moderntoss.com

Thanks

I extend my thanks firstly to all the designers, scientists and artists who allowed us to use their brilliant work. Gathering designs from a variety of fields was very inspiring, and I thank everyone who supported this open approach. Paolo Ciuccarelli, Nigel Holmes, Simon Rogers and Richard Saul Wurman contributed their own pieces to this book, and being allowed to work with them was a great privilege.

On the part of the publishing house, Benedikt Taschen and Julius Wiedemann's enthusiastic support for the subject made this publication possible. With his wealth of experience and circumspection, Daniel Siciliano Bretas brought together all the publishing threads, and provided superb project leadership. Jutta Hendricks and Chris Allen edited the book with great feeling and sensitivity. Praline Design have created a fabulous layout for this complex subject. In the print production department, Frank Goerhardt's execution of the design has been magnificent, and Stefan Klatte in pre-press is the person responsible for the outstanding visual quality.

Technical advice was forthcoming from numerous designers including Joachim Sauter, Jan Schwochow, Boris Müller, Jing He, Monika Hoinkis, Danqing Shi, Axel Pfänder, Anja Lutz, Peter Ruschel and Sven Assmann. Ole Häntzschel has fully supported the project from the beginning. I would also like to thank Julia Guther for all her help, which went beyond creative matters. My deepest thanks go to Ursula Rendgen and Andrej Rendgen and also to Clemens von Lucius for his professional and patient encouragement.

© 2025 TASCHEN GmbH
Hohenzollernring 53, D-50672 Köln
www.taschen.com

EACH AND EVERY TASCHEN BOOK PLANTS A SEED!
Each year, we offset our annual carbon emissions
with carbon credits at the Instituto Terra, a reforestation
program in Minas Gerais, Brazil, founded by Lélia
and Sebastião Salgado. To find out more about this
ecological partnership, please check:
www.taschen.com/institutoterra.
Inspiration: unlimited. Carbon footprint: (almost) zero.

Want to see more? Visit taschen.com to view our current
publications, browse our latest magazine, and subscribe
to our newsletter.

Original Edition © 2012 TASCHEN GmbH
Original Design Praline (Al Rodger, David Tanguy)

Printed in Bosnia-Herzegovina
ISBN 978-3-8365-9966-5